Catholic Higher Education

Catholic Higher Education

A Culture in Crisis

MELANIE M. MOREY

JOHN J. PIDERIT, S.J.

OXFORD
UNIVERSITY PRESS

2006

OXFORD
UNIVERSITY PRESS

Oxford University Press, Inc., publishes works that further
Oxford University's objective of excellence
in research, scholarship, and education.

Oxford   New York
Auckland   Cape Town   Dar es Salaam   Hong Kong   Karachi
Kuala Lumpur   Madrid   Melbourne   Mexico City   Nairobi
New Delhi   Shanghai   Taipei   Toronto

With offices in
Argentina   Austria   Brazil   Chile   Czech Republic   France   Greece
Guatemala   Hungary   Italy   Japan   Poland   Portugal   Singapore
South Korea   Switzerland   Thailand   Turkey   Ukraine   Vietnam

Copyright © 2006 by Oxford University Press, Inc.

Published by Oxford University Press, Inc.
198 Madison Avenue, New York, New York 10016

www.oup.com

Oxford is a registered trademark of Oxford University Press

Library of Congress Cataloging-in-Publication Data
Morey, Melanie M.
Catholic higher education : a culture in crisis / by Melanie M. Morey and
John J. Piderit, S.J.
     p.   cm.
Includes bibliographical references and index.
ISBN-13 978-0-19-530551-7
ISBN 0-19-530551-5
1. Catholic universities and colleges—United States.   2. Catholic Church—Education
(Higher)—United States.   I. Piderit, John J.   II. Title.
LC501.M65 2006
378'.0712'73—dc22   2005023086

9 8 7 6 5 4 3 2 1

Printed in the United States of America
on acid-free paper

*Dedicated
to our families*

Acknowledgments

In the course of this project, we have had the privilege of working with extraordinarily generous and wise people, and we would like to thank them for their contributions.

The first people we would like to thank are the other members of our research team. All three of these talented colleagues and dear friends left the project at various points to accept new, exciting, and challenging positions in the arena of Catholic higher education. Rev. Dennis Holtschneider, C.M., the president of DePaul University, was one of the two original designers of the study and one of its lead investigators. Dennis and Melanie were research colleagues and collaborators for ten years, and this project emerged out of their previous work together. Dennis believed in the importance of this research and found ways in the midst of a challenging schedule as executive vice-president at Niagara University to collaborate on the creation of the project and to help interview, analyze, and bring clarity to the data. Dennis took full responsibility for the execution of the first-phase questionnaire and was the coauthor of the report on that phase of the study entitled *Lay Leadership in the Age of the Laity*. Dennis moved on from the project when he accepted the presidency at DePaul and his duties no longer permitted ongoing involvement. Without his original insight and passion, however, this project would never have been conceived, let alone completed. The research was the culmination of ten years of wonderful collaboration, and what is a loss for us is a tremendous gain for DePaul.

Mary Lou Jackson joined the project in its early days and helped in project design, as well as interviewing and data analysis. Mary Lou brought a wide array of gifts to this project and to the team, but her greatest contribution was her expertise in qualitative research.

She painstakingly worked with us as we coded fifteen hundred pages of raw data. Whenever the rest of us got ahead of ourselves, she called us back to the data to clarify what we thought we knew about what administrators had said. We were all careful researchers when we entered the project. We became meticulous researchers because of Mary Lou. She also provided warmth, humor, and hospitality that kept us going when there was no end in sight. At the end of the analysis phase, she too, accepted a wonderful new position and is now the chief of staff in the president's office at Stonehill College. Her wisdom and insight helped us to see things we otherwise might have missed, and now we just miss her.

Paul Gallagher, the former executive director of the Association of Catholic Colleges and Universities, joined our team as we crafted the interview protocol. He brought his vast knowledge of the landscape of Catholic higher education to bear on this project, and it was invaluable. He also participated in the interview phase of the study. Paul has truly seen it all during his career in Catholic higher education, and he provided a perspective that was thoughtful and balanced and utterly informed. At the end of the interviews, Paul returned to his work as a search consultant and is now a principle in Gallagher-Fennell, a higher education search firm.

The presidents and senior administrators at all thirty-three interview sites participated enthusiastically in this study. They gave time, energy, and thoughtful reflection to the questions we posed and engaged warmly in the interviews themselves. Without them and the information they were willing to share, this book could not have been written.

While the presidents and administrators gave us the raw data for this study, the staffs of the presidents coordinated the interview process, collected questionnaires, set up interviews, made phone calls, and went about the business of juggling the schedules of six or more different people in order to make it all happen. Despite the demanding coordination of multiple schedules, at each and every site these individuals made us feel welcome while they attended to all we needed with great enthusiasm and nary a complaint. They were the heroes, and far more often the heroines, who helped us accomplish our work in the field.

Although the views expressed in this book are solely our responsibility, they emerged from interaction with a wide variety of colleagues, friends, and both personal and institutional patrons. The project received foundation support, including a grant from the Louisville Institute. Their belief in the project and generous support made it possible to include a large number of institutions from all across the country in this study. Their funding also made it possible for a group of researchers who were not located in one state to spend time together crafting the study, analyzing the data, and writing the first phase report.

Two people gave us technical support in this process. Michael James, the vice president of the Association of Catholic Colleges and Universities, helped provide much of the institutional information in our original data base. Nathan

Blecharczyk helped us develop ways to handle large amounts of data more effectively and efficiently during the analysis phase of the project. Their work simplified a complex process and saved us countless hours of work.

A number of women religious supported our work, answered a myriad of questions about religious congregations of women in the United States, gave us much-needed advice, and read and commented on our cautionary tale about culture and the sisterhoods. The critical comments, advice, and support of Sr. Marylouise Fennell, R.S.M., Sr. Margaret Crowley, R.S.M., Sr. Colette Mahoney, R.S.H.M., Sr. Mary Oates, C.S.J., Sr. Margaret Wick, O.S.F., and Sr. Patricia Wittberg, S.C., enhanced our understanding and appreciation of the complexity of the story of American nuns. Their contribution helped us to see much that we might have missed if left on our own. Each of these women is in her own right a heroic exemplar in our tradition, and their witness, as well as their wisdom, inspired us.

Bishop Joseph M. Sullivan, the now retired episcopal vicar for human services of the Diocese of Brooklyn, was a willing conversation partner throughout the project. He shared useful information about the challenges other institutional ministries face in sustaining and supporting Catholic culture. Bishop Sullivan also helped us to sort out how their challenges are similar to or different from the issues facing Catholic colleges and universities.

Thomas Levergood, the director of the Lumen Christi Institute at the University of Chicago, gave us pertinent information about how Catholic centers at nonsectarian colleges and universities operate and the services they provide. David Breneman, the dean of the Curry School of Education at the University of Virginia, shared strategies for writing a book based on a multisite qualitative research study of colleges and universities. His reflections on the realities of the higher education market and how colleges adjust to market pressures were also quite instructive.

In the earliest stages of this project, Fr. Richard P. McBrien of the University of Notre Dame cautioned us about two things. He urged us to be wary of the pernicious habit of self-censorship and encouraged us to be evenhanded and generous about the motives of any individuals with whom we might disagree. We took that advice to heart and earnestly tried to be faithful to it throughout. We are grateful for both his wisdom and encouragement.

The law of the Church is as important as civil law for Catholic institutions because they are subject to both legal codes. Fr. Robert T. Kennedy, a canonist from the Catholic University of America, has generously spent time over a number of years helping us more fully appreciate canon law and its particular role in the institutional life of Catholic colleges and universities. He has served as an excellent guide through the canonical legal thicket that surrounds sponsorship and institutional Catholic identity. His instruction has always been clear and compelling, his patience unflagging, and his sense of humor a blessed relief. We appreciate his working with us on this and other projects and hope he will be willing to continue the tutorials for many years to come.

Research projects benefit tremendously from excellent librarians, and this work is no different. In our case, Betty Garity, the head of acquisitions at the Fordham University libraries, provided that expertise, and it made a great deal of difference for our work.

The research project was housed at Niagara University, and Maria Hamilton provided us with superb administrative support. Her diligence and cheerful spirit in the face of hundreds of questionnaires and many rounds of mailings and phone calls kept the project on target. She also tracked expenses, provided support service, and was always delighted to hear from us, no matter the reason we called.

Niagara was also the site of a number of our research team meetings, and our unofficial social host was Bro. Augustine Towey, C.M. An emeritus professor of theatre at Niagara, Augustine is truly a renaissance man. His wit, wisdom, and warmth cheered us at each meal, and his witness as a gifted and thoroughly Catholic artist was an inspiration. We are also grateful to the president of Niagara University, Fr. Joseph Levesque, C.M. He, too, was committed to this work and demonstrated that commitment by extending hospitality to the team and, more important, by encouraging and supporting the involvement of his executive vice-president in the project.

A group of our professional colleagues gave generously of their time discussing this work with us. They listened to our long stories about the project, offered their own insights, asked questions that gave us new insights, and proved excellent sounding boards when we just had to talk to someone about it all. Timothy Schilling, a freelance writer about things Catholic, Catherine Hill, the associate academic dean at Villanova University, Fr. Timothy Lannon, S.J., the president of St. Joseph's University, Fr. John M. McDermott, S.J., Laghi Professor of Theology at Pontifical College Josephinum in Ohio, and Fr. William P. Grogan, system director of ethics for Provena Health System in Illinois, all helped us sort out thorny issues and tease out nuances, while bringing their own personal insights into the mix. Their advice and counsel made this a better book.

Fr. Andrew Greeley has been a good friend, strong in his personal support and quick with insightful criticisms. Fr. Lou Pascoe, S.J., provided expert guidance on the material relating to medieval universities. Fr. Gerry Egan's extensive experience working with senior management made important contributions to our own strategic analysis at the senior level of Catholic institutions. Helpful insights about Catholic education were provided to Fr. Piderit over many years by Larry Braskamp, Tassos Malliaris, Tom Meenahan, and Steve Englund. With the benefit of two very successful presidencies at significant nonsectarian institutions behind him and motivated by an abiding interest in Catholic education, G. Dennis O'Brien offered urbane, witty, and critical comments about our approach, for each of which we are grateful.

We both also had the benefit of good personal friends outside the field with whom we could share the work of this project. Each proved to be wise and often witty as he or she helped us navigate the twists and turns inherent in the work. Coming at things from a different perspective, they pushed us to clarify our assumptions, and they shared insights from their own professional cultures that brought our research into clearer focus. We have been doing this for many years, and never during all that time did they find our preoccupation and interest in this work tiresome. At least if they did, they never told us. We are grateful for the generous friendship and insights of Vince Cook, Chris Bell, Alicia Ianiere, Peggy Bryant, Frances Acosta, Fr. Bill Bergen, S.J., John Connorton, Jr., Sr. Diane Driscoll, S.S.J., Fr. Dan Flaherty, S.J., Katy Feeney, Fr. John Haughey, S.J., Bishop Roger Kaffer, Fr. Mark Massa, S.J., Fr. Don Rowe, S.J., and Fr. Joe Kelly. Also very important for the development of Fr. Piderit's thoughts were the administrative staffs at Fordham University, Marquette University, and Loyola University Chicago. He is especially grateful to senior administrators and the trustees during his presidency of Loyola University Chicago for their assistance in exploring the contours of a modern Catholic university culture, as well as to Francis Cardinal George for his personal support and national intellectual leadership. Sister Ann Ida Gannon, B.V.M., also provided important insights from her long experience as college president and her service on many national governing boards.

Last, but certainly not least, we are grateful for the families of our research team. Jane Gallagher generously supported the effort by transcribing tapes, scheduling trips, and putting up with numerous phone calls and extended site visits. Bill Jackson was ever gracious to the team. He supported our work, sorted out technology complications, and was often willing to pitch in to make things work when Mary Lou had to travel. Their children, Ben, Josh, and Sarah, put up with us when we invaded their home and coped in their mother's project-related absences. John Morey asked hard questions, listened while we tried to sort things out, hosted the team, and never complained about his wife being gone, preoccupied, or tied to a computer for weeks and months on end. Last but not least, Elizabeth Morey was a trooper. She helped tabulate responses to the first phase of the study, made lists, copied documents, collated dozens of color-coded analysis reports, and learned the skills of qualitative research she later applied in her own senior thesis project. Elizabeth listened enthusiastically when we had interesting things to say or good news to share and rolled her eyes when we got carried away. During the whole four years of this project, Elizabeth never stopped thinking we were worth her time or stopped making for us the best chocolate bourbon balls one could ever hope to taste.

The work for this project was challenging, but always invigorating, and the people who helped and supported us were a blessing. We are deeply grateful to them all.

Contents

PART I

Context

I

Introduction

A crisis is looming within American Catholic higher education. As Catholic colleges and universities analyze their position and set a course for the future, they are faced with a structural reality that threatens their ability to continue as institutions with vibrant religious cultures. Institutional Catholic culture is changing and adapting at all Catholic colleges and universities. Laypersons have assumed the vast majority of the leadership roles in all of these institutions, and few have the depth or breadth of religious formation and education possessed by the religious men and women who preceded them. Without nuns, brothers, and priests to depend on in the future, Catholic colleges and universities must find laypersons whose religious commitment and knowledge can sustain their institutions' religious cultural legacy and enhance it for the future. They must do this without the benefit of a sustained effort in the Church to educate and form laypersons to assume the responsibilities that are being laid at their feet. Catholic educators have struggled mightily over the better part of the last forty years with a knot of complex issues. Much has been said and written about such questions as: What constitutes the "Catholic identity" of Catholic colleges and universities? Is it inevitable for Catholic colleges and universities to follow the historical trend and lose their religious identity? What does it mean to be an authentically Catholic institution and is there only one way to do that? What is the appropriate balance between the secular and religious missions of Catholic colleges and universities? Will the loss of nuns, brothers, and priests as a vital and visible presence on campus prove fatal for institutional Catholic character? These are important questions to define carefully, describe accurately, and confront effectively, and this book attempts to do just that. The findings from a national study of Catholic higher education that focused on 124 senior administrators from thirty-three Catholic colleges and universities provides the descriptive data that informs the book. (See appendix A for a list of the participating institutions.)

In interview conversations, the administrators shared their own convictions about the enterprise of Catholic higher education. Many administrators were clear that Catholic colleges and universities are privileged places to work. As one administrator said, "We have the gift of being able to educate the whole person in a better way." They also believe they have a unique and noble mission

> that goes to faith and reason. It goes to developing leaders in a
> world and context where you need values—in a context where you
> need a faith dimension—in a context where you need someone who
> understands that there is a God and that God is good. We are re-
> sponsible for understanding that and responsible in the Catholic
> faith for transmitting those beliefs as a living witness of the Gospel
> message. To do any less than that is not sufficient.

Administrators appreciated that the Catholic approach to education and the search for truth is open and broad, not narrow and constrained. As one academic vice-president put it, "Thomas Aquinas said, 'Beware of the man with the single book.' The Catholic tradition is not an educational heritage with a single book. It is free to explore, but always with the underlying question of 'Why?' " The Catholic educational tradition was understood by administrators as rooted in the liberal arts, which were originally seen as "tools to train the mind and the heart to be able to deal with the big issues of the day and apply Christian faith to them." While they admitted the liberal arts often exist within curricula today in some contracted form, administrators still championed them as at the heart of what makes Catholic higher education unique and compelling. It is safe to say that, on the whole, senior administrators are quite satisfied to be part of what they see as a very important segment of American higher education. "Even though we get involved periodically in these self-assessments or kinds of appraisals of how we are doing, the evidence is in anecdotally. There is a great sense of satisfaction and reward [in what we do]."

Administrators also described the reality of Catholic collegiate culture as they experience it every day, a reality that frequently did not measure up to their own convictions about how things should be. Many of the administrators said their own institutions until very recently had distanced themselves from their Catholic heritage. "There's a history where many colleges in the sixties and seventies kind of put the Catholic [part] off to the side because if you said you were Catholic you weren't going to get students. There was almost an apology about being Catholic." The majority of respondents agreed with one president that this reticence about things Catholic is changing. "Three years ago, to talk about Catholic identity threatened people, and now it's part of the discourse of the college. We've created a mission division. We're looking at Catholic identity and what that means. Generationally the students, for whatever reason, want to talk more about religious issues."

While the colleges themselves are more comfortable with the Catholic dimension of their identity and mission, many administrators fear that faculty are still quite dubious. A president noted:

> On campus faculty members now have conversations about spirituality and what that means and what role it plays in their lives. I challenge the conversation about spirituality by saying it brings peace of mind to faculty. I really think that spirituality becomes a comfortable way for all of us to avoid the harder discussion of what does it mean to be Catholic.

Generally speaking, most administrators in the end admitted that their colleges and universities had rather weak Catholic cultures. A fairly typical description of the cultural climate was given by one university president.

> The Catholic culture and character of my institution is not at all thick on the ground. There are people for whom it is a nice thing, but it's not something that's meaningful to them. For the Catholic faculty, some of them have said to me it's like coming home. You know, they really feel like this is the place that will allow them to fulfill their own life vocation. There are other ones for whom this is a nice feature in the environment, but it isn't really important for them.

Administrators reported that, among faculty, responses to things Catholic run the gamut from enthusiastic to hostile and often admitted, with frustration, that "some of the folks that find it most difficult to support the mission are Catholics who are either not practicing or really have issues with the Church." Students at Catholic institutions, according to the administrators, also run the gamut, but among Catholic students, most know little about the tradition in which they were raised. For the most part, administrators agreed that it was pretty unlikely that "a student who spends four years here can remain untouched by the Catholic character of the university." However, few students would experience Catholic culture in any robust way. One administrator offered a description of what the students get out of their experience at the university that was typical of what a majority of administrators described as happening at their own institutions:

> We achieve the larger goals of trying to make or expose our students to ways of thinking that are more caring, compassionate, and civic-minded, to encourage belief in social justice, and in community service—those things. They may not at the end be able to articulate any more clearly than they did at the beginning what this has to do with Catholicism. Then there is a group of students, who may be thirty or forty in number, who come here, become involved in campus ministry, go to Church regularly, become Eucharistic ministers, become lectors, become very involved with a Catholic worker commu-

nity; we become the channel for their nascent religious and spiritual commitment, and those are the students that you see so clearly and you are proud to say they are a part of our university.

Given what they experience daily, many administrators gave voice to real concerns about what is happening in Catholic higher education in this country. Administrators were concerned about what would develop in the next ten years. They worried that Catholic education "is being viewed increasingly by students as irrelevant. How do we make ourselves relevant to the world in a time when everything's a sixty-second sound bite and when ethics seem to be totally relative?" Another administrator voiced the frustration of many who claim to be shaping the consciences of their students and then are confronted "by students doing something diametrically opposed to what we stand for. The students go off campus and they are out driving, having gotten roaring drunk. . . . You say to yourself, 'How can this happen after they had had so much Catholic education?' It's disheartening." Others were concerned about market pressures they see as undermining any possibility that the university will really address Catholic moral tradition with students.

> Faculty will say, "Well, my kids go to this Church of Christ school and they pray every day and there is no sleeping together and there are no drugs." Well, there probably is, but it is at a much lower level. This is one of those trade-offs and tensions in a school like our own. Sure we could enforce that everybody prays every day and does this, this, and this, and our enrollment would drop significantly. And we are in a hand-to-hand struggle financially to keep an institution like this afloat.

Administrators also had concerns about how effective their institutions were in engaging the Catholic tradition in the academic arena. They often suggested: "We could do a better job program-wise of finding ways to integrate people's academic experiences in courses and colleges less traditionally influenced by Catholic thought." They also admitted there were no guarantees that students learned anything about Catholicism even in theology courses. "If you have a theology requirement at a school and students can take any theology course they want, which might be comparative religions, et cetera, that hardly is rootedness in the Catholic tradition." There was a sense among some that scholarly work about Catholicism at Catholic institutions was lagging behind work at nonsectarian institutions.

> The tragedy is that the best studies of the impact of religion on society are coming out of secular universities. Now in part that's a function of their size, [their] wealth, and their interest and commitment to research. But, the Catholic universities are not doing enough. We're doing more of it than we used to, but we're not doing enough.

Finally, the senior leadership of this wide variety of colleges and universities offered their own views about general directions that need to be pursued to ensure that Catholic colleges and universities remain vital. Interestingly, very few administrators were able to come up with particular programs that would actually accomplish the goals they seemed to set. The disappearance of nuns, brothers, and priests, many administrators agreed, would drive Catholic institutions to make changes to assure the vitality of their Catholic institutional culture. "In ten years there may not be any nuns on campus who are recognizable. What will happen is that we'll have to make more concerted efforts to make Catholicism present in the classroom, present on campus." In order to do that, hiring for mission will become a top priority. "The way we turn things around," a president insisted, "is by bringing in new blood and *more* new blood. We've hired twenty-five new faculty members over three years." Administrators believe that many Catholic colleges and universities will be forced to close and those that survive will be ones that "educate students about what it means to be a Catholic in our modern world." They will be institutions that "find broader ways of strengthening [themselves] as Catholic institutions, besides simply a focus on justice. . . . If justice is the primary focus that is going to emerge over time, Catholic higher education will be missing some richness that is available."

The most successful institutions in the future will be those institutions that, as a mission vice-president characterized it, adhere to the virtuous middle.

> The virtuous middle is a place where people would be coming to the
> university with a clear understanding that it is denominational and
> that the values espoused are out of the Catholic tradition. These peo-
> ple, coming from whatever faith tradition they bring, will be really
> respected. There really will be a respect for the Catholic tradition,
> however, and people will be unafraid to talk about it and celebrate it
> and feel as much a part of it as they can—even if that might not be
> one hundred percent inclusion. The faith traditions of others would
> be celebrated also, with the recognition that doing so makes us
> richer. Students will be able to come and actually know that they are
> getting orthodox teaching, not that that's all they are going to get.
> They will know, however, they are getting what the Church teaches
> and they can feel comfortable with that, as well as the other theories
> and traditions that real education ought to be about.

Not surprisingly, the major themes and issues administrators raised revolve around the most important groups in any university: faculty and students. They spoke most frequently about the Catholic intellectual tradition, a tradition that, in the words of one administrator, "has over the centuries had such an accumulated ability to make a connection between faith and reason" and that has bearing on both faculty and students alike. The administrators also explicitly confirmed the dual emphasis on faculty and students as central to the way Catholic identity, character, and mission is sustained and advanced.

Senior administrators used a second framework that we term "broad impact" to articulate particularly Catholic aspects of their institutions. This framework encompassed ways their institutions have a positive Catholic impact on students, not only in academic courses but also in student living, student activities, and campus ministry. A vice-president talked about this approach to education as "an effort to develop an environment and create an ethos and a culture that invites young people into a transformative experience in their lives so they can be instruments of transformation to the world." The administrators themselves described and discussed cultural realities and very frequently used the word "culture" in their responses. The concept of culture is the main building block that supports this book. Unlike "Catholic identity," a term so vague it has little analytic utility, "culture" has a variety of dimensions that can be explored concretely. Along with "culture," we also use the term "institutional culture" to refer to the integral impact of various activities within the university on the Catholic formation of the student.

Senior administrators maintained that, at the minimum, it was very important for the people in their positions to be Catholic and committed to the Catholic project. As one administrator said about a key hire, "There was no doubt in my mind about what I wanted. I wanted someone who was familiar with and comfortable with Catholic traditions and I stated that. I hoped I could find a practicing Catholic, someone who was a role model for eight hundred students—someone who lived a Catholic lifestyle. I got that person." Senior administrators also cited the importance of the vowed religious on campus whose commitment to the Catholic faith at their institutions was so evident to various groups—faculty, students, and staff. Consequently, the importance of commitment in creating and sustaining a Catholic culture plays an important role in this book.

The fourth important perspective of what will follow is analytical. Our highlighting of distinguishability as an essential characteristic of a Catholic culture requires that we keep our eye on a number of cultures. One is the Catholic culture at each particular institution, another is Catholic culture at Catholic institutions in general, and a third is religious culture—Catholic or non-Catholic—at nonsectarian institutions.

Each Catholic institution has its own Catholic culture. But that culture subsists and is maintained within two broader cultures of academic institutions. One is the group of all Catholic institutions, and the other is the very large group of nonsectarian colleges and universities. The Catholic group of institutions is heterogeneous, but not so varied that it cannot be identified by characteristics rather than just names of institutions. We have tried to describe the shape of this group by identifying four models of Catholic institutions. The larger group of institutions—the nonsectarian colleges and universities—is gathered into a single generic model that we feel is sufficient for the purposes of the book.

Noting what senior administrators at Catholic institutions say as a group is important, but taken alone it hardly provides an adequate picture of the state of Catholic culture on their campuses. Since distinguishability is important for the long-term survivability of any culture, it is important to examine whether administrators' claims about what is unique to their "type" of institution is in fact different in any important and relevant way from claims about goals and procedures made by nonsectarian institutions.

This comparative emphasis on distinguishability led us to question the significance of three themes frequently mentioned by senior administrators— social justice, a caring Catholic culture, and the actual role of faculty in promoting the Catholic identity, mission, and character of the institution. These themes were indeed frequently addressed by senior administrators. However, in most instances we were unable to uncover any significant differences between how the Catholic colleges and universities approach social justice issues in practice and how they are addressed at nonsectarian institutions. Both types of institutions take social justice seriously. A handful of Catholic institutions have extensive programs that relate social justice to the general moral teaching of the Catholic Church and to its sacramental practice, but we did not see much evidence for this from senior administrators, even after they were prodded for examples of specifically Catholic contributions.

Senior administrators also noted how caring the Catholic community was and frequently used as examples the type of supportive outreach that occurred in the weeks and months after September 11, 2001. The stories here were indeed detailed, but once again we were unable to identify features of these stories that were in any way central to Catholic identity or different from the many similar reports that had appeared in the press about institutional reactions at nonsectarian institutions. Consequently, we muted these issues in our overall analysis of the comments of senior administrators.

The final theme that appeared to be suspect was the emphasis that senior administrators placed on faculty as the people who actually transmit knowledge and appreciation of the Catholic faith to students. Again, when senior administrators were asked to identify particular programs illustrative of how students were being educated in their faith, only a handful of them were able to point to programs at their institutions of which they were particularly proud.

Cultural Context

A period of great cultural polarization in the United States and the American Catholic Church is the context in which this study was undertaken and the book written. The nation, separated into Democratic blue states and Republican red states, is, many say, more polarized than any time since the states were color-coded blue and grey. The Catholic culture of the nation is also divided, and probably more so than any time since the great uproar surrounding the "Americanist" controversy of the nineteenth century.[1] In a gross oversimplification of a complex and varied phenomenon, this very public divide can be described as centering around two opposing views of what ails the Church and how it should be corrected. The view from the left tends to approach these questions with a deep appreciation for the reforms of the Second Vatican Council and a sense that problems have emerged because the reforms were not fully implemented. The view from the right is less enthusiastic about Council reforms and their implementation, believing they went too far and need cultural correction that is long overdue.[2] In public perception there are a number of things that distinguish these two cultural camps within the Church, including the popes with whom each side strongly identifies; Pope John XXIII for the liberals and Pope John Paul II for the conservatives. The divide is also evident around the big issues with which both groups are publicly identified. Conservatives are particularly strong advocates of a prolife position and frequently speak out on issues of personal morality and family morality. Liberals are far more likely to raise their voices against capital punishment, and they are outspoken advocates for justice. Conservatives are concerned about an increasing inclination toward "Catholic lite" that robs the tradition of its richness and heritage. Liberals, on the other hand, are equally concerned about "Catholic tight," a tendency to limit the tradition in the name of orthodoxy in ways that narrowly define the boundaries of Catholicism for the purposes of exclusion rather than inclusion. The left and the right are also increasingly segregated in the public square. They listen to different theologians;[3] belong to different organizations within the Church;[4] identify with different political parties and candidates;[5] and even read different periodicals.[6] Both sides read weekly Catholic newspapers known by the acronym *NCR*, but the conservative *National Catholic Register* and the liberal *National Catholic Reporter* are as different as chalk and cheese, and neither contributes substantially to broadening Catholic common ground.[7]

Catholic colleges and universities exist within the cultural context of the United States and the American Catholic Church. The porous boundaries of their religious collegiate cultures constantly bump into these larger umbrella cultures and the culture of secular American higher education, as well. There is an osmotic cultural exchange between and among all these cultures that impacts and influences how Catholic colleges and universities understand themselves, adjust to the times, and shape their futures.

In the spring and summer of 2002, during the initial stages of the work that led to this book, the kind of polarization so evident in American political culture and Catholic culture was also evident in the arena of Catholic higher education. Catholic colleges and universities were emerging from an often rancorous ten-year discussion of the apostolic constitution *Ex Corde Ecclesiae*. This discussion had kept the question of Catholic identity and culture center stage in rather contentious fashion. Two factions had emerged within the community of colleges and universities around a series of complex questions that included how best to implement the mandatum,[8] which policies should be established to determine what constitutes appropriate activities and speakers on Catholic campuses, and finally, how best to establish criteria for determining who should receive honorary degrees. Institutions coalesced around two different visions of what constituted authentically Catholic higher education.[9] These factions increasingly distanced themselves from each other, and respectful exchanges between these factions about critical issues concerning the identity, role, and mission of Catholic collegiate institutions became rare. The academic ideal of vigorous debate about competing ideas was suffering as these groups took refuge among like-minded institutions and colleagues and abandoned efforts to engage in what was becoming an increasingly acrimonious exchange.

Catholic colleges and universities operate in an atmosphere of cultural antagonism and must compete successfully with all other higher education institutions in the United States in order to survive. Many, if not most, of them feel under siege in one way or another. Some are operating on the margin financially. Others are waging internal battles over just how religious they should be. All these institutions are trying to juggle frequently conflicting pressures that include the need to "keep up with the Joneses" in order to stay competitive, the never-ending quest for funding and advancement dollars, alumnae with burnished memories about their own "Catholic educations," consumers who want the best return on their investment, parents who are looking for "authentic" Catholic institutions, boosters who insist on winning teams, administrators who are often more loyal to their professions than their employers, faculty who must answer to the dictates of their own disciplines and handle the pressures of scholarship and publishing, and bishops who have their own ideas about how Catholic colleges and universities should conduct themselves.

Many of these institutions feel they are trying to do business in the eye of a hurricane of competing demands. For them, the need to engage in an in-depth analysis of their religious culture is often seen as a baroque exercise, not a strategic necessity. Such a focus often appears to be a religious luxury akin to the eight-day spiritual retreats so readily available on an annual basis to priests, brothers, and nuns. "Wouldn't it be nice?" say the lay administrators, but by "nice," they do not mean either necessary or even possible. Knowing how they are faring in terms of their religious mission is not, however, a luxury Catholic colleges and universities can sidestep if they hope to survive as distinctive institutions.

Catholic collegiate enterprises make competitive claims to distinctiveness in terms of their educational programs. As one president put it,

> The heart and soul of these institutions are transformational in
> nature, not just transactional. They are not just credit bearing, but
> life giving. These institutions teach people not only how to earn a
> living but how to live a life in a moral sense, an ethical sense, in a
> value sense. They give a moral compass that enables students to get
> through life's crisis situations. If you look at the mission of these
> institutions versus [a nonsectarian university] they are not the same.
> I hope the day never comes in this country when the only alterna-
> tive for students is public higher education. If you closed the book
> tomorrow on all these Catholic institutions, sooner or later you
> would have to reinvent them because of how good they really are.

These claims are tied to the idea that, similar to other colleges sponsored by Christian denominations, they provide an educational alternative that is steeped in a unique religious legacy, identity, and mission. The legitimacy of these claims demands getting a better idea of what is going on with the religious mission and identity of Catholic colleges and universities. Because the milieu in which they operate is so polarized, the marketplace in which they compete is so demanding, the structural difficulties they face so daunting, and the religious sensitivities so acute, much of the discussion about the institutions is market conscious, if not market driven, and understandably tailored to put a positive spin on the story. Attempts to get beyond the spin and to analyze how these institutions are faring are often met with suspicion and more than a little resistance.

Cultural polarization contributes to the dearth of conversation between and among institutions with different visions of what it means to be an authentic Catholic institution, but it is not alone in bearing responsibility for this situation. Since the 1970s, the religious congregations that sponsor most colleges and universities have been involved in extensive discussions about this topic, but until recently they kept the conversation pretty much to themselves. In the past ten years that has begun to change, as many religious sponsors invite lay colleagues into the dialogue. While this improvement adds some breadth to the conversation, in most cases it remains intramural—focusing on institutions sponsored by the same religious group. Apart from casual contact or personal reading, most laypersons working at Catholic institutions have had limited experience with how other Catholic colleges and universities operate and what makes them distinctively different. Consequently, the faculty and staff simply do not have sufficient familiarity with other Catholic institutions to accurately assess whether the approach to Catholic culture at their institution is liberal, conservative, or middle of the road. Besides, other issues often appear more pressing to those involved in Catholic institutions and receive the lion's share of attention most of the time.

The Emerging Trends in Leadership Study, or ETL, as the project came to be known, was limited in scope. It focused on institutional Catholic culture, identity, and mission and how one group of individuals involved in the enterprise of Catholic higher education—those providing administrative leadership—understand these realities and what they mean for the work they do. Because much of what goes on in a culture is all but invisible to those who have spent any significant amount of time in it, some strategies were adopted to make the cultural components more visible and available to those involved. These attempts enhanced the ability of this particular set of cultural actors to reveal the particularities of their institutions' religious culture and the specifics of their own behaviors, attitudes, and assumptions in relation to them. Like all large investigations, this project developed over time, and initial questions led to others as information was gathered and the issues addressed became more refined.

The pressures on Catholic colleges and universities are not restricted to larger institutions or ones located in certain regions. Yet very few studies of

Catholic higher education look at the full range of institutions in all their rich variety. From small two-year colleges to major research universities, from institutions founded by religious congregations of men and dioceses to those founded by sisters and lay Catholics, from religiously conservative institutions to self-proclaimed liberal ones, from rural universities and colleges to suburban and big-city institutions, from residential colleges to commuter schools, from regional colleges to national powerhouse universities, Catholic colleges and universities are a richly diverse set of institutions. That fact is often masked by the narrow scope of much of the research that addresses them. This project attempted to get beyond this pattern of narrow exploration by studying the full range of types of Catholic colleges and universities across the length and breadth of the country.

This study was an interview-based qualitative research investigation awash in stories. Like other interview-based studies, this one ultimately produced three major story lines, each of which deserves attention. The first of these story lines was the product of the cooperative interchange between researchers and respondents and consisted of what the administrators had to say about their understandings and experiences or, in other words, the data. The second story line emerged from the data once it was fully analyzed, and that story line is being shared in this book. The third story line is the methodological narrative that describes the project itself and explains how it was conducted. It relates the understandings, strategies, decisions, and the experiences of the researchers in the field. Appendix B contains many details of that story.

Phase 1—Foundational Study

From the outset, the ETL study was conceived of as a two-phase project. The first phase was intended to set the stage for the second by providing a snapshot of the leadership landscape in Catholic higher education. Because the portrait was going to be a snapshot in a time of transition, it was structured to contrast religious leaders, the leadership model of the past, with lay leaders who represented the model for the future.

The data-gathering instrument used to create the leadership snapshot was a twelve-page, open-ended questionnaire.[10] The first part of the questionnaire elicited information about degrees, areas of study, religious preparation and formation, and other specific data points. The questionnaire also asked a series of open-ended questions about how individual leaders understood the enterprise of Catholic higher education and what its unique religious identity meant for the future of this sector of higher education and for their own positions. Surveys were sent to all the presidents of Catholic colleges and universities in the United States at the beginning of the summer of 2002, and a total of 55 percent of presidents responded.[11]

Two types of results emerged from the first phase of the ETL study. One type was almost purely factual and statistical while the other was more interpretive. The seven major factual findings of the Phase I study were as follows.

1. As a cohort, Catholic college and university presidents increasingly resemble their presidential peers elsewhere in U.S. higher education.
2. Laypersons infrequently emerge as presidents from finalist pools containing members of the founding religious congregation.
3. Women are disappearing from the presidency in Catholic colleges and universities.
4. There is a significant lack of formal theological and spiritual preparation among presidents. There is also widespread agreement among presidents that inadequate lay preparation presents a problem for the future of Catholic higher education. Despite this, few lay presidents report that they personally feel ill equipped to lead the religious mission of their institutions.
5. Forty-one percent of religious and 26 percent of lay presidents find the phrases "Catholic identity" and "Catholic intellectual tradition" to be fuzzy concepts that lack sufficient vitality on campuses. They want clearer definitions so they can develop strategies to effectively enhance this unique identity on their own campuses.
6. Presidents desire a more supportive working relationship with the hierarchical church but find such a relationship elusive and complex. Female presidents identify this more often than male presidents, and lay presidents identify this more often than their religious counterparts.
7. Presidents all acknowledge the central role faculty members play in their institutions. Nevertheless, many presidents, both lay and religious, report the faculty is an obstacle to effective leadership in the area of Catholic character, mission, and identity.

The two interpretive findings were:

1. Boards of trustees who hired the presidents have not yet identified minimum standards of religious education and training they deem essential for all Catholic college and university presidents.
2. The increasing dominance of laypersons in the leadership of Catholic colleges and universities has had an ambiguous impact, at best, in terms of the ideological divides in Catholic higher education. Conservative, liberal, and middle-of-the-road laypersons are assuming leadership positions in institutions that represent the full range of the ideological spectrum. The involvement of laypersons has resulted in neither a general trend toward any one type of leader nor a tilt toward a particular institutional ideology.

The findings of the first phase of the ETL study demonstrated that a new generation of lay leadership has arrived in American Catholic higher education. These leaders have come to their positions within a Church that traditionally has identified future leaders from its religious ranks. The Church prepared successive generations of leaders through seminaries, formation programs, and guided career moves and granted moral credibility and leadership through the structures of vows or ordination. Even the informal conversations of leadership between bishops and college presidents were traditionally conducted in the comfort and context of shared religious profession. With the exception of those who spent time in religious life or seminary, none of the lay presidents have had access to this organized and legitimating process of leadership cultivation.

Along with making clear that laypersons are increasingly running Catholic institutions of higher education in the United States, data from phase 1 of the ETL study also indicated a deep commitment among presidents to maintaining the Catholic identity of Catholic colleges and universities. Their views about that Catholic identity, however, covered a broad spectrum of attitudes and assumptions, and the presidents varied greatly in the ways they promote the Catholic faith in their own institutions. Presidents did not agree about the best and most practical means to promote the Catholic culture of their sector of American higher education, and many were at a loss about where to begin such a process.

Data indicated that many lay presidents genuinely struggle with their own lack of clarity about the Catholic intellectual tradition. They were also unsure about the degree to which they can assert moral and religious leadership over other lay professionals at their institutions. They worried about how much explicit focus on religion the market will bear, now that the true market for Catholic higher education is broader than just Catholics. They were also unclear about the particular ways Catholicism might be instilled when Catholicism itself is divided ideologically. The profile that emerged from the first phase of the study indicated that presidents at Catholic colleges and universities increasingly resemble their peers in non-Catholic institutions, and in so doing, it raised questions about their claims that Catholic colleges and universities are truly distinctive from the rest of American higher education.

This leadership profile provided valuable information, and it pointed to issues of Catholic identity, culture, and leadership as areas that needed further exploration. The phase 1 questionnaire was ineffective, however, in terms of eliciting responses about these issues that had depth, breadth, and clarity. An opportunity to question and probe respondents seemed the best approach to getting richer responses from administrators, and that realization determined the format of the second phase of the project as an interview-based study.

Site Selection

There are about 220 Catholic colleges and universities in the United States. Like the rest of American higher education, institutional diversity is a hallmark of this sector. The broadly representative sample of institutions that comprised the thirty-three sites for the study included colleges and universities among all Carnegie Classifications,[12] with a balance among institutions founded by laypersons, dioceses, and men and women's religious congregations. The latter category was comprised of a broad array of sponsoring religious orders. Sites were chosen in all geographic regions and included institutions in cities large and small, rural areas, and suburban locations. Roughly equal numbers of institutions with lay presidents and religious presidents, including both men and women, were chosen in each category.[13]

Administrators who had responsibility for shaping the religious culture of students in both the curricular and extracurricular sectors of the collegiate life were the subjects of the study. At most sites, four administrators were interviewed.[14] This group included the president, the senior academic officer, the senior student life officer, and the executive vice-president or another officer chosen by the president. The fourth slot ended up being filled by people from a number of different administrative posts that included the senior officers in charge of campus ministry, communications, finance, and admissions, as well as a number of executive vice-presidents.[15]

Protocol

Research teams of two interviewers made site visits at the colleges and universities between January and May of 2002.[16] The teams spent time prior to their arrival at the sites researching both the colleges and universities and their founding religious congregations. Different interview teams had different patterns once on site, but they all spent time in places where students gathered, visiting the chapel, and chatting with faculty, staff, and students they met walking around and during meals. These forays outside administrative offices were not systematically designed to gather specific information, but were rather opportunities to encounter some aspects of the institutional culture at each site.

The interview conversations were designed to last approximately one hour and were structured around the following five questions.

1. Imagine that you have been asked to speak at a policy institute at the Harvard Graduate School of Education about the enterprise of Catholic higher education in the United States. It is your job to say what this sector will look like in ten years, how it is unique within American higher education, and why it is essential that it continues to thrive. What will you tell them?

2. Imagine that after you retire, your institution is going to create an award to honor your contribution to the enhancing of its Catholic character and mission. What are the specific things you have done they would be honoring?

3. Most things in life are both a blessing and curse, and leadership in the unique area of Catholic character, culture, and mission is surely no different. Sometimes we have moments when things come together and are clear and coherent and we fully understand what we are about and why it is important—the blessing part. Could you describe a time when you most fully appreciated the blessing part of

your work here? Likewise, our experiences can be very difficult—the curse part. Can you describe a time when you felt most discouraged, pessimistic, or conflicted about leadership in the area of Catholic character, culture, and mission?

4. Imagine that you get to pick the next president of a Catholic institution similar to yours, but located in a different city. What two or three things would you look for among candidates to assure the new president would be qualified to meet this challenge?

5. The higher education of Catholics takes place across the landscape of American higher education. Catholic colleges and universities have a significant role to play in educating Catholics. Increasingly the Catholic tradition is being presented and engaged on non-Catholic campuses across the United States, as well. Catholic studies institutes, scholarly research and course offerings, creative and engaging campus ministry programs, and a variety of other initiatives are ways non-Catholic institutions make their mark. Over 80 percent of all Catholics who receive higher education do so at these non-Catholic institutions. Now, imagine that you have been granted an interview with a foundation that is committed to investing $500 million in higher education. The foundation wants this gift to have a significant impact on the education of Catholics for the twenty-first century. How would you convince this foundation that the most effective way to invest the money is in Catholic colleges and universities, not in programs at secular institutions?

Assumptions

Every knowledgeable researcher or research team makes certain methodological assumptions on the basis of what they already know about the topic being studied or where they choose to position themselves in relation to that topic as they begin the study. The six methodological assumptions that informed the starting point of this study are.

1. Almost all Catholic institutions are currently examining ways to be more "Catholic."[17]
2. Each of the participating Catholic institutions was striving to serve the Catholic Church and prepare Catholic students to be mature believers and good citizens.
3. Catholic colleges and universities are not the only places attending to Catholic students. Non-Catholic colleges and universities have Newman centers or other types of Catholic centers. They also strive, perhaps in a more limited way, to prepare the students who come regularly to them to be mature Catholics and good citizens.
4. The responses of any individual administrator are objective, despite the possibility of slight or substantial "spin."[18]

5. Prior to the 1970s and 1980s, Catholic colleges and universities succeeded as unambiguously Catholic institutions. Beginning in the late 1960s, and for a variety of reasons, the colleges and universities had to make large adjustments. While they are still fulfilling their mission with respect to the Catholic Church, that mission may have shifted.

6. One factor contributing to the success of Catholic institutions until the 1970s was the ability to develop a coherent, consistent culture that helped mold and confirm the religious aspirations of their students.

A seventh and last assumption emerged as the research team read the interview reports, exchanged perceptions with one another, and began to recognize an interesting trend in the responses of nonpresidential administrators. The assumption is: Many senior administrators have little knowledge of the Catholic culture in institutions other than their own and are therefore unable to locate themselves within the broader Catholic culture of higher education. They are eager, however, to see exactly where they fit in this landscape, and to become more knowledgeable, not only about religious culture at other Catholic institutions but also about the views of their colleagues at these institutions. After responding to a given question, a significant group of administrators frequently asked, "Was that about right?" or "Did I give a reasonable answer?" Initially we considered it merely a curiosity, but the pattern kept reappearing in interviews. Also, at the conclusion of interviews, many administrators wanted to know when "the book" would appear so they could compare their views with those of senior administrators at other Catholic universities. Gradually it became clear to us that many senior administrators do not know how to situate themselves in the Catholic culture of higher education. Although they may know other administrators at Catholic institutions, they do not know enough about the various Catholic approaches in higher education to determine where they or their own institutions fit in this universe. Put another way, senior administrators had surprisingly little in-depth "insider" knowledge about the Catholic sector in American higher education.[19]

Organization of the Book

This book is organized into three distinct parts. The first part establishes the analytical framework for appreciating, describing, and exploring the major themes that emerged in the study. As we reflected on the comments of senior administrators, it became apparent that their points would receive the nuance they deserve only if they were articulated using concepts they frequently employed as they passed on to other things.

Many senior administrators used the term "culture" to make their points. In addition, even more were quick to situate their Catholic institution in comparison with another local institution. They would say, "Well, we are not like university X or Y." Consistent with what we said previously, if the comparison was with a Catholic institution, in practically all cases it was confined to issues of size, academic quality, programs, or facilities, not religious emphasis. They made this point not by way of apology but simply to explain who they are. Chapter 2 examines what culture is, identifies its components, and identifies two necessary conditions for a culture to prosper among competing cultures. Chapter 3 takes seriously the diversity among Catholic colleges and universities and identifies four Catholic models, that is, four ways for institutions to be truly Catholic colleges or universities.

Part II uses the data to critically evaluate the perspectives offered by the administrators. Chapter 4 examines the academic environment, and it is here that we review the prominence given to the Catholic intellectual tradition by senior administrators. This tradition is so rich and yet so vague in the minds of the administrators that we devoted most of chapter 5 to providing some detail to the Catholic intellectual tradition. We situate it historically and then explore how it appears in various modern academic disciplines. In chapter 6 we reflect on the candid comments by senior administrators about how students actually live on their campuses and whether that type of living is compatible with the Catholic intellectual tradition. Most parents fret about how their sons and daughters maneuver through the social realities of their college experience, and our findings suggest their anxiety is well founded. Perhaps the most visible Catholic activity on any Catholic campus is campus ministry and related religious activities, which is the focus of chapter 7. One clear assertion of administrators is that talking openly about the Catholic heritage and commitment of their institution and using this language in their literature is far more prevalent than it was in the recent past. Chapter 8 explores how detailed the language is and the types of measures senior administrators use to gauge whether their institutions are having a greater "Catholic impact" on their students.

The third part of the book draws conclusions we believe are warranted by the data. It also provides insight into the current opportunities for Catholic institutions, and offers practical ways to help students grow in their knowledge of Catholicism and, at least for Catholic students, their commitment to the faith as well. All of this is done using the interpretative framework that emerged from our interviews with senior administrators.

Cultural change is always a risky business, and not all attempts at adapting institutional culture are successful. Chapter 9 presents a cautionary tale about cultural change that highlights the inherent difficulties in the process. We analyze what, until about twenty years ago, was one of the biggest success stories in Catholic culture, namely, the achievements of Catholic institutions through the influence of religious congregations of women. In discussing what has happened in religious congregations of women since the Second Vatican Council, the chapter illuminates some of the strategic choices that can ultimately erode, rather than enhance, an organization's culture. This simultaneously exhilarating and depressing story yields three cautionary principles and ushers in a discussion about how Catholic colleges and universities should assess their current situation and move forward strategically.

Chapter 10 discusses the role of leadership in cultural change and provides practical approaches to assessing and enhancing Catholic institutional culture. Our story is basically one of competing cultures. In order to adjust to the constant challenges presented by more dominant cultures and survive, all cultures need a broad group of people who support their culture and another perhaps fairly small group that provides direction. For generations of Catholics, the sisters, brothers, and priests were the ones that gave direction to the culture. Chapter 11 explores who their modern equivalents are and what type of knowledge and commitment they need to successfully fulfill their role.

There is a goodly amount of theory in this book. It is included because it provides the foundation for appreciating the current religious cultural situation in Catholic colleges and universities and for understanding how best to respond to the cultural challenges these institutions face. If the discussion should at times appear excessively theoretical, we hope to compensate by concluding with specific and particular ways for institutions to be more Catholic and have a greater "Catholic impact." Catholic institutions are quite diverse. Even two institutions that identify themselves as adhering to the same approach to Catholic mission and culture can have very different traditions. We acknowledge this diversity by offering many ways we think could be effective to strengthen Catholic culture so that it can survive and thrive at Catholic colleges and universities, enabling them to even more successfully compete in the higher education marketplace.

2

Mission and Culture

An Essential Connection

There is no single way for a Catholic college or university to understand and actualize its Catholic mission. How *mission* is understood and implemented, however, will be greatly affected by the culture from which it emerges and the depth and breadth of the Catholic character of that culture. Culture is the medium from which organizational identity grows and mission flows. Effective management of the mission of a Catholic college or university requires attention to all the dimensions of Catholic culture.

Culture in general, and organizational culture in particular, results from the interaction of *actions* and *inheritance*. *Actions* are the present choices people within a culture make about activities—what to do and how to behave. *Inheritance* is the operative context for actions that resulted from previous choices made. To be sure, culture is significantly more complicated than actions and inheritance, and the complexity of the components of organizational culture will be explored more fully later in this chapter.

Actions and inheritance suggest the general dynamic features of culture, indicating the manner in which culture changes. Inheritance emphasizes that at any point in time a culture is given or fixed, at least for the moment. Actions suggest that culture is always liable to change or reinforcement. When cultural actions are consistent with cultural inheritance, the culture intensifies. Should the actions be tangential or directly contrary to the inheritance, inheritance is challenged. Significant changes in a culture require repeated actions consistent with a desired goal over a long period of time. The length of that time is determined by the strength of the inheritance—the stronger the inheritance, the longer it will take to change it.

The question of institutional Catholic identity has taken on greater urgency of late for a number of reasons. Heightened attention to the topic came in response to the promulgation of the Apostolic Constitution, *Ex Corde Ecclesiae*. While the most forceful discussions of *Ex Corde* have swirled around the topic of application of the General Norms, and more particularly the mandatum, the larger focus of the document brings the question of Catholic cultural identity to center stage. Pope John Paul II frequently emphasized the importance of Catholic culture, both for the life of the Church and for the Church in society in his writing. In this document the pontiff laid out a vision of authentic Catholic culture for the arena of higher education. Under the section entitled "Nature and Objectives" the pontiff suggested:

> it is evident that besides teaching, research and services common to
> all universities, a Catholic university, by institutional commitment,
> brings to its task the inspiration and light of the Christian message.
> In a Catholic university, therefore, Catholic ideals, attitudes and
> principles penetrate and inform university activity in accordance
> with the proper nature and autonomy of these activities. In a word,
> being both a university and Catholic, it must be both a community
> of scholars representing various branches of human knowledge, and
> an academic institution in which Catholicism is vitally present and
> operative.[1]

Among leaders in Catholic higher education, the pervasive Catholic culture of which Pope Paul II spoke has become a persistent concern. Increasingly over the last quarter century a number of developments, both internal and external to Catholic universities, has threatened the vibrancy of Catholic identity and culture. In his preface to the book *Enhancing Religious Identity: Best Practices from Catholic Campuses*, John Wilcox frames the problem.

> Concern about linkages between Church and academe is intensified
> by several . . . developments. Among these is the rapid decrease in
> the presence of founding religious orders and diocesan clergy in the
> classroom, on the campus, or in the boardroom. Furthermore, the
> high cost of private higher education, competition for a diverse stu-
> dent body, and the imperative of educational excellence, lead Catho-
> lic higher education today to be more competitive with the other pri-
> vate colleges and universities and the lower-costing public schools.
> As an unintended consequence, Catholic institutions may emulate
> secular standards in hiring and scholarship without regard to the re-
> ligious vision intrinsic to their identity. Retention of a critical mass
> of administrators and faculty committed to maintenance and en-
> hancement of Catholic identity has thus become another dimension
> of the problem.
>   The admission of a high proportion of Catholic students who
> are unchurched or theologically ignorant of their own faith as well
> as many non-Catholics has also made attention to religious identity

an imperative. Most undergraduate students in American Catholic colleges and universities are still Catholic, but it is questionable how long this preponderance will last. Furthermore the depth of the religious commitment of the Catholic students who choose these institutions is of great concern.[2]

Organizational Culture

Culture deepens or changes as participants act—either in ways that conform to the inherited culture or in ways that effectively modify the inheritance. The actions themselves are decisive, but it is helpful to identify how the actions are motivated, how they are connected, and by whom they are undertaken.

Actions are influenced by three separate but interrelated components—*content, symbols,* and *actors. Cultural content*—attitudes, beliefs, values, and norms—motivate and guide actions people take within a culture. *Symbols*—including symbolic acts and narratives and stories, as well as beautiful images and rituals that make present components of the tradition—are the connective tissue and graphic presentation of the culture to itself and its members. Both the content and symbols provide the motivation for action.

The third component of culture is the *actors*. Because it is so obvious that people sustain culture and because people are the ones with the beliefs, attitudes, images in their minds, ritual practices, and stories, it may appear redundant to highlight the people as a third element in our analysis of culture. The types of people who act within a culture, however, are very important. Every vibrant culture includes two types of people—those who lead by undertaking changes and those who sustain the culture by their regular activities. The actions of both sets of actors are motivated and driven by the same cultural content and symbols.

Cultural change, however, is associated with *cultural catalysts* who, as the sociologist Robert Wuthnow tells us, are "actors who have special competencies" to lead and spark changes within a culture.[3] Perhaps because they have more knowledge or greater insight or simply more moxie, these leaders are the catalysts for change. They are the ones who make adjustments to reinforce the culture in altered circumstances. They are also the group that promotes the new activities that lead the culture in a different direction, which may or may not be consistent with its past.

Cultural stability, on the other hand, is dependent on a different group of actors, the *cultural citizens*. Cultural citizens are principled and high-minded actors, motivated and inspired by the beliefs, norms, stories, and rituals. These actors make almost daily decisions to do things in ways that reinforce the existing culture.

In Catholic colleges and universities, the Catholic cultural catalysts might include a significant dean, the president, a key department chair, an influential member of the religious order that sponsors the institution, or a dynamic and persuasive faculty member. Cultural citizens would be faculty members, staff, students and others who reinforce Catholic culture through their own practice of the faith or by ongoing acceptance and support of their institution's religious culture in all its dimensions.

The three components of culture have different functions within organizations. *Content* is the bedrock of culture. It defines and differentiates cultural boundaries and establishes organizational constraints. It comprises the body of what new members of the organization are taught "as the correct way to perceive, think and feel."[4] This content drives the patterns of behavior that render culture perceptible.[5] *Symbols* remind, reinforce, and refresh the content of culture by sharing cultural history, exploring cultural ideals, beckoning the community beyond its history and present circumstances to the arena of heroic possibility. Symbols tell the cultural story, linking together the different strains of a culture, highlighting the beauty of the tradition, and reinforcing an overall commitment to all its components. A culture's *actors* implement and orchestrate the interplay of all cultural components. They are the people who allocate and apply the resources necessary to secure cultural transmission and, in the case of some iconic individuals, provide a living witness of cultural coherence and vitality.

Cultural Content

Beliefs, shared assumptions, values, and norms are the building blocks of culture. These elements do not exist, however, as discrete entities that can be analyzed and explored independent of the patterns and relationships existing among all cultural components. In organizations these elements come together in what Gerard Egan refers to as the "thinking" side of culture that drives the "doing" side of culture—observable patterns of behavior.[6] Egan points out that beliefs and shared assumptions create the foundation of culture. The noble core concepts are often found in corporate mission statements, but there are also more "crass" or practical realities that determine how things really are. It is not hard to imagine a university whose official statements focus on academic excellence and admitting students on the basis of merit that at the same time admits a pool of less talented legacy students they are less likely to publicly trumpet. The "what you know" that drives admission brochures can sometimes be trumped by the "who you know" when it comes to actual admissions decisions.

The more noble beliefs of an organization are publicly stated, and the more ignoble, while obvious, are seldom touted. Cultural assumptions are not always shared by everyone in the organization but rather exist within organizational subcultures. From group to group within an organization, the shared assumptions can differ markedly or even be in direct conflict. While publicly and privately unacknowledged, these cultural assumptions—contrasting, conflicting, and covert—go a long way in shaping an institution's cultural context.

Values provide the criteria for decision-making in an organization. They "are the ideas the company or institution prizes and therefore acts on."[7] While ideally these values serve the goals of the organization, they can be in conflict. Once again, it is not difficult to imagine a financially fragile college seeking to educate underserved students yet having to price-out the same students in order to survive. There is no values formula, and each institution has to establish and nourish values that serve its mission.[8]

Norms are important, "because they sit on the edge of behavior."[9] They are the "immediate drivers of the patterns of behavior that constitute culture."[10] Norms define what is appropriate, inappropriate, accepted, and taboo in organizational behavior. The beliefs, shared assumptions, and values of the organization influence what is acceptable behavior within any given institution—in other words, what is rewarded, tolerated, and punished. Rewards and punishments emerge from beliefs and values, but they also provide a window on what an organization truly believes and values. The interplay of these components brings culture into view and shapes how an organization lives out its mission.

Content is the given of culture, but it is also subject to decay and forgetfulness. There is a vast array of cultural content in any organization, and the more complex the culture, the greater the array. If cultural content is clear and present in the forefront of the organization and in the minds of those who work there, the culture will be vibrant and affect the life, behavior, and tone of the organization. If, on the other hand, the content is too distant or vague in the minds of cultural citizens, the culture will gradually, but inevitably, slip into desuetude as the norms and practices of competing cultures become stronger.

The content of organizational culture exists within two realms, the espoused realm and the shadow realm. Espoused beliefs, values, and norms appear in public statements and represent the ideals, best intentions, or hopes of the organization. Unfortunately, as Egan points out, they are often "fanciful," only masking the shadow realm, where the real structures of culture operate and drive behavior. In the best of all possible worlds, clarity, consistency, and coherence reign, and the shadow culture serves as minimal distraction from accepted cultural attitudes, beliefs, and norms. More often than not, however, what lives and lurks in the cultural shadows is a far cry from what is publicly endorsed.[11] Neither espoused culture nor shadow culture holds a monopoly on behaviors and values that are good for the culture at large. When espoused culture operates against the best interests of the organization, shadow culture can be a helpful and useful cultural correction. On the other hand, shadow culture can exist on the margins in ways that erode cultural coherence and diminish organizational effectiveness. It also may be difficult to uncover because it is more covert and unspoken than clearly and openly identified.

Symbols

Alfred North Whitehead asserted that "symbolism is no mere idle fancy or corrupt degeneration: it is inherent in the very texture of human life."[12] Symbols, including rituals, images, narratives, and heroic exemplars are the imaginative means by which organizational cultures are transmitted and newcomers socialized. Symbols are not cultural accessories but, in fact, essential cultural components that express and transmit content.

Particular Symbols and Rituals

Symbols take a variety of forms. Language, symbolic acts or rituals, and some specific concrete items are open-ended and richly revelatory symbolic forms. They are not fanciful but realistic and characterize what group members hold in common or understand about themselves. Art and material artifacts, architecture, logos, publications, and the layout of physical space are common symbolic forms that communicate, shape, and transmit cultural understanding in any organization. At their best, symbols and rituals are beautiful, and they remind cultural citizens and cultural catalysts of the great beauty of their culture in the past. They can also dispose the same actors to recognize and experience cultural beauty in the present, while perhaps stirring them to create new images that capture cultural beauty for the future.

Rituals are expressive acts that dramatically communicate meaning and values.[13] In organizations, rituals both shape culture and reveal it. They proclaim the espoused meanings, beliefs, and values of an organization, and expose the lived contours of that culture as it is experienced in countless small symbolic acts. Some rituals are large public celebrations, and others are more akin to small practices, often repeated and seldom noticed. Whatever their form, their import cannot be denied. As Terrence Deal and Allan Kennedy insist,

> without expressive events, any culture will die. In the absence of ceremony or ritual, important values have no impact. Ceremonies are to the culture what the movie is to the script, the concert is to the score, or the dance is to values that are difficult to express in any other way.[14]

Some rituals, such as commencement exercises at colleges and universities, emerge from within the culture. Others are introduced by *cultural catalysts*. At times of change, it may be necessary to introduce, adapt, or modify rituals. In cultures that are coherent and function well, the practiced rituals, be they emergent or novel, are perceived not as imposed or new but as authentic, fitting, and appropriate.

Narrative and Storytelling

Stories are primary cultural vehicles that convey cultural content and meaning. They help us appropriate history, contextualize the present, and anticipate the future. Narratives also help one to interpret experience and one's place in it. Symbols crystallize and catalyze culture, and rituals dramatize it. Stories are the connective tissue of culture, giving it its depth, breadth, and texture. Stories also suggest why certain rituals are appropriate and apt. Narratives connect various components of culture and suggest why they play an important role in that particular culture. Even historic narratives and "war stories" reinforce the significance of certain ways of doing things. We cannot know ourselves outside of the stories and narratives that are part and parcel of the very interstices of our lives. Stories and narratives play an integral role in the cultural life of organizations. When first-year students arrive at college, for example, they are told stories about the university, how it has developed over time, and why certain customs continue to be observed. Faculty members regale one another with stories of colleagues and administrators. These stories can be about battles for power, wonderful accomplishments, or warmly humorous exchanges that illustrate the nitty-gritty of cultural encounters and survival. These stories are filled with cultural content and either reinforce the culture or challenge it.

Sagas and epic myths are rich narratives that speak to the history of an organization, pulling the thread of heroic accomplishment through the different epochs of corporate experience. These kinds of stories become templates for corporate aspiration, as well as records of an organization's glorious past. Not all organizational narrative is on the dramatic level of the saga. Some narratives are simple stories that facilitate recall, generate belief, and encourage commitment among members of an organization. Tales told at the water cooler also form part of an organization's narrative. While these tales are frequently reflections of shadow culture, at their best they serve as cautionary tales. They can remind others, particularly management, of how the organization previously lost its bearings by failing to remain faithful to some agreed-on way of proceeding. Narrative complaints can undercut culture, but at other times are simply comments on incongruities in the organization, and when they sound a much-needed warning, they represent a thoroughly positive aspect of organizational storytelling. Whether epic saga, basic story, or cautionary tale, narratives shape and reveal how an organization understands itself.[15]

Dramatic Exemplars

Within the symbolic realm of culture, characters larger than life are found. The lives and antics of heroes, antiheroes, and villains define the parameters of cultural virtue and vice. Each embodies distinct beliefs and values, and in the interplay among them, what is truly estimable and valuable within a culture, as well as utterly contemptible, comes to life. Heroes are cultural exemplars, those people whose lives courageously personify the most deeply held values and beliefs of a culture. Antiheroes are significant players in cultural history, filled with good intention but lacking extraordinary virtue. These individuals often have unique opportunities to act yet do not or cannot, remaining bland and mute on the cultural stage. Villains are as dramatically drawn as heroes but in the role of cultural enemies, not only lacking virtue but embodying treachery and posing a significant threat to all the culture holds dear.

Dramatic exemplars—people from the past who personify the culture in an extraordinary way—play an important role in organizations. Heroes are praised, and their stories serve as a constant reminder of what excellence in the culture really looks like. The former president of Notre Dame, Father Theodore Hesburgh, is a dramatic exemplar who looms large in Catholic higher education. A president in the study defined what Catholic institutions need in the future by harkening back to this dramatic exemplar.

> We have to shape our own future and we have to be doing it better.
> I'm not doing a good enough job, nor are my peers. Perhaps some
> champion will come along or a couple of champions will come
> along—Ted Hesburghs—who can intellectualize the academy for us
> and champion the future of Catholic higher education.

Dramatic exemplars can also be misused. Cultural catalysts can invoke historic figures authentically, but they can also manipulate their legacy by selectively telling their stories or relating their messages. Cultural catalysts can build on the stories of dramatic exemplars to support convincing arguments, or they can use the memory and power of the historical figure as camouflage for ill-conceived proposals. When college presidents claim to be boldly following in the footsteps of heroic predecessors as they unveil new initiatives that are simply lackluster or quite risky, they are trading on the cultural treasure of their institution and weakening the power of its dramatic exemplars.

Antiheroes represent the triumph of weakness rather than virtue within an organization. They are more pitied than reviled, their path seeming all too possible and looming at the edges of corporate consciousness—a constant reminder of what it means to be truly "inadequate." While most respondents to the study saw members of their boards of trustees in a positive light, one saw them as today's antiheroes who were squandering opportunities to act heroically on the part of the institution. "The most discouraging thing for me," this administrator said,

> has been the board of directors and their understanding of the mis-
> sion. This is a board that just doesn't have a strong sense of that.
> The board is going through a lot of changes right now and that
> might improve, but right now the board has a real hard time even
> getting their hands around the mission. . . . In the first place, the
> mission is what you sell. And that's what brings in money if you sell
> it right. And our board right now has no clue. Even our alumni on
> that board, in particular, have a hard time understanding that. They
> know what's happened to them and that's fine, but they sort of miss
> what the possibilities are.

Villains are a strong cultural force; standing in bold relief against heroic virtue, they serve to unite the organization around the threat they pose as cultural enemies of all the organization espouses. Villains may or may not posses the characteristics their opponents ascribe to them. A number of respondents saw villainy in the actions of archconservative groups in the Catholic Church and agreed with a president who said:

> My biggest discouragement is the right wing of the Catholic Church. I'm sick of them. In fact, sometimes, I tell myself it's time for me to retire when I start getting angry and defensive. These are the people who have their network out there and the way they just pick up little stuff that they don't even understand and then they attack us publicly. I'm sick of these people. In fact, I can't even be civil to them anymore. They're constantly assailing our commitment to our Catholic identity, and they're clueless about it. To them, Catholic identity is one issue or two issues, abortion, one or two other issues and that's all they can see. They're blind.

The Actors

Culture may seem like it is part of the atmosphere, but it is created and sustained by the action and interaction of human beings and cannot be transmitted without them. Some actors are *cultural citizens,* who live and process the culture. Others are *cultural catalysts,* who take on much more import in times of significant organizational change and also operate as cultural analysts. In the latter role, they indicate which things should be retained and which must be changed in order for the institution to be more faithful to its goals and heritage. Role models, knowledge experts, and heroic leaders are the *cultural catalysts* essential to any organization hoping to sustain, enhance, and transmit a vibrant culture. Without them, an organization's culture will surely dissipate and drift.

Role Models

Role models are the people in a culture who "walk the talk," in their day-to-day behavior, in formal and informal settings alike, operationalizing what an organization is really about. Their way of being in the organization is testament to what really matters, and by constant interaction with them, others begin to internalize the cultural attitudes and values they epitomize. Without role models, widely broadcast value claims and statements of purpose ring hollow, and in their seeming hypocrisy, they lay the groundwork for disillusionment and cultural erosion. Role models are the permeating agents of culture, and if a culture is going to be vibrant, they cannot be rare and must appear in different groups. People will not search out role models. If they are seldom seen, others who are more proximate will take their place, imparting beliefs, values, and norms of their own that could well be countercultural. In interviews, senior administrators frequently pointed with admiration and pride to various members of the sponsoring religious congregation as role models for Catholic academic culture. For one academic vice-president, the nuns epitomized much of what was attractive about her college.

> The presence of the Sisters is like a balm. They are part of why I took this job. They had me hooked when I interviewed. I thought, "I've come back to be near them and they are just wonderful. Their charism, their tradition of hospitality, their interest in social justice— those things are the very important things and I like being with them."

Knowledge Experts

Cultural acquisition requires investment; it is not just an absorption process.[16] The end product of this long-term investment is cultural proficiency: when a person becomes a knowledge expert. Organizations interested in sustaining, supporting, enhancing, and transmitting culture cannot do so unless they have knowledge experts. Knowledge experts share the knowledge content of culture and also give voice to it. A culture can neither exist for long nor be conveyed without a significant number of proficient knowledge experts. Until recently the main knowledge experts at Catholic universities were the members of religious orders. As they decline in numbers, replacements among laypersons will have to be found.

Heroic Leaders

In organizations, leadership and cultural development are intertwined; enhancement and transformation are mutually dependent.[17] Leaders are the gatekeepers of cultural change in an organization. If the content of culture has, over time, slipped into desuetude and the linking stories are no longer told and the organization's culture has become maladaptive, "it is ultimately the function of leadership to recognize and do something about the situation."[18] Heroic leaders know when cultural change is in order so the institution can remain true to its heritage and mission. Heroic leaders are also able to discern what needs to be retained and what changed in a process of effective cultural adaptation. Heroic leaders also have the courage to act when necessary, even in the face of strong resistance. And perhaps most important of all, heroic leaders, by definition, lead others to the realization of their stated goals.

Heroic leaders are premier, multifaceted *cultural catalysts*. They operate as cultural diagnosticians and analysts within the culture. They are knowledgeable experts and role models par excellence. These leaders invest time and energy in learning, understanding, and remembering cultural material, an investment that pays off in cultural proficiency. They demonstrate what is needed to perform well and encourage people, by word and example, to implement necessary cultural change in their daily routines.

Dramatic exemplars are people whose extraordinary ability to exemplify the best of the organization's culture has become the stuff of legend. Role models are the men and women in the present who most effectively embody the best of the culture and who inspire others to emulate them. Heroic leaders are those individuals who determine what a culture needs in order to be vibrant in the present and for the future and act decisively to actualize those needs. All of these cultural actors can be found in truly distinctive and vibrant organizational cultures.

Distinguishability and Inheritability

We present two minimum conditions necessary for the existence and continuance of organizational cultures and subcultures: *distinguishability* and *inheritability*. *Distinguishability*, defined as the readily apparent differences between a specific culture and other competing cultures, is a necessary condition for a vibrant culture. So, too, is *inheritability*, or the ways of acting in a specific culture that assure authentic cultural assimilation by new groups that enter the culture. Clearly, distinguishability and inheritability are intimately related. If an organization's culture cannot be distinguished by new actors joining the institution, there is no hope that these new actors will be formed or socialized by it. In fact, in an indistinguishable culture, it is more likely that the process will work in reverse, with the content and symbols of the culture eventually being influenced by these new actors.

Distinguishability and inheritability are primarily used to evaluate an overall culture. However, the concepts can also be applied to particular policy changes being considered. For example, a college may contemplate requiring all first-year students to take a one-credit seminar in rituals of the Catholic faith. One could debate the extent to which this makes the Catholic culture on campus more distinguishable, and one could debate whether future groups of students will be enthusiastic about or at least go along with this innovation. The more important question is whether the overall Catholic culture on campus is both distinguishable and inheritable.

Inheritability is a function of the dynamics of culture. Clifford Geertz points out that any existing culture is a system of inherited concepts expressed in symbolic forms through which actors communicate, perpetuate, and develop their knowledge and understanding about life.[19] The two-part process of inheritance includes authentic transmission by one cultural generation and cultural receptivity and adoption by the next generation. If the culture is not transmitted consistently and effectively, the next generation will be at a loss to adopt it. If the cultural transmission is inauthentic, a contiguous cultural inheritance will elude the next generation, no matter how receptive they are. Thus, for Catholic universities, the Catholic culture has to differ in important ways from the secular academic culture.

Cultural Intensity

All organizations have cultures, but the intensity of those cultures varies, and that variance, generally speaking, has an impact on the ability of an organization to live out its mission or achieve its stated goals. Although not everyone concurs, most organizational theorists agree with Terence Deal and Allan Kennedy that

> the future holds promise for strong culture companies. Strong cultures are not only able to respond to an environment, but they also adapt to diverse and changing circumstances. When times are tough, these companies can reach deeply into their shared values and beliefs for the truth and courage to see them through. When new challenges arise, they can adjust.[20]

In other words, strong or intense corporate cultures are an organizational asset.[21]

Distinguishability and inheritability are two necessary conditions for any vibrant and durable culture. Cultural intensity is a descriptor of organizational culture, albeit a descriptor that depends on the goals of the organization. The overall goals of an organization—how they are framed and the context in which they are implemented—dictate the appropriate level of cultural intensity for any organization. Each organization has to decide what level of cultural intensity is most appropriate for the successful accomplishment of its goals.

Cultures, no matter their vibrancy, may have to make significant adjustments over time. These adjustments are not always necessitated by a weakening of the culture or by deficiencies in it. Rather, other competing groups or competing cultures can change the cultural landscape by making adjustments that obscure cultural difference or limit cultural effectiveness. During such periods of transition, vibrant cultures will of necessity pale as they transition to new desired levels of cultural intensity. Vibrant cultures in transition paradoxically appear tepid, even though they are moving from one type of vibrancy to another, a cycle of adjustment prompted by things happening in the broader culture that includes the marketplace.

The concept of cultural intensity provides some useful insights, but distinguishability and inheritability offer a more robust way of understanding cultural vitality. Each concept encompasses cultural content, symbols, and actors. Each concept also presumes that fundamental decisions about goals and the means used to reach the goals are the driving factors behind any culture. Especially when examining competing cultures, such as secular and Catholic university culture, attention to context and goals is essential.

Catholic Culture

In the arena of Catholic higher education, the issue of organizational culture has great currency, particularly as it pertains to Catholic culture. Books and articles abound that explore and analyze the dimensions of Catholic identity and culture within Catholic higher education and offer suggestions about "best practices" for sustaining and enhancing that culture.[22] Echoing much of what has been written in the literature, the 124 collegiate leaders interviewed for the ETL study also focused attention on organizational culture, particularly in its Catholic character. They were concerned about finding ways to enhance and support the Catholic culture of their own institutions and wondered about the vibrancy and durability of Catholic culture across the enterprise of Catholic higher education. Many of those most interested and involved in Catholic higher education believe a vibrant Catholic culture is an organizational asset for Catholic colleges and universities.[23] They also believe that without attention and careful management, culture will dissipate. These assertions and claims about Catholic culture and its import for this sector of American higher education are laudable and encouraging. To have any lasting value, however, this avowed interest and commitment must move beyond discussion and debate in the theoretical realm and into the arena of effective action and better management. If it fails to do so, the religious culture that Catholic colleges and universities cherish and champion will evaporate into the larger and more secular academic atmosphere in which these institutions exist.

Faith, belief, and discipleship within the Catholic Church are closely connected with, but not the same as, Catholic culture. Faith is a gift freely given by God. Belief is the articulated expression of faith, and discipleship is faith thought about and acted upon. Catholics everywhere, including Catholics who teach, administer, and serve at Catholic institutions of higher education, are called first and foremost to respond to God's gift of faith in belief and action and to follow Christ in the Church. But faith in Christ that inspires discipleship is a pure gift from God assisted and sustained by God's grace. Faith is God's gift and invitation, and human beings, with the help of grace, respond by believing and becoming disciples.

Catholic culture is a human creation. Since it is a way of life that is sustained and supported by a believing community, the human creation is touched and influenced by God, but through human actors. Catholic culture is comprised of the group of practices and behaviors, beliefs, and understandings that form the ever-deepening context that nourishes the community of believers and energizes their commitment to Christ through the Church. At its best, for those who are not yet Christians, Catholic culture provides some plausibility for belief in Christ. For Catholics who have been baptized in the faith, Catholic culture reinforces their beliefs and extends their comprehension and appreciation of the teachings of the Church.[24] In a study of Catholic universities that strive to form and educate students in their faith, Catholic culture is an obvious and appropriate focus of attention.

Distinctions among faith, belief, discipleship, and culture are important for understanding the practical importance of religious culture in sustaining a believing community.[25] They also inform the work of this book. Faith and belief in Christ and discipleship are of primary importance, but this relationship and response between God and believers takes place and is sustained within the context of Catholic culture. The more vibrant that culture, the more supportive it becomes of the community responding to God's gift. That is also the case at Catholic colleges and universities. The faith of Catholic students, their following of Christ, and their service in the Church precede Catholic culture in importance, most certainly. From an institutional point of view, however, Catholic universities pay close attention to Catholic culture on campus and beyond in order to enhance the educational and formational impact on their Catholic students.

Catholic culture and faith are related and interdependent. Catholic culture emerges and develops in response to faith and is animated by faith. Faith is nurtured, reinforced, and, at its best, deepened within the context of Catholic culture. This interdependence means that the distinguishability criterion involves faith as it is culturally manifested. Cultural distinguishability is perceived through the actions and practices that make it visible. Catholic cultural distinguishability is perceived through the "practice" of the faith. When practices connected to the essential functions of a university reflect or are closely related to important Catholic beliefs and occur with sufficient frequency, Catholic culture becomes distinguishable. Faith and practice of the faith play the pivotal roles in sustaining Catholic cultural distinguishability. If the practice is not associated with a significant belief of the Church, it may indeed be a very helpful support to the Catholic culture but not sufficient in itself to distinguish the culture. Having reflection rooms available in various buildings on campus distinguishes a spiritually or religiously sensitive culture, not a Catholic culture. Since these spaces are not clearly related to the Catholic faith, they cannot visibly distinguish Catholic culture. People can pray in such rooms or spaces, but they need not. While having the spaces may be worthwhile and helpful, they do not add to distinguishability.

To secure distinguishability at a Catholic university, proposed activities have to be significant in two senses. The activity must play a central role in the life of the university as university, and the activity must be related to a central activity of Catholics. Activities not central in one of these two senses may contribute to the Catholic culture, but be insufficient to establish distinguishability. For example, having Stations of the Cross in the Catholic church or a chapel on campus is related to the central mystery of redemption but is not related to a central activity of the university. Furthermore, if the chapel is frequented by only a small percentage of the Catholic population on campus or students rarely make the Stations of the Cross, the practice is not frequent enough to contribute to distinguishability. In this example, it is possible to substitute praying the rosary, attending Mass, taking courses on the Christian faith, or engaging in conversations about the Catholic faith with other students for the particular example of Stations of the Cross, and the analysis would be similar. Each practice has value, and some are central to the Catholic faith. But unless the activity is also central to the core activities of a university, the activity does not establish distinguishability, though a frequently performed activity may contribute to distinguishability.

The desired impact of religious culture at Catholic colleges and universities is not limited to Catholic students alone. Catholic universities strive to be inclusive, welcoming, and appreciative of students who do not embrace the Catholic faith. All students are received in the Catholic community, which shares its gifts and practices freely with them. Some participate to a greater extent in this community, and some are more profoundly shaped by it religious culture. The education of each student, however, takes place within a Catholic context that shapes his or her experience and life. By enhancing and strengthening Catholic culture, Catholic universities can prepare students to better understand and appreciate their faith and more fully act on it. This is a worthy, noble endeavor. In addition to being the focus of Catholic universities, it is the focus of this study.

Analyzing Culture at Catholic Colleges and Universities

In terms of Catholic colleges and universities, the concept of boundary points is useful. If the boundary points are clearly marked, then any part of the line inside those points can be occupied by institutions that have a Catholic identity and operate as recognizably American institutions of higher education. One boundary point represents rigid cultural intensity. At this point, the Catholic culture is so dominant that the institution is no longer a college or university. In other words, the level of Catholic culture is so dominant, fundamental, exogenous, holistic, and homogeneous in these institutions that it effectively overwhelms the cultural realities of American higher education. The opposing boundary point is Catholic cultural disappearance: the boundary a purported Catholic institution crosses when it abandons its Catholic character, disappearing entirely into the culture of secular academe. Between these boundary points of rigid stability and cultural disappearance lie various cultural points across the spectrum of cultural intensity.

These two boundary points are crystal clear and represent points of no return for any institution that calls itself a Catholic college or university. When an institution crosses beyond one of these points, it simply falls off the American Catholic collegiate map. If the institution becomes too overwhelmingly Catholic, it will no longer be a university. If, on the other hand, it becomes too academically secular, it will cease to be Catholic in any meaningful sense. Using these warning tracks allows colleges and universities themselves, not some arbitrary or externally applied set of criteria, to establish which institutions comprise the universe of culturally Catholic American higher education. The institutions that place themselves between these boundary points understand that their Catholic cultural can dissipate and that in most cases over the last forty years it has. All these institutions have found their cultures impacted by forces external to themselves. These institutions are interested in maintaining and, generally speaking, enhancing the Catholic culture they claim. A number of Catholic institutions seem to think their Catholic culture has become tepid and needs enriching to become a more flavorful brew. Others find their cultures so strong that they are palatable to only a rare few.

The boundary points delineate the area within which Catholic universities can operate, but the institutions alone choose where they operate. Their location within the viable cultural terrain depends in part on their market situation and the goals they set for themselves. The complex of factors leading to a decision about where to position themselves will be analyzed in the following chapter.[26] At this point, it is sufficient to note that Catholic institutions have reasons, which can be criticized, for locating themselves at some point "within the pale."

By analyzing Catholic collegiate culture in terms of distinguishability and inheritability with attention to context and goals, it is possible to understand that Catholic culture will look different, for instance, at an urban Catholic university that has a major research agenda, a huge endowment, and a multicultural and multireligious student body and faculty from the way it looks at a small, suburban, financially strapped liberal arts college that is overwhelmingly Catholic in both student body and faculty. Each one of these institutions can publicly claim a Catholic identity and seek to enhance the vibrancy of their Catholic culture. Each one can be involved in ways that support Catholic culture, and each can be a victim of culture-leaching activities that subvert their best hopes and intentions. This approach also makes it possible to engage more effectively in critical assessments about where exactly each and every institution stands and how it can best enhance its own Catholic culture. This approach also supports applying the same analysis within institutions whose departments will certainly show equal diversity in terms of cultural intensity.

Managing Catholic Culture

Cultural competition defines the milieu in which Catholic colleges and universities find themselves. The overall university culture is determined to a significant extent by the larger and more prestigious institutions in the United States. Competing with that culture—sometimes opposed to it and other times in creative tension with it—is the Catholic culture of Catholic universities. These Catholic cultures are in part determined by the cumulative impact of prevailing patterns at Catholic institutions, patterns determined to a large extent, once again, by the larger and more prestigious institutions. Strong as they are, however, these cultural forces within American higher education and American Catholic higher education do not entirely determine how a Catholic college or university will be Catholic. Each college or university has its own actions and its own inheritance. Part of the inheritance comes from the university culture at large, part from the broader Catholic culture in higher education, and part of it from the specific inheritance at the particular institution. By forethought, happenstance, or intuition, actions are undertaken at a particular university that set it on a path that may coincide with, but more likely will diverge somewhat from, the overall university culture as well as the broad Catholic culture.

Catholic culture as it finds expression in Catholic colleges and universities is comprised of an ensemble of components that are observable, tangible and, in most cases, manageable. Some of these are very positive, while others, though also observable, tangible, and manageable, leach away the very Catholic culture that the institutions claim to support and sustain.

Roman Catholicism is a religious tradition rich with mystery. But mystery can be inappropriately invoked. In the arena of Catholic culture, there is a pronounced tendency to resort to vague language redolent of mystery when discussing it. That tendency is evasive, elusive, and unhelpful. Comments such as "Culture is taught, not caught" or "There is something 'in the air,' a certain atmosphere, at a Catholic school, that our students can somehow inhale"[27] suggest culture exists through some mysterious alchemy that defies any systematic efforts at management.[28] That kind of thinking is unfortunate and can lead to managerial paralysis, poor planning, and an insufficiently strategic understanding of the relationship between Catholic culture and mission effectiveness, as well as a lack of accountability for how it fares. Prepared, committed and skilled leaders should be able to measure or, at the very least, accurately assess their institution's Catholic cultural depth and breadth, manage the components that both support and dissipate its vibrancy, and monitor the impact of their efforts. Failing to do so is tantamount to abandoning their responsibilities as cultural leaders.

If there is to be a future for Catholic culture in Catholic colleges and universities, those concerned and involved must be able to do three things. First, they must differentiate the elements that constitute a rich, coherent Catholic culture from those that dissipate it. Second, they must be adept at identifying new actions or strategies that will strengthen the Catholic culture. And third, they must be capable and willing to promote these new actions and strategies over a long period of time within their own institutions.

Cultural Change

Cultural change is difficult and often painful. The older the culture and the more entrenched, the more difficult change will be. Some organizational change is revolutionary or in response to crises, often involving significant pain. The kind of change that is under consideration in enhancing collegiate Catholic identity is certainly not revolutionary, but it is not entirely evolutionary either. Evolutionary change is "gentle, incremental, decentralized and over time produces a broad and lasting shift with less upheaval."[29] It requires careful preparation and serious planning and an implementation process structured more like a web than a straight line. To some extent the Catholic cultural adjustments being considered here do operate at this kinder, gentler, evolutionary pace, but that is by no means always the case.

Many Catholic colleges and universities, particularly the smaller institutions, face financial challenges that force adjustments. Senior leaders at these institutions do take Catholic culture into consideration in responding to these financial forces, but, with the exception of allocations for campus ministry or the theology department, financial decisions rarely entail systematic discussions of Catholic culture. Furthermore, these leaders make decisions year after year without having the luxury of knowing what impact they have on the institution's Catholic culture. Simply put, because of the pace of life in the collegiate sector, most colleges cannot fully evaluate the Catholic cultural impact of prior decisions before they are forced to act again. Collegiate change frequently happens in a rapid-fire and scattershot way that leaves leaders hoping, but not sure, that the cumulative effect of these changes is heading in the right direction.

Because the concept of inheritability deals with the dynamics of culture, it pertains directly in situations of cultural change. A culture has to be able to absorb and form new members entering it, while retaining the commitment of those presently within it and remaining faithful to the ancestors who came before. If cultural changes are to make sense, they must be authentic in terms of previous cultural inheritance, gain acceptance by the existing group, and be sufficiently persuasive and intuitive that subsequent generations of participants in the culture will accept and be shaped by them. Cultural changes that are inauthentic or not contiguous with what has been inherited will create a cultural disconnect that disrupts rather than modifies cultural inheritance. Proposed changes that are likely to be accepted by only the current group of actors in a culture are not inheritable and consequently will not yield a modified culture.

Inheritability is a serious cultural consideration before decisions are made and as part of any process to evaluate the effectiveness of change after policies and procedures have been in place for a number of years. In anticipating change at a Catholic college or university, leaders should be confident the contemplated actions or policy shifts will be positively received by the next generation of students and faculty and will result in activities that are consistent with the cultural inheritance to date or with the cultural guidelines of the Catholic Church. Similarly, when a change or policy made some years ago at a Catholic college or university is being evaluated, leaders need to determine whether it is still in practice in some form and whether its associated activities are consistent with the cultural guidelines of the Catholic Church, as well as the norms of higher education in the United States or the rest of the world.

In order to evaluate the inheritability of any cultural change or modification, it is necessary to have at least a general idea about how long it will take for new actions and activities to become truly generative. Actually determining what that time period is depends to a great extent on the type of organization involved. For a baseball team, for instance, the period of time might be as short as two or three seasons. After that it is probably not realistic to adhere to a successful strategy because it is too easily copied by competing teams. In a university, on the other hand, targeted cultural changes in undergraduate culture have to last at least five to eight years to assure that inheritability is fulfilled. In undergraduate life, a new wave of students arrives every year, and every fifth year the undergraduate cycle is complete and an entirely new group of students is present. Undergraduates influence and are influenced by other undergraduates. To be sure that any change has taken root, it has to be adopted by least two different cultural cohorts. This suggests that a five- to eight-year period is reasonable if the focus of the change is undergraduates. Since faculty retirements, resignations, and dismissals occur at a far slower rate, an even longer time frame will be necessary for determining inheritability as it impacts faculty.

An Applied Example

Organizations contemplating a cultural course correction must first get a sense of where they are culturally. They also need some idea of where they are going, that is, they need a useful set of coordinates, not a detailed map. At Catholic institutions, a careful assessment of Catholic cultural components—content, symbols, and actors, with particular attention to their covert or shadow side—is the best strategy for determining the general starting point. An example with various features of Catholic colleges will show how a Catholic college interacts with the larger culture and manages its own culture.

Consider the following realistic, but still imaginative, description of a Catholic college. The College of Saint Joan is a midsized Catholic college founded sixty years ago by nuns. There are presently only three nuns working at the college, and only one of them is a full-time faculty member. The congregation has a number of hospitals and other health-care ministries, and they are finding it increasingly difficult to supply the college with sisters who are prepared to serve effectively on the board of trustees.

Fifteen years ago, the trustees of the college approved coeducation. However, like many women's colleges that became coeducational, St. Joan's is still primarily serving women students. The college has a very small endowment and is largely tuition driven. The college is financially stable but just barely, and it worries about its financial future.

The disappearance of sisters on campus demanded that the college confront some clear realities. First, with the decline in contributed services over the years, the salary expenses related to faculty have steadily increased. Second, the faculty members hired over the last thirty years are clearly less knowledgeable about Catholic issues than the sisters whose ranks they filled. Finally, the college needs to increase the size of the student body in order to cover costs.

As a result of much consultation among faculty, administrators, and trustees (key members of these groups are the cultural catalysts), the college has decided to address the reality of its situation by placing an emphasis on recruiting students and by adopting curricular changes. In its enrollment effort, the college is choosing a new target—more students—many of whom will certainly not be Catholic. The college has adopted a broader approach to attracting students and is using a slogan—*Lead a connected life!*—to signal their new direction. This decision flows out of the culture as they currently experience it. The current culture is a product of the actions of the many cultural citizens, who are motivated and connected via beliefs, norms, stories, and rituals.

The curricular change, supported by the faculty, is designed to make connections and will be initiated in the next year. All new students will be required as either first-year students or sophomores to take a course about the Catholic tradition and the teachings of the Church. All other courses at the College of Saint Joan will make some connection with this one course to show how knowledge itself is connected and how living truthfully leads to the fulfilled life. The college understands it will take awhile for faculty to connect with the course on Catholicism. Taking that into consideration, they have established a plan to offer in-service workshops and seminars to 10 percent of the faculty per year to help them become familiar with the Catholic intellectual tradition. Once faculty members are reasonably facile with the tradition, they will need additional time to retool course offerings in ways that make the critical connections the curricular initiative is designed to highlight. In the best of all possible worlds, the curricular effort envisioned by the faculty and administration at the College of Saint Joan will take a minimum of ten years to become fully integrated.

In the complex process by which the primary decision was reached to introduce the "connected life" changes at the College of Saint Joan, a number of important contributory decisions were made. First, the community decided not only that it could not continue financially within the framework of its current culture but also that the college would not be faithful to its heritage and tradition if it did not find effective ways to reinforce its Catholic heritage. In effect, whether it was formally stated or not, the community recognized that various changes in the marketplace and in the Catholic culture had put the Catholic culture at the College of Saint Joan in an unsustainable position. In terms of our analysis, the community—or at least significant segments of the community—realized that their Catholic culture was headed in the direction of becoming indistinguishable from cultures at colleges or universities that did not claim to share in the Catholic culture. Perhaps without knowing exactly where they stood with respect to their own culture, the cultural catalysts of St. Joan's realized that they were losing their distinguishability.

A second contributory decision made by the cultural catalysts within the institution was that the changes linked to the "connected life" project would help redirect the institution and lead over time to a clearer delineation of Saint Joan as a Catholic institution. This evaluation was made even as the decision group acknowledged that more non-Catholic students would be necessary for the college to operate on a financially sound basis. Yet a third contributory decision was that both students and faculty would adjust reasonably well to the announced changes. How current students and faculty react is important. An equally important factor for the cultural catalysts is how future faculty and students will "receive" the changes introduced at this time. By announcing the "connected life" program, the decision-makers are saying that they are reasonably confident that the changes introduced now will be not just tolerated but accepted as very reasonable by the next generation or two of students and faculty. Thus, as far as the decision-making group could determine, the changes are inheritable.

Whether the response of the College of Saint Joan will be enough to revitalize its Catholic culture cannot be known at the time the changes are introduced. As the example suggests, the cultural catalysts believe that, at a minimum, these changes point the institution in the right direction. In the real world, the cultural catalysts will closely monitor changes of this type and try to gather evidence that the new culture that is emerging is one that is both distinguishable and inheritable.

It is noteworthy in this example that it took cultural catalysts several years either to note the need of change or to persuade the community of its necessity—a common occurrence in real world higher education. Many colleges and universities spend years culturally coasting, even while peripherally aware that dramatic changes are occurring or already have undercut their previous vibrant and durable culture.

Cultural Adjustment

The historical roots of Catholic colleges and universities and their espoused values are deeply Catholic. Catholic values are not, however, the only values that shape culture at Catholic colleges and universities. The imposed values of secular university culture also hold considerable sway at these institutions, shaping the landscape in which Catholic colleges and universities compete. Sometimes the two sets of values enrich each other, sometimes they are in tension, and sometimes they conflict. When the values conflict, Catholic institutions feel real and imagined pressure to adopt secular values that will, over time, lead to Catholic cultural drift. In attempting to arrest and remedy this cultural drift, Catholic colleges and universities need to reshape collegiate culture. In reality, this process, while essential and significant, is not a process of dramatic cultural change. Rather, the revitalizing of Catholic collegiate culture is a process that entails a series of continuous cultural adjustments focused on revivifying what has become more latent than apparent and attending to internal resistance, particularly among faculty, to certain aspects of Catholic culture as they understand it.

Preparation and planning, along with good management, can help assure that the cultural course correction at Catholic colleges and universities is accepted and sustained. Newly emerging and entrepreneurial organizations readily adapt to change and modification, much of which is spontaneously generated and operates at a fast pace. Because of their organizational maturity and complex nature, however, the internal culture of Catholic colleges and universities resists modifications and variations. This conceptual tendency necessitates a process of adjustment that is carefully considered and consciously managed.[30] The process also needs to be appropriately paced for each institution. That pace will depend in part on where a particular Catholic college or university is culturally and where it wants to be. It will also be affected by the speed and direction of cultural change in the broader secular academy.

Although cultures change slowly, culture adjustments happen fairly regularly. Because the substratum of culture is comprised of people inextricably connected to each other, no culture can exist in isolation or independent of other cultures. The bonds that connect people across cultures can be as personal and strong as those in a tightly knit community. They can also be as loose and impersonal as those of the internet and news media. Regardless of the nature or strength of these human bonds, they all serve as conduits for cultural exchange. In most situations, a dominant culture provides the framework in which other cultures operate. In the United States, there is a general and prevailing culture that establishes customs and expectations for most people across the nation. As is true of all prevailing cultures, America's national culture is both strong and extensive. There are many other cultures that operate under the umbrella of our national culture, but none is either as potent or thoroughly pervasive. For instance, a culture in a small rural town can be very strong, but it does not spill out beyond rather narrow geographic boundaries. The connective tissue that renders the umbrella culture of the United States so strong and extensive is provided by the well-developed media and entertainment sectors in the United States. The raison d'être of media is communication, and simply by engaging in that endeavor the media molds perspectives and expectations, regardless of any intent to impose standards. In other words, inculturation is simply an unavoidable byproduct of sophisticated and effective mass communication. To the extent that communicated perspectives and expectations are shared by people, the media reinforces them by offering more in a similar vein, with the hope of selling more media and entertainment services. The consequence is a strong culture propagated and reinforced by the media that impacts all Americans, as well as millions of people abroad.

Within a powerful overall American culture, various subcultures exist, and some thrive. There is a sports culture, an arts culture, a fashion culture, distinct education cultures at the primary, secondary, and tertiary level, a civic culture, a general religious culture, and so on. Catholic culture operates as one of a number of religious subcultures in the United States. Like many other American religious subcultures, Catholicism relates to a larger cultural community that extends beyond the boundaries of the United States. One important feature distinguishing Catholicism from other Christian religions is governance exercised over the Church by the pope. The primary role of the pope is to assure unity and the authentic transmission of the apostolic tradition that stretches back to Jesus and the apostles and contains the central doctrines and dogmas of the faith. Because Catholics follow the lead of Rome with respect to Catholic teaching, the Catholic culture in the United States has some essential bonds with the bishop of Rome, who teaches on behalf of the Church.

In this book, our claim is that Catholic universities in the United States share a particular and distinctive subculture. This culture has important connections to the dominant U.S. culture, to the culture of university life in the United States, to the Catholic Church in the United States, and to the Catholic Church worldwide. Like cells in a living organism, these cultures live side by side and interact. They also influence and are influenced by one another.

Continuity is a component of cultural inheritability, but its relative importance within cultures and subcultures varies. In some cultures, continuity with the past is not a significant concern. This is particularly true in the cultural milieu of fashion. With unwavering attention to what is "in" and "out," couture is defined more by what is au courant than what endures. Styles change radically from year to year, creating demand and fueling the next wave of creative design. On the other hand, there are cultures, such as educational cultures, that put a high premium on cultural continuity. Initiating annual changes in teaching methods or content creates confusion that undermines an optimal learning environment. The value of cultural continuity is prized even more in religious cultures, whose foundational writings and traditional beliefs define cultural understanding and the limits of cultural adaptation.

For universities and religions, cultural consistency counts, even though that is not the case in many other aspects of American culture. The requirements and proclivities of the various cultures in the United States create a complex and often difficult dynamic. As ideas, technologies, and tastes change, as immigrants continue to flow into the United States, both the overall American culture as well as the subcultures change. In the organic way that cultures interact, changes in the broader American society put pressure on Catholic universities, but the universities, because they are both universities and Catholic, have a twofold reason to respond to these pressures in ways that ensure cultural consistency over time.

With respect to Catholic culture, cultural consistency has two aspects: core and proximate. Core consistency requires that cultural change not tamper with the major doctrines of the faith. Rooted in Scripture, they are handed down from generation to generation within the Church, subject to the authority of the pope, in cooperation with bishops around the world. While the pope protects the integrity of Church doctrine through the exercise of his Petrine ministry, theologians and laypersons with information and skills in areas relevant to the faith support the teaching authority of the Catholic Church, or the magisterium as it is termed, in important ways. Theologians play a particularly important role in exploring the relation of doctrines to Scripture and to one another. They also explore whether it is appropriate to alter how a doctrine is expressed in the midst of changing cultural realities. Words and concepts exist within a cultural framework not completely controlled by the Catholic Church. As the framework changes, it may be important to modify the way the doctrine is expressed or explained in order to maintain its significance for the believing community. Theologians also play an important role in helping elucidate aspects of doctrines that arose primarily because of the cultural context and that are judged to be no longer significant in the modern culture. Core consistency within Catholic culture assures the authentic transmission of the faith over time.

Proximate consistency applies not only to Catholic culture but to all cultures in which people voluntarily participate, and it refers to dramatic changes that clash with current practice and threaten to disrupt cultural inheritability. Simply put, people will not accept cultural changes they perceive as too disconnected from their current experience. Some changes that might be met with great resistance, however, can ultimately be adopted without too much difficulty, as long as cultural citizens understand them and receive adequate preparation for accepting them. In Catholic culture, many things can change because they are not related to core continuity or essential to the "deposit of faith."[31] Whether or not changes in these elements are ultimately acceptable is another story that depends to a large extent on how the faithful are introduced to them. As noted earlier, in order for a cultural change process to be successful, it must be managed and people must be prepared to accept it. The liturgical changes introduced after Vatican II, for instance, were accompanied by a preparation process shaped by bishops, pastors, and theologians. Some parishes, however, were more successful than others in adopting the changes. When great care was given to the preparation process for change, resistance was minimized. When a pastor chose to resist the change himself or to just announce it was going to happen, resistance among parishioners intensified. For the most part, the Church went to great lengths to educate the people about why the changes were being introduced and how people could best appropriate them. With the benefit of hindsight, it is probably true that some of the changes could have been omitted or modified, but most were accepted by the faithful and are now considered part of the Catholic cultural norm.

Ideally, all changes introduced into Catholic culture are within the boundaries of core and proximate consistency. But, as a matter of fact, inauthentic elements do creep into Catholic culture because its cultural boundaries are porous. Both the hierarchy and the faithful are constituents of multiple cultures, and they are influenced and conditioned by other cultural loyalties. Because cultures are usually in the process of adjustment or subject to adjustment pressures, the cultural consistency criterion has to be interpreted with a realistic view of changes. A change might appear initially in a particular institution or group of institutions within the culture, only to be rejected later, because it did not satisfy either core or proximate consistency. As long as the change is present, especially if it is a dramatic change, it will suggest that the criterion of consistency is not satisfied. In fact, however, in time (perhaps a few decades), the change will either have been modified to bring it into conformity with the culture or it will have been rejected. Because the pope is so important to Catholics and symbolizes the Church's unity, people might think the pope generally rejects "inauthentic elements" that are contrary to the doctrine of the Church. The pope may indeed decide to speak out strongly against some development in the life of the Church. But, because Catholic culture exists in many different Catholic communities, it is equally likely that inauthentic elements or elements contrary to the faith will be challenged by other Catholic cultural catalysts whose heroic leadership will unleash a broader corrective that in time is fully endorsed by the magisterium. Catholics' embrace of anti-Semitism, racial slavery and discrimination, and the subjugation of women are examples of inauthentic cultural practices that were eventually seen as inconsistent with core cultural beliefs of Catholicism and in time were authoritatively disavowed.

The pope himself also lives in a culture, and he both initiates and experiences the impact of change. Pope John Paul II introduced many changes. Some of them were technological, like an impressive Vatican website. Others dealt with doctrine. Pope John Paul II, for example, highlighted the importance of human rights as no previous pope has done. This changed emphasis likely resulted from his own family life growing up, his studies, his experiences in a communist-controlled Poland, the writings of many Catholics and non-Catholics around the world, and from the many bishops or foreign leaders with whom he met. Cultural change happens, even to the pope.

Obstacles to Cultural Enhancement

Cultural course corrections need to be undertaken at Catholic colleges and universities if they hope to sustain a vibrant religious character. In order for that to happen, certain obstacles to the adjustment process must be overcome. Once an institution selects a culture—by intent, action, or inaction—there is a tendency to praise the virtues of its prevailing culture. This is understandable, since colleges want to attract students, and students want to go to a place where faculty, staff, and other students are enthusiastic about what the institution offers. Of course, the shadow tendency in these circumstances is to deride any cultural stance of other institutions which poses a danger to the Catholic enterprise as a whole. Both of these tendencies blind institutions to their own cultural weaknesses, creating an atmosphere of arrogance on the part of some institutions and defensiveness among others. Neither stance is conducive to the kind of honest appraisal necessary for cultural modification. In fact, these tendencies often create more energy around defending the status quo than moving things forward.

Some theorists believe evolutionary cultural change follows a linear path to a specific goal—lean, efficient, and seldom derailed.[32] Clifford Geertz offers a different perspective, noting: "Culture moves rather like an octopus—not all at once in a smoothly coordinated synergy of parts, a massive co-action of the whole, but by disjointed movements of this part, then that, and now the other which somehow cumulate to directional change."[33] The process Geertz describes offers useful warnings about approaches to enhancing Catholic identity that could be unproductive. High visibility, centralized initiatives introduced with much fanfare under banner headlines will not necessarily lead to movement in an orderly process to a predetermined goal. In fact, this approach will frequently derail. Often the harder the push, the greater the resistance it encounters. At Catholic colleges and universities, Catholic identity quests often create defensiveness and suspicion. People wonder immediately about threats to academic freedom, narrow parochialism, and litmus tests for determining fidelity. The desired "clamor to get on board" that such an effort is supposed to engender can easily be met with resentment and a profound lack of enthusiasm. This approach often sets back rather than advances the enhancement of Catholic culture.

A New Approach

Part of effectively managing the mission at Catholic colleges and universities is supporting, sustaining, and enhancing institutional Catholic culture. Approaches to cultural enhancement in recent years have often been stymied by a poor understanding of the content, symbols, and actors that, operating together, comprise culture. They also have been unaware of obstacles that polarize discussion and undermine effective action, and ineffective or one-dimensional approaches to organizational change. Any attempt to find a more productive approach to cultural enhancement will have to address all these areas of concern. In laying out a realistic process for managing the culture question at Catholic colleges and universities, our model will address all of these critical issues. Because we believe insistence on absolute clarity about where Catholic institutions are now and where they should be in the future is unhelpful and will lead nowhere, our approach will avoid those discussions and focus more fruitfully on how to move forward on the cultural front.

Catholic colleges and universities are a heterogeneous group of institutions both in terms of their mission and goals and the breadth and depth of their Catholic culture. Our approach seeks to provide a considered and eminently useful approach to Catholic cultural enhancement for this diverse group of institutions that attends to a variety of practical considerations. The next chapter names the diversity we observe in Catholic institutions of higher education. Then, in the subsequent chapters, we first describe the current spectrum of cultural intensity at Catholic universities, as seen through the eyes of senior leadership. We will also indicate in which direction along this spectrum Catholic institutions are already moving and which direction they might consider for the future. Because culture lives in the particulars—its content, symbols, and actors—we will indicate which of these should be attended to, being specific about how their present form either supports and enhances or undermines and dissipates Catholic culture. An organizational culture cannot be vibrant if it is not distinguishable and inheritable. Our approach will use these categories as ways to assess the Catholic cultural vitality or intensity of Catholic colleges and universities. Cultural intensity is not unrelated to the goals of the institution. We do not believe it possible for organizational culture to exist independent of institutional goals and purposes. In fact, to a large extent, the goals determine what range of cultural intensity is appropriate for a given institution. In addition, the results or lack of results influences the appropriate range of intensity for a given institution. Reasonable goals that have practically no impact on students suggest that new policies need to be introduced, and it is likely that such new policies will result in a deepening of culture.

This approach assumes that an ensemble process for enhancing Catholic institutional identity has the best chance of success. Hard-driving linear processes for change can be problematic in attempts to modify or enhance culture. That does not mean, however, that a more subtle approach based only on the interconnection of small initiatives and groups of individuals is sufficient for building a broad-based and sustainable shift in religious culture. Much can be accomplished at colleges and universities by instituting voluntary programs in which students and faculty participate. By themselves, however, these initiatives are not sufficient. A vibrant Catholic culture requires some things that will impact practically all people at the institution. Identifying initiatives and modifications that respect diversity yet promote Catholic identity is a challenge, but an unavoidable one. Without far-reaching Catholic cultural initiatives, Catholic colleges and universities will have Catholic subcultures, not Catholic cultures. Consequently, we will identify modifications with the potential for broad-based impact, as well as collections of more discrete activities and initiatives that can be woven together across departments and within institutions to strengthen the fabric of a college or university's Catholic culture.

The Catholic culture at Catholic colleges and universities is porous and bumps up against other cultures. The cultural constituents at Catholic institutions are also constituents of other cultures that shape and inspire them. In this dynamic environment, cultural adjustment of some kind is inevitable. Whether that adjustment erodes or contributes to Catholic cultural enhancement will depend on a number of things, not least of which is leadership. Catholic cultural catalysts must recognize other cultural influences and assess their impact on Catholic culture. They must also introduce cultural modifications intended to enhance Catholic culture. The changes they introduce will only succeed if they demonstrate core consistency and proximate consistency. Inauthentic changes will wither over time. Changes that are sharply divergent from current practice and for which cultural citizens are not adequately prepared will be rejected. In both cases, such ill-conceived cultural adaptation will prove uninheritable. If change in the Catholic culture must take into account the octopus-like tentacles of Catholic interaction with other cultures, purposeful movement forward requires a combination of flexibility and firmness with respect to the direction in which one moves. Each Catholic university needs firm goals, linked to the broader Catholic culture, but cultural forward movement is likely to occur only if leadership displays dexterity in adjusting strategies to reach the fixed goals.

The main task of this book is to explore where Catholic colleges and universities understand themselves to be at this point in terms of Catholic culture and to evaluate in a sympathetic but critical manner the plans these institutions have to strengthen their religious cultures. In order to accomplish that task in a manner that does justice to the variety of Catholic colleges and universities, the next chapter identifies a number of different ways for institutions to be Catholic and develops those characteristics into formal models.

3

Models of Catholic Universities

In interviews with senior administrators, as well as in various books and articles on Catholic higher education, administrators and researchers note diversity as a hallmark of Catholic higher education. "Diversity" refers to a number of things—the variety of students served in Catholic colleges and universities, the array of cultures and material studied, and also the variety of approaches Catholic institutions use to pass on the Catholic heritage to their students. It is reasonable to expect if one institution has a predominantly Catholic student body while another has an undergraduate student body less than half of which is Catholic, its educational, religious, and social programs will differ.

Senior administrators made it clear they intended their institutions to be fully Catholic, but in ways tailored to their own particular circumstances. They also indicated their eagerness to find out how they were doing in this effort compared with other institutions.[1] The administrators certainly knew other Catholic institutions and were aware especially of how regionally proximate Catholic colleges or close competitors structured their programs. But for the most part, leaders did not know how competitors addressed the issue of Catholic identity. Frequently the interviewees voiced eagerness about the results of the study, which they hoped would help them more accurately locate where they stand in the landscape of Catholic higher education.

This chapter examines the different approaches Catholic colleges and universities take with respect to sharing the Catholic heritage. It also examines how the economics of higher education steers Catholic institutions toward one approach rather than another. Sketching what the market in Catholic higher education looks like with particular reference to Catholic identity will provide a context for analyzing the comments made by senior administrators and understanding some of their major challenges with respect to Catholic identity. The first part of the chapter examines basic economic requirements and assumptions. The remainder of the chapter uses the conceptual framework of culture from the previous chapter to position Catholic colleges and universities across a spectrum related to their Catholic identity.

Before discussing economic realities and assumptions, however, it is important to make a fundamental distinction between undergraduate education on the one hand and graduate programs, be they professional, business, or practical programs, on the other. Practically all Catholic institutions started as undergraduate institutions. Even as most Catholic colleges added graduate programs, practically all of them continued to focus on undergraduates as the group most intimately linked with their institutional identity. At various points this study addresses the issue of sharing the Catholic heritage with graduate and professional students, an important role for Catholic institutions. Nonetheless, since most Catholic institutions see undergraduate education as primary in terms of identity, legacy and tradition, this analysis will follow their lead and focus on this sector of the educational enterprise.[2]

For many Catholic colleges and universities, undergraduate education refers mainly to full-time traditional aged students. However, an increasing number of Catholic institutions have reached out to part-time students and students of a nontraditional age. It is important to acknowledge such institutional differences by structuring our models in a way that includes institutions that reach out to nontraditional students. While many institutions include nontraditional students, the undergraduate culture is formed primarily by the activities and processes that engage traditional undergraduate students. Thus, the focus of our analysis, unless otherwise noted, is traditional full-time undergraduate students.

The Catholic Mission and the Economics of Higher Education

Every college and university faces economic constraints. As is the case in almost any market, the most important economic constraint can be formulated generally as the ability to attract customers for a particular product at a given price. In the case of higher education, the product, the price, and the customer all have specific features that make the normal terms used in economic analysis more problematic than helpful. Each term, in fact, does not have a single referent, and for this reason using such terms without qualification can lead to confusion.

A "customer" is normally the person who uses or consumes the product. In higher education, the student would normally be seen as the customer. In the case of typical traditional-aged undergraduates, however, in many instances the "customer" includes a parent or parents. Parents make a substantial financial contribution to covering the costs charged to the student. Many also enjoy participating in the life of the university with or alongside their sons or daughters. Furthermore, most universities acknowledge parental interest, providing at least some services to the parents. Not only do most parents now participate in the orientation of students to the college, they are also invited back occasionally for special events, including sports events, social interactions with faculty and staff, and even some educational opportunities. Parents at many institutions are also encouraged to extend their involvement beyond their own children by joining parents' clubs and becoming active fundraisers for the institution.[3]

The "product" of Catholic higher education certainly includes the formal instruction that a student receives in the classroom, the informal interaction with faculty, students, and staff outside the classroom, the experience of residential living, the array of organized sports and student activities offered at the institution, the specifically religious events made available to students, various services provided—such as health services, employment services, and psychological counseling—and also the recognition that each student enjoys as a result of being associated with the particular institution.[4] Consequently, even if only the activities that the college or university offers to students are considered, the "product" is multifaceted and cannot be reduced to a single dimension, not even the Catholic dimension.

Not all institutions include the same array of activities and services as part of their educational experience. Simplistically, the more prestigious institutions offer a greater array of services and/or services of higher quality.[5] Although this is true, the emphasis on the quantity and quality of services offered masks a decision that each institution makes, either after formal engagement in a decision process or, more plausibly, by constant adjustment in practice. Any institution decides what type of education it wants to provide for its students and what type of student it wants to graduate. Because specifying the type of graduate desired is difficult among faculty with varying and sometimes conflicting views, institutions frequently choose to focus not on the outcome but rather on the process of the students' education, which allows ample room for differences of emphasis among different academic disciplines. The process of education should be driven by what the faculty and administration judge to be important for an educated and well-formed student in modern society. Some institutions demand greater academic achievement from their students, in part because they attract students who are more academically gifted. To be sure, this is a chicken-and-egg issue, but it gets resolved by the institution adjusting its educational process as it reviews its graduates. Over the long term, each institution chooses an educational process, and students come to that institution because of that process.

An education is more that the sum total of various activities offered at an institution. Many liberal arts institutions and practically all Catholic institutions claim the education they offer will impact a student for a lifetime. Using economic terminology, education, or more specifically Catholic education can therefore be classified as a capital good or an investment good that produces benefits years after the good has been purchased. Rather than speak of education as a capital good or an investment, which might suggest a predominantly capital or financial activity, it is more helpful to view Catholic education mainly as a process through which students, at times accompanied on campus by their parents, pass during a period of four or more years that yields benefits for all subsequent years.

The "price" of higher education includes both the payments that the student and/or parent makes to the institution providing the process of education, as well as the foregone income the student could have earned in gainful employment during the time spent in the process of education.[6] However, the "sticker price," or tuition, that a parent or student pays is usually less than the actual cost of providing the education to the student, even when the student is a "full-pay" or has been awarded need-based, athletic, or merit scholarship aid. In these cases, the amount of the cost not covered by the student or parental contribution is made up by the annual donations to the institution by alumni/ae and friends.[7]

The focus in this chapter is on the average or typical student (and his or her typical parents) at a type of Catholic institution. Consequently, although the distinction between the actual and sticker price is well understood, issues of discounting, merit, and need are set aside. As important as it is for all institutions to have a fair and well-constructed student enrollment strategy, as long as such strategies are deemed fair, they are unimportant for our analysis. Thus, reference is made simply to tuition, which for simplicity's sake refers to the annual amount that the average student actually pays to a particular institution for the process of becoming educated there.

How many services and of what quality can an institution offer? In order for a college or university to be financially viable, a sufficient number of students have to find the process of education attractive at the price set by the institution. Colleges or universities can use advertising, sports programs, and public relations to enhance their profile among prospective students in local, regional, and national pools. Whatever the impact of such programs, the process and price must be such that sufficient students both desire to attend the institution and can afford to do so. The number of students is sufficient if the revenues generated by their paying tuition, when combined with other revenues, are sufficient to cover the annual cost of providing the educational process to them and to generate a supplemental amount to cover special projects.[8]

All colleges or universities choose a tuition level and a process of education designed to attract a sufficient number of students. How this decision is influenced by the commitment to provide a Catholic process for students is the focus of what follows.

A Catholic college or university offers a Catholic process of education. As is the case for any institution, the Catholic process of education is determined by the type of student the institution wishes to graduate. But what the institution "wishes" is constrained by the economic reality just outlined. What the Catholic college offers in terms of Catholic process and price must be attractive and affordable to a sufficiently large group of students so that tuition revenues, when added to other regularly recurring revenues, are sufficient to cover the cost of providing the Catholic process of education. This criterion is a necessary condition, though not a sufficient one, to run a Catholic college or university. This necessary condition is encapsulated in the aphorism "No margin, no mission."[9] That is, unless an organization generates sufficient revenue to cover all costs and something extra (the margin) to invest in upgrading the institution for future students, the institution cannot be successful over the long run. So a necessary condition for a Catholic institution is to attract a sufficient number of students to the Catholic process so that the institute generates a financial margin that allows it to upgrade the institution each year.[10]

The fulfillment of the margin condition still permits an institution to choose a particular way to fulfill its Catholic mission. In principle, there are many "Catholic educational processes" that can be attractive and affordable to a sufficient number of students. Because there is more than one way of being Catholic, each educational institution has to decide what type of student it wants to attract and graduate. The college or university has to decide what type of Catholic (or Christian or generally educated person of Catholic sensitivity) one wants to produce so that she or he will have a beneficial impact on the Catholic Church and society at large and also achieve personal goals. Part of the Christian calling is to become a "saint of God." A Catholic institution should have processes that encourage the student to develop as a holy person who is grateful for legacies and insights from the past and can articulate important spiritual movements in his or her person. Many strategies exist to attain such lofty goals, and each Catholic college or university has either implicitly or explicitly chosen one overall strategy from the set of possible strategies that satisfy the criterion of generating a sufficient margin.

In earlier times, the choice of how an institution lived out its Catholic mission was determined in large part by the founding religious order or congregation.[11] Each group of sisters, priests, or brothers had a particular approach to education, a particular process in which they engaged the students. The orders had operated schools in other countries, and they had some idea of what could work in the new American setting. The particular educational process of a religious order or congregation became known, if only through the shorthand of the name of the religious order or congregation, and students and their parents chose accordingly. However, it is not accurate to single out the order as the main determinant of the Catholic process offered at a Catholic institution, since some religious orders ran multiple colleges or universities with noticeably different Catholic processes of education.[12] Distinct processes of Catholic education resulted because even orders had to make adjustments on the basis of a number of factors, including the region of the country in which they were operating or what they perceived to be the needs of the Catholic Church and their prospective students at that time. Some orders shifted their educational approach over time, but generally speaking an order's approach remained constant, until large changes were instituted beginning in the mid-1960s. It is remarkable that for many religious orders a decision made at a single point in time determined the future path of their educational institution for several decades to come.[13]

Four Goals of Catholic Colleges or Universities

Interviews with leaders at Catholic colleges and universities confirmed that Catholic institutions have different strategies and different goals. These goals emerge from the particular history of an institution or are determined because the institution, either thematically or implicitly, saw some need that the Catholic Church had and the institution chose to fulfill. Over time, the original goals and strategies have been modified, and the current Catholic mission in most institutions has a different hue than the one that prevailed during the initial founding phase of the institution. Each institution picks its own goal and strategy, but there are some common approaches. The goals formulated and considered in the discussion that follows are applicable to a group of institutions, and perhaps only approximately applicable to any particular institution. Nevertheless, they are useful because, in our judgment, they encompass what is to be found in Catholic colleges and universities in the United States, as they share the Catholic heritage and provide service to the Catholic Church and society.

We articulate four Catholic goals that seem to apply to a variety of Catholic colleges and universities. These goals are not set forth in any order of preference, as if one goal is in principle better for a Catholic institution to pursue than another. In addition to the specifically Catholic goals, every Catholic institution has the goal of transmitting information and cultivating critical thinking about topics pertinent to student's lives and our world. In Catholic universities, the overall goal with respect to students is to educate young people with respect to the Catholic faith. More particular goals are that students should be: informed, well-disposed and, in at least some cases, good, practicing Catholics; adept at thinking critically; prepared to act ethically; and open to new ways of seeing and understanding things in future years. In short, a Catholic college or university is a way of being a college or university.

In what follows, four goals are articulated that identify four ways of being a Catholic college or university. Identifying a goal is the first step in describing four models of being a Catholic institution of higher education. A set of strategies will be linked to the goals, and the goal and linked strategies together specify a particular way of being a Catholic college or university. As we note later, the number of ways of being Catholic is certainly greater than four, but these four models help us make sense of the various ways to pursue the Catholic mission in Catholic higher education.

Some Catholic colleges or universities seek to provide undergraduates with an education that prepares them to be well informed and significant leaders not only in society but also in the Catholic Church. This goal is pursued in a culture steeped in the Catholic tradition and in association with a community of faculty and fellow students who have similar goals. An institution that has selected this first goal, the *Catholic immersion* goal, tries to attract a large majority of students who are already committed Catholics or are open to becoming knowledgeable and dedicated Catholics, or students whose parents want it for them.[14] A second goal, the *Catholic persuasion* goal, seeks to give all students knowledge and appreciation of the Catholic tradition, regardless of whether they are Catholic themselves. This type of institution seeks, usually in a gentle fashion, to persuade. This goal assumes that the majority of students attracted to the institution are Catholic, even though many of these students are unfamiliar with basic teachings of the Catholic Church. A third goal, the *Catholic diaspora* goal, is directed to two things. First, ensuring that, in a region or situation in which Catholic students are a minority, all students become more open and accepting of religious beliefs. The second focus is on making sure that Catholic standards are observed in various activities in which students engage. This goal would seem most appealing to a religiously diverse population of students that includes only a small minority of Catholic students. A fourth goal, the *Catholic cohort* goal, seeks to influence the formation of two student groups. The first group consists of those who seek to advance in business, the professions, or public service, and the institution provides them with an appreciation for religious diversity. The second group is a smaller cohort of students who, through the formation they receive at the university, also pursue similar careers but have both the knowledge and commitment to actively advance broad segments of the Catholic tradition. Such an institution may attract a majority of Catholic students, but the primary goal is not to generate specific Catholic knowledge or commitment in most of the students. Rather, this type of institution attracts students of above-average academic talent, many of whom have good leadership skills. The goal is directed toward inculcating in these students a sympathetic response to a widely perceived Catholic agenda in society. It is focused at the same time on offering specific knowledge and skills to a group of well-informed and highly motivated Catholic students.

These goals are implicitly selected from a broader set of goals that a particular Catholic institution could theoretically set for itself. In fact, each institution has already made its choice. The choice may have been made a hundred years ago by the founding religious congregation or sponsor, or it may have evolved by tentative steps and strategies over a longer period of time. Some Catholic institutions currently find themselves in a strong situation where, at least theoretically, if they had not already chosen their goal, they could select any one of the four goals mentioned. Such institutions have an elevated profile, and a large number of students with sufficient family financial resources are attracted to these institutions. Presumably, such institutions could theoretically select any one of the four goals and at least for a period of time continue to attract sufficient students to satisfy the margin criterion.[15] Other institutions, however, find themselves so hemmed in by geography, history, and economic factors that only one goal is viable for them at this point in time.

Whatever the specific situation of a particular Catholic college or university, with respect to our models, we presume that Catholic colleges and universities in the United States, after shrewdly and carefully evaluating their market situation and after having made many adjustments to find their market niche, have selected one of the four goals as a primary goal. We assume that the institutions chose their model in light of financial realities and also because they truly desire to have their institutions make an important contribution to the overarching mission of the Catholic Church in modern society. In the framework of the model, we also presume that all Catholic institutions are well disposed toward the Catholic Church, that they wish to do as much as possible, given their circumstances, to help the Catholic Church thrive as an institution, and that they are working to help young people be better informed and committed Catholics.

Catholic educational reality is, of course, more complicated. Instead of four discrete goals that characterize the set of Catholic institutions, there are probably many more, and linked to each goal there can be a variety of strategies. Nonetheless, however many distinct models are needed to capture the diversity of Catholic higher education, the four goals we have briefly sketched offer a streamlined way to characterize a good number of actual Catholic colleges and universities. At the very least, these four models serve as orientation points for actual Catholic institutions of higher educations.

Distinguishability and Social Justice

In the previous chapter, distinguishability, inheritability, and coherence were singled out as important criteria for evaluating cultural change. Distinguishability means a culture has properties that make it distinctive from other cultures. At a particular Catholic college or university, that means its culture can be distinguished from the broader, but not necessarily dominant, culture in which it functions, the culture of higher education.[16] Catholic institutions compete with this larger set of institutions for students and must therefore offer processes and programs similar to nonsectarian institutions, but with identifiably Catholic components.[17] Analyzing service and justice programs at Catholic colleges and universities is particularly helpful in terms of understanding the demands of distinguishability at a Catholic college or university.

In our experience, all Catholic colleges and universities, no matter what their primary goals, emphasize the importance of social justice. Practically all colleges have extensive programs that encourage students to participate in activities that promote service and social justice. These include weekly volunteer activities; immersion trips during Christmas break, spring break, and even on weekends during the regular semester; service learning projects in which academic courses are linked to participation in projects in which students have firsthand experience working for justice; summer programs in which students travel to poor countries to lend assistance for a longer period of time, and so on. Some colleges have an extensive array of academic courses that treat issues of social justice or include some of these issues in the syllabus of topics covered in the course. Many faculty members undertake research projects because they are motivated by social justice. Professional schools encourage their students to commit time to working for the less fortunate. Nurses are encouraged to work in inner-city settings, aspiring engineers are given projects that help the disadvantaged or protect the environment, aspiring lawyers and educators are encouraged to give some of their time to the less fortunate.

All of this is impressive and clearly part of the Catholic heritage of service to others. Most Catholic colleges emphasize this focus in their literature. Students considering a particular Catholic college are informed of programs that invite students to engage in social justice issues in systematic ways. Alumni/ae magazines highlight outstanding commitments of current and past students to service and justice.

Social justice, in fact, stirs great interest not just in Catholic colleges and universities or in sectarian colleges and universities but in American universities across the spectrum. Most four-year colleges—be they public or private, sectarian or nonsectarian—have extensive programs emphasizing service and justice. Although the nonsectarian institutions do not relate individual service and justice projects to the teachings of the Catholic faith, as frequently happens in Catholic universities, the programs, both academic and nonacademic, are impressive for their breadth. Among students in the United States, service and justice programs appear to be as popular at nonsectarian institutions as they are at Catholic ones.[18]

The challenge with respect to our examination of the Catholic culture at colleges and universities is that the programs at the Catholic institutions, with the important exception of programs that link social justice specifically and in some depth to the Catholic faith, are very similar to social justice programs at nonsectarian institutions. Although a detailed comparative study is not available, the scope of the programs and the enthusiasm of faculty, students, and administrators appear to be very similar. Indeed, many nonsectarian institutions have programs that are more extensive than those at similarly sized Catholic institutions.

The important exception to this general observation is that many Catholic institutions specifically link their social justice programs in a substantial way to the teachings of the Catholic faith. They do this through the theology or religious studies department, campus ministry, or people in student affairs who are knowledgeable about the connection between the Catholic faith and social justice. For social justice at a Catholic institution to be the carrier of the Catholic intellectual tradition, courses that stress social justice have to have an impact on a large segment of the student body, and the course content must relate social justice to the other significant parts of the Catholic heritage, such as the New Testament, the doctrinal teachings of the Church, and its social teaching through papal encyclicals and other documents. A few Catholic institutions link social justice to the Catholic heritage in many academic sectors of the educational program.[19] If the link between social justice and Catholic teaching is strong in the academic and other sectors of the institution, this type of program is definitely distinguishable from social justice programs at secular institutions. In the absence of strong links, social justice programs do not create distinguishability for the Catholic culture at a college or university.

Another aspect of service and justice is providing access to students who would otherwise be unable to attend college. Traditionally, Catholic institutions have educated children of immigrants by providing them with an affordable education, but one within the Catholic tradition. Up until the latter part of the twentieth century, such education included a goodly number of courses in philosophy, Christian literature, and the Catholic faith. In our current age, the courses may differ, but most Catholic institutions are still motivated by a desire to welcome the poor and marginalized into their college or university community.

One important reality has changed, however, over the past fifty years. Now, even the very poor have reasonable access to college both through community colleges and through well-financed four-year state institutions. Catholic universities are no longer a last resort for higher education for most poor students. Nonetheless, many Catholic colleges have good reason to believe their campuses are more welcoming and supportive of students from poorer backgrounds and provide them with a better education than they would obtain at a state institution.[20] The distinguishability criterion requires a clear difference between what happens at state or other nonsectarian institutions and what happens at Catholic institutions. To the extent that the poor are incorporated into a distinct Catholic culture that helps educate and form such students in the Catholic tradition or in their own faith tradition, the distinguishability criterion is fulfilled with respect to at least one important activity of the institution. In sum, offering access to the poor is not a distinguishable criterion, but offering access to the poor and educating them in the Catholic tradition or in their own religious tradition is distinguishable.

Thus, social justice can be different in three ways at Catholic universities. First, academic courses that treat various aspects of social justice can relate the issues to the teachings and practices of the Catholic Church and show how types of social projects flow from faith commitments and understandings within the Catholic tradition.[21] Second, students who engage in service projects might do so with the encouragement and assistance of campus ministry that helps them relate these experiences to the Eucharist, private prayer, and God's action through individuals as well as institutions. Third, Catholic institutions may seek students from poor or marginalized families and offer them knowledge, training, and experience in living the Catholic faith or their own religious tradition.

In each approach, the Catholic component has to be clear and prominent in order for this activity to be distinguishable from what happens in nonsectarian colleges or universities. It has to be strong because nonsectarian institutions are engaged in these activities, though without the specific link to the Catholic tradition. The Catholic link makes the activities distinguishable. The Catholic aspect of the academic component must be especially pronounced if the academic aspect of social justice is the main way in which the college or university introduces its students to the Catholic heritage. Of course, a Catholic institution still performs something that is very laudable if it chooses to pursue the study of social justice somewhat separate from the Catholic faith. In the latter case, however, the activity of engaging in social justice is very similar to what occurs at nonsectarian institutions and may cease to be truly distinguishable.[22]

In our subsequent analysis, where we explore the Catholic tone and content of various sectors of Catholic universities, social justice is not treated as a separate distinguishable factor. Rather, to the extent that it is linked to Catholic faith and teachings, it is included in the academic sector or the other sectors we examine.

Inheritability and an Economic Margin

Distinguishability deals with cultural components, while inheritability focuses on how a culture is accepted or modified over time as new participants—faculty, students, and staff—join the university community. Inheritability means cultural change has to be acceptable in the present and viable for the future.[23] Cultural change is an enormous undertaking in any setting. Pursuing such change would make no sense unless there was reasonable assurance it would galvanize current students and faculty and also survive in the future, being accepted by subsequent groups of students and faculty.

In an economic analysis, inheritability cannot be analyzed fully without attending to the margin criterion. No college or university, no matter how wealthy it is or whether it is religious, secular, or public, has an endowment large enough to cover all the expenses for the various programs, activities, and research projects the institution would like to undertake. Every institution relies on annual tuition payments plus other fees—such as room and board—to finance its desired array of activities. The array of activities and the tuition level and fees have to be set appropriately so that each year the institution attracts the minimum number of students needed to avoid running a deficit, a pattern that must be replicated year after year. In this sense, the tuition level and the array of activities must be inheritable, that is, present students and their families must accept it and future students must be attracted to the package, which is affordable to their families, as well. Tuition, fees, and activities must be set at a level that ensures that students enroll in the future. Because colleges and universities have contingency funds, the margin criterion need not be met every single year. However, tuition, fees, and activities must be such that the institution generates at least a modest surplus over a period of three to five years. The exact time frame will depend on the size of the endowment and available contingency funds. This margin will then be used to build or refurbish existing facilities or programs or to introduce new ones.

The margin criterion is therefore an economic aspect of inheritability. Unless the margin criterion is fulfilled, the institution cannot sustain itself. After running up persistent debts in the short term, an institution will have to close its doors if it cannot generate at least good margins in subsequent years.

Linked to the margin criterion is programmatic appeal, which applies equally to all components of the educational program, including Catholic components. No program, no matter how excellent, will appeal to all students, and that is certainly the case when tuition and fees are charged. Because students have various backgrounds, as well as different hopes and expectations, any particular program appeals to some students but not to others. Colleges realize this and therefore try to offer as many particular programs as they can to enhance the breadth of student appeal.[24] Additional programs cost money, however, and in order to justify such programs, a sufficient number of students interested in each particular program or process offered must enroll. In order to justify extensive programmatic offerings, institutions must attract large numbers of students.

Catholic colleges and universities usually require some set of liberal arts courses, referred to as core courses. In many cases students are also encouraged to participate in projects promoting service and social justice, regardless of their majors. The educational philosophy of these Catholic institutions is rooted in the belief that all students should learn important things about various aspects of Western culture, as well as having some exposure to other cultures. In some Catholic colleges, "required courses" comprise almost half the courses taken during the undergraduate years. Many faculty and administrators believe in the long-term value of such core courses because this type of process generates education that is indeed valuable for a lifetime. But even dedicated faculty and administrators are cautious not to impose too many course requirements on the students, in large part because students can choose the college they attend from a broad array—from local private and public institutions, to regional institutions, to national institutions. If the Catholic program, including core courses, is perceived as too onerous, students will simply choose to go elsewhere. When that happens, the particular Catholic approach that relies on a large number of required courses will cease to be inheritable. In the rough-and-tumble economic environment that surrounds Catholic higher education, both faculty and administrators must be strategic and create programs that satisfy the margin criterion and are inheritable.

Educational Strategies of the Four Models

At this point, we do not yet have full models of the Catholic components of Catholic universities. Rather, we have lapidary descriptions of goals that have been used to suggest a model. The goals indicate the type of student the Catholic university would like to graduate. However, the goals are fairly general, and none of the four models contains enough specifics to determine whether the particular Catholic culture realized at an institution is distinguishable from the larger culture.

Any Catholic college or university has a variety of programs, approaches, and processes that are distinguishable from corresponding programs at nonsectarian universities and that make the Catholic culture distinguishable from the sectarian culture in higher education. Undergraduate life at universities has at least four distinguishable sectors: the academic program, residential living, student activities (including the sports program), and religious activities.

The activities in these four sectors, however, are molded primarily by faculty and administrators. It makes sense, therefore, to consider a fifth sector—personnel—as a potentially important differentiating point among Catholic colleges when compared with their nonsectarian counterparts.

In the previous chapter we analyzed the three major components of culture: the content, the symbols, and the actors. Academics, residential living, and student activities are all part of cultural content. Religious activities, because they also involve shared assumptions, beliefs, norms, and standards, are also to some extent part of cultural content. Religious activities motivate students who participate and tie together the various components of a Catholic education. Consequently, these activities also are rightly described as symbols. Faculty and administrators, the actors, are ideally either cultural catalysts or cultural citizens, depending on their role and position. The five sectors we now explore in detail cover the three basic components of culture, and it is primarily through these five sectors that specifically Catholic culture makes its presence felt.

In order to effectively analyze the spectrum of Catholic colleges and universities, we have already identified four models. So far we have only described the goals. Fuller models include a variety of strategies and activities for each of the five defining sectors of the education process—academic program, residential living, student activities, religious activities, and personnel that can help actualize the primary goal. The approach taken here with respect to each overall goal is minimalist, meaning the strategy listed under each sector applies to most institutions adhering to the given model. The strategies are also minimalist in the sense that they are the minimum necessary to satisfy the distinguishability criterion. With respect to the Catholic activities, Catholic colleges may do more, and we are interested in additional activities carried out at Catholic colleges. For now, however, we wish to understand what types of activities for each model are minimally necessary for the model to pass both the distinguishability and inheritability criteria.

For each of the four models, the minimal Catholic activities undertaken in the five sectors are presented. Once these strategies have been presented for each of the four models, we will examine the models and strategies to see whether indeed the distinguishability and inheritability criteria are fulfilled. Any particular institution adhering to any one of the four models may have many more particular practices and processes than those enunciated here. Our desire is to identify the "bare bones" minimum for each model. But "bare bones" means something fairly substantial, since we are looking for the minimum necessary for each type of Catholic institution to reach its stated goal and to satisfy the distinguishability and inheritability criteria. Due to this "minimal strategy," it may be that in a particular sector what we describe is very similar to what would be present in a nonsectarian culture of higher education. Nonetheless, we claim that for any of the four models, when all five sectors in a Catholic institution are jointly considered, the features listed hereafter are sufficient to ensure distinguishability.

Four Expanded Models of Catholic Colleges or Universities

In this section the four models are further specified by identifying educational strategies.[25] When one compares models, as we do in this section, the important differences are the stylized descriptions of the models, not the differences among actual universities that more or less closely approximate the models.

The assumption embedded in each of the models is that whatever model the college follows or attempts to follow, the institution as institution is faithful to the Catholic Church. The college or university develops programs and activities that are in accordance with Catholic teaching with the intent of educating Catholics who support Catholic teaching. In reality, some Catholic colleges or universities struggle to achieve this goal. At any given time, such universities may be making adjustments to better position themselves toward reaching their goal of sharing the Catholic heritage with their students, even as they adjust to new market realities that make the achievement of the goal more or less difficult. If an institution as institution has slipped from fidelity, we assume that cultural catalysts exist within the community who in collaboration introduce changes to regain it. The desire for the institution to be faithful to the Church and the willingness to take the steps to make it so are embedded within each of the four models.[26]

In order to be able to explore the Catholic culture in each of the four models, it is important to analyze the content and symbols, as well as the actions of cultural catalysts and citizens. We have selected five areas where the fundamental cultural components operate primarily: academics, residence life, student affairs, religious activities, and personnel, with particular attention in the last category to faculty and administrators. We fill out each of the four previously sketched models with descriptions of those activities across the five areas. These more detailed descriptions indicate what is minimally necessary for a school adhering to a particular model to satisfy the distinguishability criterion.

Catholic Immersion Universities

Some Catholic institutions emphasize being pervasively Catholic, the first goal outlined earlier. In this model, the goal is to attract committed Catholic students, to educate them more deeply about the Catholic tradition, and to both encourage and actively support their practice of the faith. Because the institution's strategy is to immerse its students in Catholic culture, this model is called the Catholic immersion model. A number of particular policies and practices across all five sectors of the educational program identify this model. In the academic sector, such institutions require students to take four or more courses in Catholic theology, philosophy, and also perhaps Catholic literature and/or the history of the Catholic Church. Since the academic sector is the core of any Catholic college or university, in the Catholic immersion model it is logically the most prominent sector in terms of distinguishing Catholic cultural characteristics.[27]

In residence life, the moral teaching of the Catholic Church, with its focus on relationships and responsibilities, is reviewed and reinforced. Students are expected to live in a manner that is consonant with Church teaching and leads them to living lives of character and virtue. In this type of university, there is an effective process for monitoring compliance and clear and appropriate consequences for students who violate the most important Catholic norms. In the student activities sector, the students and administration actively invite groups to campus who articulate Catholic social, moral, and religious commitment. Universities adhering to this model may allow speakers on campus who espouse views at variance with Catholic teaching, but the university makes sure that the Catholic position is explained in the same or a similar context. Such a university offers many opportunities for worship, including liturgical worship, particularly the Eucharist, and a variety of options for prayer that include affective devotional forms. Students are strongly encouraged to participate in the Mass at least once every week, if not daily. Administrators make sure religious activities receive a priority with respect to scheduling. Students are kept aware of all these spiritual experiences through frequent and prominent campus-wide announcements. Finally, in the personnel sector, an emphasis is placed on hiring committed, practicing, and knowledgeable Catholic faculty and administrators. Some non-Catholics may well be hired in these colleges, but there is a clear expectation that there is a strong cadre of Catholic faculty who are well informed about the Catholic tradition and that faculty members in general, whether Catholic or belonging to some other faith tradition, truly appreciate and actively support educating students in the Catholic tradition.

As described, *Catholic immersion universities*[28] have a clearly distinguishable Catholic culture. Since this type of institution intends to turn out students who can provide priestly, religious, and lay leadership in the Catholic Church, each of the five educational sectors is characterized by a strong Catholic culture.

Catholic Persuasion Universities

The second type of Catholic institutions intends to instill in all students, whether Catholic or not, a certain religious maturity in knowledge of the Catholic faith. If the students are Catholic, this effort will extend to their practice of the Catholic faith. Though limited in scope because the institution is expected to appeal to both Catholic and non-Catholic students, the academic sector has a clearly identifiable Catholic component. Because faith is comprised of content as well as attitude, all students are expected to take a course related to Catholic teachings.[29] Another theology course including treatment of some facets of the Catholic tradition is required, and students are either strongly encouraged or required to take one or more courses in philosophy. In residential life, students are educated about Catholic moral teachings and expected to live in a manner consonant with them. Programs or practices such as parietal hours or separate residential facilities for men and women are in place. These arrangements are designed to support students in living moral and virtuous lives and to increase the likelihood they will abide by the rules.[30] In addition, resident assistants and other supervisors in the residence halls are expected to address violations of the ethical rules in an appropriate and firm manner. The student activities sector does not sanction student groups advocating political or ethical positions at variance with official Catholic teaching. Occasionally students are permitted to extend campus invitations to speakers or groups who espouse positions contrary to Catholic teaching but only within a framework that allows the Church's position to be given similar prominence.[31] *Catholic persuasion universities* offer an impressive array of Catholic Masses and other liturgies and devotions. These institutions do not establish privileged time slots for these activities or cancel classes or activities to support them. However, faculty and administrative leaders encourage regular student participation in such activities by means of public statements and official publications. In terms of personnel, Catholic faculty and administrators are actively recruited and prominently engaged in the full educational program. There is also an identifiable group of faculty and administrators, well trained in the Catholic faith, who promote and nurture academic, social, and religious components of the Catholic culture.

Catholic Diaspora Universities

The goal of the third model is to orient students to the Catholic Church without requiring much knowledge or practice. These colleges are constrained, in terms of the Catholic dimension of their educational program, by the type of student body they can attract. The majority of students are non-Catholics who are open to the religious teachings of the Catholic faith. The leadership would be pleased to attract a greater number of Catholic students, but it is constrained in some way. In many instances, these colleges are operating in predominantly Protestant or unchurched areas of the country. Because they are small institutions without national reputations among students and/or parents, they draw from a regional, and primarily non-Catholic, student pool and must operate within that constraint. As a result, the proportion of Catholics in the undergraduate student body is less than 50 percent.

In the academic sphere, students are encouraged, but not required, to take a course on Catholic teachings. However, all students are expected to take a single course in Scripture as a work of theology and literature. Students living in residence halls conform to Catholic ethical teachings in a general way. The student handbook indicates what types of behavior are expected with respect to addictive substances and relational intimacies, but supervision and review of such activities is restrained. Only in flagrant cases do residence life staff compel compliance or impose penalties. In the student activities sector, the public profile of the institution is clearly Catholic. As with the first two models, students are not permitted to take positions or promote activities that are contrary to official Catholic teaching, nor are they permitted to invite groups to campus who take public positions at variance with official Catholic teaching. Catholic religious activities are offered on campus, but participation is modest. More generically nondenominational religious services in which administrators encourage all students to participate are more common.

These universities aim for religious sensitivity. One of the strongest aspects of their culture is that student activities and residential living conform to Catholic moral and religious teaching. This type of university has clear rules and guidelines to which all students are expected to adhere. Though their goal is to generate religiously sensitive graduates, students do not necessarily learn much about the content of the Catholic faith in courses. Policies at the university do, however, provide a strong orientation toward the Catholic faith. The shorthand title for this group is *Catholic diaspora universities*.[32]

The majority of faculty in Catholic diaspora universities are neither Catholic nor often well informed about Catholic issues. They are consequently not in a good position to help students develop greater understanding and insight, and this presents a challenge for these colleges. These institutions do, however, have a cohort of Catholic administrators and faculty who are clear about what is expected of Catholics, as well as what is unacceptable according to Catholic teaching and tradition. They also delineate how these different distinctions promote the Catholic culture at the institution. Because the group of knowledgeable and committed Catholic administrators and faculty is small, senior administrators are alert to replacing people in this group who leave the institution with people who have similar knowledge and commitment to the Catholic faith.

Catholic Cohort Universities

The goal of the fourth model of Catholic higher education is to graduate talented students with the potential to operate in important sectors of civil, business, and cultural society in the United States and in other countries from which some students come. *Catholic cohort universities* seek to attract academically talented students, whatever their religious background, who, upon graduation, will use their influence to promote Catholic viewpoints, although not always to advance Church positions encountering resistance in wider society. That is, such graduates are likely to promote official Catholic teaching that does not encounter stiff resistance among the population at large, but they may be reluctant to support official Catholic teaching when it requires them to push views accepted by only a small minority in society at large.[33]

At Catholic cohort universities, a substantial number of students are Catholic, but the focus of the institution is less on attracting a fixed percentage of Catholic students and more on attracting an eager and dedicated group of Catholic students who wish to deepen their knowledge of and commitment to the Catholic faith.

Unlike the other three collegiate models, this model has a clear dual objective. The first and broadest objective is to promote the practice and general knowledge of religion. Within an identifiable, usually small subgroup of Catholic students, however, these universities actively pursue a second objective: promoting a clear understanding and appreciation of the Catholic faith as well as its practice. The size of this subgroup is influenced by two activities of the university. First, it depends to a large extent on how proactive the institution is in attracting students who wish to develop their Catholic understanding and commitment. Second, the size of the subgroup is influenced by the package of programs the university offers undergraduates who are interested in advancing their Catholic faith. In this model, the institution is not passive with respect to students who want to advance in knowledge of and commitment to the Catholic tradition. Inheritability requires that the institution be alert to new ways to attract a sufficient number of students wishing to grow in these areas. It can secure such students by offering special programs and activities that are appealing to them.

Separating the two programmatic approaches at this point will help clarify the components of each and how, when combined, they operate within one institution. In the academic sector of the broader program, students are not required to take any course with an emphasis on Catholic teachings. Rather, students are expected to take a course or two that addresses the importance of religion in the history of various societies and its perduring influence, if not prominence, in modern society. In residential living, students are expected to be civil to one another, maintain a general studious atmosphere, and not violate any civil laws. However, only nominal attempts are made to encourage the type of intimacy in human relationships that is consonant with Catholic teaching.[34] This teaching is made available to students through written materials. Students are expected to abide by the teachings, rules, and norms, but they are not institutionally enforced. In the sector of student activities, student groups are expected to abide by official Catholic teaching. Students may invite people espousing contrary positions to official Catholic teaching, and administrators generally try to ensure that over time students who have an interest are exposed to both the Catholic and the non-Catholic position. Students are deemed sufficiently intellectually curious to determine what position they will take on issues in which there are views opposed to Catholic teaching. In the religious sector, Catholic practice is favored, but other religious traditions also receive institutional support and have representatives within campus ministry or in similar settings. Securing Catholic faculty is deemed important only for certain positions within theology, philosophy, or for special chairs or institutes that explore aspects of Catholic thought. Catholic administrators are valued, but there are no policies favoring administrators who are well-informed and committed, practicing Catholics.

The second programmatic approach focuses on students who are committed (or want to be committed) to the Catholic faith and who want to become well informed about the Catholic intellectual tradition and how the teachings of the Church relate to modern ethical and political issues. These institutions offer courses and resources that enable this kind of student to become well educated about the Catholic heritage in all its various aspects. For example, such students are given resources to bring people and groups to campus who are forceful defenders and proponents of the Catholic tradition. The focus of this particular programmatic initiative at Catholic cohort universities is on making resources available to interested students, not on directly influencing what happens in the residence halls or among faculty and administrators.

The Catholic cohort at the university is expected to be an effective leaven for all students in the university. That is, the committed group of Catholic students is expected to raise religious issues and questions in their regular classes with other students that help inform and sensitize the broader student body to Catholic teachings and sensitivities.

Implicit in all four of these models is the assumption that in the sectors of residence life and student activities, administrators make sure students do not engage in illegal activities. It is also presumed that authorities in each of the four types of institutions attempt to regulate the extent of alcohol consumption by students on campus and in the surrounding off-campus environment.

Using shorthand names has shortcomings. The names of the four models take one prominent aspect of each model and use that aspect as a mnemonic device. This does not suggest, however, the names identify exclusive characteristics of each model. For example, all the models use persuasion when speaking about the Catholic faith. However, the Catholic persuasion universities rely mainly on persuasion: they offer the material and hope most students will benefit from it. They try to give most of their Catholic students enough knowledge (and encourage sufficient practice) so that they are persuaded to take their faith seriously and practice it regularly. For this type of university, it is sufficient that the students know enough about the faith not to embarrass themselves or the institution by lack of knowledge. In fact, Catholic immersion universities, Catholic diaspora universities, and Catholic cohort universities all attempt to persuade students that Catholic teachings promote the full human person and are worthy of attention and belief. Thus, the names indicate an emphasis, but not an exclusive one.

In the area of leadership and governance, we assume that each type of institution has suitably Catholic leadership and governance. In other words, for the purposes of this study, we do not assume significant differences among the degree of commitment to the Catholic project by the senior leader and the trustees. Each of the models assumes the president is an informed, committed, and practicing Catholic.[35] Presidents set the tone and determine the general direction of the institutions in which they serve. They are also highly visible standard-bearers who lead the colleges and universities in their most important activities. In order to fulfill these roles in a Catholic institution, a president must be clearly perceived as enthusiastically committed to the Catholic tradition. That commitment cannot merely be to the Catholic faith tradition as an intellectual heritage. It must also extend to the practice of the faith, praising God by celebrating the life of Jesus, particularly in the sacraments and in the pursuit of the virtuous life. Being a figurehead simply does not suffice. Similarly, we assume that the trustees are sufficiently Catholic in their commitment and perspective that they can provide policy guidelines for the president that ensure the institution satisfies the criteria of distinguishability and inheritability with respect to the Catholic mission.

The four models are descriptive of how Catholic institutions create Catholic culture at their institution. Sufficient details with respect to Catholic activities are provided to determine whether each model is distinguishable and inheritable when compared with nonsectarian counterparts. However, our approach does not imply that the Catholic strategies pursued in actual institutions are the most efficient strategies, in an economic sense, or the most effective strategies, where effectiveness relates to the needs of the Catholic Church. Because the market (in the strict economic sense) for Catholic education is not what economists call a perfectly competitive market, economic inefficiency may exist in some or all institutions. Also, because the way the Catholic Church expresses its "market demand" for services from Catholic colleges and universities is so diffuse, Catholic institutions may not use the most effective means or even moderately effective means to attain their stated ends. Some Catholic institutions may allow too much confusion about what constitutes the Catholic faith. Some institutions may seek their identity through their sponsoring religious congregation and may distance themselves from the institution and leadership of the Catholic Church. Institutions adhering to one of the models presented here may graduate students who are properly prepared for many of life's experiences but are not prepared or motivated to provide service to the Catholic Church. These types of institutional deficiencies are compatible with the models presented here. However, it is assumed that each type of Catholic institution has an adequate number of cultural catalysts with knowledge and commitment to the Catholic faith to correct deficiencies and improve the Catholic effectiveness of the university.

The starting point in this analysis is the way Catholic colleges and universities actually operate. Beyond this factual orientation, it is assumed that Catholic universities have good will and a readiness to make changes that produce "better results," where "better results" refers to a greater number of graduates who more closely conform to the goals set by each type of university. An underlying assumption behind each model is that Catholic institutions of higher education adhering to that model, by graduating students who have been formed by the Catholic culture at that institution, are producing at least some of what the Catholic Church is looking for in young graduates. Finally, it is important to note that nonsectarian universities also produce Catholic graduates, some of whom are also motivated and prepared to serve the Catholic Church. With respect to imbuing students with knowledge of the Catholic faith and helping form them in Catholic practice, there is true competition between Catholic and nonsectarian universities, as well as among Catholic universities themselves.

Some might wonder why the goals of some of the models are relatively modest with respect to the transmission of Catholic knowledge and practice. A partial answer is that any model that captures how actual Catholic universities function depicts an equilibrium process between supply and demand. The supply side of the equation stems from what a religiously oriented group (formerly these groups were exclusively religious congregations of men and women or diocesan clergy) is prepared to offer to young students. The demand side of the equation is determined by how strong the interest is on the part of students and parents in various types of Catholic education. Catholic universities can be assertive and offer very strong programs emphasizing the assimilation of the Catholic heritage, but in order for such programs to be inheritable, a sufficient number of Catholic and non-Catholic students (and parents) have to be attracted to the programs. If, to the distress of some Catholics, many institutions offer students only the highlights of the Catholic tradition, one part of the explanation is that market demand, which includes both students and parents, for a deeper immersion into the Catholic heritage has not made itself felt. An alternative explanation is that sponsoring groups have not found ways to make substantial Catholic immersion more appealing to prospective students.

Distinguishability and Inheritability

The previous section presented a general description of the five key sectors in each of the four general models of Catholic colleges and universities. Having articulated the models more fully, it is now possible to analyze them in relationship to the criteria of distinguishability and inheritability.

Distinguishability refers to the ability of students and other observers to see clear and significant differences between the Catholic culture that exists at a Catholic university and the more general academic and social culture existing at a nonsectarian college or university. In the absence of clear and significant differences, the outside observer will see a general nonsectarian culture that is as prominent at the Catholic institution as it is at nonsectarian institutions. In those circumstances, it is legitimate to have doubts about whether a Catholic culture that educates and forms students actually exists at the Catholic college or university.[36]

Related to distinguishability and in some tension with it is the criterion of inheritability. A culture that is clearly distinguishable may prove less inheritable than one that is less distinct. That would certainly be the case if future generations of students perceive what is being offered at Catholic institutions less favorably and in a different light from current students and consequently reject or shun those institutions with a clearly Catholic approach. Similarly, Catholic cultures that are barely distinguishable from their nonsectarian counterparts might have significantly more cachet with future generations of students, who are easily influenced by their peers at such institutions. If that is the case, these less distinct collegiate cultures would have considerable stability. The appeal of these less distinctive institutions could be precisely that their indistinguishable culture is so similar to that prevailing at nonsectarian institutions. It is certainly true that Catholic cultures at current Catholic colleges and universities have passed the inheritability criterion until the present. After all, they have survived. However, inheritability, like distinguishability, is an ongoing issue in any culture, Catholic or nonsectarian,[37] and, therefore, it, too, will be addressed for each of the four models. Inheritability is not completely malleable. In many instances, however, inheritability can be secured if the institution is willing to expend sufficient human and financial capital to persuade prospective students that the type of religiously based education offered at a particular college or university provides them with important advantages for life.

Before reviewing each of the four models to determine whether, as described, they fulfill the criteria of distinguishability and inheritability, it is important to examine what is being compared in the area of campus ministry when distinguishability is being examined. We earlier described what is required for an emphasis on social justice programs at Catholic institutions to be distinguishable from a similar emphasis at nonsectarian universities. A similar comparison is required for campus ministry, because many nonsectarian institutions have centers that are roughly comparable to campus ministry at Catholic institutions. Newman or Catholic Centers are longstanding institutions at many nonsectarian private and public universities. The Newman center[38] is the Catholic place on campus where Mass is regularly celebrated and where Catholics gather for other religious, educational, and social activities. Although Newman centers also conduct ancillary educational and social activities, the emphasis at these centers is on making available Catholic religious services to the Catholic undergraduate and graduate students attending a nonsectarian institution. Depending on the size of the student body, the array of religious services offered can be quite broad and very impressive. It might even happen in a few cases that the regularity with which Catholic students participate in the religious services at the Newman center is greater than prevailing patterns at some Catholic institutions. It is also possible that the frequency and percentage of students participating in the services at a Catholic institution and at a Newman center or its equivalent at a nonsectarian university are quite similar.[39] Thus, for each model, campus ministry at the Catholic institution will have to be examined in relation to Newman centers in general.

Because the level of services and frequency of participation might be similar at the nonsectarian institution, there might be grounds for claiming that the Catholic religious services sector at some nonsectarian institutions is approximately the same as that at some Catholic universities. If that is the case, the Catholic institutions would certainly not fulfill the distinguishability criterion in the sector of campus ministry. However, another role of religious services at a Catholic college or university is to express the faith convictions not simply of individuals but also of the institution. In most Catholic colleges or universities, Eucharistic services and other rites are used at commencements, convocations, moments of loss, or other important events. While such services would similarly be offered at Newman Centers on those kinds of occasions, they would not be an expression of the faith and orientation of the secular college or university. In order to inform the Catholic culture, religious events such as these should emphasize Catholic prayer and belief. Attempts at Catholic institutions to be very inclusive may dilute the culture, with the result that the liturgies at Catholic universities have approximately the same impact on the institution as those at Newman centers. Prominent Catholic liturgies have to express the Catholic character and convictions at the institution. The Newman center, even though it may occupy a central position on a nonsectarian campus, is not central to the life of the college or university in the way campus ministry is at any Catholic college. The issue of whether religious ministry on a Catholic campus is distinguishable from the Newman center at a nonsectarian institution is an important one that will be considered with each of the four models.[40]

In the remainder of this section, each model is probed in five areas—academics, residence life, student life, campus ministry, and personnel—for the extent to which it fulfills the distinguishability criteria. For each model, we also offer some observations about the inheritability criterion. Comments about inheritability, however, can only be surmises about what will or will not prove attractive to students during the next fifteen to twenty years. They are included more as cautionary notes than definitive predictions.

The *Catholic immersion university* is clearly distinct in substantive ways from the general nonsectarian culture of higher education. Academic courses focus on the content of the Catholic faith or tradition, or they frequently include Catholic topics. Residence life and student activities teach and support the Catholic moral tradition, which helps students determine not only who they should be but also what they should do. These activities do so through positive and challenging programs and through clear and unambiguous behavioral standards, while supporting students and granting them space to make mistakes. Faculty and administrators in this type of university call attention to clear failures to abide by university policies that support Catholic teaching. Campus ministry focuses on prayerful, aesthetic, and regular celebration of the Eucharist. Finally, the cultural catalysts at this type of institution are traditional, committed, and informed Catholics, and indeed most of the cultural citizens are also informed, committed Catholics.

In short, almost any single one of the five important sectors would be sufficient to distinguish the Catholic culture at this type of institution from the general culture of higher education. The only sector that conceivably could be comparable with the culture at a nonsectarian college or university is the area of religious practice or campus ministry. However, as mentioned earlier, activities at a Newman center do not officially express the orientation of the university as a whole. Because of the size of some Newman centers, they might offer a greater array of liturgies and other religious programs than does the typical Catholic immersion college or university. Nonetheless, in practically all cases, the percentage of students actively participating in liturgical functions is almost certainly greater at the typical Catholic immersion university than at a typical Newman center.

Catholic immersion universities have well-articulated programs to develop Catholics who are informed and committed, and the Catholic component is strongly emphasized in each of the five sectors. The goal of such institutions is to provide knowledgeable and committed leadership, not just to society but to the Catholic church as well. We conclude the Catholic culture in this model clearly passes the distinguishability criterion.

While Catholic culture at Catholic immersion universities is clearly distinguishable, its inheritability can be questioned. Future generations of students, faculty, or staff at such institutions may lose interest in very Catholic programs if society becomes increasingly secular or if the traditionalist movement in the Catholic Church wanes. Whether society, especially American society, is becoming increasingly secular is a point disputed by some scholars.[41] Even if there is a general drift toward secularization in public society, reactions by individual students and their parents will differ. A more secular society might have fewer public displays of religious belief, but the impact of public religion on personal commitment is uncertain. Despite increasing secularization, committed individuals might experience greater attraction to churches and religious organizations, or student interest in the Catholic intellectual tradition and heritage may wane. In the latter case, Catholic immersion universities, unless they make changes, might fail to attract a sufficient number of students to satisfy the margin criterion. To remain viable, this type of institution would then have to introduce changes that compensate for changes in the religious outlook of students who are thinking about attending Catholic immersion universities. They might also have to adjust for the amount of religious knowledge possessed by most students who enroll at the university. Alternatively, they may need to welcome Catholic approaches not as closely linked to traditionalist movements. Most universities only reluctantly change their core academic approach. However, even Catholic immersion universities, who would like to maintain their academic, religious, and cultural program as fixed stars in an increasingly secular constellation of higher education, might have to make significant changes to satisfy the inheritability criterion.[42]

The *Catholic persuasion model* has a Catholic presence in all five sectors. However, the Catholic emphasis in some sectors is fairly narrow and targeted. In our view, the distinguishability of the Catholic culture in the Catholic persuasion model relies on two features of the model: clear Catholic components in a few of the sectors and interaction among the personnel in the sectors, so that Catholic features get reinforced by cultural actors who are knowledgeable about and committed to the Catholic faith.

The fact that all students have to take two courses both of which are related to the Catholic faith is the strong Catholic cultural component of the academic sector. With an eye to what Catholic institutions actually offer in such courses and cognizant of identifying what is minimally necessary for each model to offer a distinguishable Catholic culture, we describe these courses as "related to the Catholic faith." In fact, at many Catholic persuasion universities, the Catholic content of such courses is variable and depends to a large extent on the instructor. If the instructor is a committed Catholic and is also committed to sharing a Catholic perspective with the students, the content may convey substantial information about Catholic faith and practice, content that is made more persuasive and memorable by the personal commitment of the faculty member. But some instructors, for a variety of reasons, handle only a few

Catholic issues explicitly and prefer to address more generic religious or Christian issues. In such courses, students may emerge with a good sense of the overall religious landscape but little knowledge of things specifically Catholic. If at a particular institution a significant fraction of courses or sections of courses could be described in this way, the institution would likely not satisfy the distinguishability criterion.

Catholic policy guides the general way in which residence life is structured at Catholic persuasion universities, but in order for residential life to have a distinguishable Catholic component, Catholic moral teaching is assumed to be operational in this model. If at an actual university that might wish to think of itself as a Catholic persuasion institution students flagrantly disregard policies, such as those involving intimacies in relationships among undergraduate students, with impunity, it will in no way be apparent to students how their residential living differs in any significant way from what their friends tell them is the way of life at nonsectarian colleges and universities. Without a serious commitment among residence life staff to educate students about Catholic moral teaching, to consistently support it, and to call students to accountability when they breach its tenets, the claim to a distinctively Catholic residential culture at such a university is unfounded.

In the student activities sector in this model, the importance of institutional integrity and witness is underscored with students. In light of this institutional responsibility, the students are not allowed to sponsor activities that deny, dismiss, disrespect, or disregard the official teaching of the Catholic Church. Because the prohibition and the reasons for it are clearly expressed to students and student organizations, and because the constraint is frequently addressed in student publications and other interactions with and among students, the student activities sector at these universities is clearly distinguishable from counterparts at nonsectarian institutions.

Religious activities on campus at Catholic persuasion universities are overwhelmingly Catholic, and all students, regardless of their religious background, are encouraged to participate. Like religious activities at Catholic immersion universities, religious activities in this model are also part of the important symbols of the Catholic culture at these institutions. At nonsectarian institutions, the Newman center, or its equivalent, may sponsor very similar religious activities, and some Newman centers may also achieve participation rates among Catholic students that are comparable. Nevertheless, because the Catholic persuasion universities incorporate the Catholic religious activities into the symbols of the culture and nonsectarian institutions do not, the Catholic culture is distinctly different with respect to religious activities.

Identifiable groups of faculty and administrators at this type of Catholic institution assume responsibility for promoting the Catholic character of the institution. Faculty focus mainly on the Catholic intellectual tradition as it relates to various academic activities: required and elective courses, research projects and interests, special Catholic institutes, symposia, conferences, and so on. Although hiring is a delicate issue, this identifiable faculty group also makes sure a sufficient number of faculty members are knowledgeable about the Catholic tradition and are committed to it. Because academics are at the core of any college or university, the institution cannot satisfy the distinguishability criterion unless the regular activities in the academic sector are influenced in significant ways by faculty with Catholic knowledge and commitment. A similar cohort of knowledgeable and committed administrators is not only present but required, in order to protect and develop the Catholic tradition in residence life, student activities, and religious activities. These faculty members and administrators are the cultural catalysts and cultural citizens on whom the strong culture relies.

Reviewing Catholic persuasion universities indicates that they have fairly clear content and symbol components in residence life, student activities, and the religious activities sectors. Cultural catalysts and citizens among the faculty and administrative personnel play a significant role. The only cause for hesitation in concluding that these institutions are culturally distinguishable is the depth and breadth of the Catholic character in the academic component. Because the academic sector is the part that drives or should drive any institution of higher education, its activities must communicate clearly the important foci of the institution. If, in fact, most students do not learn much about the content of the Catholic faith in the crucial academic sector, the distinguishability criterion can hardly be fulfilled, no matter how strong the other factors are. This model of Catholic persuasion universities assumes that a good percentage of the students are Catholic and that the universities wish to continue attracting a sizable proportion of Catholic students in the future.

Inheritability among both students and faculty plays a significant role in this model. As is the case with the other models, the Catholic academic mission at this type of institution relies on having a significant percentage of Catholics among the students. The Catholic students are both recipients of the Catholic intellectual tradition and purveyors of it to both their Catholic and non-Catholic friends. Were the percentage of Catholics to shrink considerably, the impact of courses in the Catholic faith would diminish, and this sector could become indistinguishable from the academic sector in nonsectarian institutions. To avoid moving in territory that harbors dangers to the Catholic mission, Catholic persuasion universities have to proactively recruit Catholic students and offer them appealing, exciting courses in the Catholic tradition. Strong academic programs in the content of the Catholic faith increase the certainty that the inheritability criterion will be fulfilled.

Committed Catholic faculty recognized by their peers as protectors and promoters of the Catholic tradition play an essential role in the Catholic persuasion model. In the very challenging area of faculty hiring, some process needs to be worked out such that committed Catholic faculty members with appropriate expertise in their discipline are hired, nurtured, and respected by other faculty, especially when they encourage actions to support or shore up the Catholic academic and intellectual tradition at the university.

The *Catholic diaspora* model reaches out to non-Catholic students in a way that invites them to see the Catholic faith as reasonable and, perhaps, even attractive for themselves at some point in their lives. The academic component requires all students to take a course that takes the Bible seriously and presents some tenets of the Catholic faith to students. Furthermore, all students are encouraged, but not required, to take a course on Catholic teachings. The students educated by Catholic diaspora universities are predominantly non-Catholic, and the institutions, avoiding a proselytizing stance, reach out to these students but do not compel them. To the extent a single course with some Catholic or Christian content is required by most, if not all, students, this requirement is a clear point of differentiation from nonsectarian institutions, although perhaps not a significant difference. It is hard to claim that one course, out of the approximately forty courses undergraduates are expected to take, constitutes a significant cultural difference, especially since the course does not specifically treat Catholic doctrines. For this reason, in the all-important academic sector, the distinguishability criterion appears not to be fulfilled. But we withhold final judgment until a consideration of the four other components has been undertaken, with special emphasis on how these other sectors are aligned to the academic component.

Catholic teaching guides both the policy and operation of residence life at these colleges. Since this requirement is the same as that in Catholic persuasion universities, similar observations are pertinent. There is, of course, a danger here that a shadow culture prevails over the publicly espoused culture in the residence halls. Much of what occurs in residential living need not be noted by authorities. Therefore, it is possible for clearly stated collegiate policy to be overlooked by resident assistants and others involved in follow-through. If students, who in justice have a right to expect support in trying to live an ethical and chaste lifestyle as defined by the Catholic tradition, get the message that they themselves are the problem, the official culture is undermined, and the shadow culture clearly dominates. While shadow cultures can appear in principle in any one of the four sectors (academics, residence life, student activities, and religious activities) and in any one of the four models, experience suggests residential living is particularly vulnerable to the development of a shadow culture.

In the student activities sector, the importance of institutional integrity and witness is underscored with students. In light of this institutional responsibility, the students are not allowed to sponsor activities that deny, dismiss, disrespect, or disregard the official teaching of the Catholic Church. Because the prohibition and the reasons for it are clearly expressed to students and student organizations, and because the constraint is frequently addressed in student publications and other interactions with and among students, the student activities sector at these universities is clearly distinguishable from counterparts at nonsectarian institutions.

In Catholic diaspora universities, college authorities are clear and direct in the area of student activities. Student groups are simply not permitted to sponsor or host events that permit students or people from outside the institution to espouse views that directly contradict official teaching of the Catholic

Church, and they are consistently reminded of the policy and the reasons for it. This is a clear, significant difference from policies at nonsectarian institutions.

Religious activities in these colleges function in a similar way to Newman or Catholic centers at nonsectarian institutions, with the significant difference that the Eucharist and other Catholic services at Catholic institutions occur in public celebrations or rituals and therefore constitute part of the symbols of this culture. As previously noted, this is a role that Newman centers cannot play in their institutions. With respect to participation in liturgies, it is likely that many Newman centers will achieve greater participation among Catholic students than will be achieved at Catholic institutions adhering to the Catholic diaspora model.[43]

A strong feature of this model pertains to personnel. Senior administration is attentive to having a cadre of dedicated faculty and administrators who espouse the Catholic mission and who find effective ways to promote the mission in the institution. Since the institution likely operates in a geographical region where Catholics are in a minority, special efforts are made to hire Catholic faculty and administrators who constitute the cultural catalysts and citizens for the institution.

In order to compensate for their weakness in the academic sector, Catholic diaspora universities must provide significant supporting strength. Campus ministry or personnel could well provide a strategic supporting role. If the Mass is celebrated in ways that regularly focus on the Catholic academic heritage of the university, involves the faculty, or involves a good number of the students on some regular basis, the academic sector can be strengthened through religious practices that emphasize the Catholic academic and intellectual heritage. Alternatively, significant Catholic voices occupying important positions among the faculty and administration can repeatedly emphasize the Catholic mission of the institution and highlight Catholic themes that have an important influence on the way modern people think and act. If the focus is on the Catholic academic and intellectual tradition, these significant statements will promote distinguishability in the academic sector as well. Since the other sectors are already distinguishable, the boost to the academic sector from personnel or religious activities may be enough to ensure the overall distinguishability criterion for the university.

The strategy thus far has been to propose models that are minimal, in the sense that they embody the smallest set of activities enabling the institution to pass the distinguishability criterion. In this model, something more is required to satisfy the distinguishability criterion in academics. Hence the "more" should be related to the academic sector. In fact, most diaspora institutions offer more Catholic activities than those we identify. Two examples are offered. A university might sponsor one or two major academic symposia a year that emphasize some aspect of the Catholic intellectual heritage. If such symposia attract a good number of students and faculty, they will be distinguishing characteristics in the academic sector. A second alternative would be to use a faculty member who has a broad knowledge of the Catholic intellectual tradition to meet with individual academic departments on a regular schedule to talk to them about aspects of the Catholic intellectual heritage in their academic disciplines. Such an expert would encourage faculty members to address aspects of the Catholic intellectual tradition in their classes. Whatever the specific program is, it must make the academic sector at the Catholic university clearly distinguishable from its nonsectarian counterpart.

In Catholic diaspora universities, the key people who are promoting and protecting the Catholic mission and identity comprise a relatively small group of Catholic faculty and administrators.[44] If the inheritability criterion is to be satisfied, this type of university has to have a set of operating procedures that guarantees that the Catholics on the faculty are knowledgeable and committed to the Catholic faith and that appropriate knowledge of and commitment to the tradition also exists among a core group of administrators.

The fourth model, *Catholic cohort*, has a dual approach. In the academic sector, all students are required to take two courses that emphasize the role of religion in society. One such course may be in Catholic theology or in sacred writings, which include the Bible, or it may be some course that emphasizes some aspect of the Catholic intellectual tradition. For the general group of students, however, the overall goal is to make them familiar with and sympathetic to the role that religion plays in society, not to make them familiar with the content of the Catholic faith. If this model consisted only of this academic segment, it would not satisfy the distinguishability criterion in the essential area of academics. However, a second goal in this model is to produce some students with strong academic ability who are committed to and, in the course of their studies, become very well informed about the Catholic faith. All students at these institutions are invited to pursue courses in a Catholic studies program. Specific courses in theology, philosophy, literature, ethics, history, political theory, and social teaching explore the breadth of the Catholic intellectual tradition. As long as the group of students pursuing such courses remains identifiable, enjoys a respected place in the academic community, and has a high profile within the college or university, this creates a strong Catholic academic cohort and distinguishes it in the academic sector.

The crucial role this subgroup of students plays merits further discussion. This group and its impact on other students at the university set this university apart from similar nonsectarian institutions, some of which offer Catholic studies programs. In both Catholic and nonsectarian institutions, it is typically a relatively small group of students who avail themselves of the courses available in this program. In the nonsectarian institution, the institution takes little note of the students. They are students who happen to have an academic interest in Catholic issues. The Catholic cohort university, on the other hand, not only seeks students who will avail themselves of these courses but also gives them a significant profile within the institution. The institution wants these students to be recognized and acknowledged by other students as striving for the best that this Catholic university has to offer. The university takes delight in the impact that students have on the overall student and academic culture and even highlights their achievements to other students, alumni, and the public in general.

In the area of student activities at Catholic cohort universities, students are permitted to host events at which positions contrary to Catholic teaching are promoted. This type of institution believes that students should be exposed to different points of view and that they should be able to interact directly with people who espouse views different from official Catholic teaching. Administrators are expected to use their influence to make sure that the Catholic viewpoint is enunciated sufficiently frequently so that students have an opportunity to hear intelligent presentations of the official teaching of the Catholic Church concerning controversial topics.

Catholic cohort universities choose to look the other way in residential living. Students must obey civil laws, and administrators do not allow blatant transgressions of Catholic moral teaching, such as cohabitation. But the Catholic moral teaching is not imposed in the residence halls. As in student activities, faculty and administrators who are articulate about the Catholic moral position address these issues in student forums, but students are left to make their own choices in the residence halls. In residence life, the distinguishability criterion is not fulfilled.[45]

In the religious sector, Catholicism is favored, but the emphasis is on providing religious support to all students, whatever their religious heritage. Thus, campus ministry has Catholic priests and informed and committed Catholic laypersons, but it may also include Protestant ministers, rabbis, and imams. The celebration of the Eucharist as well as other Catholic activities occurs at important points throughout the academic year, and because such events are celebrated with great dignity and beauty, they play an important role as a symbol of the culture.

Since this model includes an extensive Catholic studies program, there is a significant group of faculty with knowledge of the Catholic faith, and some of them are strongly committed to the faith. At these universities, administrators are expected to have some knowledge of the Catholic faith and to lend general support to the Catholic mission, but they are not expected to be committed Catholics. Perhaps only at the highest level—president or academic vice-president—are administrators expected to be committed and practicing Catholics.

As indicated, this model satisfies the distinguishability criterion in the academic sector. Both the student activities sector and the religious activities contribute content and symbols to the culture. Although the role of Catholic administrators is weak, they are committed to supporting and creating special institutes and programs that promote the Catholic identity of the institution. The role of committed Catholic faculty is stronger, in large part due to a well-developed Catholic studies program. Considered as a single component, student activities would not satisfy the distinguishability criterion. However, the whole complex of the five sectors does, in our opinion, fulfill the distinguishability criterion.

The inheritability criterion requires that recently introduced new approaches or contemplated new approaches in various sectors of Catholic institutions be received and accepted by future generations of students, faculty, and administrators, that is, by cultural catalysts and citizens.[46] If students lack knowledge of the Catholic faith, they could respond by seeking more knowledge. In this case, any of the four Catholic models would not face inheritability issues. On the other hand, a possible weakness of the Catholic cohort model is its heavy reliance on a cadre of Catholic students who are committed to and want to understand better the Catholic faith and its implications for society. Unless such students are attracted to the university, the faculty teaching courses in the Catholic studies program will not have sufficient students registered for their courses to make them viable. The primary reliance on attracting a visible cohort of committed and informed Catholic students in this model contrasts with the first two models, which rely fairly equally on Catholic interest on the part of students and Catholic interest and expertise on the part of some faculty and administrators.[47]

Graduate and Professional Programs

We noted at the beginning of this chapter that comments would be made primarily within the framework of undergraduate education, which for most institutions—Catholic and non-Catholic—is the sector that has traditionally provided the institution with its dominant culture and character. Despite this focus, graduate programs offer excellent opportunities to address significant aspects of the Catholic intellectual tradition.

Graduate and professional programs in particular academic disciplines are remarkably well focused. In many programs, most of the courses that students must take in their first full year of studies are prescribed by the faculty; graduate students enjoy less choice in their first year of studies than undergraduate students. Because faculty members have a very clear idea of what students must know and experience in order to be properly prepared to function in their discipline, they limit choice in this first year. Both knowledge and training are important in graduate studies, and academic programs are structured to reflect this dual emphasis. It would be unusual if Catholic graduate programs did not offer some courses relating to the Catholic tradition or offer treatment of some themes about which Catholic thinkers have made important contributions over the centuries. Having a Catholic culture at the graduate and professional level requires some significant analysis of the Catholic intellectual heritage at a level consonant with graduate and professional study.[48]

At the graduate level, the emphasis is on preparing students for applying the knowledge of their particular discipline. As research in disciplines explores areas in increasingly greater depth, faculty members exert pressure to introduce more required courses to cover relatively new areas of exploration. Consequently, there is a natural tendency for disciplinary demands and developments to crowd out treatment of academic issues related to the Catholic tradition. But in many instances the strength of the Catholic intellectual tradition comes to the fore most clearly when specific issues are addressed, particularly with respect to ethics and social organization but also with respect to religion and the public practice of religion. Thus disciplines such as law, history, ethics, art, philosophy, sociology, literature, education, social work, and, of course, theology include broad areas where Catholic thinkers—along with many others—have contributed important insights over many centuries.[49]

As faculty and institutions increasingly emphasize research and publications, it is appropriate that Catholic institutions find reasonable ways to favor research related to the Catholic intellectual heritage.[50] Not only does such research contribute to the ongoing development of the Catholic tradition in a particular area, but at a particular university it usually also involves graduate students working with faculty. The more significant the research undertaking of an institution is, the more appropriate it is that special institutes or research projects be undertaken that explore issues in various ways related to the Catholic tradition.

It is possible to offer variations on the models presented here to create a context for understanding Catholic culture in graduate and professional education. In fact, however, only a few Catholic universities have staked out territory within the Catholic intellectual tradition where they publicly state that they would like to make a significant contribution. Those who make a claim to specializing in various Catholic issues usually do this through special research institutes and centers. These universities have interesting programs relating aspects of professional disciplines to the Catholic intellectual heritage, and the trend of having special Catholic institutes as loci for research on Catholic issues may develop in the coming decades. As worthwhile as a thorough exploration of Catholic graduate education would be, the focus in this study is on undergraduate learning in and outside the classroom.

The Nonsectarian Model

Each of the Catholic models presented earlier should be interpreted within the larger framework of a general nonsectarian or secular model of education at the college or university level. Indeed, the secular model is the dominant culture, against which various types of Catholic institutions distinguish themselves. Nonsectarian dominance results not by force but by the manner in which both students and faculty are formed by the secular model. Not only do the great majority of students study at nonsectarian institutions but also most faculty teach and do their research at such institutions. The most highly esteemed institutions at the tertiary level are also nonsectarian institutions. Many faculty who teach at Catholic institutions are educated at the undergraduate and/or graduate level at secular institutions, and they understandably use such institutions as their guides for what truly constitutes higher education.

Because the nonsectarian institution of higher education forms the dominant culture in higher education, it will be helpful to have a characterization of the undergraduate component of secular universities. Since the variety among nonsectarian institutions is at least as great as, if not greater than, that among Catholic institutions, it is possible to develop a number of different models of nonsectarian institutions. In this study, however, a more modest undertaking will better serve the analysis of Catholic institutions. For the sake of contrast, it will suffice to have a single referent *nonsectarian model* of universities. In describing this model, we take particular note of the way the nonsectarian institution accommodates or fails to accommodate the religious interests of students and faculty.

The overall goal of the nonsectarian model is twofold. First, these institutions seek to educate students to be intellectually curious about a variety of significant topics. Second, they seek to train students in a particular academic discipline and to develop within them the knowledge and competence to contribute to society in a manner so esteemed that they are offered gainful employment. Nonsectarian universities frequently want students to be ethically sensitive, and although their students are expected to obey society's laws and university rules, these institutions avoid presenting any ethical system as preferred.

The academic sector in the nonsectarian model is similar to the academic sector in the Catholic diaspora model. In the nonsectarian model, students may have to fulfill certain distribution requirements, but they are not required to take any course in religious faith. While one of the academic disciplines in which a student may major might include a religious discipline such as religious studies, Catholic or Christian studies, Jewish studies, or the study of Islam, the number of faculty members in these disciplines is small compared with other departments. More significantly, these academic areas or disciplines are not expected to influence other departments in the university.

Residential living in the nonsectarian model emphasizes rules, not the ethical or religious underpinning of such rules. In general, students are permitted to engage in activities involving whatever degree of personal intimacy they choose, as long they do not act contrary to civil laws and do not cause irreconcilable disruption to other students. The general atmosphere encourages students to explore and possibly experiment in their relationships with other students in order to discover what type of relationship and activities works best for them. This model also assumes that students are provided with a wide variety of sport and fitness facilities, and that support is provided for many types of student activities.

Student activities are guided by rules in the nonsectarian model, but the rules focus on good order, a respect for racial, ethnic, and gender diversity, and an almost absolute commitment to freedom of speech. The boundaries of good order are defined by the expectation that students will neither hurt one another nor compel another to engage in activities against his or her will. Such colleges and universities generally support engagement in activities that promote social justice as an option for students but not usually as a requirement.

Campus ministry, of course, is not a structural component of the nonsectarian model, and parareligious rather than religious rituals are associated with university celebrations. There is, however, a longstanding tradition that various religious groups have facilities on or close to campus. These groups are allowed to operate their facilities, so they both meet the religious needs of undergraduates and do so in a manner that fits well within the normal patterns of undergraduate life. In the nonsectarian model, the university may offer some benefits to religious groups, but such institutions take pains to offer these benefits in an evenhanded manner. Nonsectarian institutions want the religious needs of students to be satisfied, but the colleges and universities neither are directly involved in meeting those needs nor favor one religious group over another.

In the nonsectarian model, the religious knowledge and commitments of faculty, staff, and students play no role in the way the university organizes its core activities. In this model, administration and staff are not concerned about a minimum number of Catholic faculty, students, or staff at the university. Nonetheless, a good number of nonsectarian universities are eager to provide estimates of the number or percentage of students who are Catholics or belong to other denominations enrolled at the university, in part because they wish to show how inclusive they are and also because they want to reassure parents that their children will find religious companionship and be treated well at the university.

Distinguishability and inheritability are also important in nonsectarian universities. Distinguishability in this case refers to what students acquire during the period of their undergraduate studies.[51] Nonsectarian universities catering to commuting students, for example, must be able to show that the student commuter suffers no disadvantage when the student enters the job market as a result of having attended this type of institution. Some students have needs that prevent them from spending large amounts of time on campus, and commuting institutions accommodate these needs. For distinguishability and inheritability, commuting institutions, as an example, must provide knowledge and training that is at least equal to the training received by the young man or woman of the same age who works in the private sector, serves in the military, or surfs the web forty hours a week seeking to improve his or her knowledge.

When dealing with a broad category such as education for adolescents and young adults, an educational institution cannot ensure distinguishability simply by pointing to what most people count as educational institutions. Novel alternatives for educating oneself, such as the web or training through participation in "courses" sponsored by corporations, must be considered. Modes of education do change over time. Rather, the model must be able to point to clear differences, and actual universities must have (and many universities do have) data that show that their approach to education is both distinct and effective when compared with what students could obtain by following other paths. Many employers seek the credential of a degree in higher education. But the credential of an undergraduate degree is always subject to challenge by some new group that provides effective higher education in a novel way, without necessarily offering a bachelor's degree.

Some adherents to the nonsectarian model might wish to claim that the distinguishability criterion is fulfilled because the university has no fixed ideology and, as the name "university" implies, is open to a broad range of views. Such openness, however, is shared by many other institutions in American society. One might be able to get a good education (though not a degree) by surfing the web with discipline. Certainly the web is as nonjudgmental and open to as great, if not greater, variety of views than any university. In general, if other institutions are open and find ways to educate students better—such as doing it in the workplace over a period of five to ten years—the nonsectarian university model could become indistinguishable from the nonsectarian employment and education model.

The distinguishability criterion is satisfied provided the nonsectarian model includes an academic program that is of sufficient breadth to provide students not just with preparation for reasonable after-graduation employment but also with the skills that translate into better performance in other non-work-related situations in their lives, such as family and civic community, and in terms of making economic contributions in a variety of ways in modern society. No attempt will be made here to specify such an academic program; it is simply assumed to be part of the nonsectarian model.

In the nonsectarian model, inheritability means the academic program has to be sufficiently appealing that students will continue to want to pursue degrees. For example, if nonsectarian institutions became much more academically rigorous, the time students spend studying would have to increase, and the amount of time they could spend in extracurricular, social, or work-related activities would necessarily decrease. In this situation, any number of students would likely opt out of universities as their educational preference, and the universities would become something distinctly different from what they are now. As portrayed, the nonsectarian model is judged to be inheritable, partly because students perceive that they receive skills that are important for the entirety of their adult lives and partly because students realize that academic demands are balanced by an impressive array of facilities and programs that help advance their physical, social, and health needs.

Because the nonsectarian model fulfills the two criteria of distinguishability and inheritability, it possesses some stability. The four Catholic models exist as subcultures of the dominant nonsectarian university model. In many ways the Catholic models follow the nonsectarian model, and in some important respects they are distinctly different. It is these distinctly different aspects, however, that give Catholic colleges and universities their long-run stability.

In subsequent chapters, the comments and views of senior administrators at Catholic universities will be reviewed. Many of these administrators—be they laypersons or religious—received their formative education at nonsectarian institutions. It is likely, as well as plausible and acceptable, that many of them admire and seek to emulate broad segments of the nonsectarian model. In analyzing how they describe their own lived experience, whether their comments speak to one of the four Catholic models or fit more easily into the nonsectarian model will have significant implications for the distinguishability and inheritability of Catholic higher education—a distinction well worth noting.

Models as Interpretative Frameworks

This chapter identified an overall goal for each of the four models of Catholic colleges or universities. It described a set of strategies for achieving those goals while maintaining a Catholic identity, assuming that each Catholic college selects one goal and develops a strategy that includes, as a minimum the outlined strategy.[52] Whether actual Catholic institutions pass the distinguishability and inheritability criteria can only be determined by examining each institution in detail. The goal in proposing these models is more Kantian than empirical, in the sense that the models identify the conditions of possibility for four types of Catholic universities.[53] Our working assumption, based on experience, is that many Catholic institutions not only fulfill the conditions of possibility but also exceed them by some margin. Nonetheless, it is important to be clear about the conditions of possibility. We will continue to speak as if there are indeed only four models, even as we acknowledge that some institutions are positioned in some proximity to two of the four models, though not identical with either.

One of the benefits of focusing on four models is the opportunity it affords Catholic institutions, and especially their cultural catalysts and citizens, to identify approximately where they are and better understand what cultural components need emphasis in their institution. In addition, the models offer a way to capture the great variety of Catholic colleges and universities, while allowing cultural catalysts to train their gaze on other institutions pursuing similar strategies.

Educational institutions are not inert. They adjust, they launch new initiatives, they allow former ways of doing things to fall into desuetude, they seek new types of students, whether at the undergraduate or graduate level, and they constantly attract new students and new faculty members. Such changes might be intentional; however, it is also possible for mission drift to occur. An institution can let out its lines and drift far from its original mooring. This can occur for many particular reasons, but the general explanation is an unwillingness or inability on the part of administrators and other cultural catalysts to insist that innovations pass the distinguishability and inheritability criteria in terms of their Catholic mission. Administrators are under constant competitive pressure with respect to the number and quality of students, faculty, and staff, but the preservation of the Catholic identity, culture, and mission of the institutions demands that they manage the pressure and manage it well.

Significant change in collegiate institutions can come dramatically with one set of decisions and actions, or incrementally as small changes build on each other to radically shift institutional direction. In the first instance, for example, an institution may come to the realization that its economic margin criterion is no longer being satisfied and will not be satisfied unless significant changes in orientation are undertaken. At such a juncture, since the very mission of the college or university stands in jeopardy until the margin criterion is satisfied, dramatic adjustments are required. In the latter case, cultural catalysts and citizens may not have been alert to the cumulative effect of smaller annual changes that have already had a significant impact and disadvantaged the Catholic identity of the institution. Should that be the case, administrators might make a relatively small change that could seriously marginalize the Catholic culture of the institution. This is not, however, the end of the story. Once the cultural catalysts and citizens realize what has occurred, they can start to recommend adjustments. The adjustments might return the focus of the institution to the original Catholic goal, or they might redirect the institution to a new Catholic goal, a variation on the four presented here. If Catholic culture is to remain vital and viable, changes as a group must satisfy the criterion of distinguishability, its subrequirement of economic margin criterion, and inheritability.[54]

These four models of Catholic colleges and universities, with their associated strategies, will help to position the comments made by senior administrators in the subsequent interpretative chapters. None of the institutional sites of the study will be identified by name with any of the four models—a task more appropriately left to the cultural catalysts and cultural citizens at each institution. Rather, the models are used as ways both to understand and critically evaluate the foci, concerns, hopes, and strategies revealed in the comments of senior administrators.

PART II

Themes

Senior administrators who participated in the study cared deeply about the Catholic identity and culture of their institutions and had spent a great deal of time thinking about issues related to religious identity and their own performance and experience. Assured of anonymity—both personal and institutional—participants were more than willing to be candid about their own perceptions and experiences. This part of the book addresses the themes that administrators raised in those conversations. The assurance of anonymity surely enhanced the depth and reliability of interview data. It created some problems, however, regarding how to present the data in a manner that had coherence and was not just a collection of undifferentiated individual responses.

The first fruits of chapter 3 is the approach we adopt for identifying administrator comments. We fit each of the institutions that participated in the research into the model we think most appropriate and then use those model designations to identify individual quotations. This approach gives the reader a sense of the type of institutional experience that informs the comments.

The chapters begin with a judiciously chosen selection of observations that indicate how senior administrators situate issues.[1] Not surprisingly, their comments display a mixture of *conviction, reality, concerns,* and *future directions,* and these four categories are used to structure chapters 4, 6, 7, and 8.[2]

In one sense, each individual comment expresses a conviction or opinion about a certain aspect of Catholic character, identity, and mission at the college or university at which the administrator serves. Nonetheless, certain convictions are more fundamental than others, and administrators give emphasis to those that are particularly important to them. For example, one administrator might say that the university can only be Catholic if most students take one or more courses in Catholic theology. Another administrator may express an opposing opinion that it is not necessary for most students to take a course in Catholic theology in order for the institution to be Catholic. In both instances, the administrators are speaking about their convictions. These important views and opinions appear in the first part of each chapter under the heading "Convictions."[3]

Administrators also emphasized certain realities about their institutions or about the culture in which they operate. In some cases, administrators highlighted cultural circumstances that were fairly permanent and required long periods of time to adjust. At other points, administrators emphasized cultural realities that were intended as starting points that would lead to future changes. The emphasis in both these cases was on how things are, and those comments appear in what follows under the heading "Reality."

Administrators often spoke of aspects of their current reality that were troubling. In some cases, these areas of concern entailed basic tensions or even contradictions between personally or institutionally espoused convictions and what really happens—be that on their own campuses, in the broader Catholic culture, or more generally in the culture of higher education. Comments reflecting this type of angst or worry appear under the heading "Concerns."

Finally, most administrators are full of plans for the future, and those interviewed were no exception. In fact, when the current reality was not particularly to their liking, many of administrators emphasized a future time when they thought their local circumstance would improve. Some of the comments reflecting expectations or indicating future directions were healthy indicators. Others reflected some underlying disturbing aspect of lived reality. These comments appear under the heading "Future Directions."

After we present a representative sample of the observations of senior administrators, we will analyze them in two ways. First, we will explore how the comments mesh with the Catholic culture at Catholic universities in general. After that, we will make a determination about their "fit" with the basic requirements of each of the four cultural models of Catholic colleges and universities. We use the basic cultural requirements for each of the four models to critically highlight and review realities, concerns, and convictions of Catholic universities as they are now. We also use these requirements to evaluate the types of changes that will be required to move Catholic colleges and universities in the directions that administrators indicated they desired for the future.

The thumbnail sketch of the models that follows will help position both the administrator quotations and subsequent analysis that together comprise each of the theme chapters in part II.

Four Catholic Models

Model	Characteristics
Immersion	Vast majority of students are Catholic Vast majority of faculty and administrators are Catholic Broad array of Catholic courses in the academic sector Very strong nonacademic Catholic culture
Persuasion	Majority of students are Catholic Significant number of faculty and administrators are Catholic Small array of Catholic courses in the academic sector Strong nonacademic Catholic culture
Diaspora	Minority of students are Catholic Few faculty and administrators are Catholic Minimal number of Catholic courses in academic sector Consistent Catholic culture in nonacademic areas
Cohort	Two-pronged model: a small cohort of well-trained and committed Catholic students and faculty, and a much larger group of students educated to be sensitive to religious issues with a view to influencing policy

4

Faculty and Students Engaging the Catholic Intellectual Tradition

The Catholic intellectual tradition was the theme senior administrators most frequently mentioned during the course of their interviews. They spoke of the tradition and its historical legacy with pride. Even when their knowledge was sketchy, they praised the integration of faith and reason as the hallmark of Catholic intellectual life. Many administrators believed the tradition was reflected in the academic components of their institutions. Others, while no less laudatory, were clear that their institutions had much ground to cover in order to more fully incorporate the tradition as a tangible and formative force in their institutions.

Convictions

Administrators from all four models of Catholic colleges and universities believe that Catholic institutions make a significant contribution to the landscape of American higher education because they offer the richest intellectual experience available to students seeking a college education. An academic vice-president from a diaspora institution insisted that "Catholic higher education is unique in both the richness of its roots in the Catholic tradition, and in its openness to explore." A cohort university president added that the traditional "marriage between liberal education, liberal arts education, and Catholic institutions has been such a good fit because it's about the development of each human being." The power of the Catholic approach, according to an immersion university administrator, "is not to be underestimated." This kind of education, according to another immersion administrator "is the best possible combination of things

... the combination of faith and reason, the world view the religion brings in a search for truth and the search for truth in scientific empirical means and philosophical means." These institutions are built on a legacy that unites the Catholic intellectual tradition and the liberal arts. "In terms of the Catholic intellectual tradition," according to a mission vice-president from a persuasion university, "although many Christians would say they try to bond faith and reason, our tradition has been doing it longer." A cohort academic vice-president underscored the fact that "liberal arts education started in the Catholic universities of Europe and was protected through the Dark Ages by Catholic monasteries and eventually universities." But the universities, according to a cohort administrator, have a long tradition of melding the liberal arts base with "professional schools because they were important to working class Catholics. That model has served us very well, and it has created the type of university in the United States that is not only career oriented but also solidly based in the liberal arts and theology and philosophy." A persuasion university mission vice-president suggested that

> Catholic education brings a holistic approach to education that encompasses the Catholic intellectual tradition and the Catholic social teaching where the least is reverenced and combines it with a commitment to the common good. With the connection of faith and reason, these institutions are free to integrate the academic, the scholarship, the research with the larger Catholic ideals. When at its best, it is a great gift for the world.

Senior administrators agreed that American higher education would lose something significant if Catholic colleges and universities ceased to exist because, as a diaspora provost pointed out, "these institutions offer an alternative and do things that public institutions simply don't." In so doing, this administrator pointed out, Catholic higher education "keeps the public institution in check by teaching and allowing people to experience their faith." A persuasion university mission vice-president observed that "it's healthy for the American higher educational system to have a reference beyond itself that calls the intellectual life back to some of its foundations. It would be just a tragedy if Catholic colleges and universities lost their niche in the higher education system in the United States."

Senior administrators praised not only the roots of Catholic higher education but also what a diaspora academic vice-president called its "openness to explore." An immersion president explained that because of that openness, the Catholic tradition that informs colleges and universities "will always rely on reason in addition to faith and so will always have thought out positions." Unlike evangelical universities that, according to many, are "pulpits rather than universities, Catholic institutions will "be the only places you can go if you want to talk seriously about religion."

Because Catholic universities are not churches, as a persuasion university administrator points out, the "job of Catholic higher education is to teach, to inform, and to help answer questions. These institutions need to guide students and faculty to resources so they can understand and delve down into the issues. . . . These institutions must do this while keeping a respectful conversation going." Diaspora, persuasion, and cohort administrators pointed out that "the commitment to the Catholic intellectual tradition requires focus on what the tradition is, handing it on, and helping it to develop." It also, "in many ways, brings people into a more adult understanding of what it means to be a Catholic." These administrators want to develop intellectuals who have a strong religious intellectual tradition "and really try to get inside the issues that the Catholic Church is dealing with." A cohort provost insisted that "there must be Socratic dialogue so that when people leave these institutions they leave with the sense there is a lot more to the Catholic Church than they ever appreciated before."

A number of administrators agreed with a diaspora administrator that for quite some time

> Catholic colleges have hidden their spiritual tradition under a bushel
> basket because they were afraid it would be offensive to people.
> They also did not want to cram Catholicism down the throats of kids
> who had had it all their lives and they certainly did not want to cram
> it down the throats of people who are not Catholic.

A cohort president spoke for many when saying that "intellectual authenticity calls for a Catholic university to have a Catholic commitment across the board in every aspect of its functioning; in its academic curriculum, in its student life programs, in the way it handles its financial affairs." The soul of the enterprise, in the mind of an immersion president,

> is a combination of the kind of education that is connected to
> having an undergraduate core curriculum, having strong programs
> in philosophy and theology, having a particular research focus, and
> having particular institutes and centers all with a close affinity with
> the Catholic intellectual tradition.

Senior administrators were in agreement that Catholic higher education should be open and inclusive. There was little agreement, however, that Catholic colleges and universities have a particular commitment to Catholic students. Immersion administrators strongly supported this position, which is not surprising, since the goal of immersion colleges and universities is to attract committed Catholic students, to educate them more deeply about the Catholic tradition, and to both encourage and actively support their practice of the faith. Although few administrators from the other institutional models articulated any such institutional commitment, a persuasion university president was quite forceful in his defense of it. According to him, if Catholic colleges and universities

> had no Catholic students they would have no reason to exist, be-
> cause one of the reasons these institution exist is to pass on the tra-

dition to believers. Part of what these institutions do is to educate Catholics, not just Catholics, but if they are not educating any Catholics, it's not clear they are doing what they need to do.

Not all senior administrators were convinced that Catholic colleges and universities have a responsibility to educate students about the Catholic tradition, either. The preponderance of those in agreement were immersion administrators, but a rare persuasion university mission vice-president also insisted that

a student leaving a Catholic college should have a good understanding of the tradition through the manner in which he or she studied the literature. There has to be a core curriculum and an assessment at the end that indicates we have indeed integrated the tradition into all aspects of the core body of knowledge and that there is a greater understanding and formation in the life of the student.

Reality

A persuasion university president maintained that

in general, our Catholic institutions put a rich academic intellectual experience out there for students, a challenging one, and they do this in an environment where faith and intellect can be integrated, and integrated in a more intentional way than what can happen at our public or nonsectarian colleges.

The reality other senior administrators described at their institutions, however, did not always support such an optimistic assessment.

A persuasion university administrator stated quite bluntly that "the last two presidents here, both of whom were lay people and good Catholics, have been essentially unable to distinguish within the curriculum and with the academic part of the house anything Catholic about the institution." Another persuasion university academic vice-president admitted that he "cannot do a very good job defining the elements of Catholic identity" and knows that at that institution, "many colleagues are struggling with the same issue." Most administrators did not point fingers at presidents or even themselves, but they did echo the assessment the academic realities at many Catholic colleges leave much to be desired. A cohort administrator said that "Catholic literacy is very weak, and it is weakest among those with the highest educational attainment." Many colleges find themselves in a situation similar to that of a persuasion university that "does not have people who were formed in the tradition." According to the mission vice-president,

the college has wonderful lay people but they have been educated for the most part at secular universities. The college is asking these people to integrate into the curriculum the same kind of thinking and teaching that had been so natural for the nuns and priests and they're not prepared to do that.

Immersion university administrators generally thought their faculty did a great job integrating the Catholic intellectual tradition across all disciplines. One was less enthusiastic and admitted the institution "was doing less than a great job integrating the Catholic intellectual tradition." In terms of the other collegiate models, two cohort administrators provided apt descriptions. "In areas like religious studies, philosophy, communication, sociology, and psychology and the like, [faculty] are conversant in the Catholic intellectual tradition." However, "in areas like computer science, business, and education, the majority of faculty are not conversant in the Catholic intellectual tradition."

Most administrators suggested that theology, religious studies, and philosophy departments were the places where the Catholic components of the intellectual mission were most vibrant. It is in these areas, they said, that students who "don't seem to understand what it means to be Catholic" and whose "Catholic intellectual and cultural literacy is low and probably not much above the eighth-grade level," were engaging the tradition most fully. Their descriptions of what was actually happening in these departments, however, suggested that student encounters with the Catholic intellectual tradition were either weak or infrequent. Immersion universities have strong programs in theology, and administrators in these institutions agreed that their methods and approach "make sure students are intellectually alive and learning so they are better equipped to problem-solve and to go out and engage the world." At one of the immersion institutions, "a whole Catholic doctrine-based curriculum is required. The students can ask questions at the end of every class and probe and learn [about the faith]."

In the other Catholic colleges, "fewer students are taking religious studies courses because of changes in the general education requirements." This is a far cry from what used to be the rule in Catholic institutions, according to one president.

> I went [to my Catholic undergraduate college] because I wanted a wonderful, liberal arts education. The experience was wonderful—twenty-eight hours of philosophy and sixteen of theology, which everybody took. It didn't matter what your major was. Few schools today in these United States can say that. For better or worse, they can't say it.

Today at that diaspora president's own institution, "maybe six credits are required of everybody in philosophy and one or two in religion." The president at another diaspora university saw a need to require some theology and philosophy. "It's a weird thing. We require six [credits in] theology and philosophy, and I think if we didn't require it, the students simply would not take it." A persuasion university administrator was not at all interested in requiring Catholic theology courses, saying: "even the nuns wouldn't want us to require Catholic theology. We just require one religion course and the students can choose Catholic if they want." A cohort administrator pointed out that simply offering the option of Catholic theology can be a problem.

> We really don't have a Catholic theologian, and the reason is depart-
> mental hiring. You know, the department needed someone in East-
> ern religions, the department needed someone in Jewish studies, the
> department needed someone certainly in Scripture. We have some
> really solid people in biblical scholarship, but we don't have a Catho-
> lic theologian teaching systematics, only a Catholic theologian who
> deals with justice and issues of death and dying.[1]

Attempts to address this kind of theological weakness are emerging, but they are just getting going. A diaspora administrator said his institution is "beginning to take Catholic theology and actual religion teaching more seriously." This institution has decided "to develop a major in theology." It does not, however, require students to take more than one course in religion.

Senior administrators reported that hiring for mission and initiatives for faculty development are two major ways their institutions attempt to shore up the Catholic intellectual mission. A cohort academic officer pointed out: "most of our faculty is coming from graduate school experiences that are not Catholic," making hiring for mission quite difficult. A diaspora provost hires for mission,

> primarily by listening to candidates in terms of whether they have a
> strong sense of values or justice, a sense of equity in the things they
> have been doing in their scholarly lives. [This administrator] asks
> candidates to give examples of what they would do in their class-
> rooms to further the mission.

An immersion president thinks it is terribly important "to hire a lot of really good religious people. They are not all Catholic, but they take religion seriously." That institution's academic officer has a mild approach and merely "tries to determine if they would feel compelled to speak against the Catholic Church or against the tenets of the Church in a disrespectful way. Those candidates would not fit or be happy [at the university], the administrator insists." A cohort university mission officer said that she "interviews every professor who is applying for a job, all of the candidates. The purpose is to give them a chance to ask questions about what Catholic means and what it doesn't mean and to dispel some myths." This administrator was pleased that hiring for mission was getting greater emphasis, but said she believed "there is a lot more to do." There is great caution in most of the hiring for mission approaches because, as one cohort university administrator pointed out, "when the question has been raised with the faculty, they are not too ready to hear it."

Once faculty are on board, many institutions focus on orientation as a good way to enhance their understanding of the religious mission of the college or university. At a cohort university, new hires spend "a whole morning in a

session committed to understanding more about the Catholic and congregational nature of the institution." At a persuasion university, the orientation is
relatively new, because for so many years "the sisters were so prevalent, orientation was just sort of by osmosis." Now the commitment is "to helping
people understand the mission of the institution and the charism of the founding order." At another cohort university, they "have four meetings with first-
year full-time professors on Catholic identity that is more of a dialogue and a
colloquium than anything else." That approach is replicated at a persuasion
university where the academic officer "meets once a month in seminar session
on the Catholic intellectual life, the congregational heritage, the ethical component of the entire curriculum."

Efforts to enhance mission awareness are also underway with more senior
faculty. At a diaspora university, all full- and part-time faculty are invited to
participate in a series of dinner discussions; the group "reads a chapter from
a book, and then they simply talk about the major themes in the Catholic
intellectual tradition." The mission officer at a cohort university "spends a lot
of time mingling with faculty, influencing faculty, working through key departments to get more courses that are Catholic in nature and that focus on
the Catholic tradition." This administrator tries "not to leave too many finger-
prints on the process, so that it's faculty themselves who get it through."

Assessment is not a tool the vast majority of Catholic colleges and universities use to move their religious mission forward. One persuasion administrator, however, found assessment quite helpful.

> Accreditation can sometimes be a blessing, and I think that this ap-
> proach, where it is expected that you will define student outcomes,
> has forced a very meaningful conversation among the faculty. When
> we had to write those learning outcomes and those performance in-
> dicators, we had some of the best conversation about what it means
> to be Catholic and what it means to be sponsored by a congregation.
> It is our responsibility, and finally we shared it.

Concerns

When asked about their experiences at Catholic institutions, many senior administrators expressed concerns. One of their worries is that Catholic higher
education could well abandon its unique culture and mission. A persuasion
administrator insists that "we have a responsibility to teach students about
Catholicism, and to a limited extent we do. But we aren't overt enough with
that particular piece of what we do on campus." A diaspora mission vice-
president thinks it is "an obligation of our Catholic institutions of higher education to educate about the Catholic tradition. We assume that people know
about it, but they really don't." The big universities need to do some real soul
searching, according to another persuasion president, because "in terms of
considering Catholic culture and the Catholic intellectual tradition, the smaller

institutions have paid more attention to it." A diaspora administrator suggested that the threat to Catholic identity is quite real and the colleges and universities themselves must resist becoming indistinguishable from other institutions.

> If we're not careful, all our institutions can start looking alike. It's very competitive, and if you're not attentive, you'll end up with a typical degree, and you won't have any room to put theology in there. You've really got to put your foot down and say "No, we're not going along. We think this is important."

The transition to lay leadership also concerns a number of administrators. A persuasion university academic officer pointed out:

> lay people are in the ascendancy in terms of controlling stewardship. It's also very clear that the vast majority do not have formation and preparation and are theologically far less literate than the sisters. I think today the danger is that we could be what I call UNU, United Nations universities, where we believe in brotherhood, goodwill, human rights, and we can articulate those things, but we cannot articulate them in a Catholic context or articulate them as our Church has articulated them. There are just very few of us who have the same kind of education the sisters have and the same kind of commitment.

Another persuasion university administrator believes the religious "know how to do this, they have been trained to do this. How many of us really have? I am worried, truly worried." A diaspora administrator does not "think we have engaged the congregation numbers decreasing. People on campus think we are Catholic because congregation members are here—even if their only experience is seeing retired religious driving around campus collecting paper and cardboard." "The sisters certainly have a lot more in-depth knowledge of the Church," according to a persuasion administrator, and "the enterprise will have a very difficult row to hoe over the next ten years because there is the lack of some kind of plan to fill the congregation void. That's a problem."

With the nuns and priests gone, Catholic colleges and universities must find people who can fill their shoes in terms of the Catholic mission of their institutions. A persuasion administrator said he is "worried about the future of the institutions because I don't know that we all know enough." Another persuasion administrator thinks "it is going to be an ongoing effort to attract, identify, and retain the right kind of faculty," and wonders: "where are we going to find them? It seems easier to draw in faculty to build up our diversity quotient, so I worry about how to attract faculty to build up our Catholic culture component." A persuasion president is concerned that

> as a group we have not come to terms with the fact that ninety percent of the faculty we hire don't even come from a liberal arts tradition. Even if they come from a liberal arts tradition, we still have the

additional problem of integrating the Catholic intellectual, social, theological traditions of the faith. Where are those things in our humanities programs?

The increasing use of adjuncts also worries administrators. "We hire adjuncts to do something. They come in quick, they do it, they leave . . . they never know what the true mission of the institution happens to be," and that is of great concern to a persuasion administrator. An immersion president sees an indifferent faculty as a real threat to religious identity.

> If you end up with a large enough faculty who are indifferent and don't know from their own life experience what you are talking about, then you are in a precarious position, because over time that will just eat away the things that you take for granted. And you can't let it all revolve around campus ministry or things that are peripheral to the academic enterprise.

Faculty indifference to mission is one concern, but faculty hostility to the religious mission of Catholic colleges and universities is an even bigger worry for senior administrators. A cohort president pointed out that "in an intellectual environment where people are committed to postmodernism, some carry that to an extreme and say there can be no truth and there is no real knowledge. That is antithetic to the notion of the Catholic institution, and it is a particularly powerful problem." A persuasion mission officer finds some faculty who see "our being Catholic as just an extra burden upon them and something they have to pay lip service to. They don't share our values, and they are not walking the path with you." At one institution, according to the academic vice-president at a persuasion university, "two people in the philosophy department got up and told their colleagues that they were atheists." In almost all the colleges and universities, some faculty "are really hostile and ask what right we have to even gather faculty and talk about Catholic identity." They also, according to a persuasion president, can be difficult "if they think anybody is checking up on whether they are doing enough Catholic stuff in the curriculum. They go crazy!" In this mix are also "disgruntled Catholics." A cohort president admitted she would "much rather work with non-Catholics than the disgruntled ones," who undermine all attempts to address the real issues that threaten Catholic identity and mission.

A wide array of senior administrators is deeply concerned about Catholic illiteracy. One persuasion administrator said: "we've really become such a well-educated society with a lot more degrees than ever before, but faith literacy, religious literacy, tradition literacy is disappearing." The faculty is often illiterate in terms of Catholic culture and the students are in even worse straits. A persuasion president stated what many administrators believe—that "one of the crises facing the Church, especially with the upcoming generation of young people, is that they are losing the sense of Catholic culture." According to a cohort academic officer,

the America Catholic Church has really abandoned religious education in the parish communities, and as a result, we have a population of Catholics today who are illiterate in terms of their Catholic
faith. When the Catholic schools really dropped out, we in American
Catholic education did not come back with the same vigor that we
did when we created those schools. We're just seeing the results of
that today.

Many administrators want to address these issues and don't know how.
Some believe it is either too late or not the mission of Catholic colleges and
universities to attend to remediation of Catholic illiteracy. A mission officer at
a persuasion university has "always maintained that Catholicism is just a religious culture. If you don't grow up in your own culture, you don't get it. In
the Catholic Church we've lost people because we haven't given them that
tradition and that information. But I don't think Catholic higher education can
do it." Another persuasion administrator thinks "education needs to start earlier than colleges. By the time you get into college, the college can only take
what you have learned and possibly help mold it, and help you to live it."

Senior administrators worry about whether their institutions are prepared
to face the challenges to institutional Catholic culture, identity, and mission.
Some see the boards of trustees as major players who are not really prepared
for their role. An immersion president said:

> many board members don't have a clue. They relied on the religious
> to guide them, and they are vanishing from the scene. I think that's
> the area that needs the most attention as we're growing Catholic col-
> leges. They don't have any idea, I can tell you, I deal with them all
> the time. They are nice people, but they don't have a clue about how
> to keep a place Catholic.

A persuasion university administrator concurs. "The most discouraging
thing for me has been the board of directors and their understanding of the
mission." The president of the same institution echoed this sentiment, saying:
"the really discouraging thing to me is that we have people faithful to the
institution, every Sunday Church-going Catholics who are clueless about the
justice aspects of our mission." A cohort president wondered: "How do you
cultivate boards that really govern and do we really teach them to do it well?"

Future Directions

In looking to the future, senior administrators are convinced that there will be
fewer institutions. Some think the institutions that remain will be diverse and
more vital. A persuasion university financial officer thinks "that ten years from
now Catholic higher education is going to be inevitably smaller, but stronger."
Another persuasion administrator says that "certainly the premier Catholic
[institutions]—Notre Dame, Georgetown, and probably Boston College—are

going to still continue to get high-end kids. A lot of the liberal arts and sciences colleges are going to continue to attract kids not coming from wealthy families." Another persuasion university's academic officer sees the smaller Catholic colleges as "comparable to parochial schools of the old days, and those with less than three or four thousand students are going to have a hard time going forward." Issues such as "finances, location and a lot of demographics in terms of shifting populations will determine which institutions will survive," a cohort administrator maintained. He also said that "most Catholic schools tend to be relatively small with very small endowments. That means they're going to find it difficult to weather tough economic times and the competition for students." As a result, he sees a possible 35 percent of Catholic institutions closing in the next ten years.

A large number of administrators maintained that greater attention to what differentiates Catholic colleges—their religious mission—is essential if this segment of American higher education is to survive. In order to do that, a persuasion administrator recommended that Catholic colleges and universities should "put our cards on the table and say explicitly who we are. I'd like us to be a little bit more forthright in our Catholic identity in a way that is not provincialized or ghettoized." Another persuasion administrator said that this emphasis would require institutions to "clearly explain what it means to be a Catholic college and to be upfront about that."

No matter how much the colleges and universities want to be religiously distinctive, they will not be unless they hire cultural actors who are capable of sustaining and supporting their religious identities. "As the leadership of colleges—not only top administration but the faculty too—passes into the hands of lay people, it is terribly import that we hire very, very carefully," a persuasion administrator cautioned. Another persuasion administrator believes that "there are people out there, but we don't view nurturing lay leadership as critical. It may well reach the point that we start saying, 'What were we thinking? Who did we think would take this over?' " An immersion president said: "there is nothing that absolutely assures we couldn't end up becoming secularized. So it is essential that we make sure the baton is passed and are attentive to assuring the faculty hired share our vision. We also have to make sure the board members share the vision." The provost of another immersion institution believes that "if you really want to build the right infrastructure for mission, you have to have the right people. Focusing on the initial hiring of faculty is so important in Catholic institutions." Another academic officer at a persuasion university is convinced that "to enhance Catholic character, I'd really love to hire deans who know that tradition well." She noted that "if somebody in the leadership role doesn't have that understanding, it compromises the institution." Two persuasion presidents are looking for national leadership in handling the staffing challenges. One maintains "you have to have a core group of prepared people in the institutions. The Catholic higher education community in this country is beginning to understand the problem, but so far there isn't any kind of national leadership or strategic movement to fix it." The other president is looking at future presidents and realizes the chances are they won't be theologians. Maybe that is one of the national challenges that Catholic higher education through the ACCU should consider taking on—providing a way in which those presidents who do not have a theological background can be helped to reflect upon the special nature of the Catholic university. Just reading is not enough. It has to be a developmental process.

Senior administrators want to start taking action within the curriculum to bring the Catholic intellectual tradition to life in their institutions. A number of administrators think efforts should start

in the core curriculum and the manner in which we teach. How we impart and educate students, the sources we use, the text and the opportunities for discussion, the Catholic social teaching and Catholic intellectual tradition thoroughly integrated in all areas of curriculum—especially core curriculum—that's where it has to happen first.

A diaspora academic officer is looking to "develop courses students might take as electives or even as general education courses that have a religious or Catholic focus." An immersion administrator wants to "try some creative projects for all colleges, business, engineering, science, arts and letters, and to try more effectively to integrate faith and values of students who take advantage of those curriculums." This administrator also suggested "socking away money in endowments so you could offer faculty fellowships to try and do creative stuff and incentives for new courses and new programs." A really successful program would be one, according to an immersion administrator, in which

you could honestly say there had been a conscious effort to have identity and mission through the core curriculum, as well as in the majors, focus on ethics and how that relates to society—all of it a real part of the educational experience. That is what's going to be unique about the institutions that thrive ten years from now.

A diaspora provost articulated a common desire among administrators that institutions should "breathe fresh air throughout religion departments. Get some good people in, get some excitement in the department." Another diaspora administrator wants to "offer courses like: *The Roman Catholic Church* or *Faith and Tradition* where students would be able to learn." A number of administrators think it is time to require courses with Catholic content, but most think it will take some time before that is a reasonable possibility. A diaspora administrator said she "would consider putting in a requirement immediately if it weren't for a lot admissions staff and everybody else saying that would scare away prospective students. That'd probably be a deal-breaker more for non-Catholics, but our admission people even think it would be a deal-breaker for some Catholics." Another persuasion administrator said that when the religion department is energized, "then I'll require the courses. But to require it with people that will drive the students out of the institution is to defeat it." Some of the administrators are simply opposed to requiring theology—no matter the circumstances. As a persuasion administrator put it, "you can't obligate people to take Catholic 101. The universities that try force-feeding religious courses end up alienating people." A diaspora administrator concurred that "great things are accomplished by attraction rather than promotion. Over a period of time, if we offer things and make them attractive and desirable through the feedback of students who experienced them, we can build on that."

In the next ten years, administrators are looking for an increase in enthusiasm for things Catholic. "I am very hopeful, a persuasion administrator said, that in the next years our faculty will not only be disposed to understanding the Catholic tradition, they will actually have an understanding of it." Developing the faculty will be a necessary first step if that goal is to be realized, however. A persuasion university provost hopes "to design really relevant but locally delivered faculty development programs about the Catholic intellectual tradition, the Catholic social teaching, and the history of the founding religious community." Another persuasion university administrator agrees and hopes

> to establish an institute for instructing faculty in Catholic topics. We would require faculty to participate in the work of that institute or program so they would learn about the Catholic tradition. They would learn about issues of faith and morals as taught by the Catholic Church, and become comfortable with the pedagogy of teaching that in their discipline.

Other administrators agreed with a cohort mission officer that something bigger and on a national footing is required to get Catholic institutions up to speed.

> I think there have to be summer-long formation programs that are a mix of Catholic intellectual tradition—like Collegium; spiritual formation; really good grounding for administration that you learn at the BC [Boston College] Institute for Administrators. But you can't do it in four days. Maybe it is the ACCU that would need to do this. You need it every year, and it has to have cachet and pizzazz. Think about it—the sponsoring congregations. Where do they put their best people? Formation work, if they are smart! And they go through years of training. We need some really first-rate summer experiences that include not merely the intellectual, cognitive side but also the liturgical and affective side. That doesn't mean that everybody has to be Catholic, but it really has to be Catholic in more manifestations of the Catholic tradition than merely the cognitive.

In looking to the future, a persuasion university president suggested the breadth of preparation necessary to accomplish the goals senior administrators outlined.

We can articulate what should be different about our institutions because they are Catholic. Also, I would like to be able to say that all of our Catholic university graduates could critique many of our cultural institutions from the perspectives of the values of our faith. I don't think we're doing a very good job of that in most places because it would require—on the part of the faculty—a pretty intensive hard study. That doesn't mean just going to workshops, but hard study. It would take maybe even five or six consecutive summers at least of hard study to begin to get their arms around the Catholic intellectual tradition.

Analysis of the Data: Desired Characteristics of Faculty

As the previous quotations indicate, senior administrators at all four types of Catholic colleges and universities have expectations when hiring new faculty members. The knowledge, dispositions, and personal skills faculty members need to successfully contribute to and support the Catholic mission of their own university depends in part on the kind of institution at which they teach. For example, among the four Catholic models, a faculty member teaching in a Catholic immersion institution in a nontheology academic discipline is expected to have greater knowledge of the Catholic intellectual tradition than a teacher in the same discipline at a persuasion or diaspora institution. Before examining what constitutes the threshold level of preparation and disposition appropriate for faculty members in each of the four classes of institutions, it is helpful to indicate the requisite faculty skills, characteristics, and dispositions for all four Catholic models.

In their interviews, a number of senior administrators were wary of going overboard in "hiring for mission." This is clearly a sensitive topic, and suggestions for addressing the sensitivity will be presented later in this chapter. For the moment, however, it is important to note that we examined all four Catholic university models in terms of their ability to satisfy distinguishability and inheritability criteria, and each of the models has a set of minimum requirements for meeting that standard. Because faculty members play such a significant role in accomplishing the mission of the institution, it is reasonable to assume that faculty peers and senior administrators will hire "the best" candidates for those positions. In fact, senior administrators claim that is precisely what they do. At a Catholic institution, the mission has a unique religious character; the "best candidates," therefore, will be those individuals who, along with bringing disciplinary distinction to their academic work, also are able to contribute to the Catholic mission of the university and support its institutional distinguishability and inheritability.

The characteristics that suggest that a potential faculty member will be a positive addition to a department and make a strong contribution to a secular university are commonly understood in academe and widely discussed. Catholic colleges and universities are keenly aware of these characteristics and look to find candidates who embody them. Unlike secular institutions, however, Catholic colleges and universities have committed themselves to educate in a particular religious tradition and must find candidates who will also contribute to that wider mission. In effect, the models of these institutions have refined what the term "best candidate" means for them, and only by including characteristics that indicate capacity for contributing to the Catholic mission will they find and hire faculty members who truly are the "best candidates." At least four general characteristics suggest a faculty member's capacity to fully contribute to the mission of the Catholic university:

1. An appreciation of and willingness to support the central role that theology and philosophy play in the academic life of a Catholic university
2. A willingness to acknowledge and support the Catholic university's responsibility to serve the Church, as well as the academy and society
3. A willingness to help students make the connections between the Catholic tradition and the issues that emerge in a given discipline
4. A willingness to support and encourage the deepening and maturing of faith among all students, Catholic and non-Catholic alike

Theology and philosophy are central to the mission of a Catholic university.[2] Theodore Hesburgh reminds Catholic educators that the presence and privileged place of these disciplines, and especially theology, in the Catholic university "completes the total field of inquiry, raises additional and ultimate questions, moves every scholar to look beyond immediate questions, beyond the immediate field of vision, to the total landscape of God, human beings, and the universe."[3] It is from these theological and philosophical roots that the Catholic intellectual tradition emerges, and all disciplines in a Catholic institution are in some way in conversation with them. This conversation can be greatly facilitated within a Catholic college or university if faculty members across disciplines are involved in fruitful discussion with members of the theology and philosophy departments who serve as willing resources.

All universities serve the academy and society in direct and indirect ways. Catholic institutions share in serving these publics, but they also exist within and serve the Catholic Church. In educating undergraduates, Catholic colleges and universities render two types of Church-related services—one intellectual and the other formational. The intellectual service demonstrates to students the historical roots of Catholic theological understanding and also helps them appreciate how the teachings of the Church sometimes fit into the modern world and at other times challenge its presuppositions. The formational service assists young women and men in becoming generous, ethically sound, loving, theologically mature, and service-oriented members of society.

The Catholic intellectual tradition does not reside solely in the theology and philosophy department, and its vibrancy in any Catholic college or university is dependent on the eagerness of faculty to pursue related academic and intellectual issues that arise within their academic disciplines. The following chapter explores where these important issues appear in the modern constellation of the humanities and sciences. Such related issues need not be the focus of any individual faculty member's research, but all faculty members play an important role in helping students make Catholic connections. Along with providing knowledge and good training in a given discipline, faculty members render an important intellectual service by helping students discover the nuance and implications of the Catholic tradition. Making the connections within their own discipline is perhaps the most natural way for faculty members to render this service.

All people of faith are called to holiness, and at Catholic universities students are encouraged to seek holiness in their lives. As befits an intellectual institution, encouragement is first and foremost related to the intellectual mission of the institution and emphasizes important intellectual virtues. Faculty members are witnesses and role models whose own honesty witnesses the kind of honesty they expect from their students. By their personal commitment to truth, faculty members also indicate to students their unwillingness to compromise the truth. Holiness also includes just and ethical actions on the part of believers, and in appropriate ways faculty members encourage their students to act justly and ethically. Faculty members also encourage all students to participate in their religious traditions with fidelity and Catholic students to deepen their faith and to commit themselves in service to the Catholic Church.

The Problems

Administrators frequently referred to theology as the heart of the Catholic intellectual tradition on campus. They cited two problems, however, that militate against theology playing as significant a role as they think it should. Theology requirements at most Catholic colleges and universities are minimal, and at many Catholic universities there is little Catholic content in many of the theology courses that are offered. This makes it possible for students to graduate from many Catholic colleges and universities without being exposed to much Catholic theology. Most students take no more than one or two introductory courses in theology, and only a few senior administrators affirmed that theology faculty actually link the content of an introductory course in theology to the Catholic intellectual tradition. Whatever the content of the introductory courses in Catholic theology, professors of theology are probably content to present a theological perspective on important teachings of the Church but have neither the time nor, perhaps, the expertise to show how Church teachings have an impact on other academic disciplines.

Traditionally, philosophy played an important role in imparting the Catholic intellectual tradition to students. While many admired the traditional framework of the Catholic intellectual tradition, the role of philosophy in communicating that tradition to current students is hazy in the minds of many senior administrators we interviewed, who simply did not point to philosophy as a major vehicle for presenting aspects of the Catholic tradition today.[4] In fact, only one administrator suggested that current philosophy courses address themes that are linked by faculty members to Catholic theology or other aspects of the Catholic intellectual tradition. Since it is an argument from silence, this is admittedly a weak point. Nonetheless it is important to note that, with the exception of senior administrators at immersion institutions, when it came to discussing the role philosophy plays in the Catholic intellectual tradition, administrators were silent.

Some institutions require an introductory course in the history of philosophy. This is an ideal setting for examining topics from theological and philosophical perspectives, but if faculty members are capitalizing on this opportunity, it was not singled out by senior administrators as something distinctive about their type of Catholic education. Apparently, faculty members teaching required courses in philosophy at nonimmersion institutions do not explore connections between material covered in the classroom and Catholic theology. With philosophy no longer playing a pivotal role in exposing students to the Catholic intellectual tradition, this burden falls more heavily on theology and other nontheology disciplines. Administrators admitted that theology was not always shouldering that burden effectively and nontheology disciplines were faring no better.

Senior administrators were quite clear about what students should learn in relation to the Catholic intellectual tradition, but in many instances they were not confident that the faculty could situate Catholic teaching in the complex array of modern academic disciplines. While administrators were not despondent, they were also not confident and indicated that much remains to be done. Currently, a large percentage of faculty members have only modest knowledge of the Catholic intellectual tradition. Senior administrators understand that this reality requires offering in-service programs for current faculty members.[5]

Some administrators emphasized the need to find faculty members who are more knowledgeable about the Catholic intellectual tradition as it relates to their academic disciplines. Although most institutions have adopted some "hiring for mission" processes with respect to faculty, many administrators judged these procedures to be weak. While these approaches do make prospective faculty aware of the institution's Catholic character and mission, for the most part they do not suggest ways in which new faculty members can or ought to contribute to the specifically Catholic mission of the institution. With the exception of some administrators at immersion institutions, no senior administrator spoke about evaluating nontheology faculty on the basis of their contributions to the specifically Catholic mission or indicating that such evaluation would take place after the faculty member had been teaching for two or three years.

Implications within Models

Each of the four Catholic models differs in its target population of students and its strategies, and these differences determine the desirable characteristics their faculty members embody. Senior administrators identified problems in all four types of Catholic institutions that erode institutional Catholic character, identity, and mission, and they made suggestions for improvement. Analyzing the suggestions for each of the models reveals what changes are required to achieve the improvements mentioned by senior administrators. Having identified the necessary changes for each of the four models, we will address the issue of realism, or exactly what would be required to make desired changes likely in each of the four models.

The Catholic immersion model promises the greatest student exposure to Catholic theology, Catholic philosophy, and the Catholic intellectual tradition. To achieve these goals, theology faculty must have sufficient time and expertise to teach Catholic theology and indicate how Catholic teaching informs the Catholic intellectual tradition. Similarly, philosophy must address important Catholic themes in a critical, but fair, manner. Finally, current and new faculty members in nontheological disciplines need in-depth knowledge about the nontheology Catholic intellectual tradition so that they can share this with their students. A good number of immersion institutions may feel that they are doing all this, but comments from senior administrators at these institutions indicate that they are apprehensive about being able to hire faculty with the necessary qualifications for satisfactory performance in their type of institution. In addition, a number of these institutions constantly question whether they can help their students to be more critical of the underlying perspectives in the secular culture, as well as the Catholic culture. Elevating critical reflection and helping students to "challenge the assumptions" as they explore the Catholic faith and other worldviews are seen as essential ways for students to enhance their knowledge and deepen their faith. Senior administrators at immersion institutions want to be sure they are providing students with reliable skills that will enable them to respond to all the challenges they will encounter after they graduate, particularly challenges to their faith.

Some Catholic immersion administrators indicated that a significant fraction of their nontheology faculty would have difficulty relating the Catholic intellectual tradition to material they ordinarily present in their courses. Faculty members in specific academic disciplines require targeted, in-depth knowledge so that they can begin to address at least a few Catholic issues in their classes. Without particular knowledge, faculty will feel unqualified to address important Catholic issues in their own academic disciplines. Senior administrators in immersion institutions correctly point to many talented faculty members who know their academic disciplines well and are also well acquainted with the Catholic intellectual tradition. Nevertheless, administrators remain concerned about faculty who are experts in their academic field and well disposed to the Catholic faith but do not know much about the relationship of their discipline to the Catholic intellectual tradition.

Comments of senior administrators about faculty unfamiliarity with the Catholic intellectual tradition pose challenges when applied to the persuasion model. In the persuasion model, students are expected to become familiar with the teachings of the Catholic faith and the Catholic intellectual tradition through required courses in theology. But senior administrators acknowledge that the Catholic content of theology core courses is uneven. As a result, students—Catholic and non-Catholic alike—may fulfill requirements without having significant exposure to Catholic theology. The problem is complicated by the fact that philosophy is seemingly no longer a carrier of the Catholic tradition at many persuasion institutions.

Something has to give here. Some senior administrators already suspect that, despite core requirements in theology, many students avoid any substantial interaction with Catholic theology. In the absence of any strong Catholic themes in philosophy and with some students avoiding Catholic theology, what is the primary channel for allowing students to understand the contours of Catholic theology and the Catholic intellectual tradition? If Catholic academic content is to be transmitted partially through Catholic theology and primarily through individual academic disciplines, which, aside from philosophy, are the only other available channel at these institutions, faculty members from a great variety of disciplines need to become better informed about the relationship between the Catholic intellectual tradition and their own academic discipline. Senior administrators and faculty need good data about which aspects of the Catholic intellectual tradition are currently being shared, or not, with students.

In Catholic persuasion institutions, Catholic theologians at most institutions cannot realistically be expected to transmit even the greater portion of the Catholic intellectual tradition to faculty in nontheological disciplines. With strong faculty leadership and support, some knowledgeable faculty inside the institution and some outside experts must begin to prepare other faculty in their institution so that they have sufficient knowledge to address "Catholic issues" in their own academic disciplines. Catholic theology certainly should play a prominent role in this undertaking, as Catholic theologians share with their nontheology colleagues how they can draw on the Catholic intellectual tradition in their own discipline. Depending on the current departmental knowledge base, each department chair has to be alert to hiring new faculty members whose training and expertise includes knowledge about how their specific disciplines relate to the Catholic intellectual tradition.

Because Catholic diaspora institutions have a large proportion of non-Catholic students, their religion requirement is frequently just a single course in religion that includes some treatment of, but not a major emphasis on, Catholic theology. As in the other models, the Catholic intellectual tradition at a diaspora institution is communicated not only in the academic sector but also through campus ministry. Since students are not required to take much Catholic theology, any attempt to have faculty share the Catholic intellectual tradition with students at diaspora universities means this must largely take place in nontheological subjects. The other alternative would entail faculty finding ways to make elective Catholic theology courses much more attractive to students. As admirable as such an approach is in theory, however, it is not very practical in the short run. In the best of circumstances, these innovations could be attempted for years on end without substantially increasing the number of students taking Catholic theology courses.

More faculty at diaspora institutions need to address Catholic issues in their regular courses, whether they be introductory courses or advanced courses for undergraduate majors in specific disciplines. Senior administrators recommended this approach during their interviews, but implementing it requires educating the faculty about how the Catholic intellectual tradition impacts their given academic disciplines. Since the number of faculty teaching theology at diaspora institutions is not large, outside experts will most likely have to be brought in to educate the faculty. A complementary process of hiring in each department over the next several years with a view to acquiring full-time and adjunct faculty with expertise in the Catholic intellectual tradition in a number of academic disciplines is also a strategic necessity.

Comments by senior administrators about the minimal exposure of students to the Catholic intellectual tradition raise important issues for Catholic cohort institutions. If senior administrators wish to make more students familiar with the Catholic intellectual tradition in cohort institutions where philosophy plays only a minor role, the most effective place to do so is through the theology requirement. The requirement itself need not be changed, but the required course can be adjusted to focus more specifically on Catholic theology. It is true that cohort students have available to them particular elective courses outside of theology that explore aspects of the Catholic intellectual tradition. Comments by senior administrators, however, indicated that although they are not bereft of faculty who are knowledgeable both in their field and the Catholic intellectual tradition, the number of individuals with these dual competencies is limited. For example, the institution may have a faculty member who can offer a course on Christian literature, but it does not have faculty who can offer courses that provide a good perspective on Catholic philosophy, Catholic social teaching, Catholic legal theory, the Catholic understanding of the regularity of laws of nature, or the Catholic approach to marriage and children. A solid program in Catholic studies should be able to offer courses that address all these topics, providing cohort students with what they want and need, but that is not enough. All students should have the opportunity in their majors to learn how the Catholic tradition handles certain topics currently discussed by faculty in scholarly journals. In the absence of faculty with expertise in these areas, there are only two options—the institution either educates the existing faculty about the Catholic intellectual tradition or hires adjunct or full-time faculty with dual competency.

Sensitive Hiring Issues

A good number of senior administrators indicated a reluctance to be confrontational or very forthright during the hiring process with respect to issues of Catholic identity, character, and mission. Whether for legal reasons or because both faculty and administrators wanted to hire the most qualified people, the inclination, according to senior administrators, was to handle lightly issues relating to Catholic identity.

Catholic identity is indeed a sensitive issue. No goal is served by upsetting potential or current faculty members about matters of little moment, but Catholic identity is certainly not such a matter. Catholic identity is of great importance and impacts all areas of university life. Because the faculty plays the primary role in the institution, ways have to be found in the hiring process to address the issue of Catholic identity in a manner that communicates what the Catholic institution is looking for and how prospective faculty members can satisfy the religious and academic expectations of the institution.

The four general characteristics sought for in faculty members are a commitment to the centrality of theology and philosophy (or its equivalent), an appreciation of the institution's responsibility to serve the Catholic Church, a willingness to secure greater knowledge about the Catholic intellectual tradition, and acceptance of the role to encourage students in faith and virtue. These characteristics appear to have great specificity, which is potentially intimidating. On closer examination, however, it becomes clear they are rather general and manageable, and they have the potential to be quite useful for faculty. By attending to them in the hiring process, a Catholic institution indicates an expectation that faculty members will provide academic support to the Catholic project at the university and personal support to students that includes helping them grow in their commitment to the faith. While these expectations certainly require time and effort from faculty, they need not be onerous.

Following through on the expectations by developing a supportive framework that builds on the general characteristics will demonstrate their reasonableness and importance and can be a source of satisfaction for faculty entering the collegial community. Comments by senior administrators indicated that many Catholic universities establish colleagueship seminars for new faculty hires. These groups meet several times during the course of the year to discuss issues of interest to faculty members and could become the locus for information sessions that help new faculty members understand and fulfill their mission at a particular Catholic institution. For example, newly hired faculty members might be told that during the course of their first two years they will be asked to attend three or four presentations on Catholic theology and philosophy by members of these departments. Newly hired faculty members might also be given a presentation about various types of Church service that students currently perform or the various ways the institution itself renders service to the Church. Prospective faculty members could also be asked to attend two sessions per year in which departmental faculty explore issues related to the Catholic intellectual tradition. Establishing a process to support and encourage new faculty to find in their personal research intersection points between their academic disciplines and the Catholic intellectual tradition provides an advantage to faculty while also serving the needs of the institution. Finally, members of campus ministry might suggest concrete ways new faculty members could encourage student development in faith and virtue through their normal faculty-student interactions. A faculty member who is positively disposed to teaching at a Catholic institution could well find such sessions reassuring, informative, and a helpful orientation to constructive interactions with students and other faculty members.

A challenge to hiring for mission is that relatively few people are trained with discipline-specific knowledge about the Catholic intellectual tradition. Even students who do their doctoral studies at Catholic universities frequently learn little about "Catholic themes" in their academic disciplines. As a result, there is a shortage of people in the nontheology disciplines who have this kind of dual competence. Nevertheless, some people have extensive knowledge about how particular disciplines address issues that have long been part of the Catholic intellectual tradition. Once identified, these knowledgeable individuals can be a resource; they can be invited to conduct miniseminars for faculty at particular institutions in a specific discipline. A more long-term approach to the problem relies on the principles of standard economic theory. As Catholic universities increase their demand for doctoral students who are knowledgeable about both a specific discipline and how that discipline intersects with the Catholic intellectual tradition, the shift will be detected in the market, and over time an increased supply of such candidates will result.

Challenges to Modern Academic Culture

Senior administrators at Catholic institutions emphasized the special responsibilities inherent in claiming institutional Catholic identity. They expressed pride in Catholic higher education because it presents an alternative to the general nonsectarian model of education. If Catholic higher education is to be a true alternative to the nonsectarian model, Catholic colleges and universities should enable students to exercise critical reasoning beyond what can be achieved in nonsectarian institutions.

In the nonsectarian model, students are encouraged to think critically about each topic that is raised. Critical thinking of this type has its roots in the logic component of the traditional liberal arts trivium of grammar, logic, and rhetoric and demands justification for any assertions that are made. To the extent that both nonsectarian and Catholic institutions rely on the liberal arts, they both encourage this type of critical thinking by their students.

In the nonsectarian approach, critical thinking results in a general skepticism with respect to the validity of any significant claim regarding the way the world is. Relying on philosophical analysis, the Catholic approach also questions the assumptions underlying every assertion, but its skepticism does not preclude drawing some positive conclusions. Unlike the nonsectarian approach, the Catholic position affirms the reality and objectivity of significant values that are esteemed and honored by practically all human beings. In the Catholic approach, skepticism is a marker along a way that extends beyond skepticism and eventually arrives at a comprehensive appreciation of significant human values.

Some examples illustrate the two different end-points reached by secular critical reasoning and Catholic critical reasoning. In a postmodern environment, many academics either assert truth is unattainable or are skeptical about the possibility of reaching it. In this environment, although a perspective may appear to be true, asserting so with confidence is not possible. Therefore, truth in this intellectual milieu is not an attainable value. Truth for a period of time, truth from a certain perspective, truth for a certain group—all these are possible. But truth in some absolute, perduring sense is not possible. Despite this, the modern viewpoint holds that the pursuit of knowledge is always worthwhile, no matter how trivial the knowledge sought and, furthermore, many hold that the best way to advance understanding is to explore limited aspects of reality with great precision. For many academics, critical exploration of the larger issues such as truth, freedom, or God is unlikely to result in useful knowledge, much less truth.

Consider another area of inquiry. In modern society, although billions of dollars are spent on creating and maintaining beauty, beauty is considered to be in the eye of the beholder, not in any sense objective. Seeking beauty is considered to be a futile pursuit, but—strangely at variance with a skeptical evaluation of viewpoints—the critical evaluation of art and beauty is deemed genuine, real, and worthwhile. Freedom is another value esteemed in modern society. Academe places a high premium on individual freedom, which is viewed as absence of constraint and considered the highest expression of liberty. According to the modern mentality, the freedom from constraint, an individual good, trumps the welfare of the group, a communal good. Finally, many people believe in a God that is transcendent, yet immanent, and seek to live lives of holiness in obedience to the will of God. A number of modern thinkers maintain that there is nothing beyond what appears in this world and those who cling to belief in God are merely deceiving themselves.

According to Catholic critical reasoning, secular reasoning cannot account for significant things that practically all people value in their lives. As one senior administrator noted, a secular postmodern approach to truth is diametrically opposed to the approach taken in the Catholic intellectual tradition. Consequently, for each of the issues raised earlier, the Catholic philosophical tradition arrives at a different conclusion. In the Catholic tradition, the pursuit of truth is worthwhile and eventually leads to God, if the pursuit of knowledge is not restricted to small, confined issues. Beauty is a fundamental human good, sought by all people. Although individuals make different judgments about how best to participate in the value of beauty, at least within certain cultures, most people can agree on general guidelines for beauty. Furthermore, parents instruct their children about what is beautiful in life and how to make things more beautiful. By exchanging beautiful things, human beings participate in the value of beauty. The Catholic intellectual tradition appreciates individual freedom and believes it is important. However, the freedom of the individual does not always trump the welfare of the group, and in some instances individual freedom should be subordinated. Finally, in the Catholic tradition, critical thinking points its practitioners in the direction of God as both the source and the subject in the search for truth.

The Catholic approach to philosophy can certainly learn very important things from the nonsectarian approach. Yet one wonders to what extent the nonsectarian approach can seriously criticize the presuppositions that allow its adherents to arrive at conclusions so much at variance with the practice of most individuals and societies. The Catholic intellectual tradition has something valuable and different to offer to modern students and, through them, modern society.

Students and Content of the Catholic Intellectual Tradition

Administrators typically spoke enthusiastically about the Catholic intellectual tradition in its broadest sense, and in many cases they identified as a desired outcome for undergraduates the fact that the students took some required core courses in religion and/or philosophy. No administrator, however, offered any evidence beyond course grades that students were actually appropriating any significant aspect of the Catholic intellectual tradition that could be called upon after graduation. Many administrators expressed the hope that students were assimilating the Catholic intellectual tradition, just as they themselves had done when attending Catholic colleges or universities. But they shared no systematic data that focused on the extent to which the tradition was being received in theology, philosophy, the liberal arts, or the newer academic disciplines outside the liberal arts. They also did not give any indication that there was any such data available.

Administrators often focused on hopes and aspirations for students and spoke in the optative mood.[6] They indicated a desire for better performance on their own part and on that of their institutions in terms of acquainting students with the Catholic intellectual tradition. In a number of cases, they explicitly acknowledged that they were not doing enough in this regard. A few administrators articulated impressive plans for introducing more aspects of the Catholic intellectual tradition into the curriculum at their institutions. These administrators pointed to particular academic disciplines outside of theology and philosophy as target areas for more serious efforts by faculty to share the Catholic intellectual tradition with their students.

Administrator comments in this tone evidence a commendable concern about the centrality of the Catholic intellectual tradition at a Catholic university and a desire to make that tradition more accessible to students. However, because curricular matters are so sensitive, most administrators making these comments acknowledged that any improvements would have to proceed slowly and with considerable caution. It was very clear that administrators realize that the success of new academic programs with Catholic flavors is dependent on persuading, not commanding, faculty to introduce them.

The data from the interviews indicate that most institutions want to do more to help students appreciate the contours of the Catholic intellectual tradition. The administrators' comments also suggest they understand why this greater exposure to the tradition is significant for the students, the Church, and society in general. The implications of that desire are important for each of the models of Catholic universities.

That senior administrators desire to see the Catholic intellectual tradition receive greater attention in Catholic higher education is truly refreshing and initially very encouraging. However, a more careful analysis of the expectations of senior administrators with respect to a heightened emphasis on the Catholic intellectual tradition at their institutions is more sobering. By carefully examining the expectations senior administrators shared, it is reasonable to conclude that many institutions are underperforming in this area. As a group, senior administrators indicated that their single most important issue and priority was the Catholic intellectual tradition. A review of their comments, however, showed that most were phrased in the optative mood, suggesting what administrators would like to accomplish at their institutions, not what they are currently doing. This analysis shows that, apart from the Catholic immersion institutions, a number of institutions in each category likely fail to educate their students about the Catholic intellectual tradition at even the minimal levels prescribed by their given institutional model.

Many administrators noted that when new students arrive at their institutions, their knowledge of the Catholic faith is modest. Although the topic of tradition illiteracy is broader than ignorance about the Catholic intellectual tradition, even construed narrowly, initial knowledge of the Catholic tradition among students is decisive. Providing students with insight into the Catholic intellectual tradition when the students at Catholic institutions have very little knowledge of the Catholic faith is a Sisyphean task. Indeed, it is unclear how students can understand introductory theology if they are largely ignorant of Catholic culture and unfamiliar with the major tenets of Catholic teaching. Even introductory theology presupposes basic knowledge about the Catholic faith, which, according to many Catholic administrators, traditional-aged students lack when they arrive on campus as first-year students.

Faculty members at all universities have recognized the importance of determining whether students have sufficient skills to engage in regular university courses. For this reason, many universities administer a math skills exam, a writing skills exam, and a modern language exam. With respect to mathematics and writing, the results of these "placement tests" determine whether students have sufficient preparation to engage in technical subjects on the collegiate level or need supplementary preparation. Following a similar approach at Catholic institutions to knowledge of the Catholic faith or the Catholic intellectual tradition appears fruitful, even necessary.[7]

Implementing any new academic program to bring aspirations to fruition is always a challenge, and in this case, there are substantial hurdles affecting both students and faculty. Despite the hurdles, the Catholic intellectual tradition and its assimilation by students are central to the mission, identity, and character of Catholic universities. Unless students in the four models of Catholic institutions become more knowledgeable about the Catholic faith as a result of their study, their education will be indistinguishable from that available through the nonsectarian model. Administrators at Catholic institutions are paid and trained to face and address these kinds of challenges. If they are successful in overcoming the hurdles related to student knowledge of the Catholic tradition, they will move their institutions closer to fulfilling what is minimally necessary for satisfying the distinguishability criterion.

Inheritability in Different Catholic Cultures

At a time when Catholics were less influential and in general not as well educated as other groups in society, Catholic education was very confident that it was offering students something superior to what they could obtain at nonsectarian institutions. Anecdotal reports, many from alumni/ae who graduated in the first half of the twentieth century from Catholic institutions of higher education, indicate their enthusiasm, years after their graduation, about what they deem the specifically "Catholic content" of their education. In that time period, theology was not taught, though students took some courses in Catholic teachings. According to their recollections and evaluations many years later, more significant for their development were the courses they took in philosophy. Anecdotally, many alumni/ae cite these courses as being important at the time (even though, as many acknowledge, they may have struggled to comprehend the material covered in the classes) and even more significant for their later lives. Many alumni/ae of this era also believe that through their philosophy courses they received perspectives and skills that served them well in their business, civic, and personal lives. A number of senior administrators who themselves had been educated in Catholic colleges and universities echoed these sentiments.[8]

The anecdotal data from Catholic alumni/ae suggest an important nexus between what students learned in some classes at Catholic institutions and what they were able to use to their own benefit in their later lives. To the extent that this nexus actually existed early in this era, it was likely communicated to subsequent generations of students via the university itself, as well as in familial and business settings. If, indeed, the type of instruction received by undergraduates in the first half of the twentieth century was useful to their lives lived outside of academe, it enhanced the inheritability of the practice of requiring Catholic philosophy courses for undergraduates.

If the preceding tentative analysis is plausible, the philosophy courses, in addition to contributing to inheritability, seem to have become narratives for students; they were part of the symbols of Catholic culture. That is, the courses were certainly part of the intellectual content of Catholic culture at Catholic universities at that time. In addition, teachers of philosophy, by relating somewhat abstract issues to important developments in the lives of their students, enabled students to grasp what in their education was distinctive from that of their counterparts at secular institutions. The knowledge they acquired in this fashion was presented and perceived as having esteemed value for society, the Church, and the day-to-day lives of students as they matured. What could have been perceived as merely a dry and burdensome set of requirements took on an almost heroic dimension, becoming a kind of intellectual "boot camp" that rendered a competitive edge to all those who emerged from the experience.

For a half-century or more, Catholic collegiate culture was relatively impermeable to the pressures of the dominant culture with respect to Catholic philosophy courses. Administrators took a firm stance when it came to holding the line on these requirements. Their ability to strike that pose and be effective was not, however, based solely on the force of their firm determination. Administrators can decide not to yield on important issues, but their resolve will eventually crumble if what they insist on is not received in a positive way, that is, inherited, by subsequent groups of students. Administrators at Catholic colleges and universities in an earlier time could be firm about philosophy requirements because the students and parents both expected and accepted their stance. Bolstered by the views of their parents, students expected faculty and administrators to be clear and persistent about policies at Catholic colleges and universities, and much in the culture supported general compliance with positional authority. Student acquiescence was a contributor to the stability of philosophy requirements in Catholic colleges, but it was certainly bolstered by a sometimes grudging student respect for the effectiveness of the courses, as well. According to this analysis, administrative resolve in curricular policy was sustainable because it was bolstered by student acquiescence but also, more important, by their appreciation.

Most of the preceding is based on fragmentary evidence. In order to establish whether philosophy courses or other facets of Catholic culture "worked" for Catholic universities in the first half of the twentieth century, an extensive empirical investigation and careful analytical critique are necessary. They are tasks for future research, not our present concern. The point in raising these issues is not to resolve a historical question but to highlight a challenge for those desiring in the twenty-first century to give the Catholic intellectual tradition greater prominence on Catholic campuses. Whatever way Catholic universities choose to emphasize the Catholic intellectual tradition, the actual program launched by the university must have traction with students. If the Catholic intellectual tradition is to positively influence the campus culture, current and future students and their parents have to find merit or benefits in studying such courses. For this to happen in our modern society, where positional authority holds diminished sway and individual freedom is most frequently exercised for personal advancement, the benefits have to be clear to students and not lie in the too-distant future.

What are the benefits from studying the Catholic intellectual tradition? Faculty and administrators at Catholic institutions are the ones who must answer this difficult question. If faculty are convinced there are benefits for students, faculty also have to structure the courses—whether they are required or elective—so that students perceive their benefits. Understanding the reasonableness of one's Catholic faith in a world where fundamentalism in Christian and non-Christian sectors is on the rise might appeal to some students. Understanding the changes Catholic faith and practice have experienced over time might attract others. However, these are intellectual insights that are unlikely to excite many students in the present. Whether these outcomes would have a lasting impact beyond graduation is, at the very least, questionable. Although some students get lasting satisfaction from taking courses that only raise (and perhaps resolve) interesting intellectual questions, most do not. Getting students to engage in the Catholic intellectual tradition in the twenty-first century will likely require that faculty members emulate their predecessors from the first half of the twentieth century. They will have to find some way to demonstrate to students that the knowledge and insights drawn from the Catholic intellectual tradition can contribute directly to the quality of their lives once they graduate from the university. In other words, these courses will have to have a powerful appeal through symbols to the imagination of students.

Emphasizing the beneficial import of the Catholic intellectual tradition may appear to subtly undermine the tradition itself, which focuses on issues much loftier than self-interest. Self-interest, however, is not a value or emotion confined to the modern era. Even in the Middle Ages—that golden period when some would have us believe students were interested in learning for learning's sake—university students realized that a university degree would secure them a position in life they could not hope to achieve otherwise. Presumably one reason for the many changes occurring in university structure and programs over many centuries is the attempts by administrators and faculty to satisfy the demand for useful knowledge that contributes to social success and upward mobility. Administrators and faculty at Catholic universities cannot hope to succeed in making an increased emphasis on the Catholic intellectual tradition inheritable by appealing to claims of intellectual insight alone. They will also have to demonstrate that the knowledge is useful.

Inheritability is closely linked with the way cultures, like living organisms, interact with one another. As these permeable cultures bump up against each other, there is cross-boundary seepage that produces internal cultural adaptations. In cultures these adaptations are initiated by cultural catalysts, but they only become lasting features of a culture if cultural citizens are somehow induced to accept them. For most modern adults in the United States, active participation in a particular culture is a matter of choice, and most people choose to participate in a number of cultures. By definition, the dominant culture has the greatest impact on people, especially young people. All other things being equal, a significant majority of students are not inclined to opt out of the dominant culture. Most young adults who attend Catholic institutions and eagerly prepare themselves for work in service professions such as education, health care, law, or social work hope to pursue those professions, which require focus, selflessness, and commitment, while also enjoying the benefits of the dominant culture. Understandably, they want the best of both cultural worlds. They are more likely to welcome deeper immersion in a Catholic culture if they get a glimpse of how this will enable them to achieve goals they have set for themselves with respect to the dominant culture. The possibility of having a more lasting and fulfilling marriage, of being more effective parents, of being more articulate, wise, or intellectually agile—these are tangible benefits. Whether there are features of a renewed Catholic culture that are sufficiently compelling to the modern generation and whether they can be offered through a greater emphasis on the Catholic intellectual tradition are issues that must be addressed by faculty and administrators at individual Catholic institutions.

Nondominant cultures have an impact because people choose to remain connected to them. People may have many reasons for remaining connected to a culture, but at some level they must perceive the attachment as beneficial. Effective cultures make these benefits apparent to even casual seekers or experimenters, especially if the culture demands extra work or commitment. Catholic collegiate culture has to show some "proximate coherence" both with a previous Catholic culture and with other cultures, all of which point to benefits accruing from association with it. Catholic culture should be perceived by students as having a positive impact on them, and although they still have not reached full maturity, students should glimpse the benefits of engaging the Catholic intellectual tradition. Sisters, brothers, and priests in an earlier Catholic academic culture managed to weave together the content components of the Catholic intellectual tradition with religious and personal benefits in convincing enough ways that students, with support from their parents, found the process compelling and useful. Something similar, that is appropriate for the modern culture experienced by students, must occur today. Giving greater emphasis to the Catholic intellectual tradition on campus cannot be solely or even primarily an academic exercise if it is eventually to be inherited by students. Today's faculty must understand the hearts and minds and hopes and fears of their students and respond to them if attempts to revitalize a demanding Catholic culture are to take root.

Related to the need to have an approach appealing to students, administrators noted they wanted to present an upbeat version of the Catholic intellectual tradition, one that is true to the tradition but which also is optimistic and engages new learning in science and other disciplines. Administrators spoke of the tradition as being "open and developing." Is this optimistic attitude consonant with the actual Catholic tradition that must maintain core cultural coherence?

Alasdair MacIntyre has written insightfully about the intellectual tradition in the realm of ethics and morals.[9] He argues that there are only three main ethical traditions: the scientific-pragmatic tradition, the tradition of radical free choice with minimal constraints, and the natural law tradition.[10] His analysis and justification of the three traditions is not germane to the discussion here. More pertinent is his discussion of how one decides whether a moral tradition is true. After an extended analysis, he concludes that each of the three distinct traditions is logically consistent. That is, given where they begin their fundamental analysis and what they identify as most deeply human, each tradition is coherent. Thus, according to MacIntyre, none of the three traditions is theoretically or logically wrong. Assuming that his analysis is accurate, one wonders how to choose the "true moral tradition" or indeed whether any one of the traditions can be shown to be true. MacIntyre argues that there are two additional criteria for determining whether a tradition is true. One criterion relates to the community that lives the moral tradition, and the other refers to the ability of the tradition to handle new moral issues or problems as they arise.

An ethical tradition that lasts for centuries is one that is not only reflected upon and modified by an ongoing community of scholars but also is actually lived in a community. People commit themselves to a way of life based on a particular ethical position. In fact, people are always raised in one of the three ethical traditions or some combination of them long before they learn to name the ethical norms or values central to the tradition. A factor influencing which tradition is correct is the experience of those communities (and individuals, although the individuals always live their tradition in some community of like-minded individuals) as they live the tradition over a longer period of time. Ethical communities observe one another and make judgments. The experience of the community may not be sufficient to decide which tradition is correct, but it certainly plays a role.

The second factor that influences whether one tradition is judged "better" than the other is the ability of a tradition to handle new challenges that arise in society. Currently a plethora of new developments pose moral questions about how to proceed: cloning, stem cell research, environmental issues, gay marriage, preemptive military action, terminally ill patients and "brain death," euthanasia, and so on. Each issue challenges the ability of each of the three traditions not simply to offer advice, guidance, or directives but also to make statements and offer rationales that make sense to communities and are consistent with the principles inherent in that tradition, that is, that fulfill core coherence. The "response" by a tradition to these issues comes both in theory and in the lived practice of the community, and all the while that communities and scholars are formulating coherent responses, life moves on, and additional moral questions arise. Overall judgments about moral systems are made on the basis of, in part, their theoretical ability to handle new issues and the experience of the community in handling issues new and old.

Many senior administrators were concerned that the Catholic intellectual tradition actually be and be perceived as being open and developing. If MacIntyre's approach is not confined to an ethical tradition but extended to a broader tradition of intellectual inquiry, it follows that the only way for the Catholic intellectual tradition to remain viable and compelling is for it to be attentive to new developments and address the new developments with as much core coherence as possible. Core coherence means that nothing belonging to the core changes; it does not mean that nothing significant changes. The difficult task is distinguishing which are core components of a tradition and which are not. The latter can change in response to societal change, the former cannot. One way for teachers to engage their students is by using long-standing principles from the Catholic intellectual tradition to handle new developments in society. Doing this well can prove the vitality of the Catholic intellectual tradition and entice students to become familiar with the tradition because it enables them to think more clearly and consistently than people adhering to another, perhaps less disciplined, tradition.

The Catholic Church places an extraordinarily high value on core coherence, as was pointed out earlier. Consequently, any "new" approach that seems to deviate from what has become "accepted tradition" invariably undergoes long periods of discussion, development, and scrutiny as part of what many think is a glacial vetting process. It has been thus for much of the Church's history, and many theologians of good will have suffered in their honest attempts to develop more inheritable approaches. The positive aspect of this process is that, as new moral approaches are developed, the criticisms of fellow theologians help those working within the new moral paradigm to arrive at conclusions that moral theologians of both the old and new school agree are longstanding components of the Church's teaching. Clearly, in terms of the Catholic moral tradition, the Catholic Church is presently adjusting to a threat to cultural inheritability, and if history is any indicator, that adjustment period will be long and difficult.

The Margin and Strategy

A particular concern for a number of administrators was the financial pressure smaller Catholic institutions will encounter in the coming years as they try to attract a sufficient number of students. Specifically noted was whether emphasis on the Catholic component of the mission would deter students from applying to the institution.

This issue is best interpreted in terms of the four models for being a Catholic institution of higher education. On the basis of its geographical location, its competitors, and its own religious and academic history, a Catholic university has to choose a way of being Catholic that satisfies the margin criterion. In this study, there are four ways to be a Catholic university. Although other possibilities exist, these four ways, or some mixture of them, are currently the four most common ways to organize an institution that is distinguishably Catholic and one is likely to remain that way for decades to come—in other words, to be inheritable.

Some administrators noted that smaller Catholic liberal arts institutions will face increasing financial pressures. With an eye to developing effective strategies to meet this challenge, the Catholic character of the institutions comes under some scrutiny. One group of administrators indicated that Catholic institutions should be proud of their Catholic heritage, and, according to some of them, this forthright approach would enjoy a good response from interested students and their parents. Indeed, this positive view of the appeal of being a clearly Catholic institution was the most frequently mentioned.[11] Another group of administrators, however, noted that directors of admission and public relations and communications people often shy away from the Catholic dimensions of the institution, particularly when it comes to the thorny issue of theology requirements.

What lies behind this concern about an institution being "too Catholic" is worth some attention. All institutions—no matter the model they follow, including the nonsectarian one—face almost constant economic pressures. Some, however, are in a more precarious position because the number of students they annually attract is close to the minimum required to support the infrastructure and the modest array of academic courses and other student services offered. In precarious circumstances, any institution has to consider alternate ways to proceed. In the structure presented here, the president, after having secured the approval of the board, may decide that the Catholic institution must change its focus. Instead, say, of adhering to the Catholic persuasion model, it may have to switch to the Catholic diaspora or cohort model in order to remain economically viable. Changing models will always involve risks, because the process concerns fundamental changes in the institution's culture. That said, the best path for an institution to pursue might still be to switch models. Changing from one Catholic model to another is one thing. Opting for the nonsectarian model is quite another. Switching between Catholic models should not be undertaken lightly, but as long as the adjustment is made prudently and senior administration is attentive to the basic requirements for distinguishability and inheritability, the institution can continue to be viable.

There is another strategic approach an institution might take that could ostensibly satisfy the criteria for distinguishability but would threaten inheritability. In this approach, an institution attempts to remain a Catholic institution while downplaying its Catholicity in its advertising. In this scenario, students enroll at the institution under a set of expectations generated by information that was intentionally and significantly incomplete. Of necessity, student expectations will not be fulfilled. These students might adjust once they arrive or they might not. If they do not adjust, they will communicate their disappointment to future students, and the very students the university had hoped to attract with this stealth strategy—those who are skeptical about the religious dimension—will start avoiding the institution. If students adjust once they arrive on campus and experience the Catholic culture, this information will likewise be communicated to future students. In the latter case, the institution avoids emphasizing the Catholic culture, but students continue to attend because they find the Catholic culture rewarding. Any rational administration would recognize that being forthright is the best policy and start emphasizing the Catholic culture in their advertising.

The final area of emphasis related to the Catholic intellectual tradition addresses the degree to which theology at a Catholic institution is regarded as open and developing. This is one aspect of the strategy an institution chooses. Those administrators who raised this issue were interested in portraying theology and the requirement for all students to take a theology course in its most positive light. Every Catholic model assumes that the university desires to serve the Church through its mission. Although students require deeper understanding as they mature in their Catholic faith, each model assumes that institutions do nothing to mislead students about Catholic teaching or the nature of Catholic theology. It is within this context that the comments about the openness of Catholic theology should be interpreted. Administrators emphasizing the openness and breadth of Catholic theology want students to be aware of the ability of theology to address a complete array of relevant issues for modern students. This group of administrators spoke glowingly about the positive reaction students have when they see how theology can help them approach issues that are important to them now and that likely remain important to them throughout their lives. A positive approach to the power of theology to help students must be sustained over many years and appear in different university settings, not merely in the classroom. Such a positive approach might not be sufficient to energize students in great numbers to elect to take theology. It could, however, help students approach a required course in theology with anticipation of personal gain, as well as with a higher expectation they would appreciate the strengths of the Catholic intellectual tradition.

5

The Catholic Tradition

Intellectual, Moral, and Social

During the course of their conversations, senior administrators made frequent shorthand reference to three particular umbrella terms, the *Catholic intellectual tradition*, *the Catholic moral tradition*, and *Catholic social teaching*, but did not specify their components. Given the time constraints of the interviews, this lapse is not entirely surprising. Nevertheless, any attempt to appreciate what senior administrators were saying about their experience of institutional Catholic identity will certainly be enhanced by a clearer understanding of these terms. As an aid to the reader, this chapter offers a brief introduction to the three areas. Although totally insufficient for the breadth and depth of the three traditions, it does give a context in which to interpret the concerns and hopes of senior administrators at Catholic institutions. The latter part of the chapter explores the significance of cultural illiteracy and shadow cultures.

The three Catholic intellectual traditions are related to one another by inclusion. The Catholic intellectual tradition refers to all contributions made to the intellectual development of the West stemming from Catholic theology and philosophy. The Catholic moral tradition is one component, albeit a very significant one, of the Catholic intellectual tradition. One very large sector within the Catholic moral tradition is Catholic social teaching. Thus, Catholic social teaching is contained within the Catholic moral tradition, which in turn is embedded in the Catholic intellectual tradition. Relying on internal dependence, the fullest description in what follows is given for the intellectual tradition, while briefer presentations illustrate the moral and social components.

The Catholic Intellectual Tradition

Interestingly, fifty years ago, Catholic faculty members and intellectuals did not speak about the Catholic intellectual tradition as if it were an identifiable body of knowledge. At that time, people knew what the Catholic tradition was in their subject—philosophy, history, ethics, literature, political science, and law—but they saw no need to group the "Catholic content" of these academic disciplines into some larger intellectual body of knowledge. The term "Catholic intellectual tradition" and its contemporary use indicate how tenuous the grasp has become of Catholic issues within individual academic disciplines.

The Catholic intellectual tradition refers to themes that permeate many academic disciplines, and a preliminary task is to provide an ordering or taxonomy of where the salient components of the Catholic intellectual tradition appear in the extensive array of modern academic disciplines currently studied at Catholic universities. The Catholic intellectual tradition extends from the early Church to the present. Since the vast majority of modern academic disciplines have emerged since the early 1900s, we have to explore the framework in which these disciplines emerged. After a historical analysis and grouping of disciplines, we explore where significant Catholic themes arise in various disciplines. We then give a brief presentation of the Catholic moral tradition and an even briefer presentation of the Catholic tradition in social justice.

The Emergence of Universities

The foundation for Christianity is divinely inspired Scripture. Since Jesus Christ was seen as the fulfillment of Scripture, early Christianity regarded the Old Testament as sacred text inspired by God and recognized the continuity between the Old and the New Testaments. The New Testament is both the fulfillment of the Old and something markedly new; it is revelation of the Good News.

From the beginning, the Catholic intellectual tradition has had a broad base, which was expanded during the first few centuries of Christianity as important figures in the Church such as Origen, Ambrose, Augustine, Gregory of Nyssa, and Gregory Nazianzen used the great philosophers of Greek and Roman society to explain why faith in Christ and membership in the Church were consistent with human wisdom. From the vantage of the early Church, the great philosophers of old—Plato, Aristotle, and Plotinus among them—did not have the fullness of wisdom as it was contained in Jesus Christ. Nevertheless, the theoretical analysis of many secular philosophers was seen as useful for explaining the meaning of the gospel and not antagonistic to it.

The liberal arts developed out of classical Greek and Roman culture. Since these arts had been designated important areas of knowledge, the earliest education of young Christians involved learning the liberal arts.[1] Classical learning acknowledged two branches of the liberal arts: the trivium, consisting of grammar, logic, and rhetoric, and the quadrivium, consisting of arithmetic, geometry, astronomy, and music. The liberal arts were considered the foundation for the study of philosophy and theology. The reflections of the best thinkers in classical society, most prominently Plato and Aristotle, were embedded in the liberal arts, philosophy, and, with the emergence of Christianity as the state religion, theology. After the eclipse of Roman society in the sixth and seventh centuries but prior to the development of universities in the twelfth century, young boys would study the liberal arts with tutors, often monks in monasteries or priests in cathedral schools associated with the more prominent cathedrals in Europe.[2]

As medieval society developed, its need for well-educated people expanded. Universities emerged to satisfy this need and did so with a liberal arts curriculum as the foundation. Since these universities were new structures, often licensed centrally by the pope though arising in different cultures, there was great variety among them. Nonetheless, certain patterns prevailed. The liberal arts were still considered the foundation of learning, but much of the training in the trivium took place prior to the student arriving at the university. When students enrolled, they were about fifteen years old, and they normally spent four to six years getting their primary degree in the arts, which emphasized the study of philosophy. The highest degree in the arts was the *magister artium*, or master of arts. After receiving the master of arts degree and a *licentia docendi* (see hereafter), some students would pursue a second degree in theology, medicine, or law. Each of these other degrees required the master of arts degree plus six or seven additional years of specialized study. Upon successful completion of the program of studies, they again received a *licentia docendi*, as well as a master's or doctor's (the terms "master" and "doctor" were used almost interchangeably, but "master" was the more commonly used term) degree.[3]

Full universities in the Middle Ages had four faculties: arts, theology, law, and medicine. As the institutions matured, much depended on the strengths of the faculty at a particular university, but philosophy or logic was the main focus in practically all the faculties of arts. With the introduction of Aristotle into the curriculum, most of the courses students took for the master of arts degree were philosophy courses or courses in logic. Interestingly, students in the arts faculty did not take courses in Scripture or theology, though, in fact, included in philosophy of the day were what today would be considered theological subjects.

By the time students began their arts curriculum at the university, they would have studied grammar, rhetoric, and some logic, and they would know Latin well enough to speak, read, and write it. Classical history was not a separate subject. Rather, it was embedded within the Latin curriculum, in which students read the classical authors and learned the history of Greece and Rome. With this foundation in place, students would attend lectures in philosophy and some parts of the quadrivium.[4] Upon successful completion of the course of studies in the arts, students received two authorizations: the *licentia docendi* (literally, freedom to teach or authorization of teaching) and the master of arts degree. If the *licentia* was issued by a major university with a papal charter, such as Paris, Oxford, Cambridge, or Bologna, it was a *licentia ubique docendi*, a license to teach everywhere (more precisely, at every university that had a papal charter) and was consequently more valuable. Since all teaching at the university level was done in Latin, this certificate created important possibilities for adventuresome academics. As a means of personal advancement for someone who was a *magister*, the *licentia ubique docendi* was particularly important, since most universities, in whatever countries they were located, even if they were founded originally by the king or other nobility, sought and were granted a papal charter. The second authorization was the actual master of arts degree, which was granted by the guild of professors at the university, and it made the master a member of the guild of masters.

From the Renaissance and Reformation and through the Enlightenment and Romantic Movement, the intellectual development of western Europe brought with it significant changes in the traditional university curriculum.[5] The liberal arts and philosophy, however, continued to be the foundation. From the beginning of the seventeenth century onward, new academic areas emerged and were considered worthy of serious study. As significant discoveries were made in this scientific era, they were usually fitted into some aspect of the philosophy curriculum, such as natural philosophy or moral philosophy.[6] Not until the latter half of the nineteenth century did the faculty teaching a single one of these new subjects—such as mathematics, chemistry, physics, and philology—constitute a new academic unit or department in the college or university. Eventually the advances in the new sciences became so complex that they could no longer be accommodated as special lectures in the area of philosophy. By the latter half of the nineteenth century, in the leading German universities, professorial chairs were being established in chemistry, physics, and mathematics as well as in philology, which at that time consisted of the classical studies of Latin, Greek, and the history of the societies associated with these languages.[7] Many Americans interested in pursuing science in the mid- and latter part of the nineteenth century were attracted by the strong reputation of the German universities. Upon graduation from American colleges, a number made their way to German universities to pursue doctoral studies in one of the new scientific disciplines.[8] These students, imbued with the research approach that dominated higher learning at German universities, eventually returned to the United States and exerted pressure on American institutions to establish similar courses of studies.

Although research studies in science were initially deemed suitable only for students studying for the doctorate, the new disciplines gradually appeared as optional courses in the undergraduate American curriculum. At a number of American colleges in the second half of the nineteenth century, chemistry and physics were introduced as important fields of study, political science emerged from the shadow of moral philosophy, history and English literature appeared as separate academic disciplines, and, along with Greek, Latin, and Hebrew, some modern languages were added to the university curriculum as potential areas of study. In the latter quarter of the nineteenth century, some American institutions followed the lead of the German institutions and made research, especially in the sciences, a focus of their efforts. By accumulating a sufficient number of research faculty who had obtained their doctorates abroad, some American institutions were themselves able to offer the doctorate degree, thereby transforming themselves into universities.

In the latter part of the nineteenth century, institutions that did not become universities also began to incorporate many of the new disciplines into their undergraduate curriculum. They remained committed to religious and ethical learning as the most important knowledge to be transmitted to the younger generation and therefore grafted the new disciplines onto the existing American college system. This necessitated that some previously required subjects be given less time in the curriculum.

In the twentieth century, additional academic disciplines such as psychology, economics, sociology, engineering, business, comparative literature, computer science, and even American studies and education were introduced.[9] With the exception of engineering and computer science, most new disciplines had antecedents within the traditional liberal arts or the general realm of philosophy. Issues treated in philosophy or theology had implications for particular topics treated in the new academic disciplines, and these topics, though fairly narrow, had been addressed within various branches of philosophy over several hundred years.

During this transformation of higher education in the United States and abroad, Catholic colleges and universities adjusted their curricula to accommodate new academic disciplines. In doing so, however, they were careful to retain what they deemed to be the most important components of traditional Catholic learning. Since this study treats modern Catholic universities, which are now characterized by a plethora of individual academic disciplines, it is helpful to relate the current array of disciplines to the Catholic intellectual tradition.

Four Components of the Catholic Intellectual Tradition

Following modern terminology, we distinguish four separate but related components of the Catholic intellectual tradition. Theology is the first, most obvious component and is the heart of the Catholic intellectual tradition. The second component—philosophy—explores the foundations of human knowledge and experience.[10] Although it is no longer considered the handmaid of theology, theologians still regularly draw upon philosophy to present and reconcile various streams within the Catholic theological tradition. Also, because of its broad scope, philosophy is able to address large issues that often are neglected within individual disciplines. In Catholic universities up until the mid-1960s, it was in philosophy, rather than theology or religion, that students became acquainted with principles that embodied a Catholic worldview.

Closely related to philosophy is one academic discipline with an anomalous position in the modern university structure of academic disciplines, namely, ethics. In universities up until the beginning of the twentieth century, ethics was a component of philosophy called moral philosophy. Furthermore, at most American colleges and universities, ethics was the most important course, taught in senior year, often by the president of the college. During the last few decades, ethics has become more compartmentalized, and academics now talk about ethics as a category within disciplines that is distinct from philosophy, albeit closely related to it. Thus, business ethics is considered a field in business, medical ethics a field within medicine and nursing, and legal ethics a field within law. This focus on individual disciplines and the increasing need and demand for ethicists with significant competence in an academic discipline other than ethics is most likely responsible for severing ethics from its original moorings in the philosophy department. Whether treated as subsets of individual disciplines or as part of philosophy as a whole, these particular ethical disciplines address the larger philosophical issues involving practical reason.

The third component of the Catholic intellectual tradition is the traditional liberal arts. In this third group, we do not include theology and philosophy, which we placed in separate categories earlier, even though modern terminology usually includes them among the traditional liberal arts. Calling them "traditional" is, however, a bit of a misnomer. The liberal arts referred to in the literature of Catholic institutions are certainly not taught in Latin and Greek, and the original trivium and quadrivium no longer exist intact within any college curriculum. There is, however, a derivative known as modern liberal arts that consists of English literature, including subjects formerly covered in grammar and rhetoric; mathematics, including arithmetic, geometry, and logic; and history, including the study of Greek and Roman society; and music and astronomy. In the traditional hierarchy of academic disciplines that prevailed until the beginning of the twentieth century, philosophy and theology ranked above the liberal arts and were considered apart from them. We maintain this distinction in our four levels of the Catholic intellectual tradition.

As we noted earlier, the hard sciences—physics, chemistry, biology, and their derivatives—were slowly introduced as components of natural philosophy. However, they are not considered part of the modern liberal arts.[11] Even though specific topics in the hard sciences had traditionally been covered in natural philosophy, modern usage of the term *liberal arts* usually excludes the sciences.

The fourth component of the Catholic intellectual tradition is a collection of all remaining academic disciplines other than theology, philosophy, and those belonging to the modern equivalents of the traditional liberal arts. For the purposes of this book, this group will be referred to as the extended liberal arts and will include such subjects as the natural and life sciences, psychology, the social sciences, and newer disciplines such as computer science and the professional areas, the latter of which includes law, medicine, business, and education. Issues important to Catholic thought appear in many of these subject matters from the Middle Ages onward and were addressed in collegiate institutions up to and after the emergence of the German scientific research universities. For example, the relationship between Church and country was a central focus of legal studies for centuries, and since the Middle Ages medical ethics has developed side by side with the development of medicine.

Which academic disciplines should be included in the modern liberal arts and which should be included in the extended liberal arts can be debated. Two characteristics distinguish classification in the two groups: the historical point at which they emerged as separate disciplines and the depth of their relationship with theology and philosophy, which constitute the heart of the Catholic intellectual tradition. The modern liberal arts have been influenced by theology and philosophy for many hundreds of years. The extended liberal arts category, on the other hand, includes academic disciplines introduced after the mid-nineteenth century. As academic disciplines, they have only been exposed to the influence of theology and philosophy for 150 years and, accordingly, are disciplines less infused with the knowledge of revelation or philosophy than the modern liberal arts.[12]

Theology is done within the community of believers and for the benefit of believers. Modern Catholic theologians study, discuss, and interpret the foundational issues of faith, particularly God's revelation in the Old and New Testaments, and the major doctrines of the Catholic Church. They explore how human beings should behave in light of revelation and the mission of the Church in the world. By attending to the way the Church, through the popes, bishops, and theologians, have interpreted sacred Scriptural texts, by exploring the various traditions that developed in the Church, and by examining the living tradition of the Church as it appears in the Church's official pronouncements, activities, and her major writers and thinkers, theologians carefully note continuities, as well as some discontinuities, among important Christian themes through the centuries. Their work is, and always has been, shaped by differing interests and approaches that emerge in varying cultural contexts. Theologians engage, interpret, and elucidate the data of revelation, all the while attempting to reconcile conflicting viewpoints and expressing traditional doctrines in modern terms. They do so in an effort to make more clearly manifest the truth at the heart of Church teaching.

While there has always been some tension in reconciling the approaches of philosophy and theology, their estrangement is a relatively recent phenomenon that emerged gradually. Prior to developments in the Middle Ages, philosophers were deemed thinkers about all significant issues, which certainly included religious questions. For most theologians and philosophers in a pre-medieval world, all knowledge was in service of the highest type of knowledge, theological knowledge. Philosophers did not consciously try to bracket their belief in the existence of God when evaluating knowledge from different sources. Early Christians saw the faith as the culmination of philosophy. The work of Augustine in the fourth century built on neo-Platonic philosophy, and the philosophy of Aristotle was employed by Aquinas to demonstrate and more fully illuminate theological understanding. Even for Descartes and Pascal in the seventeenth century, the reality of God operating in the lives of individuals was not questioned. The alienation of the two disciplines grew from the sixteenth century on, as Renaissance scholars wrestled with nascent issues of textual criticism in the Bible and as the Reformation challenged the revelatory capacity of human reason. Finally, when the Enlightenment was in full bloom during the eighteenth century and cast doubt on the claims of faith, people started to distinguish clearly between Christian theology, which presupposes faith in God and Christ, and philosophy, which does not.

Faculty and administrators in Catholic higher education often use the term "Catholic intellectual tradition" to refer to that part of the Catholic intellectual tradition that does not specifically rely on theology.[13] In using the term this way, people do not intend to deny the relevance or influence of theology in the tradition. Rather, they merely wish to point to those areas that do not fall clearly within the ambit of theology, namely, all the academic disciplines in philosophy, the modern liberal arts, and the extended liberal arts. The Catholic aspects of these disciplines arise from Catholic teaching and theology. Though there can be a mutual interdependence of the theology and the nontheology disciplines, the nontheology disciplines have their own dynamism. In sum, the Catholic components of nontheology disciplines are influenced by faith and theology but are not determined by them.

All this necessitates making a confusing distinction that conforms to the two ways the term "Catholic intellectual tradition" is currently employed in university circles. In its fullest and strict meaning, the Catholic intellectual tradition includes the four components mentioned earlier: theology, philosophy, the liberal arts, and the extended liberal arts. However, the term is also used to refer to the subset of these components that excludes theology.[14] When the term is used in this more restricted sense, theological concepts and themes are acknowledged to play an important role in topics addressed, but theological analysis is either absent or much diminished. When senior administrators spoke of the Catholic intellectual tradition during their interviews, they most often were referring to the nontheology components, which made good sense. Senior administrators wanted more of their faculty to be involved in transmitting these parts of the tradition in their particular academic disciplines, but they were well aware that most faculty members are not interested in or knowledgeable about theology.

Prior to 1960, the Catholic intellectual tradition (excluding theology) at Catholic universities was presented to students most prominently through philosophy.[15] Since the Catholic tradition in philosophy is extensive, the very breadth of the Catholic contributions in this area makes it difficult to suggest which contributions are more important than others. Nonetheless, the Catholic intellectual tradition has its impact on other academic disciplines through both theology and philosophy, and it is important to suggest some principles that play a pivotal role.

Four Theological/Philosophical Themes in Modern Academic Disciplines

It is possible to approximate the influence of faith, theology, and philosophy on other academic disciplines by identifying four important themes stemming from theology and philosophy: the dignity of the human person individually and in community, sacramentality, sin, and mediation.[16]

The first characteristic or theme is the dignity of the human person. Every human being—whether beautiful to behold or physically impaired, whether brilliant or ordinary in intellect, whether living in poverty or wealth, whether Christian, Moslem, or atheist—is made in the image and likeness of God, has infinite value, and finds fulfillment in living and cooperating harmoniously with other human beings. Human beings, as the creation story reveals, are "good" and share in the very nature God assumed in the Incarnation. Both the Old Testament relationship of covenant and the New Testament relationship of infinite, self-giving love indicate that God's unwavering love of the people God created endows them with infinite value. Although the dignity of every human being is expressed in the creation stories of the Bible and in the New Testament, another slightly attenuated version of this characteristic, shorn of its theological provenance, can be argued on philosophical grounds: every human being has infinite value, and no one should act contrary to the natural dignity of the human person.

Sacramentality, the second characteristic, means that God is present in this world through signs and symbols that allow human beings individually and collectively to appreciate God in knowledge and beauty and approach God in love. Sacramentality means that reality is suffused with the presence of God and is sacred and that the seven sacraments of the Catholic Church are occasions for intimacy with God through Jesus Christ. Any person or culture can find God as long as he or she remains open to and inquisitive about truth, beauty, and goodness. Human beings are favored by God, that is, are graced by Christ sharing human nature. Nature and grace do not stand in opposition to each other. God is present in human experience and, although fallen, the world is essentially good, and everything is potentially a window on the experience of the divine. Jesus Christ, the Son of God, is the fullest possible revelation and presence of God in the world.

The third characteristic, sin, is primarily a break in our relationship with God and a turning away from God and what God wills for us in love. Sin breaks and damages our relationship not only with God but also with self, others, and the world. Human beings are made in the image and likeness of God and are, therefore, good. Human beings also have freedom, which is the capacity to say either yes or no to God. Temptation to sin, or to say no to God, exists because all are affected by the first sin of Adam and Eve and because human persons are influenced by evil surrounding them. This evil is perpetrated and reinforced by people. Human beings can be tragically self-absorbed, striving to reach goals they set for themselves, rather than trying to actualize God's loving plan for them. Although the world as made by God is good, human beings have turned away from God in sin and continue to do so. The Catholic intellectual tradition acknowledges sin, as well as grace and redemption, as part of the human story.

Mediation, the fourth characteristic, is a corollary of the principle of sacramentality. Mediation means God is not only present in all things, but God actually works or accomplishes God's plans through creation. God's action in creation may be ordinary (the birth of a baby) or extraordinary (a miracle or a special historical event), and both are important. Through creation God communicates God's own presence and will to human beings; the infinite God is mediated through finite creation. Creation can never be separated from the God who is its source and who sustains it.

God's ordinary, patterned actions produce the laws and regularities of science, and these ordinary, patterned actions also establish norms, which, when critically evaluated by human reason, are the basis for natural law, also referred to as natural moral law. The Catholic tradition maintains that people can derive their moral wisdom and knowledge through the use of their reason reflecting on human nature and experience. Using reason in this way produces moral knowledge and truth and is called natural law. Natural law reflects the divine order and is available to all through reason, regardless of personal beliefs or whether confirmed by divine revelation.[17]

Mediation accounts for God's presence and saving activity being specifically and uniquely focused in particular actions, individuals, or communities. Seen over the course of hundreds of years, the interpretation of God's actions within individuals and communities is referred to as salvation history.[18] According to Christian belief, the singular, most revelatory mediation in history is the Incarnation. For Christians, all events and all devotions within the church find their ultimate meaning through Christ. For example, Catholic devotion to Mary stems from her relationship to her Son. Mary is a particular example of this principle of mediation, since as a result of cooperation with God's offer to become mother of God-made-man, she fully receives God into her being. Mary in Catholic intellectual and iconic tradition is a symbol and instrument of God's grace, a focal point of God's action worthy of veneration.

In what follows, some nontheological disciplines are reviewed briefly to point out where one or more of the four themes—*sacramentality, sin, mediation,* and the *dignity of the human person*—have made an impact. Acknowledging at the outset an occasional arbitrary assignment of a specific topic to a modern discipline, we highlight in the nontheological disciplines those topics that have been informed or influenced by theological and philosophical considerations in the past. Even a cursory analysis like this helps in understanding the general contours of the Catholic intellectual tradition in subjects other than theology.[19]

Some academic disciplines focus on the expression of the three human values of beauty, truth, and goodness, and we refer to these here as expressive disciplines. (Philosophy, of course, critically examines these concepts, explores how they are used, and probes their relationship to one another and empirical data.) The expressive disciplines include literature, art, drama, music, and architecture. Because people are attracted by beauty, it is not surprising that Catholic themes have played significant roles in the development of drama, music, art, and architecture. Fitting worship is realized in beauty, in simplicity, and also in grandeur, and all these disciplines are ways believers can praise God by creating beautiful things. From a Catholic perspective, literature seeks to explore the human condition and human experience, which includes the human inclination to both good and evil. Literary explorations produce self-understanding or appreciation. Many writers and poets address important human issues from a Catholic perspective or in ways that illuminate a Catholic perspective. The number of high-quality works in the expressive disciplines that illuminate the Catholic tradition is staggering. Most academic disciplines can offer entire courses on Catholic themes, or they can treat great Catholic works in the same context that they treat other similar works.

The antecedent to modern psychology was rational psychology, a branch of philosophy, which, prior to the modern emphasis on experimentation and clinical observations, examined how the human mind grasps reality and the relationship between thought, will, and the emotions.[20] Modern psychology has become more empirical, clinical, and experimental. But the Catholic tradition in this field addresses important issues that are either not treated in modern psychology or framed in such a way as to avoid important philosophical issues. Catholic philosophy was always interested in the unity of the individual and the principle of his or her life, the human soul, and the mind as the center and substantive unity of the intellectual life. It studied the formation of conscience and how distortion of conscience could occur. The exploration of human emotions dates back to Aristotle, and the relationships among mind, emotions, will, and spirit were explored at universities from the Middle Ages onward. Catholic philosophers, in particular, noted that human beings, despite their basic goodness, have an inclination to evil. Psychologists examined how people could choose evil and what steps they could take to maximize the likelihood of avoiding evil choices. Although these issues may not lend themselves easily to experimentation and empirical analysis, they either involve empirical issues or are reflected in human behavior. Here it is enough to note that there are important issues bordering the religious and philosophical that for many centuries were considered part of the ordinary content of rational psychology.[21]

The Catholic moral tradition encompasses the natural law approach, which explores the ethical principles needed to make good decisions. Two principles with their foundation in the natural law tradition are the principles of solidarity and subsidiarity, both of which have broad ethical applications and implications for Catholic social teaching. Both principles stem from the convictions that all people are made in the image and likeness of God, enjoy a natural dignity, and should be able to pursue the fundamental values. Solidarity assumes the empirical reality that people are born into, are raised in, and live in is communities of people. An individual in the group, as well as the group as a whole, has a responsibility to promote the welfare of all people. Pure self-interest is incompatible with this intellectual tradition as a basis for making important life decisions. Individuals are not permitted to adopt rules that disadvantage members of the group without providing them with compensating benefits. Subsidiarity assumes the empirical reality that human communities should be arranged in such a way that the smallest possible group of people is responsible for those affairs that directly impact them. When given an option either to arrange society in a way that grants centralized authority to a small group making decisions for a large group or to give smaller groups authority to make decisions directly affecting their welfare, the latter option is preferable—that is, unless the small group solution results in decisions that damage the larger group in significant ways. Solidarity and subsidiarity are powerful principles that have important applications in business, economics, political theory, and medicine. We will discuss both these principles again in our discussion of social justice.

Most modern business schools have courses in business ethics, and most undergraduates who major in economics at Catholic institutions are encouraged or required to take a course in social ethics. Catholic ethics, which has a long, vibrant tradition reaching back to the Old Testament, offers a consistent approach that requires keeping the issue of justice and fairness in mind when considering economic and business arrangements. It is illegitimate to justify economic activity by simply saying "This is the way the system works." Justification requires providing a reasonable argument, or citation of another's good argument, as to why a particular way of proceeding is fair to all involved. Over the past 150 years, popes have issued encyclicals that address important social issues of the time. This group of social encyclicals embodies a good part of the Catholic intellectual tradition as it applies to issues normally treated in economics, sociology, and political science. The broad issue of social justice will be treated in a later section.[22]

In political science, Catholic ethics addresses important global and local issues. While the Church does not offer precise answers to complex political questions, it does attempt to establish a framework of values, principles, and responsibilities in which discussion of such issues can be carried on. The just war theory sets moral conditions for the declaration of war and the conduct of war. Over many centuries, the Church has developed ethical principles relating to appropriate punishment and length of incarceration. In modern times, the Church has developed an almost complete prohibition against capital punishment. In the realm of political theory, the Catholic Church has developed nuanced teachings about relationships between church and state, in which the responsibility of the state to respect legitimate activities of independent religious bodies is emphasized. Also germane to political science is the issue of when national law should yield to international law or conventions among nations, which is related to the principle of subsidiarity.

Catholic themes have been prominent in many of the professional disciplines. Before Anglo-Saxon case law was established, the Catholic Church had appropriated Roman law and joined it with aspects of tribal law to form a code of Church law referred to as canon law. In the eyes of the Church, order is necessary for society to function well, and citizens have a moral obligation to obey all just laws. According to Church teaching, neither civil nor criminal law should violate the principles of natural law. On the other hand, the Catholic approach to law acknowledges that not all things that are morally wrong must be proscribed by law. In the Catholic intellectual tradition, law is an instrument to protect people and enable them to flourish. Tolerating some wrongdoing by not making it subject to legal prohibition can be justified if the morally evil actions are not susceptible to effective control by the state.

For over a thousand years, hospitals and sanatoria were run by Church groups, usually religious orders or congregations of women. The Church has a well-developed system of medical ethics, which is regularly modified to take into account new medical findings and procedures, as well as new ways of understanding how the human body and psyche function. Issues of in vitro fertilization, stem cell research, human cloning, special feeding (intubation) and other assistance when people are nearing the end of life, tubal ligations, and abortion have an impact on millions of individual lives as well as on society in general. The Catholic Church has positions on these issues that flow from reason, not primarily from revelations or directives appearing in the Old or New Testament. Catholic ethics are in accordance with the principles of natural law, and every attempt is made to apply these principles objectively and with appropriate nuance as new medical issues develop. By appealing to natural law, the principles of which are accessible to both believers and nonbelievers alike, the Church attempts to persuade people of various religious or nonreligious traditions to agree upon reasonable ways of addressing modern issues. A strength of the natural law approach is that it not only has the benefit of hundreds of years of reflection and refinement but also exists within a community that has tried to live consistently by its principles.[23] Especially when new medical procedures are developed, it may take time to sort out the best way to apply the principles of medical ethics. During this period of adjustment, various people of good will may differ in their judgments. However, the Church's position is that if the principles of natural law are carefully applied, eventually people will be able to agree on a position that promotes the values of life and dignity without acting contrary to other important values.

Because religious sisters often were nurses in hospitals and assisted at the bedsides of patients, there is also a close connection between nursing care and spirituality. In fact, some contemporary Catholic institutions of higher education offer degrees in nursing and spirituality. Since nurses were frequently in positions where patients and hospitals had to face serious moral dilemmas, nursing education also included strong courses in medical ethics—the application of Catholic moral tradition to medical issues.

For many centuries, education in western Europe was synonymous with religious education, since there was no other variant. While most education today is secular, Catholic schools at the primary and secondary level are still admired for their combination of high academic standards and the ability to motivate a great majority of their students to perform well. Catholic schools show how religious conviction and a nurturing religious culture can help students learn better. Another caring discipline is social work, and the Catholic Church, as well as many other religious groups, has a long history of providing social work and educating and training social workers.

The Catholic intellectual tradition among the natural, life, and other sciences (physics, chemistry, biology and all its derivatives, astronomy, engineering, computing, etc.) poses challenges of interpretation. On the one hand, committed Catholics—such as Roger Bacon (scientific method), Copernicus and Galileo (astronomy), Descartes and Pascal (mathematics), Gregor Mendel (genetics), Madame Curie (chemistry), and Louis Pasteur (bacteriology)— played key roles in many important advances in the natural sciences and mathematics. Their interest in these issues and dedication to discovering "how things work" flows from a broad Catholic commitment to knowledge and from the conviction that truth can never be in contradiction to Scripture or to essential Catholic belief.[24] On the other hand, in many instances what turned out to be important advances—such as those discovered by Galileo or presented in Darwin's *The Origin of Species*—were either initially rejected by the Church or, in the latter case, viewed for some time with considerable skepticism.

These clashes contrast with the nonreaction of the Church to mathematical or computer advances in the past two hundred years, and the contrast provides a good indication of where the friction is. When a discovery is made that, at least prima facie, appears to contradict Scripture or what the Church has previously taught over a long period of time, the Church, maintaining core and proximate consistency, is extremely skeptical and moves with great caution, resisting any change to its established view. In other cases, such as startling mathematical advances, where the advances do not conflict with established Church teaching, the Church need not and does not offer an opinion. While the Second Vatican Council viewed modernization as a unique opportunity to be embraced, in practice the Church is often quite skeptical about developments in modern culture. The Church's hermeneutic of suspicion is triggered either when developments outpace the Church's ability to thoroughly analyze and review them or when developments in modern culture seem to undermine or contradict what the Church teaches. The Church moves slowly in the face of innovation because the Church brings with it a tradition of religious teaching over two millennia, onto which the innovation must be grafted and through which it must be vetted. Culturally the Catholic Church is conditioned to move slowly in a process that seeks to appropriate only those things that enhance authentic human experience, enrich understanding of the tradition, and can endure. As a culture that places a high premium on cultural coherence, the Church is deeply concerned about significant or extensive change and strenuously resists adaptation.

The friction point between Church teaching and scientific findings suggests fruitful modern areas of dialogue among natural scientists, theologians, and philosophers. The line between the various disciplines may at times be jagged or indistinct, but dialogue among the disciplines can help locate helpful boundaries. Students at either the undergraduate or graduate level would learn much by hearing presentations by theologians, philosophers, and natural scientists about the boundaries of theology and natural science. Even though there is no Catholic way of doing science or mathematics, Catholic themes and philosophical reflection can be used to help situate these sciences and point out their strengths and limitations. Science contains within itself a drive toward unified theories, which is a traditional focus within Catholic philosophy.[25]

The Catholic Moral Tradition and Social Teaching

The Catholic moral tradition is rooted in the natural law, which was first developed by Stoic philosophers in the first century B.C. Like any intellectual tradition, the natural law approach is in fact a plurality of approaches. Within the broad natural law approach, groups of thinkers disagree with one another. These differences can be substantial and lead to different conclusions about what is permitted or mandated under natural law teaching.[26] We pick one approach to natural law—the "new classical natural law" approach that relies on fundamental human values—as our point of departure to explore the Church's teaching about morality.[27] By singling out this approach, developed by John Finnis and Germaine Grisez, we are not saying that a natural law approach is necessarily the best approach for capturing the richness of Catholic moral teaching. Nor are we arguing that this is the only valued natural law approach.[28] We are saying that the Church regularly teaches from natural law; thus, trying to explain and explore that approach makes sense in the context of what Catholic colleges and universities are trying to do. As to which natural law approach is most valid or adequate, we leave that to experts in this area to decide. We follow Finnis and Grisez because their approach can be explained and presented in a straightforward manner, because it arrives at conclusions that are consistent with the teaching of the Catholic Church, and because this approach avoids what is known as the naturalist fallacy. This fallacy takes the patterns in the physical world, the functioning of the body, and the functioning of other live organisms as the sole norms for what constitutes proper moral behavior. Natural patterns can reveal important underlying tendencies, but these patterns have to be critiqued by human reason. The new classical natural law approach also is strongly supportive of the hierarchical magisterium's teaching on sexual and medical issues, many of which are of critical import to college-age students.

While the Catholic moral tradition does highlight what behavior and actions are unacceptable—the "Thou shalt nots" of human action and interaction—it is equally attentive to the realm of "Thou shalt." The Catholic moral tradition emphasizes the cultivation of virtue, as well as the avoidance of vice and sin. Christians are called to be people of character whose relationships with God, self, others, and the world are freely chosen and life-giving and who take responsibility for their actions and choices. The Catholic moral tradition is an ethic of responsibility that goes beyond simple rule-following and attention to specific acts and embraces more fully the people who are involved in the actions. This tradition is concerned with the orientation and direction of a person's life that is shaped rightly by virtuous practice.

Virtues are dispositions to accomplish good, and they are rooted in the presence of God and grace. When encouraged and practiced, these virtues point human beings in the right direction in their lives—a direction that leads them to respond positively to loving union with God.[29] Faith, hope, and charity are virtues that affect all human relationships—with God, others, and self— and are often referred to as theological or general virtues. The other virtues are often referred to as cardinal, moral, or particular virtues, and they affect particular relationships. Humility and gratitude affect our relationship with God. Mercy, forgiveness, justice, and truthfulness affect our relationship with others. Temperance and fortitude affect our relationship to self.[30]

For Christians, natural law has its roots in classical civilization and emerges in Christian tradition with Paul's letter to the Romans:

> When Gentiles, who do not possess the law, do instinctively what
> the law requires, these, though not having the law, are a law to
> themselves. They show that what the law requires is written on their
> hearts, to which their own conscience also bears witness; and their
> conflicting thoughts will accuse them or perhaps excuse them on
> the day when, according to my gospel, God, through Jesus Christ,
> will judge the secret thoughts of all. (Romans 2:14–16)[31]

Augustine, the first great figure in Christian moral theology, addressed questions of natural and revealed law in the early part of the fifth century. He believed Christian morality was a means to eternal union with God and that it required an obedient response to the Christian law of love. Augustine focused on external behavior, but he also paid great attention to psychological concerns such as the internal attitudes. In interpreting natural law philosophically, theologically, and doctrinally, Thomas Aquinas proved particularly influential within the Catholic tradition. He understood natural law as the participation of the rational creature in God's eternal law or plan. Aquinas believed that the principles of natural law reflect the good to which human beings are naturally inclined. Natural law as Thomas understood it was intrinsic and not extrinsic and focused on what God intends for human beings that they can know through reason.

A fairly general consensus about the validity of the natural law approach existed in the United States until the mid-twentieth century. At present, that consensus has broken down.[32] The Catholic Church continues to support the natural law approach, even as ethicists and philosophers committed to this tradition struggle to make it more coherent, convincing, and appealing to a modern generation of thinkers and students.

Like other moral approaches, the natural law tradition has had to respond to a variety of challenges stemming from social developments, new understandings of how the body functions, new perspectives on how the universe reached its current formation, and new technologies in health care. Many theologians accept the natural law tradition as essentially valid and important in terms of moral understanding and formation. Many theologians also explore new ways to express the natural law tradition or to use approaches that are more appealing to Catholics, though the approaches usually do not have the precision of the natural law approach.[33] Pope John Paul II often analyzed issues such as marriage by first examining the human dynamics of interrelationships. He clearly thought that addressing the issue in this way was more persuasive. However, lacking an approach that is both more persuasive and also supports positions held by the Catholic Church and other religions over many centuries, the natural law approach remains important at the same time that it is explored, debated, and refined.

The new classical natural law claims there is a core of universally binding moral precepts or values that can be discerned through reason and are therefore binding on all people. The identification of particular human values as *fundamental* human values is what distinguishes this approach. These fundamental human values are deemed valid and important for all human beings of whatever culture, and it is this universal validity of the values that separates the Catholic moral tradition from other current ethical approaches. Most nonnatural law approaches in contemporary Western society allow each person to decide which social goods are most important for him or her and also to acknowledge that all "goods" are historical and cultural, rather than fundamental, and are therefore subject to change over time. The Catholic tradition, on the other hand, identifies the common good and what people should be seeking.

According to the approach to natural law taken by Finnis and Grisez, human beings know in their minds and hearts the most important things in life. Arising out of the training children receive by living in a broader community are goals that all human beings respect or personally strive to reach.[34] Finnis and Grisez refer to these central goals and convictions as fundamental human values. These values, which should be broadly conceived, are: friendship, life, beauty, knowledge (general and personal), playfulness, religion, and practical reasonableness, which can be considered a particular form of common sense. Equally important, human beings living in their own society understand when they offend against these core precepts or values. Killing someone (acting directly contrary to life), telling lies (acting directly contrary to knowledge), and betraying the fidelity of marriage (acting directly contrary to friendship) are understood by all reasonable people to be seriously wrong because "they fundamentally contradict human flourishing and God's goodness."[35]

Each value is to be respected, in the sense that human beings should not act directly contrary to these values. Also, each value is individually a fundamental human value. They are not organized in some hierarchy, even though life is necessary for the other values. While there is no hierarchy among the values, within each value there is a hierarchy. Thus, marriage is a higher realization of the fundamental value of friendship than citizenship, being a neighbor, or a business relationship. Care has to be taken in interpreting what it means that no one should ever act directly contrary to a fundamental value, and this admonition must be applied with nuance. For example, people should respect truth and not act contrary to it by telling lies. However, it can be perfectly legitimate to maintain that some things are private and need not be divulged. Because there is no obligation to share private knowledge with others and because the values of life and friendship should be respected, it would be morally permissible, for example, for a person to be deceptive in responding to a Gestapo-like unit regarding the whereabouts of a Jewish friend. The strength of the requirement to respect the fundamental values is that it highlights those human values that almost all human beings can acknowledge as fundamental and compelling.

Catholic Social Teaching

Catholic social teaching draws heavily on two previously mentioned principles, solidarity and subsidiarity. Both of these have broad application in society, and both derive from the natural law conviction articulated earlier that all human beings should be able to pursue the fundamental human values of life, friendship, knowledge, beauty, fun or playfulness, religion, and common sense or common reasonableness. The principle of solidarity merely expresses the conviction that all people should be able to pursue the fundamental values and each adult of sound body and mind should make a contribution to that pursuit. More formally, the principle of solidarity is that all people in society should desire to create conditions so that people can flourish by pursuing the fundamental values and that all people should contribute, according to their talents or position in society, to making this possible by working inside or outside the home to produce goods and services.[36]

The principle of subsidiarity is a principle of effective organization of rights and responsibilities, and it articulates a strategy to enhance the likelihood that most people will in fact be able to pursue the fundamental values. The principle of subsidiarity is that rights and responsibilities should be assigned to the smallest unit in society that can effectively fulfill them, where "smallest" refers to the unit with the fewest number of people who have the most interest, motivation, and knowledge to fulfill the assigned rights or responsibilities. For example, responsibility for running primary and secondary schools should be assigned so that parents have as much direct responsibility as possible for the schools their children attend. Responsibility for local schools should not be given to the county, state, or federal government unless there are important things that only those governments, and not the local government, can accomplish.

One corollary of the principle of solidarity is that special concern should be given to the poor of society. Because the financially disadvantaged have the least resources available to them, they are most constrained in the pursuit of values such as life (including health and recreation, the raising of healthy children), knowledge (through schooling, access to libraries and the internet), beauty (through clothes, home, neighborhood, art, music), and fun (entertainment, sports). The preferential option for the poor means that social policy related to the generation and distribution of resources should have as a very high priority improving the long-term situation of the poor. Large numbers of modern students seem to be particularly sensitive to what is commonly referred to in the Catholic Church as the preferential option for the poor. These young men and women readily volunteer to participate in programs that provide direct benefits to the poor living in their neighborhoods or regions, in poorer parts of the United States, or in other countries of the world.[37]

The Moral Tradition in Catholic Universities

One responsibility Catholic colleges and universities take on as part of their mission to educate students of character is the work of helping them form their personal consciences. Students at Catholic colleges and universities are bombarded via popular media with the values of a secular culture that is often at odds with the Catholic understanding of what constitutes the virtuous life. Casual efforts or subdued attempts at creating a space for moral dialogue at Catholic colleges are usually overwhelmed by the din of competing cultures whose volume and pervasiveness cannot be ignored. Only carefully crafted and serious attempts to engage the Catholic moral tradition, both persuasively and pervasively, throughout all aspects of collegiate life have any hope of capturing the attention of students on today's colleges and university campuses.

Integration of the Catholic moral tradition takes place in the academic sphere but also within residence halls and in other areas of student life, and it is in this arena that senior administrators often find themselves most challenged and frustrated. In *The Idea of a University*, John Henry Cardinal Newman described the experience of residential living at Protestant universities in nineteenth-century England. What he describes as a goal of student living is an academic community: "Independent of direct instruction on the part of Superiors, there is a sort of self-education in the academic institutions."[38] The self-perpetuating and formative collegiate culture Newman describes has its modern parallels in residence halls in Catholic colleges and universities. Senior administrators would acknowledge, however, that in many instances, modern residence hall living is a far cry from the positive reinforcement Newman describes. What appears to prevail in many residence halls is a shadow culture that is antithetical to Catholic teachings.

Cultures in modern residence halls are shaped and adjusted and passed on to subsequent generations by their cultural catalysts and citizens—the students and student life staff. These student cultures live and thrive in the shadows of collegiate Catholic cultures. If senior administrators are to be believed and media reports accepted, in some Catholic institutions, residence hall cultures run counter to a good deal of Catholic moral teaching, particularly in terms of sexual activity among students and drug and alcohol use and abuse. Finding effective ways to address residential and social shadow culture is one of the most difficult challenges that administrators at Catholic colleges and universities face. We present an application of the natural law approach to the two areas of substance use and sexual intimacy in the residence halls.

One reason shadow culture may be so strong, particularly in residence halls at some universities, is that it is cultivated by student cultural catalysts and accepted by student cultural citizens who very quickly realize what it takes "to belong" and "to get along" in the culture. Countering this shadow culture requires leadership on the part of administrators and at least some faculty in the face of student resistance, parental opposition, and faculty and staff indifference. Absent administrative and faculty leadership, residence halls are prone to become "lord of the flies" cultures in which students define and sustain the operative culture. In their interviews, many senior administrators critiqued the compartmentalization that distances the academic sector from student life. They spoke appreciatively of the system that existed in Catholic residence halls when nuns and brothers and priests lived with the students and interacted with them in classes and in their residences. This system still exists in modified fashion in a few Catholic colleges and universities. And a number of administrators cited these institutions as exemplary.

If a negative shadow culture has developed at a Catholic institution, administrators can call upon Catholic moral teaching to try to regain consistency in the Catholic culture. A variety of steps can be taken. First, universities can communicate and demonstrate what constitutes exemplary behavior. Within an institution committed to the Catholic moral tradition this includes the cultivation of virtues—the "Thou shalts" that shape attitudes and norms. Second, Catholic colleges and universities can be much more specific about what is unacceptable behavior and explain why that behavior is culturally corrosive—the "Thou shalt nots." This certainly includes enforcement of civil laws regarding drug and alcohol use, but it also calls for a thorough explication of the "why" behind the commitment to temperance and fortitude that honors the freedom of will human beings should cherish and exercise in their relationships with God, others, and self. Shaping the culture also requires a clear explication of how the Church defines sexual intimacy and its role in a life-giving love that is not just warm emotion but rather a willing of good—not just comfort and pleasure—for the other and the self. Finally, Catholic universities facing a challenge in this area should demonstrate that certain behaviors are unacceptable by administering sanctions and, when patterns of behavior are egregious, removing individuals who pose a threat to the culture and to the common good.

Sustaining *no* is one of the most difficult things staff and administrators have to do. It is also essential for supporting and sustaining a vibrant organizational culture. In terms of the academic sector, there is little resistance among faculty and administrators to a deafening *no* in the face of cheating, plagiarism, and the failure to understand academic material presented in a course. Each of these constitutes breaches of the academic culture and is handled forthrightly. In a Catholic culture, patterns of drug and alcohol abuse and sexual intimacy outside of lifelong commitment are equally corrosive of a culture grounded in love of God, neighbor, and self that respects the sanctity and dignity of every human life and honors the gift of freedom and will that belongs to each individual. A clear *no* in the face of behavior that corrodes the nature of the educational endeavor as it is defined at Catholic colleges and universities is necessary and appropriate.[39]

A university that wraps itself in the mantle of Catholicism cannot turn a blind eye or a carefully covered eye to some activities of students that fly in the in the face of the Church's moral teaching. Nonetheless, both prudence and courage are required. Depending on where the university currently finds itself with respect to moral issues concerning students, it may take considerable time to change the culture so that students are informed, persuaded, and compliant with respect to the Catholic approach to substance abuse and sexual intimacy.

Substance Abuse

Drinking has become a rite of passage in the minds of many college students. The consumption of alcohol by adults is consonant with Catholic moral tradition; drunkenness is not. Human beings are rational agents. As part of their commitment to the fundamental values of life, friendship, and practical reasonableness (common sense), human beings are supposed to protect the lives of others and care for their own health and well-being. Catholic teaching about drinking obliges persons to practice the classical virtues of temperance and prudence. Individuals are not allowed to put themselves in a situation that impairs their ability to act rationally.[40] Depending on personal stature and constitution, individuals vary in the amount of alcohol they can consume without impairing either their ability to ward off a threat or their ability to act with reason. In the Catholic tradition, drunkenness does not refer to blood-alcohol content or specific amounts consumed but to the effects of alcohol consumption. In a state of insobriety or semisobriety, individuals can unwittingly make decisions that do lasting damage to themselves and others. In that state they may also be unable to take reasonable steps to avoid harm threatened by or to others. For this reason, the Catholic moral tradition teaches that getting drunk is seriously wrong. It is seriously wrong because of its potential to cause harm to oneself, another person with whom one is intimate, or members of the surrounding community, regardless of a person's access to an automobile. A similar analysis applies to taking recreational drugs.

The use of drugs or alcohol by individuals imposes some obligations (via the principles of solidarity and subsidiarity) on their friends to coordinate their activities and take reasonable steps to prevent harm and injustice from occurring. The Church understands this as a moral obligation that flows from the fundamental value of friendship and from the particular reality of being brothers and sisters in Christ. A not-infrequent occurrence at the typical student-frequented bar illustrates how irresponsible activity on the part of one person should galvanize responsible behavior by the person's friends. Suppose a young man goes to a student bar with his friends. After being with his friends for a time, suppose he notes some young woman whom he is interested in getting to know. While continuing to drink alcohol, he spends time speaking with her. After a while, the friends of the young man perceive he is getting drunk and is no longer capable of making a rational decision. If he returns to the residence hall with the young woman, he is in danger of doing something that could have serious deleterious effects on her life and his. Clearly he is not in a position to make informed, rational, or loving decisions about how to proceed, and, because he is drunk, it would be difficult for him to even remember what he did or why he did it. Good friends would not hand this young man a set of car keys. Friends who understood Catholic moral tradition would know they had other obligations, as well. They would realize that their understanding of the natural law requires that they escort their friend back to his room or their room in the residence hall, making sure that he does nothing that is potentially harmful to the young woman or himself. Friends protect friends, and this young man is in a situation that is dangerous for him and for the young woman to whom he is attracted. In addition, the friends of the young woman have a similar responsibility to assure she is in a setting that is conducive for her good as well as that of the young man.

In a strong Catholic culture, student responsibilities in examples like this one are explained clearly to students. In addition to legal considerations, students should also understand what, according to the Catholic tradition, constitutes charitable and just behavior in such situations. The Church's teachings concerning alcohol, drugs, or other addictive substances do not rely upon the state declaring use of such substances to be illegal. The Catholic moral tradition, even if the state allows the sale of addictive agents, is clearly opposed to the use and abuse of them when they impair an individual's ability to reason. While recognizing that Catholic institutions have responsibilities independent of civil law, the Catholic moral tradition also teaches that Catholics and Catholic institutions have a responsibility to obey all laws that are not themselves immoral. As an educational institution, a Catholic university informs students not merely about the rules and what the teaching of the Church is, but why the Church teaches the way she does and why Catholics are expected to live in a way that is faithful to those teachings.

The Catholic university is an institution of knowledge and formation; the goal is not to condemn students for their actions or their views. Rather, it is to persuade them that the Church's position is a reasonable one. To the extent that students understand the basis for the Church's stance, they will also understand why it is so important to use alcohol in moderation and addictive drugs not at all. This type of formation is almost certainly what parents expect to happen at Catholic institutions, and it is one of the reasons why many parents opt for Catholic universities over other non-Catholic institutions. The rules of a Catholic university should reflect the moral teachings of the Church, and the formation programs should invite students to understand the wisdom of these teachings.

Sexual Intimacy

In the Catholic tradition, the highest form of friendship is marriage between a man and woman, a relationship sealed by a lifelong promise to remain true and faithful friends. In some ways, friendship in marriage grows and matures much like other close friendships. Husband and wife spend time together; they do imaginative things for one another as they surprise, reassure, and console one another. Two distinctive aspects of marriage between a man and woman are that marriage involves a solemn, lifelong commitment and that the couple seeks to make their love fruitful through the sexual act, which expresses love and commitment. The act of love sometimes produces new life, not just for the couple but for society. The child is conceived within the woman, carried by her, and nurtured physically and emotionally by the woman until the point of birth, after which both husband and wife express their love and commitment for their child. The love and commitment of parents for their child that begins in the act of love should accompany the child as long as the parents live. According to natural law, all this is part of God's plan and the commitment made in marriage, and the nurturing love of parents for their child or children deepens their own love for one another and makes an enormous contribution to society.

Marriage is an important social institution that requires generosity, self-lessness, and discipline in both word and action on the part of people who are both spouses and parents. One commitment made in marriage is that both husband and wife bind themselves to a sexual relationship only with each other. Loving sexual expression certainly helps marital love to grow. The exclusivity of sexual expression between spouses is also a sign both to them and to others in society of their deep mutual commitment.

The Catholic Church teaches that sexual intercourse and close sexual intimacy between a man and woman are actions reserved only for a man and woman bound by the marriage commitment of love until death parts the couple. According to Church teaching, making love is an act that is essentially open to procreation and also an act that, by being restricted to marriage, confirms the couple's mutual commitment and helps nurture that commitment.

The Church's teaching is based primarily on the natural law teaching that sexual intimacies outside of marriage are not permitted. The implications of the Catholic Church's position are also quite clear. Young people, whether or not they are Catholic, who are attending universities, whether or not the institutions are Catholic, are not allowed to explore the realm of sexual intimacy, whether it be for experimentation or fun, even with willing partners. In order to promote a consistent Catholic culture on campus, Catholic colleges and universities inform students about Church teaching, offer positive reasons for the teaching, encourage students to abide by the teaching, develop policies that support the teaching, and appropriately sanction those students who violate university rules.[41]

The Church's teaching about sexual intimacy is about limits as well as possibilities, and that makes it a difficult message for college students to hear. Students are at a stage in their lives when they are testing limits. They are also at a stage in their lives when sexual attraction and desire are both very intense. College students are in the process of sorting out just who they are as individual human beings and how they—independent from their families—are going to constitute themselves and their relationships with other people. In this time of discovery, it is not surprising young people might be inclined to explore who they are as sexual beings. The Church's message for them is that their discovery of self and others should not include sexual intimacy outside of marriage.

At most Catholic colleges and universities, the personal moral issues involved in students being sexually active are accompanied by critical justice issues that emerge as a result of dormitory living arrangements. The students who entertain sexual partners, for the most part, do so in their dormitory rooms. This fact has led to the development of a sexual social etiquette within the residential shadow culture that creates serious justice issues. Students are expected to accommodate the sexual activity of their roommates by discretely leaving the room and finding another place to sleep. Others in the dorm know the drill, and they do what's necessary to make the system work. These disruptions can occur occasionally. They can also become patterns that result in students being displaced from their own space for extensive periods of time and left to fend for themselves with little or no recourse other than figuring it out on their own. For the most part, these cultural adjustments are accepted by students as "the way things are done." In many cases, universities passively accept the status quo, fail to support displaced students, avoid confrontations, and are silent in the face of behavior that offends against justice and the moral teaching of the Church.

Clearly, a Catholic university should act against such abuses, both to educate students about the teachings of the Church concerning intimacy and to uphold those teachings. A second motive for action is doing justice, since violations often involve injustice to roommates. University authorities at non-sectarian institutions may turn a blind eye to such activities, dismissing their importance with phrases such as "Kids will be kids" or "They have to live and learn," but such avoidance is not compatible with what the Catholic university says it is. The Catholic university educates the whole person, and an important part of that educational mission involves helping students understand and appreciate relational justice, what constitutes appropriate limits and boundaries in relationships, the true meaning of relational intimacy and friendship, and the importance of a lifelong commitment as the context for loving sexual expression between men and women. When students disregard these norms, university authorities should act to support the Catholic culture.

Addressing Cultural Illiteracy

As can be seen from the foregoing account of selected aspects of the Catholic intellectual tradition, even when it is understood more narrowly to include topics impacted by theology but not theology itself, the extent of the tradition is vast, and its potential impact on the lives of young students is enormous. Comments of senior administrators in the previous chapter revealed that some administrators were concerned that many Catholic students were not being informed and formed by significant components of the Catholic intellectual tradition. As our review of the tradition suggests, however, one can be ignorant of vast swaths of the tradition and still be a practicing Catholic who has received a good education at a prominent Catholic college or university. In this section, we address the issue of illiteracy within the Catholic culture.

The topic of Catholic cultural illiteracy was not among the ten that senior administrators most frequently raised in their interviews. The administrators who did address the issue, however, were quite adamant that illiteracy is a serious and pervasive problem and among the most important issues administrators at Catholic institutions must address in the coming years. The breadth of the challenge they described was also noteworthy, including as it did students, faculty, administrators, and trustees. We are not suggesting that the lack of Catholic cultural knowledge is equally distributed across institutions or constituents or that it is acute at most or all Catholic universities. Nevertheless, we do believe that the perception of a significant group of administrators that those who teach, govern, and administer lack sufficient knowledge about the heritage they are trying to share merits careful analysis.[42]

Many administrators believe students are ill informed about the Catholic tradition, both when they arrive as first-year students at the university and when they graduate as seniors. There actually is some evidence that supports that belief, but not nearly enough.[43] Moving forward effectively to address this problem, however, requires further exploration. First, faculty and administrators need to determine what constitutes the important religious knowledge students should have mastered by the time they arrive and by the time they graduate. Once these performance outcomes are determined, getting the data that indicates the extent to which students possess the knowledge will define the dimensions of the Catholic literacy challenge being addressed. Only when that information is made available can appropriate strategies be crafted.

It is striking that senior administrators reported having little data concerning essential Catholic knowledge outcomes. One obvious contributing factor is the lack of agreement among those involved in Catholic higher education about what constitutes "essential knowledge" of the Catholic tradition.[44] Catholic knowledge goals for graduation from Catholic colleges and universities lack useful specificity. Higher education has, of course, many components. Students are expected to graduate with specific knowledge in one field, their major, as well as broad knowledge in a variety of fields, generally introduced through the core curriculum. Students are also expected to demonstrate good writing, reading, and computation skills that enable them to perform well in work settings and to pursue advanced degrees in a variety of fields, such as business, law, medicine, and education. These expectations are common among all universities, and they do not contribute to distinguishability in educational outcomes. The expectations that would produce distinctive educational outcomes for students compared with the secular model would come in terms of Catholic knowledge and preparation. The average Catholic university strives to communicate the Catholic tradition in courses and more broadly in other religious, social, and intellectual activities. Since a wide range of people is involved in this effort, specifying desired outcomes would be important and helpful. Senior administrators reported an increase in the demand by accrediting agencies for such outcomes analysis, but Catholic institutions appear reluctant to urge faculty and others to identify desired "Catholic" outcomes for students. Regardless of whether students are Catholic or not, colleges and universities are not inclined to assess outcomes in terms of knowledge of the Catholic faith, knowledge of the Catholic intellectual tradition, or the extent of student religious practice.

While this hesitance, at least in the academic sector, may seem curious, it is not entirely surprising, stemming as it does from the way any university is academically structured. The academic sector is organized by academic disciplines, such as history, English literature, biology, and theology or religious studies. Academic departments, including theology or religious studies, establish a sequence of courses that all students in the major are expected to take. In recent years, many departments have instituted capstone courses or special fourth-year seminars that review the major themes and skills in a specific academic discipline to make sure all the essentials appropriate for undergraduate majors have been learned. Minimum norms for "Catholic knowledge" applicable to all students do not fit easily within this structure.

Students are fairly flexible and pragmatic, and they readily adapt to meet expectations. If they are told what they need to know about a particular subject in order to graduate, they will learn the required material. It might be relatively straightforward for faculty members in theology, philosophy, and perhaps history to determine what Catholic subjects they think students should know. Whether the material was covered in a single required course, jointly taught by faculty from various departments, or in a number of required courses, evaluating student appropriation of the material would create a major cross-departmental logistical and coordination challenge. While such coordination is certainly possible, it is countercultural in a setting where individual faculty are accustomed to working out requirements that impact their own academic discipline alone. The core curriculum does not provide an easy answer to this problem either. The core requires students to take courses in general academic areas, and usually does not specify minimum standards of required knowledge acquisition. The latter is left to particular academic departments to decide. All in all, establishing minimum standards for Catholic knowledge among undergraduates is a formidable project.

Formidable or not, determining what constitutes minimum Catholic knowledge is an issue of central import that universities adhering to each of the four models must address.[45] Without some ideal outcome for students relative to their Catholic knowledge and practice, it is impossible for administrators and faculty to gauge whether the institution is successful in reaching its educational goals. Indeed, we believe that one reason why administrators did not speak more frequently about tradition illiteracy among students is the very vagueness of the notion. Nonetheless, with faculty and administrators working together, it is possible for institutions to establish minimum or ideal norms that conform to their type of university, and it is essential that they do so. The realistic and pressing need for such standards exceeds the scope of this book; consequently, it is noted here but not developed.

In their various conversations, senior administrators mentioned that often faculty and administrators involved in Catholic higher education lack the requisite preparation and skills to be effective in terms of contributing to the institution's religious mission. However, they were not particularly forthcoming about what knowledge, preparation, or skills were necessary or desirable. In the course of their interviews, senior administrators were asked about qualities a candidate being considered for their position at another Catholic institution should have. Some indicated that the person should be knowledgeable about the Catholic tradition, but they did not specify what that knowledge would entail. Many indicated that the person should be Catholic, but did so without qualification, and only a few went so far as to specify that the successful candidate should be a "practicing Catholic," itself an ambiguous term.[46]

One important reason administrators in Catholic higher education may be unable or unwilling to specify the characteristics among candidates they deem important for creating, sustaining, and sharing a Catholic culture is that, until relatively recently, there was no need to do so. For the history of most of these institutions, there were enough nuns, brothers, and priests on campus in various key positions to take the lead in developing, sustaining, and sharing the Catholic culture, with students as well as with faculty, administrators, and trustees. In most instances, the religious did take the lead, but their dwindling numbers, particularly over the past ten to twenty years, have disrupted this pattern and shifted the responsibility to their lay colleagues.

Knowledge of Catholic culture is not gained most effectively through purely intellectual means. At its heart, the Church is the community of people who experience and bear what Robert Imbelli refers to as "the multiple riches of the mystery of Christ," who is the center of the Christian tradition. The relationship between the imaginative and conceptual components of the faith is circular. The usual path to greater understanding of the content of Catholic culture is through symbols, particularly the celebration of the seven sacraments. Of the seven sacraments, the Eucharist is the preeminent liturgical expression of what the Church knows in faith. The mystery of the faith comes to privileged expression in the Eucharistic liturgy, which is the "*theologia prima*, the living theology which nourishes and sustains our second order reflections. Liturgy is the primary bearer of tradition, because here, in sacramental fullness, Jesus 'hands himself over' for the life of the world."[47] It is through this living theological experience that the content of Catholic culture is integrated, experienced, and lived. Participation in the Eucharist, for example, gives rise to further exploration and explication of content and then circles back once again to the symbols—liturgy, ritual, narrative, and objects—now more deeply understood and profoundly experienced.

This normal route to appropriation of cultural content poses a dilemma in an academic culture, since in the groves of academe the preferred approach to understanding is purely intellectual, focusing on reading, study, and research. Nonetheless, academics appreciate the importance of alternative ways of knowing and have increasingly become champions of experiential learning for their students. As researchers, they have had firsthand experience in learning by doing, since most doctoral students become researchers in apprentice fashion by being with their mentors or other researchers, seeing how they do it, and then getting their own feet wet in the field. Research method for a particular academic discipline is seldom appropriated in the library stacks. It is a learned art, picked up primarily by accompanying accomplished researchers along the path of research.

The mutual reinforcement of Catholic content and symbol was the instinctive approach for developing religious knowledge in religious congregations and served as the structural foundation for religious formation. During and after formation, liturgy and paraliturgical practices constituted the most important activities of congregation members as individuals and as members of a community of believers. Even those who were most advanced in their intellectual understanding of cultural content were reminded by their religious superiors of the preeminence of communal celebration of the Mass, as well as other rituals and symbolic acts that constituted the foundation for the particular religious congregation (Franciscans, Jesuits, Benedictines, Mercy sisters, etc.). Collegiate Catholic culture entails religious understanding and religious practice by cultural catalysts and many cultural citizens, including faculty, administrators, and students.

The Shadow Culture

Like a plant that does not prosper in direct sunlight, a shadow culture is not strong enough to exist when it is subject to the full glare of critical review in the broad university community. But it can thrive nicely in the shadows. The shadows may consist of comments made in the recesses of the academic culture. They may be the skeptical and sardonic comments of faculty or administrators who question either the methods or goals of other faculty or administrative leaders. Or the shadows may be an agreement not to directly challenge certain university policies but to take advantage of normal academic or administrative procedures to subvert them. The shadows might also take the form of a strong, challenging atmosphere in which faculty and administrators articulate positive challenges to unrealistic university policies they believe have little chance of success.

At any given time, the shadow culture may work positively to strengthen the culture as it develops or it may weaken the culture as it questions the validity of certain approaches or strives to frustrate others. Most cultures have a shadow side. What is important, though difficult, to do is to identify the distinct components and strengths of the shadow culture and take them into consideration as part of fortifying or developing the broad culture of the institution.

A few senior administrators observed that some faculty members and administrators resist a sharper focus on institutional Catholic identity, character, and mission. This resistance could thwart attempts to enhance Catholic culture if it is rooted in a preference for secular collegiate culture. On the other hand, if the resistance is in response to flawed strategies, attending to its root cause could prove beneficial for overall cultural goals. Administrators have to understand the depth, root cause, and intent of the shadow culture, as well as its capacity to derail cultural growth and development. Those involved in the shadow culture may not intend to undermine the efforts of senior administration to strengthen Catholic culture on campus, but their impact is what matters, not their intent. The shadow culture may have some positive impact, but if the impact is primarily negative, senior administrators will need to defuse it. If an intent to undermine seems likely, strategic administrative responses to shadow culture should be initiated.

When the shadow culture consists mainly in skeptical complaints or derisive comments about the way things are handled with respect to Catholic issues at the university, it is probably best for senior administration simply to note it, monitor the degree of discontent, and move on with their work. Skepticism and derision are staples among intellectuals, and such comments often focus on inconsistent administrative policies. As most senior administrators know, it is very difficult, if not impossible, to have completely consistent policies at complicated institutions such as universities. Despite the most sincere efforts, some inconsistencies are impervious to removal. Although this reality is recognized by many faculty members, pointing out inconsistencies can be healthy or just fun. Even if it is not, suffering some derision and skepticism for such inconsistencies is part and parcel of an administrator's job.

Persistent questioning or dismissal of university initiatives regarding Catholic identity, however, should be addressed by senior administrators. Even if the senior administrative team has a coherent package of policies, questions undermining the approach of the president or senior team may continue to surface. Cultural citizens or potential cultural catalysts are not obligated to examine the big picture. Being out of the limelight allows faculty and some administrators to address limited aspects of a policy and emphasize its weaker points. Connecting the dots between one initiative and the larger plan will address some of the cause for complaint. This is especially important if harping continues over a period of time. It is equally important to remind the community why policy initiatives are being implemented and how they fit into the university's efforts to live out its religious mission in ways that are expected to help the institution prosper in the coming years. Addressing the major issues in a forthright manner will not make the shadow culture disappear, but it can drain some of its power by making it more difficult for the discontented to pick and choose only those parts of a policy that give credence to their critical perspective.

One type of shadow culture threatens the institution itself if it is sufficiently widespread. Some faculty and administrators may reject initiatives to strengthen the mission of the institution. These members of the university community may clearly understand that the Catholic mission of the institution has eroded substantially in recent years. They may also acknowledge that some changes are required to help the university make the Catholic culture more present to and effective among students. Nonetheless, this group of faculty or administrators may reject changes introduced by senior administrators because they prefer to see the institution shift its Catholic mission to a nonsectarian mission. The larger this group and the stronger their convictions, the harder senior administrators must work to see that the new policies supportive of Catholic culture are effectively implemented. In such a situation, senior administrators should provide greater prestige and benefits (not related to financial compensation) to faculty and administrators who support the new policies. Senior administration should also increase the number of people at the institution who support the mission of the institution by assuring that new hires in both the administrative and faculty ranks clearly support religious cultural enhancement.

6

Student Culture

The academic sector is not alone in determining the success of the educational mission of any college or university. Students spend a small fraction of their time in classrooms and far more of it in residence halls and engaged in student activities. While the Catholic intellectual tradition was the most important theme discussed by senior administrators during their interviews, they also placed great emphasis on student culture as both an indicator of and a contributor to each institution's truly distinctive Catholic culture and identity.

Convictions

Senior administrators insisted that their institutions educated students within pervasive and transformative Catholic cultures whose reach extended far beyond the classroom experience. According to a diaspora administrator, "the way we deliver [education] is life changing." "The heart and soul of these institutions are transformational in nature, not just transactional," a diaspora president claimed. They "teach people, not only how to earn a living, but how to live a life in a moral sense, in an ethical sense, in a value sense." The goals Catholic higher education sets for students are also unique. According to a cohort administrator, "when you're a student at a Catholic institution, you're not just supposed to learn, you're supposed to learn how to live."

Most administrators distinguished values as the component of a Catholic higher education culture that has a transformational impact on students. "If a student graduates from one of these institutions in four years and they are not different and better," a cohort administrator insisted, "then they've wasted their money. If they haven't found a value system or enhanced a value system or saved a value system, it's a waste because that's the role we have."

All colleges and universities claim to educate the whole person, but most administrators said a commitment to value neutrality at nonreligious institutions casts doubt on the ability of those institutions to make that claim. The vice-president for mission at an immersion university worked in a state university and said, "it is next to impossible to educate the whole person in a value-neutral ambiance." An immersion student affairs officer claimed that "Catholic universities influence the whole person [because] they teach values." The commitment to values at these institutions, according to a persuasion administrator, is distinctive and ongoing. "There will always be an ethical and value component to Catholic education that you cannot find in public institutions." A cohort university administrator suggested that Catholic institutions should accentuate this commitment and practice when talking about their mission. "Catholic education is unique in our society today where public institutions tout themselves as being value free. We should tout our religious institutions as value laden and argue that our society is desperately in need of programs that provide a higher set of values." "In our society," according to a persuasion president, "parents and families are looking for institutions that are value oriented." A cohort administrator agreed that "in a world where everything seems to go, where there don't seem to be any limits, including in higher education, people are looking for some rootedness and some boundaries and some assistance in helping them in these formative years—some faith-based and value-based education." In this climate, another cohort president insisted, "what is unique about Catholic institutions is the linkage of ethics, values, and spirituality. Consequently, we're more important than ever, and that will become more and more clear."

While most administrators were convinced that the values education at Catholic colleges and universities was transformational for students, they did not agree about which values were part of that education. A persuasion university student affairs officer focused on integrity as a premier value. "As a Catholic institution, whatever we do should be done with integrity. We are honest, straightforward and if we make a mistake, we say we made a mistake. If we do something very well or don't do it well, we acknowledge that and we fix it." This administrator insisted that Catholic colleges "need to have the courage of our convictions," but she could not specify the exact nature of those convictions. At a diaspora university, the vice-president for student affairs focused on "the value and worth of human nature and very high standards."

The president of another diaspora university admitted to having trouble defining the values that shaped her institution's culture. "This is hard. As I think about Catholic values, I think about those things that have to do with how we live. It just has to do with something students build on that is connected to the values of the founding congregations and their serving of those that others don't." The mission vice-president at a cohort university said that "educating from a Catholic perspective means recognizing the dignity of the whole person and seeking to educate the mind and the heart . . . as people of justice working for dignity, the dignity of human beings, and also being faithful stewards of creation." A student life officer agreed that education at Catholic institutions

> seeks to shape the minds and hearts and souls of students to become agents of change, agents of service in a larger society. We're trying to get our students to become what we hope to model, which is people who are compassionate, who care about the world, who care about the poor, who care about the needs of the globe.

In order to qualify as a university in the United States today, according to a persuasion university administrator, "the modern university has to have a certain diversity; it has to have an openness whether it's cultural, racial, economic, geographic, whatever. It has to be encompassing." An immersion university administrator suggested that secular institutions are not really faithful to the commitment in practice, however. "Diversity and openness may be a goal for secular universities. It appears in their literature—usually to a slight extent." "Frankly, it is primarily lip service. If you judge these institutions by their actions, it's very difficult to document." Other administrators agreed that Catholic institutions are uniquely welcoming communities that respect all people. A persuasion university president said that "cultural richness and diversity is very much a Christian tradition." She added that Catholic colleges display "openness to all—a welcoming aspect toward many different kinds of individuals from different races, and creeds and students from international communities and foreign countries." An administrator from a diaspora college added that the "unique contribution of Catholic higher education is Christian values, particularly the respect we show for one another. Black and white and international students—we are all good and we are all loved by God."

Many senior administrators also thought the Catholic colleges and universities demonstrated the values of openness and respect for diversity more effectively than other religiously affiliated institutions. As a diaspora administrator explained,

> Catholic institutions have a way of opening their arms in a nonjudgmental way and in an open way to diversity and people of different faiths. They do so in ways that other faith-based institutions, which are more heavy-handed, do not. At those institutions there is a certain pressure to fall into line with the majority. Catholic universities, on the other hand, have the kind of mindset that can be open to all. It's not about proselytizing to make more Catholics. It's about being catholic with a small c.

"There is a big difference in residential life at Catholic universities—or at least there should be," a vice-president for mission at a persuasion university maintained. The values that make that difference for a student life officer at an immersion institution have their roots in St. Augustine.

I'm with St. Augustine that the way you behave and the way you live really effect your openness, first of all to the truth, but then also to a happy life. Happiness doesn't consist in always doing whatever you want. Happiness lies in the path of virtue. That's hard for kids to understand, but that's the truth. So, if a Catholic college asks students to live in an orderly way and if it offers them the truth, it is offering them hope. . . . Holding kids to a high standard works. They're dying to be held to standards.

While some enthusiasm for high behavioral standards was voiced by a number of administrators, most went to some lengths to explain that Catholic standards should not be invoked in judgmental ways. A vice-president for mission at a persuasion university explained the importance of pastoral support in Catholic higher education.

As Catholics we walk the path with people, and that path is sometimes straight and even, and at other times it is difficult. Everyone who has lived long enough knows that life has its ups and downs. As Catholics we are with people through all these moments. People are struggling with who they are and their identity and they end up in situations that don't reflect gospel values. We don't walk away from these people. If a person ends up in a relationship where they are acting out inappropriately in terms of sexual practices and they end up getting themselves in trouble, we don't walk away. We're not scared. Rather, we walk with that person and try to help them come to understand what is best for them by sharing our values. Our way of life calls us to an ideal and to reach that ideal takes a lot of effort. You don't live the ideal right away.

Reality

While senior administrators insist that Catholic culture should permeate the entire educational experience at their institutions, the reality on campus that they described suggests a religiously tepid student culture. The academic vice-president at a persuasion university pointed out that

for many of our students, particularly because we are about forty percent commuting adults, they love the school because it is values oriented. However, they are not engaging the Catholic tradition in any particular way. . . . It's very possible to just feel good about this being a small college with warm values and a humanistic sort of feel without being able to identify it as specifically Catholic.

The president of another persuasion university described his university a bit differently, saying that it is "Catholic in every sense of the word and very much driven by our mission. Also, we are very ecumenical in nature." A cohort administrator focused on the importance of interreligious dialogue as a way in which the campus embraces its Catholic identity.

> [Our] Catholic identity is intermixed with our identity to have a campus that really starts to have a dialogue among other faiths . . . we have kids from so many religions that one of the best things we need to do is fortify how the Catholic religion can lead in embracing other religions, creating interfaith dialogue and making sure our kids are appreciative, aware, and articulate of their own values and ethics coupled with the ability to see the vision and the beauty and merit and worth of other peoples' faiths.

The importance of promoting religious tolerance was also echoed by a diaspora administrator who is "working with campus ministry and the students to get them to understand . . . there is a certain Catholic way that you go about things where you can embrace your Buddhist brother or a Muslim or Protestant religion at the same time being fully Catholic."

Diaspora administrators were particularly focused on their unique situation in which "more than half of the students are not Catholic." One administrator said:

> we're trying to interact with and serve and deal with students whose faith tradition is not our own and provide a place for them to come and have the kind of experience that is consistent with our values and our spirituality and our mission. At the same time we are being pressured to conform to doctrine in teaching and in an informal way to play out an identity that most of our students don't recognize or connect with.

The values of openness and religious tolerance are so heightened at one diaspora university that the vice-president for mission announced: that

> this is an ecumenical college sponsored by the Catholic Church. We will reach out to more students [by] being ecumenical than we would if specifically identified as a Catholic institution. Students have come here to discover their spiritual center. Many do not know or even want to know and care about God when they come here. Here they are introduced to God in a way that is not forceful or judging or even really institutional. It's actually experiential.

Senior administrators insisted that Catholic colleges and universities have value-based student cultures that transform the young men and women who encounter them. They also described campus situations that only dimly approximated these ideals. A cohort president was quite frustrated by the response she gets when discussing formation and student culture.

> So, I talk about formation rather than education and I really get creamed for that because some say we're only about intellectual for-

mation. I say, "No, we're not! We have nineteen-hundred-plus kids living here. They're in class 15 hours a week. We hope they are studying another thirty hours a week, but they are here for another 120 a week, and what are we doing with them during that period of time?" The faculty doesn't like hearing that, but we chose to build all these dorms and create a residential campus, so let's deal with it.

In describing their residence halls, many senior administrators admitted that they encountered real obstacles to creating pervasively Catholic cultures. As a cohort administrator pointed out, "residence halls and student areas will always be messy places." Most administrators were clear that their institutions took strong action in situations involved with drugs. A persuasion university president said: "we have some semblance of rules, and we really don't tolerate any drugs, and we're very hard on marijuana." Another persuasion administrator pointed out that "residence life people are very actively on guard about drinking and drugs and any student caught with drugs on campus is immediately expelled from residence. If you are caught with drugs, you're out. That's the only way to send the message that we are not going to tolerate drugs." Dealing with alcohol-related issues was more complicated for administrators.

> Our students drink pretty much along with most American higher education, and if you look at the first-year student studies, Catholic colleges drink at a higher rate than non-Catholic ones. On campus the alcohol culture is pretty minimal, but we've got a lot of students living in the immediate surrounding neighborhood, and there are occasional rip-roaring parties.

A persuasion administrator worried about the depth of the drinking problems on campus. "Alcohol is a terrible drug, a terrible problem here. There is a lot of underage drinking, a lot of drinking and binging."

There is a great deal of variety in how Catholic colleges and universities deal with the issue of sexual intimacy among students. One immersion university president speaks directly to student sexual mores in his opening talk with students in their early summer orientation.

> The president does the welcome and covers the social, as well as the academic and spiritual. He says to these people at orientations who are deposited and actually planning on coming here, "You will not cohabitate together. We do not do that here. If this is what you thought, then you have several months to change your mind and to find an institution where you would be happier."

A vice-president for students said her institution is direct, clear, and consistent. "If students violate policies, there are consequences and they know it. We're consistent. We don't harangue, we're just consistent."

All of the immersion institutions take a strong position about the limits of appropriate relationships, and they also insist on single-sex residence halls. Only a few persuasion institutions follow that policy. However, the president of one of these persuasion institutions felt strongly about the message that certain policies send to students.

> Institutionally there needs to be some kind of line in the sand that says this is acceptable and this is not. I have said no co-ed dorms for the simple reason one of the messages we as an institution are trying to send is that some behaviors are acceptable and some are not. Simply to be able to walk in and out of bathrooms and rooms with no constraints whatever at this point in a young person's life would be a failure on our part from a moral point of view.

Most Catholic colleges have adopted a different approach. A cohort president described the situation that exists at most Catholic colleges. "Every residence hall is co-ed by floor or suite, and it has been that way since they built the townhouses. It is really difficult to legislate morality, but we don't even have parietals. We don't have anything."

A number of administrators talked about efforts to set standards in residence halls that reflected their Catholic values. A persuasion administrator's institution "had a program trying to clarify Catholic identity with resident hall staff, because some are not Catholic; the Catholic ones have great fear of anything dealing with sexuality." At this institution, they "are not afraid of addressing these issues, but are doing so in a very quiet way." At another persuasion university, the vice-president for student affairs admitted that "sexual activity is the experience of some of the students, and a lot of the kids became sexually active in high school. We've seen an increase in sexually transmitted diseases, and we're concerned about it. We're trying to strategize about how to address it." At another persuasion university, the vice-president for mission was clear that "it is fairly common on most university campuses to have safe sex talks in residence halls at freshman orientation. On this campus there are no programs on sex or sexuality that do not take in moral theology."

Most administrators admitted that making the Catholic connection in terms of student behavioral expectations is a struggle, but they still work at it. Surprisingly, one cohort administrator was quite clear that her institution made no effort to do so.

> We haven't done anything related to Catholic identity in student affairs, and I purposely stayed away from it. I don't want to be perceived as the person designated to clean up the residences and stop all this drinking and sex and stealing. I also stayed away from it because a dialogue had begun on Catholic identity, and I thought if I were to have that conversation on another level I would be muddying the waters. Now that recommendations are going to be public, hopefully we will look at ways to integrate them into student affairs.

Concerns

Administrators generally agreed with a cohort administrator about the difficulty they face in creating transformative Catholic student cultures.

> Our society is becoming so secularized that the real danger is our Catholic institutions will become secular. We need to be institutions that aren't secular, institutions that are trying to fight the trend—to be mission driven, faith oriented, value oriented and to be training and helping people in the formative years of their lives.

Not all students will either get the message or be willing to be shaped by Catholic culture. Nevertheless, most administrators believe they must try to reach as many students as they can. They tend to agree with a persuasion student life vice-president that there are three groups of students: first, "people that no matter what you say or do, they're not going to listen. A second group, no matter what you say or do, they are still going to do the right thing. And then there is this large group in the middle that you try to push away from that small first group."

For some administrators, the greatest difficulties Catholic colleges face come in terms of conflicts about extracurricular activities. "It is difficult," a persuasion university president pointed out,

> to reconcile appropriate levels of academic freedom and the teachings of the Church or what is the kind of propriety we should be exhibiting as Catholic institutions. We had a limited production of *The Vagina Monologues* this year, which I absolutely did not want to see done on this campus. How do you handle those things? At what point do you say to faculty "No! This is totally out of alignment." When do you say, "All right, it is certainly contrary to the Church's views but we do lots of other things that provide alternative viewpoints?"

Another president from a cohort university had no difficulty or ambivalence about the same production. "For a Catholic university to use *The Vagina Monologues* in a public venue flies in the face of what we are about. There is nothing in any biblical tradition I know that portrays women's bodies in that way."

Other administrators voiced real concern about the role of alcohol and inappropriate sexual relationships in Catholic residence halls. As one persuasion university administrator put it, "Our residence halls, for the most part, are bastions of everything the Church tells us not to do. They are shocking for people my age, they are just shocking." A cohort president agreed that while "our university mission programs are effective, residence life is really a center that needs a lot of attention. It does not have the general interest or respect of the faculty, which diminishes its perceived value." That president went on to say: "I worry greatly about alcohol and drug issues." A persuasion mission offer agreed, saying:

> we try to deal with the alcohol abuse, which is rampant here, as well as what results from it—the fighting, the sexual unions where people are drunk, the damage to the buildings, bringing people to the hospital for alcohol poisoning. A lot of things happened in the seventies and eighties, and if we could go back we would probably do things differently. We blew it on some things, and pulling back now or knowing how to pull back is just very hard.

For many administrators, "the sexual activity of students is actually shocking—that students would have someone in bed with them and their roommate would be still sleeping in the room with them." A persuasion university administrator verbalized great frustration about the experiences students have prior to coming to college that makes the work of residence life staff all the more difficult. "I mean some kids really should just sue their parents. They were just not raised properly and they come away with ideas. What are we going to do if parents, who probably consider themselves good Catholics, are saying to their daughters, 'As you go away to school, here's a prescription I got you for the pill'? How are we going to undo that? What are we going to tell the student? 'Your mother who loves you is a jerk!' That's not going to work."

A cohort president pointed out that "the majority of Catholic students in everything but sexual matters adhere rather closely to church teaching. In sexual matters they don't. They have such a sense of liberation when they come and I worry greatly about it." Parents are not imparting Catholic values, and once the students get on campus, there are few intellectual supports for the Church's moral positions. A persuasion administrator pointed out: "it's not like in the old days when maybe there were four theology classes—one for each year. One of them was morality or one of them was marriage, and they would cover sexual morality."

Student life administrators at most of the colleges felt under siege and unsupported. A persuasion administrator "often feels caught in the middle between trying to help people understand what the Catholic teaching is and dealing with the student body who doesn't buy it." A mission vice-president pointed out: "we have student life people who are not well versed. They feel very incompetent and very unsure and they have no confidence." Amid a great deal of concern, however, there was one cohort administrator who thought all the worry was just a tempest in a teapot. This administrator thought that clamping down on students only succeeded in making them more defiant of Church teaching.

> We have Students for Choice who would like us to give out condoms. We're expected to hunker down and not do that, and I have to say from where I've been and where I've lived, my own gut reaction is to say "Why hunker down?" An efficient way to provoke a nega-

tive reaction is to impose a negative sanction or expectation. I'm inclined to say, "Chill!" Relax, okay?

Future Directions

In the area of student culture, senior administrators admitted to having many concerns, but few had suggestions about how to proceed in the future. One diaspora administrator said that Catholic colleges and universities

> are at a dividing of the water. In ten years, if we are still going to be in existence, we're going to have to be what we say we are. If we say we're Catholic, it shouldn't be because of the few Catholics scattered around. This generation and generations coming up are hungry for values and formation, and we have to understand what it means to deliver Catholic education and formation.

A president of a persuasion university said that "trying to incorporate Catholic values more openly and directly into the lived reality of the students will be something that happens over the next ten years."

In anticipating the future, some administrators looked to issues of hiring. They tended to agree with a cohort president that, when hiring, "number one is somebody who understands that it is important not to just be in the Catholic tradition but to be inside Catholicism. I'd be looking for someone who sees the school in terms of formation, as well as information that shapes people in applying their moral values." A persuasion administrator would seek individuals who have "a commitment to the faith and an understanding of the role of lay leadership in perpetuating student development." This means getting "somebody who is more than just familiar with Catholic education. It should be someone who lives it—who is fundamentally committed to the values of our religious tradition and the Church's teaching and is willing to lead in student affairs and in enrollment." A persuasion university administrator who was terribly concerned about the failures in residence life also relied upon a "good hire" to make a difference. "Our new resident director is a daily communicant. He is very religious. He is a person I hope will have more of an effect on our residences."

An immersion administrator insisted that

> all of us in Catholic higher education, or at least in student affairs, are saying to ourselves, "Okay, we've got to get at what our mission statement is. We want to say where we are and act according to that mission statement." I have a number of young people on my staff now, all good Catholic kids raised in solid families. They are a dedicated generation.

The president of an immersion college said that students in the future will "expect the college to be committed to the moral principles of the Church. If colleges don't understand that, they will not know how to exercise authority or leadership." A cohort president believes that being sensitive to how residence halls are staffed will be crucial. "I think the answer is in the training of residence hall assistants. I am also very interested in what they do at colleges where they have adults in every residence hall. And by adults I mean people who are priests, or sisters, or families who have this [Catholic piece] as a commitment." An administrator at another cohort institution had a different approach.

> We're going to have policies that say no overnight guests. No Sex! We won't, however, be having what I would call a sleepover patrol. No! When those things come up we'll enforce them, but I'm realistic enough and my tradition in student life tells me that we are never going to get eighteen-to twenty-two-year-olds to just all roll into line and say, "Boy, you guys are right and we're so happy you're enforcing these policies." We simply have to have some sort of policies that respect the Catholic moral tradition; we have to educate our staff and make sure we have folks who are comfortable with the moral tradition and enough Catholics in the mix so they can help explain that tradition.

Analysis of the Data: Student Formation through Catholic Culture

Senior administrators stressed that the student culture at their Catholic institutions is distinctive and transformative. They also consistently emphasized that a thoroughly Catholic culture should be inclusive. Catholic student culture, in their view, embraces everyone and is tolerant of each person, including those not raised in the tradition, as well as individuals who may not entirely accept it.

Senior administrators revealed that many of their institutions find it difficult to create the distinctive, transformative, and Catholic student culture they desire and they struggle with all this implies. The difficulties are exacerbated by the pervasive presence of the broad, dominant American culture, which Catholic colleges and universities both try to accommodate and counter.

Administrators admitted that at many Catholic universities, clear patterns of expected student behavior, especially in activities where Catholic culture competes and conflicts with the broader secular culture, are frequently not clearly articulated. Furthermore, even when such rules are stated clearly and forcefully, students who deviate from the norm are usually not sanctioned in meaningful ways. Related to this, many colleges and universities do not effectively employ Catholic moral theory, in any of its many formulations, to explain why certain patterns of behavior—including the use of drugs and excessive alcohol consumption—are incompatible with Catholic teaching. One reason for the latter phenomenon may be ignorance of the Catholic moral tradition on the part of student personnel staff and administrators. Whatever the reason, rules and explanations for them are part of the cultural content and establish the norms that are integral to any culture. Catholic culture is suffused with moral norms and the rational explanations that support them. While these rationales and explanations may not convince everyone, they appeal more to reason than religion and are, at least in principle, accessible to all students, whatever their religious background. In the absence of moral stories or reasoning, behavioral rules still support the culture. When combined with the symbols and narratives of Catholic culture, the explanatory and connective power of the rules is greatly enhanced.

In many ways, American culture is a positive force for the good, and it is important to acknowledge its many sterling characteristics. American culture, of course, has another side, a darker side, that society in general and religious groups in particular acknowledge and often criticize. Senior administrators identified many of the most worrisome aspects of modern youth culture, including the inclination to seek status, acceptance, and comfort in drugs, alcohol, and intensely sexualized relationships. The Catholic Church objects to these behaviors because they are contrary to full human flourishing. Human life is sacred, and everything people do should cultivate, rather than diminish, that sacredness.

The purpose of Catholic colleges and universities is not to change American culture, though they hope to have an impact on it. Instead, Catholic universities structure their own culture to compete with the broader American culture for the hearts and minds of its students. In analyzing student culture at Catholic universities, it is important to recall that the university is in competition. A Catholic culture can affirm many aspects of the broad American culture, but other aspects it rejects. Competition occurs at the point where Catholic culture clearly rejects an element of the broader culture and proposes in its stead something Catholics believe is more authentically human and ultimately fulfilling.[1]

If Catholic culture at colleges and universities is to have any hope of being a successful competitor, it has to have an approach that is cohesive and appealing to young people. Real competition must be vigorous, not tepid. The competitive message must be sharply differentiated and well crafted. The tolerant whatever-you-choose, my-way-is-as-good-as-yours, live-and-let-live message of American culture is enormously appealing, especially for young adults. Developing a truly competitive alternative message requires relentless repetition of a coherent message in a variety of venues. This is a tall order but not an impossible one for Catholic colleges and universities. The degree and limits of that cohesion in various situations are worth exploring.

Every culture engages content, symbols, and actors. In cohesive cultures, these components reinforce one another in both significant and small ways. Parents, for example, know that rebellion is a natural and healthy part of young adult development. With that in mind, many parents take principled stands that they consistently apply about both big issues and relatively small things, like chores or curfews. This approach creates a space for their sons and daughters to rebel without putting themselves in jeopardy. It is far better for a young person to declare his or her independence around taking out the trash than drinking and driving. A similar approach may or may not work among students and student infractions. What is transferable, however, is the value of consistent application of norms for student behavior both with respect to very important and less important matters. Through this process, students come to understand the values of Catholic culture, as well as what constitute small and large violations of it.

Conveying degrees of importance to students is crucial when establishing a culture that challenges the dominant American culture. Prior to arriving at the university, students have been negotiating their way amid the persuasions of two different cultures—the dominant American culture, which has few constraints, and their considerably more constrained family cultures. Many students arrive at the Catholic university yearning for fewer constraints even as their parents pay considerable sums of money in the hope the Catholic university will impose firm, reasonable constraints endorsed by the Catholic tradition.[2] This sets up an inevitable clash of wills, the tension points of which are usually well understood by those involved in student culture.

An important issue confronting Catholic universities in terms of student culture is inheritability. That is, to what extent is the culture proposed by the Catholic university assimilated by students? The university selects the content and symbols of the Catholic culture according to the specific model it adheres to. The university administration has the benefit of understanding the background of students and the situation into which they are being introduced, and it employs this information in selecting content. The administration, however, is never just working with one cohort of students and must consider that annually one group of students will graduate as another wave of freshpersons enters.

Every year at a Catholic university, the Catholic culture meets the American culture and competes for attention and long-term inheritability. This is preeminently true for first-year students, but it is also true for sophomores, juniors, and seniors who return from a long summer subject to the persuasions and customs of American culture. The Catholic university establishes the content and symbols of its culture, with particular attention to those areas where the two cultures compete.

In this scenario, the human actors are more complicated than in the simple model of culture examined in chapter 2. In the student culture at a Catholic university, students, administrators, and faculty are all engaged in the culture and play a role in sustaining it. Each one is called to support the culture by being a citizen or catalyst, even as experience indicates that many, including some administrators, faculty, and students, are disinclined to lend their support. The students have to be introduced to and affirmed in the culture, and the administrators have to be alert to changes in entering students that make cultural adjustments imperative.[3] In addition, although administrators establish the culture, the culture is not successfully "inherited" by students unless a good number of the citizens and catalysts are themselves students. So, while culture is imposed, it must also persuade students to become cultural citizens and catalysts if it is to survive over time.

The content of culture includes standards and norms. Both in student and other types of culture, rules help define the contours of culture. Even in what are considered the predominantly and more purely intellectual components of a culture, rules play a powerful role. Within a few weeks of their first classes at a university—Catholic or otherwise—students understand what is expected of them in their classes. Exams, quizzes, papers, class attendance, participation in class discussions, individual meetings with the professors, acceptable excuses, unacceptable use of the web or other resources—all these become clear both because faculty explain what they expect and because they impose sanctions that enforce (or fail to enforce) their standards.[4]

In addition to beliefs, explanations, norms, and shared assumptions, the content of culture includes sanctions. In order for the rules or norms to be effective in a culture, they have to be interpreted and enforced. Unenforced rules become putative standards, not real ones. For example, some professors might insist that students are required to complete all reading assignments prior to exams. If, however, the reading material is always covered in class or if on the first two or three quizzes or exams the professor never poses any questions about the reading materials, students quickly conclude that doing all assigned reading is not a norm but only a putative rule.

Students arrive at the university with their own ideas of what constitutes appropriate rules. They are, however, open to new rules, since they are entering a culture determined predominantly by others, not themselves, and they understand that. Faculty members set the academic rules and establish the norms. Students either adhere to the rules and prosper, or selectively dismiss them and suffer the consequences. There are no contract negotiations between students and faculty about academic rules, although there is mutual testing of one another with respect to rule enforcement.

At one level, the comparison between academic rules and rules for student living and student activities is apt. In student culture, administrators and students in the sophomore, junior, or senior years set the rules, and first-year students either adhere to them and prosper, or selectively break them and suffer the consequences. However, there are two significant differences between academic and student culture at Catholic universities. First, with the exception of course requirements related to the Catholic tradition, the academic rules set by professors do not have a particularly Catholic tone. With some exceptions, the rules reflect a broader consensus among faculty at most institutions of higher education about what constitutes a prudent framework for learning. Typically, so there can be no misunderstanding about what is required, these requirements are detailed in the student's academic manual. Since the course requirements and norms for plagiarism or cheating are rules set by the faculty, most academic administrators are scrupulous in adhering to them. Similarly, there are few, if any, putative course requirements in Catholic universities; one either takes the required courses or one does not graduate. Setting aside the exception of required Catholic courses, faculty rules at a Catholic university are very similar to those prevailing in the nonsectarian model. Also, faculty rules need not conflict with standards set in the dominant culture.

Superior performance in the dominant American culture requires discipline, honesty, expertise, and imagination, whether it be in the field of sports, entertainment, or business. Faculty requirements fit fairly easily in the dominant culture that places emphasis on discipline, honesty, expertise, and imagination. Because of this congruence between the dominant culture and the academic culture, academic rules do not appear to students to be problematic or unduly onerous.

The second important difference between academic and student culture involves the degree of clarity of rules and the consistency of their enforcement. Judging from comments made by senior administrators in the first part of this chapter, the extent of both enforcement and articulation of expectations with respect to nonacademic student behavior is questionable at many Catholic universities. The fact there are rules does not seem to be the issue. Rather, the difficulty emerges from a lack of clarity about rules that are poorly articulated, insufficiently motivated, and inconsistently enforced.

Some might object that because student culture involves both personal privacy and public acts, the university must avoid intrusion in the private sphere. But the academic sector easily handles private views with sensitivity. After all, how much knowledge a person has of a particular academic discipline or what a student's views are on some political, social, or family issue does not inhibit professors from posing questions on exams and evaluating student knowledge on the basis of their answers. Faculty members respect privacy but still require class participation. It is equally possible for administrators in student affairs to respect privacy while at the same time requiring adherence to certain rules that reflect Catholic teaching.

Faculty members in the classrooms of Catholic colleges or universities are usually not required or encouraged to be antiseptic purveyors of objective information. They are expected to convey objective knowledge, but they can teach passionately and share their own convictions. In the end, students determine their own views concerning particular issues covered in the classroom. This situation is analogous to student culture with respect both to Catholic teachings and Catholic practices, be they permitted or prohibited by the university. Catholic culture does not and cannot compel student belief in the Catholic faith or Catholic moral principles. Nor can Catholic culture compel compliance with its norms once students graduate. The best a culture can do is present to students as normative a particular way of living and do so as attractively as possible. During their time at college, or upon leaving the institution, students choose their beliefs and their way of behaving. Even a very cohesive Catholic culture cannot compel students to change their personal beliefs or convictions. The Catholic culture can, however, constrain students to behave in certain ways while at the university under penalty of sanction. In the sphere of personal conviction it simply cannot compel, it can only persuade.

Even though the students would never select some academic rules on their own, imposed rules play a vital role in academic culture. They enable students to become educated. Since the academic culture has devised rules that students do not perceive to violate privacy, in principle at least, administrators or mold-ers of student culture can do likewise. For this reason, it appears the main challenge for student culture at Catholic universities is one primarily of conviction—a conviction that insists that senior administrators in student affairs establish norms and consistently enforce them.

The comments of senior administrators show that rules in student culture are neuralgic, both for students and staff. Because of the developmental phase young students are passing through during their undergraduate years, some students will always challenge rules pertaining to nonacademic student behavior. If, however, these rules are properly formulated, explicated, and enforced, they will contribute to the creation of a culture that that helps students mature. These structured norms can also teach students perspectives for life that will have great value after they graduate.

If rules are to be effective, whether they pertain to student academic behavior or student social behavior, they must be clear, limited in number, pertinent to the student's development, and consistent with the identity, character and mission of the institution. Many senior administrators acknowledge they clearly state and enforce some expectations about student behavior, especially in terms of drugs. However, with respect to alcohol, the expectations are often clearly stated but inconsistently enforced. And, judging from administrators' comments, when it comes to sexual intimacies and liaisons, expectations are vaguely stated, poorly explained, and at some institutions never enforced.

Inconsistent enforcement of rules conveys a message of what really counts in a culture. For example, rules against excessive consumption of alcohol apply at many Catholic institutions only to on-campus consumption. Enforcement of the no-alcohol rule on campus is strict. Not surprisingly, the result is that most drinking takes place off campus. No attempt is made by university authorities to monitor off-campus consumption, and enforcement of penalties against students who return to campus intoxicated is feeble at best, if such penalties exist at all. The alcohol problem is handled clearly and forcefully only in a fairly restricted area.

The limited enforcement of rules forbidding drinking may be technically consistent, but that is not how it appears to students. Because easy ways to avoid the application of university rules are available to students, they interpret the broader university policy as saying drinking on campus is unacceptable, but drinking off campus, even excessive drinking, is not seriously wrong. The result, as evidenced by various surveys, is that many students at Catholic institutions frequently drink to excess, but choose carefully where they get intoxicated. These results are disturbing, and the situation with respect to drinking was acknowledged with regret by many senior administrators at Catholic universities. Many Catholic universities have instituted programs to diminish the amount of drinking, but the problem persists. Whether any of the programs to dissuade students from drinking at Catholic colleges and universities stand out by their reliance on the Catholic moral tradition is simply not known, and no senior administrator claimed any special distinction for his or her institution's own enforcement or motivation program with respect to student drinking.

In their interviews senior administrators lauded the Catholic tradition and said it is, or at least should be, distinctive. To achieve this, student norms at Catholic institutions should reflect the tradition, and the Catholic tradition should win out over the nonsectarian tradition in successfully molding student behavior. If senior administrators want better results than those of their counterparts at nonsectarian institutions, the path must include greater emphasis on pertinent aspects of the Catholic tradition. Clarity in the enforcement of rules and appropriate penalties for even small violations are ways to lend an emphasis that is easily grasped by students. Many, but not all, Catholic universities follow the lead of secular institutions and ground their policy in civil law. Students are told that underage drinking is against the law and that it is not healthy. Other reasons may also be stated, but the emphasis is frequently on two realities—civil legal prohibitions and the threat that excess drinking poses to the health and future well-being of students. Students are informed of the consequences with respect to their standing in the university should they violate the law of the state, which the university appropriates as the law on campus.

Excessive drinking is indeed unhealthy and, when indulged in by underage students, against the law. However, such an explanation does not put the full weight of a Catholic university against abusive drinking, either on or off campus. In many Catholic institutions, authorities in student affairs do not draw on traditional Catholic teaching to explain why excessive drinking is morally wrong and how it is corrosive to an individual's authentic humanity. In our view, Church teaching in this area can be very appealing to young people. Church teaching addresses the essence of what it means to be human, namely, to possess natural dignity and infinite value and to be a rational moral agent with the capacity to make choices. It also highlights the demand that young men and women always respect their own dignity and that of others and avoid situations where they can unwittingly do damage to themselves and others or in which their ability to choose is compromised.

Personal relationships are also an issue of concern. Many senior administrators acknowledged that expected student behavior with respect to interpersonal and social relations among students is not addressed. In many institutions, if these norms are stated, they are included in the student handbook. Unfortunately, they are not emphasized, and sanctions are neither threatened nor imposed.[5] This leaves students without real guidance about the appropriate role of sexual intimacies in their lives or what is expected of them in a Catholic culture. This deprives them of being effectively exposed to the very distinctiveness of the Catholic tradition with respect to lasting relationships. And this in an area of great importance to students at a significant stage of their maturation that will also have serious consequences for any future relationships they develop.

An unintended and unfortunate outcome of a policy of benign neglect is its impact on students who seek to live in concert with Catholic tradition. Many students at Catholic universities, by virtue of their past training and parental guidance, are inclined to abide by traditional Catholic norms.[6] These students want to reserve sexual intimacies to marriage, but they do not receive the kind of support they need from administration at some Catholic institutions.[7] Such students have to fend for themselves and figure out what they should do when, for example, their roommate announces that a sexual partner is coming to their room for the night. At the same time, students who act contrary to Catholic teaching in matters of sexual intimacy receive tacit approval for their actions. At some Catholic institutions, the message is unfortunately quite clear. As long as students act discreetly and follow the etiquette of proper notification of a roommate, from university authorities they receive neither notice nor penalty.[8]

Administrators are resourceful people who have an extensive array of levers they can use and adjust to influence student behavior. If student outcomes with respect to drinking or personal relationships are not consistent with the Catholic mission, administrators should act.[9] First-year students enter a university community that already has certain standards. While the university must be judicious in establishing these standards, they should not be at variance with the mission of the institution. Judging from comments made by senior administrators during their interviews, standards are at odds with the Catholic mission at a goodly number of Catholic institutions. In order to achieve greater congruence between Catholic mission and actual practice, administrators responsible for student culture will have to be much clearer about what they expect in terms of student behavior, as well as what students can anticipate if they fail to meet clearly articulated standards. A justification for the standards that takes advantage of the considerable explanatory and motivational resources available in the Catholic intellectual and moral tradition would also contribute significantly to persuading students of the inherent value in what the Catholic tradition holds dear.

Comments from our interviews with senior administrators indicate that the minimum desirable norms for student behavior at many Catholic universities are not operative. In terms of our treatment of culture in chapter 2, this means the minimum requirements for distinguishability and inheritability set forth in the four models are not fulfilled in some institutions. Senior administrators candidly admit that much work needs to be done to shore up the Catholic culture at many Catholic campuses, but they are unsure how to proceed.

With respect to clarity of standards and consistency of enforcement in matters pertaining to social drinking, addictive substances, and appropriate levels of sexual intimacy, there should be no substantial differences in norms and sanctions among the four Catholic models. Each one of these areas involves activities in which the Catholic moral tradition has been consistently clear. Each area also involves some danger that students will make poor decisions that will have deleterious consequences on their own lives for years to come, as well as on the Catholic culture on campus. Finally, to reach maturity, students need to perceive the norms associated with these three activities as essential and then appropriate them as their own.

Students have an uncanny ability to accurately read a culture when it pertains to behavior that interests them. Drinking, drugs, and sexual intimacy are issues that grab the attention of traditional-age undergraduates. Catholic universities cannot afford to send a confusing institutional message about where they stand in regard to all three. Students interpret activities that are not clearly prohibited to be permissible. They also interpret the failure to punish certain behaviors as an institutional wink and nod signaling tolerance if not all-out permission.

The centrality of these activities, the critical need for restraint, and the potential danger to students who experiment with them all call out for a unified approach among Catholic institutions in setting and managing behavioral boundaries. This stance sounds harsh and unyielding, even to us. While admittedly unyielding, it is harsh only because clarity about the responsibilities of Catholic universities in treating this sensitive issue is so important. Catholic universities who wish to act in concert with and in support of the Catholic Church cannot be ambiguous about issues that are so important for the formation of the full human person. Many factors play a role in the education and formation of young Catholics, and the Catholic university is only one of them. What path a particular student takes after graduation depends in part on the student's family background and personal disposition. The motivation and encouragement to virtue provided by the university will also have an impact. Certainly part of the motivation and encouragement comes in providing students with a clear idea of what the Catholic tradition requires, recommends, and promotes. At least with respect to practices required of or prohibited for Catholics, the same consistent message should come from all Catholic colleges and universities.

As noted in an earlier chapter, the moral tradition forms one significant part of the Catholic intellectual tradition, and senior administrators were quite clear that they think their institutions should provide greater emphasis on the Catholic intellectual tradition. The Catholic immersion institution already places significant emphasis on the Catholic intellectual tradition. Many immersion universities already draw upon Catholic moral teaching when explaining university policy with respect to student behavioral norms. There is, on the other hand, less emphasis on the Catholic moral and intellectual tradition at Catholic persuasion, diaspora, and cohort universities. One way for institutions adhering to the latter three models to expand student exposure to this tradition is by linking the moral tradition to student rules, norms, and standards and spending time exploring its implications. The array of rules exists because they have a bearing on significant matters of student development. Clearly no explanation will be persuasive and convincing to all students. Nevertheless, linking activities of great interest to students to the Catholic intellectual tradition will at least guarantee that the tradition gets a hearing from them.

If linking the Catholic moral tradition to rules is a promising strategy for Catholic persuasion, diaspora, and cohort institutions, it is important to determine the best way to go about it. Most universities currently arrange mandatory attendance sessions for new first-year students to introduce them to the rules, norms, and standards of the university for students. While issues relating to sexual intimacy are not usually covered in such sessions, there is no reason why they should not be, and time can be extended in order to treat this and other important issues. The benefit of such sessions, whether they take place at the beginning of the school year or at various times throughout the school year, is that they are clearly outside the academic structure. In such a venue, it is quite appropriate for session presenters to speak both with conviction and without adornment about what is required and why it makes sense within the Catholic moral tradition.

The goal of these initiatives is to strengthen the Catholic culture by employing both symbol and content. In order to do that, people who are part of the culture and believe strongly in it must be part of the process. Someone who presents university norms for students in a halfhearted or noncommittal manner will undermine rather than strengthen the culture. Cultural citizens with an appreciation of the wisdom of the Catholic moral tradition will be the most effective communicators of what is expected in terms of students' interactions with each other at the university.

Outside Speakers and University Awards

With respect to some other types of student activities, it is appropriate for the four types of Catholic universities to have different approaches in explaining and motivating activities prescribed or proscribed by the Catholic faith. Two characteristics distinguish when and what type of diversity of approach is appropriate. First, in activities that engage students in responding to intellectual challenges to the Catholic tradition, different strategies can be pursued, with some institutions favoring one strategy over another. Second, whatever approach is taken, the university cannot undermine the teaching of the Church.

Once they graduate, students at Catholic colleges and universities will have to engage and respond to ideas and viewpoints at variance with Catholic teaching that are prominent in American culture. It is, therefore, important for them to be exposed to these perspectives and to learn how to engage them while they are students. In attempts to persuade students about the correctness of the Catholic approach, support for Catholic teaching can be demonstrated through a *pattern* of activities rather than in *each particular* activity. For example, each of the four types of universities might have a different approach to handling such activities as invitations to outside speakers and the conferral of university awards and honors that provide opportunities to elevate and explicate the Catholic perspective.

For the types of activities involving persuasion, each path has an array of advantages and disadvantages associated with it, and prudent people will differ about which best fits the situation of a particular institution. Both a positive and negative standard can serve to define the best approach. The negative standard avoids undermining the Catholic culture, and the positive standard reasonably advances Catholic understanding.

Consider the issue of inviting speakers to campus who disagree with significant moral teachings of the Catholic Church. Some speakers are invited to address the moral issue itself, while others are invited to speak on another topic or receive an honor from the university. In each instance, matters of prudential judgment are involved. The Catholic university as an institution cannot appear to endorse a position at variance with Church teaching. That does not mean, however, that only people who completely support Church teaching can be invited on campus. There are, in fact, a number of ways institutions can distance themselves from policy positions taken by invited guests. Some current practices illustrate the general principle.

Suppose the university invites a speaker to campus who will advocate the prochoice position in a talk, and the university knows beforehand that the speaker will take this approach. This usually happens when the invitation is extended through a student group. Some universities confronted with this situation would prevent an invitation from being extended, no matter the source. Others would allow the occasional invitation to be extended. In the latter case, the universities then make arrangements to have the Catholic viewpoint presented in a suitable forum, which may well be as part and parcel of the event in question. Whatever forum is chosen, it should be so arranged that it garners at least as much attention and interest as the prochoice speaker. Education is a primary activity of universities, but for Catholic institutions so, too, are persuasion and leadership. As long as the university does not mislead students about the basic commitment of the university to the Catholic message, it has leeway in choosing the most effective manner in which to get that message across to its students. The fact that views contrary to Catholic teaching are presented by a speaker in an isolated incident is less important than the patterns of speakers who come on campus and the impression they convey. The pattern of speaker invitations should not undermine university support for Catholic positions.

In choosing speakers, Catholic colleges and universities have a public obligation, but they must also exercise leadership in choosing the best way to educate and persuade their own students. Provided there is no pattern of support for positions contrary to Church teaching, a Catholic college or university can choose the ways it deems most effective in helping students understand the position of the Catholic Church. If, for instance, the institution believes it can be more effective by arranging a special student forum on an issue in which a speaker controverts Church teaching, so be it. The university can allow the invitation to be extended and then arrange for an appropriate student forum that presents the Church position with acumen and verve. University administrators exercising their own good judgment should make these determinations.

Catholic colleges and universities frequently find themselves on the horns of a dilemma when choosing individuals on whom to convey a university honor, such as an honorary degree. At times the person the institution hopes to honor may have taken a public position against some important teaching of the Church. The applicable principles in this case are the same as in the previous case: there should be no appearance that the university supports positions at variance with Church teaching, and the university must make sure students are exposed to Church teaching and the reasons for it. With respect to the first principle, what counts, once again, is the pattern. A Catholic university may honor a person for accomplishments and not the person's position that is at odds with Church teaching. Provided the university can make this distinction crystal clear, this principle is satisfied. The second aspect of positive cultural support should also be fulfilled. University practice must assure that students have received good exposure to Church teaching and the reasons for it.

Commencement exercises are a public, solemn act of the university. The university should make sure it honors people whose lives are for the most part consistent with Catholic university values. Catholic colleges and universities are not confined to honoring only saints or those individuals who have never made a public statement deemed wrong or controversial by the Catholic Church. Honorary doctorates are awarded in part to people because they stand out from the crowd in an exemplary way. Many people stand out without ever distancing themselves from Church teaching, and they are excellent candidates for honors and honorary degrees. Other individuals are also both outstanding and exemplary even though, for a variety of reasons, they disagree with the Church on one or more of its significant moral teachings. Just as it is not expected that everyone honored at a Catholic commencement be Catholic, so, too, it is not expected that everyone honored support all significant moral teachings of the Church. What is expected, however, is that the pattern of honorees makes clear to most people involved that the university does support the teaching of the Catholic Church. It is equally important that the university be clear about those things it is not honoring.[10]

Overall, the responsibility of the university is to advance Catholic culture and to avoid undermining it. The approach it takes in these matters depends on a number of issues related to its own circumstances.[11] However, which type of Catholic university has more latitude in establishing its faithfulness to the Church turns out to be counterintuitive. Because Catholic diaspora and cohort institutions have more religiously diverse university communities, it might seem obvious they should have the greatest leeway in terms of presenting oppositional views or honoring controversial individuals. In fact, the opposite appears to be the case, in our judgment. These institutions may well be compelled more frequently to disallow speakers advocating positions seriously at variance with Church teaching. Both principles play a role in increasing the likelihood of such an approach. Positive support requires the university to be clear about its stance in support of Church teaching. Because the number of students taking courses on Church teaching is relatively small, it may be more difficult for the university to speak clearly about its support to the university community. In addition, because diaspora and cohort institutions have fewer forums in which religious issues are regularly discussed, they have less opportunity to educate students about the actual teaching of the Church. For both reasons, these institutions have to be more judicious in determining whom they honor or invite to speak on campus.

Inclusion and Mutual Support

A recurrent theme among senior administrators was their belief that Catholic colleges and universities should embrace students of different ethnic, socio-economic, and religious backgrounds and treat all students with dignity and respect, whatever their sexual orientation or political leanings. This theme receives much attention at institutions of higher education, be they religious or nonsectarian. The desire to welcome all students and encourage them is a hallmark of modern universities. At an institution with a particular religious identity, understanding the contours of that identity is a first step to being authentically inclusive. After all, inclusiveness implies that the embracing community has a clear identity.[12] In the case of Catholic higher education, Catholic colleges and universities are trying to strengthen their Catholic identity, but not at the expense of nonparticipants and nonbelievers. Requiring people of different faith traditions to change their beliefs in order to be truly welcome is unacceptable to those involved in Catholic higher education.

The identity of a Catholic university has a number of central targets. The education and formation of students are the overarching goals. At a Catholic institution, these are accomplished by introducing all students to the Catholic tradition and sharing it with them. Goals are outlined for students, and they are encouraged to exceed the goals by learning the Catholic tradition on their own. Catholics students are also encouraged to allow themselves and their activities to be formed by the tradition. Students who are not Catholic are certainly encouraged to sample various aspects of the tradition.

It is important for Catholic colleges and universities to avoid compelling belief or requiring students to engage in religious practices at variance with their own faith tradition. Students should never be compelled to act contrary to their religion. On the other hand, they can be required to abstain from practices that, though not contrary to their religion, are contrary to Catholic teaching. All students are welcomed into a Catholic culture, which includes both beliefs and practices. As indicated earlier, because the culture includes practices, the university proscribes and prescribes certain activities that play an important role in personal development. In addition, activities that violate teachings of the Catholic Church are either discouraged or disallowed. This still allows abundant room for students of various outlooks. In their interviews, senior administrators affirmed their desire to maintain that degree of room within the specifically Catholic culture for students of various orientations to develop and to feel valued.

Certain types of inclusion pose challenges, though not insurmountable obstacles, for Catholic colleges and universities, because some activities associated with student groups are not consonant with the teachings of the Catholic Church. Catholic universities, for example, want to welcome all students, no matter their sexual orientation. The Catholic tradition maintains that every person is a child of God and should be treated as such. Consequently, at a

Catholic university there should be no second-class citizens—students, faculty, or staff. Students with similar concerns form groups to organize activities on behalf of their members and for the benefit of the university community. At Catholic institutions, student organizations can be encouraged, as long as they do not publicly advance policies at variance with the teachings of the Catholic Church. University authorities have reason to intervene with these groups only if they publicly advocate positions inconsistent with Catholic teaching. So, for example, gay and lesbian students can organize for mutual support and to develop various activities on Catholic campuses. They cannot, however, advocate for the moral legitimacy of homosexual practice.

Senior administrators rightly hesitate before making changes, even changes they understand are required by their status as a Catholic institution, because they are concerned about the inheritability of the changes. Many senior administrators at Catholic institutions, for example, would like to manage institutions whose students consume below-average amounts of alcoholic beverages. They also worry that greater restrictions on student behavior may result in fewer student applications.[13] For this reason, administrators at Catholic institutions feel caught. Reinforcing the Catholic moral position is necessary, but it is perceived by senior administrators as an approach that is unappealing to many and strategically dangerous because it could well lead to a loss in students and revenue.

Most significant traditions have positive ways to induce necessary or desired restraint on the part of young people. Many young people willingly discipline themselves in order to enhance their performance in sports or dance or to enhance both their health and their appearance. In these situations, students understand the gains that accrue from self-discipline. Some Catholic universities need greater restraints on student behavior at their institutions. The pressing question is how these institutions might manage the Catholic culture so as to introduce such restraints without alienating a large number of prospective students.

Senior administrators understand that whatever changes they undertake will occur in smaller steps over a longer period of time. Changing cultures quickly is a hazardous undertaking, only to be considered when the very viability of the culture is threatened. But slow change is still change, and administrators rightly worry about the cumulative effect of such changes, not only on the culture but also on inheritability—how attractive future students find the gradually changing institution. It is important to find ways to introduce the changes that diminish the danger that prospective students will be wary and less interested in seriously considering the institution as a collegiate option.

A dual strategy, we believe, is available to administrators at Catholic institutions. One aspect of the strategy is to stress the benefits to students of being encouraged and prodded to live a life of virtue. Virtue prepares young people to be good husbands, wives, mothers, fathers, citizens, and friends.[14] Students are strengthened through the Catholic culture, and stressing the benefits of changes is part of any effective strategy a Catholic college should employ.[15] This strategy cannot succeed, however, unless the colleges and universities have administrators and staff members who are themselves both convinced of the efficacy of Catholic culture and reasonably certain the changes they anticipate will be effective and inheritable. The second aspect of the strategy is to form an alliance with two or three other university competitors. These institutions may be Catholic places, they may have a generally Christian tradition, or they may be nonsectarian but convinced of the importance of higher standards for student culture. After mutual discussions and deliberations, such institutions might be able to agree upon various guiding principles for student life. All institutions in the alliance would have to agree to abide by the principles. To the extent that the institutions attract similar applicants, such an alliance would diminish, but not eliminate, the likelihood that students would opt for other institutions because of their less demanding student cultures. It would also be possible for Catholic institutions with a broader national appeal to create alliances around types of institutions. Catholic immersion, cohort, diaspora, and persuasion universities could work together within their particular groups to create similar agreements to support a shift in student culture.

Senior administrators face important constraints, but they are resourceful, and they find ways to secure needed resources. They do this both by training and by forming binding agreements that encourage students to abide by reasonable standards that enhance personal development. This dual strategy is not offered as a panacea. Rather, it is presented in order to suggest one approach that senior administrators might adopt to address the significant issues in student culture they identified with such great concern.

7

Religious Activities

In their conversations senior administrators spoke directly about the religious culture of their institutions. They described what religious culture looks like, who molds it, and how they do so. Religious activities are vehicles that both express and nurture this culture on campus, and campus ministry is the center of much of that religious activity. Consequently, campus ministry and mission staffs bear an extraordinary responsibility for how Catholic institutions demonstrate and understand their Catholicity.

Convictions

Senior administrators understood Catholicity in their institutions as a pervasive reality that extends far beyond classroom and academic experiences. "At a Catholic university," a persuasion university president pointed out,

> Catholicity is a lived reality, not just a learned subject. In this lived reality there is also development that comes in class with prayer, in liturgy every day, the opportunity for sacraments, a lively campus ministry program and chaplain, community service assistance to Catholic institutions, as well as to other nonsectarian ones, and the celebrations of many feasts.

About a third of the interview sites in the study did not have campus chapels, were in the process of renovating existing chapel spaces, or had begun efforts to construct them. The symbolic importance of a chapel to the religious imagination of Catholic colleges and universities and as a setting for centrally important religious activities was much touted by those struggling to build or enhance them. A persuasion president at a university without a chapel said she "could not conceive of having a capital campaign and not building that symbol of Catholicism. Our religion is highly symbolic and the chapel is the symbol of our Catholicism on campus." Another persuasion president saw the chapel space as the cornerstone of Catholic activity on campus. "If one doesn't have a good place to worship, it's hard to do much else. It just emphasized the real value of our Catholic colleges and the importance of trying to make this integration of faith and intellectual work." A diaspora president desperately wanted to have a chapel.

> The chapel is a high spot for our campus. It's where all will be constantly reminded what kind of institution we are. We can have Mass there at our choice. It would give me my greatest pleasure as I leave here to have that as the pinnacle of this campus. . . . That's my dream, my rock solid dream.

Most administrators pointed to campus ministry as the "go-to" office for religious activities and those things pertaining to religious imagination. Campus ministry is responsible on most campuses to be, as an immersion administrator put it, "a powerful integrating force." Besides being a force for religious integration, campus ministry departments serve a wide variety of specific functions and administrators prioritized those functions quite differently. A vice-president for mission at a persuasion university insisted: "campus ministry is the best job on campus, because [those who work in it] get to be the Gospel to the whole community. . . . It's a great opportunity to walk in and out of people's lives and make a difference by who they are." The mission vice-president at an immersion university believes the job of campus ministers

> is to make sure the Catholic culture of the institution gives permission to students and provides opportunities for them to practice their faith. . . . We need to knock on the door of every heart here. Our task is to be faithful in offering the Gospel. As far as how many respond, that's God's responsibility.

Some, like an administrator at a cohort university, see campus ministry as a religious refuge for students. "If you are being bombarded on campus with things that are contrary to the Catholic tradition, campus ministry is a haven rather than part of what is general and taken for granted."

A number of administrators maintained that a primary role of campus ministry is in the area of campus sacramental and liturgical life. As a persuasion mission officer said,

> liturgical life is extremely important [to Catholics], and it is part of my job to explain what that means in students' lives. The Eucharist is the center of our lives that both expresses the faith of community and also challenges them to be the community of faith that they possess.

While any number of administrators touted the importance of liturgy and sacraments, few had any illusions about how easy it was to attract students to participate in religious rites and rituals. As a persuasion university administrator put it, "for whatever reasons, the sacramental life is not perceived as relevant enough for students." Most administrators regretted student apathy in terms of worship and sacraments. One, however, was convinced "students can be brought there by Scripture, by the Word, whatever their tradition or their relationship with God at that moment."

Senior administrators saw many roles for campus ministry, but by far the most common understanding they had of this sector of Catholic collegiate life was as a center for justice and service projects. "If you look over the last ten, fifteen, or twenty years in Catholic higher education," a persuasion administrator said, "there is increasingly a sense that social justice and outreach is a very rich aspect of the Catholic tradition that people try to embed in the universities." A persuasion university administrator said: "students need to realize that we have been blessed in this country at this time. We have a responsibility to take advantage of our blessing and transfer them to people who are less fortunate." The president of another persuasion university claimed that "a commitment to justice is a distinguishing characteristic of Catholic higher education. We've been pretty good at making the world better in many different ways." The president of a cohort university made the case that what makes social justice at a Catholic institution unique

> is that we speak about it from a much firmer and longstanding basis. We've been doing it under the guise of Catholic action. We've been doing it under the guise of teaching students to look at their Catholicity not simply in terms of an intellectual enterprise but as something that you do, something that you live.

The academic vice-president at a persuasion university suggested: "the reason why we serve is different. I believe that service is part of what I am called to do as a Christian."

Many administrators saw social service as the doorway that leads to greater participation and appreciation of the religious culture and mission of Catholic institutions. A mission vice-president at a cohort college pointed out:

> someone in a parish worships on Sunday and hears the Gospel and then volunteers in a soup kitchen. With us, students volunteer in a soup kitchen, and hopefully that will bring them into Church. Consequently, we have to work at why they do service. Is it just to be a good neighbor? Or, is it really that this is part of who you are as a Christian person?

The vice-president for mission at an immersion university thinks this approach puts the cart before the horse.

> From prayer there always flows a deeper social awareness because the soil is ready, yearning for what God wants of me because there

has been this moment—a "to the mountain" moment, if you will. So that's the way we go—giving permission for people to practice their faith and providing opportunities that are age appropriate for them to feed them and from that flows the social awareness and action.

The president of a cohort university suggested that "a lot of Catholic institutions are able to appeal to people who aren't Catholic if they come in through the service and community social justice door. Those are ways in for people. It is a way of sharing the mission with people who aren't Catholic." The mission officer at a persuasion university was also concerned about how non-Catholics can fit into the religious mission of Catholic colleges and universities. "Part of our work in campus ministry is to help non-Catholics understand what it means to be Catholic. You are not going to make them Catholics, but they need to reach a certain level of comfort and knowledge. . . . But they cannot feel it's an imposition." A diaspora university administrator was also concerned about non-Catholics.

> Let's forget about Catholics for a minute. There's a lot to be said about whether as an institution we can teach people how to [be better in their own faith]. Let's face it, the world would be a lot better place if not only Catholics were better Catholics, but Lutherans were better Lutherans. I think we can do that through work, service, through tolerance and understanding.

While administrators were clear that campus ministry played a vital role in cultivating the religious culture of their campuses, they also put a premium on leadership and witness among the laypersons who are the new stewards of Catholic higher education. "We need somebody in the administration, preferably at the top, who understands what the mission is," a persuasion university administrator insisted. "It has to be someone who understands that they, too, are fallen creatures and sinful, but someone who can call us back to be what we are supposed to be about—someone who can articulate it. Otherwise, there is no there there."

Another persuasion university administrator pointed out that the leadership necessary "is not standing up and dictating to people. It is actually getting underneath the people and working with them. It's being their servant." A diaspora administrator is convinced that people should be able to look at Catholic institutions and say: " 'they don't just talk the talk, they walk the walk. They actually put into action some of the things they say.' It is, of course, all interrelated. To be able to walk the walk, you have to have people who can talk the talk. So we have to do it all."

Religious men and women provided this kind of leadership for most of the history of Catholic higher education in the United States. Many administrators insisted that this is no longer necessary. "It is not necessary," a diaspora university president made clear, "that a person be a member of the sponsoring or founding religious congregation if the Spirit is leading us as a Church."

Another diaspora university's student life officer felt sure that at his institution: "we live the mission here. I'm not just talking about the nuns, either. I'm talking about everyone. I think people live the mission. They really embrace it or they don't come here."

Reality

An administrator at a cohort university spoke for many administrators when she said: "How you experience Catholicity here is most probably in residence life—residence halls have chapels with many Masses, the church, retreats, et cetera. Whether a student experiences that in the context of the classroom is questionable." Campus ministry in most universities, and residence life in a few, bears the lion's share of responsibility for campus-wide religious culture. This pervasive responsibility is exercised quite differently at various institutions, according to senior administrators. At one particular persuasion university, "everything [in student life] is somehow related to our mission and to the Church and to Jesus. We couch everything and place it in the holy, no matter what kind of a program it is, so students can see the goodness in it."

Senior administrators focused many of their comments about specific campus religious activities on sacramental and liturgical events, particularly the Mass. Mass participation at immersion universities—over against the whole landscape of Catholic higher education—is unusually high. At one immersion university, for instance, "the same number of people come to Baccalaureate Mass as come to commencement." At another, "sixty-five percent of students go to Mass every day." Student participation at Mass at other kinds of colleges and universities is far less gratifying to senior administrators. A persuasion university administrator reported: "the president is worried about students and the Eucharist." At a cohort university the president was chagrined to say:

> At the end of my first year, I thought Baccalaureate Mass could have been held in the chapel, so few people came. We did a terrible job of letting people know it was important. If it's not important to us, it won't be to the students. Our graduates didn't know why they should be there. It was a cultural piece.

A diaspora administrator was quite distressed to announce: "We don't have Mass here on Sunday. The sisters go to the infirmary Mass, and we don't have Mass for the students."

While most administrators agreed that Mass attendance and liturgical life were not where they hoped they would be, a few seemed to take it in stride. A vice-president for mission at a persuasion university reported low numbers in terms of Mass attendance but was not overly discouraged.

> About thirty percent of our on-campus students who are Catholic go to Masses every week. I think that's higher than most Catholic uni-

versities, except for maybe a few where you have twenty-seven Masses in the dormitories every week. In terms of the others, we're doing pretty well.

A cohort administrator hoped he had "really contributed through the liturgical life of the place so that we have a vibrant university ministry program. I think we have a good one, but it's not great."

Liturgical life is not limited to Mass, and campus ministers are involved in offering other sacramental and worship experiences. The vice-president for mission at an immersion university "focuses on more than liturgy. It's Catholic fellowship, prayer groups, it's being okay to be Catholic, openness with all different kinds of liturgical moments to feed people where they are. This approach has helped us to have a much less divided and marginalized campus." At a persuasion university, the priest who is the mission officer, "has spent five hours for two straight days" administering the sacrament of reconciliation. He experiences students in this sacrament as "very thoughtful, very reflective, in-depth, relational. Something is happening. Ask me do they know the catechism? They don't have a clue."

A number of obstacles impinge on liturgical experience at some campuses. A cohort mission officer sensed that "the flavor of campus ministry is that we operate out of a theology that is very intellectual, definitely liberal, and it is difficult for us to appreciate the diversity of expressions of the faith. We're very Western, very intellectual, and we're certainly afraid of public piety." The same cohort mission officer was frustrated because his own campus ministry team did not want adoration of the Blessed Sacrament, which, according to the campus ministry team, smacked of unsophisticated piety. "I don't think this does a service to anybody," the mission officer said. "It's really important for students to have Eucharistic adoration, to come before the Blessed Sacrament, to be invited to do that. We just don't do that regularly." At an immersion university, the president said: "we've tried to depoliticize liturgy." That institution now makes an effort to offer liturgical worship that appeals to a broad range of liturgical tastes. According to a persuasion university student life officer, her university has "certainly increased the number of liturgies. However, we have a huge handicap in the campus ministry area. We have great visions for what we could do in campus ministry, but we just don't have the staff." An administrator at the same persuasion university reported an attempt to give graduates religious medals at graduation. In the end, it did not become part of the ceremony, however. "Curiously, it was the folks coming from campus ministry and student development that found it most difficult. The balance between including everybody, while not diluting what you are trying to accomplish, is very challenging."

Administrators from almost all institutions echoed the observation of an immersion president that "social outreach is a big part of how students explore spirituality." Some of that outreach takes place in secular settings. At a persuasion university, "students became affiliated with Habitat for Humanity.... We learned it cost fifty-five thousand dollars to sponsor a house, and we dedicate the house the first part of March." An immersion university "started an outreach program working with elderly shut-ins, doing things like visitations, house cleaning, small projects and those types of things. It's been really, really nice." Other institutions have focused on service to the Church. A persuasion university "just attracted a two-million-dollar grant that seeks to reinvigorate the Catholic-based experiences on campus and put into practice with surrounding parishes what students are being exposed to and learning in the classrooms." A diaspora institution that "is very conscious of being the Catholic university for the region" has established a program that involves "a group of students who do retreats for high school youth across the state. In eleven years they've probably worked with forty thousand kids." A wide variety of colleges and universities are involved in international programs like one at an immersion university. "Four years ago we started our mission program. And we've dedicated every spring break since to that mission program. We encourage our students to make a sacrifice, and during their spring break, or sometimes summer breaks, they provide service in different places in the Western Hemisphere."

Concerns

Senior administrators expressed concern about the religious culture of their institutions primarily in two areas. The first revolves around Mass attendance by students. The mission officer at a cohort institution said:

> one of the things that really concerns me here is the lack of participation in liturgy on Sunday. It's only a few students who participate in the liturgical life of the Church. Seventy percent of the students recognize themselves as Catholic. Eighty percent are baptized, and only sixteen to eighteen percent come to Mass.

Even at institutions where students participate regularly in weekly Mass, administrators worry. "One of our problems," a cohort administrator reported, "is the students all go to Mass here and then they go home at Christmas break and don't go. In that case we haven't done a very good job." Whatever the worries about student Mass attendance, concerns about what happens after graduation are even greater. Unfortunately, most institutions have no data about what happens in the spiritual lives of their graduates, so they are left to imagine, and they often imagine the worst. The president of a persuasion university said: "I don't even want to bring up the issue of whether the students from Catholic universities go to Mass regularly after they graduate. I would dance around that question because I wouldn't even want to stop and think about it."

The second most significant concern administrators articulated focused on filling the shoes of the nuns, brothers, and priests who are disappearing from campuses. An administrator at a diaspora university pointed out:

The sisters are all professionals. There might be twelve or fifteen of them and they're beloved. Their problem is that they're old. They're not getting younger. I wish I knew what this means long term. One of the things I would like to do is spend the rest of my life recruiting nuns. I see their values. I see their commitment and their love of people. They just give so much, and we're going to miss that. I don't know what it means in the long term for the Church, other than maybe they'll have to find a different way. I don't know.

A persuasion university administrator worried that

in many Catholic institutions the last of the Mohicans is that one cleric or religious who is still there and who understands where the Ark of the Covenant is buried, so to speak. When that person is gone and if the cultivation hasn't taken place, there won't be anyone who can call us to accountability. It will become a school in the Catholic or congregational tradition, and there won't be anyone there who can say "This is what it means. This is why we teach these courses and this is how we behave." There has to be someone in the institution who can call people to accountability in that way.

A number of administrators were quite comfortable with the preparation, leadership, and witness of laypersons, but many were far from comfortable about the implications of having no religious on campus. They agreed with an administrator from a persuasion university that

lay people are in the ascendance in terms of controlling stewardship in this institution. It is also very clear that the vast majority do not have formation and preparation and are theologically far less literate than the sisters. There is far less ability today than there would have been thirty years ago to articulate the religious roots of our mission and to speak about Gospel connections. What inspired these sisters to establish an institution like we have today is rooted in their faith and in their commitment, and that is really rooted in the gospel and in their belief.

A number of administrators also were concerned about whether the unique congregational identities of many Catholic colleges and universities could survive without members of the congregations exercising leadership on campus. A diaspora president said:

too many new presidents make the mistake that because they are able and capable and willing to work that is sufficient. It is insufficient. You have to be in sync with the charism of the founders. You need to be able to understand it, to speak it, to express it, to live it. You have to try to go to the founding ground of the founders. Once that happens, you are transformed and you can transform.

The role of campus ministry also gave some administrators pause. A cohort president said: "this moment in time requires a reimagination of what it means to be a religiously oriented person. . . . For the last many, many years, we've taken the identity question and pushed it into campus ministry, and I'm right now essentially taking that apart." A vice-president for mission might not have agreed that the preeminence of campus ministry should be taken apart, but he did think how it operated in the nonsectarian model was in many ways healthier.

> I envy the non-Catholic school and the Catholic satellites that build up around them—the campus ministry chapel, the Newman clubs, the Catholic studies program, the chair in Catholic studies. It seems a simpler context within which to place a Catholic piece, because you can just be Catholic. I actually envy that you can jump in and get to it, and not have to carry with you the baggage of the whole institution, the Church and the Catholic Church as it is in the United States. It seems that Catholic schools like our own are freighted with that baggage and much more. We can't get a real quick jump off the block because we have so many things we have to pay attention to, whereas a non-Catholic school—the sprinter— can just go.

Future Directions

Senior administrators had little to offer in terms of future directions as they pertain to religious activities and culture, beyond "more opportunities for spiritual direction, more opportunity for Bible study, more opportunity for retreats, more opportunity to affirm and acknowledge other religious traditions," and a sense, as a persuasion university mission officer put it, that prayers and spirituality and the worship side of things is the challenge for the future. They did, however, feel strongly that leadership would be crucial to the vitality of religious culture.

Administrators with responsibility for mission were asked to identify qualities essential for a successful campus minister or vice-president for mission. Since this question looks ahead to someone who will be active over the next five to ten years, the responses provide a glimpse of important issues in the future. In a comprehensive listing, the vice-president for mission at a persuasion university articulated several qualifications that echoed comments by most of the administrators with responsibility for mission.

Almost all the administrators agreed with this administrator that "there are several qualities necessary, in order to be credible for this position." Among them were a knowledge base in the Catholic tradition and, when the college or university was founded by a religious congregation, a knowledge of congregational culture, as well.

First is a strong formative background in the Catholic tradition and
then the congregational tradition—how the Catholic understanding
of the gospel is interpreted through a congregational lens. That way,
our uniqueness as a Catholic congregational institution is not lost.
And I'm not saying that they have to be congregational, but that
they embody those qualities that distinguish a congregational worldview.

Many administrators also talked about the importance of personal commitment to the faith and some kind of religious formation. "The person needs
personal conviction and formation—some good background in theology and
a contemporary view of the Church, which is, I think, a very critical time that
we're in." None of the administrators were interested in having people in
charge of ministry who were not open and willing to engage with people who
were often suspicious about the Church. The same vice-president for mission
at the persuasion university said: "they need openness to what is the best of
what the Catholic tradition can offer. There's suspicion about this Catholic
morality and a narrowness that doesn't allow inclusivity and openness to
healthy dialogue." Knowing how intense Catholic campus life can be, some
administrators also thought that "the person would need a good sense of humor because when the curses come, then you'd be able to weather those situations. I believe you need to be a bridge builder." There were mixed feelings
among administrators about whether the person who leads in the area of a
university's religious culture needs to be a nun or priest, but all agreed that
these leaders must live their religious beliefs with integrity and be witnesses
for the faith. "They don't need to be vowed religious, but they need to be a
practicing Catholic, and I believe there are some nonnegotiables to being a
Catholic. They include, I would say, a commitment to the basic tenets of the
gospel message."

Some administrators focused on a leader's view on issues of life, and others were far more likely to focus on the social Gospel and how it is lived out
on college campuses.

A mission person must have deep respect and reverence for the dignity of human life—and I'm not just talking about abortion issues,
I'm talking about life in all its stages and how is that lived out. I
think that's the Catholic social teaching. That somebody has an understanding of that and not just in the head, but in how we deal
with issues that affect life and life on this campus.

Campus ministry and mission offices are responsible for offering opportunities for students to practice their faith and, consequently, administrators look
to this person who leads in these areas to have a commitment to spiritual
practices, especially to the sacraments and the Eucharist.

There is a nonnegotiable about our relationship to our prayer life,
that there's some commitment to deepening a relationship with God

out of the Catholic tradition. . . . The person would need to be open to having to learn more about that and be open to a greater understanding. They would need some commitment to the traditions of our Church, to our faith tradition—things like the liturgy and devotion to the Eucharist and how we understand the Incarnation. God did come among us as a human person, not because we were sinners, but God would have come among us if we had never sinned because God loved us so much—that understanding of Incarnational theology—John's Gospel. And I believe some of the traditions, devotions of the Church, that make sense for who we are, they should know.

And finally, a number of administrators talked about a Catholic way of approaching life that gives rise to great possibility and the desire to serve in ministry. "I believe that somebody needs to have an appreciation of the Catholic imagination. And in order to survive and be credible for the job, I believe fundamentally the person has to have a ministerial heart to know we're not in it for ourselves."

Analysis of the Data: Liturgy, Service, Inclusion, and Congregations

Religious activities fall within the category of symbols of Catholic culture at Catholic colleges and universities. The stories, objects, rituals, and other symbolic acts are the connective tissue and graphic presentation of the culture to itself and its members. Symbols and content provide the motivation for distinctive action within the culture. They remind, reinforce, and refresh cultural content by sharing cultural history, exploring cultural ideals, and, as was indicated in the chapter on culture, they also invite the community to imagine and participate in creating what is yet to be. Liturgical acts and symbols tell the cultural story, create linkages, and reinforce broad cultural commitments. As the symbols of Catholic culture, the religious activities on a Catholic college campus are essential to the vibrancy of the institution's religious culture, for without them the religious beliefs, values, and norms that make the culture distinguishable and inheritable cannot be expressed, fully understood, or effectively transmitted.

In talking about cultural symbols on campus and how effective they are, senior administrators remarked frequently about the important contributions being made by campus ministers. With a few exceptions, the religious activities sponsored by campus ministry appear to be substantial, and the adaptations recommended by senior administrators focused primarily on increasing resources to enhance and extend what is already happening in this area.

The effectiveness of religious activities in contributing to the Catholic culture on campus will be analyzed in terms of the three significant areas emphasized by administrators—liturgical life, service programs, and the demonstration of religious tolerance and inclusion. As part of the analysis, we will use as a comparison the corresponding religious and symbolic activities available to Catholics at nonsectarian institutions of similar size through Newman or Catholic centers. We do not cite specific data for such a comparison, but instead review the type of data that would demonstrate campus ministry initiatives in all three significant areas are indeed making a distinctive and effective contribution to the Catholic culture at Catholic colleges and universities.

The final topic treated in this chapter is a complex of contested topics swirling around the question of who will be the heroic cultural leaders at Catholic colleges and universities when religious congregations are gone. In particular, we examine whether these new knowledgeable experts and role models will emphasize Catholic culture or congregational connections as they lead the institutions forward. The topic is contested, because neither senior administrators nor members of religious congregations are of one mind about these central issues. In the final section we address the issue and offer reasons for stressing "Catholic" culture rather than "congregational" culture.

Effectiveness and Distinguishability in Liturgies

At most Catholic colleges and universities, Eucharistic liturgy is the premier religious ritual around which the community comes to celebrate and more fully understand its Catholic culture. As a number of administrators pointed out, the Catholic imagination is sacramental at its core, and the celebration of the Eucharist is the ultimate communication of the faith and how the Catholic community understands itself and its purpose. With that in mind, it is no wonder that Eucharistic liturgy was the ritual that most interested senior administrators who talked about the symbols of their institutions' religious culture.

Within any culture, there are rituals that are large public celebrations—rare events designed to focus the organization and the stakeholders on the publicly proclaimed purposes, values, and beliefs of the organization. At Catholic colleges and universities, these high-profile liturgies are most notably liturgies that open the academic year and the Baccalaureate liturgy from which seniors go forth at the end of their collegiate experience. A number of administrators at diaspora, cohort, and persuasion universities indicated that these liturgies were poorly attended by both faculty and students alike, which concerned them greatly.

At immersion universities, Eucharistic liturgy is well attended, no matter where it is celebrated or how high-profile or intimate the venue. At all of the immersion universities, the symbols of religious culture hold a prominent place, and religious rituals draw the community together in celebration of the faith that is shared in common. Because these major liturgical celebrations are designed to focus the community on the publicly proclaimed purposes, values, and beliefs of the college, they are less culturally critical at immersion universities, where the vast majority of the community shares the tradition and celebrates the Eucharist on a daily basis. At these institutions, the community is often enthusiastic about high-profile liturgies, but they hardly need them as a reminder of what the institution stands for. On the other hand, at diaspora, cohort, and persuasion universities, large portions of the community, including the faculty and staff, do not share the religious tradition, and the daily Eucharistic liturgy is seldom well attended. At these institutions, high-profile liturgies are extremely important, because in dramatic and public ways they affirm what the institution is about. Yet it is at these very institutions that high-profile liturgies are so often poorly attended, according to senior administrators. Diaspora, cohort, and persuasion universities would be well served by elevating the importance of these liturgies across all sectors of their collegiate communities.

In terms of the standard of comparison, large liturgies do happen at non-Catholic universities, but they are not sponsored by the university itself. There are usually Masses of the Holy Spirit and graduation Masses at the Newman center, and many are extremely well attended by the Catholic membership. Many administrators pointed out in their conversations that one of the unique differences between Catholic and non-Catholic institutions was the fact that the institution itself was grounded in faith. When only small groups attend what are supposed to be public liturgical events, Catholic colleges and universities miss one of the most distinctive opportunities available to demonstrate their unique religious culture. If the Mass of the Holy Spirit and Baccalaureate become "boutique" liturgies, there is little to distinguish them from ceremonial liturgies at nonsectarian university Catholic Centers.

One outcome measure of the strength of Catholic culture on campus is its lasting impact on students after they graduate. Campus ministry assumes significant responsibility for creating transformative Catholic culture on college campuses. Undergraduates typically spend four or five years at universities, and after receiving the baccalaureate degree, few alumni/ae have any ongoing connection with campus ministry or liturgical life at the university. As senior administrators said frequently in their interviews, Catholic education is supposed to make an impact on students as undergraduates that lasts a lifetime. If that is the case, what young alumni/ae do in the first years after graduation should give evidence that their education truly was transformative. Catholic colleges and universities take seriously their responsibility not only to inform students about Catholicism but also to form them in their faith. In light of that commitment, one of campus ministry's goals should be that Catholic alumni/ae participate regularly in the life of whatever parish they choose as a worshiping community. Administrators indicated, however, that active involvement in the well-planned and effectively executed religious activities at Catholic universities often "spoils" students for regular parish life. Careful planning is, therefore, required to make sure campus liturgical life encourages, rather than discourages, students from participating in local parishes once they graduate. Alternatively, campus ministry should have preparation programs for graduating students that point them in the direction of regular participation in parish liturgies.

At most Catholic universities, Eucharistic celebrations for Sunday worship are beautifully arranged. The music, the ritual, the devotion, and the homilies are exemplary. Campus ministry teams work hard to make liturgy the center of religious life on campus, and most plan even the weekly liturgies meticulously. Hard work, attention to detail, along with prayer and reflection, produce good liturgies. Homilists at these liturgies have the opportunity to speak directly to the experience of the undergraduates, because the university congregations, unlike parish congregations, are comprised of people of a similar age, with common interests, attitudes, and shared experiences. Issues can be confronted directly, with humor, via example, or by allusion to important events on campus. Common, shared experiences enable the homilist to be direct and to effectively motivate the students.

All in all, the experience of the Eucharist in an almost entirely undergraduate community is a wonderful, special series of celebrations. The experience is so powerful that many young alumni/ae are underwhelmed or even depressed by the Eucharist they encounter at their local parishes. In the parish, the music is not as moving, the homilies are more general, the worshiping community is much older, and the former students have few friends, if any, who join them in the pews. Experienced campus ministers are aware of the problem, and many establish programs that help seniors transition to parish life and overcome whatever initial aversions they might experience on their way to becoming regular worshiping members of a parish community.

Unfortunately, at some Catholic colleges and universities, students avoid liturgy because they are as underwhelmed by what is happening on campus as they might be in some parishes. Prior to coming to the Catholic university, some students have been buoyed by wonderful parish or high school liturgies. Such students are disappointed in what they encounter at college, as one senior administrator made very clear. Even with the golden opportunity of preaching to a relatively homogenous congregation, many celebrants perform poorly. This phenomenon, however, appears less common than the reverse, in which students appreciate campus liturgies and are disappointed in their parish experiences after graduation.

It is important for Catholic colleges and universities to evaluate the effectiveness of their liturgical life, but finding the appropriate standard can be tricky. Newman and Catholic centers at non-Catholic institutions have similar kinds of liturgical experiences to those of Catholic colleges and universities. They have excellent and well-planned liturgies and experience the same "real-world" implications regarding parish life. There are also Catholic centers whose liturgies are less than exemplary. The standard for determining whether liturgies and religious activities at Catholic institutions of higher education are distinctive (distinguishable) is not the quality of the worship experience at nonsectarian institutions but rather the array of liturgies and religious activities and the extent of undergraduate participation in these activities. Because little or no data are available at either type of institution, the standard is a virtual standard. Nonetheless, it offers helpful virtual comparisons.

With some variation across geographical regions, attendance at Mass in the average parish is, unfortunately, very low.[1] Attending Sunday Mass is a sacred responsibility of all Catholics, and a Catholic university plays a significant role in helping students understand why that is so and encouraging them to embrace the responsibility. It is both commendable and culturally distinguishable if campus ministry programs at Catholic colleges and universities have higher rates of participation than either the average parish or Catholic center at nonsectarian institutions.

The big issue for campus ministry at both Catholic universities and Catholic centers is having reasonable data to document rates of regular participation by students at Sunday Mass. While collecting such data is not simple, it is not prohibitively difficult either. Required is a list of students who are at least nominal Catholics and some method of determining the number of these students who regularly attend Mass on Sunday, either on campus or at a parish. Distributing self-reporting student questionnaires is an obvious first step in the process. Self-reporting is, however, notoriously inaccurate, and it is useful to compensate for this difficulty with occasional counts of actual participants at on-campus liturgies.[2]

In quite a few instances, senior administrators suggested estimates of regular Catholic student Mass attendance rates. These amounted to no more than guesstimates, however, because they never referred to any data or process for determining a number about which campus ministry personnel had confidence. Nor did campus ministers cite evidence that during the past few years the percentage of students participating in on-campus liturgies had increased, remained the same, or decreased by a lower percentage than the corresponding rate for parishes.

Expecting miracles in the area of Mass attendance is unfair to campus ministry. Getting young people to attend Mass regularly is difficult in general in the American environment. However, when a culture is in crisis, it is essential to focus unwaveringly on central cultural goals. We believe the Catholic culture at Catholic universities is threatened, a case we develop more fully in the final three chapters of the book. That threat makes it imperative that a unit as vital to Catholic culture as campus ministry simply must articulate clear goals and monitor progress toward those goals. One task of campus ministry at each of the four types of Catholic universities is to form Catholic students in the practice of the faith. Part of that responsibility is first conveying to them that the university and the campus ministry staff take very seriously every Catholic's responsibility to attend Mass on a weekly basis. Beyond that, in any of the four models of Catholic universities, one reasonable measure of the strength of the Catholic culture is regular Mass attendance. In order to gauge their own success in reaching their goals in this area, campus ministry should collect appropriate data about attendance rates. Even if Catholic culture at a particular Catholic university is not threatened, campus ministry personnel should be interested in liturgical participation rates and whether their work in structuring and positioning liturgies is having a positive impact on students.

Changing Mass times, adjusting liturgical settings, introducing different music—be they informal or formal, more progressive or more traditional—can improve attendance, with some changes more effective than others. Without collecting appropriate data, however, no one will know for sure.

Comments by senior administrators at universities sponsored by sisters indicated that they experience special challenges in arranging for Mass to be celebrated on campus. Many religious congregations of women have close relationships with different men's religious orders and diocesan priests who make themselves available to celebrate Mass for the sisters and the students. However, since the number of priests available for parish and other ministry has steadily declined since the 1970s, many Catholic universities find it difficult to arrange for priests who can both connect with the students and celebrate liturgy on a regular basis. All too often, students at these institutions only experience circuit-rider priests who drop in to say Mass occasionally and then move on. At present this situation is most acute for institutions sponsored by nuns, but over the next twenty years it is likely to become a challenge for all Catholic colleges and universities, as the number of priests available for active ministry continues to fall.

Campus ministry personnel are resourceful, and resourcefulness will be required to find workable solutions to the challenge presented by a decreasing number of priests. Some of the solutions may move students out of the protected environment of the campus to parishes located close to campus, where they can rub shoulders with the very Catholics they will worship with in the future. Others may require leadership on campus to "hustle" in an effort to find priests whose parish experience and pastoral style will challenge students to make connections between campus liturgy and parish life—between their faith lives in the present and what they might be in the future. The same parish priests will also be enriched by the opportunity to serve young Catholics who are the future of the Church. The number of liturgies available on campus will undoubtedly decrease, but campus ministry personnel, working in collaboration with other offices on campus, can arrange events around a weekly Mass in such a way that students are more inclined to attend. It would also be possible to pair Mass with other activities that further enhance the appeal and the likelihood that Catholic students would regularly participate in Mass on campus. Whatever the solutions, most will require an increase in financial resources made available to campus ministry. They will also require, in most cases, a commitment to hire more campus ministry staff.

At a number of Catholic universities, senior administrators described a campus ministry team that was shouldering a disproportionate share of the responsibility for religious culture on campus. Such comments may reflect the personal views of administrators or be a judgment shared by the entire senior administrative team. Since the comments were made numerous times, however, it seems fair to conclude that in the recent past, campus ministry has not received sufficient support from other sectors of the university. We refer here both to financial support and to activities undertaken in other sectors of the university that promote Catholic culture. It seems reasonable to expect that these patterns will continue for the next few years, until adjustments can be implemented. This issue of balanced cultural support among various sectors of the university has serious implications for the long-term sustainability of Catholic institutional culture, and we will address this again in the final chapters of the book.

In previous chapters, we noted the need to amplify student exposure to the Catholic intellectual tradition. We also noted that the Catholic moral tradition is not being effectively shared with students at a number of Catholic institutions. Many senior administrators in this study were convinced that, all too frequently, campus ministry is expected to be almost the sole bearer and purveyor of the Catholic tradition at Catholic colleges and universities. If Catholic culture is to survive, this simply has to change. To do that, however, will require that the university make greater efforts and secure more resources to share the Catholic intellectual and moral tradition with students in academic and student affairs. Any initiatives in these areas will take some years to plan and implement. Until such initiatives bear fruit, it will be campus ministry's task to shoulder the disproportionate burden. Campus ministry remains the sector most capable of strengthening the Catholic culture on campus and presenting to students more of the wealth of the Catholic liturgical, spiritual, and service traditions.

In the Catholic immersion model, it is unlikely that campus ministry carries a greater burden than other sectors, because the Catholic immersion model expects strong Catholic components in everything—academics, student activities, residential life, hiring, and the public conduct of the university. In each of the other three models—persuasion, diaspora, and cohort institutions—organizational imperfections or lack of staff who are educated and formed in things Catholic may prevent various units from contributing as effectively to the Catholic culture as their model optimally demands. In such situations, the senior management team should acknowledge the problem and analyze how long the anomaly is expected to persist. If the lack of support to the Catholic culture from key sectors is expected to last for more than two or three years, the senior team should identify precipitating reasons and have a plan to correct the situation. In the meantime, campus ministry will need to develop a plan and accompanying budget, with input from senior management, to increase either the intensity or the scope of its own activities. Just throwing money at the problem, however, will not guarantee desired results. Campus ministry will need an effective strategy, and it should be invited to justify why any strategy and activities it proposes is most likely to strengthen the Catholic culture or catalyze cultural adjustment during this period of transition. Campus ministry also should submit what it is looking for in terms of outcomes and benchmarks, as well as target rates of student participation in various religious activities.

Effectiveness and Distinguishability in Social Justice Programs

In discussing religious activities on their campuses, senior administrators frequently talked about social justice and service programs. Although some of these programs are service learning opportunities, the inclination of administrators to include them among cultural symbols rather than cultural content seems most appropriate. Justice and service programs, as they are designed and experienced in universities, can aptly be described as ritual experiences. As Robert Wuthnow points out, rituals are ways of expressing beliefs. Rituals integrate belief and action in such a way that the belief shapes the action and the action reinforces and affirms the belief. Universities believe that public service is a part of good citizenship, and they encourage students to get involved in service projects.[3] Most students involved in community service find the experience enriching, and through their experience they, too, come to believe in the importance of service and thereby adopt for themselves the university's ideal.

Most colleges and universities in the United States offer and highly tout service opportunities for students. Senior administrators in this study overwhelmingly agreed that there is something distinctive about the service programs at Catholic institutions that sets them apart from those offered at nonsectarian institutions. In order to evaluate this claim, however, some standard for determining distinguishability among service programs needs to be adopted. Chapter 3 described five models—four models of Catholic universities and a nonsectarian model as well. Chapter 3 also detailed the appropriate role of service activities in Catholic institutions and their contribution to a university's distinctive Catholic culture. Many institutions sponsor volunteer activities for undergraduates. To the extent that these activities at Catholic and nonsectarian institutions are the same, they do not contribute to a distinctively Catholic culture on campus. If, however, the volunteer activities are linked to specifically Catholic beliefs, values, norms, and assumptions, the activities become distinct from similar activities at nonsectarian institutions.[4]

One of the ways Catholic institutions distinguish their service programs is in terms of whom they serve. Few nonsectarian colleges or universities commit energy and time to creating service opportunities that meet the needs of the Roman Catholic Church in the United States. Catholic institutions are the main higher education institutions in the country that can forthrightly address this need. Doing so certainly distinguishes the service programs at these institutions, and senior administrators described a number of such programs at their colleges and universities. By working through programs in local parishes, diocesan service organizations, and Catholic schools, university students have the opportunity to make a significant contribution in religious education programs, youth programs, or other activities that serve the needs of Catholics and others living in the diocese. This work also offers the opportunity for student transformation, as students overcome their own reticence about how parishes operate and become more disposed to continue their parish involvement as both leaders and cultural catalysts once they graduate.

Developing students to be exemplary leaders is part of the distinctive mission of all Catholic institutions, a goal mentioned by many senior administrators. Part of the identity, character, and mission of Catholic universities is to serve the Catholic Church, which is at once a human organization and one that mediates a supernatural relationship with Christ. As a human organization, the Catholic Church needs various types of leaders, not just bishops and priests. The Second Vatican Council emphasized the baptismal call to ministry of all Catholics, and in the last forty years laypersons have assumed positions of leadership in almost all areas of Catholic life. As the number of priests and religious men and women has decreased, necessity has added momentum to this leadership transformation. Through a strong Catholic culture, Catholic universities are in an excellent position to develop future Catholic lay leaders. By forthrightly presenting to students the needs of the institutional Catholic Church, Catholic universities sometimes motivate students to offer their lives in special service to the Church as priests or religious. Campus ministry has a wonderful opportunity to elevate the sights of eager, idealistic young people so they understand what exemplary Catholic service entails, both to society and to the Catholic Church. As a result of the clergy sexual abuse scandal, the American Catholic Church is in the midst of possibly the worst crisis of its history. If service programs are intended to meet the critical needs of the age, surely future faith-filled leadership is a crying need in the Catholic Church that Catholic colleges and universities are uniquely positioned to address.

Besides programs that serve the Church, campus ministry at some Catholic colleges and universities designs programs to serve those in society in greatest need—the poorest among us. Most service programs across the landscape of higher education are focused on serving the least fortunate in the society. This focus in and of itself, however, does not distinguish Catholic service programs. Some administrators claimed that what distinguishes volunteer activities at Catholic institutions is not what is done, but rather the motivation of the students doing it.

The motivations of Catholic students, they indicated, had a religious orientation that would not be found among students at nonsectarian colleges and universities. A few senior administrators even went so far as to impute less-than-noble motives to students engaged in volunteer activities at nonsectarian institutions. For example, they said students at other institutions are more interested in building resumes than really committing themselves to helping the poor. Of course, it is equally possible that students at Catholic universities are polishing their resumes rather than promoting the Kingdom of God or that students at nonsectarian institutions are motivated by a desire to promote justice and serve their brothers and sisters. The exact motivation behind any individual student's involvement in volunteer service is difficult to determine. It is at least plausible to suggest that students who participate in service at Catholic institutions have a similar mixed bag of reasons for getting involved in voluntary service to those of their counterparts at nonsectarian institutions.

In a vibrant Catholic culture, what should truly distinguish service programs at Catholic colleges and universities is not the motives of the students who join them but the beliefs and values of the university that shapes the ritual of service work. The distinguishing motivation behind the institutional commitment to justice and service at a Catholic university is a belief that the bishops have described: "Action on behalf of justice and participation in the transformation of the world fully appears to us as a constitutive dimension of the preaching of the Gospel, or, in other words, of the church's mission for the redemption of the human race and its liberation from every oppressive situation."[5] Service and justice work are actions compelled by the beliefs, values, norms, and shared assumptions that are the bedrock of Catholic cultural understanding. Justice and service programs at Catholic colleges and universities are designed to create experiences that form and transform students by reinforcing these core institutional beliefs and commitments in the lives of students.

Because students are young, during their undergraduate years their attitudes toward belief in God or in Christ can undergo significant fluctuations. At some times students are more open to participating in the saving mission of Christ. This is a decision to be made by the student, and it is a decision that is likely in flux. It is made one way perhaps for a few months, after which some experience prompts reconsideration. One of the most powerful things about a cultural symbol is its ability to beckon members of the community to embrace the heroic possibilities beyond the moment. A realistic and self-confident culture anticipates a range of possible responses to the transforming power of culture when presented to younger members of the community.

The academic sector offers a good example of a forthright but flexible array of response possibilities. Faculty members seek to engage students in the academic enterprise. Ideally, students become fascinated with the material covered by the professor in class. In the absence of compelling intellectual curiosity, however, a faculty member provokes student engagement with a number of methodological tools such as group projects, analyses of books and articles, quizzes, grades for class participation, and so on. The professor uses grades to motivate students with different abilities and interests. Excellent grades are given to students who demonstrate mastery of the material. Apart from grades, faculty members speak in the classroom about the importance and significance of what is being studied. They also hold out to students the prospect of achieving academic expertise by attending prestigious graduate schools for disciplinary study at the highest level. Academic culture is self-confident and realistic. It knows that students have different levels of interest and ability. Faculty members therefore speak to all students about a variety of levels of engagement, and they also use a variety of levers (grades, prestige, and professorial affirmation) to induce students to perform at the highest level appropriate for them. Some students go on to good graduate schools, perhaps to do a doctorate; others engage in the subject material and master it. Still others perform in a satisfactory manner and move on to other more engaging studies or pursuits.

The same kind of approach can work well with respect to community service or any other area pertaining to Catholic culture. Adept campus ministry programs offer an array of starting points and gradually offer deeper involvement. They do this through the service projects themselves, through religious reflection on the Christian message, and eventually through deeper religious commitment. The service opportunity may begin with a mere toe-dipping but eventually include immersion in service. Similarly, the religious offer may begin with a nod to the social teaching of the Church and extend to a full embrace of the call to discipleship and participation in the saving mission of Christ. A broad array of possibilities accommodates the different experiences, inclinations, and aspirations of students who might be interested in a service project.

In their interviews, a number of senior administrators acknowledged that Christian spirituality is part of the distinctive approach that campus ministry takes to service activities. Campus ministers find ways to present the ideal of Christian service to students who are believers and wish to deepen their commitment to Christ. Since all Catholic institutions have as a goal preparing students to be leaders, it is appropriate that all campus ministry programs at Catholic institutions find a way to present to students interested in service the goal of participating in Christ's saving mission by bringing hope and faith in Christ to those in need. Presenting to students the highest ideal of Christian service is important at all four types of Catholic institutions—immersion, persuasion, diaspora, and cohort—precisely because each type of Catholic institution strives to form an elite group of leaders. It is the hope and firm intention of Catholic institutions that a good number of their graduates will be leaders in society, leaders with both a theoretical and practical knowledge of the Catholic faith, and leaders with a commitment to serve others as the gospel attests Christ demonstrated by his words and works.

Service was singled out by administrators as the religious activity with the greatest potential to change students. For this reason, when presented to students as a significant activity in their lives, service should embrace not only a great variety of activities but also various degrees of participatory engagement and various ways to incorporate the central mysteries of the Christian faith in service to other people. Catholic students, as well as others, should be encouraged to give themselves over to service in its highest Christian form. Campus ministry only strengthens the Catholic culture on campus by presenting to students the best ways to unite Christian belief with service to others.

Different approaches to voluntary service programs within a Catholic institution expand opportunities for different kinds of students. Some variation in approach to structuring service programs is also appropriate among the four types of Catholic universities. The Catholic immersion model has the broadest approach to Catholic culture, since it attempts to inform and motivate all students through the academic, student affairs, and religious sectors. For this reason, religious activities do not need to compensate for other sectors at these institutions. At the present time, a reasonable assumption is that for many Catholic institutions in the other three models, campus ministry and religious activities are generally relied on to compensate for some underfunctioning in other sectors. Therefore, these institutions need to amplify their justice and community service programs. The target strategy for Catholic persuasion, diaspora, and cohort institutions should be to enhance the Catholic connection in these programs by creating or strengthening links with Catholic spirituality, theology, and social teaching.[6] Catholic institutions seek to transform students, according to senior administrators, and transformation is best achieved in a strong Catholic culture. By helping students relate their service experience to the Christian mystery of salvation and by helping them integrate service with their private and public prayer, campus ministry deepens institutional Catholic culture and enhances the likelihood of student transformation.

While the religious activities of immersion institutions do not need to compensate for Catholic culture, they should complement and deepen the culture by offering students a fuller experience of the tradition. Institutions that take a pass when it comes to involving students in the social ministry of the Church avoid strong cultural symbols and do not share with their students a major part of the Catholic intellectual tradition.

Whatever the faith tradition of students who volunteer for service, all students engaged in these activities should learn about the ways committed Catholics link service to the mystery of salvation through Christ, because that is what makes these experiences culturally distinctive. Whether students try to live the Christian mysteries through service depends on the inclination of each student, but exposing them, whatever their inclination, to what compels Catholics to serve could hardly be construed as offensive. Since the goal is to strengthen the Catholic culture and enhance the possibility of student religious transformation, service opportunities should be linked to the Catholic tradition. As is the case in volunteer work, service learning courses can be linked to Catholic theology, the Catholic moral tradition, the social teaching of the Church, or even the history of the Catholic Church.[7]

Getting the data about what actually is happening is as important in the area of service opportunities as in other activities, and collecting different types of data will help in the assessment of how things are progressing toward stated goals. Especially at institutions where the distinguishability of the Catholic culture is questionable, senior administrators should establish clear short-term goals that include linking service activities to the Catholic tradition. They should also develop a process for monitoring whether adequate progress toward the goals is being made. Campus ministry should establish specific goals for student participation in different types of service projects. Once the goals have been reviewed and approved, and prior to implementing the initiatives, an appropriate group should determine what type of data should be collected so that progress toward the goals can be monitored regularly. What constitutes "regularly" depends in part on the activities, but for most activities, "regularly" should be more frequently than once a year. Only if feedback is frequent will administrators know the extent of progress toward the goals. Frequent feedback enables the institutions to make adjustments when initiatives do not yield desired outcomes.

In pressing their need to strengthen their Catholic culture, universities will likely focus on short-term goals. However, Catholic institutions at which the distinguishability criterion is comfortably satisfied will want outcomes data that measure both the short and long-term impact of service projects linked to the Catholic tradition. Graduation surveys that probe the impact of service projects on student's faith and practice are very helpful. Many institutions undertake alumni/ae surveys at various intervals. Such surveys can usefully include questions about the extent to which alumni/ae still engage in service projects. Depending on the longitudinal spread of the survey, it may also explore whether the attitudes and motivation of alumni/ae to service—to society, to the Catholic Church, and to other religious organizations—have changed over the years. Many senior administrators expressed the conviction that service projects at Catholic institutions are more genuine, complete, or fulfilling than comparable activities undertaken at nonsectarian institutions. This conviction can be tested. It is important for Catholic institutions to provide some data, which may be suggestive more than probative, indicating that the quality of service projects at their institutions has a more long-lasting, faith-related, or transformative impact on students. In the absence of such data, nonsectarian institutions can credibly make the same claims as Catholic institutions with respect to community service and social justice programs.

In formulating, striving for, and reaching its goals, campus ministry can provide an educational service by insisting that its program be integrated into university-wide plans. Because the effort to strengthen Catholic culture should engage all aspects of the university, the determination of whether satisfactory progress toward the goals is being achieved should be reviewed by people from different sectors of the university. People serving on the oversight committee should get good data and ask demanding questions. Service opportunities linked to the Catholic tradition appear to be effective ways to strengthen the Catholic culture on campus. To be successful, however, a sufficient number of additional students must be willing to participate in them, and a good number of students must also be willing to explore the connection between service of others and the saving message and deeds of Jesus Christ.

Effectiveness, Distinguishability, and Inclusion

In their interviews, many senior administrators emphasized the importance of being welcoming to students of different religious backgrounds. Students of a variety of religious backgrounds are welcome at Catholic institutions, and it appears they know this. In a country that emphasizes religious tolerance at the same time it promotes religious practice, such inclusion fits well within the larger culture. In addition, there is a significant practical reason for Catholic colleges and universities to be religiously inclusive: most of these institutions need non-Catholic students to survive and thrive.

Religious inclusion can be primarily a matter of style, or it may entail the allocation of financial resources. In their interviews, some administrators emphasized the importance of a welcoming tone and introducing religious topics to the university community in ways that emphasize shared perspectives and beliefs. As style, inclusion is appropriate at all Catholic institutions, since in raising religious or ethical topics it seeks as much common ground as is consistent with representing the Catholic identity, character, and mission of the university. Even at specifically Catholic events or activities, adept administrators find ways to respectfully acknowledge religious traditions other than the Catholic tradition. Without compromising Catholic teaching or liturgy, other religions are treated with respect and acknowledged for their power in educating and transforming people.

Understanding the importance of religious appreciation, some Catholic universities commit substantial financial resources to religious inclusion. In a variety of ways, funds are made available to support various non-Catholic religious groups. Support ranges from funds and facilities being made available to student religious groups to annual salaries to pay for religious ministers representing different faiths. Typically, large prestigious Catholic universities allocate resources to non-Catholic groups, and they do so with funds generated by a large number of students, substantial donations, or high tuitions. Catholic institutions with constraining pressures on their budgets make sure that campus ministry is adequately funded for the objectives it is expected to achieve. In these circumstances, usually there are not enough funds to allocate for outreach to religious groups other than Catholics. Occasionally funds are available for more religiously inclusive activities, but most funds are targeted to sustaining or enhancing the Catholic culture on campus.

Senior administrators in this study spoke specifically about religious inclusion in interreligious terms. Religious tolerance at Catholic colleges and universities also has implications for how Catholics treat each other within a religious communion that is increasingly polarized along ideological lines. Administrators frequently spoke about the difficulties they encounter between and among Catholics who have little respect or tolerance for Catholic styles that differ from their own. The issue of "in-house" religious intolerance is a challenge for all four models of Catholic colleges and universities and one that causes them the particular pain of a house divided.

Universities adhering to the nonsectarian model are the most inclusive of all the articulated models with respect to religious denominations. If funds are made available at these institutions, the financial resources are allocated to religious groups on a totally impartial formula that is deemed fair by the university community. Typically, limited resources are allocated by the nonsectarian university to the primary religious groups, while additional money to support programmatic efforts is the responsibility of each religious group. This approach is appropriate for a nonsectarian institution where there is no "host religion" or no "institutional religion" that shapes institutional culture. According to any one of the four Catholic models, Catholicism is both the host and institutional religion, where "institutional" means that the university as institution does not sponsor activities contrary to the Catholic faith and, on the positive side, promotes the Catholic heritage through a variety of activities the cost of which is borne by the university. "Host" emphasizes cohesive style and content provided by the host, but includes graciousness as well. A host welcomes guests to his or her home and takes pride in encouraging them to enter into the spirit of the house. A host would not hide a piece of furniture, though he or she might rearrange furniture to make the experience for his or her guests more enjoyable and stimulating. Analogously, the Catholic university welcomes people of various faiths to the university community, takes pride in sharing its Catholic heritage and culture with them, and invites them to enter into the ways and spirit of the house. It does not hide religious convictions, but presents or arranges them in ways that are likely to produce helpful exchanges.

One area where Catholic universities can be more respectful of inclusion than nonsectarian institutions is in terms of exposure to the breadth of the Catholic heritage. The Catholic tradition is expansive, and in any given era, some Catholics identify themselves as conservative, others as liberal, and others as moderate. As was already indicated, among these three groups, there is friction, competition, and arguments. Catholics constitute a fractious family, but a family nonetheless. Because the underlying issues within the tradition are contended and because a university helps students explore important intellectual issues, campus ministry operations at Catholic universities should properly explore the tension and promote respect for all people. Jesus reached out to people where they stood and through the power of inclusion transformed their lives. So, too, Catholic institutions can meet individuals where they stand and invite them into a transformative experience that is at once wholly other and utterly respectful. In that the university will be both respectful and transformative—clear about who it is, but ever hopeful about embracing all who seek to know and follow Jesus Christ in the Catholic tradition.

All Catholic universities have to teach and preach in conformity with what the Church teaches. Nevertheless, they do so in their own way and in loving imitation of Christ. The Catholic imaginative tradition is universal, but it is also particular and can have different styles. Campus ministry rightly encourages students to respond to the call to discipleship while experiencing different styles. This approach allows students to select an approach that fits their own religious backgrounds and aspirations. It also encourages them to explore alternative approaches that will stretch their religious imaginations.

What and How Much Knowledge?

A vibrant organizational culture cannot exist without the cultural citizens who inherit the culture, live it, shape it, and pass it on to the next generation. Within this group of culture-bearers are role models, knowledge experts, and heroic leaders who sustain and support cultural integrity and coherence. For much of the history of American Catholic colleges and universities, nuns, brothers, and priests operated as the premier and multifaceted cultural catalysts who shaped collegiate Catholic culture. Within their ranks were the dramatic exemplars who founded the institutions and saw them through the necessary cultural adaptations that assured their survival, coherence, and vitality. Congregation members were also the highly visible role models who personified on a day-to-day basis what it meant to embody culture. They were the knowledge experts capable of passing on the cultural legacy to the next generation. Finally nuns, brothers, and priests were the heroic leaders responsible for monitoring the religious culture of their universities. They made sure the institutions remained true to their cultural heritage and mission, but they also initiated and managed necessary cultural changes that allowed them to realize their stated goals.

Since the early 1980s, religious congregations have understood that they were passing the torch of cultural leadership to laypersons, but exactly what it would mean for laypersons to be role models, knowledge experts, and heroic leaders remained unclear. The final section of this chapter and the whole of the following chapter focus on how laypersons will fill these important roles that determine the contours of the collegiate Catholic culture they have inherited from founding religious congregations.

In their interviews, many senior administrators were ambivalent about exactly which cultural emphasis should dominate in their institutions—Catholic or congregational. Some administrators thought it strategically best for faculty, staff, and administration to emphasize and be well informed about the sponsoring religious congregation. They also thought the congregational focus was more particular to their institutions and more inclusive. The stories and cultures of the Mercies, the Charities, the Jesuits, or the Franciscans are stirring and can easily be shared in appropriate ways with students. Congregational culture, though quite specific, is easily accessible to people with many different backgrounds and, just as important, laypersons are enthusiastic about congregational heritage and goals, and equally enthusiastic about sharing this information with students.

A second group of administrators stressed in their interviews the importance of focusing on Catholic culture directly and becoming more knowledgeable and familiar with the Catholic faith. Without being ungrateful for the powerful contributions of the sponsoring congregation, they see that phase of their institution's history coming to an end. In some institutions it may linger for a decade or more. In a few experiencing a vocational resurgence, the active involvement of the sponsoring congregation in the life and culture of the university may continue for generations to come. Most Catholic universities, however, are nearing the end of significant active involvement by congregations beyond the exercise of modest governance and oversight and limited participation in a few specific positions at the university. In practically all cases, sponsoring religious congregations are no longer able to actively shape the religious culture on campuses, though many congregations still retain cultural influence.

Administrators who emphasize Catholic culture accept that the role of the laity is eclipsing that of religious congregations in all areas of American Catholic life, including at Catholic universities and colleges, and they believe Catholicism is the significant identifying characteristic that these institutions should embrace as they move forward. Whether the institution is a Josephite, Vincentian, or Dominican university is of less significance today, largely because American Catholics are less familiar with distinctions among religious orders and congregations than they once were. In order for Catholic institutions to prosper, faculty, staff, and administrators in appropriate proportions need Catholic cultural knowledge and fluency that they can then share with students just as easily as they could share cultural knowledge of congregations. The Catholic tradition is much broader than any congregational tradition. Nevertheless, in the view of administrators with a Catholic cultural focus, it is much more important for students to become familiar with it than with the tradition of any particular sponsoring group that is fading in numbers.

Some might ask whether students prefer the Catholic or the congregational cultural focus, but a reflective response would note that such a question is misplaced. The university must decide its cultural focus, and then, in the free market of higher education, students will make their decisions. Cultural content is properly a university decision, but because inheritability is vital to any institution, it is appropriate for a university to consider how student preferences with respect to religious culture might develop over time. Predicting even general developments is risky, but a negative criterion is important. Administrators should not institute programs that they are fairly sure will be rejected by the type of student who usually applies for admission to their institution. According to the (insufficiently documented) current wisdom, modern undergraduates know very little about either the Catholic faith or the history and charism of any particular sponsoring religious congregation. Students could benefit from increased knowledge of both, and emphasizing one over the other is unlikely to enhance or diminish satisfaction of the inheritability criterion.

Consider a thought experiment involving the choice of religious cultural identification at a Catholic university. Suppose a Catholic university were, in some public way, to commit itself solely to communicating the culture of the sponsoring congregation to undergraduates. By choice of words and programs, the university would publicly indicate that undergraduate students should learn more about the sponsoring congregation. The academic curriculum and an array of student projects and activities would make it possible for students to attain this knowledge. Although the word "Catholic" would be retained and used in certain contexts to indicate historical legacy, the emphasis in this institution would be on its Augustinian, Charity, or Benedictine culture.

Such an approach might be attractive to faculty, staff, and administrators at some Catholic universities. In our view, however, it would neither be intellectually honest nor serve the mission of the Catholic Church. We also suspect that it would not last more than a generation, since its appeal relies on the attractiveness of a religious congregation that over the next twenty-five years will no longer have a significant presence or impact on Catholic culture nationally. In our view, if the emphasis on the sponsoring congregation and its charism proves attractive to students, the likely reason is that it deemphasizes a Catholic connection.

Members of sponsoring religious congregations are dramatic exemplars of Catholic culture at Catholic colleges and universities. But, as was pointed out in chapter 2, dramatic exemplars who remain vital to the organization may be presented in ways that are not culturally authentic and that manipulate their legacy through a selective telling of their story. Any attempt to isolate religious congregations from the Catholic culture in which they are embedded would be tantamount to misusing and manipulating the legacy of the institution's dramatic cultural exemplars. Every religious congregation arises out of the Church and is motivated by a deep commitment to serve the Church. Although some think that a number of religious congregations were founded to challenge governance structures in the Catholic Church, in fact they all emerged from founders who themselves were committed to serve the Church in more effective ways, and they attracted people who felt likewise. Cultural authenticity and intellectual honesty require that the religious culture of congregations be understood and transmitted as arising from within the Catholic Church through the efforts of men and women committed in lifelong service to it.

While it is possible for Catholic universities to give precedence to transmitting congregational culture over Catholic culture, this approach clouds the religious cultural issue on campus. Emphasizing knowledge of the congregational sponsor means the university is convinced that Catholic culture on campus is best captured through the prism of the sponsoring religious congregation, not through the teachings and practices of the Catholic Church itself. This approach appears to be coherent and faithful to the historical tradition because it has clear links with the sponsoring religious congregation. However, by downplaying the Catholic connection, the strong links between the sponsoring religious congregation and the Catholic Church are neglected. Thus, in our judgment, the decision to emphasize congregational identity and heritage proves inconsistent and unworkable.

Cultural vibrancy in any organization is impossible without a significant cluster of knowledge experts, and Catholic culture at Catholic universities will not survive and thrive without a sufficiently broad cluster of knowledgeable faculty, staff, and administrators. Some members of the university community, including students, will surely be interested in exploring the foundations of the university and understanding the ethos and élan of the sponsoring congregation. The university itself will continue to point to the founding religious congregation and its heroic leaders as the most powerful dramatic exemplars of the meaning and lived reality of Catholic culture at the institution. But in an era when Catholic universities struggle to make sure that Catholic students are adequately formed and informed about their own Catholic heritage and culture, the institutions' primary cultural emphasis must be Catholic.

One senior administrator commented that "there will always be people of Catholic faith who will gravitate to Catholic universities as a home; so [the Catholic universities] will continue." The administrator may be correct, but we would not bet on it. Many religious sisters were similarly optimistic about their own congregations. Even in the 1970s, most congregations of sisters, brothers, or priests could not imagine a situation in which hundreds of religious congregations would become moribund by the year 2000 because young women and men ceased to enter. And yet it happened. Catholics will likely gravitate to Catholic universities provided they see them as a home or as a place where they can better come to know their own religious roots and heritage. To be either, these institutions have to be a source of Catholic knowledge and practice. To be a welcoming home, they have to be a source of Catholic knowledge and practice. To be a Catholic resource, administrators, staff, campus ministers, and most especially faculty members must be able and willing to transmit the Catholic culture by explaining it to curious undergraduates. In order for that to occur, they have to become sufficiently knowledgeable about and fluent in Catholic culture themselves that they can bring it to bear appropriately in all sectors of university life.

8

Institutional Culture

Institutional Catholic culture at Catholic colleges and universities is the context in which educational goals are defined and outcomes secured. When talking about institutional culture, senior administrators frequently did so in terms of ideal constructs that focused primarily on hopes and possibilities. The previous chapters focused on individual sectors of the university. Those area portraits were far less enthusiastic about what is really happening on Catholic college campuses than these descriptions of institutional culture. While the whole is always more than the sum of its parts, it is seldom this much more. In this chapter, the senior administrators speak confidently of the pervasive character of the Catholic culture and the transformative impact it has had on many of their students. Yet, in earlier chapters they acknowledged that at their institutions the conceptual components of Catholic culture were not being effectively shared with students through adequate exposure to the Catholic intellectual and moral traditions. Administrators also described a situation in which dependence on the symbolic components of religious culture was expected to compensate for weaknesses in cultural content. On many campuses, the office of campus ministry was shouldering a disproportionate share of the responsibility for transmitting Catholic culture, and even this sector faced obstacles as a result of insufficient resources and understaffing that has limited the breadth and depth of its initiatives.

The contrast both in tone and content expressed by senior administrators can be explained in large measure by the context in which both kinds of responses were offered. Each interview consisted of five formal questions. The first question and the last question served as interview bookends and asked for a public defense of the Catholic higher education sector, both in terms of its contribution to the landscape of American higher education and as a superior educator of Catholics for the twenty-first century. The three questions in between were designed to elicit information about what is actually happening at Catholic colleges and universities in relation to their religious identity and mission. The bookend questions provoked "marketing responses" that were more general in nature, and put the very best face on what makes these institutions significant contributors to society and to the Church. The questions that focused on what is actually happening at the institutions elicited responses that were much more specific and dealt equally with the strengths and weaknesses administrators observe and encounter.

Many of the comments that form the narrative of this chapter came in response to the last of the five questions. This question focused on the contrast between a Catholic education at a Catholic university and Catholic education available to students through a Catholic or Newman center at a nonsectarian institution. In the scenario given to the senior administrators, a wealthy donor was prepared to make a very large donation ($500 million) to promote Catholic education at some university. The donor wanted to put the money where it would have the biggest impact on the education of Catholics in the United States, and was considering two possibilities: the senior administrator's Catholic university, or a nonsectarian university with a good Catholic center.[1] After being reminded that over 80 percent of Catholics are educated on the tertiary level in non-Catholic institutions, the senior administrators were asked to present the best possible arguments for why the Catholic university should receive the gift, and they rose to the challenge. So spirited were some of their responses that a few asked, after having made the case, "Well, do we get the $500 million?" Not all administrators, it must be said, were convinced the money should go to Catholic institutions. Some thought that on the issue of numbers alone, justice demanded that the gift be split between the two types of institutions, or given to the sector with the most Catholic students. A few administrators indicated that Newman and Catholic centers had very difficult work to do and few resources available to do it. This group said they would urge the donor to give the money to the centers.

Many administrators were convinced that the donor would get a much bigger return by investing the money in a Catholic university. Frequently they returned to responses they had given to the first question of the interview, in which they were asked to describe Catholic higher education ten years in the future and to explain to a Harvard policy institute why this sector was both unique and essential in the landscape of American higher education. Having gone through the entire interview and wrestled with questions that probed the contours of their actual experience, administrators' return to earlier arguments was often somewhat muted. After making their pitch to the virtual donor, many of the same administrators acknowledged that the reality they had earlier described in responses to other questions was often a far cry from the idealistic picture they had painted for the benefit of either Harvard or the generous donor, and a far cry from their own ideals about Catholic higher education as well.

During their interviews, senior administrators were able to point to many instances where their Catholic universities perform extremely well, but they also realized that much more needs to be done to extend and deepen the impact of Catholic culture on students at their institutions. Like most of us, however, when asked to talk to outsiders about the enterprise, senior administrators focused on success, not failure; potential, not problems; the best of all possible descriptions, not the worst. For this reason, the comments concerning the pervasive presence of a transformative Catholic culture at Catholic universities are conviction statements interpreted in this chapter as epitomizing what senior administrators hope for their institutions to be, rather than as actual descriptions of how they experience them.

Convictions

Senior administrators across all the models insisted that Catholic colleges and universities offer the best possible educational experience for Catholic students. An administrator from a persuasion university captured the view of most administrators when he said: "institutes and think tanks and training programs in isolation do not have nearly the [same] effect [on students] as a traditional undergraduate experience at a Catholic institution." Administrators said they believe Catholic colleges and universities offer superior education primarily because, as a diaspora president asserted,

> Catholic education is not just in the classroom; it is a cultural experience. While a secular institution or an institution of another religious tradition might have a very fine set of courses on the history of Catholicism or even in some Catholic theology, Catholic higher education is a much more complete and comprehensive experience.

"Catholic education is an integrated education," a cohort administrator insisted, "that joins issues of faith, faith development, morality, moral development, the calling of the gospel, and being in service to each other—and not service in a strictly humanitarian, secular way, but in a way which is guided by Jesus' message in the Gospel."

When asked what constitutes the Catholic part of the university, an immersion president said: "it's multiple things, it's not just one thing. It's curriculum, programming, academic research, liturgical life, and support for faith development with a huge investment in campus ministry. It's service—social concerns and outreach. It's hiring for mission." The unique kind of education that is available at a Catholic college or university comes not only from classes but also, as a persuasion university administrator pointed out, "from the environment. The whole environment has to speak to what the university is teaching." The environment or culture at Catholic universities is so pervasive, according to a diaspora administrator, that

> students are going to experience it throughout their educational experience. Students get more focus on ethics and values in their courses. They are surrounded by people who care about the mission and values of the institution, and they use that mission and those values to guide the way they interact.

A cohort administrator said that her university has "constant reminders for students, inside and outside the classroom, in working with administrators and others, that they are at a Catholic institution." This administrator felt strongly that

> there should not be many moments when students forget they are at a Catholic institution. This does not mean waving the flag. But everything that happens during the day—how we treat each other, how we listen to each other, how we behave toward each other, how our discipline is meted out, our code of conduct in dealing with one another as children of God—all this defines us as a Catholic institution.

Many administrators insisted that not only do students experience a pervasively Catholic culture on a Catholic college or university campus but also they are transformed by it. "My sense," a cohort administrator said,

> is that we are about changing people's lives, and we have an influence on changing their lives, almost more than any other factor that adults have in society today. When I talk to people who have graduated from our programs and say "Tell me about your experience," in almost all cases people describe life-changing, inward life-changing experiences.

Catholic colleges, according to a persuasion administrator, are

> not just preparing students for jobs, which is what the public institutions do. We are preparing students for how to live a life. And that means more than just book knowledge and x number of credits taken and passed. That means it's about questions like, "What do I do with the knowledge? Also, what is my commitment to society, to service, to others?"

As an immersion university administrator pointed out, "We believe that forming someone well humanly actually makes them capable of performing well."

A significant number of administrators were quite clear that the unique thing the Catholic sector has to offer higher education in general is its particular religious identity and culture. As a diaspora administrator put it, "the reason for a Catholic institution is that the Catholicity means something." Administrators critiqued attempts by some Catholic colleges to distance themselves from their religious roots. "Many of us in Catholic higher education are trying to do what everyone else is doing," a persuasion administrator pointed out, adding: "that approach will kill us." Administrators also pointed out that Catholic colleges have begun to more fully appreciate and publicly claim their religious identity of late, seeing it as a marketing plus. The academic vice-president at an immersion university has seen "in the last ten years a big change in Catholic higher education away from an obvious drift to be exactly like the secular institutions. Some Catholic colleges and universities tried to be different than what they were founded to be and what they really were," he said.

> They held out excellence in academics, not in their own image, but in the image of what secular education said it ought to be. If, on the other hand, institutions have excellence in their own image, they meet the demands of secular education and have the same standards and then have the added dimensions.

The president of a persuasion university was proud that the institution had made a determination to reclaim its Catholic heritage and mission. The new mission statement "makes it very clear that we are a Catholic college," the president announced. "We thought it was important to be very clear about being sponsored by a religious congregation and that we are a Catholic college. The first goal in our new strategic plan is deepening our understanding of the Catholic tradition and clarifying the identity of this college as a Catholic college." The president of a cohort institution regretted what he saw as a misbegotten attempt to distance Catholic colleges from their religious identity for the sake of secular legitimacy. "One of the worst things we did in the sixties was to give up distinctiveness under the guise of gaining credibility with our secular counterparts."

Administrators also maintained that Catholic colleges and universities are uniquely capable of cultivating people of faith within their collegiate communities. According to a persuasion administrator,

> the faith, like most things, grows best in rich soil, and the Catholic heritage and traditions you find on Catholic campuses are that rich soil. You see it in multiple areas, not in any one area. You see it in the curriculum, in the faculty and administrators, in extracurricular activities, in the types of organizations and clubs that have support, in campus culture, in the presence of prayer, the architecture, the art—all the things on campus that create a culture that is a faith-embedded culture.

It is really important for Catholic colleges, a persuasion administrator said, "as a faith community . . . to try to instill in everyone—our faculty, our students, our staff—an appreciation for discovering not only the Truth of Jesus Christ but all the other truths and their relation to that one." At some institutions there is a strong commitment to enhancing the faith life of Catholic students.

"The one thing that we try very hard to do," a persuasion president said, "is to make students better Catholics by the time they leave." It is equally important, as a diaspora administrator pointed out, that the faith be so alive within the organizational structure of a Catholic college that "everything we do, every decision we make, is based on our faith."

Senior administrators want their institutions to have distinct and vibrant Catholic cultures. They also want them to be excellent and respected academic institutions and well-run organizations that are welcoming to those of different faiths. Administrators also recognized that the people who teach in these institutions and who lead them in the presidency and in senior administrative posts will largely determine whether these institutions survive as respected universities with vibrant religious cultures. In talking about hiring for mission and qualifications for leadership in various administrative positions, administrators had to address to what extent being Catholic should be a consideration in hiring. Many talked, as a persuasion university administrator did, about needing "a critical mass of people who embody the tradition in order to say that it is Catholic." A cohort administrator agreed, saying: "in any Catholic institution, if you don't have a core of people who are practicing Catholics, you've missed the boat."

In terms of the faculty, most administrators agreed with the academic vice-president at a cohort university that

> as a faculty member you don't necessarily have to be Catholic to share in our mission and to further it. We do believe that people we hire have to be people of faith, that faith means something in their lives, because otherwise they will never have any commitment to the type of teaching we would like to see here and especially the responsibility for service.

An immersion university president concurred.

> If you're going to be a religious institution, you can't be hiring faculty on the basis of their intellectual capability so that they'd fit in great at a secular place. They're going to be at a religious institution. You have to find people who are intelligent, have the reason, but they also have to have the faith part. They don't necessarily have to have Catholic faith, because you want other religions to enter into the dialogue. It's got to be clear they are part of a faith tradition and take it seriously, and you can find that out very easily if you are attuned to it.

When it came to their own positions, most administrators were at first hesitant about suggesting they should be filled by Catholics, and many were themselves not Catholic. A persuasion university administrator pointed out that

> as a non-Catholic who spent all these years in Catholic higher education, obviously I believe that you can be in these jobs and do these

jobs and you can be a non-Catholic. But I also think you can only be successful to the extent that you are willing to embrace and understand the Catholic dimensions of the institutions. I would be hard pressed to work in an institution where my own personal values were not in concert with the values of the institution I work for.

As they began talking about religious qualifications, administrators followed the lead of a persuasion university administrator who made it clear that "you have to have some key people who are committed to the belief or it will become watered down. It will be a good institution with values, but the Catholic [part] won't be as important." Other administrators focused on having people in administration—regardless of their own personal religious tradition—who had professional experience in a Catholic institution. For one persuasion administrator, that meant that "somewhere along the line [they] have to have gotten to understand not just the culture but the profound faith that is at the heart of a Catholic institution." A cohort administrator expected the kind of familiarity with Catholic culture that he described as immersion. "Immersion is the only way you can become familiar with the Catholic culture. So, if somebody really hasn't been part of a Catholic community at some level, I think that whether they are Catholic or not, they are not really going to understand all the issues and they aren't going to be very effective."

After spending some time talking about what it takes to be successful and really contribute at a Catholic university in a senior administrative position, most administrators decided that "a person has to be a Catholic." A persuasion university administrator explained quite well what most administrators meant when they made this statement.

> I do believe that in an institution like ours the person has to be a Catholic, and it's more than just that you go to your parish every Sunday. I think they need to have some education about the character and mission of an institution like ours. And that requires some background in theology or religious education. I do think there are key roles in the institution where the person not only should be Catholic but ought to be able to articulate for others what it means to be a Catholic institution. In order to be able to articulate it effectively, honestly, and clearly, the person has to have some education and familiarity with the language.

There was almost universal agreement among administrators that, as a persuasion university president put it,

> the president has to be a practicing Catholic. She must be comfortable addressing the Catholic nature of the institution. She must be able on many occasions, to interpret, explicate, or even defend a decision and show how it is aligned with the Catholic and congregational values of the college.

An administrator at another persuasion university simply could not imagine how a non-Catholic person would be effective as the president of a Catholic institution. "I don't know how you could comfortably be a leader of a Catholic college without being a Catholic, unless it is really not a Catholic college which values its Catholicism. How could you lead a Lutheran college unless you were a Lutheran?" "It's important for somebody to be a practicing Catholic in the position of president," another persuasion president insisted. "It's very important because it's hard to fake it. I believe [the president] should be someone who is truly devoted to the Catholic Church." Most administrators not only maintained that the president of the university should be a Catholic but also said the president had to live in ways that reflected what the Church teaches. A persuasion university president was adamant that

> absolutely, the president cannot be in flagrant violation of some teaching of the Church. He can't be living with some woman to whom he is not married! I don't take that position with faculty, and I've never been confronted with it with a senior administrator. But the president of an institution has got to model what we think is appropriate behavior within this tradition. I know that's hard, and none of us is perfect and we all make mistakes. In our positions we're not always going to carry that out faithfully. But I don't think a Catholic institution could have such a visible contradiction.

Administrators in Catholic colleges have lofty religious goals for their institutions and rigorous standards about the religious knowledge and commitment they think must be in evidence among faculty, administrators, and the president. Very few, however, said anything about assessing whether what they hope is happening at their institutions truly is. In fact, only three administrators raised the topic. One persuasion mission officer said:

> there has to be an assessment at the end that indicates we have indeed integrated all aspects of this core body of knowledge and that there's a greater understanding and a formation in the life of the student. We should have given that person—not just the knowledge headwise, but an ownership for the tradition.

A cohort university administrator warned that

> the president who shakes the graduate's hand should be assured that questions about who I am and who I am in relation to God and what is my responsibility to other beings who are made in the image and likeness of God as described in the Gospel, have been addressed, and these perspectives have been incorporated into his or her learning and lifestyle.

"Having data that shows our Catholic students are more involved in the Church after graduation, a persuasion university president insisted, "would be absolutely critical, and we need to really give some attention to that."

Analysis of the Data: Articulating Religious Identity
and Mission

Many senior administrators thought that how Catholic colleges and universities claim and articulate their Catholic identity and mission impacts Catholic culture. They also maintain that institutions are becoming increasingly direct and clear about their religious character and purposes, reversing a trend toward ambiguity that had been dominant from the mid-1960s onward.[2] Other administrators made it clear that their institutions are still grappling with how they want to present themselves to prospective students and their parents, government funding agencies, alumni/ae, and possible donors. They talked about a commitment to enhance Catholic identity; but they also pointed out that many in the institution are nervous about the possibility that this emphasis could cost their institutions students, funding, or prestige, and consequently they are moving very slowly in that direction.

While many administrators understood that how an institution presents itself has implications for its religious culture, that appreciation was not universal. Historically, in the 1960s and 1970s, Catholic colleges and universities operated in ways that flew in the face of this understanding. Catholic colleges made a decision to mute their religious self-identification beginning in the late 1960s in order to survive. At the time there was a general consensus that such a move had great utility in terms of attracting government monies and had little down-side. The shift in public emphasis was seen as a "purely symbolic" gesture that would have little or no impact on their institutional Catholicity. For a group of institutions steeped in Catholic sacramental understanding to believe that a symbolic gesture will have little impact seems almost naïve. Nonetheless, during the 1960s, with great optimism and innocence, many symbolic changes were initiated within the Church, with little real understanding that there could be a discrepancy between their intended meaning and what they actually conveyed. The unintended cultural impact that results from this kind of discrepancy can be profound.[3] Although it was not intended to do so, the deemphasis of religious self-identity at Catholic colleges and universities was interpreted by many as religious cultural erosion, and in time that perception contributed to actual cultural drift. It is possible that if men and women religious had remained in large numbers and highly visible on Catholic college campuses, the effect of deemphasizing religious identity and mission in public statements would have been less culturally corrosive. In the face of dwindling congregational presence, however, the decision to mute public affirmations of institutional Catholicity over time contributed mightily to the leeching away of religious culture at many of these colleges and universities.

Most Catholic colleges and universities have returned to readily self-identifying as "Catholic" in their mission statements. Senior administrators also appear to be gaining confidence as they address different groups about the Catholic identity, character, and mission of their institutions. Many said they speak out more frequently and forcefully about the Catholic identity of their institutions and the importance of emphasizing that identity programmatically. This may well be true, but in terms of their interview conversations, administrators were still religiously timid, avoiding the use of richly evocative Catholic language, thereby abandoning one of the tradition's richest symbol sets. Administrators frequently used the term "Catholic" and the name of the sponsoring religious congregation. They also comfortably referred to God's presence among us or in all things, as well as to the "Mass" or "Eucharist." Only a few administrators talked about the "gospel," and almost all completely avoided the words "Christ," "Jesus Christ," "Lord," sacrament, sanctity, virtue, holiness, or sin. No one spoke of the Holy Spirit, the Trinity, or the Blessed Virgin. There was no expectation at the beginning of the study that respondents would use particular religious language, but upon reflection, its tepid use was striking. As Edgar Schein points out, "critical conceptual categories are usually built into the basic language a group uses."[4] The almost universal resistance to using rich Catholic language suggests that institutional self-identification with Catholicism is still less than robust at many Catholic colleges and universities.

On numerous occasions, administrators were at pains to distance themselves from the evangelical colleges and universities that use religious language quite openly and do so as part of a process that actively seeks converts. One president talked about these evangelical groups as "shout to the Lord" Christians. An academic vice-president, in saying that "a lot of evangelicals are very involved and believe that they must bring other people to their way of believing, whereas tolerance and acceptance is much more a value or virtue in Catholicism," provided some useful insights about the values that might tempt administrators to shun a particularly Catholic vocabulary. Administrators are trying very hard to negotiate the boundary between overt religious identification and off-putting religious triumphalism that is disrespectful or offensive to people of different faith backgrounds.

Just as striking as the paucity of particularly evocative religious language in interview conversations was the breadth of the phenomenon among so many administrators, serving at quite different types of universities, with such distinctly different backgrounds. At times it seemed as if senior administrators were all using the same script when speaking about religious culture—a script that had been sanitized for the sake of offending no one. It recalled the pattern of religious congregations of women amid the changes from the 1960s through the 1990s. Once a national leadership group for women religious was established with provincials as members, they developed a particular way of talking about religious life that was unifying but culturally bland.[5] It provided a common language that framed an even more common understanding of congregational mission and culture, but it worked against cultural distinguishability among congregations and served to dampen entrepreneurial initiatives. Even when their situation turned very bleak, an entrepreneurial spirit did not quicken, and these women did not choose to introduce a little competition into the mix, in the sense of trying different approaches to attract at least some vocations. It was as though once they determined a particular path for renewal, these congregations became more committed to the particular path than to finding the best way to get where they wanted to go. Their language was similar, their cultural analysis never varied, and their strategies about how to proceed were identical.

The senior administrators who participated in this study are locked into a language pattern they believe is respectful, and consequently there is not much variety in the way they speak about the religious identity, character, and mission of their institutions. Even in the face of a weakening institutional Catholic culture they clearly want to strengthen, many senior administrators are seemingly more committed to the religious sensibilities of non-Catholics than they are to reclaiming symbolic religious language that is clearly "Catholic." Perhaps this verbal timidity is just one of the last remnants of the trend toward ambiguous self-identification that is soon to give way to a wider use of more culturally provocative language in the coming years.

Specifying Transformation

Senior administrators insisted that Catholic higher education is unique and superior to other kinds of educational experiences for Catholics. Because these institutions have pervasive religious cultures that provide transformative experiences for students that are unmatched at non-Catholic colleges and universities, their performance and product is superior. Although senior administrators' passionate assertions were convicted, they were seldom very convincing. The same administrators also described institutions that are somewhat hesitant about articulating the depth of their Catholic identity, mission, and culture. They admitted that the Catholic intellectual tradition and moral tradition are not presented as effectively as they could be to students and the religious activities on their campuses are often poorly attended or less extensive than is necessary for assuring a vibrant Catholic culture that is both distinguishable and inheritable over time. The kind of student transformation many senior administrators spoke about with approval and admiration touches the core activities of Catholic universities. The challenge for administrators, faculty, and alumni/ae is to demonstrate that institutional practice measures up to passionate public appraisals that Catholic higher education has a truly distinctive culture that is, in fact, transformative. As a first step, these institutions must be specific about the type of transformation they desire and then estimate the type and degree of transformation that is actually achieved.

"Transformation" is a general concept, and people engaged in higher education at nonsectarian universities readily use the word to describe positive, fundamental changes that take place in students during their undergraduate years at their nonsectarian institutions. Traditional-aged college students are in the throes of significant developmental change that brings them into full adulthood. It is, therefore, hardly surprising that interaction with faculty members and administrators, experience in service projects, camaraderie with fellow students, and living away from their homes and families produce substantial changes in the outlook students have on life and what they deem important.

Almost every parent will attest to the transformative nature of his or her son's or daughter's collegiate experience.

Faculty and administrators at Catholic universities would likely agree with their counterparts at nonsectarian institutions about the types of transformations that would be highly esteemed by both groups. Students who become independent and articulate problem-solvers, who make the less fortunate a priority in their lives, who become attuned to the importance of making careful distinctions in arguments, who arrive at a deep appreciation of arts and culture, who learn to deal with adversity through their experiences at college—these types of students are admirable, and universities rightfully point to them as examples of the type of transformation that is wrought by putting talented individuals in close contact with one another under a demanding academic regime in their universities.[6]

In their interviews, a number of senior administrators mentioned student transformation as "the blessing" they experienced as a result of working in a Catholic institution, and shared anecdotal information that illuminated their experience. The particular examples they gave of transformation most frequently dealt with students from the social and economic margins. Administrators lauded these often-first-generation college students who had achieved a measure of "success" that was extraordinary given their personal circumstances. Whether the student was a young man who might otherwise still be on the streets of the inner city, or the single mother coming out of an abusive domestic situation who finally received an academic degree, or the young woman raised in rural poverty who graduated with a scholarship for a doctoral program at a top university, the transformation stories administrators shared were almost all Horatio Alger stories of striving, opportunity, and "making it" in the real world. Most administrators claimed the distinctive transformational success of their institutions on the basis of entirely nonreligious outcomes that were indistinguishable from stories that faculty at countless institutions could just as readily relate. In hour-long interviews that focused on Catholic institutional identity and leadership and in the face of a specific question that asked about where a donor should invest to provide for the best education of Catholics, administrators most frequently based their claims of institutional superiority on predominantly secular outcomes.

The hypothetical donor in the case presented to senior administrators in their last question had a very particular interest and wavered between making a donation to the Catholic university and the Catholic or Newman center at the nonsectarian university. The uncertainty in the donor's mind was about where the investment would be more productive in terms of the education of Catholics in the United States. To appeal to the particular interest of the foundation or donor, the administrators had to use some norm, perhaps only implicit, about what constitutes "the education of Catholics in the United States." Only a few administrators addressed this aspect of the question. Rather, in their attempts to cooperate with the interview process, by far the majority of administrators tried to persuade the donor to choose a Catholic university as a gift recipient[7] because students would be educated by a more pervasive Catholic culture there than anything they might experience through a Newman or Catholic center. In many cases, the administrators realized that the Catholic culture at their university was neither as strong nor as pervasive as they would like. They assumed, however, that whatever its weaknesses, it was more compelling than anything Catholic students would encounter at non-Catholic institutions.

Young Catholics interested in pursuing a degree can be educated in a number of ways. They can attend a public or nonsectarian private university with a Newman center but with no Catholic studies program at the university. They can attend a public or nonsectarian private university that has both a Newman center and a Catholic studies program. They can attend a nonsectarian university located within a parish attuned to the needs of students and eager to involve Catholic students in the life of their parish. They can also be educated at a Catholic university. Catholic universities have been the mainstay of Catholic education, but they now compete with a number of institutions that provide some Catholic education for young Catholics. Catholic universities are used to competition. Good competition improves the regimen at each type of institution. As a result of this competition, Catholic universities are compelled to more clearly outline the type of undergraduate—Catholic and non-Catholic—they hope to graduate. They also need to specify the steps they are taking to increase the likelihood that their Catholic graduates will be active in their faith, committed to participate in the life of a parish community, well informed about matters integral to the Church and society, and contributors to the mission of the Church.

Catholic institutions maintaining their religious distinguishability will claim cultural distinctions that are appropriate to the model of Catholic institution to which they subscribe. Immersion and persuasion institutions have a much greater commitment to educating Catholics in the faith and preparing them for participation in the life of the Catholic Church in the United States than do diaspora and cohort institutions. As a Catholic operation, each institution has its own attractive features, and these features can be presented to prospective students in appealing ways. A number of Catholic universities already articulate what they hope is the value added for any Catholic student graduating from them and also their minimum hopes and expectations for those students in the years after graduation.

Many Catholic universities have not yet specified particular religious goals or designed effective programs to achieve the goals or established minimum "transformational" rates for graduating students. This is understandable, considering that until fairly recently there was general agreement about what it meant to be a committed and knowledgeable lay Catholic in the community, in the parish, and in family life and how that supported and sustained Catholic culture and identity. Religious congregations of women were largely responsible for sustaining and transmitting this cultural understanding in the myriad settings of their apostolic works. The cultural collapse of religious congregations of women is so important within Catholic circles precisely because these women had such a strong religious culture and because they taught us all what it meant to be Catholic. In the culture of the 1940s, 1950s, and 1960s, it was much easier to run a good Catholic university than it is today, and that was due, in large measure, to the solid cultural infrastructure put in place by women religious in most parishes in the United States.

The pervading Catholic culture that was sustained and promoted by religious sisters and nourished and cultivated by religious brothers and priests exists no more. Many find it curious that the religious women and men who anticipated the evaporation of vocations for two decades were not more aggressive in preparing their lay successors to cultivate Catholic culture. Congregations were, for the most part, blindsided by their own cultural crisis. They did not anticipate that their ranks would almost disappear at Catholic colleges and universities so quickly. They also had not fully appreciated the witness power and impact of their own visible presence on campus in terms of enhancing Catholic identity and culture. For reasons that remain somewhat mysterious, religious sponsors systematically overestimated the depth and breadth of Catholic knowledge and faith commitment among faculty, staff, and administrators at the colleges and universities. Some of the miscalculation can be ascribed to wishful thinking, since the sponsoring religious congregation wanted to believe that a recognition of the baptismal call of all people was all that stood between laypersons and their appropriate leadership in the Church. Congregations also were vested in the people they had hired and optimistic that just a little time on their own was all laypersons needed to get their bearings and assume religious leadership without assistance from congregations. The sheer magnitude of the problem also distorted the congregational assessment of what exactly needed to be done to prepare the next generation of leadership for Catholic institutions. Whatever it was that clouded perception and interfered with proper assessment of the task at hand, many laypersons admit that they are ill prepared for the responsibilities that have been thrust upon them in their stewardship roles at Catholic apostolic works, despite their deep commitment to the institutions at which they serve.

How this critical moment came to pass is an interesting question. What it means for the future and how laypersons and institutions should proceed is of far more critical import. In terms of contemporary Catholic universities, two major issues must be confronted. The first concerns the type of substitute cultural reality that might emerge in our new circumstances. This new cultural entity will need to be effective in educating and forming young adult Catholics and to make good use of the talents of laypersons who are currently active or willing to become more active in the Catholic Church in the United States. The second issue involves the education and identification of faculty and administrators who can support and shape Catholic culture within universities. At this transitional moment, the critical question is how to prepare faculty and administrators to be the religious cultural catalysts and citizens at Catholic universities.

Catholic Knowledge and Commitment

An adapted or revitalized American Catholic culture, just like any institutional culture, has knowledgeable and committed actors, that is, cultural catalysts and cultural citizens, as well as content and symbols. Catholic cultural catalysts need to be not only knowledgeable about the Catholic faith and tradition but also committed to the faith and to sustaining Catholic culture.[8] Faith and culture are closely linked at the institutional level, even if at the individual level there are important and appropriate distinctions. The majority of Catholics do not have to be committed to sustaining the Catholic culture, but at any Catholic university there must be some group that commits itself not merely to living the faith but also to monitoring, adjusting, and, where necessary, strengthening the Catholic culture.

Senior administrators emphasized the importance of having faculty and administrators on campus who are knowledgeable about and committed to the Catholic faith. In terms of the knowledge component, the decision about who should be knowledgeable and just how knowledgeable they should be depends on the Catholic institutional model the university adopts. In addressing the knowledge issue at Catholic colleges and universities, it is reasonable to begin with the faculty. As Terence Murphy reminds us,

> the chief providers of a Catholic education are the faculty. No amount of rhetoric from the president's office, or statements of mission, or religious symbols, helpful as these may be, constitute a Catholic university or a Catholic education. What goes on in the classroom day after day determines whether or not the educational experience has a religious or value dimension. The faculty is the key. They must understand the religious element of the mission of the university.[9]

Faculty members teaching Catholic theology at any Catholic college or university must necessarily be well informed about the Catholic faith and able to respond to questions about the faith that might be posed in classes, on campus, and in public forums where their professional opinion is sought. The appropriate knowledge base for faculty members who are not teaching theology will vary. However, it is important that in each of the four Catholic models, some faculty members in all areas be well informed about issues—historical as well as contemporary—that are critical to understanding the Catholic tradition. Having at least a small group, or disciplinary cluster, of such knowledgeable faculty is important for two reasons. All faculty need mutual support from a community of scholars, and a disciplinary cluster will provide that support. Even a small group is also far more likely than an isolated individual to have an impact within a department. Second only to theology, philosophy engages much that is foundational to Catholic tradition, and it is consequently particularly important this kind of cluster be part of the philosophy department.[10]

Chapter 5 identified desirable characteristics for faculty teaching at Catholic universities. These included commitment to the centrality of theology and philosophy, appreciation of the institution's responsibility to serve the Catholic Church, acceptance of the responsibility to encourage students in faith and virtue, and willingness to secure greater knowledge about the Catholic intellectual tradition. These are general traits that ideally apply to all faculty members teaching at any Catholic university. The first three characteristics are sufficient in themselves for making a direct contribution to Catholic institutional culture. The last characteristic is not. Faculty members who are willing to secure greater knowledge about the Catholic intellectual tradition are certainly properly disposed to contribute to the Catholic culture in their disciplines. Until they actually have the knowledge, however, they simply cannot deliver.

According to *Ex Corde Ecclesiae*, non-Catholic faculty should not constitute a majority of the faculty.[11] *Majority* here may refer simply to anything more than 50 percent of the full-time faculty. Alternatively, as we propose hereafter, a smaller group of Catholic faculty could functionally constitute a majority, in terms of determining the Catholic culture of the university, if so empowered by other faculty members. In effect, a rather small group of faculty could have leadership status and particular authority with respect to issues involving Catholic culture.

Most people in Catholic higher education circles shy away from numerical quotas, even as they acknowledge that Catholic institutional identity requires a critical mass of people who are knowledgeable about the Catholic tradition and, as James Provost terms them, "people who are Catholic in full communion."[12] There is less agreement about what number actually constitutes this critical mass. Richard P. McBrien defines critical mass as "(not necessarily a large majority, or even a simple majority) of faculty and administrative leaders who are committed and active Catholics and of non-Catholics who respect the Catholic tradition and who support the university's intention to be and to remain faithful to that tradition."[13] The interests of faculty are frequently focused on their own academic discipline and not on core requirements or the general academic curriculum. If the entire faculty respects the judgment of "Catholic specialists," faculty members may be willing to defer to the Catholic group in matters pertaining to Catholic academic content."[14] Critical mass is not the same hard-and-fast number for every Catholic college or university in the United States, since it is dependent on a number of factors. In terms of this analysis, the type of Catholic university—be it immersion, persuasion, cohort, or diaspora—will determine what constitutes a critical mass of active, committed, and effective Catholics necessary for sustaining a vibrant Catholic culture.

In considering critical mass and Catholic knowledge, it is important to first recognize that all faculty members at Catholic colleges are responsible for the academic culture and its integration with the Catholic tradition. Immersion institutions are committed by their mission and goals to having a large number of faculty members who are well informed about the Catholic intellectual tradition in particular, as well as the broader Catholic tradition. The goals of Catholic persuasion universities also require a significant number of faculty members who are knowledgeable about the Catholic tradition in general, as well as how the tradition pertains to their own disciplines. The number of knowledgeable faculty at persuasion universities should be sufficient to exert influence in the guidance of the appropriate Catholic culture in academic matters. It should also be adequate to provide instruction and guidance for students, many of whom are Catholic. The Catholic group should also be sufficient in number and prominence that colleagues will actually listen to them and accept their guidance. In order to have such influence at persuasion universities, we tentatively propose (this proposal will be critically reviewed later) that the cluster of Catholic faculty knowledgeable in the Catholic intellectual tradition should be no less than 25 percent of the faculty. At diaspora and cohort institutions, the cluster of faculty knowledgeable in the Catholic tradition can be much smaller than at immersion and persuasion universities, and in some cases it might not exceed 10 percent of the faculty. Because of these low numbers, however, there is a pressing need for the Catholic cluster to enjoy even greater legitimacy with faculty colleagues. If the knowledgeable cluster speaks clearly and with legitimate authority concerning what the promotion of Catholic culture at the institution requires, other colleagues should be willing to respect their expertise and, in most cases, accept their judgment.

Teacher interactions with students in a classroom comprise the most fundamental work of the university. This is the primary way practically all students become educated. From their earliest formal educational experience, students learn how much what is taught is affected by the teacher—a pattern that continues unabated in college. In most courses, faculty impact students by the way they teach and the material they select for student mastery. As first-year students quickly learn, two courses with the same title taught by different people are different learning experiences. Teachers all have distinct pedagogical styles. Some are better practitioners than others, more adept at clarifying complex material. Teachers attend to and emphasize topics differently in their classes, and because they have differing degrees of conviction about the importance of certain issues, the tone, temper, and trajectory of their classes vary widely. Faculty members are the people on the front lines of collegiate education, and senior administrators understand how important they are in advancing the religious identity and mission of the university. Consequently, administrators put great emphasis on the extent of the Catholic knowledge and commitment. Although many administrators cited non-Catholic faculty members who also made excellent contributions, Catholic faculty members were seen by administrators as a sine qua non, not only for the Catholic intellectual tradition to be transmitted but also for the Catholic culture to appear in the classroom.

Having a critical mass of faculty who are knowledgeable about the Catholic tradition is essential for colleges and universities to retain Catholic identity and support a vibrant Catholic culture. As important as religious knowledge is, however, it is not sufficient unto itself to sustain religious culture. Richard McBrien and James Provost both point out that for an institution to call itself Catholic, committed Catholics in significant numbers have to be part of the critical mass of individuals who are knowledgeable about the tradition. Most of the senior administrators interviewed in this study praised Catholic higher education for its unique capacity to integrate faith and reason. Talking about the integration of faith and reason, however, is not the same thing as actually integrating them. In order for this claim of Catholic colleges and universities to be legitimate, faculty members must actually bring faith and reason together in their own lives in a manner that is authentic and provocative for the entire community. The power of lived witness to catalyze culture and authenticate claims cannot be overestimated, as Pope Paul VI reminded us in *Evangelii Nunciandi*:

> Above all the Gospel must be proclaimed by witness. Take a Chris-
> tian or a handful of Christians who, in the midst of their own com-
> munity, show their capacity for understanding and acceptance, their
> sharing of life and destiny with other people, their solidarity with
> the efforts of all for whatever is noble and good. Let us suppose that,
> in addition, they radiate in an altogether simple and unaffected way
> their faith in values that go beyond current values, and their hope in
> something that is not seen, that one would not dare to imagine.
> Through this wordless witness these Christians stir up irresistible
> questions in the hearts of all those who see how they live. Why are
> they like this? Why do they live in this way? What or who is it that
> inspires them? Why are they in our midst? Such a witness is already
> a silent proclamation of the Good News and a very powerful and ef-
> fective one.[15]

In the intellectual community of Catholic colleges or universities, the pro-vocative questions that emerge in response to the lived witness of committed and knowledgeable faculty must go beyond silence and become part and parcel of the intellectual and formative conversation of the academy. The conversation that ensues, however, will be altogether different from how it might have been, because it was provoked by the authentic experience of witness in the faculty ranks. It will also have great currency in terms of enriching institutional Cath-olic culture.

Just as they did in terms of Catholic knowledge, the goals of each type of Catholic college or university give a general indication of the desired proportion of active and committed Catholic faculty members in the university and in particular disciplines. For Catholic immersion institutions to achieve their goals, a large proportion of the faculty will need to be Catholic. As noted earlier, in *Ex Corde Ecclesiae* Pope John Paul II says the proportion of Catholics should be no less than a majority. That number would seem to be an appropriate lower limit for the number of Catholic faculty at immersion universities. Students in immersion institutions are disposed to focus on "Catholic questions," and they are anxious to make connections or surface disagreements between sec-ular knowledge and Catholic teachings. Teachers who are knowledgeable, com-mitted Catholics can convey to students how they should integrate secular and religious knowledge.[16] There are some immersion universities whose faculties are comprised almost solely of Catholics, which poses some difficulties for the vitality of their intellectual culture. It is no more desirable for immersion university faculty to be universally Catholic than it is for the institution to lose its Catholic majority.[17] As the canonist James Provost points out, as long as they are among an active, committed and effective core of Catholic cultural catalysts, the presence of non-Catholics on the faculty can enrich the genuine, universal, "catholic" character of a university. The largest proportion of committed Catholic faculty is at immersion universities. In view of their stated goal that practically all students regularly have professors teaching their courses who are committed and practicing Catholics, setting a high percentage for informed Catholic faculty members is reasonable. Because Catholic culture is so stable at these institutions, the inclusion of some non-Catholic faculty contributes to the liveliness of their institutional religious culture, and assures that it remains responsive and attentive to new issues.

The majority of undergraduates at Catholic persuasion universities are Catholic, and the institutional religious goals of these institutions include educating Catholic students about Catholicism and the Catholic intellectual tradition. This necessitates that theology and philosophy departments (alternatively, the departments in which philosophical issues are addressed) at persuasion universities take the lead in terms of having a significant number of faculty who are committed and knowledgeable Catholics. Senior administrators at persuasion universities described their institutions as having a broad commitment to the Catholic intellectual tradition across disciplines. This commitment requires that a sizeable percentage of active and effective Catholics be teaching in the academic disciplines other than theology and philosophy, with presumably a higher percentage in the liberal arts-related disciplines.

By their design, Catholic diaspora and cohort institutions have a narrow connection to the Catholic tradition. In order to meet their religious goals, they must make sure that what this connection lacks in breadth is compensated for in terms of intensity. In order to demonstrate the vital integration of faith and reason, most tradition-knowledgeable faculty members at diaspora and cohort universities should be living witnesses of that tradition. That means that primarily Catholic faculty should be teaching Catholic theology and philosophy courses, as well as courses in specific disciplines with particularly rich Catholic connections and themes. This by no means necessitates that all faculty offering courses in these areas are Catholic. It does mean, however, that for courses in which Catholics are expected to dominate or for courses in which non-Catholics seek exposure to and greater insight into a Catholic worldview, knowledgeable and committed Catholic faculty should predominate. Simply put, because the academic connection to the Catholic tradition in both diaspora and cohort institutions is narrow, it also needs to be intense. It is important that students in these courses be exposed to a knowledgeable and committed Catholic teacher, who may well be their only personal contact with the Catholic faith in the academic sector.

At many Catholic universities, undergraduates enroll in business schools, schools of education, and programs or schools of performing arts (including music, drama, art history, and performance art). The Catholic intellectual tradition and the Catholic moral tradition have made important contributions in all three professions. It is important that knowledgeable faculty within these schools present and build on these Catholic contributions. Since the tradition is ongoing, it is also important that students hear from faculty members who are committed both to Catholic faith and to expanding the Catholic culture in their discipline.

At academic institutions, students learn by listening, reacting, imitating, and engaging their own creative intellectual faculties. For their part, faculty members find great satisfaction when students take their courses seriously and delve into the material with élan similar to their own. The dynamics of the relationship between student and teacher creates outstanding learning. In a Catholic university, students can learn much by interacting with faculty members who are knowledgeable about the Catholic faith, are informed about Catholic themes in their academic disciplines, and have a personal commitment to living their Catholic faith. In this kind of formative mentoring relationship, students come to learn about the faith interpersonally, and the knowledge and commitment that is shared contributes not only to their growth and development but to the depth and breadth of Catholic culture on campus as well.

As mentioned before, *Ex Corde Ecclesiae* says that non-Catholic faculty should not constitute a majority of the faculty. Arguably, the reason for this norm is that committed Catholics should be able to direct and influence the Catholic culture on campus, especially with respect to the curriculum. In fact, many Catholic colleges and universities in the United States of the persuasion, diaspora, or cohort variety do not currently have a majority of Catholic faculty.[18] For these institutions, it is important for the Catholic cluster of informed and committed Catholic faculty to work in a structure that permits this group to have asymmetric influence on the Catholic culture at the university. We return to this issue in the following two sections and offer one possible way to safeguard the Catholic culture with a predominantly non-Catholic faculty.

Visibility and Stature Count

In an academic environment, professional components of secular knowledge and commitment become known through publications, service on campus, and teaching. There is no comparable system that signals religious knowledge and commitment. In the present environment, faculty members with knowledge of and commitment to the Catholic faith and culture may be universally indistinguishable from anyone else on the faculty. An important challenge for the modern Catholic university is to enhance its distinguishability by elevating their visibility.

At the institutional level in a Catholic university, passing the distinguishability criterion means the institutional actors, content, or style differ in important ways from what is available at nonsectarian institutions. If the distinct ways are carefully designed, they result in different student outcomes that are, at least in principle, measurable. Distinguishability is a characteristic of an institution. Because it is very difficult to distinguish what you cannot find or identify, an important aspect of distinguishability is visibility. In order for a Catholic university to be distinguishable, there have to be some visible differences—some easy, fairly superficial things (which may point to much deeper realities) that people can identify that indicate that the institution is indeed Catholic.

Visibility can also be applied on a micro level, where it can refer to some easy, superficial way to identify someone belonging to a particular group within an institution. With religious sisters, for instance, the habit they wore identified them as belonging to a certain religious order. In the medical profession, for years, the traditional white coat easily identified some men and women as physicians. And in a situation that has more currency, a team uniform visibly distinguishes one sports team from another on the playing field.

Consider the example of baseball team A and B. Both may have the same strategy, the same culture, yet to anyone who can see their uniforms, they are visibly different entities. In comparing the two teams, it is quite possible to conclude that their cultures are fundamentally the same or indistinguishable. But because they wear different uniforms, they are visibly different and, at least in this superficial sense, they become distinguishable. Although visibility is only a superficial distinction, it can be a crucial one.

On Catholic campuses, sisters, brothers, and priests were known in three ways: they had distinctive titles, they wore distinctive garb, and many of those who worked at the university knew them personally. Even if people did not know a sister, brother, or priest personally, they understood that these individuals had distinctive training that gave them extensive knowledge of the Catholic faith and culture and had committed their lives to fostering that faith and culture.

In the twenty-first century at Catholic universities structured according to one of the four models, Catholic faculty with knowledge and commitment need to be visible in some appropriate manner. This is not to suggest that laypersons dress in any distinctive fashion. It does mean, however, there should be some way, short of personal knowledge, for faculty and students to know which persons of their group have accepted an extraordinary responsibility for nurturing Catholic culture through personal knowledge and faith commitment. Unless the university community has some easy, superficial ways of knowing which faculty members are informed about and committed to the Catholic faith, it is difficult for cultural catalysts and cultural citizens to emerge within a predominantly lay faculty at a Catholic institution. Visibility for such a group of informed and committed actors communicates to the university community at large that without religious knowledge and commitment, the university will not continue to flourish. Visibility also indicates that one group of people on campus legitimately holds a privileged place, in terms of helping the broader university community maintain its Catholic culture.

The visibility of religious congregations forty years ago enhanced their witness value at Catholic colleges and universities. These men and women stood out as religious exemplars whose vowed lives of service were a testament

to the power of their faith and the depth of their commitment to Christ and
his Church. When undergraduate students encountered them in the classroom
and on campus at Catholic institutions, they were often stunned that such
extraordinarily faith-filled people could hold their own and then some in the
rough and tumble of competitive academe. Their dual competency was compelling.

Today the situation is entirely different, but the potential witness value of
a cluster of religiously knowledgeable and committed faculty is equally great.
Laypersons on the faculty and in the administration are clearly talented professionals with all the requisite competencies that are expected in the academy.
What would be stunning to today's undergraduates is that these gifted higher
education professionals are also religious exemplars whose own lives of faith-
filled witness and service speak volumes about the power of their faith and the
depth of their commitment to Christ and his Church. They, too, have dual
competency, and when it is witnessed by undergraduates and others in the
collegiate community, it can also be compelling.

One type of visible characteristic for this new group of cultural exemplars
may be an asterisk in a listing of faculty and administrators, or perhaps something more extensive, such as membership in a certain society on campus that
brings together faculty and others who are committed keepers of the Catholic
culture. In addition to being noted on some list, members of this group might
wear a special pin or other insignia so that students know they can approach
these faculty members with faith issues. If a Catholic university is to retain a
vibrant Catholic culture, the Catholic faith and knowledge of faculty and administrators cannot remain a purely private affair—a light hidden under a
basket. There must be some appropriate way to make this group institutionally
visible and a cultural focal point for the whole community. The witness group
should also "give witness" visibly and publicly by involving itself in some particular practices. By being publicly associated with events that include faith-
related intellectual activities and service, as well as prayer and worship, and by
inviting other members of the university community to participate, this knowledgeable and committed cluster will provide essential witness to the full dimensions of the Catholic mission of the university.[19]

In the Catholic university culture of the twenty-first century, one further
characteristic, beyond knowledge, commitment, and visibility, is required. People who are informed, knowledgeable, and visible must enjoy some stature in
the institution with respect to advancing Catholic projects or modifying the
Catholic culture on campus. In this context, "stature" means that the group is
deemed legitimate by faculty, who are disposed to listen to them appreciatively
and to follow their advice when the group addresses important issues related
to Catholic identity, character, and mission. In a particular instance, there may
be good reasons for the faculty to choose not to follow the advice of this group,
but the assumption here is that the faculty members who do not belong to this
Catholic witness cluster are inclined to follow their advice, because members
of this group give authentic witness to the Catholic tradition at this college or

university and because the broader faculty are committed to retaining the Catholic mission of the institution.

As a practical matter, the group of informed and committed men and women must also have reasonable resources to function effectively. The group should be provided with some resources that enable them to monitor the Catholic culture on campus and make recommendations. Different ways to effectively accommodate this need depend in part on the particular organizational structure at the institution. Perhaps in conjunction with one of the senior administrators, the group can request and be provided with data, and a modest budget can be established to consult with experts on Catholic culture at Catholic universities.

The group of informed and committed Catholics is not identical with the combined group of cultural catalysts and cultural citizens. For one thing, it is easy to think of cultural catalysts or citizens who are not Catholic. While not Catholic, these individuals are strongly committed to maintaining the university as a Catholic institution. Second, not everyone who is informed about and committed to the Catholic faith will be a cultural catalyst or leader. Catalysts, be they faculty members, administrators or staff, have to be willing to speak up, float ideas, receive reaction and criticism, persuade and cajole. Leadership is never easy, and it is particularly challenging at an institution where the group of informed and committed Catholics is a fraction of the overall faculty and staff. Cultural citizens, following the lead of cultural catalysts, sustain the culture and support important changes that enhance the Catholic culture. They also use their imagination and skills to implement cultural changes in effective ways. In general, the number of cultural citizens is much larger than the number of cultural catalysts, and cultural citizens also need not be committed to the Catholic faith as their personal persuasion.

Although many non-Catholics with some knowledge of the Catholic faith and culture and a deep commitment to the Catholic culture on campus are excellent cultural citizens and some can be outstanding cultural catalysts, it is still important to have an identifiable group of dramatic exemplars who are both informed and committed Catholic faculty. Catholics who actively participate in their faith develop a deep appreciation for the liturgy. They are also in an ideal position to perceive opportunities to strengthen the faith formation of young adults. Actively involved Catholics can also speak from personal religious experience about what promotes a lifelong commitment to living the faith. Informed and committed Catholics should not have the only say about cultivating Catholic culture, but they should have similar legitimacy around issues pertaining to Catholic identity, culture, and mission to that once enjoyed by the sponsoring religious congregation.

If there is an identifiable group of informed and committed Catholic faculty, the group cannot function effectively without visible support from other members of the university community.[20] As senior administrators noted in their interviews, the role of non-Catholic leaders, either among faculty or administrators, can be decisive. Because they are not Catholics themselves, they have a certain distance from whatever project is being proposed. If the project meets their approval, many faculty members may be persuaded that it is good for the university. In this type of academic culture, all members of the faculty have an important say, whether they be Catholic or non-Catholic. Some legitimate authority regarding knowledge, experience, and commitment is necessary, however, and this expertise will emerge from the distinct group that is prepared and willing to assume that responsibility.

In small institutions with fewer than one hundred faculty members, the need for a witness cluster might not appear to be great. After all, at such institutions, new faculty members are invited into a rather small community in which it is relatively easy to learn "who's who" and which faculty are the religious cultural leaders and mentors for their peers. Claiming that young faculty at smaller institutions soon learn "who's who" in terms of Catholic culture, however, neglects an important feature of modern academic culture. Even at colleges where faculty regularly spend most days in their offices interacting with colleagues, the majority identify closely with colleagues in their own academic discipline or related disciplines. Ideally, because Catholic universities claim and show that knowledge is interconnected, young faculty members develop an interest in learning the interests and projects of other faculty members. Realistically, however, most young faculty are focused on tenure and likely to commit available free time to doing research and writing papers, not chatting informally with colleagues about various aspects of the Catholic intellectual tradition and how it might relate to the classes the new faculty member is teaching.

In modern society, religion is assumed to be exercised in the private sphere at a discrete distance from any professional commitments. Within this larger cultural reality, faculty members have a natural tendency to recoil from any system that identifies individual faculty members as particularly prepared, committed, and responsible for the religious identity, mission, and culture of the institution. In this milieu, religious witness is seen as an unspoken force that beckons purely by example without clear explanation, articulated invitation, or institutional support. The delicacy of this approach conforms closely to the prevailing American culture, but by failing to assert a place of privilege for the defining religious tradition, it undermines institutional distinctiveness and compromises religious culture. The Catholic culture on campus is a precious and always vulnerable asset that needs attention and care.

In most nonimmersion universities, the majority of lay faculty members simply choose to sidestep Catholic identity and culture issues at their institutions. This pattern was well established during the long history of Catholic institutions, when sisters, brothers, and priests were in charge and laypersons deferred to their "expertise" in things religious rather than taking the lead themselves. The sisters, brothers, and priests are, however, no longer able to provide the role modeling, knowledge expertise, and heroic leadership necessary to guarantee a viable future for Catholic institutions. Laypersons are now responsible for providing this leadership. To suggest that Catholic colleges and universities reestablish a cluster of visible and authoritative Catholic faculty who embody tradition knowledge and religious commitment may seem radical to some and quite conservative to others. In truth, because this approach replicates a pattern that was deeply entrenched and well respected over a long period of time, the recommendation is in fact somewhat conservative. This system worked well in many Catholic institutions for several decades.[21] Faculty members are still the heart of the university, and it is appropriate and fitting that some able, willing, and committed faculty be entrusted by their colleagues with the responsibility to act as knowledge experts and role models with respect to Catholic culture on campus. As long as a new generation of faculty is willing to assume this role in terms of Catholic culture and mission, Catholic universities should support and encourage them, and embrace their leadership.

In recent decades, parents sent their sons and daughters to Catholic institutions in the hopes that they would receive an education that was truly "Franciscan" or "Jesuit" or "Dominican," regardless of whether they ever took a class with a member of the congregation. Since there were still members of these congregations on campus, their influence was informally judged to be sufficiently significant to produce a congregationally distinctive education. In light of the decreased involvement of religious congregations on campus, the appropriate aspirations for collegiate education are no longer well placed by focusing on the sponsoring religious congregation. Rather, the attention of students and parents must focus on the Catholic content of the education.

In our judgment, students do not receive a Catholic education if they never take a course from a Catholic faculty member who links some course material to the Catholic faith. A central activity of the university is learning about the Catholic faith and reflecting on it. A student may choose to make the Catholic faith the focus of a paper or of a course, but a Catholic student at a nonsectarian university could also choose to do this. A minimum for a student to receive a Catholic education is to learn significant things about the Catholic faith from a sympathetic and informed Catholic faculty member. It is not possible for students at immersion universities to avoid having several courses each year taught by informed and committed Catholics. To make this likely, setting a goal of 75 percent of the faculty being informed Catholics makes good sense for immersion institutions. The important issue of who gets a Catholic education arises at persuasion, diaspora, and cohort universities.

The value added by attending a Catholic persuasion university should be suspect if students could fulfill the various requirements for an undergraduate degree and never take a course from a faculty member who was knowledgeable about and committed to the Catholic faith. Students, of course, ultimately make their own choices about specific courses or particular sections of a course. If a student intentionally avoids taking courses from this group of faculty, no one but the student is to blame. That said, however, it is reasonable for students and parents to expect that at a persuasion university, it would be practically impossible for students to avoid these cultural mentors altogether. Having at least 25 percent of the faculty identified as informed and committed Catholics in persuasion institutions makes it very likely that most students will have such teachers for their required or elective courses. If with 25 percent of the faculty being informed and committed Catholics a number of students can adroitly weave their way through the curriculum without encountering Catholic role models and knowledge experts among their faculty, the university will need to make significant adjustments. The norm of 25 percent will work, in our judgment, if the special subgroup of informed and committed faculty members who assume responsibility for the Catholic culture on campus enjoy prestige on campus and, on most issues relating to Catholic culture, are permitted to set the norms.

Judging a diaspora or cohort university by the norm of every student having to take at least one course from an informed and committed Catholic member of the faculty is more problematic. The diaspora university does not claim to offer a broad array of courses in the Catholic faith. On the other hand, senior administrators at diaspora and other institutions have expressed an interest in having more Catholic themes addressed in regular liberal arts courses. At a diaspora institution, it should be fairly easy for a student to take a course offered by an informed and committed Catholic faculty member. A similar analysis would apply for a Catholic cohort institution. Of course, students within the Catholic studies component of the latter type of university should have this experience quite readily. Since the goal of Catholic cohort universities is to sensitize and inform all students about significant religious issues, all students—whether or not they are Catholic—ideally should have a collegiate experience in one course with a faculty member from this witness group. Practically speaking, however, it would be difficult to require this of students. At the very least, those students enrolled outside the Catholic studies program at a Catholic cohort institution should be able to take courses from informed and committed Catholics with relative ease.

At diaspora and cohort institutions, the number of faculty needed for students to receive instruction from informed and committed Catholic faculty depends in large part on the percent of Catholic students at the diaspora institution and the size (relative to the total number of undergraduates) of the Catholic cohort of students at the cohort university. Catholic cohort students should have most of their Catholic studies courses taught by informed and committed Catholics. If one considers student requirements alone, having 10 or 15 percent of the faculty as informed and committed Catholics may be sufficient. However, for these two types of universities, the more binding constraint is likely to be the percent of informed and committed Catholics needed to make sure that the subgroup assuming responsibility for Catholic culture on campus has the stature and prestige necessary in the broader faculty. In our judgment, a large portion of the faculty is unlikely to grant a very small subgroup general authority to determine Catholic culture on campus if a good number of them are not Catholic. Thus, for diaspora and cohort institutions, having at least 15 or 20 percent of the faculty Catholic is a reasonable criterion.

Gaining Catholic Knowledge and Stature

Comments by senior administrators showed strong support for having faculty members who can represent well the Catholic intellectual and faith tradition in the classroom. However, the same administrators expressed concern over the Catholic knowledge base of faculty, and many had an agnostic stance about the extent to which Catholic faculty were committed Catholics. Administrators spoke little about faculty members being averse to the Catholic tradition but worried deeply about what they described as their indifference. Senior administrators were clearly at a loss about where to find faculty who would be able and willing to articulate and support the Catholic tradition in their institutions.

The first issue that concerned administrators can be effectively addressed without a great deal of difficulty. If Catholic faculty are willing cultural citizens, they can develop the necessary knowledge base to effectively engage important Catholic themes in their academic disciplines. There are a number of paths they can pursue that will enhance their knowledge, including through their own reading. Faculty summer and intersession seminars conducted with expertise in the intersection of a particular academic discipline and the Catholic intellectual tradition is another more structured path that has the advantage of providing a cluster of similarly inclined faculty colleagues. While the focus of such seminars might be almost exclusively on the Catholic themes contained in a particular discipline, broader questions about the tradition would naturally arise. Over time, faculty would develop greater understanding and insight about Catholicism, as well as about Catholic themes in their own academic discipline.

The thornier issue administrators raised was hinted at more than spoken: Is there a sufficient number of faculty who are interested in becoming better informed about Catholic themes, are committed to the Catholic faith, and are willing to acknowledge to the university community that they are committed Catholics? That is a factual question we cannot answer. Apparently, the senior administrators are also incapable of answering the question for faculty at their own institution. Since they were apprehensive, it suggests that they realize that there are too few Catholic faculty members willing to sign on in any of these three categories.

Such apprehensions may prove to be unfounded, but even if they are true, the problem can be addressed, and things can turn around. Cultural indifference grows when the culture seems secure, when no one is seriously discussing how to sustain or enhance it, when leadership is ambivalent, when cultural citizens are not cultivated, and when the critical issues of inheritability are not addressed. For a good many years, Catholic colleges and universities believed that their religious culture was strong and their academic and intellectual culture was less robust. In this environment, there was great emphasis on the need to strengthen both the intellectual climate and the performance outcomes of graduates from Catholic colleges and universities. Presidents of Catholic colleges and boards of trustees, as well as sponsors, pushed the agenda of greater intellectual rigor, and the faculty bore down on the issue with tenacity, focusing energy and enthusiasm on reshaping departments through strategic hiring. It all worked, and without a doubt, Catholic colleges and universities now have a better reputation for academic excellence and intellectual rigor than they did forty years ago. If Catholic colleges and universities take it upon themselves to address the serious issues related to Catholic identity, culture, and mission that face them today as tenaciously as they addressed the problem of second-rate scholarship, the issue will be resolved. When the religious cultural issues are named, discussions about how the institutions themselves can make effective cultural changes become richer and more numerous; presidents, boards of trustees, and sponsors start driving the process of cultural adaptation; and faculty members are made aware of the critical issues involved and their serious implications for the entire educational enterprise, things will change. Once this effort is begun in earnest, dramatic and dynamic cultural adaptations will follow.

The best way for a Catholic university to move forward, in terms of strengthening the Catholic culture on campus, is to begin with what can be accomplished in a relatively straightforward manner. Many administrators asserted wistfully that to turn things around required the emergence of a brilliant new leader. They spoke admiringly of Fr. Theodore Hesburgh, C.S.C., a national figure in education and public service who provided thirty-five years of dynamic leadership to the University of Notre Dame as its president. He was also a leader for Catholic higher education in general and a national leader as well. In our hearts we all hope that once again in our lifetimes someone of Father Hesburgh's capacity, courage, stature, and creativity will come to the fore and galvanize hope and energy in American Catholic higher education. In the meantime, we need to get on with things. Catholic colleges and universities do not need to have an overarching grand plan or one dynamic leader for the entire enterprise to make cultural changes and adaptations. Each and every institution can begin by initiating some project for interested faculty focused on engaging Catholic themes in a few academic disciplines that attract a large number of students. If this is a positive experience for those who participate, it will draw additional faculty to subsequent faculty seminars or to whatever initiative for faculty is adopted.

If, for various personal or professional reasons, faculty members at a particular institution are reluctant to become better informed about Catholic themes in their academic disciplines, a hiring strategy needs to be adopted. After all, that was precisely the path that Catholic colleges and universities followed to enhance their academic reputations. As a first step in activating this strategy, the chief academic officer has to verify that faculty truly are indifferent and then the officer will need to share the problem with faculty leaders. The officer can assure faculty that their wishes to learn more about the Catholic intellectual and faith tradition will be respected. However, since the institution must have religious cultural catalysts and citizens on the faculty if its religious culture is to survive, Catholic knowledge and commitment must be considered important factors in future faculty hires at the university. This may be contrary to the personal inclinations of some faculty, but the needs of the institution have to be given appropriate consideration. It can be presented to faculty that, as a particular type of Catholic institution (immersion, persuasion, diaspora, or cohort), the university needs more informed and committed faculty in certain disciplines, and getting them will be a priority in the coming years.

For a Catholic institution functioning in this way, it is important that informed and committed Catholic faculty be clearly visible to other faculty and to students as a witness cluster of individuals who embrace the responsibility to cultivate the Catholic culture and mission of the university. The way this Catholic culture cluster is identified should be transparent and enjoy the support of faculty in general. The faculty in general must legitimate this faculty cluster's authority in terms of their expertise concerning Catholic culture, especially Catholic academic culture. The Catholic culture cluster should only speak as a group when recommending something they consider vital to the Catholic culture on campus. If the group has legitimate authority within the faculty body, when they speak in this way on such a topic their wisdom will be seriously considered and, all other things being equal, the broader faculty will be disposed to follow their advice.

The desideratum is that the Catholic culture cluster be seen as legitimate inheritors of the stewardship role that religious congregations assumed on Catholic university campuses for much of their history. With the exception of religious sponsors, at most institutions no such knowledgeable and committed group presently exists, let alone enjoys the respect of their colleagues as uniquely qualified to speak on matters that pertain to the institution's Catholic identity. For a Catholic culture cluster to serve this function, they will first have to earn the respect of the faculty over time. Faculty members who are identified in some reasonable way as being both knowledgeable about and committed to the Catholic faith have to demonstrate their competence and work respectfully with other faculty, to explain appropriately and convincingly what steps, innovations, or additions will strengthen the Catholic culture, but especially the Catholic academic culture, on campus. They also have to succeed in persuading the rest of the faculty to act.

The most challenging phase in developing a respected Catholic culture cluster will be in the first years. At many Catholic universities, some changes in the academic culture will have to be undertaken in the next few years. Faculty at large and the emerging Catholic culture cluster will have to proceed carefully, respecting one another. All the faculty will also have to be willing to trust the considered judgment of this group that is taking particular responsibility for safeguarding and strengthening the Catholic academic culture on campus.

Administration and Institutional Culture

While the chief providers of a Catholic education are the faculty, administrators play an essential role in terms of sustaining and enhancing the culture of the university. Terence Murphy describes the impact of their work on Catholic culture and identity:

> One group that certainly must have a clear grasp of the mission and identity of the university is the administration. It is so intimately interwoven with the fabric of the university that failure to understand or to believe in the mission is a prescription for failure. Since the president is the head of the administration, this may seem to be a truism. It nevertheless needs emphasis because the administration is scattered across the institution and is of key importance in setting the tone and direction. For it is administrators at various levels with whom faculty and students mostly interact. They can further the mission or possibly set it aside in their day-to-day work.[22]

Many of the same principles that determine what comprises a critical mass of knowledgeable and committed people necessary for any institution to call itself Catholic apply to administration, as well as to faculty. Administrators need to be well informed about the Catholic faith and willing and able to engage its teaching as it appropriately applies to their given sector. What constitutes an appropriate level of knowledge will vary, depending on the model of Catholic institution in which the administrators work and on the nature of the work they do. Administrators working in the financial divisions of the university, for instance, do not need to be as knowledgeable as administrators in the area of student and residence life. Much as in the academic sector, there need to be some staff members in each administrative division who are informed about the issues critical to the Catholic tradition that impinge on what makes their work authentic and faithful within the context of a Catholic institution. Administrators, like their faculty colleagues, need support, and a cluster of administrators who are knowledgeable about the tradition will provide that support. A cluster will also be more successful in terms of influencing decision-making within various units of the university.

Administrators, as well as faculty members, operate as role models, knowledge experts, and cultural catalysts at Catholic universities, and among them must be a critical mass of active, committed Catholics who bring their own lived experience to bear in the institutions in which they serve. The complexities of assessing what exactly is the number that represents a critical mass of active and committed Catholics is no less difficult in the ranks of administrators than it is among faculty, with one possible exception—the president. Senior administrators were unanimous in maintaining that Catholic college and university presidents should be active, committed, and knowledgeable Catholics.[23] Presidents are the most public standard-bearers of the university's self-understanding and its most public role models. Presidents articulate institutional self-understanding and shape institutional culture. The president sets the tone for the rest of the university and must exemplify the highest level of cultural integration. It is difficult to imagine how a president can effectively lead a Catholic institution without embracing the faith both as a personal conviction and as a professional responsibility. As indicated in chapter 10, how the need for knowledgeable and committed Catholics in all sectors of the university is interpreted by presidents hiring a senior team will vary according to the president's own leadership style and assessment of institutional need. All presidents, whatever their own approach, must ensure that each division of the university has the requisite levels of Catholic knowledge and commitment necessary for moving the institution forward and the leadership to make that happen.

Being known as a committed Catholic faculty member or administrator imposes a burden and the clear expectation of fidelity to the Church and its teachings and of active participation in its sacramental life. The willingness of some faculty, staff, and administrators to be identified in this way and held accountable in the public forum is a great contribution to the Catholic university. By their knowledge, their witness, and their visible service, they will prove apt and worthy successors to the religious men and women whose legacy of Catholic cultural cultivation they will carry on.

PART III

Recommendations

9

Cultural Collapse and Religious Congregations of Women

This chapter focuses on religious congregations of women as a case study in cultural change and its effects on organizations. While the resourcefulness of religious congregations is highlighted, their experience also offers a cautionary tale. These groups of women exist within the larger Roman Catholic Church. Throughout their history, the sisterhoods faced social and cultural realities that demanded they change and adapt. At various points, at least up until the Second Vatican Council, these women made the necessary adaptations that sustained, supported, and enhanced their organizational culture.[1] After Vatican II, however, the dramatic cultural adjustments congregations made over more than three decades resulted in the collapse of their organizational culture.

Although any number of organizations, including religious congregations of men, could serve as a case study in cultural adaptation, we deem the experience of religious congregations of women to be particularly instructive. A comparative study of cultural change in congregations of men and women would provide a more nuanced picture of how and why these groups of vowed religious approached adaptation similarly and differently. Nevertheless, for the purposes of this book, it seemed most reasonable to use a single example to illustrate the difficulty involved in cultural change, and we chose to look at women's religious congregations and did so for a number of reasons.

Arguably, nuns have been the primary transmitters of Catholic culture in the history of the United States who, through their apostolic works, shaped how Americans Catholics understood themselves. Women religious taught 30 to 40 percent of American Catholic schoolchildren in Catholic parochial schools.[2] They also founded the largest number of Catholic college and universities in the United States. The cultural vibrancy of religious congregations contributed extensively to the religious culture of the colleges they founded, and a deeper understanding of their history provides useful insights about the cultural issues facing Catholic colleges and universities today.

Lora Ann Quinonez and Mary Daniel Turner point out what makes the changes in religious congregations of women so interesting. These women deliberately chose to undertake corporate transformation, and they made this decision collectively.[3] Their organizational changes were also highly visible and provocative in the wider culture, if for no other reason than their collective decision to do away with habits, their "distinctive black-and-white garb" that Elizabeth Kuhns tells us served "as a universal representation of holiness—a mysterious and evocative cultural icon that has defined the Catholic sister."[4] The visibility of these changes was also more substantively heightened by the fact that they were the subject of a good deal of scholarly research. In exploring elements of the cultural change process, this chapter draws on a number of studies—some conducted by women religious and others by outside researchers.[5]

The story of cultural change in sisterhoods is also particularly useful to our purposes in this book. Analyzing sisterhoods' development, with heightened regard to colleges and universities, can help point to the type of knowledge and commitment needed to sustain Catholic culture in modern Catholic universities. Finally, we chose to look at the women religious because one of us has spent the better part of ten years working with and researching them. It seemed natural and appropriate to build on that foundation.

Prior to the 1960s, women in American Catholic sisterhoods were clearly distinguishable in all their ministerial works, including Catholic colleges. Easily recognizable in distinctive religious garb, these women led lives committed to making the Catholic tradition institutionally vibrant and personally transferable within their institutions. Assuring Catholic cultural clarity and cohesion, they were a highly visible witness community of role models and knowledge experts whose intense culture permeated their institutions. Even without distinctive dress, however, these women would have been a distinguishable group because their preparation, formation, and group activities rendered them knowledgeable, committed, visible, and consequently capable of transmitting the Catholic culture they personally embodied. Until about the 1940s, religious women, unlike priests, were not required and, unfortunately, not even allowed to have broad-based theological training as part of their formation process.[6] Despite this lacuna, for generations these women were arguably the chief cultural transmitters of the Catholic tradition in the United States.

Catholic higher education for women in the United States was one of the many institutional arenas in which nuns made an impact. These institutions established a foothold in the United States primarily in the first half of the twentieth century. They were outgrowths of the academies for girls that the nuns had founded earlier in the nineteenth century and that were flourishing by the end of the century. In 1900, only a handful of colleges were operating, but by 1950, the number of Catholic colleges for women numbered 116, and by 1968 there were more than 170 colleges and 70 sister formation colleges.[7] These institutions were founded with an eye to meeting the needs of local communities and the emerging Catholic Church, and they served a broad range of students in a variety of different kinds of institutions.

The sisters who founded, led, and taught in Catholic colleges received the general training common to all sisters in postulancy and novitiate programs. Religious formation was intense and tailored to serve both spiritual and apostolic goals of young sisters. It combined a congregationally infused, broad-based Roman Catholic spirituality with a pragmatic, rather than intellectually inspired, professional education. Of necessity, this formation provided the basics that enabled young nuns to get started in their apostolic ministries, which included teaching, health care, orphanages, and social work.[8] Postulancy and novitiate generally comprised a two-year formation experience that was marked by a combination of unique particularity and striking uniformity.[9] There was little cooperation among congregations, and a good deal of formation experience focused on the distinctive culture and charism[10] of each particular order. But, aside from some distinctive heritage-based differences, most formation programs were quite similar and included a three- to six-month postulancy that was intensely cohort based. This period was followed by the novitiate, "a highly structured educational experience that assimilated the novices into the community, educated them spiritually, psychologically and academically, and provided them with a . . . trial period before they took their first vows."[11]

The young women aspirants were placed in the charge of the mistress of novices, who served as a knowledge expert and a role model for religious life. As the young women moved from one stage of formation to the next, their involvement with congregation members expanded from interaction with only their own cohort to increasing contact with professed sisters.[12] Likewise, they moved from doing largely domestic work such as cooking, cleaning, sewing, and mending to being involved more fully as apostolic apprentices, who worked along with professed sisters. Although the life of novices was highly structured, most sisters found the regimen satisfying, and many sisters were grateful for their novitiate training. During this time they formed important friendships and a real esprit de corps with the cohort of young women who would be their partners in ministry for years to come. Novitiate training was strict, but it was more lively than lugubrious.[13]

Most entrants to religious congregations had a basic understanding of the beliefs, values, and norms of Catholic culture when they entered. That knowledge was reinforced and supplemented with books and articles written for religious communities. There was little flexibility in either the content or approach to learning in most formation programs. The approach largely entailed memorization of rote answers to questions about the meaning of vows and spiritual perfection and "a body of rules, and distinctions among degrees of virtue and culpability—all presented as unchanging fact."[14] This approach to formation helped create a tightly knit organizational culture and, at least minimally, prepared the sisters to do their ministerial work. Looking back, the limitations for individual sisters of this approach are clear. However, the culture of the times, internal financial stresses, and escalating demands for service to the Church gave congregations little choice but to structure formation at a very basic level.

Prepared by basic spiritual formation and rudimentary professional education that continued over many years, women religious set about the business of founding and growing an impressive sector of Catholic higher education in the United States in the years from 1900 to 1950. Women religious were motivated to found colleges and to pursue higher levels of education themselves because they were addressing a critical educational need in the Catholic population.[15]

Religious Women and Their Colleges

With the expansion of parochial schools and the rising waves of Catholic immigration, religious congregations were constantly trying to keep up with the demand for their sisters to open and staff schools. As a result, most nuns were sent out to teach directly after novitiate, and they attended college on weekends and during the summer. It was, therefore, not at all unusual for a sister to take twenty years to earn her degree.[16] Two approaches to dealing with this problem emerged. The first was a Sisters' College associated with the Catholic University of America in Washington, D.C.

This college was path-breaking since Catholic colleges for men were disinclined to accept any women, even women religious, as students, and secular institutions were considered a threat to faith and vocation and therefore an unacceptable alternative for sisters. With increasing pressure being put on Catholic parents to educate their children in Catholic schools, the idea of sisters being educated in secular institutions seemed scandalous. Consequently, with the support of a number of religious superiors, the Very Reverend Dr. Thomas Shields succeeded in opening the Sisters' College as a four-year college for sisters only.[17] This bold approach encountered difficulties.

Religious congregations of women did not wholeheartedly support the Sisters' College. Superiors and educators feared the comingling of sisters would blur congregational distinctions and weaken ties to their orders.[18] The stiff cost of educating sisters at the Sisters' College also proved problematic.[19] Faced with the possibility of weakened congregational identity and enormous financial cost, a significant number of superiors determined that the most feasible way to educate their sisters was to open their own colleges. In most cases, these were normal colleges that eventually were opened to lay women seeking to meet the increasing demands of state certification for teaching.[20]

By the 1940s, the professional preparation of sisters began to surface as a significant issue that would have serious implications for the growth of colleges in the latter part of the century. Increasing standards for teacher certification combined with the first major study, by Sr. Bertrande Meyers, D.C., of the teacher training religious women received brought the question of professional training to the fore in Catholic educational circles in the early years of the 1940s.[21] Sr. Madeleva Wolff, C.S.C., a champion of the cause of improving theological education for women in Catholic colleges, became a driving force in the ensuing debates and discussions. After Bertrande Meyers's study, Sister Madeleva shifted her focus from theological training for sisters, particularly those who taught at the college level, to the training of all sisters who taught. She recommended that all young sisters be allowed to receive degrees before beginning their teaching careers at the college, high school, or elementary level. This position represented a drastic departure from the work-study approach common among most congregations at the time and fueled congregational discussions about sister preparation over the course of the next twenty years.[22]

The debate about how best to prepare women religious for teaching in schools and colleges continued to roil, and in 1952 it entered a new phase. Three things came together that changed the dynamics around the question. First, a papal statement encouraged sisters to alter outmoded customs and meet the professional standards of their day. This combined with increasing pressure emanating from state certification requirements to improve educational standards of teaching sisters. Finally, a new type of cultural catalyst among sisters who pushed the preparation agenda emerged at just the right time to combine with the other forces to bring both urgency and action on the sister preparation question.

Sr. Emil Penet, I.H.M., of Marygrove College in Detroit, pointed out that a lack of time and resources, coupled with poor understanding about the importance of the issue, hobbled the efforts of women religious to improve sister preparation.[23] She was instrumental in providing convincing data to the National Catholic Education Association (NCEA) convention in 1953 and spearheaded the creation of the Sister Formation Conference, modeled after the National Education Association. The new commission allowed sister-teachers to have more "say" about their own professional situation. By 1954, the Sister Formation Conference was approved as a subunit of NCEA, and Sister Emil provided its leadership. The Sister Formation Movement flourished for only about ten years. During that time, however, numerous sister formation colleges were started. Because these colleges were only for religious women, they were often very small and were not accredited. By 1962, the NCEA registered concern about "the undue multiplication of new, small, unaccredited Catholic colleges." Mary Oates points out that by the mid-1960s, increasing pressure from faculty and administration to have novices and junior sisters attend classes at established colleges finally overcame the objections of many superiors to the mingling of lay and sister students. This move to include sisters in what was perceived as the "richer intellectual climate of the college campus" brought the Sister Formation Movement to an end. The Sister Formation Movement was not long-lived, but it was an important bridge that, as Mary Oates notes, "fostered intercommunity cooperation, hitherto stoutly resisted by most communities."[24]

As the number of Catholic young women seeking college education increased, sisters expanded their normal colleges to admit them, and the normal colleges gradually transformed themselves into small four-year liberal arts colleges.[25] By the 1960s, religious congregations of women had established the majority of Catholic colleges in the United States. Over the course of sixty years, these colleges developed in response to the specific needs of students for liberal, professional, and vocational education within a thoroughly Catholic milieu. The sisters encountered grave financial obstacles in building and growing these colleges, and they survived because of the enormous sacrifices women religious made on their behalf. Contributed services of sisters who taught in colleges, along with financial support from all sisters, whatever their apostolic works, gifts from generous benefactors, and the study-as-you-go plan for professional education helped these colleges to take root and grow.[26]

From the late nineteenth century to 1960, the education of the sisters developed from initial apprentice-based preparation to a requirement that all sisters have a high school education and finally to an insistence that all sisters receive a complete baccalaureate degree, with most going on for master's-level study. At the colleges, the same kind of developmental pattern was repeated in response to the needs of the students and the demands of the time. As a result, by the 1960s, most sister-faculty either had doctorates or were in doctoral programs.

The period beginning in the mid-1960s saw tremendous changes within religious congregations and within their colleges as well. The pattern of advanced study and professionalization of women religious had shifted from what Mary Daigler terms "the pragmatic to the personalized," following patterns from less to more specialization in the wider educational milieu.[27] In this period the needs of the sisters-sponsored institutions no longer drove the educational preparation of women religious; rather, sisters studied what they preferred, not necessarily what their colleges needed. Upon completion of their degrees, there was no guarantee a position would be available in the sponsored institution, and frequently sisters went to other institutions, many of them secular, where they believed their education could best be used.

This escalating enhancement of educational opportunities for women religious is not the whole story and, in fact, can be misleading. Throughout its history in the United States, the structure of religious life itself has worked against the intellectual achievement of sisters. In 1996, the Brookland Commission published the findings of an extensive study about the value of intellectual life in the sisterhoods. The sisters had reported "a complex set of factors militates against women religious doing research and writing. Among these it named lack of time, resources, solitude, encouragement, and regular interaction with top professional in their fields. [Also, they said] publishing is neither expected nor rewarded."[28] The same difficulties were even more intense and dispiriting to nuns prior to the Second Vatican Council and impeded the development of vibrant academic cultures in many colleges run by religious congregations.[29]

The change in the way sisters were prepared for teaching, especially at the college level, was followed by a cultural shift in America in the early 1960s. Tremendous social changes in the country and a call for renewal within the Church and religious congregations by the Second Vatican Council altered the cultural landscape within congregations and within their colleges as well. As women religious identified increasingly with issues of social justice and the needs of the poor, fewer sisters were available or interested in working in the colleges. Many of the best educated sisters left religious life altogether. With fewer numbers, an increased sensitivity to the shared baptismal call of the laity, and rising financial worries, women religious brought laypersons onto boards of trustees and increasingly into faculty positions and administrative posts. This trend brought great benefits to women religious and the colleges they founded, but it also had a negative impact over time, particularly in terms of their colleges' Catholic cultures. Although in many instances the laypersons hired were committed Catholics, as their number increased relative to the number of nuns, the special impact of the religious sisters was attenuated. Many congregations did not find ways to enable committed lay Catholics to have a primary influence within their unit or division of the college, as happened naturally if a nun were active in the unit. These changes were subtle in the late 1950s and early 1960s, but eventually the lack of a process for investing committed Catholic laypersons with authority at various levels and in various units of the college had important consequences, as large waves of change began to wash over many of these institutions.

The group of religious women who had once permeated the colleges they founded, as teachers, administrators, role models, and leaders, started to disappear at the same time the colleges were faced with their own upheavals. Secularizing impulses challenged the strong Catholic orientation of the institutions. A rise in consumer demand for coeducation over single-sex collegiate education swept the nation. A feminist perspective that stressed equal opportunity and the breaking down of walls that kept women in separate spheres fueled the enthusiasm for coeducation among women. Vatican II loosened the reins holding back Catholic students from attending the elite institutions whose own Protestant sectarian heritage was fading. As a result of the latter change, the broad stream of highly gifted and qualified Catholic students who previously would only consider attending Catholic colleges lost much of its force. Catholic women's colleges not only faced increasing competitive pressures during this period but also had to bear escalating costs, as new technology became de rigueur at sophisticated colleges and universities. Any one of these changes would have been sufficient to disorient a goodly number of Catholic institutions. The combined impact on Catholic colleges founded by women religious was, in most cases, destabilizing. To maintain solvency, these institutions had to scramble and innovate. They did so without sufficient time to ponder the impact that some of the changes made in haste would have, not only on the colleges themselves but also on their founding religious congregations.[30]

After the 1960s, the ties that bound religious congregations to their colleges loosened. In the process, the Catholic identity of these institutions, formerly taken for granted when religious women had been present on campus in abundance, began to erode. In response, the colleges and universities found it necessary to both reclaim and reframe their Catholic and congregational identity, but they had to do so without relying on the commitment and knowledge of the nuns. The intellectual and professional knowledge of the sisters had developed over time, particularly as they sought to compete with secular institutions, but it was always seen as uniquely connected to the religious knowledge they received as committed members of religious congregations. The emerging challenge related more and more to specialized knowledge, as well as the frameworks of religious meaning traditionally emphasized by the sisters. How religious knowledge and commitment were cultivated and sustained and how these traditional values were related to the increasingly specialized knowledge sisters were acquiring created a tension for women religious in higher education that had to be resolved.

Religious Knowledge and Commitment

Prior to the 1960s, the religious knowledge and commitment imparted and encouraged in formation prepared sisters in unique ways for their responsibilities to students in Catholic colleges and universities. These Catholic educators were expected not only to meet the liberal and vocational educational needs of their students but also to enhance their spiritual lives and prepare them for their roles as Catholic wives and mothers. Eileen Brewer points out that in the period from the late nineteenth century to the 1920s, "nuns made extraordinary efforts to instill a deep religious faith and a fervent piety in their girls by placing religious faith at the center of the curriculum and requiring attendance at numerous services and devotions."[31] The pattern continued well into the twentieth century, with mandatory Sunday and feast day Masses; encouragement to attend daily Mass; demands to observe the Lenten fast and participate in an annual three-day retreat of silent prayer; and encouragement to engage in frequent devotional opportunities, such as May processions and listen to inspirational talks by chaplains, retreat masters and other visiting clergy. Many of these activities were also part of the normal culture at Catholic colleges and universities run by priests and religious congregations of men.

One of the things that distinguished Catholic colleges founded by women from those founded by priests or brothers was their sharp focus on personal spiritual development of students. Women religious saw the spiritual formation of their students as critical to their education and, therefore, nuns took this responsibility seriously and continued to improve their own preparation and formation in this regard. The content of religious knowledge—beliefs, values, assumptions, and norms—that was transmitted to postulants and novices was important in supporting the personal path to spiritual perfection that was the religious life, but it also helped prepare young women religious for their apostolic work.[32]

Spiritual knowledge and practice formed the foundation of early training in religious life. The director of novices guided the young sisters in their spiritual reading, which was intended to inform practice. At the same time, the director of novices also modeled the cultivation of virtues and perspectives that supported religious life. This regimen was designed to ensure that candidates would have the character, commitment, and ability to meet the challenges ministerial life held in store for them. Religious congregations of women were also strongly connected to the liturgical life of the Church, and this commitment was reflected in their formation and in the spiritual life they cultivated on their campuses. Daily participation in the Mass and recitation of the Little Office (psalms, readings, hymns, and prayers were grouped together and recited in common in the morning and evening) were integral to the daily spiritual life of religious women. Along with daily Mass and the Little Office, most women's congregations also had a rich devotional spirituality that included not only the rosary but a vast array of popular religious experiences and expressions.

The formation process emphasized knowledge and practices that would foster the faithfulness of the sisters to their calling and guard them against temptations. Those responsible for the religious formation of sisters understood that many of the same religious practices could be used by young laywomen to advance their spiritual life. In this way, aspects of religious formation became effective (perhaps even efficient) apostolic tools that helped educate young laywomen in the faith and also kept them closely bound to the nuns, whose spiritual practices they often shared. The clear link between the sisters' formation process and the desired apostolic impact on young collegiate women should not be overlooked. The culture of formation was detailed, rigorous, and fundamentally apostolic. It was structured to produce committed and knowledgeable sisters who would significantly assist young laywomen to lead lives of outstanding holiness and service to the Church and society.

Until changes were introduced in the 1950s, the theological education during formation was not of high quality. It was rudimentary at best, and in most cases did not go beyond the Baltimore Catechism. This posed problems for the sisters who were teaching in Catholic colleges. Until adequate theological training was addressed in a systematic manner, religious found ways around this lacuna in their theological knowledge. As indicated earlier, the sisters emphasized practical devotions that would be helpful to young women as either single young women in society or married women raising children. Eventually the sisters found the lack of training to be a serious impediment in their work, and in much the same way religious women addressed the issue of weakness in their professional training, they tackled the question of theological preparation.[33] A particularly forthright cultural catalyst in this area, Sr. Emmanuel Collins, O.S.F., was utterly disdainful of the literature that passed for spiritual reading in convents. To her it was no better than dime novels that kept religious in "permanent spiritual adolescence."[34] She and others like her made a clear impact. By the mid-twentieth century, formation programs across the country had a far more serious theological component, as evidenced by this description of novitiate in the Congregation of the Sisters of Charity of the Incarnate Word:

The novitiate or time of intense spiritual training begins with investiture in the holy habit and lasts two full years. The emphasis in novitiate instruction today is on the biblical, the liturgical, the apostolic, while not neglecting the solid doctrinal foundation that must be laid for a full Christian and religious life.[35]

Distinguishability

The more distinct the community or culture, the greater the commitment it can command and sustain. Organizations and communities both want and need commitment from members in order to thrive and survive. Deepening commitment increases the probability that an organization or community and its culture will remain distinguishable and be passed on to subsequent generations. Commitment at ever-increasing levels of intensity was an important part of religious formation and found great expression among sisters. The commitment of women religious to both their faith and the women they educated in their colleges was sustained and made more tangible by the depth of the sisters' sacrifice and personal renunciation, as well as by their communal involvement in a life of faith, witness, and shared ministry. The kind of commitment these women evidenced required a choice, and the depth of commitment emerging from that choice was partially dependent on the distinguishability of the religious congregation.

Prior to the 1960s, women religious were very distinguishable, and not only because of their habits. Within their colleges they operated as a witness community of role models and knowledge experts who sustained the Catholic culture of the institutions and guided young women as much by the power of how they lived as by what they taught. The vowed lives in community of these women reflected a carefully organized and painstakingly sustained balance built around a deep and abiding spiritual core. In every day there was time for prayer, meals, and work. Sisters also spent time with the community in recreation and doing the daily chores of community life. Maintaining balance was part of what religious women did. They also lived in communities that spanned an intergenerational life-cycle where young women entered and were taught by those who had gone before. Each sister worked in a particular religious institution, such as a school or hospital, but each sister also had great emotional interest in the well-being of the congregation and how the various undertakings of the congregation were prospering.[36] When sisters became old, they found a place in the heart of the community, where they were honored and embraced and their fellow sisters surrounded them and cared for them as they were dying.

The depictions of religious congregations prior to the 1960s often suggest rigid organizations with highly disciplined and regimented memberships. There is certainly truth in this portrayal, but the fact that there were highly disciplined and regimented members in these congregations did not necessarily make them organizationally or personally brittle. Nor did it rob the sisters of their intellectual gifts, curiosity, and ambition. From the earliest days of their formation, religious were encouraged to develop virtuous habits, extraordinary self-discipline, and a complete submission to the will of their religious superiors. Regardless of their impact on individual nuns, these qualities contributed to the stability of religious congregations and their flexibility in responding to ministerial needs that emerged. Religious women ran organizations and moved from institution to institution—from religious assignment to religious assignment—in an apparently seamless flow, marked more by shared commitment and professionalism than the dictates of personal affection.

Religious women were also distinguishable in their colleges by the leadership and competence they exhibited in running the whole college or parts of it. In a world in which it was rare for women to have high-profile leadership positions, nuns ran institutions, handled the finances, hired lay faculty, raised funds, and accomplished all of that without sacrificing their unique roles as religious virtuosi.[37] It is somewhat surprising these orders whose spiritual formation focused on humility, self-effacement, sacrifice, and service to others managed to produce outstanding leaders with no end of entrepreneurial skills, profound courage, and a willingness to take risks. These leaders were not exceptions to the rule but frequently followed one after another.[38]

The faith of women religious and their esprit de corps gave them the courage to take risks. Whether constructing a classroom building in the middle of the depression without available funds, developing the first graduate school of theology for women, finally getting approval for a college by waiting until the oppositional bishop-chancellor was out of town, or convincing town fathers to put a stop for the railroad outside the college gates, religious women found ways to meet the needs of their time by having a broad view of what was possible, a deep trust in God, faith in their own ability to make it happen, and the willingness to act and enlist others in significant institution building.[39]

The Vatican II Experience

Prior to the Second Vatican Council, the purpose of religious life was to seek a life of personal holiness in a spiritually superior state and to work for the salvation of others in apostolic works that served the mission of the Church. The content, and symbols of religious culture supported this understanding and practical strategies abounded that supported these goals, as well. The process of religious formation was a systematic immersion in a culture so intense it had become what Peter McDonough refers to as "motivational metaphor," "an institution virtually indistinguishable from an enveloping way of life, grounded in behavioral, cognitive, and affective reinforcements."[40] The entire system had unity and coherence. The system also had generativity: cultural knowledge experts and role models ushered aspirants into these orders and transmitted to them a distinguishable culture that was imminently inheritable.

The thirty-five-year period between 1965 and 2000 produced a transformation within Catholic religious congregations of women. The ultimate outcome of this process was not something anticipated, intended, or—in most cases—desired by the sisters who undertook the initial changes. Interestingly, the earliest changes occurred in response to directives from Rome that looked to revitalize religious life. Efforts that seemed a priori likely to enhance distinguishability and promote inheritability unfortunately undermined those very qualities.

It is difficult to fully grasp what happened to produce such enormous cultural change and institutional unraveling within religious congregations, particularly in the short span of forty years. No doubt, scholars will try to sort out that question during the coming decades. However, it is safe to say that in attempting to faithfully respond to the Second Vatican Council, and to relate more fully and effectively to modern society, women religious began a process of cultural adaptation that contributed to their organizational undoing. This happened under the leadership of dynamic women religious and with the enthusiastic participation of sisters who could not have imagined, let alone intended, the end result.

Religious women responded to the impetus of the Second Vatican Council and directives from Rome more quickly and enthusiastically than many priests, congregations of male religious, and parishes. One reason they were receptive and institutionally agile is directly linked to the Sister Formation Movement in the United States, described earlier in this chapter. For religious congregations of women, the Sister Formation Movement could well be understood as, "without question, the single most critical ground for the radical transformative process following Vatican II."[41] Responding to the decline of vocations in Europe after World War II, Pope Pius XII had called upon religious congregations to adapt or eliminate the outdated practices standing between modern young people and a commitment to religious life. Although there had been little direct response among congregations to this plea, the more pressing issue of sister preparation had become a significant force for change in the United States, and out of it grew the Sister Formation Movement.

As a result of this process, American nuns became the most highly educated women in the Church, as well as one of the mostly highly educated groups of women in the whole country. This movement also led to the establishment of informal norms and similar organizational structures. In the United States at that time, there were many hundreds of congregations of religious women. The informal norms and the organizational structures connected disparate and highly individualistic orders, giving them a common language and greatly facilitating communication between and among them. The *Sister Formation Bulletin*, begun in 1954, transmitted new ideas about religious life, as well as abstracts of leading theologians of the day. Laura Ann Quinonez and Mary Daniel Turner, pivotal leaders in the Leadership Conference of Women Religious, point out that the articles of the *Bulletin* conveyed "the image of a movement underway (and gaining momentum) to make both the individual sister and the community relevant to and confident in the times."[42] When the Vatican Council sounded the clarion call for congregational renewal, women religious in the United States had the spirit, the organization, and the education to respond quickly, and they did.

The Council and Renewal

The Second Vatican Council provided the ecclesiological foundation for the revolution in religious life. The Council encouraged religious congregations to renew themselves by reflection on their mission within a Church that is a sign and means of holiness and both challenges and cooperates with secular society. Religious congregations were encouraged to become more engaged in the world by reexamining and appropriating anew the motivation and insights of their founders. These recommendations, when linked with the *Zeitgeist* of the radical 1960s, propelled many congregations of religious women in new directions. As this process gathered steam, many outsiders had the impression the sisters turned upside down or radically reinterpreted their original purpose. This was not how most sisters saw it. By and large, sisters were excited to be returning to the ideals of their founders.[43] Eventually, as the process gained momentum and even the cultural content and symbols of religious congregations were changed, resistance developed within the religious congregations themselves.

Religious congregational culture in the post–Vatican II era faced increasing external pressures to change. In hindsight, it is clear that these congregations were caught between a rock and a hard place in terms of their cultural future. American congregations realized that vocations had slowed, and the pattern in Europe was even more alarming. If they did nothing, the downward trend in vocations could well continue. On the other hand, inheritability could be threatened if they made the wrong choices about change. They believed that renewal could attract new generations of young members who would bring revitalized congregational cultures to bear in a world that sorely needed such witness. Because religious congregations of women had such a strong track record of cultural adaptation, they were confident they could meet the substantial challenges ahead. Some voices warned that the sisters were surrendering too much or making too many adjustments, too quickly. The sisters noted these voices, but the din for change effectively muted them. Perhaps leaders of the religious congregations understood that the process of change would be rocky and dangerous, but they felt obstacles would eventually be overcome.

Broad and Sweeping Change

The reforms the sisters made in response to Vatican II were broad and sweeping. The most fundamental change was a reinterpretation of congregational purpose that framed religious orders as agencies of "prophetic witness."[44] In her article "The Dynamics of Personal and Organizational Reframing," Jean Bartunek described the process of organizational "reframing," which she defined as "a discontinuous change in [an] organization's shared meaning, or culture" that took place in religious congregations after the Second Vatican Council. Although the seeds of cultural change had been growing for many years, the tipping point for congregations, or the "trigger event," as Bartunek calls it, was the Second Vatican Council.[45] The Council provided a theological framework that harnessed the winds of change blowing from many directions at the time and focused them toward a reimagining of religious life. Through the process Bartunek outlines in the article, congregations came to define their purpose as the work of justice, not the work of traditional ministries. Over time, the legacy of justice became so culturally pervasive and intense in religious congregations of women that all institutions became suspect. Institutions were contrary to their missions because they "institutionalized injustice." In the United States at the time, the feminist movement and the civil rights movement, as well as the sexual revolution, were raising critical issues of justice and individual rights in the public arena. The deep dyes of these secular movements colored reflections and decisions within religious communities of women. A large portion of the country was increasingly sensitive to issues of justice, and this sensitivity fueled a similar commitment among religious women. Although "rights language" had not traditionally been used in religious life, religious women very much wanted to show respect for their individual should be co-sisters, especially since many of them had suffered as a result of having to submerge their feelings and convictions in the face of strong-willed religious superiors. The secular lens provided a new optic through which many religious women began to see and understand their own apostolic work, their congregations, and the Church itself. Many religious women, as well as men, it must be said, looked at the Roman Catholic Church and saw an organization with a history of entrenched patriarchy, oppression of women, and discrimination against people of color and homosexuals. Horrified by what they saw as behavior contrary to the gospel message of love within their own Church and congregations—behavior they had themselves participated in—religious women set about trying to reform the injustice they saw in their own house.

The new perspectives resulted in dramatic changes in institutional behavior. After the Council, cloister was removed in apostolic communities, and separation between sisters and laypersons all but disappeared. Congregations also reinterpreted their vows of poverty, chastity, and obedience. With a new understanding of authority, congregations changed their governance, decentralizing power and opting for consensus leadership. Reacting against what Patricia Wittberg calls "incidents from their own early years in stultifying and soul-destroying 'communities'—stories of God-given talents quashed and denied, of life-giving friendships poisoned and thwarted, of self-esteem wrecked and hopes ruined," congregations placed a new focus on individual rights and freedoms.[46] This new focus allowed for educational opportunities to be defined by personal desire rather than congregational need, and sisters were allowed to accept professional work outside congregationally sponsored institutions. In a similarly less-constrained vein, women religious began creating living arrangements in apartments or small houses rather than in large, institutional convents. Religious habits were put aside, and secular dress became the accepted norm. Sisters who previously were not permitted to travel without a sister as companion were now given freedom to travel on their own.

Religious women were individually affirmed but, partially as a result of the emphasis on individual projects and approaches, also became less visible to ordinary Catholics. In earlier times, the nuns all arrived in the parish church to attend daily Mass together with the other parishioners. Even had they not been wearing habits, they would have been visible simply by their numbers and communal prayers. They moved as if they were a syncopated dance troupe. Now, they lived two or three together, wore nothing distinguishable, and frequently no longer attended Mass together in the same parish. Referring to this passage from institutional conformity to individual choice and expression, one sister, speaking about her fellow sisters, wryly notes: "Sometimes we did not recognize each other at meetings or conventions, or at the corner store. Certainly the laity could not find us. It was quite a journey from being completely conspicuous (in habits) and anonymous to being hardly noticed and individuated."[47]

The renewal that took place in religious congregations of women and its aftermath is an example of cultural change writ large. Since the changes began over thirty years ago, it is easy to second-guess the process. Hindsight does not grant the right to make judgments about how prudential religious were at the time. Hindsight does, however, provide the opportunity to analyze the situation and identify changes that proved to be unhelpful or even devastating, though they were not viewed that way at the time. Ideally this will lead to development of a set of principles institutions can use to protect themselves in times of intense cultural adaptation. By examining post–Vatican II congregational renewal over against the framework for cultural change outlined earlier in the book, it will be possible to develop those principles. But first, a recap of the framework will be useful.

Vibrant organizational cultures have well-understood goals and purposes, and their cultural content and symbols support achievement of corporate goals. Cultural citizens, motivated by cultural content and symbols, make almost daily decisions to act in ways that reinforce the culture and the achievement of its goals, and cultural catalysts are able to initiate cultural adaptation that can address perilous situations that threaten the distinguishability or inheritability of the culture.

Despite their best intentions to the contrary, the renewal process in religious congregations created a cultural crisis. The understanding of religious life changed, but the shift in understanding was not adequately thought through. The new, more modern understanding that eventually prevailed did not prove attractive to young women considering dedicating their lives to Christ in service of the Church.

In the years following Vatican II, religious congregations tried to develop an alternative distinctive purpose for religious life other than a claim for spiritual superiority. According to Patricia Wittberg, it is possible to see this discussion develop in the pages of the *Review for Religious* between 1963 and 1991. By the mid-1980s, after a significant and ambiguous period of discussion and discernment, an alternative purpose for religious life emerged. The authors of the *Review* "held that all Christians were indeed called to the same holiness, but that religious were called to *an increased level of visibility* in living out this call. Thus, they were to serve as prophets or public witnesses to the rest of the Church."[48] As a group, sisters no longer considered themselves primarily as exemplars of holiness and commitment to the Church or as models of obedience as they undertook common tasks with good outcomes far beyond what could be achieved with each acting individually. Rather, the sisters were now promoters of justice who spoke and acted on behalf of the poor and marginalized. Each sister in her own sphere of influence and the sisters collectively were to witness to the truth by speaking boldly, like the prophets of old.

Whatever attraction the sisters felt to the idea of religious life as prophetic witness, organizational adjustments (or what we have termed changes in the conceptual framework of their life) had taken root that undermined their ability to speak prophetically, at least as a group. The sisters in leadership in congregations acted as cultural citizens, not as cultural catalysts. They did not fully comprehend or attend to the increasing tension between the stated purpose of religious life as prophetic witness and the life-style changes, practices, and actions that were developing and that they themselves encouraged among the sisters. Organizational structures were designed and implemented that crippled the mechanism by which cultural catalysts could emerge and initiate essential cultural adjustments that could have stabilized the cultural crisis. Three particular aspects of renewal—the reinterpretation of the vows of poverty, chastity, and obedience, the restructuring of community life, and the reconfiguration of authority—are illustrative of how this attempt at cultural renaissance became derailed, resulting in the erosion of cultural distinguishability and the unraveling of cultural inheritability.[49]

Reinterpretation of Vows

Prior to the Council, the vow of obedience had meant absolute compliance with the will of the superior, who represented for the sister the will of God in her present situation. In the postconciliar period of adjustment, a more internalized concept of searching for the meaning of God's will that completely repudiated the prior view came to be accepted. This new interpretation was a clear attempt to address the infantilizing of adult women that resulted from older understandings of the vow of obedience.[50] While this new view supported a more adult appreciation of women religious, including their insights and religious sensibilities, it also created unforeseen problems in terms of cultural distinguishability. A salient characteristic of sisters, both in their own estimation and in the view of laypersons, was their absolute obedience to the will of God, expressed for them through their religious superior. This common discipline enabled the sisters to act and be perceived as a unified group pursuing the will of God without reference to their own personal inclinations.

The new, emerging understanding of religious life as prophetic witness called on individual sisters and congregations to become more visible in speaking out against injustice and on behalf of the marginalized. Had they been able to martial the full force of organizational unity that a vow of obedience assured, congregations could have become highly visible institutional forces for justice. Instead of one common institutional voice, there was a mixture of voices. Individual sisters spoke out strongly on particular issues related to their particular ministry. Some of their comments were reflected in positions taken by the congregation, while others were not. The main impression made on the faithful, however, was of individual sisters speaking forthrightly about matters of great concern to them. Laypersons easily interpreted such "stands" as political positions rather than justice positions taken by the congregation because they were closely related to their religious heritage.

In this new milieu, sisters were educated and prepared to be individual witnesses. While sisters acted in concert on some issues, with this new individualistic interpretation, obedience no longer allowed superiors to assess the needs of institutional ministries and prepare sisters to fill them. The inability of congregations to focus their energies in any set of highly visible organizations undermined the collective "witness" and visibility of the congregation, and that compromised congregational distinguishability. Because common action became entirely optional in religious congregations, sisterhoods developed into a community of prophetic individuals rather than a prophetic community that was highly visible and speaking with one voice.

Something quite similar happened in the reinterpretation of the vow of poverty. Prior to the Second Vatican Council, sisters were expected to renounce all ownership, as well as maintain an internal disengagement from wealth and possessions, with a trust in the God who cared for the lilies of the field and the birds of the air. Although there had always been some variance in how strictly congregations interpreted the vow of poverty, all sisters were presented with a clear vision of how the congregation they were entering lived poverty. This always included commitments to the renunciation of goods, community ownership of most things, and the limitation on goods that any sister personally controlled—the clothes she wore and the books she used—to things that were meager by comparison with any woman of moderate means.[51] After the Council, there was genuine disagreement about the external commitments to poverty. William Reiser, S.J., raises the question that continues to torment many in religious life:

> What does it mean to be poor? This question has occasioned endless debates in religious communities. Does the poverty which one vows to observe designate spiritual poverty or material poverty? With what social class or classes is one identifying? There has never been a single, uniform definition of religious poverty.[52]

During the post–Vatican II renewal, the predominant view of the vow that emerged was a resistance to consumerism and a critique of society's treatment of the poor.[53]

Once again, the reinterpretation of part of the content of religious life had its impact in the actions of sisters. Women religious suddenly had spending money. They drove cars and lived in apartments. They no longer needed a superior's permission to buy things. Some of them worked with the poor, but many more were working in secular settings, drawing significant salaries and adopting lifestyles that in terms of a vow of poverty were not distinguishable from those of many lay Catholics.[54] A study of laywomen by Sister Donna Markham, O.P., in 1981 documented the loss of distinguishability in terms of the vow of poverty.[55] The laywomen surveyed did not perceive sisters as living simple lives, and they saw no evidence of a simple life. They also maintained that nuns were not adequately serving the poor. For a community committed to being a prophetic witness, these results were not only a strong indictment but also a clear indication of mounting cultural indistinguishability.[56]

In the years following Vatican II, the meaning of the vow of chastity not only shifted but the vow itself became suspect. In the Catholic ambience prior to Vatican II, celibacy had been considered superior to marriage as a spiritual path and a sign of God's redeeming love. *Lumen Gentium,* one of the foundational documents of Vatican II, had dissolved the spiritual elitism inherent in this interpretation of chastity, and, as a result, the vow lost its aura and sisters were diminished in stature. Conceptually what remained was an awkward secular pragmatism: celibacy was important because it enabled a sister to commit herself completely to Christ and the Church, without the need to attend to a spouse and family. In this understanding, the act of living a celibate life no longer had significance in itself. Rather, the importance of celibacy was purely instrumental—it enabled one to have more time for prophetic witness and living in community. In the judgment of many committed laypersons, the meaning of the vow of celibacy had been fundamentally altered.

In the process of renewal, the question of celibacy became a source of embarrassment for many sisters because in the broader society it was often seen as a sign of psychosexual deviance rather than spiritual superiority. While it still had the potential to enhance distinguishability in the culture of religious life, it became a real threat to cultural inheritability. Like the sisters who preceded them, most post–Vatican II nuns continued to witness the value of celibacy by honoring their vow of chastity for life. Because the sisters were fewer in number and less visible in society and because the vow itself was either suspect or its fundamental significance as a way of becoming one with Christ had been undermined, the power of this lived witness was muted.

Restructuring of Community Life

The renewal process in religious life had a decidedly individualistic stamp that influenced changes in norms, values, and beliefs that had supported a highly distinguishable culture within religious congregations. Communal living, the

wearing of habits, common meals, ritualized schedules that kept women together for rest, recreation, work, meals, and prayer—all disappeared as nuns
moved out of large convents and motherhouses and into small group houses
or increasingly into apartments by themselves. The intention was noble—to
establish fruitful relationships with laypersons and assist them both in their
service to the Church and society and in the development of their spiritual
lives. What sisters did not perceive at the time was the enormous impact their
common life and prayers had on people with whom they may or may not have
had close personal relationships.[57]

Reconfiguration of Authority

The reconfiguration of authority within religious congregations also had powerful implications for the inheritability of the culture of religious life that was
facing real threats on two fronts. The first threat came in terms of the decline
in vocations. The second emerged when religious women began leaving their
congregations in droves.

Prior to Vatican II, the interpretation of authority in religious congregations focused on hierarchy, centralization, and control. It mirrored the structure of the Church and followed a top-down pattern of decision-making that
was reinforced by member obedience to superiors whose judgments were seen
as reflecting the will of God. After the Council the emphasis changed, and
collegiality, consultation, and respect for the individual became the driving
principles behind a reimagining of congregational authority, leadership, and
obedience.[58] Responding to this conceptual shift, congregations vested authority in the entire community and not within the leadership alone. Leadership
itself was turned over to teams, each member of which increasingly exemplified
the qualities of cultural citizens, rather than cultural catalysts. As the process
of renewal wore on, congregations moved beyond consultation and into a
model of consensus of those sisters elected to the consultative council. Consensus implied a demand for collective action, and this became organizationally paralyzing. This new conceptual understanding of authority and leadership
made it impossible for cultural catalysts to emerge or operate. Their absence
resulted in a complete inability of congregations to fully understand or respond
to the deepening crisis in vocations that unraveled their cultural inheritability.

If a culture is perceived to be neither distinct nor particularly attractive,
future generations will not be inclined to join, and the culture will eventually
disappear. In the years 1948–1952, 23,302 women entered religious life in the
United States. In the years 1953–57, the number grew to 27,157. The high-water
mark was reached in the period 1958–62, when 32,433 women entered religious life.[59] This rising trend reversed in the two-year period 1963–65, when
the number of entrants dropped to 18,316.[60] In the years following, the downward trend continued and soon became an emerging crisis for religious congregations, a crisis that continues unabated to this day.

Although sisters might not have perceived this loss of postulants and novices as a serious problem early on, after a few years the trend surely cried out

for decisive action. As the situation worsened, the design of formation itself tended to exacerbate the problems in cultural socialization. One of the great strengths of formation prior to the Council was the fact that large groups of young women entered together, supported each other, affirmed their mutual decision, and established a cohesive cohort of sisters.[61] As the size of entering groups markedly decreased, formation ceased to be a group process that supported specific congregational connection.

For the most part, regular churchgoers were unaware of the significant drop-off in vocations among the sisters. Many laypersons realized that numbers were down, but they did not know that many religious congregations had gone for several years with only one or two or no postulants or novices. The sisters moved into smaller communities because they wanted to be closer to laypersons, but, as noted earlier, the sisters actually became less visible in these smaller settings. Strangely, the laypersons who liked and admired the sisters and could have stimulated the nuns to initiate changes to attract more sisters did not speak up because they were unaware of the severity of the vocation problem. They also had become complicit in fueling the vocations crisis by their increasing unwillingness to support the vowed life as a viable option for their own daughters.

The second crisis in inheritability within religious congregations was a defection crisis. Change becomes a threat to the vibrancy of culture if the next generation is unwilling to accept the adapted culture in any meaningful numbers. Religious congregations after the Council were facing that threat. For change to enhance cultural vibrancy, it is equally important that it be accepted by the current generation of cultural citizens. In the case of religious congregations in the process of renewal, the revolving front doors of convents and motherhouses provided ample evidence that this was not the case. The loss of so many women from religious congregations staggered the communities. In 1950, 381 women left religious life. In 1955 that number had grown to 590. The trend continued in 1960, with departures rising to 765 women, and in 1965, 1,562 sisters left congregations. By 1970, the number of defections had almost tripled, when 4,337 women religious, 1,723 unprofessed and 2,614 professed, walked away from their convents.[62]

This flood of departures happened in the midst of two profound cultural shifts, one in the broader society and one occurring within religious congregations themselves. The broader shift granted women new stature in society, opening up to them positions that had formerly been reserved for men. This new reality and the excitement that surrounded the emerging interest in the contributions of women represented a marked threat for religious congregations. To counter debilitating, persistent threats, strong core components and clear distinguishability are required. Cultural content and symbols were still in flux in the protracted period of renewal. The women who were the cultural citizens and transmitters of congregational culture were not as clear as they needed to be about what they were transmitting. The mutual support and validation so important to community life was breaking down, and the very survival of religious life was in question. In the midst of this massive defection, religious congregations did not act decisively.

Both of these issues—recruitment and retention—threatened inheritability and cried out for cultural change that involved renewed emphasis on the distinguishing characteristics of sisters in a changed environment. As a result of changes in how congregations understood authority and leadership, however, women religious were organized in ways that prevented the emergence of the strong cultural catalysts who might have initiated the kind of large-scale changes needed to stem the tide of vocational erosion and institutional hemorrhaging. Urged to renew their congregations by Rome, women religious began that process of renewal with great enthusiasm and hope, but with little clarity about direction, goals, and strategies for change. They had not developed means of evaluating the success or failure of the process at any stage, and they chose a leadership structure that left them organizationally paralyzed—a structure that they nonetheless defended. Even during the period of free fall, sisters claimed that consensual leadership was the best strategy for forward movement and clung to it tenaciously. Consequently, when things started to get out of control, not only was it difficult to stop the process but there was no way to even mount a persuasive rationale that it should be stopped.

Principles for Perilous Times

Content and symbols support the goals of a vibrant culture, and the actions of cultural citizens who are motivated by these components enhance the culture. During the process of congregational renewal, cultural coherence and cultural distinguishability both became threatened. Because the content of congregational culture, reflected in a new focus on individual rights, freedoms, and self-determination, was at odds with their stated purposes as a united and highly visible prophetic witness, cultural insiders became increasingly confused about the purpose and meaning of religious life. The actions of sisters reflected beliefs, norms, and values that did not cohere with the congregation's stated purpose. Careful monitoring of whether or not the actions of cultural citizens support or undermine the goals of the institution is essential to assuring cultural coherence inside an organization. If there is a cultural disconnect between what an organization is trying to do and how it actually behaves, a strategy for cultural change is required in order to regain cultural coherence. At the same time, the way women religious went about living their commitment to identify with the people and operate as prophetic witnesses further eroded their distinguishability. From the vantage point of the regular churchgoer, nuns simply seemed to disappear. Yes, laypersons who worked in schools, hospitals, or agencies run by the sisters would regularly interact with nuns. But these laypersons constituted a small fraction of the Catholic population. An organizational culture has to be distinguishable to both insiders and outsiders to survive and flourish. The actions of cultural citizens are revelatory of cultural distinctions.

In order to maintain cultural distinguishability, it is necessary to monitor whether the behavior of members of the culture truly is distinctive. If distinguishability is on the wane, cultural adaptation initiated by cultural catalysts is necessary.

Organizational cultures are by their very nature dynamic and in flux. At times when cultures seem their strongest, they may in fact be at the beginning of a process of cultural decline or disintegration. At times when they seem most tepid, organizational cultures can well be structuring a process of cultural adaptation that strengthens and supports greater cultural vibrancy. Much like a sailboat on the open sea that must frequently tack in order to reach its destination, organizations that want to achieve their goals must make frequent modifications and cultural adaptations. In order for that to happen, there have to be cultural catalysts who can initiate changes and an authority and leadership structure that monitors cultural conditions, measures cultural drifts, and makes changes to assure that the culture remains vibrant, vital, and in service of the institution's goals.

In the midst of their renewal, religious congregations redefined authority in ways that paralyzed their ability to act. As part of their adjustment process, they also substantially decreased their visibility. Sisters began flying below the accustomed radar of the Catholic faithful and as a result cut off important avenues of communication with laypersons who might otherwise have offered constructive feedback about fundamental congregational changes.

Even if the sisters had been sufficiently visible to the laypersons, another development made religious life in the latter twentieth century less appealing than it had been. Sisters, who in the minds of laypersons had been distinguished by their obedience, chose to challenge the highest authority in the Church on an important but neuralgic issue. Sisters lent their voices to the growing outcry that publicly challenged the Church's position on women priests and requested a serious examination of the issue. In a very high-profile action in 1979, the Leadership Council of Women Religious (LCWR) president, Theresa Kane, greeted Pope John Paul II in the name of American sisters and appealed to him for the inclusion of women in all ministries of the Church. In discussing that interaction, Lora Ann Quinonez and Mary Daniel Turner described the reaction of major superiors of women's religious orders. Some of the superiors "applauded her courage, many agreed with her statement but were troubled by its timing, a handful were offended. Five discontinued membership in the Conference."[63] For the most part, nuns supported women's ordination, and their public support of that movement unwittingly further undermined their own way of life as distinctively appealing to prospective entrants.[64]

Just as the market for single-sex education crumbled in the wake of growing interest in coeducation, so too, women's religious life was eclipsed by interest in opening up priesthood to women. At a time when the feminist movement was focused on breaking down the barriers to women's full participation in all realms of society, opening up priesthood to women became an obvious issue for many Catholic women. By publicly supporting the full inclusion of women in all of the Church's ministries, women religious clearly did not intend to distance themselves from religious life or to suggest it was a less desirable vocational choice for women. Unfortunately, in the realm of public opinion, intention is easily overwhelmed by perception, and the call for women's ordination by nuns signaled to young women that priesthood, not religious life, was the true locus of distinctive religious virtuosity. The support by sisters for women's ordination was certainly not the only factor, or even the most critical factor, that deterred young women from joining sisterhoods. As noted earlier, women's position in all areas of society was undergoing wrenching reinterpretation. But it is difficult to attract young women to a demanding life that is not being championed as uniquely desirable by the people who are living it.[65]

There was another more personal and painful factor that inhibited religious women from championing their vocational choice to the next generation. Many religious congregations, faced with the loss of members in dramatic numbers and the complete reorientation of their self-understanding, experienced tremendous loss, grief, and pain. One sister described that difficult time when

> the congregation's world was just literally turned upside down. Who we were, what we did, didn't seem to have any value any more. Every value, everything we had held true and dear and good was immediately reversed. There were a lot of angry people in the congregations then. The life that these women had committed themselves to was thrown out, no good, worth nothing. It is a sociological wonder that religious congregations ever survived that time at all. People were leaving all the time, and I can remember the agony and the pain and the tears when I was younger and we were trying to go through these changes. It has taken us a number of years to live through the anger.[66]

The superior of this sister's congregation refused to accept new members for a number of years because she believed it was unconscionable to ask young women to join a community that was convulsed with conflict, confusion, and wrenching loss. The atmosphere was not conducive to recruitment, as vocations directors and religious superiors were well aware, and it further compromised the inheritability of religious congregations of women.

Another unanticipated contributor to the erosion of institutional culture in religious congregations was the decision, discussed earlier, to self-identify religious life as institutional prophetic witness.[67] The sisters expected that prophetic witness would yield, as a side benefit, clear distinguishability from other groups in the Catholic Church. But because sisters did not link prophetic witness in visible, discernible ways to any specific religious components of their heritage, this reidentification likely contained within it the seeds of indistinguishability.[68] In many ways, the identification of religious congregations of women with prophetic witness was more about direction than goals. The direction was away from things more than it was toward any particular end. Prophetic witness stood against institutionalized injustice, and it was very much involved in the spirit of liberation that characterized the women's movement and the civil rights movement in the midst of which it developed.[69]

This prophetic stance "away from" or "over against" organizations, institutions, and societal forces that were unjust included a distancing from the hierarchical Roman Catholic Church.[70] It also put many women religious at odds with their own history, which they began to understand as oppressive. Once nuns were ideologically cut off from their historical roots, cultural inheritability of religious congregations was in peril. In her book *Witness to Integrity*, Anita Caspary describes a kind of cultural isolation that religious faced once the renewal process became a confrontation with authority from which they believed they could no longer back down.

> Those of us in leadership positions in the Sisters of the Immaculate
> Heart knew that our stance toward renewal would mean the strain
> of making an increasing number of choices. We knew that we were
> facing the possibility of standing alone, especially when no one
> knew what "renewal" really meant. We had no pattern to follow. Yet
> we knew that this was the way we had to go if we, as women reli-
> gious, were to make any difference in the modern world.[71]

A prophetic message once received and understood completely reorients perception. Relying on the insights of Walter Brueggemann, Elizabeth Dreyer describes this moment as "the visceral experience of waking up to the truth that things are not right. The light bulb goes on, and we wonder why we did not see that before. Pretending that things are fine is no longer an option."[72] Religious congregations believed that their prophetic statements had made it quite obvious that things were not right with religious life, the Church, and the world. The "Ah, ha!" light bulb did not go off, however, in the face of their own dissipating congregational culture. Women religious either were blind to their course or simply could not accept that they were culturally off course and that mistakes had been made.

Cultures can make adaptive mistakes and recover, provided they understand that a mistake was made. Especially at times when far-reaching changes are being undertaken, it is important for groups to monitor their progress toward stated goals.[73] If sufficient progress is not being made and it is quite clear to those involved that this is the case, cultural catalysts will emerge to make changes, provided they are not blocked from exercising leadership. If dramatically different results are needed, small adjustments in strategy are insufficient. New, carefully articulated strategies with clear objectives are needed. Equally essential are the people who could formulate and implement such strategies. Unfortunately, competitive strategies to reimagine religious life were stifled by the tendency toward "group think" among leaders of religious congregations.

Through their membership in the LCWR, religious superiors created, as

Lora Quinonez and Mary Daniel Turner pointed out, "a sense of corporate power" that was focused on being a prophetic voice.[74] The opposition congregations encountered from the ecclesiastical hierarchy both in the United States and in Rome created a siege mentality that further united American sisters and discouraged internal dissent from the "party line" that was developing within the LCWR. In this atmosphere, alternative voices and competitive choices largely disappeared within women's religious congregations.[75]

None of the obstacles confronting religious congregations of women would have been easy to overcome, but by definition a crisis only threatens when obstacles appear almost insurmountable. The sisters themselves were satisfied with leadership by consensus. They were also committed to the type of prophetic witness they were bearing and largely unaware that their growing national consensus was silencing alternative voices and eroding competition among the various religious congregations. Attending to their internal actions and statements was certainly worthwhile and important for maintaining consistency and quality control. However, such monitoring has to be supplemented by attention to outcomes, including the impact that actions and announcements have on outsiders. In this context, the outsiders are laypersons and the outcomes are their perceptions of the sisters and the sisters' contributions to the Church and society. It appears that most congregations of religious women had little data on these perceptions.

By committing to consensus and collective action, religious congregations smothered the possibility that cultural catalysts would initiate necessary and appropriate cultural adaptation. They also set out on a journey dedicated to cultural change of significant dimensions with no clear goals, no process for effective evaluation, no clear criteria for measuring the success or failure of the renewal process, and no outside consultation to provide alternative perspectives on the crisis and how to handle it. Without these structures in place, it was possible for communities to be in denial about the lack of new entrants and contraction of communities and to spin it as the purifying work of the Spirit, rather than the collapse of corporate reform.

The factors mentioned earlier that prevented sisters from making sufficient adjustments in their culture can be reformulated as principles or guidelines for perilous times in Catholic universities. First, in a crisis there is no substitute for strong leadership. A leader of an institution, usually the president or someone empowered by the president, must have the authority to act decisively to adjust the Catholic culture. Second, clear targets and goals have to be established, and progress toward those goals must be closely, frequently, and objectively monitored. These targets and goals might be difficult to select, because Catholic culture does not admit of easy quantification. Nonetheless, some measures must be chosen and progress monitored. Third, lack of alternative voices and vigorous competition is a warning signal that should cause grave concern.

These cautionary principles, we believe, have applicability to a number of different Catholic institutions facing considerable obstacles. A siege mentality, excessive group think, or complacency within the system of Catholic higher education can erode spirited competition in matters of Catholic culture. Similarly, parish life faces enormous challenges, and it may be that parishes are not experimenting enough. What masquerades as generally accepted wisdom can in fact be an omen of an intensifying cultural crisis. In certain regions of the country, Mass attendance has fallen steadily over several years. Some experimentation is warranted. Pastors would never think of changing fundamentals of the Mass to make it more appealing. That is an example of good groupthink. On the other hand, pastors should be willing to experiment with everything not related to essentials, even if particular experiments do not conform to the sensitivities or preferences of pastors. Thus, if one pastor learned through various conversations and other information that people were tired of Masses lasting over an hour and were more likely to attend Masses lasting less than forty-five minutes, it would be appropriate for one or more pastors to try this approach. There is, of course, no guarantee this approach will work. However, doing nothing means the percentage of Catholics attending Mass regularly continues to decline. Bold experiments (we readily acknowledge cutting the average length of Mass by fifteen minutes only qualifies as a bold experiment in some parishes) are better than almost certain irrelevancy.

The first two principles apply to individual institutions and, in our judgment, are necessary principles for institutions to survive a crisis. The third principle applies to the system as a whole and encourages a healthy skepticism about "conventional wisdom" and its efficacy for the long-term vitality of organizational culture. A crisis necessitates a willingness to try any new approach that is consistent with personal and cultural integrity. In order for such experiments to be undertaken in a timely fashion, judgments will have to be based on partial information. A crisis does not usually allow the luxury of gathering all relevant data.

Cultural change and adaptation are a necessary part of maintaining a healthy and vital corporate culture. For change to be constructive rather than destructive, it needs to be part of a carefully monitored process that has objectives and built-in opportunities for assessment. It also requires leadership with accountability. Open-ended and unstructured cultural adaptation that is not carefully monitored by someone who bears responsibility for its success can easily veer off course and become destructive. The innate volatility of cultural change requires careful and accountable management.

The cultural collapse of religious congregations of women is complex and requires more analysis than this chapter allows. One particular aspect that has received little attention here but deserves more careful critique is the cultural implosion of all types of religious congregations of women. Several hundred congregations of religious women existed in the United States in the 1960s. Some were monastic congregations, others were contemplative, and still others were involved in apostolic ministry. Within each of these designations there were further distinctions. For instance, in apostolic communities, some were congregations focusing their ministry on education and others on health care, and some religious orders were involved in a number of different ministries. The failure of certain types of congregations to maintain cultural viability is lamentable but is understandable. The fact that practically all congregations of religious women in the United States, regardless of their composition, focus, geographical location, or apostolate, have been unsuccessful in satisfying the criteria of distinguishability and inheritability is truly confounding and distressing. As previously noted, competition among different groups in an organization was insufficient for individual congregations to attempt new approaches that were at variance from the prevailing wisdom.[76] Whatever diversity of approach did emerge in this critical period was not found to be sufficiently compelling or effective to rescue the various types of religious congregations of women from cultural decline.

Knowledge and Commitment

A final lesson we draw from our analysis of the experience of religious women in the United States is the importance of knowledge of and commitment to a culture. Knowledge of cultural content and symbols must be cultivated if any culture is to remain distinguishable and inheritable over time. To participate fully in a culture, as Rodney Stark and Roger Finke point out in their discussion of religious culture, "requires mastery of a lot of culture."[77] To become culturally fluent, a person has to master the content and symbols of the "cultural package deemed essential in their society."[78] That mastery is dependent to some degree on the existence of cultural knowledge experts capable of transmitting cultural content to the next generation. While culture is to some extent "caught," it is also, most assuredly, taught. Culture survives because it is taught to newcomers, and the absence of a group of cultural knowledge experts will threaten both the distinguishability and inheritability of any culture.[79]

The vibrancy of organizational culture certainly requires knowledge about its content, its beliefs, and its shared assumptions and norms. Cultural knowledge alone, however, is not enough to sustain the vitality of organizational culture beyond the present generation. Cultural inheritability in a group or organization requires significant levels of commitment from the community of cultural catalysts and citizens in order for there to be any chance it will appeal to the future generations required to sustain it. Commitment connects what a person wants to do with what he or she is supposed to do. That link makes it possible for an individual to make a social contribution while at the same time nourishing a personal sense of self.[80] Committed members of a community serve as the role models and living witnesses of the content of culture. As cultural citizens, their lives and everyday choices support and deepen the culture of the organizations and enhance its values while enforcing its norms. Commitment is shared and extended in the symbols of the culture in stories, rituals, and symbolic expressions that elevate the distinctiveness of the culture and make it available to the next generation as part of authentic cultural transmission.

Catholic Colleges and Universities Today

Catholic colleges and universities are facing a degree of cultural crisis of their own these days. In order for them to sustain a vibrant Catholic identity and culture, they will need to replace the witness community of knowledgeable and committed cultural icons who were the members of religious communities. No organizational culture can survive or flourish without a visible witness group, be they formally or informally structured, that has both knowledge and commitment. It is clear that no group of laypersons will have the same level of preparation and formation as the nuns and priests who preceded them. What is not clear is what the standard for knowledge and commitment must be in order to assure the vibrancy of Catholic culture in these institutions. Coming to terms with how to establish this new standard is one of the critical challenges facing Catholic higher education today.

Religious formation was a process that developed both commitment and knowledge within religious life. There are three aspects of the approach sisters took in formation and cultural enhancement that are particularly useful in describing the type and extent of knowledge and commitment needed at the current time in Catholic colleges and universities. First, the sisters themselves did not use an absolute standard for the amount of knowledge or the extent of the commitment necessary in their apostolic work. Rather, they accepted young women with the education and commitment they had and then developed and reinforced these components, deepening both their knowledge and commitment, without achieving some perfectly formulated goal. As entrants changed, the activities that formation emphasized were modified.[81] Second, the amount of knowledge a sister needed to be successful was determined in relation to two primary goals—what was necessary to strengthen the sisters in religious life and necessary to help others, laywomen and laymen. Sufficient knowledge was communicated so that the young sisters could both sustain their religious commitment and also so that they could be apostolically effective. Theological knowledge became important once cultural catalysts realized that sisters needed this knowledge to advance in their faith and also to be able to address the needs and concerns of students at their institutions. Third, for much of their history, though not since the 1970s, religious congregations developed a culture of strong leadership. The historical cavalcade of women empowered to found institutions and to build, grow, and encourage others to join them is legendary. In threatening times during those years, a clear authority structure and strong leadership by entrepreneurial cultural catalysts proved crucial to the survival and development of the congregations.[82]

As applied to Catholic colleges and universities, these reflections could be formulated in the following three guidelines. First, the quality of knowledge and depth of commitment needed to sustain and enhance the Catholic culture of these institutions depends on the existing amount of cultural knowledge and commitment that the cultural actors currently possess. Second, knowledge follows the lead of commitment and mission. The appropriate amount of knowledge is determined by what is needed to sustain commitment in faculty, administrators, and staff and what is needed to help students progress in the knowledge, commitment, and appreciation of the Catholic faith. Third, in times of crisis, a college or university needs someone with expert knowledge and deep commitment as a leader who has effective, albeit not unlimited, power to reset the course of cultural development.

In practice, a Catholic college has to make a general judgment about current faculty and administrators. This means determining the level of knowledge and commitment among most of the faculty and assessing whether a group of faculty, including some young faculty members, exists that is at least relatively well informed and very committed to the Catholic mission at the institution. The second guideline indicates that the college has to know what model it is following with respect to Catholic identity. The goal of informing students about the Catholic tradition must be described in clear terms. This description will determine to a large extent the depth of knowledge required by faculty and staff. The final guideline is only relevant if cultural catalysts at an institution judge that the institution is at a tipping point. In such circumstances, broad knowledge and deep commitment are required in a leadership group that has sufficient authority to make significant cultural change in order to move the institution forward.

IO

Leadership and Governance

Cultural enhancement and change in any organization require strong leadership at the highest level. Almost to a person, the group of 124 administrators we interviewed talked about the importance of deepening Catholic culture. Making progress on this front, however, will depend in large measure on the performance of Catholic college and university presidents. This chapter develops an analytical structure that explores religious leadership. It focuses primarily on presidents, but includes the pivotal role trustees play in religious leadership at Catholic colleges and universities.

In *Organizational Culture and Leadership*, Edgar Schein talks about the interconnectedness of leadership and culture.

> Organizational cultures are created in part by leaders, and one of the most decisive functions of leadership is the creation, the management, and sometimes even the destruction of culture.
>
> Neither culture nor leadership, when one examines each closely, can really be understood by itself. In fact, one could argue that the only thing of real importance that leaders do is to create and manage culture and that the unique talent of leaders is their ability to understand and work with culture. If one wishes to distinguish leadership from management or administration, one can argue that leaders create and change cultures, while managers and administrators live within them.[1]

One of the most important ways presidents of Catholic colleges and universities distinguish themselves is by successfully shaping the religious culture at their institutions. How they go about doing this, however, varies considerably.

Types of Presidents

Leadership styles exemplified by collegiate presidents have been the subject of a significant body of research and writing in the past thirty years. Drawing on this abundant literature, we have developed two composite types of visionary presidents—the *connective president* and the *directive president*. Both have a strong sense of where the religious university should be headed, and both can effectively lead it there. There are, of course, both advantages and disadvantages in using this analytical approach. The obvious disadvantage is that a distillation of possible presidential styles to only two necessarily blurs a great deal of nuance about how presidents lead. The simplicity and manageability of the approach, however, provides a distinct advantage in illuminating important strategic choices and their implications for religious cultural enhancement.

Connective presidents[2] resemble James M. Burns's transactional leaders, whose attentiveness to culture and trust-building create a climate in which change becomes most readily acceptable.[3] Reminiscent of Westley and Mintzberg's *bricoleur* leaders, connective presidents collect and weave together small and disparate initiatives into more complex and overarching programmatic plans for enhancing cultural identity.[4] Ideal for any university that needs revitalizing, the connective leader is, as Joseph Crowley suggests, "a strategist, a builder, a promoter who deals well with people" and infuses the university with the symbolism and the personal spirit necessary to accomplish daring goals.[5] As Jean Lipman-Blumen points out, connective presidents "easily 'get' the connections among diverse people, ideas, and institutions, even when the parties themselves do not."[6] As champions of possibility, connective leaders can find common ground. They are engaged and focused, and their style is subtle. By employing Mintzberg's quiet management techniques, connective presidents "infuse values into slow, profound change for which everyone takes responsibility while holding other things steady, [thus assuring] a natural continuous improvement."[7] Connective presidents are intuitive and persuasive, and by exercising their powers of persuasion, these presidents build consensus among centers of influence, linking them together in a supportive network that moves the institution forward.[8] As a facilitator and mentor, the connective president is aware of others and their needs and places great emphasis on broad participation and openness.[9]

Connective presidents make an impact in three ways. First, these presidents carefully assess who and what presently exists within the culture that could positively contribute to achieving their stated goals. Second, the presidents assemble a senior administrative ensemble that reports directly to them and becomes the dominant catalyzing team within the existing culture. Finally, connective presidents put time and energy into mentoring this group and strategizing with them. These presidents spend considerable time with the senior team, articulating the vision for the institution and receiving feedback about plausible ways to realize that vision.

Peter Senge points out that often "leaders spend too much time trying to remediate weaknesses and too little building on strengths."[10] Connective presidents do not fall into that trap. Appreciating the tendency of people in organizations to follow their own, the connective president builds a strategy for change on the natural leadership that has already surfaced in the university and augments this small group with carefully chosen new administrators hired to be committed agents of renewal. These new hires add balance and depth to the leadership ensemble and can reinvigorate the group with fresh ideas.

With respect to the religious dimension of leadership, the connective leader selects senior administrators who, all other things being equal, also embody the Catholic mission. Prior to appointing any senior administrator, the connective leader gathers as much information as possible about his or her past performance and makes a reasoned judgment about the new senior administrator's commitment to "things Catholic." This assures that senior administrators chosen by the connective leader are either personally informed about the Catholic intellectual tradition at a depth appropriate for the position they hold or are eager to become informed through programs the president suggests or establishes. The connective leader understands the pivotal role each senior administrator will play in establishing the Catholic cultural network at the university and consequently chooses individuals who are committed to both Catholic higher education and the Catholic faith.[11]

The impact of the connective president is realized in a long-term framework of at least six to ten years. This president works with senior administrators, jointly selects good strategies, makes connections with existing programs and potential cultural catalysts, and carefully establishes initiatives within an overarching master plan. Once the plan is hatched, the president also helps prepare the various constituencies within the institution to accept the changes that are underway or yet to come. Connective presidents rely on trust and the connective tissue of networked support to ensure successful outcomes.

While connective presidents are reminiscent of Burns's transactional leaders, *directive presidents* closely resemble his transformational leaders. Their heroic approach depends on the skillful use of personal "expertise, prestige, intelligence, charm and credibility."[12] Like Westley and Mintzberg's idealist presidents, directive presidents are pragmatic and politically astute leaders who understand that they "must crystallize the dreams of a constituency."[13] These presidents, as Joseph Crowley points out, are perfectly suited to universities in some kind of turnaround situation. Directive presidents take charge, and, like Kerr and Gade's pathfinder presidents, they "improve substantially on the performance and direction of existing endeavors."[14] This kind of president envisions change and cleverly and creatively pursues innovations and adaptations that will make a significant difference in how successful the university is in achieving stated goals. One of the hallmarks of the directive president is a future orientation and commitment to continuous improvement of current activities.[15] Directive presidents are charismatic leaders who command great loyalty among their immediate circle of senior administrators. They establish clear limits, priorities, and positions and confidently delegate responsibility to get things done.[16]

Directive presidents also make their impact in three principal ways. First, these presidents refine the vision and goals for their institutions, and they craft the message that catalyzes action. Second, directive presidents carefully assemble a senior team that is fully on board with the new vision and goals and unassailably loyal to the president. Finally, directive presidents spend some intensely focused time with their senior team laying out a specific plan to secure their goals and establishing a clear system for assessing progress.

James Fisher believes that people "simply want to agree with and to follow charismatic leaders."[17] Directive leaders understand how important a loyal team is to accomplishing stated goals. They also realize that a cohesive group of senior administrators will generate hope for the future that is contagious. Consequently, the directive leader wastes little time trying to convert skeptics and focuses on hiring senior administrators who get the message and want to be part of a team that brings the president's vision to fruition. There are distinct advantages for the directive president in having one or two team members who have history in the university. Loyalty and a sense of shared purpose, however, will always trump cultural experience when the directive president assembles a senior team.

With respect to the religious dimension of leadership, the directive leader is quite knowledgeable about the Catholic intellectual tradition and personally committed to the Catholic faith. In selecting senior administrators, however, this president is not overly concerned with their personal knowledge of the Catholic intellectual tradition or their commitment to the Catholic faith. Instead, the directive president looks for skilled administrators who are willing to take some direction from the president, implement programs, assess their effectiveness, and be accountable for securing results.

The directive president makes a decisive impact and does so in the short run. New programs or approaches are implemented quickly within a three- to five-year time frame. This approach allows little time to develop an elegant master plan or place particular initiatives within it. As a result, certain inconsistencies among programs can emerge that require ongoing corrections and emendations during the ensuing years. Directive leaders rely on personal loyalty, acceptance, awe, or polite respect by key constituencies in the institution to secure general support for the new programs and approaches they launch.

A wide variety of distinctly different qualities distinguish which leadership style is most appropriate in a given context. One of the most important of these is the length of time available to address a given leadership challenge. Connective leadership is a long-term proposition. It relies on the foundations of fact-finding and assessment for building coalitions and alliances of like-minded or similarly disposed individuals who can act as cultural catalysts within a leadership cohort. Patience is also an essential component of the connective leadership style. Not only do connective leaders need time to assemble a leadership ensemble but also they must invest significant time in mentoring their team before embarking on a mutually agreed-upon agenda. Any challenge that poses an imminent threat to an organization requires immediate and dramatic action in order to be resolved. The requirement of speedy action discounts connective leadership as the most effective or appropriate style in these circumstances.

On the other hand, organizational challenges that require broad-based support and consensus will not be well served by a leadership approach that moves too quickly. Directive leadership spends little time persuading or building coalitions, preferring instead to rely on a dynamic team of loyal administrators who act independently and creatively to secure predetermined outcomes in a timely fashion. The careful work of making connections and developing networks takes a back seat to innovation and action, as far as directive leaders are concerned. Challenges that will be derailed if acted on too quickly are ill served by dynamic and fast-paced directive leaders.

Cultural Context

In order for a Catholic college or university to move forward in terms of its religious identity and mission, it needs the right leadership. The two types of presidents described here differ sharply in style and approach, but they can both succeed in enhancing the religious culture of a Catholic institution. What constitutes effective leadership, however, depends not only on a leader's attributes but also on the context in which those attributes are brought to bear. In other words, the right religious leader for a Catholic college or university is the one whose talents match the college's needs. In her analysis of theoretical approaches to leadership, Jana Nidiffer points out that contingency theorists insist that "good leadership is situationally specific . . . [and] the nature of appropriate or effective leadership is best understood within the context of the organization."[18]

Administrators interviewed for this study almost all maintained that their institutions would benefit from efforts to enhance or invigorate the Catholic culture. What each college or university needs in order to accomplish those ends, however, varies considerably. The institutions some administrators described had reasonably strong Catholic cultures with shared beliefs, norms, and assumptions and a rich and varied array of rituals, stories, and symbols that supported and enriched cultural content. These colleges and universities employed cultural catalysts who invigorated cultural transmission. They also had cultural citizens in significant enough numbers to assure that the institution's religious culture was both distinguishable and inheritable.

Other administrators described universities with tepid religious cultures. Beliefs, norms, and assumptions at these institutions were not widely shared, except in the shadow culture that often undermined Catholic character, identity, and mission. Religious rituals were rare or poorly attended, and the stories that were intended to connect aspects of the Catholic culture more often challenged, rather than supported, Catholic identity. Cultural catalysts were only beginning to emerge at these institutions, and very few cultural citizens were successfully involved in transmitting religious culture. Consequently, the distinguishability and inheritability of Catholic culture at these Catholic colleges and universities were threatened.

Most of the institutions described by senior administrators operate in a religious cultural context that needs enhancement. Their religious cultures are adequate but not vibrant. The cultural strengths and weakness of these institutions vary widely, and many appear to stand between two of the four models of Catholic universities, poised at the point of making cultural adjustments that would bring them more in line with one model or another.

As indicated in the previous chapter, if there is a cultural disconnect between what an organization is trying to do and how it actually behaves, a strategy for cultural change is required in order to regain cultural coherence. There are any number of degrees of cultural change in Catholic colleges and universities that might be desirable or necessary to assure Catholic cultural distinguishability and inheritability. In order to simplify and clarify the spectrum in terms of its implications for leadership, it is helpful to narrow the possibilities to only two—religious cultural *adjustment* and religious cultural *correction*.

Cultural *adjustment* is appropriate for institutions that are in no immediate danger of losing cultural distinguishability and face no imminent threats to inheritability. Because organizational cultures are dynamic and constantly in flux, Catholic colleges have to make cultural adjustments just to maintain the current state of their religious culture. Much like ships at sea that are buffeted by wind and current, colleges that make no adjustments in terms of their religious cultures will soon find themselves off course and in trouble. Senior administrators at all of the colleges studied were interested in far more than simply maintaining Catholic culture. The kind of enhancement and invigoration of religious culture administrators claimed to want requires a president who carefully choreographs efforts to assure that an overarching plan is implemented in the long term.

Cultural *correction* is not only appropriate but necessary for Catholic colleges and universities that are in danger of losing cultural distinguishability and face imminent threats to inheritability. Like ships that find themselves off course and near the rocks, these institutions are in perilous straits. The survival of their religious culture will require dramatic intervention on the part of a president to turn things around. There is little opportunity for broad-based and meticulously executed plans for cultural invigoration. Quick action on multiple fronts and in the short run is the only approach that can assure Catholic culture survives at these institutions.

Outcomes and the Leadership Match

Presidents at Catholic colleges and universities are hired and subsequently evaluated in relation to a number of criteria, only one of which is religious leadership. For the purposes of this analysis, however, the religious situation of a given institution is assumed to be determinative of who should lead and what constitutes successful leadership. Effective presidents at Catholic colleges and universities are those who enhance the religious cultures of their institutions. Trustees select presidents they judge are most likely to achieve the best results in a given context and in a timely fashion.

Over the course of time, the religious culture of Catholic colleges and universities shifts and changes. Presidents are responsible for reading the cultural signs of the times, analyzing them, confronting the challenges they present, and acting resolutely to address them so the institution can move forward. At times presidents confront problems in terms of religious culture that are pressing, but not critical, and require cultural adjustment. If, for instance, an institution relies too strongly on campus ministry and social justice initiatives and the vitality of the Catholic intellectual tradition in the academic sector fades, the president must make adjustments. If the academic sector is reasonably strong and campus ministry is vital but Catholic moral tradition is largely ignored in residence halls, once again, adjustments must be made. In these situations and a variety of others, the president is confronted with clear weaknesses and gaps in the religious culture of the institution that must be addressed. Each of these problems suggests an institution in need of revitalization. Within a university facing these kinds of challenges, there are usually any number of initiatives that function well in terms of supporting and enhancing Catholic culture and identity. An overarching plan that connects these programs and creates a comprehensive roadmap for enhancing religious culture could well be missing. In this situation, the Catholic university could obviously benefit from the work of a strategist, builder, and promoter who can work well with the various citizens, link their disparate initiatives, and develop a comprehensive approach toward revitalizing the religious dimension of the university in all areas.

The religious cultural context in this setting needs cultural adjustment and will benefit from the careful planning and quiet management of a president with a connective approach. After assessing the strengths and weaknesses of the administrative staff, the president can most effectively marshal energy and enthusiasm by gathering together an ensemble of positively contributing administrators. After identifying the areas needing reinvigoration, the president makes strategic hires that complement the existing team. Seeking broad support and open discussion, the president uncovers existing strengths and begins a process of shoring up areas of weakness. Having put in place the structural pieces that support broad-based religious culture, the connective president establishes programs that train faculty and staff to engage the Catholic intellectual and moral traditions in all areas of campus life. Because the enhancement of religious culture in these situations requires adjustment and not critical correction, the president has the luxury of time to put things in place. Using that time well to create a more broadly based infrastructure that supports religious culture is well worth the time and energy it requires.

Not all presidents find themselves at institutions whose religious cultures need only be adjusted in order to become more vibrant and vital. Some Catholic colleges and universities face dramatic threats to the vibrancy of their religious culture, and perhaps even to their survival. Often these cultural crises have been slowly building over a long period of time.

Significant changes in the Catholic culture can take place at institutions in incremental fashion, as a series of seemingly innocuous modifications build on each other and culminate in a dramatic cultural shift. For instance, by definition, persuasion universities rely on a considerable number of Catholic faculty and administrators who are prominently engaged in the full educational program. They also have an identifiable group of faculty and administrators, well trained in the Catholic faith, who promote and nurture academic, social, and religious components of the Catholic culture. Suppose that for many years members of the founding religious congregation provided the largest number of people comprising this recognizable group of committed and knowledgeable Catholics who permeated all sectors of a persuasion university. As the demographics within the founding religious congregation shifted, fewer and fewer members chose or were able to be fully involved in all areas of collegiate life. At the same time, the university responded to changes in the educational market and added business and other professional programs that shifted the traditional focus on liberal arts. Over time, full-time or adjunct faculty with little or no knowledge of or commitment to the Catholic tradition were hired in increasing numbers in order to staff these new programs and meet the increasing demand of students to take them. The number of religious continued to drop precipitously, and suddenly the university realized that it no longer had the necessary cadre of committed and knowledgeable faculty and staff to assure the Catholic educational component would remain clear and its religious goals would be met. This institution has reached a crisis point, and without some dramatic intervention, it will lose its religious cultural distinguishability and inheritability.

The religious cultural context in this situation needs a cultural correction. It requires the expertise, prestige, intelligence, charm, and credibility of a directive president who can turn things around. Benign neglect allowed things to drift for too long, and the institution is in desperate need of a president who is able to clearly articulate a new vision for how it will be Catholic in the future. By bringing in a group of administrators who understand and are enthusiastic about the new goals and committed to securing results, the president can jump-start Catholic culture with a series of innovations and adaptations and make significant improvements in the short run. The directive president establishes the direction, goals, and scope of change, while delegating responsibility for action to a new and invigorated senior staff, and in so doing, brings a sense of optimism and shared purpose to the college community that is contagious. By sheer dint of personal charisma and political prowess, this kind of president can get people on board with new initiatives. The directive president's ability to take charge, set a new course, and assemble a loyal staff that is empowered and accountable will substantially improve the university's Catholic culture in relatively short order.

Directive and connective presidents will probably have different attitudes to hiring. A newly hired directive president will likely find new activities for some sitting members of the senior team and hire a number of people from outside the university. New hires will be chosen for their administrative ability, as well as their strong support for the initiatives of the president. Connective presidents are more inclined to keep senior staff as long as they show a willingness to familiarize themselves with issues the president wants to tackle. Whether or not a directive president moves more aggressively to replace members of the senior administrative team depends in large part on the skills and qualities of those individuals.

A more significant difference between connective and directive presidents lies in the type of information they share with current or prospective members of the senior team. Connective presidents give general information about the goals and share benchmark information necessary to any process involved in strengthening religious culture. This general information creates the contours of the project, and senior administrators collaborate in developing the particular strategies that will be implemented across the institution over time. Directive presidents, on the other hand, either sketch specific projects they want launched or describe them in detail, providing actual or prospective members of the senior team with a clear picture of what type of support and innovation is expected. Rather than entertaining a variety of approaches to modifying the Catholic culture, the directive president produces a plan and expects the senior team members to implement it and make whatever cultural adjustments are necessary in their own sectors to strengthen and support presidential initiatives.

Two of the most respected and successful presidents in the history of American Catholic higher education were directive presidents. Father Theodore Hesburgh and Sister Madeleva Wolff were both members of the larger community of Holy Cross. In the previous chapter, we highlighted Sister Madeleva's program for getting more professional education and training for sisters. Sr. Madeleva's institution—Saint Mary's College—sat across the street from the University of Notre Dame, where Father Hesburgh served as president. Father Hesburgh began his presidency in 1952 and retired from it in 1987, while Sister Madeleva served from 1934 until 1961. These two outstanding leaders had overlapping presidencies, and both made a significant impact not only in their own institutions but beyond their doors as well. Sister Madeleva and Father Hesburgh had the intellectual capacity, imagination, and confidence to expand the potential and extend the reach of a thoroughly intellectual Catholicism. They served as presidents during a time when there was an abundance of nuns and priests living and teaching at their respective institutions. The religious congregations set the tone on campus, and lay faculty were far more likely than they are today to defer to the president or to the judgment of the Holy Cross communities. Despite this "authority edge," both presidents faced two significant obstacles: they had to challenge their own religious communities, and they had to operate with far fewer financial resources than St. Mary's and Notre Dame have available today.

No less an authority than Sr. Madeleva herself placed her in the directive leader category. "I have," she said, "all the virtues and the defects of the autocratic personality." Sr. Madeleva might have recognized the prickly parts of that description, but she also appreciated the benefits of this particular style. "It's friction that keeps the car on the road," she said, and added in even more colorful language, "We couldn't digest our food at all if a cataract of acid didn't drench it on the way down."[19]

In his book *God, Country and Notre Dame*, Father Hesburgh made it clear that he came into the presidency of Notre Dame with a vision for where the university should be and went about hiring the team necessary to realize the vision. "I envisioned Notre Dame as a great Catholic university, the greatest in the world." A great university needs a pervading spirit, but according to Hesburgh, it also "needs a great faculty, a great student body, and great facilities." "The spirit we had," he allows, "the rest we didn't. . . . I knew that if Notre Dame was ever to become the university it is today, we had to bring in new deans and start upgrading the faculty. That was my job as I saw it."[20] Holy Cross father, James Burns, was president of Notre Dame from 1919 to 1922. During that tenure he demonstrated for Hesburgh the power of directive leadership in the short term. "He [Father Burns] proved to my mind, that one person can change the whole direction of an institution, and he did it in a mere three years in office."[21]

While both Sister Madeleva and Father Hesburgh were directive leaders in their first years of leadership, they became connective leaders who energized broad networks of convinced cultural catalysts and citizens within their respective institutions. Both were truly ambidextrous in terms of leadership style, and as a result, they radically transformed their institutions and brought to life expansive visions of what was institutionally possible in Catholic higher education in the United States. They also served as popular presidents who garnered strong institutional support over long tenures—twenty-seven years in the case of Sr. Madeleva and thirty-five years for Father Hesburgh.

Different Leadership Situations

Catholic colleges and universities find themselves in one of two situations in terms of their leadership. Either they have a sitting president involved in religious leadership, or they are searching to find the most effective religious leader for their institution. Both situations require careful assessment of where the institution stands in terms of its Catholic culture, identity, and mission. Both also present real challenges for presidents, who must maintain a good fit between their personal leadership style and the religious cultural challenges they must address over time.

Sitting Presidents

Sitting presidents are expected to sustain, support, and enhance the Catholic culture of the colleges and universities they serve so that they are better able to achieve their religious goals. Presidents are evaluated in terms of how successful they are in this endeavor. Sitting presidents will only be successful in terms of securing religious outcomes if they fit their approach to the needs of their situation and do so in an appropriate time frame. For purposes of simplicity and clarity in this discussion, sitting presidents are assumed to have a style compatible for the challenges confronting their institution. That means that if the Catholic culture needs corrective action in a fairly short period of time, a directive president is on hand to lead this change. Institutions merely needing adjustments in their Catholic culture or correctives that can be introduced in a methodical way over time have a connective president. Of course, in the real world, current presidents are not always up to the cultural task, whatever the type of leadership required. The complexities involved in this kind of mismatch will be attended in greater detail later in the chapter.

Catholic colleges and universities in each of the four models have a variety of programs, approaches, and processes in the areas of academics, residence life, student affairs, and religious activities, as well as cultural catalysts and citizens who shape the content and structure of each of these areas. In order to assure the vibrancy of Catholic culture on campus, presidents assess the strength or weakness of the cultural content and symbols and evaluate whether the cadre of cultural catalysts and citizens, particularly among the faculty and administrative staff, is appropriate to assure ongoing cultural growth and development and the achievement of stated religious goals.

When sitting presidents first arrive at their institutions, they are faced either with the need to adjust the religious culture of the institution or to correct the course the university was pursuing, and they tailor their leadership styles to meet those particular needs. Over time, circumstances change, and leaders may have to adjust their approach to meet the new challenges facing their institutions. Even before presidents modify their approach, they have to know whether cultural change is required and what type of change is most important. As Edgar Schein pointed out, leaders change, shape, and manage culture. When leaders come into institutions from the outside, they bring a clear eye to cultural observation, and if they are astute, these new presidents can take advantage of their outsider/insider status in diagnosing the cultural ills of their new organization. In many cases, boards of trustees engage in extensive analysis about institutional religious goals and culture prior to hiring new presidents. This analysis shapes the choice of president and any mandates for change requiring either cultural adjustments or corrections the new president receives.

Once presidents have been in office for a time, however, they become participants in and shapers of the cultures they lead. At that point, the cultural distance they had when first hired disappears. For all intents and purposes, presidents over time become cultural insiders. Diagnosing cultural reality and its ills from this vantage point is a complicated challenge.[22]

The religious cultures of Catholic colleges and universities either enhance or inhibit the ability of the institutions to educate students in the Catholic tradition and achieve other religious goals. As indicated earlier, changes can occur both within the organization and in the environment that require some alteration in the religious culture of Catholic colleges and universities. Sometimes a shift occurs internally that renders the culture no longer supportive of the stated religious goals of the college or university. At other times, external pressures are the impetus for cultural adaptation. An inability to meet economic margin criteria may cause a university or college to rethink its religious goals. Competitive pressures from other Catholic institutions that noticeably strengthen their Catholic culture and do so in such compelling ways that they develop a competitive advantage can also create impetus for change. Whether the pressure is internal or external, it requires the institution to make adjustments or corrections in the supporting religious culture.

If sitting presidents hope to make appropriate adaptations and changes in the religious culture of their institutions, they must be able to determine whether cultural adjustment or correction is most appropriate. Making that determination requires a clear understanding of the ideal the institution hopes to realize, an accurate depiction of present performance, and a measure of the gap that exists between the two. As important as this diagnostic information is, however, few institutions, according to the judgment of senior administrators, are gathering it.

All organizations resist change, and Catholic colleges and universities are no different. Presidents are expected to monitor progress or the lack thereof and make appropriate adjustments to keep the university on course. Over time, presidents become cultural insiders who have better insights about how to effect change. At the same time, however, they can lose critical perspective and miss the cultural clues that signal the need for change. As insiders, presidents become accustomed to having regular sources of information within the university. Unfortunately, if these sources are not sufficiently attuned to the religious culture, they may well misread what is happening and mislead the president about the need for substantial cultural change.

Presidents enhance their performance as religious leaders if they are both astute about the internal realities of religious culture and aware of important developments and trends emerging more broadly. Presidents may be fortunate to have some senior administrators who both comprehend the need for a strong Catholic culture and are alert to the trends that have diminished the strength of the culture. Presidents will be in a much better place when it comes to developing a strategic plan for change if they both trust these religiously attuned administrators more than others and are willing to be positively influenced by them.

For the most part, presidents think of themselves as responding well to the insights of their senior team. That may well be the case, but even if it is, the insights that team members offer are frequently contradictory. In the best of circumstances, some senior administrators will see a need for strengthening the Catholic culture, while others are sure that proposed changes are risky and likely to jeopardize the competitive position of the university. In matters of Catholic culture, as in all other things, presidents must listen to a variety of advice but be personally astute about what is required. In the unlikely event a senior team unanimously agrees a substantial change in the Catholic culture is necessary, the president can count his or her blessings and then commit all energy to moving forward. Otherwise, the president will have to first determine who has the most cogent analysis about what is happening and how to proceed before rallying the dissenters and getting on with the plan.

Being astute about analyzing the state of Catholic culture on their own campuses will help presidents be more effective religious leaders. They will also be more successful in that endeavor if they are attentive to what is happening elsewhere. In the collegiate world, where imitation is the highest form of flattery, keeping an eye on the performance of respected colleagues who are able presidents can be a source of inspiration that produces effective initiatives. But even this approach can be problematic. Other presidents may well be doing an excellent job in terms of enhancing Catholic culture, but if they are doing it in situations that are vastly different, their actions are probably not transferable.

A significant hallmark noted earlier that distinguishes connective and directive presidents is their approach to senior team-building. Connective presidents assemble teams largely from within their institutions and persuasively build consensus among the members, listening to them, mentoring them, and receiving feedback about the best ways to secure results. By design, this leadership style is careful, deliberate, highly interconnected, and relatively slow. In the rapidly changing world of American higher education, it is quite possible that a university with a connective president would suddenly find itself in significantly altered circumstances requiring dramatic action in the short term to produce a much-needed cultural correction. The culturally alert president may well be ready to make the necessary adjustments in strategy and even leadership style to meet this challenge, but his or her carefully assembled senior team could prove to be a significant obstacle in the process. Senior team members in a connective president's cabinet are not chosen to act quickly or be loyal lieutenants who willingly get behind a predetermined action plan that they then take full responsibility to implement. Consequently, rather than facilitating the president's change of approach, the senior team may well resist it.

The same problem can emerge just as easily for a directive president whose team comes largely from outside the university and was chosen for their commitment to the president's vision and their entrepreneurial approach to getting results. This approach creates possibilities and programs that in the short run can dramatically improve performance at the university. Eventually, however, these programs must become part of a larger plan that has broad support across the university. In order to stabilize a cultural correction, presidents need to shift gears and assume a connective approach that relies on strategizing with a senior team whose members listen carefully, provide considered feedback, and build consensus among centers of influence. Members of a directive president's senior team will probably find the pace of connective leadership irritating and will chafe under a system that prizes process as much as performance. Rather than being the president's chief allies in the process of adapting style, they may well become unwitting enemies whose resistance sabotages any attempt to try a different approach.

New Presidents

Looking at the situation of new presidents offers other useful insights about leadership and cultural change at Catholic colleges and universities. In choosing a new president, it is the responsibility of trustees to determine the religious goals of the institution and the extent of the gap between these goals and the real performance of the institution. This information is critical in determining whether an institution needs a connective president who can continue to adjust the religious culture of a given college or university or a directive president capable of orchestrating a successful cultural correction. For the most part, trustees do not have data about actual religious performance of the institutions they serve. Without it, they are hampered in attempts to assess cultural context or determine the most appropriate leadership style to look for in a president. Given this information gap, it is not surprising that trustees often fail to include the religious vitality of their colleges or universities in the leadership equation that defines presidential choice. Trustees have relied for years on members of founding religious congregations to evaluate the religious goals and culture of Catholic colleges and universities. As the number of priests and religious women who serve on boards of trustees continues to fall, trustees will be increasingly at a loss when it comes to making these crucial decisions unless they take it upon themselves to become better informed about Catholic culture and how it is changed. Developing tools that assist trustees in assessing religious performance is essential if lay trustees are to be successful in hiring the most effective religious leader when it comes time for presidential transition.

In most cases, trustees select a new president with the particular leadership style they believe will help them move the college or university forward in securing its religious goals. For purposes of analysis, it was assumed earlier that sitting presidents are stylistically suited for the challenges they face. It was also assumed that sitting presidents are willing and able to make adjustments in their strategy and leadership approaches as institutional needs demand. But, as was noted, even an alert, nimble, and talented president will find it difficult to make necessary stylistic changes because the senior staff is hired to be complementary to one approach and will naturally resist modifying it.

In the best of all possible worlds, chief executives are as agile as these assumptions suggest, but Catholic college presidents do not live or lead in the best of all possible worlds. Most leaders, including university presidents, have a dominant leadership style they have polished over the years that is not easily modified. New presidents are often hired because they have a particular style appropriate for the cultural context they will initially encounter. After assembling senior teams that complement their style, these leaders confront and address cultural challenges. Over time, the cultural tide changes, demanding a different approach on the part of the president and senior team. The difficulty senior teams have in accepting and adapting to stylistic change has already been discussed. The problem is further exacerbated by the simple fact that most presidents have a default style and are themselves less than anxious to try different approaches, particularly in critical circumstances. Consequently, unless a president assembles his or her leadership team with an eye to accommodating necessary adaptations in style and approach that might be called for in the future, the kind of flexibility that cultural theorists insist is a hallmark of successful leadership will be rare.[23]

Trustees and Presidents

Ultimate responsibility for a university rests with the trustees. Trustees are often selected to serve because they hold the university in high esteem and are willing to commit their time, talent, and treasure on its behalf. Their influence and generosity are deeply appreciated by the university and advance its interests, but their major responsibility is governance. The three most important governance responsibilities of trustees are selecting the president, monitoring the performance of the president, and establishing general policies for the university. At Catholic colleges and universities, trustees take on these responsibilities in circumstances that are made extraordinarily more difficult because of fundamental changes in Catholic culture both inside and outside the university.

Trustees at all universities, including nonsectarian ones, have grave responsibilities that have always been difficult to fulfill.[24] In accepting their fiduciary responsibility, trustees agree to make important decisions in an area—the education sector—they and most of their colleagues know about only as consumers. New university trustees realize that their role is distinctly different from that of for-profit corporate directors. The biggest difference, aside from the nonprofit status of the university, lies in the area of personal expertise and how it is applied. Corporate "directors" are chosen for their expertise in the business for which they are setting general policies. University trustees are not. University trustees are being asked to bring personal expertise to bear in a distinctly different arena, and they must learn how to do that on the job. The personal expertise university trustees bring with them is usually either in a particular industry or a more general field such as finance, management, law, or personnel relations. Some of this knowledge and skill is transferable to higher education, but what exactly or how much often eludes them because they are unfamiliar with the education sector.

After being appointed to the board, most new trustees participate in some introductory workshop or seminar that familiarizes them with general trustee responsibilities and the current situation of the university. Because they are new to the environment and operate under great time constraints, the introductory seminars are at best rudimentary. They introduce new trustees to areas that require some general knowledge and those in which they will have to make decisions. These sessions also inform new trustees how they can best participate in committee meetings, as well as full board meetings. Unless they have already served as a university trustee at another institution, most new trustees find that their first two to three years on the board serve as a kind of apprenticeship in which they become fully versed in all their responsibilities.

Being asked to set general university policies for a market sector about which you have few specifics is an unsettling experience. Nevertheless, most lay trustees are willing to accept the responsibility because they want to help the university and because they know they are no less qualified than most of the other trustees currently serving on the board. They realize that it is an honor to be asked to serve as a trustee, and most are willing to give generously of their time and their financial wherewithal, while learning the ins and outs of university trusteeship. The information deficit for trustees serving at Catholic institutions is almost certainly larger than for trustees serving on the boards of similar nonsectarian institutions, despite the fact that the general triad of governance responsibilities remains the same. This may have always been the case, but as a result of the diminished role played by the sponsoring religious congregation in the governance of the Catholic universities over the past fifteen years, the situation has become even more pronounced. That is certainly the case in terms of the first trustee governance responsibility—selecting a president.

Selecting a President

Prior to the 1970s, religious congregations owned, operated, and governed the institutions they founded and fully participated in all aspects of their operation.[25] The choice of a president in these days was a matter for the congregation provincial, whose decision was accepted under the vow of obedience. Since the 1970s, responsibility for university governance at Catholic institutions has passed increasingly to lay trustees, and with it has come the role of choosing the president. At first trustees made their choice from pools of candidates who were members of the sponsoring religious congregation. By the 1980s, many boards of trustees were looking beyond men and women religious to laypersons as potential Catholic college and university presidents. When considering only nuns, brothers, and priests as candidates for the presidency, trustees could reliably assume the candidates had the knowledge and commitment necessary for religious leadership. After all, these men and women had committed their lives to service in the Church and had spent years being educated and formed in preparation for ministry and leadership. The days when trustees could handle the thorny issues involved in assessing religious preparation and commitment by only considering religious men and women as candidates are long gone. Now, all trustees at Catholic colleges and university must determine how much "Catholic knowledge" candidates have and the extent of their commitment to the Catholic Church. They must also determine what level of knowledge and commitment is appropriate for and commensurate with the responsibilities inherent in religious leadership at a Catholic college or university.

Trustees have experience and skills in this area that can be very helpful in establishing creative and effective ways to judge the suitability of prospective presidents. Many trustees have been involved in selecting high-level executives and are familiar with different insightful and subtle ways to illicit candid information about candidates. By bringing their collective experience and wisdom to bear when evaluating candidates, trustees can go a long way toward assuring a good leadership fit between their final choice and the needs of the university.

Trustees rightly want to judge the potential effectiveness of candidates they are considering for the position of university president. As in many performance issues, the best indicator of future behavior is past performance in similar circumstances. Of course, it is often the case that a candidate's past performance is at another institution or in another position that bears little resemblance to the institution at hand. Nevertheless, trustees have to make some determination about how they think candidates will perform at their university. Part of the leadership challenge facing any Catholic college or university president will center on religious culture, and trustees need information about how able candidates are personally to provide effective leadership in this area. Knowledge of the Catholic tradition and commitment to it have been hallmarks of religious leaders at Catholic colleges and universities for most of their history, and those qualifications are essential components of effective religious leadership. Trustees will not be able to make an informed decision about leadership unless they can evaluate the depth of each candidate's knowledge of the Catholic tradition and commitment to it. Delicacy and subtlety count when trying to elicit this information, but trustees should avail themselves of any data they judge to be important. Candidates' participation in parish life, their leadership in Catholic issues, the witness of their personal lives—all of these offer information about Catholic background. It is incumbent on trustees, relying on an appropriate combination of the direct approach and subtlety, to get the information they need to make wise decisions.

Establishing Policy

The demographic shifts in religious congregations over the past twenty-five years have had an impact on both the number of religious serving as trustees at Catholic institutions and the extent of their professional experience in higher education. As a result of these changes, the burden for setting broad policies in all areas—the second governance responsibility—now rests more squarely on the shoulders of the lay trustees. One of the most important policy areas trustees must address is Catholic institutional identity and what that implies both for the university and for the type of service it provides to the local, regional, national, and global Church. The university's Catholic culture, how it deals with Church teaching, and its development of effective ways to provide service to the Church follow general guidelines set by the trustees. These guidelines, once established, then influence the determination of policy in other areas.

In the last fifteen years, trustees have had to confront policy decisions that demonstrate the governance responsibilities unique to Catholic universities. The implications of the mandatum granted to Catholic faculty teaching Catholic theology at Catholic universities, the canonical status of the university, and the sale of property as it pertains to the law of the Church (or canon law, as it is more commonly known) are all issues demanding the attention of Catholic collegiate trustees. Most lay trustees do not consider themselves sufficiently knowledgeable in these areas to make well-informed and wise decisions. But because decisions have to be made, trustees often defer to the recommendations of the president, who usually is well informed.[26] This tendency to rely on the president may be useful and expedient, but it contravenes the role and purpose of a board of trustees. A governing board is structured to give direction to the president and to the broader university concerning the Catholic identity, character, and mission of the institution. Concerning substantial policies, the board should conduct its own analysis and develop policy alternatives. Certainly the president makes recommendations, but good governance demands the trustees do their own work, make their own considered judgments, and hammer out policies that conform to their own sentiments. Even if the board eventually adopts policies identical to those the president recommends, the university is still better served if the board attends carefully to its own process. No matter how wise and trusted presidents might be, no board should simply defer to their president's recommendations.

Effective boards of trustees set general policies and the direction of the university. As part of their fiduciary responsibility, they also must make course corrections that are necessary for the good of the university and the success of its mission. Knowing when it is time to undertake a substantial course change in terms of the Catholic culture of the university is one of the most difficult challenges that trustees of Catholic colleges and universities face. Small changes in the Catholic culture happen almost every year. They can occur by consciously introducing new programs, or they may result because current programs are slightly modified or new students entering the university arrive with a different set of backgrounds and expectations. Such changes occur regularly, and often it is difficult to gauge their impact. Over time, however, the cumulative impact of these incremental changes becomes clear. Sometimes the effect is clearly positive, but it is also possible that the accumulated smaller changes have had an unanticipated negative impact on religious culture. This could mean either that the current Catholic culture no longer molds, forms, or transforms the students the way it once did or that other Catholic colleges and universities have become more effective and the university's incremental changes have simply not kept pace. In order to signal the need for a course correction, trustees must become aware of the cumulative effect that changes in Catholic culture have made at the university. How they develop that awareness is not always very clear.

Senior management usually signals the need for collegiate cultural change, by means of what Edgar Schein calls "intense communication." Because most participants in an organization resist change and will not willingly accept the need for it, something has to get their attention. In the case of university trustees, that comes from leadership and consists of "disconfirming data . . . that show[s] the organization that some of its goals are not being met or that some of its processes are not accomplishing what they are supposed to."[27] Relying on information and recommendations from the senior team, the president can come to the realization that substantial changes in the Catholic culture are imperative. The president then approaches the board and requests approval of a major plan that addresses the underlying issues in a substantive manner. If the board is persuaded by the president's analysis and plan, it gives its endorsement. Although trustees rely on senior management in this situation, they still need sufficient information of their own to evaluate the validity and efficacy of the president's recommendation.

Presidents play a significant role in assuring that university boards are truly effective. While most reports to the board accentuate the positive and reflect well on the president and the senior leadership team, they must never sidestep real challenges that face the institution. That does not mean, however, that presidents should be alarmists. As Richard Chait and his colleagues point out, "institutional leaders should convey succinct, forthright, strategic information that places the college's strengths and weaknesses in sharp relief."[28] In order to fulfill part of its governance responsibility, the board of trustees at a Catholic university needs the same kind of succinct, forthright, and strategic information about institutional Catholic culture, including reports about various Catholic activities and programs in the usual sectors of the university: academic affairs, student affairs, campus ministry, athletics, alumni/ae affairs, and so on. As is the case for most information, interpreting it requires a context, and trustees need a good understanding of the larger universe of higher education and Catholic higher education in order to be more effective. Working out a system with administration for providing the pertinent information about the university to trustees on a regular basis and through the committee structure will be most helpful. Trustees also need some additional, albeit less detailed information about what at least one other comparable Catholic institution does in this regard. Benchmarking and comparative data provide trustees with a feel for activities that some other well-respected Catholic university deems to be important and increase their understanding of the institution's relative performance.

For any given university, deciding what data are appropriate to have for measuring the intensity of the Catholic culture is difficult. Neither trustees nor administrators can make this decision on their own. Rather, the appropriate data will likely emerge from a discussion and review that may last a year or more. For example, trustees of a particular committee, say the student affairs committee of the board, may ask student affairs administrators to give their committee a sample of currently available data that will provide insight to the Catholic culture in this area. In conversation with administration, and perhaps consulting with other people, the trustees might decide that the data provided are not really helpful. Alternatively, they might say that such data are helpful but they would like additional data about particular activities or outcomes related to the Catholic identity, character, and mission of the university. Administration then attempts to gather such data for a subsequent meeting of the student affairs committee. A thorough review of the type of information that is needed to understand the depth and breadth of student culture may extend over several trustee meetings. Eventually, however, trustees should have confidence that they are receiving the right mix of data on a regular basis. The "right mix" includes the information that trustees need to judge whether the Catholic culture of the sector they oversee is sufficiently broad and intensive that it effectively contributes to fulfilling the Catholic mission of the university.

Pertinent data concerning the Catholic culture on campus provide helpful guidance for trustees.[29] The emphasis here on pertinent information is not meant to suggest that trustees become involved in micromanaging the Catholic culture of the institution. Trustees restrict themselves to setting general policies and monitoring them to verify that they are being implemented. However, good data should lead experienced trustees to reflect in greater depth on the current position of the university with respect to its Catholic identity, mission, and character.

In determining the type of data they would like to see, trustees can take into account their own talents. For example, many trustees are adept at measuring the relative importance of various activities by following revenues and expenses. They may effectively use this strength by requesting certain types of data. A university is complex, and important activities cannot always be reduced to dollars and cents. On the other hand, seeing expenditure flows for activities related to Catholic culture can help trustees understand better how committed the university is to its religious mission, identity, and character. Trustee members on the student affairs committee, for example, may reasonably request information about the amount of money spent on training university personnel in components of the Catholic tradition. Although this offers only a partial glimpse of what is being done, such data might be useful to trustees, especially when other data are also regularly studied and evaluated.

Receiving pertinent information on Catholic culture allows trustees to perceive over time whether they should continue to press the president and the senior team to strengthen the Catholic culture and devote more resources to accomplishing this goal. The data also allow trustees to see the impact of Catholic culture and to situate their university within the four models of Catholic universities. Depending on where the university stands with respect to distinguishability and inheritability of the Catholic culture, data allow trustees to consider the movement of the institution from one model to another. Finally, having access to excellent and timely data simply allows trustees to be more astute and effective in establishing policy that enhances Catholic culture.

Monitoring Presidential Performance

The last of the three governance responsibilities of trustees—monitoring the performance of the president—implies a commitment on the part of trustees to support the president they have selected to lead the university. Fulfilling this twofold responsibility requires even greater familiarity with campus Catholic culture than either of the other two responsibilities. Trustees have to have some understanding of how presidents at Catholic universities can best improve their institutions generally, and more particularly, how they can better fulfill their unique Catholic mission. They also must be aware of and develop effective ways to support presidents in their religious leadership.

As indicated earlier, one of the most important responsibilities of the trustees is selecting the president. Presidents, of course, lead universities, but they do so while following guidelines established by trustees. Both for the sake of consistent policy and the good of universities, trustees want presidents to succeed. In matters pertaining to Catholic culture, trustees can provide important assistance to presidents that can enhance their success.

The trustees have the highest authority in the university. In matters of great import, such as the Catholic culture at the university, trustees can help the president immensely by signaling first that they personally and collectively support the president and second that they particularly want to see the Catholic culture at the university strengthened or maintained. Obviously, before trustees can signal the direction they want the university to move, in terms of its Catholic culture, they have to decide where they stand in relationship to it. For example, they may decide that the Catholic culture needs strengthening in a number of areas. Alternatively, they may be satisfied with the current programs the university has to fulfill its Catholic mission but want the university to develop additional educational, social, or religious programs to strengthen Catholic culture.

If the current policy direction of the trustees represents a change from the past, the trustees will need to signal to the university community that they expect the president to lead the process of change in the direction they indicate. This support is particularly important for a new or recently inaugurated president, but it also applies to presidents who have been in office for some time. The board of trustees should, of course, avoid issuing directives preempting management or operations, which is the purview of the president and the senior team. A careful statement by the board indicating the desire of the trustees for greater emphasis on or strengthening of certain areas or activities communicates a number of things to the university community. First it alerts everyone to the fact the board expects substantial adjustments in the Catholic culture on campus. It also lets them know that they can anticipate an annual review of progress made by senior management in this regard. Unless the trustees are dissatisfied with the performance of the president and the senior team, the board should provide public backing, especially when difficult leadership steps are being taken. With respect to strengthening the Catholic culture, a statement by the board should provide a strong endorsement of the president. It should also communicate the expectation that administrators, by working collaboratively with various groups in the university, will make changes that conform to the policies set by the trustees. A clear and unambiguous statement sends a strong signal to the whole community about the importance of supporting or enhancing Catholic identity and further strengthens the hand of the president and senior management in their efforts to realize these goals.

Having access to useful data and then evaluating it are important tasks for trustees at all universities. Unfortunately, nonprofit boards are not always vigilant about evaluation and monitoring progress. As William Bowen, president of Andrew Mellon Foundation and former president of Princeton University, points out,

> corporate boards devote much more time to reviews of performance (short-term and long-term) than do boards of nonprofits. . . . [Consequently,] the boards of non-profits are notoriously subject to the problem of failing to see a fast, clearly visible train coming—even when it is moving inexorably and their organization is sitting right on the tracks.[30]

Richard Chait suggests that a lack of knowledge and agreement about "appropriate performance metrics for higher education" is largely responsible for this kind of board failure.[31] If there is little agreement among boards about performance metrics for higher education in general, the problem is even greater in the area of Catholic institutional culture. Negotiating this terrain, let alone making strategic decisions about it, is relatively new for lay trustees at Catholic institutions. In order for lay trustees to perform their oversight role effectively, however, they will have to be willing to learn about significant cultural activities that are important at any Catholic university and agree upon performance standards.

Trustee Membership Committees

Typically, one of the standing committees of the board of trustees is the membership committee. This group discusses among themselves people who might be good board members and then makes recommendations to the full board of trustees. If there is a sense that the proposed persons would indeed be good board members, the candidates are invited to become members of the board of trustees by the chair of the board and the president of the university.

A responsibility of both the membership committee and the board is to make sure that the board itself has a suitable composition of members who are knowledgeable about and committed to the Catholic tradition. Of course, the "Catholic knowledge" needed by a typical board member is not as substantial as that required by, say, a professor of English who engages the Catholic intellectual tradition in university courses. Individual members need an appropriate amount of "Catholic knowledge," and the board as a whole needs balance. Balance implies that some board members should have fairly specific knowledge of the Catholic tradition. Many boards make sure, for example, that they have a current or former faculty member or two from another institution on the board. It is appropriate that Catholic boards have some members, professors or others, who are well informed about the Catholic tradition. In addition to having adequate Catholic knowledge, the majority of the board of trustees should be committed Catholics. Every board is enriched by members who belong to other religious traditions, but committed Catholics are essential. Because any Catholic university has as part of its goal service to the Catholic Church, and because the board has a fundamental responsibility to protect and ensure the Catholic mission, identity, and character of the institution, the majority of members should themselves be committed Catholics. These issues are important topics for discussion and policy review by the membership committee.[32]

In the past, issues of Catholic knowledge and commitment were often handled by having a suitable number of religious sisters, brothers, or priests on the board. That strategy is gradually becoming nonsustainable, and good trustees remain alert to getting the proper mix of Catholic knowledge and commitment on their board.

To secure trustees who can fulfill their governance responsibilities with competence and confidence, the chair and the president must speak with clarity on the front end about the full range of responsibilities new trustees incur, particularly emphasizing the unique governance responsibilities inherent at a Catholic university. Many would-be trustees will find the expectations daunting, but by emphasizing that a learning curve of a year or more is usual, both the board chair and president can help calm their fears. While assuring new trustees that participating at regular board meetings and attending a seminar for new trustees will help prepare them to fulfill their governance responsibilities, neither the chair nor president can responsibly downplay the unique responsibilities trustees have in terms of the institution's Catholic character, mission, and identity. Governance responsibilities with respect to the Catholic mission and culture are incurred, of course, by all trustees, no matter what their religious affiliation.[33] Because trustees bear the burden of maintaining the Catholic character of the institution, it is imperative that they become informed about many things, including the extent to which the culture at their institution is Catholic.

Trustees have the authority to make many decisions on behalf of Catholic colleges and universities. They also have a corresponding responsibility to be prepared to make those decisions well, as Robert Kennedy points out when discussing shared responsibility in ecclesial decision-making.

> Plato's reminder that there is more to running a ship than just seizing the helm was not intended to discourage broadly-based participation in government, but simply to urge that such participation be knowledgeable and open to continual learning. So, too, to remind ourselves that there is more to governance in the Church than just casting a vote in the making of decisions is similarly not to discourage participative governance in the Church but to manifest concern for more learned, more knowledgeable participation. To hold the

helm of a ship, without knowledge of the sea, the winds, the tides, the stars, and one's own ship is to imperil the lives of everyone on board; so too, to participate in ecclesial governance without acquired knowledge not only of ecclesiology but also of governance and its manifold process, is to imperil the ecclesial life of the community in which one governs.[34]

Inheritability Crises

The first interview question posed to senior administrators asked each of them to imagine themselves making a presentation at the Harvard Graduate School of Education about the prospects for Catholic higher education in the United States over the next ten years. In outlining what they might say, a large majority of respondents indicated that Catholic colleges and universities would decrease in number. Some anticipated substantial closings of at least 10 percent or more. Most others agreed that there would be closings but were unwilling to even hazard a guess about how extensive they would be.

Because the very existence of the university is of great concern to both trustees and the president, it is important to review the governance responsibilities of trustees during times when the inheritability of the institution is threatened and the institution's very survival is in question.

Colleges and universities fail for a variety of reasons, but practically all the reasons are related to the inability to attract to the institution a sufficiently large or talented number of students capable of paying the fees they have been assessed. The clearest warning that signals a threat to institutional survival is a decline in the numbers of applicants over the years. In some cases, the drop in new students enrolling at the university in a given year can be precipitous. Most failing institutions, however, experience episodic crises over time, as years with catastrophically small numbers of new students are followed by years in which the numbers of new students are better or even good.

When the viability of the institution is threatened, trustees realize that they have to either replace the president or authorize the president to undertake dramatic changes to help the institution regain financial stability. In most cases, increased financial stability means regularizing at a sufficiently high level a steady flow of suitable students. When an institution is in danger of not satisfying the margin criterion, general advice is not helpful. What is important are the particular circumstances of that institution. However, because the trustees hold in trust the Catholic identity, character, and mission of the institution, it is important for them to be aware of general options that may improve the situation of the college or university while continuing to safeguard its Catholic character. Of course, these general options would have to be linked to particular initiatives that correspond to the specific circumstances in which the institution finds itself.

Trustees, working with the president, have three general options available to them in these kinds of critical circumstances: reaffirm current policy but substantially improve the way the policy is implemented, change the Catholic model that has been the guide for the institution, or move away from the Catholic character and become a nonsectarian institution.[35]

The first and third options in most circumstances are not plausible. If the institution has been unable to attract enough students by emphasizing some aspect of its Catholic heritage, it is unlikely to attract more students by downplaying or dismissing that heritage. Parents pay substantial sums of money to send their children to a private university because the education offered there is more valuable and distinctive than that offered at the relatively inexpensive local public university. Dropping the Catholic tradition is unlikely to persuade parents or students that the institution is therefore more effective and attractive.

The first option—to basically try harder with the same policy—is also unlikely to be effective. An institution, under the guidance of its trustees, only arrives at a crisis situation if it has gone through several cycles of trying harder that did not yield satisfactory results. In order for this approach to work as the institution approaches a financial precipice, the trustees would have to admit that they do not have the right president for the task, be convinced they can hire a president who will embrace their general policy, and then trust that the newly hired president is much more effective. This approach becomes less attractive as the board struggles with the same problem through different presidencies.

The most plausible option is the second one. This option involves, but is not restricted to, moving the institution away from its current Catholic model and closer to one of the other three models. Provided the move makes tactical and strategic sense, this offers the institution several possible paths to emphasize new approaches while drawing upon its longstanding Catholic tradition. Whether or not the policy is successful depends on myriad details related to the particular market in which the university operates. The main point is, however, that the Catholic tradition offers flexibility to institutions facing a grave crisis.

Leadership Implications for Distinguishability and Inheritability

In order to survive and thrive, the religious culture of Catholic colleges and universities must be both distinguishable and inheritable. Both connective and directive leaders make adjustments to enhance the distinguishability of Catholic culture. The differential impact of these two types of leaders occurs mainly in the timing of the outcomes they secure. Connective leaders catalyze cultural changes that enhance distinguishability in institutions where the religious culture is flagging, and they do so over the long term—a period of five to ten years. Directive leaders catalyze cultural changes that enhance distinguishability in institutions whose religious cultures are imperiled, and they do so, as the critical nature of the situation necessitates, in the short term—a period of three to five years.

Both directive and connective presidents can succeed in making changes that secure a more distinguishable culture at the institutions they serve. In order for any culture to thrive, however, it must be inheritable, as well as distinguishable. Connective and directive leadership approaches have different implications when it comes to assuring inheritability. Cultural inheritability is linked to two different time frames—the past and the future. In order to ensure that changes affecting the religious culture of Catholic colleges and universities are inheritable, presidents must make sure that they are consistent with the culture inherited from the past. They must also be reasonably sure the changes have a future and will be positively received, not only by the current generation of students, staff and faculty but also by generations to come. This means that a significant number of knowledgeable and committed faculty and staff members who operate as cultural citizens and catalysts embrace authentic cultural changes and are willing and capable of imparting them to students. It also means that a sufficient number of students are persuaded by the acculturation process to become additional cultural citizens and catalysts who personally accept the adjusted culture and are willing to pass it on to other students.

Directive leaders are particularly suited to assuring cultural coherence and making changes that preserve cultural inheritance. If the religious culture of Catholic colleges and universities has become inauthentic, it requires a serious and immediate course correction for the institution to get back on track. In this situation, there is little value in coalition building and long-term careful adjustment. Cultural integrity is an essential part of inheritability, and when it is lost, a strong leader must act quickly to restore it.

Connective leaders, on the other hand, most notably contribute to inheritability by building consensus about cultural change among centers of influence and linking them together to move the institution forward. Because connective leaders are aware of the needs of others and place great emphasis on broad participation and openness, their cultural changes have broad appeal among faculty and staff. They also make the connections for all citizens, including students, that allow them to become the cultural catalysts and citizens who will pass on the adjusted culture to the next generation.

All cultures, including religious cultures at Catholic colleges and universities, must change and adapt in order to remain distinguishable and inheritable. Cultural enhancement and cultural change in any organization requires strong leadership at the highest level. Presidents of Catholic colleges and universities distinguish themselves by successfully shaping their institutions' religious culture. Both connective and directive presidents contribute to the distinguishability of religious culture at the institutions they serve. The inheritability of that culture, however, requires that presidents exercise both connective and directive leadership at various times in order to assure that the religious culture is authentic and appealing to future generations.

Presidents at Catholic colleges and universities are more likely to be successful in sustaining, supporting, and enhancing the religious culture of the institutions they serve if they are culturally ambidextrous. As we indicated earlier in the chapter, however, most presidents have a particular style that they abandon with some difficulty. Nevertheless, circumstances change in all situations, and most people learn to adapt, at least marginally, to altered circumstances. Some leaders cultivate personal flexibility, and others surround themselves with trusted colleagues who can spur them to modify their preferred and more practiced style, or whose talents compensate for the leader's limits. Whatever the tactic, most successful leaders are aware of the need to adapt and find ways to make necessary adjustments that allow them to attend the needs of the institutions they serve. This kind of stylistic flexibility enables leaders to adjust their own styles to the magnitude of changes needed, the length of time over which they will extend, and the most propitious time to initiate them.

In trying to make the wisest choice in hiring a new president, trustees might assume a president will be somewhat stylistically flexible, but they should also be keenly aware of any candidate's dominant approach to leadership. Once trustees determine the university's religious goals, the magnitude of change needed to accomplish them, and the time frame for change that will be most effective, they will be able to determine the dominant leadership style called for in their present circumstance. Certainly trustees will hope that whichever president they choose has the flexibility to adjust and adapt to changes in the situation over time. Nevertheless, trustees are hiring presidents in a particular time frame to face particular challenges, and it is for those challenges that they must find effective leadership. Whether or not that leader is flexible over time is less of an issue than how that leader will deal with the circumstances at hand. Accurately assessing these challenges and finding an appropriate leadership match is the challenge the board of trustees faces in selecting a president.

Policy Implications

The creation of effective tools to measure the religious performance of Catholic colleges and universities is the most important policy change necessary to strengthen and monitor the Catholic culture on campus. Both trustees and presidents need effective tools to measure the religious performance of Catholic colleges and universities. Those tools, however, are only as useful as the information provided and unless they are carefully tailored, they will not be helpful in terms of enhancing governance and decision-making.

Higher education is strongly competitive. Universities regularly search for ways to improve their programs or offer new programs that attract a larger number and higher quality of student to their institutions. Universities keep abreast of developments not only by reading about innovative approaches in trade journals but also by maintaining close contact with administrators at other universities. This personal knowledge is enhanced by systematic comparative information or performance data about students at other universities. Three types of comparative data are particularly helpful to institutions: information about entering students, financial performance data, and data on how well students perform upon graduation and many years later.

The easiest comparative data to access concern aptitude and scholastic performance measures for entering students at various institutions. Because universities find it advantageous to advertise their prestige, they provide detailed information about the aptitude and achievement of their entering students. Data about financial performance of institutions are more difficult to obtain, although private consortia of universities now exist that share such information. Comparative outcomes data on graduating students and current achievements about students who graduated ten or twenty years ago are difficult, if not impossible, to obtain. Universities that have such data seldom share that data either publicly or with particular institutions.

Although one institution is never quite the same as another, and comparative data—either for a single universities or a group of universities—are never strictly comparable, the data offer some measure of how well the institution is doing according to certain measures. In the business of education, in which administrators must be adept, progress is most often measured through comparison with other institutions. For this reason, aside from having accurate data for one's own institution, the best type of data makes it possible to contrast performance with another comparable university or class of universities.

In order for Catholic institutions to advance and maintain their competitive edge, they need data pertinent to their Catholic culture, in addition to the normal data collected by the university. The most important data to collect is data about student, faculty, and institutional performance relative to Catholic identity, character, and mission at one's own university. Also of great value are comparative or benchmarking data pertinent to Catholic culture and performance. Unfortunately, the many competing Catholic institutions are unlikely to share such data with one another. Administrators can seek data from any comparable Catholic institutions, but they are far more likely to get cooperation from institutions not directly competing with one another.

A comparable Catholic university is one that adheres to the same model and is approximately the same size. Identifying a comparable Catholic university and securing agreement to share data are formidable, but not impossible, tasks. Because there are over 220 Catholic universities, it is relatively easy to find one that is not a competitor. Finding a partner institution of similar size and, ideally, with similar financial resources, such as endowment and tuition revenue, is the most useful, but alas, it is also far more difficult.

As a Catholic institution refines its search for a data partner, the number of comparable institutions drops sharply. The model with the largest number of adherents is most likely the persuasion model. Of the over 220 Catholic universities, about 100 might belong to this category. Among these hundred universities are institutions of various sizes, endowments, and reputations, some of which directly compete with one another. Finding a suitably comparable, noncompeting institution willing to exchange data on Catholic culture can be done, but it requires patience and persistence.[36]

Once the most important task of finding a data partner is accomplished, the institutions will want to settle on the most pertinent and useful data to exchange. Since most Catholic universities do not currently collect much data pertinent to their Catholic culture, identifying useful data points and then agreeing on parameters for their collection will be an important way in which data partners work together.

The Law of the Church

The penultimate issue for consideration in this chapter involves both appropriate data and expertise available to presidents and trustees. Catholic colleges and universities have two dimensions to their identity—one secular and one religious—both of which must be attended with care. There is any number of issues that emerge because of this dual identity, but none is more interesting, nor perhaps more challenging, than issues related to law.

Most Catholic colleges and universities are independently incorporated organizations that have legal status under civil law and have obligations under the civil legal system. Because these institutions claim a Catholic identity, they also have canonical status under the law of the Church and obligations incurred under an ecclesiastical legal system. All Catholics and all Catholic endeavors are subject, to some degree, to the governance of ecclesial authority. It is one of the defining characteristics of being Catholic.[37] However, just as there are different types of corporations under civil law, there are also different ways Catholic individuals and Catholic organizations are subject to Church authority. The laws that civil corporations are subject to are determined by their corporate status. So too, canonical status determines to which Church laws a Catholic endeavor such as a university or college is subject.

The 1983 Code of Canon Law affords a number of different ways Catholic colleges and universities and other works can be related to the Church, and each has advantages and disadvantages. There is no one best option for all Church-related institutions, but whatever that status is will determine the limits of the ecclesial obligations of the institution. Canonical status has implications for such matters as liability, autonomy, and ownership of property—all issues of grave concern for trustees.[38]

Sorting out the implications of canonical and civil law status is an exceedingly complex issue for Catholic colleges and universities and their trustees. "The issues," according to Rev. Robert Kennedy, "involve not only the conflicting claims of two legal systems, the canonical and the American, but also the differing legal provisions of two codes of canon law (1917 and 1983) and fifty-one American jurisdictions (federal and state). The complexity is enhanced by the dissimilarity of the many institutions involved."[39] No matter the complexity, Catholic colleges and universities have an obligation to satisfy the claims of both ecclesial and civil legal systems, and trustees are responsible for assuring that happens.

Universities are usually alert to fulfilling their civil legal responsibilities. They conform to state and federal statutes with respect to organization, benefits, objectivity in hiring and firing, property transactions, and so on. Any university has a number of people whose main function is making sure that the institution complies with federal and state laws pertinent to a great variety of areas and has sufficient documentation to prove that it complies with such laws. Trustee meetings at many, if not most, Catholic universities are attended by university counsel.

Senior administration and trustees at most Catholic institutions seldom are as careful about the university's obligations under the law of the Church. Most trustees are not lawyers. Consequently, for matters concerning criminal and civil legal compliance and potential suits under civil law, trustees respectfully listen to university counsel and, in most cases, follow the recommendations of that counsel. Failure to do so could well place the university and perhaps the trustees themselves in some legal jeopardy. Ignorance of the law of the Church or disregard for its obligations also can have serious implications for Catholic colleges and universities.[40] Both trustees and presidents have a responsibility to make sure the college is fulfilling all its obligations. In order to do so, they need the advice of excellent canonical legal counsel every bit as much as they need good civil legal counsel. By retaining a canon lawyer to both educate and advise them, trustees and presidents will better understand their obligations under the law of the Church and will enhance their leadership and stewardship of the Catholic university they serve.

Catholic universities occupy a position of leadership among Catholic institutions. Because Catholic universities teach people who teach or manage other Catholic institutions—such as primary and secondary schools, health care institutions, and social welfare institutions—the universities are expected to attend to details and show the way for other institutions. In addition, Catholic universities have the financial resources to pay for needed personnel. In order to exercise their leadership role within the broader Catholic culture, Catholic universities should do things correctly and be sure that they are in conformity with the law of the Church, as well as civil law.

The Current Context

Both trustees and presidents of Catholic universities operate in the context of the Catholic Church in the United States, which has been rocked, shamed, and seriously damaged by a scandal concerning sexual abuse that has devastated many once innocent children. A number of commentators have stressed that the scandal has two disturbing foci: the activity of some priests who violated their vows, as well as the trust the faithful had in them, and the activity of some bishops who did not forthrightly and honestly address unacceptable and damaging behavior on the part of some priests. As leaders of the Church, bishops are expected to protect their flock. In far too many cases, the bishops did not protect the young and abused, even after they had clear and unambiguous evidence of morally reprehensible behavior by some priests.

In the sexual abuse situation, the guardians were not guarding, and those entrusted with responsibility betrayed it. The ineffective or negligent actions of some bishops have damaged the reputation and moral authority of American bishops in general and the good standing of the Catholic Church in the United States. Once it became clear that priests were suspected of abusing children, bishops had an obligation to act more forcefully to remove them from contact with children. The damage done was not just to children who were subsequently abused and not just to the diocese to which the priest belonged. The entire Catholic Church in the United States suffers as a result of ineffective action by some bishops.

We recall this context not because we wish in any way to suggest that, beyond what has already been reported in the media, sexual abuse at Catholic universities is taking place. The point rather is to highlight the importance of responsibilities in trust—responsibilities accepted by all trustees and presidents of Catholic colleges and universities. The actions of these leaders have implications beyond themselves and the institutions they serve. Ineffective action on their part has a negative impact on Catholic higher education in general, as well as the Church in the United States. Similarly, forthright action on their part can strengthen the enterprise of Catholic higher education and the American Church, as well.

The actions and interactions of presidents and trustees provide the leadership that shapes Catholic colleges and universities in the present and defines them for the future. Both presidents and trustees must be creative and courageous in meeting their responsibilities. Although they lived in a different time and they faced different challenges, college presidents Father Theodore Hesburgh and Sister Madeleva Wolff were models of heroic leadership. What is characteristic of them and worthy of emulation by all presidents was that they saw big problems clearly, they named them in a public place, and they refused to simply hope these thorny issues would resolve themselves. While presidents cannot be expected to solve all the big problems, they are surely called upon to squarely address the ones immediately before them. Sr. Madeleva and Father Hesburgh understood that they served precisely to address the big and seemingly irresolvable issues of their day. Just as they faced significant problems in securing the future of Catholic higher education, so, too, does this generation of Catholic college and university presidents.

The boards of trustees of Catholic colleges and universities play a far more significant role than they did when Father Hesburgh and Sister Madeleva assumed the responsibilities of the presidency in their respective institutions. Today, these boards are the appropriate bodies to judge whether their institutions are sufficiently Catholic in identity, character, and mission, and they are in a good position to make that judgment. Trustees responsible for the Catholic culture at their institution have to get adequate information and then make well-informed decisions about how to modify and/or strengthen the Catholic culture on their campuses. Adjusting to a new reality in which religious trustees play less of a role and lay trustees bear a larger burden than they traditionally did, it is understandable that trustees need time to make adjustments that assure pertinent information flows to them. Trustees are guardians of

Catholic universities, and no other group has ultimate responsibility in the area of Catholic character, mission, and identity. While each university is different, all trustees at Catholic colleges and universities have the responsibility to oversee the vibrancy of Catholic culture in their institutions. They are also trusted to make changes when they judge the Catholic culture at their institution is in need of a correction.

II

Policy Packages

The thematic chapters in part 2 structured and analyzed the comments of senior administrators. Each of the chapters also made recommendations about ways to promote the Catholic culture at Catholic universities. These suggestions, however, were not integrated into general plans that individual institutions might use and adjust in addressing their own circumstances. Enhancing religious culture presents practical challenges for Catholic colleges and universities that require a solid theoretical understanding of the issues and the implementation of an integrated strategy. This chapter draws together various recommendations included in the theme chapters and develops a variety of practical approaches, as well as situation specific-plans, that Catholic universities in each of the models can adopt and adapt in developing their own coordinated strategies for strengthening their institutional Catholic culture.

As chapter 10 made clear, providing leadership for religious cultural enhancement is the responsibility of presidents and boards of trustees, not sponsoring religious congregations. It is the president and the board who must determine the current strength or weakness of institutional Catholic culture and fashion a strategy to enhance it for the future. Whatever strategy they choose to employ must accommodate the particular nuances of their own institutional circumstances. The recommendations and approaches outlined in this chapter address the components of culture and the leadership style of the president and, where appropriate, are articulated according to each of the four ways of being a Catholic university.

Data and Knowledge

There are a number of recommendations for strengthening Catholic culture that are model specific. Two recommendations, however, apply to all four models in approximately the same manner. Catholic colleges and universities in general need more data about the extent of Catholic knowledge and commitment to the faith among all constituent groups. There is also a need among faculty for more general and discipline-specific knowledge about the Catholic intellectual tradition.

Amassing more data about Catholic knowledge and commitment does not directly improve Catholic culture, but good use of the data can lead to such an outcome. Despite the increasing pressure on all higher education institutions from accrediting agencies to establish student outcome measures for various academic disciplines, few Catholic universities have developed such measures for anything pertaining to general Catholic knowledge of students, or so senior administrators would lead us to believe. Nor have these colleges and universities interpreted such pressures more broadly in terms of their mission to educate all students in some degree about the Catholic faith. Outcome evaluations may exist for students who are theology or religious studies majors, but these do not capture the extent to which the Catholic university fulfills its mission with respect to all, most, or even just Catholic undergraduates.

Generating such data at any college or university will not be easy. On the other hand, the process the university goes through in order to determine which data to collect will itself yield greater clarity about the religious mission of the university. An initial plan to collect data may confine itself strictly to academic learning. Such a plan would engage faculty in theology, philosophy, and perhaps a few other academic disciplines and ask them to specify what content should be expected of a senior graduating from this type of Catholic institution. Securing agreement on this issue would be a significant achievement and would also provide focus for the academic sector.

According to senior administrators, practically all Catholic institutions try to educate and inform students through the entire culture on campus, not merely through courses in theology, philosophy, or other courses pertinent to the Catholic intellectual tradition. Campus ministry, student activities, residential life, and athletics all make a contribution to the education and character formation of students. Eventually each unit of the university involved in shaping and transmitting religious culture would engage in a Catholic outcomes data-gathering process. Each would explain to the other units what they are trying to accomplish through their array of student programs and activities. Then this umbrella group would decide on a set of measures that, however imperfectly, provides some insight into what students know about the Catholic tradition. A second set of measures would address religious practices among students.

Determining what data will be helpful is just the first step in determining how the university is doing in relationship to its religious mission. Once those decisions are made, the data can then be efficiently gathered and carefully analyzed. As the cycle of data specification, data collection, and data analysis repeats itself, the university can gradually modify the data it decides to collect. This winnowing of data will be especially important as the university comes to understand where its performance is strong and where greater attention needs to be focused. The purpose of gathering data is to monitor performance. That necessitates two things. First, the data collected must be the most salient in terms of providing a clear picture to the various units of the university, including the trustees, of what the university is doing and how that compares with established goals. Second, in order to provide information about progress, the data collection, analysis, and reporting must be done on a regular basis.

Colleges and universities are interested in how they are performing in terms of their stated goals. They also have a competitive interest in how they are doing in relation to other similar institutions. Such comparative data about performance in terms of religious mission would provide greater insight into "value-added" outcomes.[1] For example, it makes a difference whether students entering the university are already well educated in the Catholic faith and devout in their practice or whether they know and practice little. A Catholic university that enrolls first-year Catholic students who know little about their faith and rarely practice it yet transforms many of them into graduates who have a basic knowledge of the Catholic faith and fairly regularly practice it has performed at a high level. Its "religious value added" is very significant. If, on the other hand, a Catholic university attracts mostly students from Catholic high schools who are knowledgeable and committed to their faith and upon graduation their knowledge has grown little and their practice of the faith has abated, the university will have to take a serious look at its educational program. Even though graduates from both institutions are quite similar in terms of their religious knowledge and commitment, only one institution can claim a high level of performance.

Liberal arts colleges and all other institutions of higher education that are primarily focused on undergraduates claim that they educate students for a lifetime. Most Catholic universities share in making that general claim. Making the claim and delivering on it are two different things, however. Catholic colleges have an obligation to back up their claims with data that indicate how much religious knowledge students retain and how committed they are to the practice of their faith over a lifetime. Modern American culture emphasizes the importance of data. The booming industry in college guides is just one example of how important data is for many in the collegiate marketplace. These guides have a plethora of facts about universities, and they are consulted regularly by high school students and their parents. Some institutions provide data about the percentage of their students who achieve significant levels of leadership in various professions and industry and consider such information an important indicator of the success of their educational program. Few, if any, Catholic colleges provide long-term performance indicators about their graduates' faith development, commitment, and involvement or the leadership roles they assume in the Church.[2] Although these Catholic colleges distinguish themselves as religious institutions and believe that their educational programs are transformative and build character, they seldom, if ever, seek the data that would legitimate their claims.

Religious knowledge and practice should make an impact on how students lead their lives, and senior administrators believe the impact is for the good. Greater knowledge and commitment should influence in a positive way their friendships and marriages, their service to society and to the Church, their professional lives, the way they raise their children, and the attachments they maintain with their alma mater. To the extent that these connections can be documented, the lifelong benefits of Catholic education can provide the motivation for future students to embrace an educational experience that makes more demands on them during their undergraduate years. Advertising campaigns can help spread the word about the unique benefits of Catholic higher education. Those campaigns, however, are no substitute for a rich culture that is self-perpetuating. Catholic culture puts extra demands on those who choose it over other collegiate cultures. Those who run Catholic colleges must admit that this is the case, but they must also be convinced that the costs, however gently they are imposed, are worth the added investment and will produce long-term results that are worthwhile and good. While this argument might have little impact on prospective students, it can influence parents positively, especially if it is backed up with persuasive data.

The convictions of Catholic collegiate leaders about the benefits of their educational program are essential, but students and their parents must also believe that the benefits outweigh the burdens a Catholic collegiate culture imposes. That kind of buy-in seldom comes in response to advertising campaigns and is more often the result of imaginative appeal generated through cultural narratives. Stories repeated by students themselves about illustrious graduates (the heroes and virtuosi of the culture) who exemplify the lifelong impact of Catholic faith and learning on lives lived, tales of wonderful courses or challenging professors who bring the tradition to life and demonstrate its potential for transformation, and stories shared by teachers of former undergraduates whose religious commitment had a positive impact on the community and the undergraduates of their day—all these types of narratives can fire the imagination, transmit shared assumptions and norms, and convince others of the efficacy of a collegiate experience in a vibrant Catholic culture.

The second recommendation that applies to all types of Catholic colleges and universities is the importance of increasing undergraduate acquaintance with the Catholic intellectual tradition, including both Catholic social teaching and the Catholic moral tradition. In order for that goal to be realized, faculty members themselves will first need to become more knowledgeable about this tradition. As noted in an earlier chapter, it is quite feasible to develop a program that enables faculty to become more knowledgeable about the Catholic intellectual tradition, as long as presidents are willing to commit financial resources to fund such a program. Committing resources is one thing, but most presidents first have to find the funds. Because presidents are adept at raising funds for projects they believe are essential for the university to prosper, however, most Catholic colleges and universities will have the available funds necessary to support the development of the faculty. Such programs can have a variety of formats, but the best format is one in which faculty members hear from experts but also have the opportunity to interact with their own institutional colleagues, as well as with those from similar institutions.

The foundation of academic culture at universities is the structure of academic departments. Much as academic deans and provosts would like faculty to think about the larger academic enterprise and cooperate across disciplines for the overall good of the university, in fact the focus of most faculty members is on their own discipline and the way this discipline is pursued at the national level. Faculty associate most frequently with members of the same department, their scholarly activity relates to their department, and the courses they teach are, for the most part, discipline specific. Sharing knowledge with faculty about the Catholic intellectual tradition is most effective if the knowledge is related to their own academic discipline. Faculty at Catholic institutions are intellectually curious and have religious interests, and many would likely respond positively to an invitation to join a group of their colleagues interested in learning more about the Catholic intellectual tradition and how it relates to their academic discipline. A number of formats are available for sharing this information with groups of well-disposed faculty. One approach is a reading group under the direction of someone who knows well the Catholic intellectual tradition as it relates to a specific academic discipline. Another could be a faculty seminar designed for faculty teaching at a number of regional Catholic institutions. This approach is especially appealing for smaller Catholic colleges, since it has the advantage of enabling faculty to create a number of personal relationships with like-minded colleagues at other institutions. Such seminars can provide an overall view of the Catholic intellectual tradition, as well as discipline-specific components. A third approach would be for one Catholic university to partner with a second Catholic university in the vicinity. Each institution would host reading groups, organized according to academic discipline, during the academic year or during the summer, and then the two groups would come together for a few days to interact with each other and share the approaches they developed, as well as whatever concerns they have.

Whatever format an institution selects, the goals should be narrow rather than broad. Faculty members can be encouraged to study the material on the Catholic intellectual tradition with the objective of learning material that they can present in a course they plan to teach in the following academic year. This orientation sharpens the focus of the faculty and also increases the likelihood that faculty participation in the seminar will have a direct and almost immediate, positive impact on undergraduates.

Interviews with senior administrators at Catholic universities made it quite clear that almost all Catholic colleges and universities, regardless of type, would benefit from collecting data about student outcomes with respect to Catholic knowledge and practice and also from educating faculty about the contours of the Catholic intellectual tradition. Some Catholic institutions, especially immersion universities, currently have faculty who have an extensive knowledge of the Catholic intellectual tradition. Even in these cases, however, younger faculty members are operating at some disadvantage. Very few of them have taken specific courses that link their own discipline with Catholic themes and philosophical or moral issues. That limitation will increasingly pose difficulties for all Catholic colleges and universities, including immersion institutions, that are seeking to attract faculty members with discipline-specific knowledge of Catholic themes.

Establishing a system for educating faculty about the Catholic intellectual tradition poses a political challenge. The initiative indicates a desire of the institution to present more Catholic perspectives in a variety of academic disciplines. Even though an invitation to participate in a seminar on the Catholic intellectual tradition is extended to all faculty members in a particular discipline, some may be resistant or resentful of any suggestion that specific material be included in their courses. Some faculty will claim (perhaps quite rightly) that they were not hired to teach Catholic material in their courses. The more recent hires may find the emphasis on learning about the Catholic intellectual tradition more plausible and palatable than hires from the 1970s and 1980s. The chief academic officers at many Catholic institutions indicated that they now emphasize the importance of making a contribution to the Catholic identity, character, and mission of the university with each faculty candidate they interview. They also admitted that this emphasis is relatively new and that many long-term faculty members were hired with little regard given to their interest in or knowledge of Catholicism or Catholic themes and issues. Consequently, general faculty support for such an initiative might be difficult to engender. Whatever the reluctance of some, most faculty have an admirable intellectual curiosity, and a good number will be eager to participate in a seminar that enables them to fulfill better the Catholic mission of the institution. Faculty interest and support is also more likely if a stipend, even a modest one, is provided for participants. Scheduling difficulties could also emerge. Developing a program that provides enough contact time between and among faculty whose lives are already overbooked may prove a real challenge. Despite the challenge, there are effective strategies to meet them.

If either of the two initiatives outlined here were easy to undertake, presidents would have done so long ago. In fact, both initiatives involve considerable planning and persuasion. In order to accomplish them, presidents have to identify and motivate Catholic catalysts among the faculty who are willing to become programmatic allies who support and push for these changes. These initiatives are long-term projects, in the sense that it takes both a long time to implement them and an even longer time to produce results that can be evaluated. As indicated earlier, collecting effective outcomes data involves a cycle of data collection, evaluation, and refinement of the desired data. A program that yields appropriate data, collected in a timely manner over a long enough period to indicate the best modifications for enhancing effectiveness, requires several years to develop. Similarly, several years will be necessary before a sufficient number of discipline-related faculty learning groups can be organized and developed to the point that they have an impact on faculty knowledge about the Catholic intellectual tradition or approaches to teaching the tradition to students.

The success of either initiative is dependent on leadership, but nether requires a specific presidential leadership style, although one style may prove more effective. Because student outcomes with respect to Catholic knowledge and practice and the enhancement of faculty knowledge of the Catholic intellectual tradition are both essential to creating more robust Catholic cultures on campus, presidents should feel some pressure to introduce these programs quickly. On the other hand, because both programs are long-term undertakings, they need substantial faculty and staff input so that from the outset they are well designed and supported. The connective president has some obvious advantages with respect to formulating and implementing the programs, given these challenges. While the directive president may act with greater dispatch, what truly counts is the long-term effectiveness of the program. A poorly designed program launched in haste may set the effort back a few years.

Model-Specific Ways to Strengthen Catholic Culture

Interpreting the comments of senior administrators in the context of the three components of culture (content, symbols, and actors), the four different ways of being a Catholic university (immersion, persuasion, diaspora, and cohort), and the three principles for perilous times (capacity for decisive leadership is necessary, effective assessment of progress toward clearly articulated goals is necessary, and a lack of competition should alert concern), we previously identified several ways for institutions to fortify the Catholic culture on campus. Data collection and educating faculty about the Catholic intellectual tradition apply to all Catholic universities, and none can ensure a vibrant religious culture in the future if it does not attend to both. Not all Catholic colleges and universities have the same goals, nor do they face the same challenges or have the same types of students. For each type of Catholic college and university, different sets of strategies will be required to address Catholic cultural enhancement. In this section we differentiate those potential strategies according to collegiate model and the relative strength of institutional Catholic culture.

An institution's cultural strength is gauged by the extent to which the distinguishability and inheritability criteria are fulfilled. With respect to these criteria, we consider only two formal scenarios, and we select a common weakness that is particular for each of the four models.[3] In scenario 1, the two criteria are either almost fulfilled or just barely fulfilled. In order to move into a realm where distinguishability and inheritability are safely fulfilled, considerable strengthening of the culture must occur. What type of strengthening is needed depends on the particular location of the cultural weakness. In scenario 2, the institution is perilously distant from fulfilling distinguishability or inheritability, and thus the character, mission, and identity of the institution as Catholic are questionable. In this situation, some fundamental steps have to be introduced and particular attention given to the three principles for perilous times.

We apply the two scenarios to each of the four ways a university chooses to be Catholic. The goal is not to make judgments about what individual institutions should do. Rather, the approach applies to general types of institutions in two distinct scenarios. For each type of institution, we examine both scenarios and then make appropriate model-specific recommendations.

Each Catholic college or university must decide for itself what type of institution it is and where it falls with respect to the criteria of distinguishability and inheritability. That is, each institution should be able to identify which of the four ways of being Catholic it most closely approximates. Knowing its own aspirations and general strategies, the cultural catalysts in the institution, following our analysis, should decide how the university is positioned with respect to distinguishability and inheritability. Three general scenarios are possible. The first is that the Catholic culture is very strong, and, where improvements are needed, they are fairly minor.[4] Such an institution is clearly distinguishable and inheritable. Listening carefully to senior administrators and extrapolating to the entire set of Catholic colleges and universities, we are fairly sure that not many Catholic institutions appear to consider themselves in this category. In the second scenario, the institution is just barely or almost, but not quite, distinguishable as Catholic. An institution in the third scenario is in a perilous state with respect to its Catholic culture.

For each type of institution, judgments must be made, but it is the sign of institutional strength if initial judgments are made not by outside evaluators but by the institutions themselves and, most important, by the cultural catalysts (and perhaps cultural citizens as well) at each institution. It is in the interest of cultural actors at each institution to be as honest and objective as possible, because the viability of the institution may be at stake, as well as its ability to thrive within the larger constellation of Catholic universities.

In addition to the two generally applicable policies of data gathering and faculty development addressed in the previous section, five other general policy changes emerged as important for supporting vibrant Catholic collegiate culture, as follows.

1. An increased emphasis on theology and philosophy is the most effective way to emphasize the Catholic intellectual tradition, even though there may be reasons that it is better to emphasize Catholic themes in individual academic disciplines. Whichever approach is taken, their lasting benefits should be transparent to students.

2. New faculty should be hired with the provision that, at a minimum, they are willing to take some steps to become familiar with the Catholic intellectual tradition and to give students personal encouragement to become familiar with Catholic issues and practices. Once hired, new faculty should be given more extensive orientation in Catholic themes and practices.

3. Staff in residence life and student activities should clearly inform students about the Catholic moral tradition and more consistently require them to comply with the rules that flow from this tradition.

4. In many instances, campus ministry should be allocated additional resources.
5. Catholic universities should form visible groups among faculty and staff at their institution who have knowledge of the Catholic tradition and are committed to it.

Universities with strong Catholic cultures are already engaged in many of the activities outlined here. On the other hand, Catholic universities that have not yet identified a viable way to be Catholic will likely be overwhelmed by the task before them. The challenge is great, but not as formidable as the two general recommendations and the five more particular adaptations described here suggest. A university has to respect its culture. Change usually challenges the normal way of doing things, but change should be introduced in ways that, as far as possible, are supported by the university's cultural symbols and narratives. Unless the university is close to losing its Catholic identity, change should not be too broad, too deep, or too abrupt in coming. Rather, changes should be introduced incrementally, beginning with the least jarring, followed by others once the initial changes have been absorbed and integrated into the normal pattern of university life.

Universities with weak Catholic cultures in many instances also struggle with their profitability margin. They are often concerned about whether they can continue to attract a sufficient number of students. Cultural inheritability is in question for these institutions first and foremost because of the margin criterion. Innovations to strengthen the Catholic culture could possibly weaken the financial profile of the institution. In our discussions of concerted policy responses, we assume that the margin criterion is indeed in jeopardy of not being fulfilled, and we are alert to this concern.

Each of the five particular policy recommendations outlined here and in the previous chapters will increase distinguishability at universities where the Catholic culture is weak and blends in with a general culture of higher education. Each of the innovations suggested in the previous chapter can be introduced in ways that do not threaten inheritability, as long as care is taken that changes are woven into the cultural fabric of the institution. Even though the changes may be primarily in the intellectual sector, success requires linkages to the the given university's important cultural symbols. We present here some general ways this can be done for each class of university. None of the recommended policy plans listed here should be implemented without first carefully examining the specific situation of a particular university. It is important to strike a balance between general policy recommendations and overly prescriptive directions. Giving sufficiently specific plans that provide administrators with a general way to proceed while noting that it is unlikely any of the specific policies listed are made to order for a particular university is the way we hope to strike that balance.

Policy Packages for Catholic Immersion Universities

In the first scenario considered, the Catholic culture on an immersion campus does not quite fulfill the distinguishability and inheritability criteria. A number of possible reasons are postulated for the failure to satisfy the criteria. It may be that insufficient Catholic content is being provided in the academic sector to satisfy the distinguishability criterion. This might be an emerging problem as the pool of qualified faculty to teach in immersion universities contracts. The number of Catholic graduate students earning doctorates who are also well informed about the Catholic intellectual tradition is declining. This puts added pressure on immersion institutions, many of which are quite small, financially strapped, and unable to pay the premium salaries necessary to woo topnotch faculty candidates. In this scenario, the type of faculty needed to sustain the immersion institution is not available. Another possibility is that the Catholic culture is so pervasive and homogenous that the pool of potential student applicants is very limited. If it becomes too small, the school will not likely be able to attract a sufficient number of applicants to enable the university to afford capable faculty to teach courses in the life, physical, and social sciences. It might also be that the graduates of the immersion university in scenario 1 do not render particularly good service to the Church, in part because the college education they receive is not distinguished and therefore not valued in the marketplace; as a consequence, over time graduates do not assume positions of prominence in the Church or society. Finally, the six-year graduation rate of students at a particular immersion institution might be embarrassingly low because, although some Catholic students give themselves enthusiastically to the program at the university, the program is insufficiently broad-based for students. A particular immersion university may offer only a small number of majors, or the emphasis in the majors may be narrowly Catholic and insufficiently rigorous and professional. Because of these limitations, many students switch to other institutions because they do not feel their academic preparation positions them to succeed in secular society.

Because the immersion colleges and universities are so avowedly and clearly Catholic, the crucial issues for immersion institutions are not directly related to a lack of distinguishability. They may have difficulty being as Catholic as they would like because the available faculty cannot relate their discipline with any depth to the Catholic intellectual tradition.[5] More likely, the challenges to immersion institutions come in attracting and graduating a sufficient number of students or graduating students with the requisite skills to make important contributions to the Church or society. A relatively small student base may be a continuing problem because parents and prospective students know the institution cannot afford to hire faculty members with sufficient expertise to provide a high-quality educational experience to the students in many academic disciplines. The result is that students are well trained only in a handful of subjects. In particular, they do not receive adequate training in subjects such as the hard sciences, the social sciences, or perhaps in business or education.

While no university can be all things to all people, immersion institutions want to make significant contributions to the Catholic Church. Unless their students have a strong experience in more than just the humanities, it is unlikely the schools will attract sufficient numbers of high-quality students.

Described here are aspects of a college or university that may apply to some immersion institutions. Consider the first scenario in which two of the shortcomings described appear, while not threatening institutional viability. For the particular immersion institution in scenario 1, we assume that attracting qualified faculty becomes a problem. We also assume that the difficulty of attracting a large enough base of students to make sure students receive a truly excellent education in a sufficiently broad array of academic disciplines jeopardizes the inheritability criterion.

Faculty may not be qualified for one of two reasons, both of which are germane to the challenge we have described. The faculty members may have good background in their own academic discipline but not be able to relate this discipline to important teachings of the Catholic faith or important themes in the Catholic intellectual tradition. In the second instance, the faculty members attracted to the institution do not have sufficiently respected doctoral degrees in their own academic discipline. As a result, students may become well informed about Catholic teachings and participate regularly in Mass and other religious activities, but their knowledge of and training in academic disciplines will be considered substandard. Related to this situation is the inability of the institution to attract a sufficient number of students. This occurs both because of the low prestige of the faculty and because the program, while Catholic, does not permit students sufficient room to mature into knowledgeable and articulate Catholics with the prudence to distinguish among vital Catholic issues and less important ones.

What to do? The faculty issue and the student base are directly related. Unless the institution attracts a large enough student population, the institution cannot afford to hire faculty members with solid qualifications in a sufficient number of academic disciplines. Parents, even very committed and dedicated Catholic parents who want the immersion experience for their sons and daughters, are unlikely to encourage or even allow them to attend an institution with an exceedingly narrow academic base. As first-year students and sophomores, students frequently change their majors. To accommodate the normal vicissitudes of students, institutions must have a sufficient array of majors from which students can choose. A university that graduates students in only a limited number of majors is also unlikely to make a broad contribution to the Catholic Church, one of the important objectives of Catholic immersion institutions.

The immersion university in scenario 1 must become more proactive in making sure that faculty members in a variety of disciplines receive what the institution deems adequate training, both in the general Catholic faith tradition and in that tradition as it relates to the specific disciplines taught at the institution. This is a big challenge, and it is unlikely that a single institution will be able to address the problem adequately. An immersion institution in this situation is best served by establishing collaborative relationships with other Catholic universities that can provide joint programs for current and/or prospective faculty. Ideally, the partner institution or institutions will be larger ones that have a good number of faculty, at least a portion of whom will be interested in becoming more deeply acquainted with the Catholic faith in general and the Catholic themes that appear in a particular academic discipline. An alternative approach would be to establish a link with a Catholic university that has a number of doctoral programs in academic disciplines that play an important role in the way the immersion institution plans to prosper in the coming years.

Training faculty is an expensive undertaking, and, realistically, in any partnership or linkage, the immersion institution will have to contribute some financial or human resources to the project. Even if the contribution of the immersion institution is faculty members at their institution who are already well trained in the academic disciplines of interest, the immersion institution will have to provide stipends for their own faculty members to teach graduate students or other prospective faculty members coming from other institutions. For an institution already pressured by the margin criterion, as this one is presumed to be, the ability to make additional financial resources available without some other changes is highly unlikely.

Since the resources of most universities in the United States are directly influenced by the tuition fees they receive from their students, the other important approach this immersion university could take would be to broaden its student base. By focusing on marketing, student discounting, the sports program, and programmatic changes in academics or student life, many institutions have successfully broadened their student base. Since our focus is on changes related to the Catholic identity, character, and mission of the institution, we focus on the Catholic aspects of broadening the student base. While remaining an immersion university, the institution can lower the number of required Catholic courses, increase the range of possible majors, publicize better the degrees of faculty and raise their visibility in intellectual circles and on the national scene, or link the service activities of students with local employers who value the Catholic education and formation of students. Whatever the adjustments made, prospective students must have an elevated perception that they will receive a good education at this immersion university. The institution may believe that has always been the case, and this is likely true. What is important is that the perception of prospective students changes. Normally, in order to change perceptions of a fairly large population, it is necessary to point to real differences that have changed the situation. In this case, the differences would be either in terms of programs, faculty, or both.

Two guidelines will indicate which changes are likely to be more productive. First, according to most student survey data, students attend an institution because they believe the university has high academic standards. Second, student interest in a religious education can be enhanced if students perceive that they have a good number of choices with respect to the courses they take. Both these principles provide strong guidelines for changes that should be introduced. Any cost-effective innovation likely to increase the perception of academic quality will probably increase the student base. Similarly, American culture emphasizes freedom. Although immersion institutions may be convinced that undergraduates enjoy too much freedom with respect to course selection, the amount of choice potentially available to students is a continuum. A demanding institution, measured by the number of required courses, can decrease the number of prescribed courses without adversely affecting its rigor. Without pressure to increase the student base, the institution may not choose to make such a change. But, as we showed earlier, the university has to take some measures to increase its net revenue, and the normal route to achieve this is by increasing the number of student applicants.

Scenario 2 is similar to what was portrayed for scenario 1, with the important difference that the institution in this scenario is in danger of losing its Catholic identity. Usually scenario 2 involves a failure to satisfy both the distinguishability and the inheritability criterion. Immersion universities, however, are strongly distinguishable, and it lacks plausibility to claim hypothetically that the institution is in danger of not satisfying this criterion. For the immersion institution, a plausible scenario 2 is that the inheritability criterion is not satisfied. In general, this means that the institution fails to attract a sufficient number of students. This may occur for a number of reasons. The type of Catholic education being offered may appeal to only a small pool of students. This may be because students don't like the program or because the program is not successful. Since the point of interest is the Catholic identity of the institution, we assume that the students graduating from the institution, although being exposed to the Catholic tradition in classes and other spheres of university life, are not sufficiently bright or well trained to impress future employers. In this case, the immersion institution does not graduate students who make significant contributions to the Church, much less to society. This gradually becomes known, and the pool of students interested in attending the university shrinks. The difficulty in attracting students might also be a result of increased competition among immersion universities for a limited pool of students. Many of the Catholic colleges and universities that have recently been founded in the United States are immersion institutions. For a good many years, the number of immersion institutions was relatively stable, and enough students were interested in their programs to sustain inheritability at all of them. Founders of new immersion institutions are betting that the number of students (and parents) desiring an education that emphasizes Catholic faith and its consequences for personal and civic life is increasing. If the pool of prospective interested students is not rising as sharply as the number of institutions, competition among the institutions will become increasingly intense. Those immersion institutions that are most appealing will continue to attract strong students. Those whose programs are less appealing will founder. Senior administrators at some of the immersion institutions were quite concerned about whether the influx of new institutions represented a response to an increased need among students. If not, a number of the smaller immersion institutions could face real threats to their continued survival. The focus here is on a particular immersion institution that no longer attracts a sufficient number of students to make viable a solid academic program. What to do?

The two principles for perilous times that are applicable to the institution are, first, that one person, usually the president, must have the will and authority to act decisively, and second, that after specific goals have been established, progress toward the goals must be regularly monitored. If progress toward the goals is not on schedule, adjustments in tactics should be made.

Decisive action on the part of the president means actions that will quickly and effectively reverse the decline in students admitted to the university. This may mean forming a management team with responsibility for increasing the number of student applicants, admissions, and enrollments incrementally over a specified period. It may be that the president brings together admissions, financial aid, public relations, student affairs, campus ministry, and whatever other groups are pertinent. This task force operates under the president directly or under the leadership of another person directly reporting to the president. All policies have to be coordinated, and all should work toward increasing the number of student enrollments.

Once again, because our interest is the Catholic identity, character, and mission of the institution, the person in charge of coordinating policies should attend carefully to the religious tone and requirements at the institution, provided there is evidence that tone contributes to influencing the number of applicants to the university. Practically speaking, in all cases adjustments can be made in tone and requirements that enhance the attractiveness of the university while only slightly diminishing the Catholic knowledge and commitment of the institution's graduates. Following the same analysis as laid out for scenario 1, the president or the presidential delegate in the midst of this cultural crisis will have to attend to securing better qualified faculty. And faculty, especially highly qualified faculty, are expensive. When student numbers are near historic lows, the university cuts back on new hiring, a strategy that further exacerbates and extends the inheritability issues. With the benefit of consultation, the decision-maker should draw up a plan for faculty hiring to be implemented in the coming years, with an emphasis on hiring well-qualified faculty who are good teachers. This will have a positive impact on student interest, even if the main impact occurs in the long rather than the short term. In the short term, there are other available options. Reasonably well-qualified adjunct faculty who are excellent teachers can be hired and used effectively at the institution. Adjunct faculty members are much less expensive than full-time faculty. If the adjuncts have the desired qualities and qualifications, the university can pay them a premium in order to get them to teach specific courses at designated times. It will be in the university's interest to hire engaging faculty members who can capture the imagination of students and harness their enthusiasm. Over time, as things stabilize, some of the same adjunct faculty members who have proven their ability and contributed to the collegiate program could be valuable additions to the full-time faculty.

The appointed decision-maker should also review the curriculum and, in consultation with the faculty, determine what changes can be made in the short run and what changes should be made over a two- or three-year period. Once these decisions have been made, the point person should draw up a list of current changes and a schedule for future changes. The schedule must take into consideration the ability of the university community to adjust to changes, but not be overly cautious. When there is some question about flexibility, the rule should be to err on the side of quick action. After all, the institution is in peril, and a major course correction is called for. If the institution continues to do basically the same things it has done for the last five or six years but does them just a little bit better, the results will be similar but just a little better. The university needs a dramatic improvement in the number of student applicants and enrollments. In order to bring about big improvements in a short period of time, big changes quickly introduced are needed.

In normal circumstances, cultural changes should be introduced gradually, and people should be prepared carefully for them. In perilous times, the luxury of time disappears, and quick action is required. One benefit of truly perilous times is that people understand that important decisions must be made quickly. Once the community realizes that the survival of the institution as a Catholic institution is at stake, they will be far more willing to make adjustments, take some risks, and cooperate with a plan for improvement. The president will have to level with the community about the depth of the crisis, however. Any attempt to minimize the difficulty will undermine the broad-based cooperation so necessary for effective and timely adjustments.

When a university is in crisis, one possible option for addressing the situation is to switch models. For example, instead of adhering to the immersion model, the president, with the support of the board of trustees, might decide that in order to survive, the institution has to switch to another model. This is certainly a possibility. However, if the institution has been an immersion institution for more than a few decades, switching to a persuasion or diaspora or cohort model will pose enormous difficulties with many university constituencies, including the alumni/ae. Model switching can occur with the justification that times are perilous, but there are dangers. The current faculty and student body are there because the university appealed to them as an immersion institution. They will not likely acquiesce easily to a model change. Successful model switching usually occurs gradually, over time, as an institution slowly evolves to the point where it has more of the attributes of a different model. When that "tipping point" is reached, the community is able to recognize the new model as a better cultural fit.

The third principle for perilous times refers not to a single institution but rather to the set of Catholic universities that are similar to one another. The principle says that if a group of institutions has been experiencing serious difficulties and if there is an absence of active competition, the lack of competition should be a warning sign that institutions adhering to this model are not being sufficiently active and imaginative in exploring new ways to achieve their goals. For the relevant group of immersion institutions, the third principle does not seem to apply, since, as a group, the immersion institutions are increasingly popular, even if individual institutions may struggle to attract a sufficiently high number of students. Interestingly, immersion institutions are the growth sector in Catholic higher education. There are at least five new institutions getting underway that to all appearances have chosen the immersion model, and two of these have already opened their doors to classes.[6] Furthermore, both of the new institutions plan to be considerably larger than the typical immersion institution, whose median size does not exceed one thousand students.

The foundation of new immersion colleges and universities certainly indicates that successful businesspeople with knowledge of the market are convinced that the number of students seeking this type of education has already and probably will continue to increase. Historical precedent, however, suggests caution in evaluating inheritability for this model, as well as for the other three models. Catholic colleges founded by women's religious congregations enjoyed a period of tremendous growth between 1920 and 1968, when these institutions met the emerging needs of women for a specific type of education. They also proliferated in the period from the 1950s through the 1960s, with the emergence of congregationally sponsored "sister's colleges." From 1968 on, their fortunes turned. Coeducation threatened the survival of all women's institutions, and the "sisters' colleges" no longer addressed a critical congregational need. In a very short time, a booming market died out. Only a few women-only colleges survive today, with most having become coeducational in one way or another. There presently is only one surviving "sisters' college" in the country.[7]

Policy Packages for Persuasion Universities

Over half of the institutions in this study we tentatively designated persuasion universities. The critical issues most of these institutions face, according to the comments of senior administrators, are related to distinguishability, not inheritability. Most persuasion institutions attract a good number of students, a number that is large enough to offer a program with sufficient majors and with good teachers and researchers. Some persuasion universities struggle to attract a sufficient number of students, but most are inheritable, in the sense that without too much angst, they annually bring in well-sized first-year classes. If inheritability is a problem, it is the inheritability of particular Catholic programs at the university. This type of inheritability is in turn related to how distinguishable the programs are. The focus in this section, therefore, is on distinguishability, not inheritability.

Scenario 1 for persuasion universities portrays an institution that does not provide sufficient Catholic academic content either to the Catholic or the non-Catholic undergraduates. Although the university is known in its community as a Catholic institution, the Catholic culture on campus is weak and possibly inconsistent. That is, some activities, customs, and stories convey Catholic information and conviction to the institution, but there are too many gaps in the culture for most students to graduate with a mature sense of what the

Catholic faith teaches or a good sense of what the tradition demands in terms of how people live their lives. Students would be hard pressed to write an essay outlining what Catholics are supposed to and do believe. In this scenario, Catholic moral teaching is conveyed to students, but institutional rules and norms are enforced most consistently in areas where the university is liable to legal action.

Weakness with respect to Catholic content in the academic sector poses considerable problems for persuasion institutions, since one of their goals is to provide Catholic knowledge and guidance for a large number of the undergraduate students. According to the model, this type of university has two required courses related to the Catholic faith. As we noted earlier, in effect this means that the amount of "Catholic content," even in a required Catholic course, depends to a large extent on the judgment of the instructor. In chapter 3 we noted that the distinguishability criterion could not be fulfilled at persuasion universities unless there was sufficient Catholic content covered in the academic sector.

Since the Catholic academic mission is a sine qua non for distinguishability, it has to be the primary component of a policy package that is designed to enhance religious distinguishability. The efforts of the university should be focused, in a temporal sense as well as in terms of resources, on improving the exposure of undergraduates to what the Catholic Church teaches and how those teachings apply to modern society. The second most important issue is the need to address and reinforce Catholic moral teaching in student life. This necessitates that Catholic persuasion universities establish and enforce consistent behavioral norms and communicate to students the Catholic rationale for these standards. A perfunctory statement of rules with little explanation of their religious grounding or a tepid approach to enforcement of behavioral standards rooted in the Catholic moral tradition will communicate a clear message to students that the Catholic moral tradition is inconsequential to character formation. No Catholic college or university believes that to be the case, but these colleges' ambivalence about championing this aspect of the Catholic tradition suggests otherwise. The third most important component of a policy package for enhancing Catholic cultural distinguishability would entail forming a cadre or cohort of faculty and/or administrators who are informed about and committed to the Catholic faith. This group will cultivate and nourish the cultural catalysts the university needs to move forward under lay leadership.

Changing course requirements or stipulating what material should be covered in certain required courses can be a hazardous undertaking at any university. Equally challenging is introducing courses that, if not required, are strongly endorsed by different departments as contributing to the religious knowledge and formation of undergraduates. Designating these types of changes as being of the highest priority for institutions that find themselves in a serious scenario 1 situation is essentially a stalling tactic and suggests a willingness to do nothing. The reality of university life in the United States is that faculty members engage in lengthy conversations before ever agreeing to proposals for change. Once the proposals are formulated, there usually is a further period of discussion and reflection. If agreement is finally reached, it likely will take several years before those mutually agreeable changes are implemented. Because this is the reality at most Catholic colleges and universities, a number of alternate policies focused on academics would need to be pursued. In striving to achieve goals that are vital to the Catholic identity, character, and mission of the institution, it is important for administrators to have flexibility.

Before offering alternative approaches, the a priori merits of addressing the issue of lack of academic Catholic content should be discussed. According to scenario 1, a relatively small percentage of students—Catholic and those belonging to other denominations—graduate from the persuasion institution with any confidence that they know what Catholicism teaches about central issues mentioned in the Nicene Creed, the sacraments, the structure of the Church, the social Gospel, and the moral teaching of the Church. Informed faculty members will have legitimate disagreements about the truly important things that students should know about the Catholic faith, but it is assumed that they will eventually settle on a set of issues and areas that are required for student mastery or proficiency. The areas might have a certain arbitrary quality, but only because compromises are necessary to reach an agreement on a plan of action.

The assumptions of scenario 1 indicate that the institution must strengthen its distinguishability as a Catholic institution and, in particular, must find better ways to make sure that a significantly larger percentage of the undergraduates understand the major teachings of the Catholic faith. The fact that the university is only barely distinguishable as a Catholic institution should cause consternation among the faculty, as well as among administrators and trustees. Once the trustees become aware of the problem, they can provide needed clarity of focus and energy for action by directing the president to take the necessary steps to ensure that greater Catholic content is made available in required theology and/or philosophy courses. This type of directive would only be made after appropriately broad consultation.

In the absence of knowledge about the way the institution functions, how the faculty interact with one another and administration, and what attempts have been made to bolster the Catholic content of academic courses in the recent past, our judgment is that the most direct and efficient way to address undergraduate ignorance about issues of great importance to the university is to require all students to take courses that cover the specified subject matter. Such an approach would limit somewhat the freedom of a faculty member to select topics to be covered in a certain area. However, one reason that students are not learning about Catholic culture is that too many faculty members address other religious issues and, according to the combined judgment of trustees, administrators, and faculty, leave insufficient time to cover material directly related to Catholic faith and practice. The best possible solution is for faculty to agree to specify two required courses for undergraduates with specific topics that cover material judged by them to be essential. This approach makes it possible for practically all students to master some material about Catholic faith and practice. It assures that practically all students of similar ability have a similar knowledge base. It also creates common ground for intellectual discussion across campus. With this foundation, students would be able to discuss social and political topics with greater knowledge of why the Catholic Church takes the positions it does. Similarly, a common knowledge base among students would encourage a healthy exchange of views on matters involving the Catholic faith. Because of their conversing informally among themselves about these issues, their retention of the relevant material would be better and this would also increase the likelihood that the material would continue to influence them for many years to come. If this approach were adopted, the university could legitimately claim that, as a Catholic persuasion institution, it provides a solid grounding in Catholic faith and practice to almost all students, regardless of their religious affiliation or practice.

The advantages of this frontal approach are that almost all students receive the benefit of this system while its broad application fosters productive informal conversation about the Catholic faith that can reinforce the concepts, and perhaps even the appeal, of the faith. The main disadvantage we have already noted: it is difficult to get faculty to agree on such a prescriptive solution to the challenge of educating students in Catholic faith and practice. In a medium-sized or larger institution, where many faculty members are likely to have conflicting views, this difficulty is likely to be a disabling impediment. Faculty might be more amenable to the direct approach of a course that covers the basics of the Catholic faith if the Catholic cultural cluster of faculty that we proposed in chapter 8 actually existed at this institution. In this case, the course would be strongly recommended by a cadre of faculty who are esteemed and known for their knowledge and commitment to the Catholic culture on campus. Some persuasion universities might already have such a group or a group that approximates it. Most institutions, however, do not have such a body, and it would require several years, at least, to develop one.

Because of significant practical difficulties in implementing a frontal approach, we present three alternative approaches. In our judgment, they are viable for augmenting the number of students who graduate from the university with good knowledge about Catholic faith and practice. The first involves student choice and incentives, the second approaches academics via a nonstandard unit, campus ministry, and the third encourages students to make good use of their current theology courses to prepare for a general exam in Catholic faith and practice. Presenting alternatives stems from our interaction with senior administrators. Understandably, they were wary about getting into unproductive disagreements with faculty members. At the same time, they realized the importance of increasing the Catholic content to which most undergraduates are exposed. Every institution faces different pressures and constraints. One or more of these alternatives might suggest ways for senior administrators to provide more specifically Catholic content to a broader segment of the university population.

Perhaps the most characteristic feature of modern universities, compared with their counterparts of a century ago, is the number of courses students are free to choose, both in their major and to satisfy distribution requirements.

Since most Catholic universities continue to emphasize the liberal arts, which offer educational breadth, students at these institutions still have a relatively large number of prescribed courses (between 20 and 40 percent of all their courses) in comparison with nonsectarian institutions. Even at these institutions, however, undergraduates select over half their courses. Students are accustomed to choice, but because there are so many courses from which to choose, students are also open to direction and persuasion. Accumulating multiple majors, minors, and concentrations has been very popular among students in higher education, and this offers a path to engage students.

The faculty, working with administrators, could establish a special certificate, minor, or concentration in Catholic faith and practice. Modest requirements could be established that might include two theology courses with heavy Catholic content, a philosophy course that explores Catholic issues, and a course within the major that handles important Catholic themes relevant to that major. The diploma for a student successfully completing these courses might designate a concentration in what could variously be named Catholic studies, the Catholic academic tradition, or Catholic scholarship. For a student who takes even more courses in the Catholic tradition or takes an additional service learning course in which service to a Catholic institution is provided, the designation "Catholic scholar" might be included on the diploma.[8] Individual institutions have to craft a program that students are likely to choose, both because of the course content and also because they want the recognition that comes with the designation of having a Catholic concentration or being a Catholic scholar.[9] Not all students will choose this route, but many students will find it attractive. It will be especially appealing if students understand that these courses provide them with the opportunity to appropriate their Catholic faith as adults, rather than as a childhood inheritance.

A second alternative is to work through campus ministry or through a newly designed educational arm of campus ministry. Faculty in theology or religious studies departments at some persuasion universities balk at teaching required introductory courses to students that the faculty also deem remedial. Another way to provide college-level information and insight into Catholic faith and practice is to establish a religious education function within campus ministry. In this plan, campus ministry would hire theologians to teach "courses" to undergraduates. These "courses" would not count toward graduation, but the content would be Catholic faith and practice. As in the plan discussed earlier, students could receive recognition on their diploma for various levels of involvement in these "courses." To accomplish this, more resources would have to be made available to campus ministry for taking on this service.

One might wonder whether many students would actually sign up for noncredit courses offered through campus ministry, since they are voluntary courses and do not count toward the fulfillment of their degree requirements. Much would depend on how the courses are structured. The courses might be scheduled to meet at more conveniently concentrated times than regular courses, and there might not be as many papers or exams required. It would be up to the Catholic university to design incentives that would appeal to students. Who teaches the courses would also have an impact on how many students choose to avail themselves of the offerings. There are always dynamic faculty members or visiting scholars whose courses students want to take. Frequently, because of strong demand, not all students can be accommodated in these courses, and they get turned away. If these very popular teachers are willing to spend some time teaching for campus ministry, students would be far more likely to sign up to participate.

The third alternative provides a similar array of incentives but does not add specific courses in Catholic theology or philosophy or tighten up the Catholic content of existing courses. In this approach, students are directed to one or two books, such as an introductory text on Catholicism supplemented by material available on the local university network or perhaps a text authored by faculty members that covers the most important components of Catholic teachings and practice.[10] Students are encouraged to master the material contained in the designated books or articles. Once or twice a year, an exam is offered that covers the material in these books. The score on the exam determines the degree of recognition (Catholic student, scholar, or master, for example) awarded to the student, and this recognition is noted on the graduation diploma. This approach encourages students to take advantage of their required courses in theology and/or philosophy to master the assigned material. It gives them a motive (do well on the exam) and a clear target. The more organized and motivated students would look through the required text prior to taking one of the required theology courses with the intent of asking the professor to answer questions on the material to be covered. Sample exams or previous exams can be made available to the students so they have a good idea of the level of knowledge that will be required.

Designing exams is time-consuming, but it is worthwhile when the number of students taking the exam is large. If the institution contemplating this third approach were small, it might advantageously link up with some local or regional Catholic institutions to see whether they might agree on common texts. In this way, faculty from two or more institutions can share the burden of creating an annual exam that covers the required material. Even if the exam is common, the decision about what type of designation to grant a student would lie with the local institution. In this way, the local institution would retain control of its standards.

Which alternative is best or whether, because of special circumstances, it might even be more advantageous to address the issue directly by strengthening the Catholic content in the required theology courses depends on each individual institution that finds itself in scenario 1. The obvious drawback to the three alternative approaches is that, because they all establish incentives for students and because the incentives are modest, most students will chose not to take the bait and therefore will not become better informed about Catholic teachings and practice. With the third alternative, however, one can make a simple adjustment that will eliminate this drawback. One could simply require that all students—Catholic as well as non-Catholic—take a "basic Catholicism" exam along the lines outlined here. In this approach, the exam

would no longer be optional, and, above and beyond student course requirements, students would have to attain a certain grade in this exam in order to
graduate. This is, of course, a more aggressive approach, but it provides unavoidable incentives to students to become informed about the basics of Catholic teachings and practice. The cost to the university is not negligible, since
it must either purchase an exam or use faculty to design at least one exam a
year. But if most students graduate with a basic knowledge of Catholic faith
and practice, the investment would be more than worthwhile.

An advantage of establishing a general graduation requirement is that it
provides a common outcomes-based evaluation of how well the university is
fulfilling part of its core mission. As we noted at the beginning of this chapter,
such outcomes-based data are important for administration, prospective parents, and Catholics in general, as they try to gauge how well Catholic universities are fulfilling their mission and their responsibilities to the Church and
society.

Various ways to provide Catholic content to students have been explored
here at considerable length primarily because acquainting most students with
Catholic teachings and practices is a major responsibility of a Catholic persuasion university. Although each approach has its own challenges, resourceful
administrators find ways to achieve important goals. These alternatives can
also be invoked when Catholic diaspora and cohort models are examined.

For a Catholic persuasion university that is nearly fulfilling the distinguishability criterion, the second component of the recommended policy package is
establishing and enforcing consistent standards that reflect the moral tradition
of the Catholic Church, especially in the area of residence life and student
activities. We have already emphasized that character formation is a process
that requires both positive encouragement and clear limits about what constitutes acceptable behavior. Positive encouragement to lead lives of virtue and
service to others is, and should be, the primary focus of moral educators.
Nevertheless, clarity about what students are not permitted to do is also essential. Although behavioral limitations are unlikely to motivate students to lead
good moral lives, they do clarify the boundaries of what is acceptable behavior.
Part of the developmental process that brings young men and women to full
maturity entails a testing of limits. It is impossible for them to test the limits
and explore the boundaries, however, when they cannot distinguish where they
are. Setting limits helps define what an institution expects and will not tolerate,
and enforcing sanctions makes it clear that the institution means business.

Because distinguishability is in question, the presumption here is that the
university currently has a low profile with respect to stating and enforcing
certain types of student or university behavior. In particular, a great deal of
drinking and "cohabitation" in residence halls goes on with little or no intervention by the university. Also, Catholic norms against the distribution of contraceptives and against referrals for abortion services are not always respected.
Finally, student life in this scenario does not take advantage of the normal
sessions it has with students to explain the motivation and justification for
Catholic moral teaching.

Any of these lapses seriously distorts the message of the university about its commitment to the Catholic faith and its support of Catholic moral teaching in particular. Turning what we have described as an intentionally covered eye to the sexual behaviors of students in the dormitories suggests that "it's no big deal" as far as the university and the Church are concerned. One justification given by university administration for this laissez-faire approach is that students are young adults who need to work these things out for themselves. There are two difficulties with this stance. First, this is the exact same message students receive at nonsectarian institutions, which simply confirms that there is nothing distinguishable going on at the Catholic institution. Second, although appealing to the fact that students are adults or nearly adults has merit, this approach can only work if university administration communicates university policy to students and shows them fairly straightforward ways to implement the policy. Administration should also offer advice to students about how to proceed when the policy is abrogated. That is, administration may give students the responsibility to abide by and even monitor the policy, but that does not mean the university can wash its hands of all responsibility. In fact, the university has the responsibility to communicate two things. First, exactly what according to the Catholic tradition constitutes unacceptable behavior and second, exactly what students should do when the violations everyone knows happen do in fact occur.

University administration should inform students about Catholic teaching concerning sexual behavior and also provide the moral reasons the Church gives for its teaching. How students behave in dorm rooms is not a purely personal matter. There are justice issues at stake every time a roommate is cordially invited to look elsewhere for a place to sleep because a roommate is "entertaining" a sexual partner. Students need to know that they have obligations in justice to roommates and the university takes those obligations seriously, even if the students do not.

There is a strong shadow culture at many Catholic institutions that not only tolerates "cohabitation" but also makes clear that students who take issue with this practice or with being "sexiled," as it is termed, for the benefit of a roommate's sexual entertaining, are the real problem. In this environment, students need to be encouraged both to report violations of these rules and to provide a strategy that gives some cover to the student who has been locked out for the night. It is helpful for administration to point out that students who are "invited" out of their rooms in this kind of situation are unlikely to report the incident. The appropriate person to report the situation is a friend of the displaced person. That will require acknowledgment of what constitutes the common good in a residence that is at odds with both the shadow culture on the Catholic campus and the residential culture at most colleges in the United States today. Cultivating such a view is the positive task of student life officers, and a deeper understanding of the Catholic moral tradition and reliance upon it can contribute profoundly to this cultural transformation.

Sexual impropriety in residence halls is a serious issue that can be no less than perilous for students. Much of the sexual activity on today's college campuses, including Catholic campuses, is related to alcohol consumption. Increasingly, students are engaging in binge drinking on a regular basis. Invariably this leads to sexual "hookups" that cannot possibly be consensual. When Catholic colleges tacitly accept a posture of "minding your own business" that fuels this kind of destructive and reckless behavior, they have effectively walked away from their religious mission. Now, it is true that when alcohol consumption reaches extreme levels or precipitates other very public outrageous behaviors, Catholic colleges and universities are quick to step in and enforce the law. One of the ways they do this is by dismissing students from the residence halls. While this practice simplifies life in the dorms, it creates other problems that have strong justice implications. If a student's drinking is a problem on campus, it will be at least as much a problem off campus, as well. When a university decides to expel a student from the dorms and not from the college, they are dumping the problem on the neighborhood, while avoiding further problems in the residence hall. There is nothing vaguely just about such a policy; it offends against the common good.

Catholic universities can and should treat students as adults, but the universities should also provide them with pertinent information about the rules and regulations they are expected to abide by. If voluntary compliance works in the sense that there are relatively few unreported violations, student reporting can be a very good policy. On the other hand, if, relying on voluntary compliance and student reporting, university administration learns that many students are drinking excessively and violating rules about sexual behavior, it has a responsibility to come up with an alternate approach that is more effective. Implementing such changes requires training so that the staff understands the university rules and the reasons for them. Since staff understand best of all the way students interact, staff can be very helpful in drawing up specific policies that are respectful of students yet also reflect Catholic moral teaching.

The final policy to be included in the policy package for persuasion universities in scenario 1 involves establishing a group of faculty and/or administrators who are informed about the Catholic tradition and are committed to maintaining it at this Catholic persuasion university. This recommendation could have been included with the need for data on outcomes and faculty training in the Catholic intellectual tradition as a third general recommendation. In its broad outlines, after all, it is an important component for each type of Catholic university. Because the ideal size of the cluster of informed and committed faculty differs from model to model, however, we address it as a model-specific recommendation.

The goal in a persuasion university is that most students get a basic understanding of Catholic faith and practice. In order for this to happen, policies that convey Catholic knowledge, such as required courses or even strongly recommended courses, should be in place. Such policies also need to be coupled with clearly stated, justified, and enforced rules concerning student behavior that reflect Catholic moral teaching. Furthermore, the Catholic culture at the university will change as it rubs against and interacts with the dominant culture. When this happens, perceptive faculty, administrators, and staff who know and are committed to the Catholic tradition should recommend adjustments to strengthen the Catholic culture on campus. Every university already has many such people among its faculty, administrators, and staff. Focusing just on faculty members, we note that people with the desired qualities are usually found among the ranks of the faculty and are known to at least some faculty. In bigger institutions with a large faculty, some informed, committed Catholic faculty will be known in some circles, though not in others.

There are at least five reasons for forming the group of informed, committed Catholic faculty into an identifiable cluster: first, to allow and invite other similar minded faculty members to associate themselves with the group and to allow interested faculty members to seek out the opinions of the whole group or members of the group; second, to undertake activities that reinforce the knowledge and commitment of the group; third, to review the Catholic culture on campus in view of the needs of students and faculty; fourth, to recommend to the rest of the faculty teaching undergraduates ways to strengthen the Catholic culture on campus; fifth, to provide access to students and parents who are interested in or have concerns about the Catholic culture on campus. This Catholic cultural cluster serves the university community by attending to the Catholic culture and making recommendations to improve it. They are experts in Catholic culture and in understanding, justifying, and modifying it.

The group will likely be given some name associated with the particular institution they serve. For pedagogic reasons as well as ease of reference, we call such groups CIC clusters, that is, committed, informed, and Catholic clusters (or, simply, CICs), and they are envisioned to be the groups that take over some responsibilities for promoting Catholic culture formerly discharged by members of the sponsoring religious congregation. The general norm with respect to the appropriate size of the group is that it should be large enough to fulfill its responsibilities. Their most important task is to review the various components of Catholic culture and, when the cluster deems it appropriate, recommend measures to strengthen the Catholic culture on campus. The scope of their recommendations need not be restricted to academic matters, but academics or matters related to academics are likely to be the primary focus of their activities. Each institution can decide whether the CIC cluster should have faculty only or include faculty, administrators, and staff. For our discussion, we assume that only faculty members belong to the CIC.

The CIC should be launched with however many hardy faculty members are willing to state and perhaps offer evidence for (each university will have to establish guidelines for membership in the group) their commitment to the Catholic faith, their knowledge of it, and their willingness to make the Catholic culture on campus an area of special service to the university. For planning, promotion, and maintenance of this group, it is helpful to have a desired number of members of the CIC. A starting target for the first step in arriving at such an ideal number could be derived from past experience when members of the sponsoring religious congregation were more populous on campus as faculty and administrators. Targeting the percentage of faculty belonging to the sponsoring religious congregation during a period when the university and the Catholic culture were flourishing under their leadership is one helpful approach. Thus, a ten-year interval might be selected, and then the average annual percent of faculty belonging to the sponsoring religious congregation over that interval can be calculated. Suppose this percentage turned out to be approximately 10 or 15 percent. This would then be the initial target percentage. For example, if at the current time a university has 140 faculty, multiplying 140 by .10 yields a CIC size of fourteen members. There may be many good reasons for encouraging a larger group. Those reasons can be evaluated and a decision made.

During years in which a university flourished through the presence of a significant number of faculty belonging to the sponsoring religious congregation, members of the religious congregation provided the religious direction for the institution. The CIC cluster is a replacement group, consisting primarily of laypersons who are not members of a religious congregation. Selecting a target number of members for the replacement group is a useful exercise to help faculty and administrators think carefully about what the CIC should be doing. In particular, it is important for the group to have influence on the broader faculty in academic matters related to the Catholic identity, character, and mission of the institution. Influence for such a group is achieved both through the prestige of the individual members and the number of people and the various departments and academic entities from which they are drawn. The size of the group is also related to the resources they need to fulfill their responsibilities. The calculation described here is not intended to generate an unmovable ideal number. In fact, the number is best considered as a minimum, since any faculty with the stipulated qualifications should be welcome to join the group. The danger is rather that an insufficient number of faculty would be willing or interested in serving in the CIC. This would be a signal that the university has to take some measures to increase the number of informed, committed, and Catholic faculty willing to take active leadership in nurturing the Catholic culture on campus.

Scenario 2 is that the Catholic persuasion institution is dangerously close to losing its Catholic identity because both the distinguishability criterion and the inheritability criterion are not fulfilled. The Catholic culture on campus is weak, and the pool of potentially interested students is decreasing in size. A decreasing pool of students may be caused by a number of different factors. The ad hoc assumption with respect to the student pool made for purposes of exposition is that the university has lost distinctiveness in the eyes of prospective students. This persuasion university neither is recognizably Catholic nor has any high-profile programs whose excellence is acknowledged by prospective students. The first two principles for perilous times prescribe decisive action on the part of the president or someone designated by the president, as well as identifying and monitoring progress toward clear targets.

In perilous times, the attractiveness of the institution to prospective students is the most important factor to be strengthened. This requires increased emphasis on the Catholic culture, as well as higher visibility for the institution and its programs. Various strategies are possible, but we present only one. The presentation of just one strategy is not meant to suggest that it will work for every institution. Rather, we mean to demonstrate one way of many for the university to regain its Catholic distinctiveness and also attract a broader array of students. The particular strategy described here positions the Catholic academic sector in an appealing light and links the theology requirements to a new program in a discipline in which, it is assumed, the university already has a good reputation.

As a component of a comprehensive new strategy, understanding the role of religion personally and in society can be presented as a common goal for all students in their first year. The scenario 2 university being considered might decide that all incoming students must take a course on basic Christian and moral issues in their first year as undergraduates and that this course will be linked to another required course in an academic discipline. The theology course provides students with fundamental information about Christianity and its practices and how the basic beliefs are related to Scripture. Linking means that students register for two courses that are joined together. That is, the same twenty-five students in the theology course also together take the second course, which might be in English literature or history. By linking theology to another core course, the university creates a community of students and encourages the professor teaching the second course to establish linkages with issues addressed in the theology course. The university might emphasize that basic material will be covered in a way that helps students understand the main differences between, say, Catholics on the one hand and Lutherans or Episcopalians, or evangelicals, on the other. Students will have the opportunity to clarify issues they have found confusing.[11] As a second component of the strategy, the university could introduce a new program in some particular specialty of an academic discipline, perhaps democracies in various cultures, that would be a component of political science. Aside from the regular courses in the new major or concentration, students would also take a course that provides them with ethical guidelines for issues related to the discipline and ethical ideals for students to realize in their lives.

Whatever the particular strategy developed for the university whose Catholic culture is in perilous straits, the components must be sufficiently new, both to attract the attention of prospective students and parents and to create distance between former programs and what is currently happening at the university. There are many ways to emphasize the benefits flowing from the study of Catholicism, and the emphasis on Catholic theology recalls to students and parents something distinctive and rewarding about this university. This general strategy has to be tailored to a particular institution and supplemented with specific targets and a timetable to reach them. The timetable should include dates by which different components of the strategy are introduced, as well as numerical targets and measures that give indications of progress toward the targets. The president or designee of the president should establish one or more task forces to monitor this progress and to share both progress and setbacks with the university community. By assumption, the university is in perilous straits; therefore, a total effort is required to return the institution to culturally secure territory.

The third principle for perilous times applies not to a single university but rather to a group of universities adhering to the same model. If most universities in the group face significant problems, the principle calls for a careful, critical look at whether the institutions adhering to the same model are trying different approaches to Catholic culture or whether the overwhelming majority of these institutions are following the same strategies. Most Catholic universities adhere to the persuasion model. Since it appears that a very large number of these institutions have weak Catholic cultures, Catholic persuasion universities would probably do well to jolt themselves out of following the conventional wisdom and attempt some new ways to support and enhance the Catholic culture. Many initiatives are possible, especially with respect to Catholic teachings and practice. As happens with new approaches, some succeed and some fail. The threat of cultural loss should be enough to convince such institutions that it is time to take a few risks by devising and adopting new ways to promote the Catholic culture in academe and student activities.

Policy Packages for Catholic Diaspora Universities

Catholic diaspora universities rely primarily on committed Catholic administrators and a handful of strong and high-profile Catholic faculty members for their distinguishability. By assumption, these institutions have a relatively low percentage of Catholics among their undergraduates. For distinguishability at these institutions, it was pointed out, Catholic culture in the academic sector would have to be supplemented either by special symposia or conferences that explore the intellectual provenance of Catholic policies and themes or by Eucharistic celebrations in which homilists expound and explore Catholic themes and their relationship to Scripture.

In scenario 1, a Catholic diaspora university is barely distinguishable, and its Catholic culture is barely inheritable. For the institution being considered, we assume that weaknesses with respect to distinguishability and inheritability stem from an insufficient number of strong Catholic administrators and/or faculty. This assumption is made because if Catholic distinguishability is weak in a geographical area that is not heavily Catholic, it is unlikely to result in a diminished student pool. There may be enrollment difficulties at the institution, but they are assumed to be unrelated to the Catholic identity of the university. In this scenario, the assumption is that the areas of residence life and student activities have effective policies that reflect Catholic teaching and practice.

In order to strengthen distinguishability, the first necessary step is to begin a program to hire Catholic administrators who have the requisite knowledge and commitment to make changes in the Catholic culture. As always, when new people are hired with a particular mission, they have to proceed with prudence. Despite initial difficulties, however, administrators with Catholic knowledge and commitment are needed to identify what additional cultural changes are necessary to strengthen the Catholic culture. In our original description of diaspora institutions, the weakness of the Catholic academic component was noted. In these institutions, the academic requirement related to the Catholic faith consists typically of only one course in religion or theology, and this course focuses more on the Old and New Testament than on Catholic teachings and practice. In our description of the diaspora model, we indicated that this was a thin academic reed to use as the basis for a Catholic academic culture and said that it would have to be supplemented either by university-wide liturgies emphasizing Catholic teaching or practice or academic symposia focusing on issues important to the Catholic faith. Newly hired Catholic administrators should be encouraged to explore options such as these and find ways to enhance the Catholic academic tradition that fit the particular university experiencing the difficulties. One of these options almost certainly will be that a few academic departments are chosen to focus their hiring for the next few years on getting an appropriate number of very capable faculty members who are informed about and committed to the Catholic tradition and are able and willing to address Catholic themes that are germane to their discipline in the classroom.

Service learning projects and initiatives on behalf of peace and justice are also excellent vehicles for a diaspora university to use to enhance Catholic knowledge and commitment. While most diaspora universities have small campus ministry departments, these departments are quite successful in working with faculty, students, and staff to create excellent service learning opportunities for students. Many believe that service can lead to a better understanding of faith, but it makes more strategic sense for diaspora universities to operate from the perspective that knowledge of the faith will impel service. With that in mind, the Catholic chaplain of the ministry staff can develop a program that is foundational for all service learning. This program would provide students with a basic understanding of Catholic social teaching and a reflection model that would be used throughout the term of their own service project. If this course came in a student's first year, it could also lay the groundwork for learning how Catholics understand personal and social ethics and apply them to serious issues that are debated in the public square. This program would serve as a focal point for Catholic faculty, administration, and staff who wanted to be more seriously involved in promoting the Catholic mission of the university. It could also create a foundation for common conversation by providing all first-year students with a text to read and prepare prior to their arrival on campus. The advantage of this type of approach is that it builds on a strong student interest in service learning, but also provides knowledge of the Catholic tradition, creates a venue for ongoing reflection and learning about the tradition, establishes a topic and a forum for common conversation, helps to create a cohort community, and has appeal for faculty and staff, as well as students.

Scenario 2 envisions a diaspora institution in which the Catholic culture is almost nonexistent. The difference between the policy recommendations for scenarios 1 and 2 is that the president in scenario 2 has to act more quickly and decisively and that in scenario 2 the issue of hiring more Catholic faculty who are informed about the tradition and willing to share the tradition with students in the classroom has to be addressed in a comprehensive way.

Diaspora universities also need a cadre of committed and informed Catholic faculty (CIC) who are willing to assume primary responsibility for maintaining the Catholic culture, especially in the academic sector on campus. Similar to the guideline proposed for the Catholic persuasion institution, the size of this cluster, which should be visible to the university community, should reflect approximately the influence of the sponsoring religious congregation on the overall faculty when the institution was functioning well under the guidance of the religious sponsors. One can set an initial target for the number of faculty members as the proportion of faculty belonging to the sponsoring religious congregation during a strong period for the university. If the percentage of nuns teaching at the university had averaged about 15 percent over a ten-year period of strength and stability, about 15 percent of the current faculty would be a good number of faculty to attract to a CIC. The CIC group should meet and examine the various components of the Catholic culture on campus. They should also engage in some activities, such as prayer and liturgies and perhaps symposia, that promote the Catholic culture and in which all faculty members are invited to participate.

Campus ministry is one of the most significant contributors to Catholic culture on a diaspora campus. Therefore, the president should make sure that both the chaplain and, depending on the size of the student body, a suitable number of other members of the staff have broad Catholic knowledge and the ability to reach out to students and faculty alike in a programmatic effort that grounds service learning with Catholic knowledge. An excellent campus ministry program and team can go a long way toward stabilizing the Catholic culture on a diaspora campus. A lackluster performance in this area, however, will cripple the religious culture of the institution.

The third principle for perilous times entails being alert to sufficient competition among universities in this category. With respect to competition, a particular disadvantage for diaspora universities is that they are usually geographically dispersed. Since by reason of their location they serve a largely non-Catholic population, not many other Catholic institutions have chosen to operate universities in the same geographical area. Because they are not close to one another, they usually do not compete with one another, unless they are nationally competitive institutions. The result can be that neither administrators nor faculty are familiar with potentially more effective Catholic approaches being pursued at other diaspora universities.

Whether or not diaspora universities are geographically dispersed, if their cultures are weak and their programs to promote Catholic identity are similar, they are in great danger, in our judgment. Trying new approaches in periods when the Catholic culture is threatened is essential. Catholic diaspora institutions are in an awkward situation, because the Catholic culture at the university is not supported by large numbers of Catholics among students, faculty, or staff. On the other hand, their strength is that "Catholic" is exotic and different in this region, and students as well as faculty expect that differences will be apparent, and they are often looking to find them.

Policy Packages for Catholic Cohort Universities

Because cohort universities pursue a dual strategy of extensive Catholic education for a small cohort of students and general religious, not specifically Catholic education for most undergraduates, the potential reasons that they find themselves in scenarios 1 or 2 have different sources. The reasons may relate primarily to the broad undergraduate population and, even in this case, it may be due either to the academic sector or to student activities as they impact the general student population. Alternatively, the primary issue may be the weakness of the featured Catholic studies programs that should provide excellent and extensive Catholic education to a relatively small percentage of undergraduates.

Suppose, according to either scenario 1 or scenario 2, the reason that the Catholic culture of the university only barely qualifies as distinguishable and inheritable stems primarily from the fact that the students in the Catholic cohort program at the university have practically no influence on the rest of the campus. This may occur because there are so few students in the Catholic studies program (which constitutes the Catholic cohort), because the cohort students are not given sufficient respect, or because the cohort students are not being well trained. Whichever the cause, this must be addressed by administrators. It is particularly important for the Catholic cohort group to be both visible on campus and well trained in Catholic teaching, since they are supposed to be a leaven to the undergraduates, at least in the sense of discussing, writing about, and reflecting upon issues related to the Catholic faith. Even questions they pose in their noncohort classes about the Catholic faith contribute to the Catholic education of students not belonging to the cohort. If the issue is the small number of students in the Catholic cohort, administrators should change features of the program or offer special advantages to students who are members of the cohort. If faculty members who teach in the cohort program are not well informed about the Catholic faith or their own discipline, the right type of faculty member has to be located within the university, or new faculty members must be hired. Whatever the reason for the small number of students or their lack of influence on campus, it must be addressed. In the dire circumstances of scenario 2 arising from the same lack of impact of the Catholic cohort, the president has to take decisive action. Appointing a small group of well-informed and committed faculty members to draw up proposals can be a very good step, provided the committee understands the pressing need to act in a relatively short period of time. As was indicated in the analysis of previous crisis situations, general directives from the board of trustees to the president to address the problem in a forthright and imaginative way can be extremely helpful in establishing a consensus in the university community to act. Because students in the Catholic cohort often would effectively have two majors (Catholic studies plus another academic discipline), such students might be given some preference in registering for courses each semester, since they face more difficulties than other students in coordinating their schedules. Also, to make membership in the Catholic cohort more attractive, such students might be offered special opportunities to study in Rome or some Catholic center in a less-developed country or work collaboratively with senior ecclesiastics in the United States. The task force can rather easily identify many ways to make student participation in the cohort more attractive.

A second potential source for the weak Catholic culture on campus may be the paucity of Catholic content in the distribution requirements for non-cohort undergraduate students. Although students may be required to take a course or two that touches on aspects of the Catholic faith, such courses grant considerable discretion to the faculty member teaching the course about which topics to cover in a fairly broad area. Especially in scenario 2, administrators may have to institute a new course in which Catholic teachings and practices are covered almost exclusively. Alternatively, administrators may judge that the current courses are appropriate but that they should be supplemented by an additional course in a student's major that addresses Catholic themes relevant to that major. Depending on the urgency of the situation, the president may direct the academic vice-president or provost to design a suitable program whereby most undergraduates are exposed to Catholic teachings in a required core course. The president would also direct that students must take at least one other course, either in their major or some other academic department, that explores Catholic themes. In lieu of the preceding approach, the president could direct the academic vice president to quickly design some flexible ways to reach the same goal of greater knowledge of the Catholic faith among undergraduates. The menu of alternatives could include the steps mentioned earlier as well as initiatives similar to those outlined earlier in this chapter for persuasion universities, namely, student choice among new courses emphasizing Catholic content, noncredit courses with Catholic content offered through campus ministry or some new unit, or a graduation requirement of passing a test in minimum Catholic knowledge.

The Catholic cohort model is a viable way for a university to be Catholic. The model does, however, rely on a dual strategy that, to be successful, must be carefully integrated. The question of integration is particularly important when the criteria for distinguishability and inheritability are not fulfilled or satisfied at the minimum level. A healthy Catholic culture relying on integration of various components is akin to just-in-time manufacturing: everyone has to be in the right place at the right time. For Catholic culture to flourish at Catholic cohort institutions, each component of the university has to understand the strategy and know what its specific contribution is. Components must also understand how to lend assistance to other components of the university that work to sustain and promote the Catholic culture. In particular, faculty who do not teach courses taken primarily by students in the Catholic cohort should understand that the Catholic identity, character, and mission of the whole institution depends on having a good number of students involved in that Catholic cohort. If that part of the strategy fails, although many faculty members are not directly involved in it, the Catholic culture on campus suffers and may not be sustainable. All faculty, therefore, have a responsibility to contribute, at least generally, to the strategy of the cohort university. University administration and faculty leaders should know and endorse the strategy. Faculty teaching undergraduates should know in general what has been covered in the required core course(s) in religion and, where appropriate, make reference to or build on that information.

The Catholic academic content in the cohort university is narrow, just as it is in the Catholic diaspora university. In the give-and-take of university life that respects faculty freedom in selecting required course content, it can happen that the Catholic content evanesces from the courses over time. It is not the intention of faculty and administrators that this should happen, it just does. One way to make this unintended result less likely is to adopt a system of regular reminders for both new and established faculty that reinforces that the university has a Catholic character and culture, that it shares Catholic academic content with the students, and that all faculty members—whether or not they are Catholic—play an important role in fulfilling the Catholic mission of the institution.

In view of the foregoing reflections, Catholic faculty who are informed and committed to the Catholic faith (the CIC) and are willing to assume responsibility, especially for the Catholic academic culture on campus, should be those who are primarily engaged in the Catholic cohort program. Others who are not involved in this program but want to cultivate Catholic knowledge among the broader population of undergraduates should also be engaged. Particular institutions can decide how best to attract an adequate number of faculty engaged in each of the two Catholic academic strategies pursued by the cohort university. As was the case for the persuasion and diaspora institutions, the number of faculty in the CIC should initially be sufficient to maintain the same proportion as existed when the sponsoring religious congregation had a healthy number of its members serving on the faculty.

Catholic Educational Programs for Faculty and Administrators

For each model of Catholic university, the sector where the Catholic identity of the institution must be most securely and clearly represented is the academic sector. In their interviews, senior administrators were eager to have a broad range of students be exposed to various components of the Catholic intellectual tradition more intensively than currently is the case. The comments and suggestions in the previous sections reflect that interest. At the beginning of the chapter, we highlighted the need for faculty to become better informed about the Catholic intellectual tradition, and we made some suggestions about how best to engage interested faculty in specific academic programs that give them adequate information to address Catholic themes in the classes they teach. In this penultimate section, the same issue is treated from the perspective of financial resources needed to make such programs possible.

When hired as new young faculty members or administrators at a university adhering to the nonsectarian model, most faculty and administrators come well prepared for the tasks they have to carry out. Usually fresh out of graduate school with their newly minted Ph.D. or other appropriate advanced degree, they are ready and eager to make their contribution. This applies equally to administrators and faculty, but for the sake of simplicity we make faculty members the focus of our reflections. Faculty come from doctoral programs where graduate faculty members are engaged almost daily in the activities not only of their academic department and their university but also of their profession. Faculty members teaching in graduate programs read and do research in their field, they attend various conferences every year, and they are in regular contact with their colleagues at other institutions. Even though all faculty members struggle to keep up on various branches of their discipline, they are well informed about current trends, at least in the area of the academic discipline they have carved out for their own research and writing. Students in doctoral programs encounter faculty members in the classroom, in special seminars, in informal gatherings, and they often collaborate in research projects with them. Young faculty members arrive at the nonsectarian university well prepared for their work.

This is not likely to be the case for the newly hired Ph.D. who has been hired to teach at a Catholic university. In a small number of cases, doctoral candidates take a personal interest in Catholic issues as they move through their doctoral program and read about Catholic matters related to their discipline. Alternatively, some students emerging with a Ph.D. from a Catholic university may have taken some courses that systematically treated some Catholic issues, but practically all Catholic universities that have doctoral programs in the nontheological disciplines follow the nonsectarian model with respect to courses and course content. Since students receive little systematic preparation for identifying or analyzing Catholic issues in their discipline, the newly minted Ph.D.s (in nontheological disciplines) arrive eager to serve and to learn, but not knowledgeable about the Catholic intellectual tradition in their own discipline. Some new hires may have taken an undergraduate course or two in theology or philosophy, but most would not claim that they have mastered that material in such a way that they can relate it to the courses they are expected to teach in their own discipline.

Under more suitable circumstances, the market mechanism would work, and Catholic universities could hire faculty members with some discipline-specific knowledge of the Catholic intellectual tradition. Demand for faculty so trained would nudge Catholic graduate programs to introduce such courses, thereby giving them a slight comparative advantage over their nonsectarian competitors. In fact, however, that is not the case. Perhaps the expressed demand for Ph.D.s with such qualifications is not significant enough or the demand for them is not communicated in a sufficiently clear manner, or the cost of modifying graduate programs to include courses on Catholic themes is excessive. If the latter is the case, the "cost" may be high because it is almost impossible to identity and hire faculty who have a dual expertise in their own academic discipline and Catholic themes related to the discipline. Whether due to deficient demand or supply, very few doctoral students are educated in graduate school about themes related to the Catholic intellectual tradition.

Another variation of a market solution would be the outsourcing of education in the Catholic intellectual tradition. This approach would involve an independent organization or a trade group formed by a group of Catholic colleges or universities. The trade group would offer training in the Catholic intellectual tradition to interested faculty members. Presumably the cost (either in whole or part) of participating in such a training would be covered by either the trade group itself or the Catholic university at which the faculty member teaches. Because both the trade group and the Catholic university have an interest in making sure that their faculty are educated and disposed to share the Catholic intellectual tradition with their students, they have an incentive to cover the costs of the program either in whole or in part.

The latter scenario is more likely. Even in this case, however, there is a cost involved. Since all colleges and universities have insufficient funds to do all the things they know are worthwhile, two issues should be addressed. First, it is important to prioritize how important educating faculty in the Catholic intellectual tradition is, and second, it is helpful to have a guideline for a Catholic university about appropriate expenditures in this area. To address both issues, we return to the discussion of religious congregations.

The highest priority for religious congregations of men and women was the training of their new members. Not only were financial resources (donated by congregants' families and generous donors) made available but also the best people were selected to train the young sisters, brothers, and seminarians. As we noted in chapter 9, the religious superiors selected the most talented people for teaching in seminaries or houses of formation. These teachers, even though they interacted with a relatively small number of novices, seminarians, or religious-in-training, had a multiplicative impact, since their charges went on to teach and interact with thousands of other people. Education is the core activity of Catholic universities. In order for distinguishability to be fulfilled, students must become acquainted with Catholic teaching and practice. In our judgment, among the many things that can be done to promote and nurture the Catholic culture on campus, none is more important than making sure students gain knowledge about the Catholic tradition and that sufficient faculty are prepared to present that knowledge.

How much should universities be willing to pay to achieve this goal? It is possible to derive a reasonable guideline by looking at what the practice of religious congregations was with respect to preparing new entrants to religious life for university work. Each religious congregation had a different approach, based on its own needs, goals, and tradition. The following calculation makes general assumptions about religious congregations and universities that are unlikely to apply in detail to any particular Catholic university. Nonetheless, the exercise is a helpful one, since it points out the relevant variables and also suggests an approximate annual amount that would be appropriate to spend on educating lay faculty in the Catholic intellectual tradition.

The first task is to determine the approximate amount of time congregations of teaching sisters, brothers, and priests-in-training dedicated to theology, philosophy, Church history, Catholic literature, and everything else that comprises the broad Catholic intellectual tradition. Many important Catholic issues were covered in novitiate, a period usually of two years when religious were introduced to religious life and the history of the congregation and were told what would be expected of them. Prior to the 1970s, the custom was for most young women and men to enter religious life after high school. Once they completed the two years of novitiate (including postulancy), they did their college studies, often in special colleges run just by the religious congregation for its own members. In their years of college, they would have studied some theology, philosophy, and the liberal arts. In many of these disciplines, Catholic topics would have been covered. Not only was this the custom of the day in Catholic colleges and universities but the religious were intended to be better prepared so they could respond to the needs and questions of laypersons with whom they interacted. As part of their preparation for the priesthood, seminarians studied philosophy for three years and theology for four years.

Each congregation had a distinct approach. Clearly, preparation for the priesthood involved extensive amounts of philosophy and theology. Many sisters, however, had theological and philosophical education as part of their training, particularly after the mid-1950s. Most congregations also had additional religious training for their members. Some of this focused on spiritual development, some of it focused on aspects of the Catholic intellectual tradition, and much of it happened on an ad hoc basis by way of religious regularly interacting with one another and discussing various religious topics related to modern culture or to secular disciplines in which they were being trained. The goal here is to propose an amount that should be spent on training a layperson interested in communicating the Catholic intellectual tradition at a Catholic university. Since the general approach thus far has been to look at what is minimally necessary for distinguishability, this approach will derive an amount deemed to be a minimum.

The working assumption we make in this analysis is that representative religious congregations traditionally spent four years on the Catholic formation of their novices, seminarians, and young women and men in formation. Two years of novitiate focused on the basics. All subsequent religious learning and training for the average religious sister or brother is assumed to constitute an additional two years. Thus, the cumulative impact of four years of undergraduate studies with a heavy Catholic accent, the years spent in community reading and talking about Catholic issues, plus ongoing formation that included regular talks about the Church, the spiritual life, and religious life is assumed to constitute two academic years of full-time study, with a focus on the Catholic intellectual tradition. Many religious congregations provided considerably more training to their members, but the two distilled and concentrated years are what we deem to be the minimum aggregate content of training (beyond novitiate) related to Catholic faith and practice. Thus, the two years of novitiate and the two composite years constitute four years of education with very substantial Catholic content.

Because the religious sisters, brothers, or seminarians lived simply, they did not incur many expenses. However, the costs of training also include paying for the expenses of those experienced faculty who were their teachers in the novitiate or later in their training. Compared with a university experience, expenses of religious faculty were relatively high, because the number of students taught or trained by a faculty member was low. In the convent or seminary, a teacher might only have ten or fifteen students in a class. Taking all this into consideration, we make the assumption that the total cost (in current dollars) of training seminarians, including room and board as well as expenses of faculty who are members of the religious congregation itself, is $40,000 per year. By comparison, this cost is approximately the full cost to a student for tuition, room, and board for an academic year at an elite university. Since parents also have to pay for their child's health insurance, clothes, presents, travel, and summer and other recreational activities, the actual full cost to a family not receiving scholarship aid of supporting a son or daughter is greater than $40,000 per year. Our estimate, however, of total annual expenses for a religious in training, including all the items a family has to pay in addition to tuition, room, and board, is $40,000. Since we assume that the average religious received a total of at least four years of instruction on primarily Catholic issues, the total minimum lifetime cost is $160,000 (4 times $40,000) to provide the requisite education in Catholic teaching and practice.

Consider now a young faculty member coming to a Catholic university. Magically, assume that this person, because of personal disposition and talent, is encouraged to become and would like to be a member of the campus CIC cluster. The only difficulty is that this faculty member needs more education about the Catholic intellectual tradition and Catholic themes, since practically none was offered or received in graduate school. Finally, assume that the young faculty member is well received at the university, likes it very much, is very productive, remains at the university, and ultimately provides forty years of service to the institution. Setting aside issues related to inflation or time discounting, we divide $160,000 by forty years and get a cost of $4,000 per year. That is, if the Catholic education of this modern young faculty member occurred over forty years, the minimum cost per year would be $4,000 under the simplifying assumptions of this analysis.[12]

Most faculty members do not serve in CIC, and yet, depending on the model to which the institution adheres, many faculty members should be well informed about the Catholic intellectual tradition. One can make further distinctions and assumptions and calculate how much the university should be willing to spend in principle to produce well-informed Catholic faculty members, where "well-informed" is defined by roughly estimating the average resources expended to educate young women and men religious in the Catholic faith.

We extend the calculation one more step so that senior administrators and faculty understand the order of magnitude of funds needed to support the Catholic academic portion of Catholic education for faculty.[13] We have to make a few additional assumptions. Suppose the goal is, out of a full-time faculty consisting of one hundred members, to have ten faculty members in the CIC group. The annual cost for educating this group is $40,000. Furthermore, suppose the average Catholic persuasion institution wishes, in addition, to have two faculty members in each academic discipline who are reasonably well informed about the Catholic intellectual tradition as it relates to that particular academic discipline. Suppose the institution has fifteen disciplines.[14] Finally, suppose the (2 times 15 equals) thirty faculty members in these disciplines are given training costing the same $4,000. However, this cost is not incurred every year. Since their training is not intended to be as extensive, one might think of these faculty members receiving special training on the average once every four years. This may occur through special institutes or retreats organized by the academic vice-president. The assumption is that, though the training pertains to their specific discipline and helps them explore Catholic themes and relate them to Catholic theology and philosophy, the amount of time spent in this learning is about one-fourth of that spent by members of the CIC. To put everything on an annual basis, it is assumed they receive one-fourth of their training each year. That is, the annual cost is $1,000, which is $4,000 divided by 4. Since there are thirty faculty in this group, the total annual cost to the university of educating this group is $30,000, which is the annual per faculty cost of $1,000 multiplied by the thirty faculty members. Adding the $40,000 per year for the faculty CIC members and the $30,000 per year for the thirty faculty being trained in the Catholic component of their academic discipline, the result is $70,000 per year for a faculty of one hundred full-time members.[15] Another perspective from which to view this number is as a percent of annual faculty compensation. If average compensation (salary plus benefits) for a faculty member at a representative institution is $75,000, total compensation is $7,500,000 for a faculty of one hundred members. An additional annual expense of $70,000 is 0.93 percent, or slightly less than 1 percent, of total annual faculty compensation.

Some institutions will choose to have faculty who are even more extensively trained in the Catholic intellectual tradition than this outline suggests. Some will want more faculty or perhaps every faculty member to receive at least some training in the Catholic intellectual tradition. Some will choose a less extensive educational program than the one outlined here. Each institution can make appropriate adjustments in the assumptions and develop an annually projected cost for making sure the foundational pieces are in place to foster and promote Catholic academic culture on campus.

Administrators should also be trained in the Catholic intellectual tradition, with particular emphasis on the tradition as it impacts their areas of responsibility. These costs can also be estimated, though additional assumptions have to be made. One important assumption pertains to the percentage of administrators who are hired from the faculty, since a number of these faculty members may already have received some training in the Catholic intellectual tradition at the university. The calculation proceeds in much the same way, but care should be taken to avoid double counting of costs.

Cooperation and Competition

The third principle for perilous times indicates that when Catholic universities are not very distinguishable and there is a question about whether they can continue to attract good students and faculty in sufficient numbers, an absence of effective competition with respect to Catholic identity should be a red flag. This absence should either alert people to impending disaster or prompt them to quickly launch some new initiatives that attempt to turn back the inevitable result of continuing to do the same thing as other similar institutions. If Catholic universities note that many universities adhering to the same model are facing indistinguishability, they have to try different things, or, if different approaches have no likelihood of success, it may be time to switch models.

At other points in this study we recommended cooperation. Toward the end of chapter 6 we advised that a few universities should get together, agree on a common policy with respect to Catholic morality and student life, and publicly announce that they are committed to adhering to these standards. To trustees we recommended that they request from university administration comparative data about student outcomes at comparable Catholic universities or simply from comparable Catholic institutions about programs and expenditures to promote Catholic identity.

Some of the most prestigious universities in the United States both cooperate graciously and compete fiercely with one another. Catholic universities would do well to imitate such productive institutional schizophrenia. Many administrators at Catholic universities are not sufficiently aware of various ways to promote the Catholic culture on campus, nor do they have a good sense of how much institutions spend on programs they deem important for Catholic identity, character, and mission. Sharing information means that another Catholic institution may look at the idea and imitate it. Depending on their student market, the university that shared the idea or made information about its program available might suffer some diminished student flow over several years. The more likely result is that the university that suffered somewhat because of one program imitated by a Catholic competitor will pick up another good idea from a different Catholic competitor and benefit by it. Cooperation combined with competition possibly may cause a poorly run institution to suffer and languish. Well-run institutions understand that sharing programs creates pressure on them to improve and stay ahead of the other Catholic institutions. This attitude creates an administrative staff that is always looking for ways to improve both the services offered to students and faculty and its competitive position among all universities, including Catholic ones.

I2

Flourishing Cultures

A Catholic cultural crisis is looming within American Catholic higher education. Senior administrators described the situation in their interviews but in most cases were either unable or unwilling to acknowledge its full dimensions. The majority of senior administrators approached their interviews for this study with optimism, confident that their institutions are well poised to address the challenges inherent in promoting and sustaining institutional Catholic culture. The optimism and enthusiasm seemed unfounded, however, when their responses to probing questions were finally and fully analyzed. The situation that senior administrators actually described created serious doubt in our minds about whether the religious legacy of Catholic colleges and universities will survive, let alone thrive, if present policy approaches persist. These doubts arose primarily for two reasons. First, Catholic components as they now exist at most Catholic colleges are so understated or subtle they can be easily overlooked or ignored. Second, administrators know little about the Catholic tradition they so enthusiastically champion.

Far too often it requires a sympathetic eye and careful attention to see the Catholic culture at Catholic colleges and universities, especially in the academic sector. Catholic cultural contours at many interview sites, when distinguishable at all, appeared only after senior administrators pointed them out. Even their attempts to illuminate religious culture took effort. Only after considerable time spent contrasting their institutions with nonsectarian counterparts did clear differences surface. The distinctive contribution of campus ministry to Catholic culture was cited by all administrators. Campus ministry aside, and with the exception of immersion institutions, there were few activities or aspects of campus life that were both clearly Catholic and touched the hearts and minds of most of the undergraduates. Most senior administrators pointed to student experiences related to social justice or service as distinctively Catholic characteristics. Few of these activities, however, had an explicit Catholic component, and without one, they were identical to those of nonsectarian institutions. The Catholic culture at any number of colleges and universities was like one prize-winning rose in an extensive English garden—arresting when pointed out, but all too easy to overlook.

Senior administrators are enthusiastic about the Catholic intellectual tradition and excited about sharing it with students. They frequently mentioned making it better known among faculty and more available to students in the classroom as a potential strategic initiative. Yet they themselves appeared to know little about it. Senior administrators knew that the Catholic intellectual tradition is big and significant, but their understanding of it seldom went beyond what its name clearly states, that it is both Catholic and intellectual. They knew this tradition refers to something that includes theology and is also linked to individual disciplines, but they did not know which academic disciplines might easily lend themselves to courses or components that explore the tradition. Unfortunately, senior administrators often drew a blank when it came to discussing the particulars of the Catholic intellectual tradition, and they were at a loss about how to make it available to students in the classroom.

Promoting the Catholic intellectual tradition is an enormous undertaking, and previous chapters have offered some rather general but practical ways to move such a large project forward. The importance of the project derives from the fact that it involves the core of what a university does, namely, sharing, critiquing, and developing a tradition of knowledge and inquiry. Strengthening this component will generate real Catholic character and knowledge among faculty and students in the university. And yet, even if this is achieved, an inheritable Catholic culture must also engage the imagination. As important as the intellectual sector is for a university, without engaging cultural symbols that provide liveliness, verve, depth, and richness, its distinctively Catholic character is diminished.

Catholic higher education does not stand alone in facing this religious cultural crisis, and these colleges and universities should not be faulted for failing to adequately address a problem that is afflicting the Catholic community at large. Many Catholic institutions—primary and secondary schools, hospitals, social service agencies—struggle to be identifiably Catholic. As mightily as Pope John Paul II worked to strengthen various Catholic institutions, he struggled to have his challenge to the dominant culture heard. As promising as the opening of Pope Benedict XVI's leadership is, he will face the same struggle. American culture is strong and quite conflicted about religion. This country is deeply religious and at the same time anxious that religion might constrain the exercise of individual rights and freedoms. Our media invokes religious images and themes but also disparages religious sensibilities. Many scholars and intellectuals recognize and study religion and its role in shaping American cultural attitudes at the same time that they ardently dismiss the legitimacy of religious claims. At times, the culture champions this land of believers, but far more often it is impatient with religion. Americans may have strong religious views and attend religious services regularly, but culturally religion is suspect.[1] Furthermore, the dominant culture, despite obeisance paid to cultural diversity, wants religious institutions to provide the same services as secular ones, and they expect to judge them according to the same standards. Religious distinctions are acceptable as add-ons, but they are not expected to alter generally accepted standards. In this cultural milieu, Catholic colleges and universities try mightily to offer basically the same education as their nonsectarian counterparts. The courses they offer in Catholic philosophy or literature certainly make them interesting, but they count for nothing in terms of institutional legitimacy and consequently appear more decorative than useful.

Religion in the United States is controlled, constrained, and tamed in ways that assure that it does not threaten the dominant secular culture of the land. In the early 1970s, Leszek Kolakowski noted a tendency among all American Christians to blend in as a matter of strategy:

> Fearful lest it become relegated to the position of an isolated sect, Christianity seems to be making frenzied efforts at mimicry in order to escape being devoured by its enemies—a reaction that seems defensive, but is in fact self-destructive. In the hope of saving itself, it seems to be assuming the colors of its environment, but the result is that it loses its identity, which depends on just that distinction between the sacred and the profane, and on the conflict that can and often must exist between them.[2]

This kind of cultural adaptation is certainly true for Catholics, who are as likely to "go along" to "get along" as any other group of religiously affiliated Americans. As a result, they are equally likely to end up with a religious culture that is fairly bland.

Senior administrators at Catholic universities, while not being defensive in their interviews, gave witness to the strong pressures they experience to conform to the practices of their nonsectarian counterparts. The legitimacy of these institutions as colleges and universities is claimed on the basis of how similar they are to all other colleges and universities. In a sense, Catholic colleges want to offer the same fare as every other institution of higher learning in the United States, not a new menu.[3] They are willing to put a dash of religion in their collegiate stew, but, wary of having it overpower, they put just enough to make it interesting, not enough to make it truly distinctive. Because there is so little variety available, this hint of flavor often stands out. Consequently, the courses with very modest Catholic content may appear more significant than they are because they are wonderfully different from the standard fare at nonsectarian institutions. These offerings may in fact be intriguing, but their content is not enough to be culturally substantive or make a difference in the lives of students.

Because Catholic universities are embedded in a dominant culture that is largely conflicted about religion and as a result confines it to the private sphere, a contrary strategy is required if their religious cultures are to survive and flourish. For Catholic universities we recommend the embellished form, rather than the spare; the lush, rather than the lean; a smorgasbord, rather than a snack. Catholic universities are confronting and interacting with a strong, brassy, dominant culture, and we are recommending a bold and dynamic Catholic cultural response that acknowledges and embraces the good of the wider culture, but is not crushed by it. Although Catholic universities should avoid arrogance, they gain nothing through a false humility and even less by not claiming their distinctiveness in a dominant culture that lavishes praise on diversity.

Warrant for suggesting bold and dramatic initiatives for strengthening Catholic culture on campuses comes from the heartfelt desires expressed by senior administrators to have their institutions be more Catholic. They consistently insisted that the Catholic dimension is what provides the distinctive value of their institutions within the landscape of American higher education. These senior administrators wanted desperately for their institutions to be considered legitimate by the dominant culture, but at the same time they also wanted them to be religiously distinctive, offering an authentic alternative to other possible collegiate choices. Senior administrators of Catholic colleges and universities find themselves on the horns of a dilemma that, if they fail to resolve, will result in either the loss of their public legitimacy or the erosion of their religious culture.

While claiming the value of their "religious" difference, many administrators wanted to check out the competition within Catholic higher education. They wanted to know what administrators at other Catholic universities were thinking. The verbatim comments in the theme chapters provide that information. They also wanted to know what others were actually doing in regard to "things Catholic" or what kinds of things their institutions might do to enhance institutional distinctiveness. Our reflections on Catholic culture in higher education end in this chapter with several suggested innovations for enhancing that culture, culled from the comments of senior administrators. Variants of some of the suggestions made here have been implemented at some Catholic universities. Some are ideas that emerged as we listened to senior administrators explain their hopes and desires. Many senior administrators offered one example of a practice, policy, or initiative that works well at their place, but they did not report enough potential projects to make the Catholic culture much stronger on their campus. Finally, some of these ideas are variations on suggestions presented in earlier chapters.

In the previous chapter, we noted several times that Catholic universities adhering to the same model should be apprehensive if they are all doing approximately the same thing. This was formally expressed in the third principle for perilous times. Each time we invoked this principle, we urged Catholic universities to buck the tide of conventional wisdom and to come up with different ways of going about supporting, sustaining, and enhancing their Catholic culture, identity, and mission. We are aware, however, that this encouragement was accompanied by only a few examples of particular strategies or policies that are both strongly Catholic and appropriately different from what most Catholic institutions currently do. This final chapter addresses that deficit.

In a column in the *New York Times*, William Safire drew some distinctions between conventional wisdom and groupthink.[4] Conventional wisdom refers to received wisdom and has positive connotations about information and attitudes that have stood the test of time. Groupthink, on the other hand, is a pejorative term, referring to a flawed decision-making process that entails individuals trying to conform their own ideas and attitudes to what they think is the consensus opinion of the group. Conventional wisdom is a resource that can help decision-makers be more knowledgeable and effective, while avoiding reinventing the wheel each time they deliberate. Groupthink, on the other hand, is an insidious process that masquerades as knowledgeable policymaking, while substituting conformity for deliberation and false harmony for true accord. In ordinary times, groupthink in certain areas may not put institutions at a disadvantage. Nevertheless, participating in groupthink rarely moves institutions to the head of the pack.

Despite its pejorative connotation, groupthink is a type of conventional wisdom. Conventional wisdom works in conventional circumstances and only slides into groupthink when administrators concentrate on the wrong things. When administrators focus only on what certain representatives of the competition are doing and fail to accurately assess what is happening on their own home turf and why it might be markedly different from what is happening elsewhere, they become susceptible to groupthink. There are three types of "conventional wisdom" that come into play at Catholic colleges and universities. They correspond to the three types of culture that generate such wisdom. The first is a general conventional wisdom, sometimes described as good business sense, institutional ways of proceeding, practical sense, and so on, which stems from the dominant American culture. There is a second conventional wisdom emanating from the culture of nonsectarian higher education. Finally, there is conventional wisdom within Catholic universities or the Catholic sector.

Conventional wisdom expresses important but partial truths; in our context, it presents solid advice for most institutions in ordinary circumstances. Our argument, however, is that many Catholic institutions are no longer in ordinary circumstances, but rather in a perilous state with respect to their Catholic identity, culture, and mission. In such circumstances, while conventional wisdom should not be dismissed out of hand, it may not prove to be a useful guide for what Catholic colleges and universities should be doing in the anything-but-conventional situation in which they are trying to do it. Institutions that wish to move to the head of the pack have to have well-thought-out strategies that move them smartly beyond what other institutions in their class are doing. Many Catholic universities need approaches that dramatically strengthen their Catholic cultures.

What follows is a list of possible programs or strategies that Catholic colleges and universities might adopt that challenge one or more forms of the conventional wisdom. In each instance, we identify the source of the conventional wisdom, and we outline the distinctively different way of proceeding and detail its efficacy. These suggestions are general in nature, and each would require careful adaptation to an institution's particular situation. Some suggestions will make more sense for one type of Catholic institution than for another, while others would be useful regardless of whether the institution were an immersion, persuasion, diaspora, or cohort university. Since the issue of hiring committed, informed Catholic faculty was discussed at length in chapter 8, we have included only a few faculty initiatives, more as reminders of the importance of the topic. Notwithstanding the few illustrations, many more approaches are possible. The following suggestions are divided into four groups: academic incentives, student living and activities initiatives, campus ministry initiatives, and administrative and governance initiatives.

Academic Initiatives

Cultivating Competence

The conventional wisdom within faith-based higher education suggests that focusing resources and attention on the religious "vocation" and the personal spirituality of individual faculty members and administrators is a valuable process for enhancing religious identity, culture, and mission. This approach brings peers together in an environment of mutual support and creates a cohort of colleagues interested in developing their own spirituality. This approach also can help create a powerful conversation within the university community. The particular approach is an investment in individual faculty members that could well pay off in the long run, in terms of both their religious commitment and their knowledge. In the short run, however, there is no guarantee that "vocation"-related programs have a payoff in the classroom.

A different approach would focus less on how faculty and administrators understand themselves and their vocational role and more on giving them the requisite knowledge and skill to weave religious themes and topics into their course work. This approach builds competence to engage the intellectual tradition for the benefit of students, but it also provides an opportunity that is personally enriching for the faculty and administrators who are involved. At a time when many Catholic colleges and universities are barely meeting the criteria for religious distinguishability and others are facing a religious cultural crisis, long-term cultivation efforts simply do not adequately address institutional needs with requisite speed.

Refocusing Congregational Investment

Conventional wisdom in Catholic higher education has placed a high premium on preserving the particular congregational culture of sponsoring religious orders. Many sponsoring groups have invested significant funds in the creation of congregational spirituality centers. Others have extended their order's commitment to the poor by funding scholarships for students with significant need. Both of these types of initiatives are popular on campuses, and both build on the religious foundations of the institutions for the future. By investing in these programs, congregations keep their legacy alive on campus. These programs, however, do nothing to help develop the witness community that is needed to replace religious congregations as Catholic cultural catalysts and exemplars.

The previous chapter talked about creating a critical mass of faculty and/ or administrators, termed a CIC cluster, that would step in to take the place of vowed religious and provide knowledgeable, committed, and visible religious leadership for the university. The development, ongoing formation, and support of this group would be a commitment worthy of congregational investment. Congregational funds so directed would promote a living Catholic legacy comprised of individuals within the colleges who have the requisite skills and legitimacy to assure that the educational experience offered is both excellent and distinctively Catholic.

Immersion Experiences

Conventional wisdom in American higher education is that immersion experiences are extremely effective educational experiences. During their interviews, senior administrators acknowledged that these types of experiences in the inner city and in the Third World transformed students, and they pointed to them as some of the most "Catholic" of their programmatic initiatives. At Catholic colleges and universities, these particular experiences, when rooted in Catholic social teaching, are powerful vehicles for transmitting the Church's message about the preferential option for the poor.

As another approach to the immersion experience, Catholic universities could find a way to have a good majority of their students experience Catholic culture in Rome for two or three weeks at the same time that students get academic credit for a course. The course could be offered annually during an intersession, a carve-out in the academic year, or in a special mini–summer course at the beginning or end of the summer. The course would be holistic, in that it would explore Catholic faith and the Catholic tradition through theology, philosophy, literature, architecture, art, and politics. Even if a Catholic university does not have its own study abroad program, it is easy for a college or university to sponsor a program jointly through another Catholic institution. Also, most sponsoring religious congregations have a motherhouse or major seminary in Rome, and there are people there who could provide this type of experience.

In order to enhance Catholic culture on campus, it would be important for a large number of students to take up the option. To make that possible, the university would need to make the program convenient for all students, regardless of their majors. They would also have to exert some gentle pressure to combat the all-too-common inertia that becomes an obstacle to participation. By granting a larger-than-expected number of credits for participation in the program or strictly minimizing the costs, the university could build broad enthusiasm for the program.

Although the focus on the program is student participation, it would be advantageous, provided there are available funds, to invite some faculty from the university to participate in the program by paying a minimal fee, whether or not they are able to contribute to the course material. As in the case of the students, many faculty members would discover that their stay in Rome is a transforming experience and that the time in Rome gives them a much better grasp of the Catholic intellectual heritage. The mutual exchange among faculty and students would also enhance the community aspect of the program.

Getting Students up to Speed

Conventional wisdom in Catholic higher education maintained that attempts by Catholic colleges and universities to effectively address the Catholic illiteracy of their students would prove unworkable. There is general recognition among Catholic collegiate educators that religious education programs in parishes have failed to produce knowledgeable Catholics. These educators also acknowledge that the problem will only grow worse over time, because fewer and fewer Catholics will have had the benefit of even basic conceptual education and formation as Catholics. Many administrators are frustrated by the unwillingness of bishops to address the problem at its root in local parishes. They also believe that students need a straightforward course in Catholic teachings and practice, but they maintain that attempts to institute a required introduction-to-Catholicism course for all students would be resisted on many fronts.

Catholic colleges and universities can begin to address the Catholic illiteracy of their students if they acknowledge two basic realities. First, they have to accept that educating students in the basics of Catholic faith and practice is part of the mission of a Catholic institution, and second, they have to recognize that knowledge of the Catholic faith tradition is an area that, for many students, involves remediation. All colleges and universities have recognized that some students come to them with gaps in their skill base that need shoring up before they can perform effectively in their college courses. In response, they create remedial programs and insist that the students get the skills they need to succeed. The lack of the most basic understanding of Catholicism is a similar situation that can be addressed in much the same way. All accepted students could opt either to read a basic Catholicism text as their summer reading option and pass a test on the material the first week of school, or to participate in a course on Catholic faith and practice created within an intermediate academic space and taught, perhaps, by adjunct faculty.

Student Publications

Conventional wisdom at Catholic colleges and universities emphasizes the value of careful administrative oversight of student publications. This approach assures that students do not run afoul of Church teaching in their publications and minimizes public embarrassment for the university. Students who work for the publications get a good idea of what is unacceptable in terms of the tradition, but in general this approach accentuates only Church prohibitions, not the intellectual richness of the tradition. Consequently, it is a weak instrument for influencing student opinion.

A more effective way for students to engage the tradition would be in a publication or journal that explored the Catholic intellectual tradition, particularly in relation to modern topics of interest. Although student journals may be uneven in the quality of their contributions, these publications often provide wonderful encouragement and positive reinforcement to students. The student editor, working under the general direction of a faculty mentor, learns how to evaluate different styles of writing and the way people marshal their arguments. Because most students have little detailed knowledge of the Catholic faith, student essays in one or more of these publications cannot presume familiarity with the pertinent books and articles on the topics addressed, or present original research. Rather, the publications present student perspectives, informed by some research, on significant issues that engage important theological or philosophical issues of the day.

Science and the Catholic Connection

Conventional wisdom in Catholic higher education situates learning about the Catholic tradition primarily within theology and the traditional liberal arts and humanities. These subjects easily lend themselves to making connections with the tradition. However, many of the brightest and most diligent students attending Catholic institutions are not majoring in these subjects, and they get little or no exposure to the richness of Catholic thought throughout the ages.

By focusing on increasing the exposure of students majoring in the physical or biological sciences to the Catholic intellectual tradition, Catholic colleges and universities could significantly extend the reach of Catholic academic offerings and make a valuable and lasting contribution to the education of a particularly promising group of students. These students are a special breed both at Catholic and nonsectarian universities. Accustomed to studying long hours and resigned to puzzling out relationships between laws in the natural or life sciences that they do not grasp accurately, they are fairly intense and focused. Because many are preparing for graduate work in some branch of science, they take a large number of science courses so that they are well prepared both for graduate school and for the standardized exams required for admission to good graduate programs. Some of these students are deeply religious and wonder about religious issues. At a Catholic university, they may be delighted to take the required courses in theology. Frequently, however, such students have a more practical orientation. They want to learn what the Catholic faith teaches, and they want to learn an appropriate religious perspective that helps them to understand the natural sciences in the framework of God's creation and the teachings of the Church.

A Catholic university could offer these students a special program that, within the limited options for elective courses available to them, provides opportunities to learn about the Catholic faith, understand the limits of sciences, and appreciate how science relates to Scripture and the teachings of the Catholic Church. Participation in this special program would substitute for some of the general course requirements in the humanities that science students would otherwise be required to fulfill. The program would have a significant impact on the Catholic culture if the program has substantial Catholic content and if a large percentage of science majors participate in the program.

Hiring for Catholic Competence

Conventional wisdom in Catholic universities indicates that assuring the vibrancy of Catholic collegiate culture requires hiring more Catholic faculty and more faculty members who are comfortable with the religious mission of the institution. While it is important for any Catholic college to have a critical mass of Catholics and also important that faculty are not hostile to the religious mission of the institution, this focus alone might not deliver the cultural catalysts and citizens that Catholic institutions hope to attract. Not all Catholic candidates for faculty positions are interested or are practicing Catholics. Some Catholic candidates are disaffected and could well resent or resist attempts to bring Catholic themes into the academic sector. Because this approach takes a simplistic view of what it means to be Catholic, it could easily falter.

A different approach to hiring for mission would focus on Catholic competence, rather than personal Catholic identity. Those hiring using this approach would ask candidates what they could actually contribute to the Catholic character, culture, and mission of the institution, especially in the teaching and research. Accepting the wisdom that the best predictor of future actions is past performance, those who were hiring would look for specific indications of how candidates had actually made a contribution to furthering the Catholic intellectual tradition in other settings. As many senior administrators noted, some of the most effective cultural catalysts among the faculty are not themselves Catholic. These individuals do have Catholic competencies, however, and usually have track records of accomplishment that complement their enthusiasm for the religious mission of the institution. By setting targets for new hires who have this type of knowledge and are willing to share it in the classroom, Catholic colleges and universities can assure that they have the cultural actors necessary to assure that the Catholic mission and culture of their institutions is sustainable for the future.

Hiring for Catholic Citizens and CIC Clusters

Conventional wisdom for both Catholic and general university cultures maintains that religious practice is a private issue that a university has no business probing in its hiring process. This presents a problem for Catholic universities that need faculty and administrators who are committed Catholics, supportive of the university being a strong Catholic institution, and willing to use their knowledge, talents, and commitment to that end. Simply knowing that someone is a Catholic frequently does not convey much of the information necessary to make the best hires for a Catholic institution. If it is out of bounds to ask questions in the hiring process about religious conviction and practice, following conventional wisdom makes it almost impossible for a Catholic college or university to assure that it has the cultural actors necessary for its own religious cultural survival.

A different approach to hiring recognizes that a visible faculty group that is be both informed and committed to the Catholic tradition is a nonnegotiable component of Catholic cultural vibrancy. It would support cultural enhancement through a strategic hiring process focused on attracting a generally targeted number of faculty members to be in the university's CIC cluster. Over time, university hiring would assure that the pool of faculty who could be selected to be the CIC is of sufficient size to function as a critical mass.

This approach to faculty hiring explicitly acknowledges the importance to the university community of having a reasonable percentage of faculty who are practicing Catholics. Other things being equal, evidence of a candidate being a practicing Catholic will make the candidate more attractive. In chapter 8, we noted that a Catholic persuasion institution could not really claim to offer students a Catholic education if the average student graduated without ever having a course from a Catholic professor who sympathetically presented material about Catholic faith or practice. The need for instruction provided by Catholic faculty and the existence of the CIC cluster and its function should be forthrightly explained to candidates. The university needs faculty who are informed about the Catholic intellectual tradition or willing to become informed about it. In addition, it needs strong, respected faculty members in the CIC. Without them, the institution will cease to have a viable Catholic identity. Interviewers can easily convey this information to candidates and determine whether they aspire to become part of the CIC. Either within the CIC or not, Catholic faculty members are in a position to make a substantial contribution to the Catholic identity of the institution if they are willing and interested in doing so.

Knowing What the Students Learned

Conventional wisdom indicates that universities should evaluate a student's level of knowledge when they graduate in a number of disciplines in order to determine the educational value added from their collegiate experience. These tests also provide benchmarking data that can be used in tailoring the institution's academic program. The conventional wisdom at Catholic colleges and universities is that this approach has merit in many areas, but not in terms of evaluating knowledge about Catholicism.

If a Catholic university determined that having a basic knowledge of the Catholic tradition was a reasonable thing to expect of its graduating seniors, it would be useful for the institution to adopt some form of assessment as part of its approach to actualizing that goal. Graduating seniors who could demonstrate a basic knowledge of Catholicism would be acknowledged in some appropriate fashion at graduation. Those with more extensive knowledge could be awarded some institutional accolade. A number of colleges and universities believe that it is important for their graduates, as educated men and women, to be able to swim, and students are required to pass a swimming test to graduate. It would seem equally reasonable for a Catholic college or university to maintain that men and women educated in a Catholic institution should not graduate ignorant of the tradition the university claims as foundational. Creating an assessment process to determine what graduating seniors had learned about the Catholic tradition would be extremely useful to the university and would have a positive impact on the Catholic culture of the institution.

Catholic Philosophy

Conventional wisdom in Catholic universities suggests that the price a Catholic university must pay for having a dialogue with the main philosophical currents of the day is almost the complete disappearance of Catholic philosophy within their philosophy departments. John Van Engen frames this dilemma Catholic universities face as follows:

> Overstated, the dilemma might be put this way: When Catholic philosophy pursued its own path from Aristotle to Thomas, it was treated as largely irrelevant to modern philosophy . . . though supremely relevant to Catholic intellectual formation; as it absorbs and interacts with modern philosophy, it risks becoming irrelevant to the shaping of a distinctively Catholic mind.[5]

The absence of philosophy courses at Catholic universities examining traditional Catholic themes in philosophy suggests that Catholic institutions are willing to accept the latter irrelevance.

A different approach would seek to maintain the dialogue, while attempting to sustain a Catholic perspective. One way of doing this is by creating a special program that provides an opportunity for philosophy majors to become well trained in Catholic philosophy. Any program thus designed would necessarily have to acknowledge that the pool of students interested in Catholic philosophy is small, as is the pool of faculty who might teach the courses. The best approach, therefore, would be a voluntary joint program bringing students, faculty, and resources together from different Catholic (and perhaps nonsectarian) universities. Faculty who work in fields related to Catholic philosophy would design the program and identify the courses and syllabi that would give undergraduate students the best modern training in Catholic philosophy. If this is done through a consortium of universities, the times for courses would have to be selected so that students from different institutions could attend. A summer program, intensive extended weekends, or intersession courses are all possibilities. One of the strengths of the program is its creation of an intellectual community of students interested in assimilating the material.[6]

Opening Things Up

Conventional wisdom among conservative Catholics is that because of their theological orthodoxy and intense Catholic culture, immersion institutions produce the most effective graduates in terms of their service to the Church and their distinctively Catholic contribution to society. Clearly, these institutions have an extraordinary commitment to educating knowledgeable Catholics who have great personal commitment to the faith. However, most immersion institutions remain quite small. Whether or not this approach is by design, such institutions lack broad appeal. As long as that remains the case, no matter how vibrant their Catholic culture or fine their education, the impact of these institutions will be modest.

Some immersion universities could take a different approach that broadens their appeal to students and thereby increases the size of their student bodies. Without abandoning their educational and religious goals, some of these institutions could broaden their program, add to their majors, and widen their base of support in the broader community. Some trade-offs would, of course, have to be made. The small and intense boutique educational experience would be modified, resulting in a less intense Catholic milieu but a larger pool of students whose impact over time both in Church and in society would be magnified.

Creating a Common Conversation

Conventional wisdom accepts that within colleges and universities, disciplines and departments are balkanized and knowledge is organized into what Lindsay Waters suggests are intellectual "gated communities."[7] As a result, undergraduates are far more likely to experience colleges and universities as intellectual collectives rather than intellectual communities. This particular arrangement, with its drive toward specialization, has contributed mightily to the acquisition of knowledge and the depth and breadth of research that has flourished within American higher education. The resulting fragmentation that many experience is the price academe has willingly paid in becoming the premier higher educational system in the world.

Rather than simply lamenting the loss of an intellectual community on campus, Catholic colleges and universities could attempt to enhance Catholic cultural knowledge and understanding and increase a sense of community by establishing a "common conversation" initiative. A college could invite the entire community—students, faculty, and administrators—to participate in such an experience over a limited time period. Using a common book that deals with a Catholic theme as the centerpiece, the entire community could commit to reading it and contributing to a campus-wide conversation about the book. This initiative could easily become an annual event scheduled during Advent or Lent that would bring the community together in intellectual conversation around ideas that pertain to its Catholic character and identity.

Channeling the Flow of Informed and Committed Catholics

Conventional wisdom from higher education tells department chairs, deans, and academic vice-presidents to rely on the regular job market to get the talent needed for universities. The normal process is: interview the candidates, invite some back to the university to give seminars, and then make the job offers. This process works well in efficiently functioning job markets. The market for informed and committed Catholics who, as Ph.D. candidates, are also knowledgeable in their academic discipline is hardly well developed.

Catholic colleges and universities can help define the market for excellent faculty candidates across disciplines who are committed and knowledgeable Catholics if they are willing for several years to prime the pump. A few ways to do so might include the following. A particular small Catholic university might contact a larger Catholic university that grants doctorates in fields of interest in an attempt to create a better pipeline of prepared candidates. Alternatively, a group of Catholic institutions could form a consortium that promotes learning about the Catholic intellectual tradition among interested graduate students. In addition to offering pertinent graduate courses, Catholic doctoral-granting institutions could develop what would amount to CIC training programs of their own through their campus ministry units. These developmental programs would focus on "vocation" and religious leadership for graduate students who have a desire to be practicing Catholics both as graduate students and later as faculty members. These CIC programs would then be in a position to offer letters of endorsement to prospective Catholic collegiate employers. There are many ways to structure a program like this. What is essential, however, is that the large Catholic doctoral-granting institutions signal to interested students that those completing the various Catholic components of the doctoral program will likely be far more appealing in the candidate pools at Catholic colleges and universities.

Catholic Entry Points

The usual approach to educating students in a field of study is to start broadly with an overview of the discipline and to systematically move over time to more intense study of increasingly narrow topics. The overview might consist of a survey course or, in the life or physical sciences, perhaps an introduction to some basic concepts. After taking the overview, students have a sense of what the discipline explores, what phenomena it explains, and what conundrums it tries to resolve. From that base, students go on and pick courses that concentrate on particular areas within the field in more in-depth fashion.

What is daunting about the Catholic intellectual tradition is its breadth. Certainly it would be possible to offer an introductory course entitled "The

Catholic Intellectual Tradition." However, a good tactic more consistent with the approach taken in this book would be a course that explores the Catholic intellectual tradition in a particular discipline. But even with a discipline-specific course, the possibilities can be overwhelming. One way to approach the expanse of the tradition is to turn the usual approach on its head and begin quite small, with a narrow and intense focus that eventually expands the discussion and material covered by helping students make ever wider connections. For example, a semester course on the Catholic intellectual tradition in poetry might consider four fairly short but peculiarly Christian poems. Each poem would serve as the point of entry into a much broader and richer discussion about increasingly more complex sets of interrelated core concepts that get to the heart of the Christian faith. The poems could share a common basic theme uniquely presented by each poet that, when taken together, made the broader connections. For instance, all of the poems could explore sin, but each would tease out different implications and in the process introduce and explore other significant issues such as redemption, forgiveness, grace, or the call to holiness. Alternately, each of the poems could focus on one of these four themes. Then by linking the individual explorations, one to another, students would arrive at a fuller and richer understanding of the Christian concept of sin and its effects on human persons.

The strategy of starting with a narrow focus and gradually expanding it to address larger topics can be helpful in any number of disciplines, even theology. Capitalizing on the exotic appeal to students of aspects of the faith with which they are not familiar, a theology professor can weave a web of increasing complexity that keeps interest high and reveals a great deal about more important aspects of the tradition. One approach would be a theology course that focuses on four secondary devotional practices in the Church, such as the rosary, litanies, Benediction, and wakes. In each case, an introductory exploration of the specific practice can be extended to enhance the depth and range of investigation and discussion. In the case of rosary recitation, the explanation of the devotion itself can move to a discussion of when the practice began, the ebbs and flows in its devotional use, how it is connected to the sacraments and Scripture, whether the Church always needs the rosary, and whether the rosary is a good pedagogical device. All of these questions flow from the particular devotional practice. In each of these cases, faculty members build on very particular and concrete topics that are appealing to students and move out to touch on a rich array of related issues that can help students understand broader beliefs of the Catholic Church.

Initiatives in Student Living and Student Activities

Catalyzing Catholic Culture in Residence Halls

Conventional wisdom in American higher education increasingly champions student independence and self-reliance as the model for residential living on college campuses. Institutions have stepped back from operating *in loco par-*

entis and have enfranchised students to negotiate their interpersonal living relationships within a coeducational framework with few rules beyond those imposed by civil law. This approach minimizes the role of on-site faculty and other professional staff and transfers responsibility for shaping residential culture to student leaders. This approach generally appeals to traditional-age students and encourages them to take responsibility for establishing their own boundaries. It also frees faculty members and administrators from the confines of dormitory responsibility. Unfortunately, the approach also limits contact with professors and other educators to discrete and formal interactions and offers few opportunities for casual ad hoc interactions between those in charge of the educational experience and the students. It also leaves students on their own and with limited options in terms of people to turn to when things become difficult.

Another approach that Catholic colleges and universities could take would be to reintroduce pastoral and residential responsibilities for the faculty and staff within dormitories. The rules that define residential culture at Catholic colleges and universities conform to the moral tradition of the Church, but at many Catholic institutions, almost no one in the dorms is conversant with that tradition. Consequently, the rules are almost always cast as controls rather than truly constructive supports for respectful mutual living. If Catholic colleges brought faculty and pastoral people back into the dormitories, they could help create living environments where students are mentored in the Catholic tradition, not left to their own devices to create shadow cultures that are often corrosive of all the Catholic college hopes to accomplish.

Faculty members and administrators communicate what is valuable to them by where they spend their time. When adults avoid the students where they live, distance themselves from the day-to-day struggles students have as they negotiate their nonacademic lives, and walk away from opportunities to reinforce the values of the Catholic moral tradition and Catholic social teaching, they undercut the very message of Christian community they hope to convey. Catholic colleges and universities maintain that they are supportive communities that value the students and are committed to their growth. Greater involvement by faculty, administrators, and pastoral staff with students in residence halls would demonstrate the truth of that assertion.

Thorny Issues

Conventional wisdom among Catholic bishops is that Catholic colleges and universities should avoid featuring outside speakers, performances, or events that challenge the Church's teaching. This approach helps to assure that the Catholic university does not confuse the university community by presenting views that run contrary to those of the Church. Unfortunately, this approach does little to illuminate what the Church does teach. It also can suggest that Catholics are afraid to confront other views in a public forum, even within a university community—an approach that often whets contrarian appetites, rather than satisfying them. Faced with this conventional wisdom, Catholic colleges respond differently. Some colleges carefully vet all groups and individuals that might be invited to campus and only approve those that fully support Church teaching. Others take a hands-off approach, emphasizing academic freedom and avoiding saying no to student groups.

A different approach would seize the opportunity presented by so-called objectionable groups or individuals to engage the question and provide a framework to explain, explore, and emphasize Catholic themes over against the message that is contrary to Catholic teaching. An example of this is the controversy surrounding *The Vagina Monologues*. It would be far better for a Catholic university to champion the cause that surrounds the production—repudiating violence against women—while working with faculty, administrators, and students to find or develop vehicles that more authentically celebrate women in ways highlighting strengths from the Catholic tradition.

Preparing Resident Assistants

Conventional wisdom in American higher education supports a type of preparation for resident assistants (RAs) that includes training in community building, problem-solving, and safety procedures, as well as extended sessions that deal with the legal rules they must enforce in relationship to drugs and alcohol. This training is considered appropriate preparation for their role as the responsible on-site leaders in residence halls who are expected to "set the tone," communicate what constitutes acceptable and unacceptable behavior, monitor student behavior, maintain reasonable order, be supportive listeners who give good advice, help students to negotiate their differences, and inform administrators when things have gotten out of control. This kind of training may prepare RAs for their responsibilities in nonsectarian institutions, but in Catholic colleges and universities, this training leaves much to be desired.

Resident assistants at Catholic colleges and universities have a significant role to play in supporting Catholic ethical teaching that requires they understand, support, and be able to explain these teachings that inform the behavioral norms in residence halls. Senior administrators acknowledged that these young men and women are uncomfortable dealing with many moral issues, particularly those that deal with sexual intimacy between students, and they receive no training that prepares them to assume that responsibility. As part of a plan to enhance the character formation and moral education of students, Catholic universities should require RAs to participate in programs that teach them about the Catholic approach to student issues.

Athletes and Catholic Culture

Conventional wisdom considers athletes as a group to be intellectually indifferent at best and culturally subversive at worst. Demanding practice and game schedules surely cut into the time they might spend studying. These students are often recruited more for their physical prowess than their intellectual ability, and their graduation rates are frequently a matter of grave concern. Recent stories in the media about "team cultures" that are dismissive or abusive of women have tarnished the reputation of many student athletes, and the special attention they receive further sets them apart from the rest of campus culture.

Despite the press and conventional wisdom, most student athletes more than hold their own in terms of their studies. Varsity athletes are usually a well-motivated and well-disciplined group, both in matters pertaining to their sport and also in academics. Judging from publicly available statistics, athletes at all but a small subset of universities have higher grade point averages than the general student average. For the most part, athletes comprise a group of conscientious and well-disciplined individuals, many of whom are quite religious in their orientation.[8]

Many Catholic universities do have religious opportunities specifically for athletes, most often an occasional special Mass. By focusing on athletes as potential religious cultural catalysts and providing them opportunities to grow in their own knowledge and understanding of the faith and to deepen their religious practice, Catholic colleges and universities can enhance institutional Catholic culture. Voluntary programs could target athletes who choose to make a commitment to their religious growth. These programs would call on these individuals to also commit to attaining above-average knowledge of the Catholic faith and to practice their own faith more purposefully. The fact that at most universities athletes enjoy the admiration and respect of other students further enhances their capacity to act as Catholic cultural catalysts whose commitment to deepening religious understanding and faith will both strengthen themselves and the institution's Catholic culture.

Confronting Consumer Culture

Conventional wisdom says that in order to compete, colleges and universities must provide students with the leisure amenities they have come to expect as part of the residential package at collegiate institutions. Students and their parents are consumers of higher education who often bring that mentality to the decision-making process when choosing an undergraduate institution. They appear to want state-of-the-art fitness centers, climbing walls, swimming pools, hot tubs, and saunas—all the things they would expect to find at sports clubs that charge expensive entrance fees. Students also want townhouse apartments, cable TV, and a wide array of food options no different from those they would find in any suburban mall. Even institutions with limited resources will find ways to get a fitness center before they do other things, just to be able to compete in today's higher education market.

For colleges and universities to remain competitive, they almost certainly have to conform to general student and parental tastes and desires with respect to college life. Strong words in the Gospels, recent statements by Pope John Paul II and Pope Benedict XVI, and the general tradition of religious congregations all indicate that Catholic colleges and universities should be at least partially countercultural with respect to consumerism, one of the defining characteristics of American society. A variety of programs are possible. Students could choose to sign up for an academic semester or year of simple living, where "simple living" has different characteristics at different universities. "Simple living" might include living accommodations, meals, the amount of clothes and other gadgets students bring to campus, the facilities students use on campus, and so on. Students committed to simple living might be charged a smaller amount for room and board, or they might pay the same amount and the university might contribute the money saved to a charity involving the poor in the United States or in other parts of the world.

Such a program can take many different forms, but university sponsorship is important. After proper consultation, the university can establish a voluntary program for students, and perhaps for faculty and parents as well. For the agreed-upon period of time, the students and others adopt a modest style of living. By committing to such a program, the participants make an important contribution to the life of the Catholic community on campus.

Not Just Academic Honor Codes

Conventional wisdom in colleges and universities accepts the wisdom of establishing strict academic honor codes that call on students to conduct themselves according to the highest standards of intellectual integrity. They also summarize the content of these codes and ask students to sign statements signifying their willingness to comply with these standards. Colleges and universities recognize that by focusing the issue clearly and having students sign statements of compliance, they can impress on them the importance of this set of values and be in a better position to enforce institutional guidelines concerning breaches of the code. In terms of behavioral codes, universities expect compliance with only minimal, rather than optimal, standards regarding how students conduct themselves and are often restrained in how they enforce even these minimal standards.

Catholic colleges and universities could take a different approach that calls students to a set of high behavioral standards that they acknowledge as rooted in the Catholic tradition and its moral and social teaching. They could also adapt the approach to honor codes by summarizing the content of their behavioral expectations and asking students to sign them, signifying their willingness to comply and their intention to abide by the honor code of conduct. Since this approach would require an educational and formational program, it might be that students choose to abide by the honor code only at the end of their first semester. Whatever the particular arrangements, it would clarify that Catholic institutions expect more than most colleges in terms of how students conduct themselves on campus and off campus, and it would make clear why they had those expectations. This approach would also strengthen the university's ability to enforce the norms they establish.

Initiatives Linked to Campus Ministry

Appreciating Catholicism's Diversity

Conventional wisdom in American higher education places a premium on programs that highlight diversity and appreciation of different cultural approaches and beliefs. Ecumenical and interreligious outreach programs within campus ministry at Catholic and non-Catholic colleges and universities are popular programmatic initiatives designed to enhance appreciation and tolerance among individuals and groups who have different religious traditions. Many Catholic colleges and universities are particularly sensitive about embracing members of the community who are not Catholic, and they dedicate time, energy, and resources to developing ecumenical and interreligious campus ministry programs. These efforts are important, but they often assume that Catholic students already have a rich understanding of their own tradition, which is increasingly not the case. These programs also do nothing to encourage tolerance of different religious "styles" among Catholic students.

The Catholic tradition has a diverse array of liturgical experiences and devotional practices, and most Catholic students have experienced very few of them. A program dedicated to extending the devotional and liturgical repertoire of Catholic students would address this Catholic cultural deficit. Campus ministry can offer a broad variety of experiences to the students, encourage them to experience their richness, and educate them about their history. This approach to enhancing appreciation of religious diversity issues at Catholic colleges and universities can complement ecumenical and interreligious understanding and deepen Catholic cultural understanding at the same time.

Volunteer Service

Conventional wisdom in American colleges supports service learning as an important part of the educational experience of undergraduates. Most of these programs are involved in rendering service to those at the margins of society. Educators believe that patterns of service that are developed in undergraduate years will continue after graduation, and they anticipate that such educational programs will have lasting benefit for society. Catholic colleges and universities are equally committed to service learning, especially when it involves service to the poor.

A different approach to volunteer service and service learning that has the potential to enhance institutional Catholic culture and positively contribute to the Catholic community would be an expansion of volunteer service and learning to include projects that are focused on service to the Church. Such a campus-wide program emphasizing service to parishes during the student's undergraduate years can take many forms. One approach could emphasize students volunteering to commit a certain number of hours over a two-semester interval to a particular parish. During this period of time, the particular parish would likely become the place of worship for the student, even as he or she spends time assisting the priest or some parish staff person or society. Most parishes would be thrilled to have young students volunteering and participating in some way in the life of the parish, and the students would gather a wealth of information about parish life. A second approach would be to train a good number of students to be instructors of religious education. Most dioceses have preparation programs that could be offered to students at the university. Training qualified instructors of religious education would provide a substantial boost to the diocese and also help students to be well-informed parents who can teach the Catholic faith to their own children when the time comes.

Parish Life Preparation

Conventional wisdom in Catholic colleges and universities is that as a result of excellent liturgical experiences on campus, students after graduation often become disenchanted with what parishes have to offer them and frequently disengage from parish life. Part of what makes liturgy so compelling at a Catholic university is that it usually brings together hundreds of young students, all of approximately the same age and with similar interests. It is perhaps one of the most homogeneous but also stimulating religious experiences students have in their young lives, since most liturgies in the postuniversity environment have participants who are much more diverse in age, socioeconomic status, and interests. For a priest, preaching to a group of undergraduates is a privilege and considerably easier than preaching in a typical parish, where the experiences and viewpoints of the people in the pews are so wide and varied. Catholic colleges and universities recognize that part of their mission is to serve the Catholic Church, and most of them also want to form leaders not only for society in general but for the Catholic Church as well. Leadership in the Church assumes active participation in parish life, and this presents a challenge for universities in terms of how they should prepare their Catholic students to be effective leaders in the emerging Church.

Campus ministry clearly should continue to provide excellent and varied liturgical experiences for the university community. But it can also create initiatives especially for groups of students in their final undergraduate year at the university. The program might include some Sunday trips to parishes, participation in the liturgy there, and then an opportunity to meet afterward with parishioners and the pastors. In this program, students would learn from current parishioners what they hope for the new young adult members of their parish. Parishioners could also share the most beneficial contributions young adults have made to parish life, along with what was disappointing. By participating in such sessions at a number of parishes, graduating students will form clear ideas of the expectations people have for them, and they can formulate a strategy for how they hope to make a contribution to the life of the local church once they graduate.

Relational Intimacy and the Catholic Tradition

Conventional wisdom in higher education holds that students have to sort out their relationships on their own. Beyond informing students of the health-related resources available for their protection, most colleges and universities do not insert themselves in the thicket of their students' relationships. Coming of age in a dominant culture in which few boundaries are respected and that all too often confuses sexual activity with intimacy is, at the very least, confusing. On college campuses today, young men and women struggle to negotiate who they are and how they will be with others without many wise and supportive men and women available to guide them. Their attempts to sort out relationships take place in a cultural environment that is not conducive to understanding, let alone establishing, appropriate relationships that can enhance true intimacy within appropriate loving boundaries. While this certainly is the situation at most colleges and universities in the United States, it is simply not tenable at a Catholic institution.

A different approach, while recognizing that students will ultimately decide for themselves both how they understand intimacy and what interpersonal boundaries they will respect, will not abandon them to their own devices. Instead, it will bring the wisdom and richness of the Catholic tradition to bear in a program that focuses specifically on relationships. The Catholic Church itself is in the midst of a sexual abuse crisis that at its heart is all about distorted views of intimacy and the absence of necessary and reasonable interpersonal boundaries. If Catholic colleges and universities are willing to address these issues head-on, rather than walking away from them because they are so thorny, they can render profound service not only to the young men and women they are educating but to the wider society and the Church as well.

Spiritual Outreach

Conventional wisdom in Catholic colleges and universities supports an approach that attracts students to justice and service experiences that are seen as catalyzing programs that lead to the exploration and expansion of spiritual, sacramental, and devotional practice. This approach assumes that students are more inclined to act generously on behalf of the poor and marginalized and from that experience to ask the ultimate questions that move them toward a deeper faith that seeks ritual expression.

Another approach inverts this process. It operates from the premise that spiritual, sacramental, and devotional practice, when cultivated and enhanced, will compel students to live lives in service to the poor and marginalized. This approach assumes that students have deep religious motivations and that nurturing them will heighten their desire to be of service and enrich any service experiences they have. Such a programmatic approach would establish a framework that combines special liturgies, prayer, and devotional experiences with service and a reflection component. It would also include ongoing opportunities for students to pray for the people they serve. The inspiration for the latter approach is the example of nuns in Catholic hospitals and nursing homes: they cultivated their own spiritual lives, which compelled them to serve those most in need. In serving the sick and infirm, they both cared for their patients and prayed for them.

Praying for the University Community

Conventional wisdom in Catholic colleges and universities assumes that weekly prayer and worship is primarily focused on students who live on campus, not the whole university community. The focus shifts to the whole university community only for two or three occasions during the year when there are large Eucharistic liturgies that students, faculty, and administrators are encouraged to attend.[9]

At a time when the dominant society seeks to privatize religious expression, Catholic colleges and universities can take a different approach that communicates that prayer is a central Christian activity. Certainly people can and do pray in private. But having regular occasions when a good portion of the university community can come together in prayer provides helpful support to all members of the community. Selecting a time in the weekly schedule when most students, faculty, and administrators are free to attend is very important. Various types of prayer can be used, and different universities will make different choices. Reciting a part of the Liturgy of the Hours, attending Mass, silent prayer, quiet adoration, reciting aloud some psalms and a few other prayers are all possibilities. Whatever the type of prayer selected, it should be relatively brief and focus on the needs of the university community. Having the broader university community pray in this way helps the university by keeping a constant focus on the gifts it receives from God through its Catholic faith. The participation of faculty, administrators, and staff with the students further reinforces the lifelong importance of regular prayer.

Administrative and Governance Initiatives

A Strategic Hire

The conventional wisdom in Catholic higher education suggests that if a university were to make one "hire" designed to have a significant impact on the vibrancy of its institutional Catholic culture, it would make the most sense to hire a vice-president or director in charge of mission. In fact, many Catholic colleges and universities have done just that. Often, however, the "mission" person is seen as an outsider by other members of the community. That is particularly the case when the sponsoring religious congregation holds great sway in making the appointment. When appointed by the sponsoring religious congregation, the mission director may also be more associated with the Mercies, Josephites, or Augustinians than with the mission to serve the Catholic Church. If the mission director has little or no university experience, particularly within the academic sector, that person is further marginalized. It is easy for most departments and individuals to "steer clear" of the mission office if they choose to do so, and many believe that such an appointment suggests that the president is not appropriately involved in the religious dimensions of university life.

Considering the vice-president for finance, rather than a mission director, as a pivotal "hire" in terms of shaping the religious culture counters conventional wisdom but offers unique opportunities for effecting religious mission throughout the university. Every department must work with the person who holds the purse strings. If that individual is thoroughly knowledgeable concerning the Catholic tradition and masterful about how to bring resources to bear on supporting institutional cultural vitality, programmatic efforts that enhance religious identity and mission will develop across campus, and they will be funded. In most cases, the religious knowledge and commitment of candidates for this position is not a top consideration in the final choice for who will be appointed. This office, however, plays a significant role in shaping institutional priorities, and leadership by a dynamic Catholic cultural catalyst will have significant ripple effects throughout the institution.

Enfranchising Trustees

Conventional wisdom at Catholic colleges and universities favors a general workshop approach to educating trustees about their fiduciary responsibility for institutional Catholic identity, culture, and mission. These workshops tend to be either particular and limited to a few areas or quite general in nature. The general workshops or retreats are largely introductory sessions designed to make lay trustees aware of the implications of their role in terms of the Catholic identity of the institution. The more particular sessions usually focus on founding congregational issues or specific problems that need to be addressed, often dealing with civil and canonical legal issues, the sale of property, leadership changes, and so on. All of these sessions are worthwhile and important and help trustees to develop greater facility with a component of trusteeship that has mostly been ceded to congregational sponsors or other Catholic experts. These sessions need to be repeated cyclically as new trustees are added to the board. Because of the many demands on trustee time, there is little opportunity to develop greater sophistication among board members as a result of increasingly comprehensive workshops that build on each other over time. As a result, few trustees ever get to a place where they feel comfortable assessing institutional performance in terms of the religious mission of the institution.

A different approach would redirect the focus of the trustees within their committees so that in the course of their normal oversight activities they would be able to monitor religious performance and evaluate which programs had the greatest promise for enhancing that performance for the future. Working with the president, trustees could develop the necessary tools and measures that would most accurately reflect performance across the university. Over time these measures could be fine-tuned in ways that would be most helpful to the trustees.

Partnering with the Diocese

Conventional wisdom at Catholic colleges and universities supports keeping a respectful distance between the institutions and the local diocese. This distance assures that the universities have the independence necessary to fulfill their mission as universities, not as educational arms of the Church. When difficult issues about authority and control, such as those that emerged concerning the implementation of *Ex Corde Ecclesiae,* are at their peak, independence rather than interdependence is often accentuated. Keeping some distance during these difficult times also creates a space in which the dust can settle and new and more mutually beneficial connections can be forged. Unfortunately, distance is not always beneficial, and it can contribute to suspicion and alienation that impoverishes both the diocese and the university.

If Catholic colleges and universities really are to be one of the places where the Church does its thinking, partnering with the local diocese to establish programs that are mutually beneficial could prove strategically wise. Catholic universities have resources and research capacity that they already bring to bear when attempting to address many of the pressing problems that confront society and the Church. Program series that engage the Catholic intellectual tradition and bring the moral and social teaching of the Church to bear on critical institutional and social issues could be of great benefit to the university and the diocese, as well. Programs that involve partnering with the diocese to provide education and formation for catechists and pastoral ministers also have particular merit and many Catholic universities have such programs. A partnership that respects that the bishop has more to offer the university than his presence on the stage at graduation, and that also acknowledges the contribution that Catholic colleges and universities can and do make to the diocese, can be enormously positive. These kinds of partnerships contribute to a healthy interdependence that enhances the work and contributions of both.

Becoming More Catholic through Trustee Competition

Conventional practice is that, depending on location and the type of programs offered, Catholic colleges and universities energetically compete with one another for students, faculty, and administrators. Typically, the boards of trustees at one Catholic institution may acknowledge and even revel in this friendly competition among institutions. But usually the boards do not see themselves competing with each other to take the best approach to monitoring the Catholic performance of their institution.

Some trustees are CEOs of large corporations, and they have all participated in various training seminars—to be better leaders, to manage their corporations better, to handle their staff more effectively. Some CEOs speak highly of particular programs in which they have participated. We encourage one generous trustee of a Catholic university to challenge both his own board and the board of some other Catholic college or university to participate in a leadership or management program designed for corporations. The generous CEO or other executive would cover the expenses of the two boards to participate in the program. But instead of the boards collaborating with each other, they would compete. Both boards would attend the same sessions together. But each board would have the task of developing trustee policies that would strengthen the Catholic identity of their own institution. All this would occur in the course of a two-or three-day corporate environment in some nice, cushy corporate vacation spot. Toward the end of the seminar, each board would present its program for governance, and two or three impartial "judges" could decide which approach was stronger or which components of an overall strategy made more sense. The point is not to secure agreement but to get boards to think of themselves as competitors. This is familiar and comfortable terrain for most trustees, who believe that competition leads to more efficient institutions.

Final Thoughts

We have presented many potential programs. One may wonder why these programs have not already been instituted at various Catholic universities. First, we note that a number of universities have programs similar to some of the programs we have described. Nonetheless, it is true that many of the proposals are distant relations to what most Catholic universities have on their campuses. Second, some of these proposed programs may not be good ideas, or they may not fit the current circumstances of many Catholic universities. But, assuming that at least some of the programs might work well at some Catholic institutions, it is curious that more of them have not been implemented in some form.

Each institution has its own reasons for offering its current array of programs. Two reasons for some hesitancy in developing Catholic programs emerged from the interviews with senior administrators: lack of comparative data and fear of turning away students because of Catholic content.

No institution wants to be too far ahead of the pack, and many Catholic universities are having a difficult time finding the pack. With little information about what other Catholic universities are doing, a type of paralysis can set in among many Catholic institutions. Information from senior administrators has been provided in this study, and it has been given a context by identifying the type of Catholic institution at which the administrator serves. The proposals discussed are ours, although they were inspired by the comments of senior administrators as well as by actual practice in some universities. These programmatic suggestions are graphic, realistic ways to enhance competition among Catholic universities, but they are not intended as a blueprint for success that institutions should merely adopt. They are proffered as intellectual and inspirational stimulus packages that can be altered, adapted, and improved upon to make most Catholic institutions better all-around universities, as well as better Catholic institutions.

Appendix A

Participating Colleges and Universities

Ancilla College	Indiana
Barry University	Florida
Catholic University of America	District of Columbia
Christendom College	Virginia
Christian Brothers University	Tennessee
College of Mount Saint Joseph	Ohio
College of Notre Dame of Maryland	Maryland
College of St. Elizabeth	New Jersey
DeSales University	Pennsylvania
Fontbonne University	Missouri
Gannon University	Pennsylvania
Georgetown University	District of Columbia
Immaculata University	Pennsylvania
Mount Mary College	Wisconsin
Mount Mercy College	Iowa
Neumann College	Pennsylvania
Our Lady of the Lake University	Texas
Regis University	Colorado
Saint Anselm College	New Hampshire
Saint Catharine College	Kentucky
St. Edward's University	Texas
St. Francis University	Pennsylvania
St. Gregory's University	Oklahoma
St. John's University	New York
St. Thomas University	Florida
Stonehill College	Massachusetts
Thomas Aquinas College	California
University of Notre Dame	Indiana

University of Portland	Oregon
University of San Diego	California
University of the Incarnate Word	Texas
Villanova University	Pennsylvania
Wheeling Jesuit University	West Virginia

Appendix B

Methodological Narrative

Selection

Much of the scholarly work and literature concerning Catholic colleges and universities focuses on particular segments of the sector— not on the whole range of diverse institutions that make up the enterprise known as American Catholic higher education. One of the purposes of the second phase of the Emerging Trends in Leadership Study was to provide a rich description of how Catholic identity and mission were understood by those people who are exercising leadership at the senior level across the Catholic collegiate spectrum in the United States. This goal required a broadly representative sample of institutions, and that in turn necessitated a rather large sample. This relatively large sample made it possible to include many different kinds of institutions, but it also made the selection of which institutions to visit rather complicated. A number of factors went into determining the final list of sites for the study, including geography, institutional size, founding bodies (be they women's religious congregations, men's congregations, local dioceses, or groups of laypersons), Carnegie Classifications, finances, and student body composition. Attention was also given to a balance among presidents, in terms of gender and congregational and lay status. Ideological differences are quite distinct within the landscape of Catholic higher education, and few studies look at institutions across that divide. The final list of sites included institutions that run the gamut from those perceived to be quite traditional or conservative to those known as liberal or progressive and everything in between.

Thirty-five colleges and universities were contacted and asked to participate as one of the thirty-three sites in the interview phase of the study. Two institutions declined, citing their accreditation process as the limiting factor. Although the study was designed to be broadly representative, 80 percent of institutions founded by Holy Cross priests and brothers were included among the sites for this study. We originally intended to look at similarities and differences among institutions founded by one religious congregation. This group of institutions was manageable in size, unlike other groups such as those founded by the Mercy Sisters, the Jesuits, or the Josephites, all of which comprise a far greater number of institutions. As the data mounted, the complexity of the project increased, and time marched on, however, the wisdom of that original plan was questioned. In the end, the research team determined that a comprehensive study of similarities and differences among institutions operating under the umbrella of one congregation was a study unto itself, and reluctantly put it aside for another time.

Bridge Questionnaires

The thin descriptions that emerged in the first phase of the project were a bit of a puzzle for the team. It was possible that administrators with limited time and a twelve-page questionnaire staring them in the face gave shorthand responses to the questions. If that were the case, interviews would provide the time and opportunity necessary to unpack the spare responses, getting below the surface and revealing the rich descriptions to which the shorthand referred. It was also possible, however, that terms like *Catholic identity, Catholic intellectual tradition, Catholic moral tradition,* and *Catholic mission* were generally not well understood by the administrators. There is little specificity about them in current literature about Catholic higher education, even though authors refer to them reverentially and quite frequently. That being the case, it seemed safe to assume that most administrators did not have a clue what these terms actually signified. Consequently, the team decided to use a multiple-choice questionnaire as a strategic device to facilitate the next phase of the research.

Multiple-choice questionnaires can be helpful or frustrating for respondents. Regardless of which way participants in this study reacted, the research team intended to use the tool as a bridge that would lead to more in-depth conversations about the theme of Catholic identity, culture, mission, and leadership. For administrators who lacked in-depth knowledge or experience, these instruments could suggest unimagined possibilities previously not considered. In so doing, they would help break open elements of participants' own experience that otherwise would have gone unattended. If administrators were quite knowledgeable and fluent with Catholic culture, and consequently found the questionnaire confining, their reactions and descriptions would serve as a jumping-off place that could be used to deepen and enrich the interview conversation. In either case, the questionnaires had the potential to add breadth and depth to interviews and push beyond pat answers that could not capture the heart of the matter.

Protocol

A copy of the interview protocol and the multiple-choice questionnaire for each administrator was sent to the president's office prior to the site visit. Allowing time for respondents to reflect on the material before the interview increased the likelihood that interviewees could provide the rich descriptions of their lived experience that the study sought. Each interviewee was also invited to call a member of the visiting team with any questions they had about the study, the questionnaires, or their forthcoming interview. While the team was committed to creating the most hospitable environment for the interview phase of the study, it was under no illusion that every interviewee would prepare for the conversation. To increase the likelihood that administrators would give some thought to the questions prior to the actual interview, the research team requested that the multiple-choice questionnaires be filled out and made available to the researchers in the president's office before the interviews.

In drawing up the interview protocol, the research team focused on eliciting from the interviewee what he or she thought was particular about Catholic higher education, what types of contributions he or she made that specifically contributed to the institution's Catholic mission, and what degree of personal and professional commitment to the Catholic project he or she deemed was required for Catholic higher education to succeed. The questions did not seek to gauge differences between lay interviewees on the one hand and male and women religious on the other hand. Responses from phase 1 had indicated that though there were significant differences in prior education and training between these two groups, there did not appear to be important differences in viewpoints with respect to Catholic identity, mission, and character. Any significant differences would be captured in responses to the multiple-choice questions.

Analysis of Phase 2

Interview analysis in any study is a continuous process, and that was certainly the case with phase 2 of this project. The design phase determined the basic structure of the interviews, and analysis began with interviewer reactions to the first interview conversations. Additional reactions during the interview phase furthered this kind of preliminary analysis and suggested ways to probe the interviews beyond the standard evaluation techniques. Once the interviews were completed, the team met to agree upon first steps in formal analysis of the interviews.

Analysis Sheets

In order to provide an accurate text of interviews that at a distance would convey what was actually said, the research team decided to audiotape the interactions and have them transcribed.[1] The transcripts captured language accurately, but they were blind to the conversational dynamics. These essential elements were captured in a series of careful notes each researcher wrote immediately after the interviews. These notes were reviewed later during the site visit in debriefing sessions with site partners. At the sites where a single interviewer conducted conversations, the debriefing sessions took place via telephone with another member of the research team.

In about a quarter of the interviews, interviewees had prepared either talking notes or "thoughts" for each of the questions. People with such notes indicated that they had looked over the questions and just wanted to get a few thoughts down on paper. In practically all cases, what the interviewer said during the interview was much clearer and pointed than what was written in the prepared "talking notes." Even when interviews gave the researchers the talking notes, the main reference remained the interview itself, not the talking notes.

Ongoing conversations among researchers and extensive field notes captured the dynamics of what happened in each interview and proved useful in constructing the outlines of the broader story told in each conversation. The text transcriptions assured that there was an accurate accounting of what was said in a particular interview, and at times provided necessary correctives for unfounded researcher impressions that had been unduly influenced by the dynamics, rather than the content, of their interview interactions. The analysis report was one methodological tool that helped keep the dynamics and the text of interviews in a productive tension, promoting a reliable interpretation.

The analysis reports clearly stated the questions researchers asked of the data. These reports were filled out at some distance from the interviews and after many subsequent interviews, necessitating both a careful reading of the text and review of the audiotapes by researchers. In filling out the report, the interviewers summarized their general impressions of their conversation and any details of the process that were particularly noteworthy or could have had an impact on the interaction itself. They described what was termed "a peek at the performance," noting general tone, demeanor, body language, and/or emotional overlay they had observed. Because the interviewers were cocreators of the interview, they talked about how they reacted and anything else about themselves or their demeanor that might have been contributory to what ensued.

The research team for this project consisted of five interviewers, each with a unique interview style and approach, who did varying numbers of interviews. The interview protocol provided one mechanism for keeping this diverse group within boundaries that were broad enough to capitalize on their own individual styles without sacrificing necessary consistency across interviews. The analysis reports also helped assure a useful, albeit flexible, consistency across interviews. The reports asked a series of questions about each of the protocol topics that categorized whether responses dealt primarily with people, programs, events, or faith and values. Interviewers also wrote headlines and provided one-word feeling descriptors for each response, a technique that surfaced impressionistic reactions to both the essential content and tone of the interchange. Interviewers indicated what was most surprising in the interview, what was most positive or persuasive, and what was most negative or depressing about each interviewee's responses. Interviewers also recorded two or three quotations that best told the story of the response to the question at the end of each question analysis segment. This particular feature was designed to assure that quotations from interviews were truly representative of the interview as a whole and were not snippets taken out of context to justify researcher positions.

With an eye always on the larger story to be told, the analysis report posed questions that moved back and forth from the particular details of a response to the story it told, from the informational content to the emotional overlay, and from the interviewee's words to the interviewer's reaction. This design kept both the dynamics of the cocreational interview conversation and its textual accuracy fruitfully engaged. At the end of each interview analysis report, researchers were encouraged to include comments and quotations that did not fit into any particular category but captured something significant. Sometimes these were outlier comments, and other times they represented conceptual developments for the interviewee that resulted from having the conversation.

Interview conversations often have a meandering quality about them. In responding to questions in this study, interviewees frequently circled back to previous questions, added information, changed their minds, and sometimes contradicted themselves. As they went through this process, and were attending to direct or clarifying follow-up questions, senior administrators often developed greater insight about their own ideas. Researchers paid careful attention to the changes, avoiding emphasis on decontextualized statements that truncated the sense of the conversation as a whole. Each interview began with an opportunity for the interviewee to react to the bridge questionnaire, and in many instances respondents took the lead in using the introductory phase of the conversation as a jumping-off place for comments that got right to the heart of the protocol questions. Others shared information and perceptions that provided insights that did not fall into the protocol categories but shed light on the interviewee's lived experience and understandings. At the beginning of the interview, some researchers asked the administrator to give a thumbnail description of the college or university. Even when this was not addressed at the beginning of the interview, a number of interviewees included such information in the course of the interview. Any tangential comments that added to the story or provided context or richer description, as well as any responses that particularly struck interviewers as threads worth pulling during analysis, were included in a final open-ended section of the analysis report.

As a next step in the process, each of the researchers received a copy of every interview transcript and every analysis report. After reading them, the team had an opportunity to discuss, ask questions, and share their different interpretations about what had been said during the encounter. At times, these conversations led to a shift in perspective, but more frequently they added dimensions to the analysis. In a few instances, the researcher who conducted the interview rejected alternative interpretations. When this occurred, the other team members deferred to his or her judgment, because they recognized that the interviewer had the benefit of the whole experience, whereas they were conversing with only the transcription text.

At this point in the process, with analysis reports completed and fully discussed, a shift took place in the research team. One of the members of the team was only available to participate through the design phase and for a limited number of interviews.[2] Once the analysis reports were completed, it became necessary for the remaining four researchers to reconstitute themselves as a new group responsible for analyzing the study data.

Interpretation

A significant piece of interpretative work in this study emerged prior to the formal analysis component of the project. In kaleidoscopic fashion during the interview phase of the research study, patterns among responses began to emerge, blur, and shift, with new patterns emerging, replacing the old. At the start of this project, it was clear that there are many different kinds of Catholic colleges and universities that understand their Catholic identity, culture, and mission in a variety of ways. This rather inchoate picture of variety began to take some form relatively early on, as interview teams began seeing connections among the responses of interviewees at some colleges and real differences among others regarding how they understood the purposes and goals of a Catholic college or university. As they moved from one site to the next, those connections became clearer, and the discontinuities came into greater relief, eventually coalescing around four distinct ways of approaching collegiate Catholic mission, culture, and identity. Not all the institutions were exact fits with these models, but most either fit or were close enough to one or the other of the prototypical types of institutions to render them useful for understanding the enterprise as a whole. The rough outline of the models sprang from site conversations and became more structured as researchers shared their impressions with each other, building on what they learned as they crisscrossed the country. These models came into even bolder relief when the researchers moved from the immediacy of the interviews to reviewing transcription texts and were fine-tuned prior to the multifaceted and systematic analysis of the major themes embedded in the interviews.

Themes

After they completed the first relatively small batch of interviews, researchers noticed that interviewees were striking a number of common themes in their conversations. They chatted about them with their site partners, carefully noted them as they moved from site to site, and recorded them when they wrote their analysis reports. Over the seven months of interviewing and report-writing, some themes that early on seemed prominent began to fade. Others originally of little note took on greater prominence, as more and more interviewees discussed them. A fair number of themes claimed attention consistently across institutions, no matter their size or geographic location. During this period, the research team did not have formal meetings together. Consequently, aside from ad hoc conversational sharing among researchers, the emergence of themes was tracked by researchers in their field notes and analysis reports.

Once the interview season was over, the four members of the team met for an extended three-day session. During this session, they spent time getting a general overview of the study, discussed each of the interviews in some detail, and began listing the themes that had surfaced during their site visits. One of the outcomes of these discussions was an "impressionistic list" of themes that served as the basis for a subsequent, more detailed thematic categorization.

The impressionistic theme list was derived from analysis reports, impressions recorded in field notes, and the most vivid recollections of the researchers themselves. The field notes represented the most immediate, raw, and uncluttered appraisal of the interviews. The analysis reports were more thoroughly percolated appraisals because they were written after a significant lapse of time and after the impact of subsequent interviews. The recollections and stories that came to the fore at the extended group session were the farthest removed from the actual interviews themselves, and represented only a fraction of what had transpired. Also, the reasons why stories and themes loomed larger for interviewers at that point was not always linked to their prominence in the original interviews. The passion of the respondent, the focus or interest of the interviewer, the elegance of the description all could have contributed to making these themes memorable to an interviewer. Because they knew the impressionistic list of themes could be somewhat soft, the researchers compensated by expanding its breadth and cataloguing an extensive list of themes. They then used the analysis reports and, when necessary, interview transcriptions as the basis for corroborating or disproving the impressionistic list and drilling down to the most essential themes in the study.

Another step was taken to get an overview of a large amount of data. As indicated earlier, two kinds of quotation were listed in analysis reports. The first group contained quotations that best typified the story each interviewee was telling in response to protocol questions. The second group contained quotations that were richly descriptive and significant in terms of context or the overall story the study was trying to tell, but were in some way not typical of the interview as a whole. All of these quotations were assembled and categorized by the team, using the theme categories surfaced in the earlier impressionistic discussion, with the addition of the category "other." The addition of the "other" category allowed for themes not anticipated by the researchers. Once the categorizing was completed, the researchers pulled out all quotations that had fallen under the category "other" and analyzed them for dominant themes. These new theme categories were then added to the original list. At that point, the researchers discarded theme categories they had anticipated would be significant factors but were not broadly represented in the quotations.

A number of themes emerged very strongly out of this process, but not all of them received attention in this study. The team judged that in terms of some themes, there was little variation in how they were understood by those interviewed. They also judged that in all likelihood these themes would have emerged just as strongly in interviews with senior administrators at secular institutions.

The preliminary list that resulted from this first weeding-out session included significant themes. These themes had a general point of view and were not merely "topics raised." The review of the quotations was an initial step but, of course, not an unbiased one. Some of the senior administrators interviewed were more facile with words than others, and they generated more quotations. Any attempt to simply count responses at this stage would have been misleading, confusing emphasis with frequency. As a result, another step was undertaken to provide a more reliable picture of what was actually emphasized across sites and interviews. The team undertook a second review focused on the interviews themselves and not just on the quotations. Two researchers reviewed the analysis reports of every interview, and when necessary for purposes of clarification, they went back to original transcripts. Each researcher made a decision about how important each particular theme was in the interview and ranked it. When disagreements occurred, team members had discussions after which, in cases of doubt, priority was given to the view of the person who actually conducted the original interview.

For each of the 124 interviews, a judgment was made by the group about the importance of each theme. For each of the twenty-six tentative themes, the researchers had to agree whether the theme was (1) heavily emphasized, (2) mentioned but not emphasized, or (3) hardly mentioned at all. (Depending on the specific theme, the wording of the three choices varied, but for each theme the researchers had to make a decision whether for the person being interviewed it was emphasized, addressed but not emphasized, or hardly mentioned.) On the basis of these group judgments, the mean response over the 124 interviews was calculated for each theme. For example, a mean of 1.25 indicates that the theme was heavily emphasized in many interviews, while a mean of 2.75 indicates that overall the topic played almost no role in the conversations. Basic statistics (means and standard deviations) were collected on these themes. The ten significant themes (their means are given in parentheses following the theme) can be grouped as follows.

GROUP I
Academic
1. Catholic intellectual tradition is key to Catholic character, identity, and mission. (1.19)
2. Faculty plays important role in maintaining Catholic character, identity, and mission. (1.89)

Student Culture
  3. The theme of values as a component of Catholic character, identity, and mission is emphasized. (1.56)
  4. Student transformation through Catholic culture is emphasized. (1.70)
Religious
  5. The sponsoring religious congregation continues to be vital. (1.51)
  6. Catholic commitment is important for senior administrators. (1.69)
  7. Social justice and service are important ways of living out Catholic character, identity, and mission. (1.70)
  8. Liturgy and other things as encouraged and managed by campus ministry are mentioned as ways to promote Catholic character, identity, and mission. (1.90)
Institutional
  9. The theme of "enveloping Catholic culture" is an important component of Catholic character, identity, and mission. (1.78)
  10. The theme of a caring community as a component of the Catholic character, identity, and mission is emphasized. (1.70)

An intermediate group of themes that received some or relatively little emphasis in interview conversations were noted.

GROUP 2
  11. The necessity of priests or religious on campus is mentioned. (2.05)
  12. Solutions offering particular ways to promote Catholic identity are presented. (2.07)
  13. In looking at the future of Catholic higher education, the responder is optimistic. (2.08)
  14. The responder is positive about Church and service to the Church. (2.11)
  15. The theme of being illiterate about the Catholic tradition is emphasized. (2.12)
  16. The theme of having faculty unconnected to the Catholic mission or Catholic intellectual heritage is emphasized. (2.27)
  17. Difficulties concerning moral issues among students, in general or specially in the residence halls are emphasized. (2.49)
  18. The interviewee uses religious language on a number of occasions. (2.60)
  19. Difficulties concerning types of student activities or outside speakers representing views counter to Catholic teaching are raised. (2.82)
  20. Lack of assessment tools is emphasized. (2.84)

Because these themes were not mentioned frequently or with emphasis by most senior administrators, they have an in-between status.

Some themes were mentioned by only a few of the participants, and they did not directly relate to the models that were developed. One might designate these themes as hypothesized but not validated by the data, and they are not treated specifically in the text. They include the following.

GROUP 3
21. The special situation of women or institutions originally founded by women is emphasized. (2.25)
22. The view is expressed that a number of Catholic colleges will face severe financial challenges in the coming years. (2.31)
23. The theme of the sponsoring religious congregation as a problem or obstacle in maintaining Catholic character, identity, and mission is emphasized. (2.59)
24. Complaints that conservatives are making things difficult for administrators are raised. (2.65)
25. Difficulties with bishops and *Ex Corde* or other difficulties with the Church are emphasized. (2.67)
26. Complaints that liberals are making things difficult for administrators are emphasized. (2.75)

Of the themes in group 2 that have an in-between status, some we do treat, and some we do not. A methodological analysis provides justification for our selection among them. We used three general justifications for including one or more of these themes. First, if only a small percentage of administrators focused on one of these themes but did so with great intensity, we included the theme for treatment. Second, if the themes were implicated in the cultural framework and/or the four Catholic university models used in our analysis, they were also included. Finally, for the most part, we included themes whose treatment by administrators stood in stark contrast to the expectations that the research team had going into the field or after our initial rather cursory review of the data. In one sense, each of the twenty-six proposed themes represented an impression we had. They were, however, of a general nature, and many were not strongly held. The reason for including them in the overarching list of themes was to avoid neglecting any topics that various administrators addressed a number of times. In terms of our "surprise" category, we felt justified in including those themes that were in marked contrast to either the confident expectations or vivid impressions of our research team.

In our judgment, only some administrators spoke with a degree of intensity about themes 14 (optimistic about future of Catholic higher education), 15 (illiteracy about the Catholic tradition), and 17 (moral issues among students). With respect to theme 14, the future of higher education, most administrators expressed optimism, though a number did so with one large proviso. Their optimism was contingent on colleges and universities in the coming years making the hard decisions necessary to emphasize their Catholic character and doing so in ways the administrators themselves considered to be correct. Since this is the central dilemma of the book, it receives ample treatment. Themes about Catholic illiteracy and moral issues among students are included in our analysis, both because some administrators insisted they were important issues and, as we see hereafter, they also are implicated in the cultural framework and the four models of Catholic universities.

The second criterion that justifies addressing a secondary theme entails a process of fitting themes into our analytical framework of culture and the four Catholic models. Many administrators mentioned the central role the Catholic intellectual tradition should play in a Catholic college or university. As a result of using the framework, it became important to explore the role of the faculty (theme 16) in sharing that tradition. Similarly, because each model assumes a commitment to the Church and, in particular, a commitment to avoiding activities incompatible with Catholic teaching, we needed to explore issues related to speakers and activities at variance with Catholic teaching (theme 19). Using a cultural framework and set of models we devised could suggest to some that we biased the data. On the contrary, because the framework emerged directly out of what senior administrators reported, it reflects, rather than skews, the data.

The third justification we use is the surprise factor. Considering we were conducting hour-long interviews on the subject of Catholic identity, we expected senior administrators' conversations to be peppered with religious language. We also expected that there would be considerable variation in how administrators used the language that depended on which of the four different models of Catholic universities their institution represented (theme 18). From the outset, we were not looking for certain words or phrases. However, we did think we would find greater frequency of use and more variety. Because this initial expectation (an informal null hypothesis) was not fulfilled, we thought the actual situation should be described and reasons for it explored.

We were also surprised by the lack of data relevant to Catholic outcomes (theme 20). Determining whether Catholic universities are achieving their goals or whether one model is generally better than the others in that regard requires data. Senior administrators made claims about the effectiveness of Catholic education in general and their institution's approach in particular, but they pointed to no data that demonstrated those claims. The research team was also surprised by how little interest administrators focused on the mandatum theme (theme 25) in group 3, but we did not include it for treatment. Senior administrators spent very little time even discussing, let alone emphasizing, the mandatum. Much has been written about the mandatum in the last ten years, and the topic will certainly receive some prominence again during the five-year review of the *Ex Corde* implementation taking place in 2006. For now, however, administrators seem to have moved on and are addressing other issues. We decided to follow their lead.

Although only a few offered new, practical, and effective ways to emphasize the Catholic tradition (theme 12), we thought it would be helpful to offer our own, and we present potential initiatives in chapter 12.

Using the three justifications results in five themes being added to the list we have labeled group 1. For ease of reference, we provide the following expanded list, in which each additional theme from group 2 is noted with an asterisk.

EXPANDED GROUP I

Academic

1. Catholic intellectual tradition is key to Catholic character, identity, and mission. (1.19)
2. Faculty plays an important role in maintaining Catholic character, identity, and mission. (1.89)

*15. The theme of being illiterate about the Catholic tradition is emphasized. (2.12)
*16. The theme of having faculty unconnected to the Catholic mission or Catholic intellectual heritage is emphasized. (2.27)

Student Culture

3. The theme of values as a component of Catholic character, identity, and mission is emphasized. (1.56)
4. Student transformation through Catholic culture is emphasized. (1.70)

*17. Difficulties concerning moral issues among students, in general or specially in the residence halls, are emphasized. (2.49)

Religious

5. It is emphasized that the sponsoring religious congregation continues to be vital. (1.51)
6. Catholic commitment is important for senior administrators. (1.69)
7. It is emphasized that social justice and service are important ways of living out Catholic character, identity, and mission. (1.70)
8. Liturgy and other things as encouraged and managed by campus ministry are mentioned as ways to promote Catholic character, identity, and mission. (1.90)

Institutional

9. The theme of "enveloping Catholic culture" as an important component of Catholic character, identity, and mission is emphasized. (1.78)
10. The theme of a caring community as a component of the Catholic character, identity, and mission is emphasized. (1.70)

*18. The interviewee uses religious language on a number of occasions. (2.60)
*20. Lack of assessment tools is emphasized. (2.84)

The penultimate step of the process laid out a detailed map of what senior administrators said in their interviews. Under the four general categories, one author (Morey) provided a written analysis of each theme and noted ways administrators emphasized different aspects of the theme. These were then passed on to the second author (Piderit), who in extended essays critically evaluated the comments within the framework of culture and the four Catholic models. These essays were then reviewed jointly by the authors, modified, and rewritten. By this time, however, quotations from senior administrators exceeded any reasonable limit, and some step had to be taken to reduce the volume to a manageable size. The final adjustment reduced senior administrator comments both in number and length to those that most aptly and effectively reflected the primary interview data. These modified quotations were incorporated into the analytical discussion in each of the theme chapters.

Ethical Issues

Confidentiality

For much of this project, creating the boundaries of confidentiality was a work-in-progress. In the end, those boundaries were largely determined by the way the research team chose to illuminate how various administrators understood their own circumstances in the final report. In thematic and design discussions, the research team explored the various threats the research posed for individuals and institutions and how best to minimize them. After many go-rounds, the initial determination was to make public all of the institutions that participated in the study, to blind all critical and contentious or controversial comments, and to cite all other quotations, particularly those that offered useful insights that other institutions might find helpful.[3] Each interview participant was informed of the guidelines and also assured that he or she would have the opportunity to review any quotation attributed to him or her and intended for use in the final report. In each instance, interviewees understood that the researchers would honor any request to delete quotations or remove citations.

As the analysis of data unfolded, the research team became less certain that citing particular individuals would be useful. Without a clear conviction that this practice would add value and not create problems for individuals or institutions, the team decided not to attribute quotations. Instead, the quotations were identified by the model each respondent's university most closely resembled. This approach protects individuals and institutions, while still providing readers with some useful guideposts about the kind of institutional experience that might have prompted the response.

Transcription

The standards regarding transcription of interviews do not exist in terms of a specific form or code. Rather, they revolve around choices that researchers make in order to ensure that the text does justice to what was said in an interview conversation. Three different professionals were involved in transforming the interviews into text documents for this project, and they all worked with tapes of varying quality. Each followed a simple set of common instructions in their work that were dictated by the fact that these transcriptions were only intended to assist the interviewers in remembering what had gone on. Because they were not intended for a larger audience of general readers, the transcription texts included everything that was said by both the interviewer and interviewee in the text—including short notations about pauses or other distractions. Sidebar comments about emotive expression such as laughter were also included, to be helpful to other researchers who had not experienced the interview firsthand. Tapes were available for use by the whole research team if any questions emerged about the exact content or tone of responses.

A different set of choices came into play when researchers transferred quotations from the text of the interview to the analysis reports. It was clear as early as the design phase of the project that the quotations in the analysis reports would be the pool the research team would draw from when writing the final report of the study. Doing justice to the intent of an interviewee in a report written for general readership is a different enterprise from recording all that was actually said in the interview and requires a shift in focus from linguistic accuracy to intentional accuracy. Verbal exchanges are far less carefully constructed and graceful than written exchanges and are often filled with pauses, run-on sentences, and redundancies that writers have the luxury of editing out. By taking into consideration how a person might write a response, rather than how they would share it verbally, researchers are better able to present quotations in a manner that highlights meaning rather than detracting from it. This often necessitates some condensing, rephrasing, and editing of text. The researchers in this study employed these techniques in this report in order to render text that accurately conveyed the speakers' meanings in a way that would prove neither embarrassing to interviewees nor distracting to readers of the final report.

Responding to Subjects

Interview research is based on a human interaction that at its best not only expands the knowledge and understanding of the researchers but also impacts those interviewed. As part of the give-and-take of this research experience, senior administrators openly shared how they understood what Catholicity means at their institutions and for their own leadership—the giving part of the interaction. They also were clear that they wanted to take something away as a result of their participation. First, many expressed an interest in what other people who were interviewed had said. They also wanted to know if their own comments were "good" or "appropriate." Such comments indicated that the administrators, particularly lay administrators, often do not know where they or their institutions; fall within the spectrum of Catholic universities and collegiate leaders in terms of Catholic culture and identity.[4] Second, many administrators were very eager to find out about best practices, or at the very least, common practices that could help them be more knowledgeable and better practitioners in their own settings. Although there certainly is contact between and among administrators across Catholic institutions, those interactions have not translated into a solid sense among this group of interviewees of what works best in terms of supporting, enhancing, or enriching institutional Catholic identity, character, and culture.

Notes

1. The Americanist controversy was a movement associated with efforts to adapt Catholicism to American culture. It was condemned by Pope Leo XIII in the apostolic letter *Testem Benevolentiae*, issued on January 22, 1899. In the last decade of the nineteenth century a series of issues divided the American Catholic Church. One side of the divide sought to accommodate Catholicism to American culture and to "Americanize" Catholic immigrants, believing that American principles were not only compatible with the truth of the Church but pointed to a more authentic way of living out that truth. The other side saw these efforts as a dangerous abandonment of Catholic principles that ultimately elevated American cultural truth over divinely revealed religious truth. As a result of this controversy and the condemnation of Americanism, American Catholics were broadly suspected of being less than enthusiastic supporters of the First Amendment—a view that held considerable sway until the Second Vatican Council. American Catholic intellectual life was also stifled in this atmosphere—a result that was intensified by the condemnation by Pope Pius X of modernism in 1907 in his encyclical *Pascendi Dominici Gregis*. See Gerald P. Fogarty, *The Vatican and the American Hierarchy from 1870 to 1965* (Collegeville, Minn.: Liturgical Press, 1985), and Thomas T. McAvoy, *Great Crisis in American Catholic History, 1895–1900* (Chicago: Henry Regnery, 1957).

2. Peter Steinfels provides a more complex and richly nuanced discussion of the divide in terms of reactions to the Second Vatican Council and the implementation of its reforms. See Peter Steinfels, *A People Adrift: The Crisis of the Roman Catholic Church in America* (New York: Simon and Schuster, 2003), 32–39.

3. The conservatives find faithfulness and orthodoxy in Hans Urs von Balthasar, formerly Cardinal Joseph Ratzinger and now Pope Benedict XVI, Cardinal Avery Dulles, Germain Grisez, and George Weigel, while the liber-

als find encouragement in Karl Rahner, Cardinal Walter Kasper, Richard McBrien, Charles Curran, and Lisa Sowle Cahill.

4. The Voice of the Faithful and the Knights of Columbus are two such organizations. Members of the former tend to be liberal in their outlook, just as members of the latter tend to be more conservative. The speakers both groups invite to address them provide an indication of the level of this polarization. The Voice of the Faithful frequently invites more liberal speakers with a reformist agenda. The Knights of Columbus, a self-professed nonpolitical service group within the Church, invited George Bush to be a speaker at their 2004 annual convention. The din created by delegates chanting "Four More Years!" left little doubt of the ideological preferences of the group. Conservatives find hope in newer groups such as the Legionaries of Christ and its lay arm, Regnum Christi, Opus Dei, and other congregations that promote the Tridentine Mass and traditional Catholic devotions. Liberals take consolation in groups known for their critical thinking and stances, such as the Jesuits, the Mercy Sisters, the Women's Ordination Conference, Call to Action, and Catholic politicians who oppose the death penalty and are committed to U.S. and global justice.

5. If conventional wisdom and media reports are to be believed, Catholics disenchanted with the implementation of Vatican II reforms are more likely to support Republican candidates, particularly in presidential elections, and those frustrated by what they see as the reforms not fully realized are far more likely to support Democrats in presidential elections.

6. The more right-leaning periodicals include *First Things* and *Crisis*. The more left-leaning include *Commonweal* and *America*.

7. This idea of Catholic common ground is strongly identified with the late Joseph Cardinal Bernardin. He believed that a statement entitled "Called to be Catholic: Church in a Time of Peril" that was the product of three years of discussion among laypersons and clergy accurately described the polarized state of the Church. The Common Ground Initiative was brought to life to address this polarization.

8. "Mandatum" is a Latin word signifying a charge or mandate given to someone. In this instance, it refers to a mandate given by the local bishop to Catholic theologians who are involved in Catholic activities in three ways: they are themselves Catholic, they are teaching courses in Catholic theology, and they are doing so at a Catholic college or university. A theologian fulfilling the three conditions is expected to request the mandatum from the bishop (the primary bishop or archbishop of a diocese or archdiocese is more technically referred to as the ordinary) of the diocese or archdiocese in which the Catholic university operates. The mandatum signifies that the Catholic theologian is committed to presenting the official teaching of the Catholic Church in his or her teaching.

9. While colleges and universities were certainly not evenly divided in terms of allegiance to these visions, both received equal attention in the media that played a big role in defining the poles. It often did so in terms of two associations deeply concerned with Catholic higher education—the Association of Catholic College and Universities (ACCU) and the Cardinal Newman Society. By far the largest number of Catholic colleges and universities are either members of the ACCU or sympathetic to the organization's point of view. The Cardinal Newman Society, on the other hand, operates rather like a political action committee and does not formally represent Catholic collegiate institutions. It does have a relatively high profile, and its perspectives are often juxtaposed to those of the ACCU by the press.

10. A survey instrument was the logical choice for this phase of the project because the basic purpose of survey research is to describe a population and explain the

variability of certain of its features. See Catherine Marshall and Gretchen B. Rossman, *Designing Qualitative Research* (Newbury Park, Calif.: Sage, 1989), 84.

11. For a complete discussion of the methodology and findings of the phase 1 study, see Melanie M. Morey and Dennis H. Holtschneider, "Leadership and the Age of the Laity: Emerging Patterns in Catholic Higher Education," in *Lay Leaders in Catholic Higher Education*, ed. Anthony J. Cernera (Fairfield, Conn.: Sacred Heart University Press, 2005), 3–27.

12. Carnegie Classifications originated with the Carnegie Foundation for the Advancement of Teaching whose website describes them as, "the leading typology of American colleges and universities. It is the framework in which institutional diversity in U.S. higher education is commonly described."

13. The sample was designed to be broadly representative with one notable exception. A number of religious congregations sponsor more than one institution. The colleges and congregations often claim there is something distinctive about this congregational identity that shapes Catholic culture in all the sponsored institutions. The Jesuits have twenty-eight institutions and the Mercy Sisters sponsor twelve. The size of these large congregationally sponsored pools made it impossible to interview at a majority of them while still broadly sampling all of Catholic higher education. Holy Cross priests and brothers, on the other hand, sponsor only five institutions in the United States. Including 80 percent of these institutions in the sample allowed an opportunity at some future point to explore this claim of congregational imprint on Catholic identity with a manageable number of institutions that did not limit the breadth of the sample.

14. There were some exceptions to this general rule. At one institution, only two people were interviewed. At seven institutions, three people were interviewed, and at two institutions, the president requested that five people participate in the study.

15. At two of the sites, presidents requested that five administrators be interviewed, and their wishes were respected. At one institution, four administrators were selected for interviews but on the day scheduled, one was seriously ill and another was unable to keep the appointment due to a campus-related crisis. It was not possible to schedule phone interviews with either of these administrators. A number of presidents provided rosters of only three administrators, and at one institution the president ended up choosing not to be interviewed.

16. Due to unforeseen circumstances, it was impossible for a two-member research team to visit three of the thirty-three sites. At those particular institutions, all the interviews were conducted by a single researcher.

17. Practically all senior administrators said this is very important and they are looking for ways to be Catholic that fit their student population and the faculty resources they are likely to have available to them.

18. In the rare cases where individual administrators contradicted one another on a significant issue, researchers were forced to choose the more objective view. Once all the interviews were conducted and the views of the administrators across many institutions were known, occasional inconsistencies in expectations and policies were noted.

19. Almost all senior administrators—presidents as well as vice-presidents—made one particular distinction that placed them within the broader context of other Catholic institutions. Administrators at some of the smaller and more traditional colleges and universities made it quite clear their "brand" of Catholic education was significantly different from that offered at the majority of other Catholic institutions. Administrators at the very institutions the more traditional colleges placed at arm's

length were equally eager to make a similar distinction in reverse. Little appreciation for this apparent diversity of religious approaches was in evidence on either side.

CHAPTER 2

1. *Ex Corde Ecclesiae*, pt. 1, sec. A, para. 14, in *Catholic Universities in Church and Society: A Dialogue on Ex Corde Ecclesiae*, ed. John P. Langan, S.J. (Washington, D.C.: Georgetown University Press, 1993), 235.

2. John R. Wilcox, "Preface to Religious Identity: A Critical Issue in Catholic Higher Education," in *Enhancing Religious Identity: Best Practices from Catholic Campuses*, ed. John Wilcox and Irene King (Washington, D.C.: Georgetown University Press, 2000), xvi.

3. Robert Wuthnow, *Meaning and Moral Order: Explorations in Cultural Analysis* (Berkeley: University of California Press, 1987), 15.

4. Edgar H. Schein, *Organizational Culture and Leadership* (San Francisco: Jossey-Bass, 1992), 12.

5. Gerard Egan, *Working the Shadow Side: A Guide to Positive behind-the-Scenes Management* (San Francisco: Jossey-Bass, 1994), 77.

6. Egan, *Working the Shadow Side*, 77.

7. Egan, *Working the Shadow Side*, 82.

8. Egan, *Working the Shadow Side*, 83.

9. Egan, *Working the Shadow Side*, 84.

10. Egan, *Working the Shadow Side*, 77.

11. Egan, *Working the Shadow Side*, 85–88. Egan points out that the conceptual components that create the covert or shadow culture are not discussed, and therefore "they lie outside ordinary managerial processes and often have a negative impact" (88). Assessing, analyzing, and addressing the unstated assumptions, beliefs, values, and norms in any organization is a difficult process. If managers don't rise to the occasion and engage the problem, however, their efforts at managing culture will be a waste of their time and energy.

12. Alfred North Whitehead, *Symbolism: Its Meaning and Effect*. New York: Macmillan, 1927).

13. Wuthnow, *Meaning and Moral Order*, 109.

14. Terrence E. Deal and Allan A. Kennedy, *Corporate Cultures: The Rites and Rituals of Corporate Life* (Reading, Mass.: Addison-Wesley, 1982), 63.

15. Melanie M. Morey, "Leadership and Legacy: Is There a Future for the Past?" (Ed.D. diss., Harvard Graduate School of Education, 1995), 39–40.

16. Rodney Stark and Roger Finke, *Acts of Faith: Explaining the Human Side of Religion* (Berkeley: University of California Press, 2000), 120.

17. Schein, *Organizational Culture and Leadership*, 386.

18. Schein, *Organizational Culture and Leadership*, 5.

19. Clifford Geertz defines this cultural concept in his chapter on religion as a cultural system. He does so as part of a process of widening, broadening, and expanding the narrow traditions of social anthropology. See *Interpretation of Culture* (New York: Perseus Books, 1973), 89.

20. Deal and Kennedy, *Corporate Cultures*, 195–196.

21. Because strong cultures stabilize organizations, however, some theorists question whether that very quality can become a barrier to the kind of organizational flexibility and agility necessary for market success. Edgar Schein maintains that strong cultures are an organizational asset as long as the cultures are "learning cul-

tures" and "contain a core shared assumption that the environmental context in which the organization exists is to some degree manageable." See Schein, *Organizational Culture and Leadership*, 364.

22. Notable contributions to the body of literature in this area include: James T. Burtchaell, *The Dying of the Light* (Grand Rapids, Mich.: Eerdman, 1998); Alice Gallin, O.S.U., *Negotiating Identity: Catholic Higher Education since 1960* (Notre Dame, Ind.: University of Notre Dame Press, 2000); Philip Gleason, *Contending with Modernity: Catholic Higher Education in the Twentieth Century* (New York: Oxford University Press, 1995); Theodore M. Hesburgh, C.S.C., ed., *The Challenge and Promise of a Catholic University* (Notre Dame, Ind.: University of Notre Dame Press, 1994); John P. Langan, S.J., ed., *Catholic Universities in Church and Society: A Dialogue on Ex Corde Ecclesiae* (Washington, D.C.: Georgetown University Press, 1993); Terrence J. Murphy, *A Catholic University: Vision and Opportunities* (Collegeville, Minn.: Liturgical Press, 2001); George Dennis O'Brien, *The Idea of a Catholic University* (Chicago: University of Chicago Press, 2002); John Wilcox and Irene King, eds., *Enhancing Religious Identity: Best Practices from Catholic Campuses* (Washington, D.C.: Georgetown University Press, 2000). In a recent book, Mark Massa, S.J., carefully analyzes why it is appropriate for Catholics in the United States to be, in a very real and reasonable sense, opposed to the prevailing American culture. His analysis is theological and goes far beyond questions of consumerism. See *Anti-Catholicism in America: The Last Acceptable Prejudice* (New York: Crossroad, 2003).

23. "Vibrant" culture here appears to refer primarily to accepted patterns of behavior and ways of action, and less to flexibility in adjusting to changes. There is, of course, a trade-off: the stronger the accepted ways of doing things, the more difficult it is to effect change.

24. In *The Idea of a University*, John Henry Cardinal Newman notes the ambiguity of what we call culture or what he calls "the religion of philosophy," where philosophy is understood as the prevailing sophisticated mores of the time. In his day, the religion of philosophy included Christian aspects, but they pertained to style rather than substance. Although such philosophy may produce very cultured and revered gentlemen, it may miss Christian belief entirely. As he noted, gentlemen formed in a Christian society may not hold any significant Christian beliefs. For this reason, Catholic universities should strive for knowledge and learning beyond the veneer of the prevailing culture, learning that is connected to Catholic teaching and theology. See John Henry Cardinal Newman, *The Idea of a University* (New Haven: Yale University Press, 1996 [originally published 1852, 1889]), especially 140–147.

25. Further distinctions that include theology and doctrine are also important to understand, particularly as they relate to the conceptual components of religious culture. Richard P. McBrien provides a helpful treatment of these different distinctions and their importance in understanding Christian faith. See *Catholicism* (San Francisco: HarperCollins, 1994), 19–21.

26. This "decision" is really a series of smaller decisions made over a number of years.

27. The latter comment, formed as a question, appears in the text of Stephen J. Heaney's chapter "The Catholic University Project: What Kind of Curriculum Does It Require?" in Wilcox and King, *Enhancing Religious Identity*, 169. His response to the question highlights the real-world, rather than mysterious, components of culture: "If a Catholic university has a 'Catholic atmosphere,' it is not the 'atmosphere' that makes the place Catholic. The atmosphere of any university is an outgrowth of the particular project of that university. If the Catholic university has a Catholic atmo-

sphere it is due only to the fact that people involved in the project take that project, and the central truth involved, very seriously. Nor can any amount of atmosphere give students a clue as to its applicability in their particular disciplines or stations in life."

28. One Jesuit at a Jesuit university facetiously suggested that, as far as the students are concerned, the often repeated phrase "Jesuit presence" might be experienced much as a cheap cologne. It is there at the university before the students arrive and remains after they leave. How much it changes the students is unknown.

29. Debra E. Meyerson, "Radical Change, The Quiet Way," in *Harvard Business Review on Culture and Change* (Cambridge, Mass.: Harvard Business School, 1999), 64.

30. Kim S. Cameron and Robert E. Quinn, *Diagnosing and Changing Organizational Culture: Based on the Competing Values Framework* (Reading, Mass.: Addison-Wesley, 1999), 51.

31. The deposit of faith is the teaching of Jesus Christ in Scripture and the apostolic tradition that has been entrusted to the Church. According to Nancy Dallavalle, "Vatican II views the Church as the trustee of an inexhaustible treasure, and its authentic expositor. This exposition takes many forms, from study of the Scriptures, to the rearticulation of doctrine, to the faithful celebration of the Eucharist . . . [and it is] preserved by the Church only by its continuous witness to the life, death, and Resurrection of Jesus Christ." See Richard P. McBrien, ed., *The HarperCollins Encyclopedia of Catholicism* (New York: HarperCollins, 1995), 410.

32. Wuthnow, *Meaning and Moral Order*, 215.

33. Geertz, *Interpretation of Cultures*, 408.

CHAPTER 3

1. From an economic perspective, it is significant that leaders of these institutions lack comparative data. The lack of available data either suggests a market structure that is less than perfectly competitive in the economic sense, or it reveals that imperfections exist in the transmission of information that is not, strictly speaking, proprietary information.

2. Toward the conclusion of this chapter, we note some ways Catholic institutions include aspects of the Catholic intellectual tradition in their graduate and professional programs.

3. Along with these other activities, it is, of course, appropriate that Catholic institutions also have a plan to share the Catholic heritage in a fitting way with parents. For the most part, however, we avoid this factor in our treatment and focus instead on students as those who engage in a process of education and formation, a process that is designed for them by faculty and administration and that, at least in its general outlines, is known to students and parents before enrollment in the institution.

4. The prestige of an institution is determined to a great extent by the research productivity and publications of the faculty. Some of this has a direct impact on undergraduate students, but much of it an indirect impact, through the reputation that the institution enjoys among peer institutions and society in general.

5. The most important (and expensive, except for athletic coaches of high profile teams) service comes from faculty holding teaching and research positions. Among institutions of higher education, prestige is determined in large part by faculty profile, which includes the teaching, research, and public sector activities of the faculty. The more prestigious universities hire the more prestigious faculty and grant undergradu-

ate students access to them. More prestigious places may also include a wider array of student services, especially in the context of residential living.

6. Many studies show that, even after accounting for the opportunity cost of college tuition, students with college degrees have a higher present value of future discounted income streams than that expected by young people who do not acquire a college degree. See Daron Acemoglu, "Technical Change, Inequality, and the Labor Market," *Journal of Economic Literature* 50, 1 (2002), and Diane J. Macunovich, *Birth Quake: The Baby Boom and Its Aftershocks* (Chicago: University of Chicago, 2002).

7. Although much data on tuition and fees are available on individual colleges, comparatively little data are published that allow parents and students to examine the actual cost for the typical student (sticker price for tuition and fees less financial aid) attending various types of colleges. For a discussion of some of the economics of college education see Gordon C. Winston, "Subsidies, Hierarchy and Peers: The Awkward Economics of Higher Education," *Economic Perspectives* 13, 1 (1999), and, for a discussion of returns to education see Patrick L. Mason, "Persistent Discrimination: Racial Disparity in the United States, 1967–1988," *American Economic Review* 90, 2 (2002).

8. In an analysis of twelve liberal arts institutions, David Breneman offers a good analysis of the interaction between tuition level and the number of students attending an institution. See David W. Breneman, *Liberal Arts Colleges: Thriving, Surviving, or Endangered?* (Washington, D.C.: Brookings Institution, 1994).

9. This formulation, used widely in circles of Catholic health care, received prominence when Sister Irene Kraus, D.C., former president of Daughters of Charity National Health System, was quoted on the front page of the *Wall Street Journal* using and justifying this phrase. See Monica Langley, "Money Order: Nuns' Zeal for Profits Shapes Hospital Chain, Wins Fans," *Wall Street Journal*, January 7, 1998.

10. Strictly speaking, the institution does not have to generate a margin every year. However, over an interval of three to five years it should generate an average annual surplus (or margin) that enables the introduction of new programs and facilities. How large the margin should be depends on what the institution's group of competing institutions generates as a margin and the institution's own aspirations.

11. Not all Catholic colleges and universities were founded by religious congregations. Some were founded by bishops or local dioceses. However, the overwhelming majority of institutions were founded under the auspices of religious congregations. Included within that larger reality are a few diocesan institutions.

12. Most religious congregations adhered to the same educational paradigm at each location, but there were adjustments. Thus, all Jesuit colleges and universities adhered to the *ratio studiorum (plan of studies or pedagogical approach)*, that contained guidelines for pedagogy, but some Jesuit institutions developed their own emphases.

13. The relative permanence of these decisions is seen by some as a source of strength and stability. Others, however, see this long-term consistency as a sign of institutional inflexibility and brittleness.

14. In a later section we call the model following this goal the Catholic immersion model. The goal remains the same, but the name of the model is taken from the strategy pursued by this type of institution.

15. Even "strong" institutions are constrained in their choices. In the real world, each institution has a faculty and alumni/ae base that would resist a dramatic change in the Catholic mission of the institution. Modifications of the current mission are possible. Dramatic changes, however, are unlikely to be inheritable by the current faculty and will be resisted by alumni.

16. One usually looks for positive attributes of the subculture as distinguishing characteristics. Negative characteristics might exist, but they might be signs of a barely inheritable culture, rather than one that attracts a large number of students. For example, if, contrary to fact, Catholic institutions were distinguished *only* by being much smaller than other private or state institutions and having fewer financial resources, this would be a sign of weakness rather than a strength of the subculture.

17. In the course of their interview conversations, administrators consistently claimed there was something distinctive about Catholic higher education that justified the survival of this sector of higher education and made a significant contribution to the "diversity" of higher educational opportunities in the country. They firmly believed that if these institutions disappeared they would immediately be missed.

18. Published comparative data are not available. Informal comparisons of websites at Catholic universities and nonsectarian institutions indicate that the nonsectarian institutions promote justice and service opportunities as extensively as Catholic institutions. The long lists of potential sites where students can volunteer suggest also that students at nonsectarian institutions enthusiastically embrace service opportunities as part of their university experience.

19. The religious programs are also likely to be more successful. Martin E. Marty in *Education, Religion and the Common Good* (San Francisco: Jossey-Bass, 2000) argues that at the grade school and secondary level, "values programs" emphasizing the common good lack the impact that religious programs have. Similarly, Bryk argues that it is the Catholic culture in Catholic high schools that accounts for their large positive impact. See Anthony S. Bryk, Valerie E. Lee, and Peter B. Holland, *Catholic Schools and the Common Good* (Cambridge, Mass.: Harvard University Press, 1993).

20. "It is not the case anymore that public institutions have a special mission to serve lower-income and minority students, or that private institutions have a special mission to serve the rich or would-be ministers. Across the country, both public and private institutions have ethnically and economically diverse student bodies and compete for the same people as students." See Dorothy Blaney, "Who Should Pay the Bill for a Private Education?" *Chronicle of Higher Education*, April 2, 2004.

21. Linking social justice to the gospel and Catholic teaching in some instances requires a strong stance against prevailing currents in social justice. Tripole argues that promoting social justice without embedding it in the framework of the Catholic (or more broadly Christian) community belief in Christ and his saving mission may promote secularism. See Martin R. Tripole, "Secularism, Justice, and Jesuit Higher Education—Are They the Same?" *Review for Religious* 63, 1 (2004).

22. Alan Wolfe argues that religious cultures are eventually swallowed by the larger, encompassing American culture. If his analysis is entirely correct, his result implies that Catholic colleges and universities—as well as other sectarian institutions—are trying something impossible. If he is only partially correct, the Catholic way of doing social justice must be distinct and have an impact on students that is either qualitatively or quantitatively different from the impact social justice programs have at nonsectarian institutions. See Alan Wolfe, *The Transformation of American Religion: How We Actually Live Our Faith* (New York: Free Press, 2003).

23. Acceptance of cultural change is not always enthusiastic. In fact, it can often be reluctant. Insisting on the first year of calculus as a requirement for all undergraduates would surely be reluctantly accepted, at best.

24. Not everything in a university undergraduate program has to be appealing to students, in part because students are imperfectly aware of the product they are

choosing. For a good number of students core courses are unattractive, yet they choose the total package. Similarly, it may be that the Catholic component of education at a particular Catholic institution is not appealing. The important requirement is that the package be attractive to students and parents.

25. Since each of the models contains the bare minimum with respect to activities that both transmit the Catholic heritage to students and achieve the stated goal for each model, actual Catholic colleges or universities are likely to be much fuller than the spare characteristics of models presented in this section.

26. In order for a Catholic college or university to be culturally coherent, we assume conformity to Church teaching by the institution. Should individuals who are teaching or representing the institution put forward positions that are contrary to Church teaching, we assume their perspectives will be labeled as personal views not in conformity with Church teaching.

27. See "*Ex Corde Ecclesiae*," in Michael J. Buckley, *The Catholic University as Promise and Project* (Washington, D.C.: Georgetown University Press, 1998). Buckley emphasizes the key role that theology ought to play in any Catholic university. Theology is the central discipline, in that it should relate to all other academic disciplines and other academic disciplines should seek helpful assistance from theology. In Buckley's view, theology is the primary and focal discipline at a Catholic university.

28. To avoid cumbersome phraseology, we drop the couplet of "colleges and universities" and simply use "universities" when we want to refer to one of the models, e.g., *Catholic immersion universities* rather than *Catholic immersion colleges and universities*. Ease of reference, not slight of colleges, is intended when using this modestly abbreviated phrase.

29. A few institutions require all students to take a course in Catholic teachings. Many more institutions that adhere to this model require a course that includes some discussion of Catholic teachings, but leaves the decision of "how much" to the individual instructor. As we will discuss in the next section, if the Catholic content is modest, other sectors of this model will have to be sufficiently strong to ensure that the distinguishability criterion is satisfied.

30. Edward Hall speaks eloquently about the importance of what he terms "technical props" as essential supports for maintaining cultural values. In our terminology, technical props are symbolic rituals that reinforce the basic value system. He uses as an example a discussion he had in class with a group of young college women, one of whom addressed her cultural predicament in trying to maintain her sexual virtue at college. She wondered: "How could she preserve the core of a formal system (of belief) when all the important technical props had been removed?" Interestingly, most Catholic colleges supply extensive technical props for students to avoid drugs and alcohol, even if the props for avoiding excessive consumption of alcohol are less successful. When a Catholic college institutes coeducational living arrangements and turns a blind eye to violations of ethical standards, it is dismantling the technical props that can support the very kind of virtuous life it claims to prefer and abandoning young people to go it alone amid tremendous social pressure. See Edward Hall, *The Silent Language* (New York: Anchor Books, 1991), 89.

31. The purpose of this restriction is not to prevent students from hearing views contrary to Catholic teaching. In fact, in a society with readily accessible media, one cannot prevent students from accessing information, via the internet and other media, conflicting with or contradicting Catholic teaching. Rather, the purpose of preventing outside speakers or other groups from presenting views that are contrary to Catholic teaching is to signal that the particular college or university as an institution

supports the Catholic viewpoint. That this signal is important both to members of the university community as well as to those outside the university is apparent by the amount of controversy such policies generate both on and off campus. Our claim is that, despite the controversy, these prohibitions are part of a consistent policy in light of the Catholic goals the institution is striving to achieve.

32. "Diaspora" stems from the Greek and means a scattering. Originally it refers to the scattering of the Jews throughout the Middle East following the Babylonian Exile in the sixth century B.C., as many of the Jews did not return to Israel even after they were permitted to. In this context, it suggests merely that a scattering of Catholics exists in a certain region or that relatively few Catholics are attracted to this type of college or university.

33. Graduates, for example, might typically be eager to promote the abolition of the death penalty but resist discouraging the use of contraceptives.

34. A drawback to each of the models is that in student matters the Catholic heritage appears to be characterized solely by negative prescriptions. That is, sexual intimacy is not permitted in the residence halls, the university cannot make contraceptives available, and gay and lesbian groups cannot be permitted to promote positions opposed to the Catholic Church. A weak justification for this negative approach is that, in the absence of objective data provided by people outside the university, it is easier to evaluate the effect of prohibitions than of positive programs that promote a proper Catholic understanding of important issues such as intimacy.

35. In unusual circumstances, a board of trustees at a Catholic institution may choose a non-Catholic president. The circumstances might demand someone who, though non-Catholic, strongly supports and is equipped to advance the Catholic mission, and has other strong leadership qualities not available in the other candidates under consideration. However, this should be an exception to the general rule. A Catholic institution that over a number of cycles failed to attract qualified Catholic presidential candidates appears to have a model that does not pass the inheritability criterion, at least with respect to presidential leadership.

36. For purposes of comparison, the nonsectarian culture is assumed to consist of the same five significant sectors that have been singled out as the loci of Catholic content and practice. In the nonsectarian sector, one assumes that any religious activities or programming are offered on a purely voluntary basis. At nonsectarian institutions, there is no institutional promotion of a religious viewpoint or encouragement to participate in religious activities. In particular, in the academic sector, no regard is given to the religious knowledge or practice of faculty, unless they are being hired to teach a religious subject. Even in this case, the issue of whether the person practices the religion he or she teaches is not an issue. A full non-sectarian model is articulated later in this chapter.

37. Indeed, it is an ongoing issue at nonsectarian universities. As appealing as American university education is to various students, some have argued that it lacks a solid foundation. See Bill Readings, The University in Ruins (Cambridge, Mass.: Harvard University Press, 1996).

38. The centers are named after John Henry Cardinal Newman, the great nineteenth-century theologian and educator whose reflections on what constitutes a university and how a Catholic university might function had a significant impact on how Catholic institutions of higher education in the United States have been structured. See John Henry Cardinal Newman, The Idea of a University (New York: Image, 1959 [originally published 1852]).

39. Colleges that espouse the Catholic immersion model have very high rates of

participation in Sunday Mass and other religious events. Even nonsectarian universities with outstanding Newman centers are unlikely to equal the student participation rates in such liturgies as those attained at Catholic immersion institutions.

40. The distinguishability criterion requires that, in general, activities in the Catholic culture be distinguishable from activities in the broader culture of higher education. The fact that in a few cases the sectarian institution, through its Newman center, has activities that are virtually the same as those at the Catholic institution does not mean that campus ministry at the Catholic institution is not, in general, distinguishable from the comparable activity at the nonsectarian institution. Comparative student participation rates at Newman centers versus Catholic universities would be illuminating, but we are unaware of any studies that provide data enabling useful comparisons.

41. See Owen Chadwick, *The Secularization of the European Mind in the Nineteenth Century* (Cambridge: Cambridge University Press, 1975), Christopher Lasch, *The True and Only Heaven: Progress and Its Critics* (New York: Norton, 1991), and Jon H. Roberts and James Turner, *The Sacred and the Secular University* (Princeton: Princeton University Press, 2000), 107–122.

42. Those who work with students understand they need to be flexible in the way they present content, be it academic, religious, ethical, or social. Students can accept many things if they are presented in the right way. One outcome of a vibrant culture is finding new ways to present long-enduring truths. The new ways have to relate sufficiently to the youth culture to be attractive to young people, but in making such adjustments, one can remain faithful to the essential unchanging message with respect to a faith tradition or an ethical tradition.

43. Dennis O'Brien argues that campus ministry plays a vital role in celebrating the Catholic heritage of a Catholic institution. In the Catholic diaspora model, campus ministry has to achieve a complex task. It should serve the Catholic students and reach out to non-Catholics yet be strong and clear in celebrating the Eucharist at significant events, precisely because the Eucharist expresses the core commitment of the institution. See George Dennis O'Brien, *The Idea of a Catholic University* (Chicago: University of Chicago Press, 2002).

44. As is the case with the other models, the board of trustees is assumed to strongly support the Catholic mission of the institution.

45. Because the distinguishability criterion is not fulfilled in residence life, this model comes close to undermining our original claim that all four models are faithful and support the teaching of the Catholic Church. This model assumes that if the authorities are brought convincing evidence, for example, of inappropriate sexual intimacies taking place in the residence halls, those in charge would take steps to prevent such behavior from recurring. Unless some such response is assumed, this model would contradict the supposition of faithfulness made in all four models.

46. Because inheritability as a functioning criterion refers to recently introduced or future changes, it will feature more prominently in future chapters that review the comments of senior administrators concerning ways to enhance Catholic education.

47. Inheritability is equally important among faculty, staff, and students. In this chapter, inheritability among students has been highlighted, in part because the interest of Catholic students in the Catholic faith may waver. Recent studies have emphasized the narrow knowledge base among young adult Catholics. See William Dinges, Dean R. Hoge, Mary Johnson, and Juan L. Gonzales, Jr., "A Faith Loosely Held: The Institutional Allegiance of Young Catholics," *Commonweal*, July 17, 1998, Dean R. Hoge, "Catholic Generational Differences: Can We Learn Anything by Identifying the

Specific Issues of Generational Agreement and Disagreement?" *America* 181, 9 (1999).

48. Secular graduate and professional education appears to have even more stringent norms and expectations than secular undergraduate programs. Students have less choice, are expected to be more focused on collaborative work with faculty members, and, at least in many programs, are also expected to progress in their studies in small groups. Even though at many institutions the faculty members teaching at the graduate and professional level also teach at the undergraduate level, the purely secular graduate culture appears to make more specific demands, and not merely with respect to how much knowledge is accumulated.

49. Introducing Catholic subject matter into specific disciplines, where appropriate, is part of the process of coming to terms with specialization in discrete disciplines, a process that has been continuing for over a century. The history of this process suggests that separate disciplines can regain some of their "natural connectivity" through both theology and philosophy. See Roberts and Turner, *Sacred and the Secular University*, especially 83–95.

50. See John C. Haughey, S.J., "Faculty Research and Catholic Identity," in *Theological Education in the Catholic Tradition: Contemporary Challenges*, ed. Patrick W. Carey and Earl C. Muller, S.J. (New York: Crossroad, 1997).

51. Various types of secular institutions attempt to distinguish themselves, one from another. Thus, four-year universities emphasize the range of their offerings when comparing themselves with other four-year colleges. For-profit institutions pride themselves in getting jobs for a high percentage of their students (usually around 95 percent of graduating students) within three months of graduation. Major research universities emphasize this in their advertising and also note that undergraduates at such institutions have opportunities to be involved in exciting research projects with distinguished research professors. This type of distinguishability is interesting, but not of concern here, since all secular institutions are assumed to conform to the same nonsectarian model by not having an institutional religious mission.

52. Alternate strategies to the one we present are possible. In order to satisfy the distinguishability criterion, such alternate strategies must create cultures that have an impact similar to the ones generated by the strategies we have described.

53. In his philosophical works, Immanuel Kant speaks of the conditions of possibility for various types of knowledge. For an introduction to this approach see Immanuel Kant, *Prolegomena to Any Future Metaphysics*, trans. P. Carus and Lewis W. Beck (New York: Prentice-Hall, 1950).

54. By emphasizing that all models assume an institutional commitment to support the Catholic faith and a desire to assist the Catholic Church, the coherence principle with respect to the institution's core identity is satisfied in each model. Any particular college or university must attend to this coherence, as well as to coherence with respect to particular practices or ways of proceeding. The introduction of religious policies sharply discordant with the institution's tradition may offend against core coherence.

PART II

1. Each of the dominant themes was coded and separated into a series of subthemes. From these, extensive narratives comprised of lengthy and contextualized quotations were developed. These narratives were then grouped into four categories—convictions, reality, concerns, and future directions—that provide the architecture for

presenting the major findings of the study. Condensed quotations that best represented the original themes and sub-themes and which adequately reflected context were incorporated into the descriptive sections of each of the theme chapters.

2. The four categories of *convictions, reality, concerns,* and *future directions* were distinguishable within the remarks administrators made, but their comments were not necessarily restricted within single categories. In some instances, administrators' responses combined a number of these categories into a single observation. Comments which potentially could be placed in a number of categories were situated in the category that best illustrated the views of a number of administrators.

3. In reporting administrator comments we have randomly used feminine and masculine singular pronouns in order to assure anonymity.

CHAPTER 4

1. The reference is to systematic theology, which identifies themes in the teaching of the Church and then attempts to present those teachings in a coherent, integrated (systematic) way.

2. Whether philosophy should occupy a privileged position alongside theology is an important issue, and it is addressed again in the following chapter. Some faculty and administrators claim that topics traditionally treated by philosophy are now handled in a number of particular disciplines. For this reason, they claim, "philosophical issues" may be better studied in particular disciplines. If this turns out to be the correct view, in this chapter, wherever "philosophy" is given a privileged position, it can subsequently be reinterpreted to mean "traditional philosophical issues handled in particular disciplines."

3. Theodore M. Hesburgh, C.S.C., introduction to *The Challenge and Promise of a Catholic University*, ed. Theodore M. Hesburgh, C.S.C. (Notre Dame, Ind.: University of Notre Dame Press, 1994), 7.

4. The exception is immersion institutions. Senior administrators at these institutions put significant emphasis on the value of philosophy courses that address important issues from a broadly Catholic perspective. These administrators also look to philosophy to create the critical reflection that enables students to question and, where appropriate, refute broad claims made in the modern media.

5. Some national summer institutes have been instituted precisely to assist faculty and administrators in understanding and contributing to the Catholic intellectual tradition at their institutions. The two most prominent of these are Collegium and the Institute for Administrators in Catholic Higher Education at Boston College. Collegium is a colloquy on faith and the intellectual life that was founded in 1992, and its week-long summer sessions focus primarily on the formation of new faculty. The Institute at Boston College began in 2001, as a week-long seminar for administrators that focuses on the unique issues related to Catholic identity at Catholic colleges and universities, including ways administrators can contribute to enhancing the vibrancy of the Catholic intellectual tradition in these institutions.

6. In Greek, the optative mood is distinct from the indicative and subjunctive mood and refers to wishes of the form "Would that things were such."

7. At the very least, faculty members teaching Catholic theology courses should specify what degree of familiarity with the Catholic faith is expected of students taking the course, and students, prior to being registered for these courses, should provide some evidence that they have attained the minimum knowledge required. A similar approach would be useful in courses that address "Catholic topics" in philosophy.

Students deemed by faculty to have insufficient knowledge about the Catholic faith might be encouraged, or even required, to take a course that is technically not theology (though it may be listed in the curriculum under the theology or religious studies department) but rather an exposition of the basic teachings of the Catholic faith.

8. It must be said that anecdotal memories are often skewed by time and any number of other things. At best, these views are impressionistic. Nevertheless, they point to a sense that the depth of the exposure to theology and philosophy made a lasting and frequently positive impression on students that they came to appreciate more fully over time.

9. See Alasdair MacIntyre, *Three Rival Versions of Moral Inquiry: Encyclopaedia, Genealogy, and Tradition* (Notre Dame, Ind.: University of Notre Dame Press, 1990), Alasdair MacIntyre, *After Virtue: A Study in Moral Theory*, 2nd ed. (Notre Dame, Ind.: University of Notre Dame Press, 1984), and Alasdair MacIntyre, *Whose Justice? Which Rationality?* (Notre Dame, Ind.: University of Notre Dame Press, 1988).

10. MacIntyre calls these, respectively, the encyclopaedic tradition, the genealogical tradition (which refers to Nietzsche's *Genealogy of Morals*), and simply "the tradition."

11. The number of administrators expressing views on this subject was too small to make any clear determination about a dominant view.

CHAPTER 5

1. Women were not urged and usually were not allowed to become educated in this period.

2. See C. Stephen Jaeger, *The Envy of Angels: Cathedral Schools and Social Ideals in Medieval Europe, 950–1200* (Philadelphia: University of Pennsylvania Press, 1994).

3. "Doctorate" in the modern sense emerges during the nineteenth century at German universities.

4. For an account of medieval universities see Olaf Pedersen, *The First Universities: Studium Generale and the Origins of University Education in Europe* (Cambridge: Cambridge University Press, 1998), 122–188, and Hilde de Ridder-Symoens, ed., *Universities in the Middle Ages, A History of the University in Europe* (Cambridge: Cambridge University Press, 2003).

5. For a useful account of what the actual course of studies at a sixteenth-century university would have been like, see George E. Ganns, S.J., *Saint Ignatius' Idea of a Jesuit University: A Study in the History of Catholic Education* (Milwaukee: Marquette University Press, 1956). For a more detailed review of developments in the universities from the Reformation to the Enlightenment see Hilde de Ridder-Symoens, ed., *Universities in Early Modern Europe*, 4 vols., vol. 2, *A History of the University in Europe* (New York: Cambridge University Press, 1996).

6. For a good analysis of the emergence of modern academic disciplines see Julie A. Reuben, *The Making of the Modern University: Intellectual Transformation and the Marginalization of Morality* (Chicago: University of Chicago Press, 1996), especially 17–35, 61–87, Jon H. Roberts and James Turner, *The Sacred and the Secular University*. (Princeton: Princeton University Press, 2000), and Laurence R. Veysey, *The Emergence of the American University* (Chicago: University of Chicago Press, 1965).

7. See Walter Rüegg, ed., *Universities in the Nineteenth and Early Twentieth Centuries (1800–1945)*, 4 vols., vol. 3, *A History of the University in Europe* (New York: Cambridge University Press, 2004), 415–428 and 499–505.

8. The new doctorates were granted for emerging disciplines, each of whose pro-

fessors was a member of the faculty of arts and philosophy. For this reason, even doctorates in chemistry, mathematics, or physics were doctorates in philosophy, or, in Latin, *philosophiae doctor*, from which "Ph.D." is derived. Medieval universities had only four advanced degrees: the master of arts, the master or doctor of theology, the doctor of law, and the doctor of medicine. For a helpful overview of the medieval period, see Gerald L. Gutek, *A History of the Western Educational Experience*, 2nd ed. (Prospect Heights, Ill.: Waveland Press, 1972), 73–113.

9. In the earlier system, everyone studied Latin and Greek, since these were the bases of the liberal arts and required for the study of philosophy and theology. In modern terminology, prior to the latter half of the nineteenth century, every university student was a classics major.

10. Philosophy here is understood in the modern sense, not as the traditional faculty of philosophy, which embraced modern philosophy as well as the liberal arts and the inchoative stages of many modern sciences.

11. Many colleges within universities have the general title of "College of Arts and Sciences." The "arts" are the descendants of the liberal arts, including philosophy and theology, and the "sciences" are the natural, life, social, and psychological sciences that have been introduced in the undergraduate curriculum over the past two centuries.

12. The term "humanities" is not quite the same as the liberal arts, since it includes language, literature, history, philosophy, classics, and the arts but excludes mathematics, a normal component of the liberal arts.

13. Some uses of the phrase "Catholic intellectual tradition" also bracket out the contributions of philosophy and focus on components 3 and 4. In this study, theology, which is component 1 of the Catholic intellectual tradition, is contrasted with Catholic themes in the three other components: philosophy, liberal arts, and the extended liberal arts.

14. Thus the nontheology components of the tradition are philosophy (including ethics, which constitutes the Catholic moral tradition, which in turn includes Catholic social teaching), the liberal arts, and the extended liberal arts.

15. Using current norms for counting courses, most undergraduates attending Catholic colleges or universities prior to 1965 would have had more than ten courses in philosophy and theology. Most students regarded their philosophy courses as more demanding than their theology courses. See Philip Gleason, *Contending with Modernity: Catholic Higher Education in the Twentieth Century* (New York: Oxford University Press, 1995), and Paul A. Fitzgerald, *The Governance of Jesuit Colleges in the United States, 1920–1970* (Notre Dame, Ind.: University of Notre Dame Press, 1984).

16. Richard McBrien points out that the particular configuration of sacramentality, mediation, and the centrality of community is not duplicated anywhere else in the Christian community and that they are expressed in all aspects of Church life and experience, including doctrine, liturgical life, theology, spiritualities, religious congregations, lay apostolates, social teachings, and the Petrine ministry itself. See Richard P. McBrien, *Catholicism* (San Francisco: HarperCollins, 1994), 8–17.

17. Moral precepts emerge from the lived experience of communities. Since sin is a reality in every community, larger or smaller groups in the community may not live in conformity to the natural moral law. To the extent that the influence of groups living in ways contrary to the requirements of the natural moral law is great on the broader society, perceiving the requirements of human reason in this community may be extremely difficult. For this reason, perceiving the requirements of natural law is often greatly assisted through revelation in the Old and New Testaments. See Russell

Hittinger, *The First Grace: Rediscovering the Natural Law in a Post-Christian World* (Wilmington, Del.: ISI Books, 2003), xi–xlvi.

18. McBrien, *Catholicism*, 11.

19. Martin R. Tripole, ed., *Jesuit Education 21: Conference Proceedings on the Future of Jesuit Higher Education.* (Philadelphia: Saint Joseph's University Press, 2000), covers variously aggregated academic disciplines and notes ways in which they intersect with important themes in Jesuit higher education.

20. There is a distinctly different modern use of the term "rational psychology" that refers to a part of mathematics concerned with mathematical and conceptual analysis of psychological notions. Rational psychology in its traditional sense, with its philosophical mooring, is the focus in this essay, and it can be considered the philosophical precursor of modern psychology.

21. For a full discussion and bibliography, see entry "Psychology," in *The Catholic Encyclopedia,*" vol. 12 (Washington, D.C.: Robert Appleton, 1911), online ed., copyright K. Knight, 2003, available at: www.newadvent.org/cathen/.

22. For an overview of Catholic social teaching relevant to modern issues see Marvin L. Krier Mich, *Catholic Social Teaching and Movements* (Mystic, Conn.: Twenty-Third Publications, 1998).

23. In the previous chapter, we highlighted Alasdair MacIntyre's contention that one way to decide which of three ethical systems is correct is to observe how it is lived. That is, do people live in harmony with one another and do they flourish as human beings?

24. Stark shows how science developed from the theological and philosophical foundations of Christianity. See Rodney Stark, "False Conflict: Christianity Is Not Only Compatible with Science—It Created It," *American Enterprise* 14 (October–November 2003).

25. An example of philosophical issues being treated in other academic disciplines involves biology and the unity of knowledge. In a stimulating book, the biologist Edward O. Wilson proposes a unified theory ("consilience") of all human understanding and experience. See Edward O. Wilson, *Consilience: The Unity of Knowledge* (New York: Knopf, 1998). Some philosophers and scientists disagree with his approach, but because his quest for the unity of understanding is squarely within the Catholic philosophical tradition, dialogue in this area can be fruitful.

26. For a helpful analysis, see Stephen J. Pope, "Natural Law and Christian Ethics," in *The Cambridge Companion to Christian Ethics*, ed. Robin Gill (Cambridge: Cambridge University Press, 2001), 89.

27. Natural law is a tradition within moral reasoning. As a tradition, various approaches and positions are taken in natural law with respect to particular issues. The "new classical natural-law theory" or fundamental value approach that is developed in this text follows the Finnis-and-Grisez school. See John Finnis, *Natural Law and Natural Rights* (Oxford: Clarendon, 1980), *Fundamentals of Ethics* (Oxford: Clarendon, 1982), *Aquinas: Moral, Political, and Legal Theory* (New York: Oxford University Press, 1998), and Germain Grisez, "A Contemporary Natural-Law Ethics," in *Moral Philosophy: Historical and Contemporary Essays*, ed. William C. Starr and Richard C. Taylor (Milwaukee: Marquette University Press, 1989). For a Catholic approach to ethics, as well as a helpful treatment of particular moral issues from a Catholic perspective, see James T. Bretzke, *A Morally Complex World: Engaging Contemporary Moral Theology* (Collegeville, Minn.: Liturgical Press, 2004), Edward J. Hayes, Paul J. Hayes, Dorothy Ellen Kelly, and James J. Drummey, *Catholicism and Ethics* (Norwood, Mass.: C.R. Publications, 1997), and Paulinus Ikechukwu Odozor, C.S.Sp., *Moral Theology in an*

Age of Renewal: A Study of the Catholic Tradition since Vatican II (Notre Dame, Ind.: University of Notre Dame Press, 2003). For helpful account of "changes" in the natural law influenced by historical changes see Eberhard Schockenhoff, *Natural Law and Human Dignity: Universal Ethics in an Historical World* (Washington, D.C.: Catholic University of America Press, 2003), with the caveat that his "principle of intervening action" (210–223) does not, in our view, represent an accurate and consistent account of the natural law tradition. Also very helpful for both historical perspective and care analysis are Jean Porter's two books, *Natural and Divine Law: Relaiming the Tradition for Christian Ethics* (Grand Rapids: Eerdmans, 1999) and *Nature as Reason: A Thomistic Theory of the Natural Law* (Grand Rapids: Eerdmans, 2005).

28. One strength of the approach by Grisez and Finnis is they derive norms that do not allow exceptions. Revisionist natural law thinkers are sometimes called "proportionalists" by their critics because of the analysis they use to determine exceptions to norms. Proportionalists argue that no judgment of moral rightness or wrongness of acts can be made without considering all the circumstances of the actions. Proportionalism is rejected by the Grisez-and-Finnis school, which maintains that there are certain basic human goods that can never be acted against, no matter the cause or circumstance. Pope John Paul II was also critical of proportionalism in his encyclical *Vertitatis Splendor.*

29. An excellent discussion of the relationship between virtue and the Catholic moral tradition can be found in McBrien, *Catholicism*, 921–952. See also Jean Porter, "Virtue Ethics," in *The Cambridge Companion to Christian Ethics*, ed. Robin Gill (Cambridge: Cambridge University Press, 2001), 96–111.

30. Since the Second Vatican Council, the Church in its official teaching has paid more attention to personalist or person-centered ethics, particularly with regard to sexual ethics. This is especially true of the writings of Pope John Paul II. Yet, when justifying certain positions the Church takes, especially with respect to procreation and new medical advances, the Vatican and episcopal documents continue to rely on natural law.

31. Paul's thought here reflects the approach of the Stoics to natural law, which, according to them, was inherent in the cosmic order of the universe. Thomas Aquinas used this Pauline text to demonstrate that there is a natural law (*Summa Theologiae*, bks. 1–2, 91, 2, *sed contra*), and in the Pastoral Constitution on the Church in the Modern World—*Gaudium et Spes*—the Second Vatican Council also referred to this passage to support its teaching that natural law is a binding force.

32. For an interesting account of the natural law principles embedded in the Constitution of the United States, see Douglas W. Kmiec and Stephen B. Presser, *The History, Philosophy and Structure of the American Constitution* (Cincinnati: Anderson, 1998).

33. For a careful analysis of the tradition and newer approaches, see Lisa Sowle Cahill, *Sex, Gender, and Christian Ethics* (Cambridge: Cambridge University Press, 1996).

34. The Greek word for goal is *telos*. Natural law, therefore, is classified as a teleological system. Grisez and Finnis attempt to revive the natural law approach of Thomas Aquinas, although they take a distinctly different approach from that pursued by Alasdair MacIntyre, who is also motivated by Aquinas. See Lawrence C. Becker and Charlotte B. Becker, eds., *A History of Western Ethics*, 2nd ed. (New York: Routledge, 2003), 150.

35. Bretzke, *Morally Complex World*, 73.

36. Solidarity is also known as the principle of the common good, where *com-*

mon good refers to the ability of all people in society to pursue the fundamental values.

37. In the Catholic understanding, "the function of social justice is to evaluate the essential institutions of society in terms of their ability to satisfy the minimum needs and basic rights of the citizenry. . . . It is usually expected that social justice will be accomplished through organized activity rather than individual actions." See J. Bryan Hehir, *Social Justice*, in *The HarperCollins Encyclopedia of Catholicism*, ed. Richard P. McBrien (New York: HarperCollins, 1995), 1204.

38. John Henry Cardinal Newman, *The Idea of a University*, ed. Frank M. Turner (New Haven: Yale University Press, 1996), 106. Newman wrote this book to justify the course of studies to be pursued in the first Catholic university to be established in Great Britain since the Reformation.

39. The emphasis on ethics at Catholic universities should not be taken for granted. In an article in the *New York Times*, Peter Steinfels cautioned his readers not to "be fooled by those lofty commencement speeches. Not everyone thinks that a college education should have anything to do with inculcating moral values." See Peter Steinfels, "Beliefs: The University's Role in Instilling a Moral Code among Students? None Whatever, Some Argue," *New York Times*, June 19, 2004. Also, Stanley Fish, the dean of the College of Liberal Arts and Sciences at the University of Illinois at Chicago, is forceful in his repudiation of moral education as the proper purview of higher educational institutions. In speaking of students Fish insists: "You can't make them into good people, and you shouldn't try." In the same article, Fish goes on to point out that his main objection to the idea that students' moral and civic development is central to a university's mission "is not that it is a bad idea (which it surely is), but that it's an unworkable idea." "Aim Low," *Chronicle of Higher Education*, May 16, 2003.

40. There are circumstances in which individuals can elect to be in such a situation, but it requires sufficient safeguards to ensure that they can protect themselves and will not harm others. For instance, a person undergoing a major operation is administered a general anesthetic. Even though the person cannot act rationally during the operation, doctors and nurses are in constant attendance to respond to threats to the health of the person. A person under general anesthetic is no threat to anyone. Such is usually not the case with drinking alcohol to excess.

41. That is, the position of the Church should be made comprehensible to young people. James Bretzke includes comprehensibility as one of the six hallmarks of Christian moral discourse that can contribute to building moral common ground. The others are: comprehensiveness, coherence or consistency, credibility, being convincing, and being Christian. See Bretzke, *Morally Complex World*, 147–161.

42. The concern that a lack of sufficient knowledge and preparation is a serious problem across Catholic institutions in the absence of significant numbers of men and women religious has been raised in the media. In his book *A People Adrift*, Peter Steinfels addresses the shortfall many perceive in the preparation of laypersons who run Catholic institutions, over against the religious congregations members they have replaced. See *A People Adrift: The Crisis of the Roman Catholic Church in America* (New York: Simon and Schuster), 103–161.

43. The chair of the theology department at the University of Notre Dame urges a candid admission on the part of theology faculty at Catholic colleges and universities that Catholic students know little about their faith. See John C Cavadini, "Ignorant Catholics: The Alarming Void in Religious Education," *Commonweal* 131, 7 (2004). Aside from personal evaluations such as these, however, most information

about young and adult Catholics concerns their beliefs and practices, not their knowledge. See Dean R. Hoge, William D. Dinges, Mary Johnson, and Juan L. Gonzales, Jr., *Young Adult Catholics: Religion in the Culture of Choice* (Notre Dame, Ind.: University of Notre Dame Press, 2001), and William V. D'Antonio, James D. Davidson, Dean R. Hoge, and Katherine Meyer, *American Catholics: Gender, Generation, and Commitment* (New York: Rowman and Littlefield, 2001). Both these studies document steady, significant reductions in traditional practices and beliefs among young Catholics. The extent to which young Catholics know the teaching of the Church but decide not to abide by it is unknown.

44. Immersion institutions put a heavy emphasis on sharing the Catholic tradition with students. From the interviews it was clear that the requirements at immersion institutions to study theology and philosophy are greater than at persuasion institutions. However, from the interviews it was unclear whether administrators or faculty at immersion institutions had agreed on minimum standards of knowledge about the Catholic tradition and whether such standards were reached by students graduating from their institutions.

45. Some colleges or universities have undoubtedly identified certain components of "required Catholic knowledge." We are not aware, however, of any general consensus among institutions about how much or what type of Catholic knowledge should be expected of graduates. Ideally, "expected Catholic outcomes" would form part of the description of each of the four Catholic models.

46. The interview team noticed a pattern of responses to one of the five set questions (provided beforehand to the person being interviewed) posed to each administrator interviewed. The fourth question asked the administrator to consider himself or herself a consultant in the hiring process at some other Catholic institution similar in structure to the one at which the administrator currently serves. As consultant, the administrator is asked to list the most important qualities for a person to be hired at the other Catholic institution for the same level of position held by the administrator being interviewed. In most of our interviews, the response by the administrator did not initially include any requirement about whether it was important for the person hired to be Catholic. When we then explicitly posed this question, most administrators spoke about the Catholic issue for a few minutes and gradually convinced themselves that the person indeed should be a Catholic. But only a few indicated that the person should be a practicing Catholic.

47. Robert P. Imbelli, "Christ the Center," in *Examining the Catholic Intellectual Tradition*, vol. 2, ed. Anthony J. Cernera and Oliver J. Morgan (Fairfield, Conn.: Sacred Heart University Press, 2002), 4.

CHAPTER 6

1. The noted philosopher Charles Taylor emphasizes the positive developments in modern culture. He wants to retain the positive aspects, even as he notes that they have to be supplemented with important insights of an earlier traditional and more comprehensive outlook. See Charles Taylor, "Justice after Virtue," in *After Macintyre: Critical Perspectives on the Work of Alasdair Macintyre*, ed. John Horton and Susan Mendus (Notre Dame, Ind.: University of Notre Dame Press, 1994), and Francisco Lombo de León and Bart van Leeuwen, "Charles Taylor on Secularization," *Ethical Perspectives* 10 (November 2003).

2. In some instances, parents are hoping the Catholic university will impose constraints they have been unwilling or unable to impose themselves.

3. It is unlikely that adjustments have to be made every year. Rather, over time, administrators notice patterns characteristic of incoming students (and/or returning students). When incoming students display attitudes or ways of acting that are reflective of the dominant American culture, which is at variance with the desired Catholic culture, administrators make adjustments. For example, over several years, administrators might notice that entering students are less inclined to attend Mass or other religious services regularly. Administrators then have to devise ways to reinforce understanding among students of the importance of regular Mass attendance.

4. The norms in academic culture are not only consistently enforced but also linked to faculty with an important status in the university. In order for the young to acquire good habits, Bellah emphasizes the importance of authority figures articulating to the young what must be done. See Robert N. Bellah, "Habit and History," *Ethical Perspectives* 8, 3 (2001).

5. Sanctions may be mentioned in the student handbook or mentioned by a university official. "Threaten" would mean that an official warns students about severe consequences for engaging in behavior not permitted to undergraduates.

6. One of the unfortunate realities Catholic colleges and universities face is that many Catholic parents no longer support Catholic moral teaching, particularly in terms of drinking and intimate relationships. Administrators were very troubled by the fact that parents associate college social life with heavy drinking and often relate stories of their own collegiate drinking histories. The kind of "big-game" athletic weekends that bring parents to campus with their own stores of liquor that they share with sons and daughters further erode university positions. As noted in the text, in terms of sexual intimacy, many Catholic parents make sure their sons and daughters have condoms and birth control pills before they get to campus, so that if they engage in sex it will, of course, be safe sex.

7. The sociologist Edward Hall provides interesting insights about the role of technical props in helping to sustain the values of formal cultural systems. The absence of strong technical props to support sexual virtue in residence halls leaves young men and women entirely on their own as they negotiate how to behave sexually. See Hall, *Silent Language*, 89–91.

8. In most cases, apparently, invitations to spend the night are extended by women and not by men. Although feminist issues and justice concerns have great currency on college campuses, they seem not to apply when it comes to sharing sleeping arrangements. Young men are loathe to evict their friends for the night, or so it appears, whereas women are either quite willing or feel compelled to displace other women in order to entertain young men. While women seem to be being used, and the rights of roommates are trampled, no hue and cry is raised either by feminists or those who champion the cause of justice.

9. Consulting with appropriate groups on campus would naturally precede any actions administrators might take to modify student behavior.

10. There are a number of ways for the university to distance itself from the objectionable policies advocated by the person being honored. It can note the laudatory aspects of the person's life when the citation conferring the honorary degree is read and in the printed program note that the institution does not support the public positions taken by the honoree about some important topic in society.

11. A Catholic university is not always obliged to take the most effective route for supporting the Church. Rather, it must select an approach that makes clear the university's position against the oppositional stance of the invited guest, and it must provide Church teaching in an appropriate forum.

12. James Davison Hunter notes three modern philosophical justifications for inclusiveness: psychological, neoclassical, and communitarian. While there is merit to these approaches, the inclination is to avoid controversy by emphasizing norms that are not contested. Because the Catholic culture both contests certain values and approaches and competes with variant cultures, it will not be as inclusive as the three approaches mentioned by Hunter. Hunter argues for particularity in cultures. See James Davison Hunter, "Leading Children beyond Good and Evil," *First Things* 103 (2000).

13. Using the language of chapter 3, senior administrators are correct about inheritability of the Catholic tradition and the margin criterion. They understand the Catholic student culture has to be strengthened, but this will achieve only short-term gains if, as a result of the changes, the number of student applications decreases to such an extent that the margin criterion (one aspect of inheritability) can no longer be satisfied.

14. In order for human beings to flourish, they have to experience relationships in which people freely give and receive, without calculating benefits to themselves. Children and young people have to see this modeled in others, in our case, in the university setting. For a carefully reasoned argument for the necessity of virtue for human flourishing see Alasdair MacIntyre, *Dependent Rational Animals: Why Human Beings Need the Virtues* (Chicago: Open Court, 1999), especially 119–128.

15. Stressing the benefits of adherence to the culture and highlighting students who are exemplars of the culture makes the culture more cohesive and persuasive. Bernheim presents a theoretical model and notes that the desire of people for social status (in our case, social status within the Catholic culture) will make many, but not all, people conform to a standard even though their underlying preferences may be different. See B. Douglas Bernheim, "A Theory of Conformity," *Journal of Political Economy* 102, 5 (1994).

CHAPTER 7

1. Data collected in the Archdiocese of New York and the Diocese of Brooklyn for the year 2004 indicates that fewer than 20 percent of baptized Catholics attend Mass on most weekends.

2. Counting may require distinctions, since the aim is to calculate the number of Catholic students attending Masses on campus.

3. Robert Wuthnow, *Meaning and Moral Order:Explorations in Cultural Analysis* (Berkeley: University of California Press, 1987), 172.

4. The service programs at nonsectarian institutions are assumed to be run by a unit of the university, not by the Newman or Catholic center associated with the university.

5. Synod of Catholic Bishops, *Justice in the World*, cited in Timothy R. Scully, C.S.C., "What Is Catholic?" in *The Challenge and Promise of a Catholic University*, ed. Theodore M. Hesburgh, C.S.C. (Notre Dame, Ind.: University of Notre Dame Press, 1997), 318.

6. Greater intensity might mean engaging more students in service immersion experiences. "Immersion" in this context means that students spend a week or more living with and serving people in need. Many colleges sponsor immersion experiences in the inner city or internationally. The recommendation is to link these experiences more directly to the Catholic tradition in prayer and social teaching. For example, students on immersion trips can be invited to pray together every day for the people they

serve. A campus minister might also explain to the student participants one or more of the important social encyclicals. However it happens, the Catholic link to service should be operative.

7. At some institutions, campus ministry is not directly in charge of these programs. For the sake of simplicity, we refer only to campus ministry but are aware that at some institutions the analysis will apply to other university organizations that most probably work in collaboration with the campus ministry team.

CHAPTER 8

1. The complete interview question (number 5) is provided in chapter 1. The pertinent portion for the discussion here is as follows. "Over 80% of all Catholics who receive higher education do so at these non-Catholic institutions. Now, imagine that you have been granted an interview with a foundation that is committed to investing $500 million in higher education. The foundation wants this gift to have a significant impact on the education of Catholics for the twenty-first century. How would you convince this foundation that the most effective way to invest the money is in Catholic colleges and universities, not in programs at secular institutions?"

2. One of the crucial elements that contributed to the ambiguity trend emerged in the courts. In 1966, in the Horace Mann case, the Maryland Court of Appeals ruled against awarding construction grants to three church-related colleges. Included in this group were the College of Notre Dame of Maryland in Baltimore and St. Joseph's College in Emmitsburg, Maryland. Alice Gallin, O.S.U., points out that the argument developed by the court in this case "furnished a framework for the various cases that would follow, and the question of 'legal sectarianism' as defined in Horace Mann became a crucial element in the ambiguity characteristic of the church-related colleges' efforts at self-identity in the decades ahead." See Alice Gallin, O.S.U. (2000), 36.

3. Robert Wuthnow, *Meaning and Moral Order: Explorations in Cultural Analysis* (Berkeley: University of California Press, 1987), 105.

4. Edgar H. Schein, *Organizational Culture and Leadership* (San Francisco: Jossey-Bass, 1992), 74.

5. Prior to 1956, there were no umbrella groups representing congregations of religious men and women. In 1956, at the urging of Rome, these organizations were formed. The Conference of Major Superior of Men (CMSM) and the Conference of Major Superiors of Women (CMSW) were organizations comprised of the heads of men's and women's religious communities, respectively. Pat Wittberg indicates that the focus of the CMSW at about 1960 was "on the educational and spiritual reforms requested by the pope ten years earlier." See *The Rise and Fall of Catholic Religious Orders: A Social Movement Perspective* (Albany: State University of New York Press, 1994), 213. By the late 1960s and early 1970s, CMSW had undergone a significant reassessment of its goals and purposes and also changed its name to the Leadership Conference of Women Religious (LCWR). For the first time, this newly named organization "brought sisters face to face with religious life as an institution in the church [and] with generalized concepts of 'religious life.'" See Lora Ann Quinonez, C.D.P., and Mary Daniel Turner, S.N.D.deN., *The Transformation of American Catholic Sisters* (Philadelphia: Temple University Press, 1992), 109.

6. The Jesuit Richard A. McCormick outlines eight qualities that should be found in graduates of a great Catholic university that include: sensitivity to justice and injustice, appreciation of and thirst for knowledge, facility in the spoken and written

word, open-mindedness, critical capacity, ability to listen, willingness to serve, and a Catholic vision. Only the last of these characteristics would necessarily be unique to Catholic university graduates, but all eight are indicators of educational and developmental transformation among students. See Richard A. McCormick, S.J., "What Is a Great Catholic University?" in *Enhancing Religious Identity: Best Practices from Catholic Campuses*, ed. John R. Wilcox and Irene King (Washington, D.C.: Georgetown University Press, 2000), 4–11.

7. It became clear through the conversations with senior administrators that a different question would have been more helpful in terms of focusing attention on the Catholic component of education at Catholic institutions. If the foundation's interest had been expressed slightly differently by stating it wanted to commit the large sum of money to the institution (Catholic university or Newman center) that would have the biggest impact through its undergraduate program on the Catholic Church in the United States, responses might have been more illuminating. Because the legitimacy of university claims are measured by their products, a Catholic university in this case would have to indicate what things its graduates do, and do better or at a disproportionately higher rate than graduates from the Catholic center, that would contribute positively to the Catholic Church in the United States. If the Catholic university, like the Newman centers, lacked data to make a convincing case, at the very least it would have to point to the activities on campus that make it more likely that its students would be prepared and disposed to serve the American Catholic Church, as well as society at large. Certainly the Catholic Church in the United States is enriched by having talented leaders in key positions in business, government, the arts, etc. The Church also benefits, however, from active, committed Catholics who attend Mass regularly, volunteer in their parish or at the diocesan level, are well informed about issues impacting the Church, serve the poor and needy, are attentive to the needs of the universal Church, and engage the critical questions of the day in a manner that brings the best of Catholic belief and values to bear. The Catholic university would point to an array of ways their graduates serve and support the Church and invest themselves in its future.

8. This point was made by many senior administrators, and it will be examined again in greater detail in the following chapter, which explores why the culture of religious congregations of women was so strong over such a long period of time.

9. Terence J. Murphy, *A Catholic University: Vision and Opportunities* (Collegeville, Minn.: Liturgical Press, 2001), 23.

10. If topics traditionally handled in the philosophy department have migrated to other academic disciplines, at least a small cluster of faculty who are well informed about these issues is needed in those departments in which the topics are currently handled or could profitably be addressed.

11. *Ex Corde Ecclesiae*, art. 4, para. 4: "In order not to endanger the Catholic identity of the University or Institute of Higher Studies, the number of non-Catholic teachers should not be allowed to constitute a majority within the Institution, which is and must remain Catholic."

12. James H. Provost, "The Sides of Catholic Identity," in Wilcox and King, *Enhancing Religious Identity*, 23.

13. Richard P. McBrien, "What Is A Catholic University?" in Hesburgh, *The Challenge and Promise of a Catholic University*, 156.

14. Such an arrangement should be suitably formalized in the faculty charter or bylaws.

15. Paul VI, *Evangelii Nunciandi* (Washington, D.C.: United States Catholic Conference, 1976), 17, cited in Timothy R. Scully, C.S.C., "What Is Catholic?" in Hesburgh, *Challenge and Promise of a Catholic University*, 320–321.

16. Certain non-Catholics who are knowledgeable about the Catholic faith can sometimes be more effective than Catholics in presenting connections or disagreements between the Catholic faith and secular knowledge. All things being equal, however, one expects committed Catholics to speak more convincingly about the importance of Catholic faith in American society because their teaching is combined with the power of lived witness. Furthermore, the culture at Catholic immersion or persuasion institutions should be such that Catholic knowledge and commitment is encouraged and rewarded in research, as well as in teaching.

17. In light of the apostolic constitution, *Ex Corde Ecclesiae*, a universally Catholic faculty is problematic and might be described as an attempt to be more Catholic than the pope. This approach is as problematic, in terms of sustaining a vibrant Catholic university culture, as being less Catholic than Rome.

18. Most Catholic institutions do not know the percentage of Catholic faculty members they have, since they do not collect these data. Similarly, they have no data about practicing or committed Catholic faculty.

19. It is fair to say there is resistance on campuses to raising the status and visibility of any group, let alone one distinguished for its knowledge and commitment to faith. Religious congregations have spent the last forty years trying to put away the trappings of a kind of spiritual elitism that was rightly rejected by the Second Vatican Council. Attempts to create visibility for a new generation of Catholic witnesses must be carefully nuanced and explained as just what they are—efforts to develop a leavening community, not an elite and privileged society more akin to the Pharisee than the publican.

20. References here are to faculty members alone. In most instances faculty, administrators, and staff members will comprise this group—much as they did when religious congregations had full control of the institutions. In each sector, however, there will be times when issues pertain only to one group or another and persuasion and leadership must come from within their own body. The blending of these particular and more general needs for committed and knowledgeable Catholics in all divisions of university life will vary from one institution to another.

21. The one area in which it failed was in embracing and cultivating the potential of the laity in terms of religious leadership. Those lay men and women who were heroic leaders and exemplars in their own right—and there have always been some outstanding examples—were largely self-made.

22. Murphy, *Catholic University*, 83.

23. Administrators are careful to nuance most of their comments and usually said that only in extremely rare circumstances should the president not be Catholic. We believe those circumstances are so rare as to be almost nonexistent and the caveat is more an instance of never saying "never" than any indication that exceptions should be made to this functional rule.

CHAPTER 9

1. Mark Massa, S.J., points out that that cultural adaptation had always been a part of religious life: "the very 'routine' of a convent or monastery represented the institutional price for the continued life of the original anti-structural charism. In time, of course, such routinization of the monastic charismatic impulse always risks

becoming too stable, too 'safe'—a fate inherent in all institution building but inimical to the original prophetic impulse itself. Thus, as [Max] Weber himself observed, the history of Catholicism was replete with religious reform movements whose mission was to call overly rigid, structured communities *ad fontes*—that is, back to the authentic, anti-structural 'fountain,' or sources, that founded those communities." See Mark S. Massa, S.J., *Catholics and American Culture: Fulton Sheen, Dorothy Day, and the Notre Dame Football Team* (New York: Crossroad, 1999), 180.

2. Arthur Jones, "Nuns Renew Vows," *National Catholic Reporter*, March 5, 1999, cited in Elizabeth Kuhns, *The Habit: A History of the Clothing of Catholic Nuns* (New York: Doubleday, 2003), 12.

3. Lora Ann Quinonez, C.D.P., and Mary Daniel Turner, S.N.D.deN., *The Transformation of American Catholic Sisters* (Philadelphia: Temple University Press, 1992), 164.

4. Kuhns, *Habit*, 1.

5. Four among the many that are of note include: Marie Augusta Neal, S.N.D.deN., *Catholic Sisters in Transition: From the 1960's to the 1980's* (Wilmington, Del.: Michael Glazier, 1984), Quinonez and Turner, *Transformation of American Catholic Sisters*, Rodney Stark and Roger Finke, *Acts of Faith: Explaining the Human Side of Religion* (Berkeley: University of California Press, 2000), Patricia Wittberg, *The Rise and Fall of Catholic Religious Orders: A Social Movement Perspective* (Albany: State University of New York Press, 1994).

6. In fact, until the opening of the graduate theological school at St. Mary's in Notre Dame, Indiana, religious women were forbidden to earn advanced theological degrees.

7. Kathleen A. Mahoney, "American Catholic Colleges for Women: Historical Origins," in *Catholic Women's Colleges in America*, ed. Tracy Schier and Cynthia Russet (Baltimore: Johns Hopkins University Press, 2002), 26. As an outgrowth of the Sister Formation Movement, a proliferation of small colleges was founded by women's religious congregations in the 1950s and early 1960s to provide improved academic preparation for novices and junior sisters. These institutions are commonly referred to as sister formation colleges.

8. Karen Kennelly, "Women Religious, the Intellectual Life, and Anti-Intellectualism," in *Women Religious and the Intellectual Life: The North American Achievement*, ed. Bridget Puzon, O.S.U. (San Francisco: International Scholars, 1996), 65.

9. One year of novitiate is a canonical requirement. The second year the experience was structured in a more flexible manner, largely due to the fact that the novices were frequently involved in mentoring experiences with professed sisters in apostolic settings, particularly in the parochial schools. The pressures for personnel in schools also exacerbated the need for novices to begin their apostolic work as quickly as possible.

10. *Charism* is a word that came into more prominence in religious congregations after the Second Vatican Council. It refers to the particular gift and focus that is unique to a given congregation and infuses its approach to ministry. These charisms are traceable to the congregational founders and are hallmarks or signatures of each religious congregation. Some charisms are more distinct than others, and the lack of a clearly distinctive charism has been problematic for some religious congregations.

11. Carol Coburn and Martha Smith, *Spirited Lives: How Nuns Shaped Catholic Culture and American Life, 1836–1920* (Chapel Hill: University of North Carolina Press, 1999), 72.

12. Professed sisters are those who have taken final or permanent vows of poverty, chastity, and obedience in the congregation.

13. The young women who entered religious life were normal young women, filled with life and enthusiasm. Like people in any intensely structured or rigorous program, these young novices and postulants found ways, times, and places to laugh and chat and commiserate and to put things in perspective. For a description of how postulants in the Sisters of St. Joseph of Carondolet described this kind of experience and response in the early part of the twentieth century, see Coburn and Smith, *Spirited Lives*, 74–75.

14. Wittberg, *Rise and Fall of Catholic Religious Orders*, 231.

15. In her discussion of the Sisters of Mercy and their work in higher education, Mary Daigler describes a pattern replicated by scores of other religious congregations of women. "Good education often creates a hunger for more food for the mind and that is the observable pattern in Catholic education in . . . the United States. As each stage of need developed, the Sisters of Mercy acquired the preparation needed or hired others to join with them to answer the ever-rising level of Catholics' hopes and dreams. . . . Thus, from their earliest days in their new land, the Sisters had ample stimuli to educate their students and themselves to the highest possible level." See Mary Jeremy Daigler, *Through the Windows: A History of the Work of Higher Education among the Sisters of Mercy of the Americas* (Scranton, Pa.: University of Scranton Press, 2000), 71.

16. See Mary J. Oates, C.S.J., "Sisterhoods and Catholic Higher Education," in *Catholic Women's Colleges in America*, ed. Tracy Schier and Cynthia Russet (Baltimore: Johns Hopkins University Press, 2002), 183.

17. See Mary J. Oates, "Sisterhoods and Catholic Higher Education," in Schier and Russet, *Catholic Women's Colleges in America*, 178.

18. Mother Mary Cleophas, S.P., of the Sisters of Providence, was shocked when she visited her sisters at Immaculata in February 1913. Many of her sisters did receive degrees in the ensuing years. Very few of them, however, did so in Washington, D.C. See Sister Mary Roger Madden, S.P., *The Path Marked Out: History of the Sisters of Providence of Saint Mary-of-the-Woods*, vol. 3 (Saint Mary-of-the-Woods, Ind.: Office of Congregational Advancement—Sisters of Providence, 1991), 36–67.

19. Philip Gleason reports that the Sisters of Charity of the Blessed Virgin Mary sent six of their sisters to the Sisters' College in the first year of its operation at the cost of $6,000, or the total annual earnings of thirty of their own sisters. See Philip Gleason, *Contending with Modernity: Catholic Higher Education in the Twentieth Century* (Oxford: Oxford University Press, 1995), 95.

20. Normal colleges were two-year institutions that prepared people to be elementary school teachers.

21. Bertrande Meyers, D.C., *The Education of Sisters: A Plan for Integrating the Religious, Cultural, Social, and Professional Training of Sisters* (New York: Sheed and Ward, 1941).

22. Sister Madeleva Wolff, C.S.C., "The Education of Our Young Religious Sisters," *National Catholic Education Association Bulletin*, Philadelphia, vol. 46 August 1949.

23. Gleason, *Contending with Modernity*, 230–234.

24. Oates, "Sisterhoods and Catholic Higher Education," 185.

25. Gleason, *Contending with Modernity*, 95.

26. This "study-as-you-go" plan had a long life in religious congregations of women, as the Brookland Commission study on women religious and the intellectual life demonstrates. The average age at which sisters living in 1996 received their doc-

toral degrees was over forty. Interestingly, this pattern is quite consistent among living sisters, irrespective of the decade they entered community. The average age for doctoral degree reception among those entering prior to 1921, was forty. It increased to a high of 43.5 among the cohort of sisters entering in the years 1921–30. That average decreased slightly each decade over the next six decades and jumped with the cohort entering in 1991–92. The average age of those women when they received their doctorates was forty-seven.

27. Daigler, *Through the Windows*, 77.

28. Katarina Schuth, O.S.F., "The Intellectual Life as a Value for Women Religious in the United States," in *Women Religious and the Intellectual Life: The North American Achievement*, ed. Bridget Puzon, O.S.U. (San Francisco: International Scholars, 1996), 23.

29. These difficulties were highlighted in the whole set of discussions set off by John Tracy Ellis in his 1955 work "American Catholics and the Intellectual Life." Some of the writing of the day denounced the proliferation of colleges founded by women religious, which many believed were less than high-quality educational institutions. Limitations in terms of sisters' professional preparation and obstacles to their scholarly research and writing certainly contributed to the problem. See John Tracy Ellis, "American Catholics and the Intellectual Life," *Thought* 30 (autumn 1955).

30. Patricia Wittberg points out that "religious congregations derived their apostolic identity from the institutions they staffed." The decisions to move away from institutional ministry altered congregations' very understandings of who they were and what they were about. That outcome was little anticipated when these decisions were made. See Patricia Wittberg, "Reciprocal Identities: Apostolic Life and Consecrated Life," in *Review for Religious* 61, 4 (July–August, 2002), 342.

31. Eileen M. Brewer, *Nuns and the Education of American Catholic Women: 1860–1920* (Chicago: Loyola University Press, 1987), 8.

32. Cited in David Cantosta, "The Philadelphia Story: Life at Immaculata, Rosemont, and Chestnut Hill," in Schier and Russet, *Catholic Women's Colleges in America*.

33. Once again Sister Madeleva, C.S.C., was a significant cultural catalyst in this regard. She lamented the quality of religion classes in schools and colleges operated by nuns. Madeleva's interest in theology was longstanding, rooted in the belief that theology should be the integrating subject in a liberal education, "giving sequence, importance and validity to all other subjects." It was under her supervision that the first theological school for laypersons was opened in 1943 at St. Mary's College in Indiana. With this bold move, a cultural change emerged in religious formation programs. See Sister Mary Immaculate Creek, C.S.C., *A Panorama: 1844–1977, Saint Mary's College Notre Dame, Indiana* (Notre Dame, Ind.: Congregation of the Sisters of the Holy Cross, 1977), 93–100.

34. Kennelly, "Women Religious, the Intellectual Life, and Anti-Intellectualism," 63–64.

35. Sister Mary Loyola Hegarty, C.C.V.I., *Serving with Gladness: The Origin and History of the Congregation of the Sisters of Charity of the Incarnate Word, Houston, Texas* (Houston: Bruce, 1967), 393.

36. In part, this interest in the overall works of the congregation was self-serving, since any sister could be transferred to one of those works when new assignments were posted at the end of the academic year.

37. It is important to note that women religious were and are religious virtuosi. That is a term that has been applied to them and certainly does reflect a conscious attitude they had about themselves. For the most part, they lived out their vocational

choice as best they could and focused on getting on with their work—not on creating a spiritual paradigm.

38. These comments by Sr. Elizabeth Sueltenfuss, C.D.P., president, Our Lady of the Lake University, San Antonio, Texas, describe the courageous risk-taking that is a legacy of religious congregations of women in the United States. See Melanie M. Morey, "Leadership and Legacy: Is There a Future for the Past?" (Ed.D. diss., Harvard Graduate School of Education, 1995), 178.

39. The recognition of talent by superiors and the sequencing of their assignments made it possible at St. Mary's College in Notre Dame, Indiana, to have sixty-three years of administrative leadership under three different but gifted women who brought the college from infancy to maturity with spirit, imagination, wisdom, and extraordinary scope and reach. St. Mary's experience was not unique among Catholic colleges or congregations, whose histories are replete with stories of buildings built, programs crafted, donors approached, and dreams realized—all because dedicated and talented women truly believed "that if they just really abandoned themselves to this work and went in there and did it, God would not shove them off the cliff." See Morey, "Leadership and Legacy," 179.

40. Peter McDonough, *Men Astutely Trained: A History of the Jesuits in the American Century* (New York: Free Press, 1992), 9.

41. Quinonez and Turner, *Transformation of American Catholic Sisters*, 6. It also should be noted there could be alternate explanations for their comparatively greater responsiveness. It could also have been a reaction to the greater constraints placed on them by the law of the Church and also by the ministerial demands of local bishops.

42. Quinonez and Turner, *Transformation of American Catholic Sisters*, 10.

43. Tony Flannery, C.Ss.R., captures the spirit of many of the young women religious of the time. "For the younger religious it was a great time. They had freedom. They were full of heady excitement. The windows were open. All the old stale ways were going to be thrown aside. 'Relevance' was the word. The new-style religious life was no longer going to be shut off from the world. Instead it would engage with it, and bring it the message of salvation, not from the remote recesses of monasteries, convents and pulpits, but right there in the heart of the action." *The Death of Religious Life?* (Dublin: Columba Press, 1997), 42.

44. Congregations' claim of a prophetic role has its problems. As Richard P. McBrien points out, prophets stand apart from institutions and do not make claims that are self-aggrandizing. See Richard P. McBrien, ed., *Catholicism* (San Francisco: HarperCollins, 1994), 260–262. Religious congregations are organizations whose prophetic claims often serve to legitimate their own institutional choices. This motif is also antiinstitutional and cuts the congregations off from their own cultural history, as well as from the patriarchal Church they hope to critique. See Morey, "Leadership and Legacy," 99.

45. The seeds of the cultural reframing process for religious congregations of women Bartunek describes were first sown by Pope Pius XII in 1950. The pope convened the first General Assembly for Religious in 1950 that gathered together in Rome all the religious superiors in the world. Delegates received copies of the Pope's Apostolic Constitution, *Sponsa Christi*, which explained the purpose of their gathering. "We find some . . . things in the institutes of nuns which are neither necessary or complimentary; they are merely extrinsic and historical. And so we have decreed . . . to introduce cautiously and prudently those adaptations to present-day conditions which will be able to bring not only greater dignity but also greater efficacy to the institute." Adaptations certainly came, but the caution and careful pace the pontiff an-

ticipated most assuredly did not. The proceedings of this conference appeared in Latin in four volumes. For an abbreviated version, see P. Vius Gaiani, O.F.M., *For a Better Religious Life* (Staten Island, N.Y.: Alba House, 1963).

46. Patricia Wittberg, S.C., *Pathways to Re-Creating Religious Communities* (Mahwah, N.J.: Paulist Press, 1996), 88.

47. See Elissa Rinere, C.P., "Poverty: Now You See It, Now You Don't," *Review for Religious* 58, 2 (March–April 1999), 188. In speaking about the result of the renewal, she observes that "women religious became visible as individuals and invisible as religious."

48. The Vatican never formally approved this new interpretation, and congregations did not universally accept it. Nevertheless, it appealed to many sisters because it encouraged them to draw upon the tradition of Jesus as prophet who challenged the power structures of his day and to strategically speak out and act against injustice, especially situations that kept poor people marginalized in their own country and in global society. See Wittberg, *Rise and Fall of Catholic Religious Orders*, 233.

49. Patricia Wittberg's discussion of vow reinterpretation informs this analysis. See Wittberg, *Rise and Fall of Catholic Religious Orders*, 241–256.

50. JoAnn McNamara believes there is no turning back to practices that not only infantilized women religious but bored them as well. See JoAnn K. McNamara, *Sisters in Arms: Catholic Nuns through Two Millennia* (Cambridge, Mass.: Harvard University Press, 1996), 644.

51. In an article on interpreting the vow of poverty, Richard DeMaria points out that "the church has always recognized different valid ways to interpret the vows and has allowed each religious community latitude to develop its own understanding of the vow. . . . One interpretation of poverty was not considered better than another; they were different." That said, however, he makes it very clear that religious congregations need to have a clear way to live poverty that they can present to potential candidates. That clarity was certainly available to pre-Vatican II aspirants but is largely missing today. See Richard J. DeMaria, C.F.C., "Let's Talk Again about Poverty," *Review for Religious* 54, 4 (July–August 1995), 605.

52. William Reiser, S. J., "Reformulating the Religious Vows," *Review for Religious* 54, 4 (July–August, 1995), 596.

53. It is interesting to note that Reiser himself comes down quite directly in this camp. He says: "Committing oneself to living a preferential option for the poor would render the spirituality underlying religious life an essentially corporate and public matter. The option for the poor as the content of a religious vow would also underscore a profound gospel truth, namely, that the Christian search for God takes us to the side and the defense of our victimized neighbor." See Reiser, "Reformulating the Religious Vows," 599.

54. It must be said that men's congregations adopted these practices long before women religious and did so in order to be more effective and efficient in their ministerial works. While over time both men and women religious might have become accustomed to the ease that accompanied the availability of cars and spending money, and so on, their original adoption was for the sake of ministerial work, not personal comfort.

55. See Donna Markham, O.P., "Psychological Factors Influencing the Decline of and Persistence in Religious Vocations," unpublished paper. Donna Markham, O.P. 1257 E. Siena Heights Drive, Adrian, MI, 49221, 14, cited in Wittberg, *Rise and Fall of Catholic Religious Orders*, 249.

56. In the article in *Review for Religious* in the mid-1990s, Richard J. DeMaria,

C.F.C., described how religious men and women today appear to themselves and to much of the outside world in terms of their vow of poverty. "Many religious employ servants, live in high-rent apartments, drive expensive cars, dine in the best restaurants. We can be found in luxury resorts, on cruise ships. We take midwinter and midspring as well as fairly extensive summer vacations. We have personal bank accounts, personal resources. Our lives are not materially poor, nor for that matter simple." See DeMaria, "Let's Talk Again about Poverty," 600. Elissa Rinere, C.P., points out that in 1999, religious congregations were still unclear about how to understand and live out their vow of poverty in a post-Vatican II world. She asks: "How is it that I am vowed to poverty but unable to be materially poor? What has happened to this vow in my own life and my own community's life? Where has it gone? What does it look like now? What might it look like in the future?" See Rinere, "Poverty: Now You See It, Now You Don't," 185.

57. Also in 1999, Doris Gottemoeller, R.S.M., spoke directly to this issue in terms of community living. "I believe that our inability or unwillingness to answer the questions of what community living means today and what our common obligation or commitment is weakens our credibility internally and externally. . . . When we are ambiguous about this significant dimension of consecrated life, can we invite potential new members to explore this life?" See Doris Gottemoeller, R.S.M., "Community Living: Beginning the Conversation," *Review for Religious* 58, 2 (March–April 1999) 138.

58. The reimagining of authority, leadership, and obedience in the post-Vatican II environment was undertaken by religious orders of both men and women, though women shed almost completely the hierarchical structure.

59. Applications to religious orders, both male and female, worldwide, rose in the aftermath of World War II, but the phenomenon did not last. This contributed in part to the decline in applications between the years 1958 and 1965.

60. These figures came from the work of Marie Augusta Neal, S.N.D.deN., reported in Marie Augusta Neal, *Catholic Sisters in Transition,* and cited in Helen Rose Fuchs Ebaugh, *Women in the Vanishing Cloister: Organizational Decline in Catholic Religious Orders in the United States* (New Brunswick, N.J.: Rutgers University Press, 1993), 48.

61. These cohorts helped many women to keep the less appealing aspects of formation in proper perspective.

62. Ebaugh, *Women in the Vanishing Cloister,* 49.

63. Quinonez and Turner, *Transformation of American Catholic Sisters,* 157.

64. Women religious have had a longstanding interest in ordination. Doris Gottemoeller, R.S.M. indicates the breadth of that commitment, as well as the common perceptions that emerge in response to it. "The interest of women religious in ordination is shown by their longstanding participation in the women's ordination movement. The initial conference of the Women's Ordination Conference (WOC), held in Detroit in 1975, was largely organized by sisters, and the overwhelming majority of the attendees were sisters. WOC cofounder Dolly Pomerleau claims that without women religious, the organization would not exist. Over the course of years the leadership of WOC has passed into the hands of laywomen, but sisters are still disproportionately represented in the membership, on the board, and as participants at national gatherings. WOC treasurer and board member Maureen Fiedler, S.L., reports that the financial support of women's congregations and of individual sisters continues to be significant. So much is this the case that working for the ordination of women is popularly regarded as a sisters' issue. . . . The net effect of the factors we have identified

is that many Catholics assume that sisters in general want to be ordained or that ordination is a natural evolution in their ministerial commitment." See Doris Gottemoeller, R.S.M., "The Priesthood: Implications in Consecrated Life for Women," in *A Concert of Charism: Ordained Ministry in Religious Life*, ed. Paul K. Hennessy, C.F.C. (Mahwah, N.J.: Paulist Press, 1997), 130–131.

65. Attitudes within the WOC and attitudes among sisters regarding ordination are not identical. Doris Gottemoeller indicates that "the current tension within the women's ordination movement between continuing to espouse ordination to the priesthood as a goal versus working for a 'discipleship of equals' in which the priesthood is radically recast is reflected among sisters, as well." See Gottemoeller, "Priesthood," 130.

66. Cited in Morey, "Leadership and Legacy," 168.

67. While this understanding of religious life emerged in the early 1980s, it still holds sway. A number of sources have dealt with the topic in the last decade. A small sample includes Sandra Schneiders, I.H.M., *Finding the Treasure: Locating Catholic Religious Life in a New Ecclesial and Cultural Context* (New York: Paulist Press, 2000), Nadine Foley, ed., *Journey in Faith and Fidelity: Women Shaping Religious Life for a Renewed Church* (New York: Continuum, 1999), Joan Chittister, O.S.B., *The Fire in These Ashes: A Spirituality of Contemporary Religious Life* (Kansas City: Sheed Ward, 1995).

68. Gerald Arbuckle does attempt to make these linkages. See "Prophecy or Restorationism in Religious Life," in *The Church and Consecrated Life: The Best of the Review—5*, ed. David L. Fleming, S.J., and Elizabeth McDonough, O.P. (St. Louis, Mo.: Review for Religious, 1996), 295–308. Arbuckle insists that religious congregations were founded as "prophetic reactions" to abuses or corruption of power within the Church and therefore prophetic action is integral to the founding story of religious life. This particular view of congregations as prophetic witness communities requires they be distinct and that individuals join them. They are a visible witness calling forth a response from the community. In religious congregations of women, however, some of the most courageous acts of prophecy are considered to be the times when the congregations go out of existence and disappear on a matter of principle. Such was the case in Los Angeles when the majority of Immaculate Heart of Mary Sisters was willing to disband rather than accept the interference of Cardinal McIntyre in the internal renewal process of their congregation. For two views on this interaction see Massa, S.J. (1999), 172–194; Anita Marie Caspary, *Witness to Integrity: The Crisis of the Immaculate Heart Community of California* (Collegeville, Minn.: Liturgical Press, 2003).

69. Lora Ann Quinonez, C.D.P., and Mary Daniel Turner, S.N.D.deN., describe how this vision of the purpose of religious congregation burst forth at LCWR from the original mandate for renewal. "In the late sixties . . . the Conference took a fresh look at itself as an organization. Believing themselves responsible for framing and acting on the mission of the church in the world, the leaders of sisters' communities were convinced that the Conference had to be assertive. It must invest itself in fashioning a church faithful to Gospel values, responsive to the concrete historical reality, and capable of offering alternatives to unjust systems and practices. 'Participating in the transformation of the world' became, as it were, a consuming passion of leaders of American communities. Establishing a Peace and Justice Office and securing nongovernmental status at the United Nations in the early seventies are indices of the Conference's new orientation toward the use of corporate power and moral agency." See Quinonez and Turner, *Transformation of American Catholic Sisters*, 129.

70. The strain between women religious and the Church has not disappeared with time. One of the findings of the Brookland study makes that quite clear. In de-

scribing religious congregations in the mid-1990s, Katrina Schuth, O.S.F., says: "Many congregations are struggling with their relationship to the church in light of the tensions about the status of women. Energy is devoted to inclusive language and other women's concerns related to the church. These tensions are brought to bear in the kind of education that is sought and provided, and the kinds of ministries sisters are choosing." See Schuth, "Intellectual Life as a Value for Women Religious in the United States," 25.

71. Caspary, *Witness to Integrity*.

72. Walter Brueggemann's insights about prophetic imagination inspire a great deal of the writing about the prophetic role of women religious. The ideas to which Elizabeth Dreyer refers can be found in: Walter Brueggemann, *The Prophetic Imagination* (Minneapolis: Fortress Press, 1976), 13. They are cited in Elizabeth A. Dreyer, "Prophetic Voice in Religious Life," *Review for Religious* 62, 3 (2003), 256.

73. One reason monitoring and recalibration of the course of renewal did not occur may be that religious based their willingness to experiment on an erroneous assumption. According to Doris Gottemoeller, "the so-called 'experimentation' was built on an erroneous premise of scientific objectivity and control, namely, that if we could change, for example, our way of praying or relating to one another in community for a given period of time and if the results were not what had been anticipated, we could revert back to the *status quo ante*." If women religious held this belief on even the most subconscious level, it explains their willingness to engage in cultural change of massive proportions with almost no evaluative mechanisms built into the process. See Doris Gottemoeller, R.S.M., "Has the Renewal of Religious Life Been Successful?" *Review for Religious* 55, 1 (January–February, 1996), 65.

74. Quinonez and Turner, *Transformation of American Catholic Sisters*, 129.

75. This competitive erosion was surprising, since one feature of Catholic culture in the first half of the twentieth century was the very strong competition among religious congregations. Many students strongly identified with the particular congregation they had as teachers in this era and touted its unique virtues over those of other religious congregations. In any event, weak competition in the aftermath of Vatican II prevented sisters from trying distinctly different strategies to attract young women to enter religious life. Most emerging congregations have distanced themselves from operating as a prophetic voice within the Church and have focused more on being visible supporters of traditional Catholicism. This strategy is reinvigorating a competitive alternative for women who might be interested in a vocation to the sisterhood. As long as this different approach is appreciated as a competitive choice and not demonized as a false alternative in a battle for the hearts and minds of Catholic sisters, it should prove invigorating for the Church.

76. Lora Ann Quinonez, C.D.P., and Mary Daniel Turner, S.N.D.deN., give insights into how the LCWR became an organization that united sisters nationally. In our view, the cohesion gained through participation in the LCWR engendered a substantial liability; it undermined the possibility for creative competition that might have proved helpful in creating diverse approaches to renewal. Without noting any liability, Quinonez and Daniel Turner make a powerful case for the prominent role the LCWR played in the reimagining of religious life for women. "It was the LCWR, however, that brought sisters face to face with religious life as an institution in the church, with generalized concepts of 'religious life,' with a common awareness of the poor fit between formal church teaching on religious life and the life of flesh-and-blood American sisters. It was the Conference that provided an arena and tools for a collective orientation toward the renewal mandated by Vatican II. It was the Conference

that often served as a channel of information and communication about what was taking place in individual communities as they pursued the expectations generated by the Council. It was in the Conference that the heads of communities began to risk voicing to one another their anxieties about Vatican reactions to American developments. It was to the Conference that the women increasingly looked for the education, research, and reflection needed for a new formulation of religious identity. The Conference, in short, was where the women learned to talk to one another. And that talk quite literally gave birth to new women." See Quinonez and Turner, *Transformation of American Catholic Sisters*, 109.

77. Stark and Finke, *Acts of Faith*, 120.

78. Stark and Finke, *Acts of Faith*, 120.

79. Edgar Schein, *Organizational Culture and Leadership* (San Francisco: Jossey-Bass, 1992), 228.

80. Rosabeth Moss Kanter, *Commitment and Community: Communes and Utopias in Sociological Perspective* (Cambridge, Mass.: Harvard University Press, 1972), 66–67.

81. An example of this flexibility is the modification in focus that developed as educational needs changed. By the mid-twentieth century, the education levels of some young women entering religious congregations had increased. For others, juniorates provided the opportunity for nuns to receive their professional education. At that point, the emphasis in formation shifted more toward commitment, since the knowledge needs of young women were already effectively attended.

82. When the future and livelihood of the congregations was threatened after the Second Vatican Council because of the dearth of novices, having a bold, knowledgeable leader empowered to lead became a critical necessity. However, a structure to produce such leadership no longer existed. Consensus may be a fine form of governance for religious women in certain circumstances, but it proved ineffectual when decisions needed to be made to redirect congregations.

CHAPTER 10

1. Edgar Schein, *Organizational Culture and Leadership*. San Francisco: Jossey-Bass, 5. Schein's characterization of administrators as living within the culture does not correspond completely to our terminology and analysis, since we acknowledge that some administrators are cultural catalysts, that is, people actively molding the culture even though they live within it.

2. The term "connective" appears directly in the literature, particularly in the work of Jean Lipman-Blumen; see "The Age of Connective Leadership," in *On Leading Change*, ed. Frances Hesselbein and Rob Johnston (San Francisco: Jossey-Bass, 2002), 89–102.

3. James McGregor Burns, *Leadership* (New York: Harper and Row, 1978), 1–4.

4. According to the Merriam-Webster unabridged dictionary, *bricoleur* is a French word for someone who makes a sculpture out of whatever comes to hand. Frances Westley and Henry Mintzberg use the term to designate one of five leadership styles in evidence in government and corporate setting. See Frances Westley and Henry Mintzberg, "Visionary Leadership and Strategic Management," *Strategic Management Journal* 10 (1989), 27.

5. Joseph Crowley provides an excellent review of various presidential typologies, as well as detailing the literary depictions of college and university presidents that have gone a long way toward shaping the mythic understanding of this elusive office and the individuals who might occupy it. See Joseph N. Crowley, *No Equal in the*

World: An Interpretation of the Academic Presidency (Reno: University of Nevada Press, 1994), 143.

6. Lipman-Blumen, "Age of Connective Leadership," 91.

7. Henry Mintzberg, "Managing Quietly," in *On Mission and Leadership*, ed. Frances Hesselbein and Rob Johnston (San Francisco: Jossey-Bass, 2002), 75.

8. In their typology of college presidents and collegiate settings, Clark Kerr and Marian Gade present a model of shared governance and consensus whose center of influence is the president. See Clark Kerr and Marian Gade, *The Many Lives of Academic Presidents: Time, Place and Character* (Washington, D.C.: Association of Governing Boards of Universities and Colleges, 1989), 133–157.

9. According to the analysis of Cameron and Quinn, being a facilitator and a mentor are leadership roles of paramount import in organizational settings that resemble clan culture. See Kim S. Cameron and Robert E. Quinn, *Diagnosing and Changing Organizational Culture: Based on the Competing Values Framework* (Reading, Mass.: Addison-Wesley, 1999), 36–38.

10. Peter M. Senge, "Lessons for Change Leaders," in *On Leading Change*, eds. Frances Hesselbein and Rob Johnston (San Francisco: Jossey-Bass, 2002), 27.

11. This commitment to the faith does not necessarily mean belief. It is quite possible that some of the senior administrators hired by the connective president are not Catholic. It is necessary, however, that these individuals respect the faith and are committed to its being a defining force in the institution.

12. Burns, *Leadership*, 373.

13. Westley and Mintzberg, "Visionary Leadership and Strategic Management," 25.

14. Kerr and Gade, *Many Lives of Academic Presidents*, 67.

15. Cameron and Quinn, *Diagnosing and Changing Organizational Culture*, 206. These characteristics are particularly true of the visionary presidential type Cameron and Quinn describe as leading in cultural adhocracies.

16. James Fisher maintains that charismatic leadership has been viewed for centuries by philosophers as the most effective form of leadership. He also indicates that research continues to suggest that charisma effectively inspires others to follow and support a leader. See James L. Fisher, *Power of the Presidency* (New York: Macmillan, 1984), 39–42.

17. Fisher, *Power of the Presidency*, 40.

18. Nidiffer draws upon the work of a number of theorists in this group. They include: Estela M. Bensimon, Anna Neuman, and Robert Birnbaum, "Making Sense of Administrative Leadership: The "L" Word in Higher Education," in *ASHE-ERIC Higher Education Report 1, 1090* (Washington, D.C.: School of Education and Human Development, George Washington University, 1989), Jana Nidiffer, "New Leadership for a New Century," in *Women Administrators in Higher Education*, ed. Jana Nidiffer and Carolyn Terry Bashaw (Albany: State University of New York Press, 2001), 107.

19. Sister Mary Immaculate Creek, C.S.C., *A Panorama: 1844–1977, Saint Mary's College, Notre Dame, Indiana* (Notre Dame, Ind.: Congregation of the Sisters of the Holy Cross, 1977), 130.

20. Theodore Hesburgh, C.S.C., *God, Country, and Notre Dame* (New York: Fawcett Columbine, 1990), 64–65.

21. Hesburgh, *God, Country, and Notre Dame*, 62.

22. Edgar Schein points out that any team that hopes to unleash transformative change must determine the gap between the ideal future and the present reality. He cautions, however, that a change team of all insiders "is likely to misperceive the state

of the culture, or not perceive it at all because team members are so embedded in it."
See Edgar Schein, *The Corporate Culture Survival Guide* (San Francisco: Jossey-Bass,
1999), 135.

23. Kim Cameron and Robert Quinn discovered that leaders who were rated by
their peers, superiors, and subordinates as most highly effective were ambidextrous
leaders. While that may well be the ideal, most individuals have a dominant style or
mode of leadership that operates as a default position, and it takes extraordinary talent and significant discipline for leaders to slide effortlessly from one style to another
depending on the needs of the organization. See Cameron and Quinn, *Diagnosing
and Changing Organizational Culture*, 42.

24. Trustees who are nuns, brothers, and priests often have an extensive background in Catholic higher education. On many boards of trustees at Catholic institutions, one or two presidents of other Catholic institutions serve as trustees, and they
certainly have extensive knowledge of the market of higher education. However, most
presidents serving as trustees are reluctant to challenge the president of the university
at a board meeting. At best, they are willing to provide behind-the-scenes advice and
criticism to the reigning university president.

25. There are a number of institutions that were founded by laypersons or operate under the auspices of a local diocese or have pontifical status, and the historical
modifications of their governance situations are somewhat different. For further discussion of developments in governance at Catholic colleges and universities see
Morey and Holtschneider, "Relationship Revisited: Catholic Institutions and Their
Founding Congregations," Association of Governing Boards of Universities and Colleges occasional paper no. 47 (September 2000), and Melanie M. Morey, in *Catholic
Women's Colleges in America*, ed. Tracy Schier and Cynthia Russet (Baltimore: Johns
Hopkins University Press, 2002),

26. In many cases, presidents bring personal expertise to bear in these situations. In circumstances where that is not the case, they can depend on staff to help
bring them up to speed.

27. Edgar Schein, "How Can Organizations Learn Faster? The Challenge of Entering the Green Room," *Sloan Management Review* 34 (February 1993), 299.

28. Richard P. Chait, Thomas P. Holland, and Barbara E. Taylor, *Improving the
Performance of Governing Boards* (Phoenix, Ariz.: Oryx Press, 1996), 26.

29. As is the case in other areas of the university, trustees receive a great number of reports. For the most part, the reports analyze where the university is. In some
cases, administration uses such reports to justify a change in policy with respect to an
individual area. Only rarely do trustees take specific actions based on data. One such
circumstance, however, is the approval of the annual budget or multiyear budget proposed by administration.

30. William G. Bowen, *Inside the Boardroom* (New York: Wiley, 1994), 24.

31. Chait, Holland, and Taylor, *Improving the Performance of Governing Boards*, 14.

32. One could argue that a "Catholic cultural cluster" of trustees consisting of,
say, only 20 percent of the trustees would be sufficient to fulfill the Catholic board
responsibilities, similar to what we argued for the Catholic cultural cluster or CIC
among faculty. But the board is the legal governing board, and one cannot rely upon
norms of deference and prestige. If a university prefers to have a small group of
knowledgeable and committed Catholics as the Catholic guardians, there is a legal
structure that can accommodate this by reserving power to a select group over issues
pertaining to the religious mission, identity, and culture of the institution. See Morey,
"Relationship Revisited," 298–302, for a discussion of reserved powers.

33. Some Catholic universities have two-tier governance structures comprised usually of two bodies. The upper body consists solely of founding congregation members and has ultimate authority over any issues reserved to them by statute. This group is usually called the members of the corporation. The second body is the board of trustees, and it has all powers not reserved specifically to the members of the corporation. The most common powers reserved to the members of the corporation include decisions relating to amending governing documents, purchase or sale of property, dissolution of the corporation, and the mission and identity of the institution. Although mission and identity are frequently reserved powers, the board of trustees is expected to share responsibility for religious character and mission and provide oversight.

34. Robert T. Kennedy, "Shared Responsibility in Ecclesial Decision-Making," Excerpt from *Studia Canonica*, vol. 14, no. 1 (Ottawa: Saint Paul University, 1980), 5–6. Plato's parable about a ship, captain, and crew offers useful insights about the importance of knowledge in situations of shared governance. See *The Republic Book 6*, trans. H.D.P. Lee (Baltimore: Penguin Books, 1955), 249–250, 488–489.

35. As indicated earlier, the last option is viable for the trustees only after they have secured permission from the appropriate ecclesiastical authority.

36. At the present time, institutions with the same religious sponsors often share information about new or existing programs. They do not, however, share data on inputs, outcomes, and financial commitments pertinent to Catholic culture.

37. Robert T. Kennedy, "Note on the Canonical Status of Church-Related Institutions in the United States," in *New Commentary on the Code of Canon Law*, ed. John P. Beal, James A. Coriden, and Thomas J. Green (New York: Paulist Press, 2000), 172.

38. For a more in-depth discussion of the history and interpretation of canonical and civil law status, see Robert T. Kennedy, "McGrath, Maida, Michiels: Introduction to a Study of the Canonical and Civil-Law Status of Church-Related Institutions in the United States," *Jurist* 50 (1990). For a discussion of how these issues pertain particularly to Catholic colleges and universities and the religious congregations that sponsor them, see Morey, "Relationship Revisited," 287–291.

39. Kennedy, "McGrath, Maida, Michiels," 353, 358.

40. The kinds of difficulties that can emerge were well illustrated when the board of trustees of St. Louis University Hospital attempted to sell the hospital to Tenet Healthcare. Archbishop Justin Rigali of St. Louis opposed the sale because he maintained the Board had not fulfilled its obligations under ecclesial law to alienate the property. See Morey, "Relationship Revisited," 416n.

CHAPTER 11

1. It should be said that in the typical four-year undergraduate program, no Catholic university can provide the knowledge that comes from regular practice and instruction over many years in grade school and high school.

2. Long-term outcomes should be of particular interest to Catholic colleges and universities. It is quite common for young men and women to take a step back from the practice of their religion when in college as part of a developmental process that allows them to claim their faith, not just inherit it. To the extent that this is the case, data collected at graduation could appear unnecessarily alarming. If, however, Catholic colleges and universities can demonstrate that graduates mature into their faith and have greater knowledge and commitment that develops over time, developmental is-

sues not programmatic weaknesses would be the most likely cause of apparent "weakening faith."

3. This judgment is based both on the comments of senior administrators and our knowledge of higher education.

4. This scenario has a straightforward policy application: in the absence of new challenges coming from the dominant secular culture, continue to manage the Catholic culture as one has been doing.

5. This may be a future problem. The comments of senior administrators at immersion institutions did not suggest that this is a difficulty at present.

6. New Catholic University will open in San Diego. The new University of Sacramento, sponsored by the Legionaries of Christ, is in the planning stage, as is one in Thornwood, New York, also sponsored by the Legionaries of Christ. Southern Catholic College in Atlanta has accepted its first class of students, as has Ave Maria University in Florida (eventually to be located in Immokalee, Florida). Another university, probably adhering to the persuasion model, is being planned by the Christian Brothers for Sacramento, California.

7. See Thomas M. Landy, "The Colleges in Context," in *Catholic Women's Colleges in America*, ed. Tracy Schier and Cynthia Russet (Baltimore: Johns Hopkins University Press, 2002), 55–97.

8. Other appropriate words or designation that more closely fit the academic structure of a particular college or university could obviously be substituted.

9. Prestige is the coin of the realm in American higher education, and colleges are quite adept at enhancing the prestige of groups when they choose. Many universities attract outstanding students by establishing presidential scholars programs. One of the greatest attractions of these programs is the face time they provide with the president. It is certainly possible for a Catholic university president to enhance Catholic programmatic efforts by spending some time with students who choose to be "Catholic scholars." There are other ways to indicate that a student's involvement in the Catholic components of the academic experience is valued by those who run the institution.

10. Some will question why any text other than the Catechism of the Catholic Church should be used. The Catechism is certainly a comprehensive text, but it may be too detailed for some institutions. Alternatively, some universities may choose the Catechism as the reference text and only choose to examine students on some sections of it. Universities who choose texts other than the Catechism presumably will do so because the material in the assigned book is more accessible and circumscribed.

11. If the courses are advertised in this way, administrators have to work with faculty to make sure the material in each course or section is presented clearly and that the questions of students are dealt with seriously.

12. In reality, many of the costs for educating the faculty member in the Catholic tradition would be incurred in the first ten years the teacher is at the university. Introducing such plausible assumptions changes the total cost per year but, abstracting from inflation and time-discounting, not the total cost over forty years.

13. Many Catholic universities have in-service programs for their faculty members. To the extent that the faculty education programs being discussed here are distinctly different from what is currently done at the university and are retained, the total cost represents a net addition to the current expenditures on faculty.

14. If the university has a business school or school of education, each such

school can be counted as a single academic discipline, or if the school has many departments, the larger departments can be counted as individual departments.

15. This is an estimate of funds that should be made available for the annual training of Catholic faculty at an institution similar to the characteristics we have described. How these funds are expended is, of course, an important issue, though not one we handle here in any detail. It is to be expected, however, that most universities will provide faculty members with a stipend for participating in the Catholic intellectual seminars, conferences, or meetings proposed here. These stipends would cover a portion of what economists call the opportunity costs of faculty attending the instructional sessions. Providing stipends is certainly praiseworthy. However, the cost of stipends should be added to the sum of $70,000 since the example developed in the text made no provision for opportunity costs. Making this adjustment and depending on the size of the stipend, the annual expense for educating Catholic intellectual tradition would be approximately 1.5 percent of total annual faculty compensation in the example in the text.

CHAPTER 12

1. In the public square there is a fair amount of discussion about religious belief in relation to pressing social issues such as stem cell research, homosexual marriage, and abortion. The Christian Coalition has for some time been deeply involved in electoral politics. The civil rights movement in the 1960s was fueled by church leadership. Religious leaders as diverse as Pat Robertson, Jesse Jackson, Louis Farrakhan, Billy Graham, Martin Luther King, and Robert Drinan, S.J., have been prominent in electoral politics and public debate. Nevertheless, the dominant American culture still operates from the schizophrenic position of wanting its public discourse and political life to be conducted by people who have private religious convictions but who refer to them in only the broadest terms.

2. See Leszek Kolakowski, *Modernity on Endless Trial* (Chicago: University of Chicago Press, 1990), 69, quoted in Glenn W. Olsen, *Beginning at Jerusalem: Five Reflections on the History of the Church* (San Francisco: Ignatius, 2004), 151–152.

3. Of course, a richer appreciation of Catholic universities as something different from nonsectarian universities does not in any way suggest that these institutions should be less than universities. A religious heritage is not an excuse to operate in a substandard way. Nevertheless, the religious character of a university, if it is to be distinctive to the enterprise, cannot be relegated to a small area that is simply added on to an otherwise nonsectarian institution, much the way a garage is added onto a house.

4. According to Safire, the term *groupthink* was coined by the psychologist Irving Janus in 1970. *Conventional wisdom*, on the other hand, was coined in 1958 by John Kenneth Galbraith and is derived from the fourteenth-century Church term for the teaching of tradition. See William Safire, "Language: 'Groupthink' as a Collaborative Search," *New York Times*, Monday, August 9, 2004.

5. Van Engen believes that what the Catholic world today most needs are figures like Thomas Aquinas who can sort through contemporary philosophy and "rescue its most congruent features for Catholic learning." See John Van Engen, "Historic Past or Distinctive Future?" in Theodore M. Hesburgh, C.S.C., ed. (Notre Dame, Ind.: University of Notre Dame Press, 1994), 365.

6. Catholic philosophy can include a broad array of topics. For proposals about what would most appropriate to present to students in modern Catholic philosophy

see Martin R. Tripole, S.J., ed., *Jesuit Education 21: Conference Proceedings on the Future of Jesuit Higher Education* (Philadelphia: Saint Joseph's University Press, 2000), 138–159, and Martin R. Tripole, S.J., ed., *Promise Renewed: Jesuit Higher Education for a New Millennium* (Chicago: Loyola Press), 245–266.

7. Lindsay Waters, "Bonfire of the Humanities," *Village Voice*, August 30, 2004.

8. The disappointing exceptions to the rule that student-athletes are above-average students most often emerge among students participating in high-profile programs at universities that are nationally competitive in a particular sport.

9. In earlier times, when lay faculty members were predominantly Catholic, it was assumed that they would attend Sunday Mass in their parishes. Students on campus would see members of the sponsoring religious congregation attending Mass on campus or engaged in other types of prayer. Especially as the number of sisters, brothers, or priests on campus decreases, occasions for students to worship together with other members of the university community are becoming increasingly rare.

APPENDIX B

1. In a small number of cases (about 6 percent), there was a malfunction of the recording apparatus, and interviewers had to rely on notes they had taken during the interviews.

2. This researcher completed analysis reports but did not participate in the rest of the structured analysis phase of the project.

3. This last provision was rooted in the researchers' hope that the study report would provide enough information so that administrators could contact each other to discuss various insights that might prove interesting, provocative, or helpful.

4. The piqued interest in comparative performance and understanding of other institutional experience was much more pronounced among lay participants in the study. Men and women religious seemed to have a more reliable network for exchanging information about these issues. A comparable network does not seem to exist for lay administrators at Catholic colleges and universities, or if it does, they do not rely on it for information concerning leadership and practice in the area of Catholic identity.

Bibliography

Acemoglu, Daron. "Technical Change, Inequality, and the Labor Market."
  Journal of Economic Literature 40, 1 (2002).
Arbuckle, Gerald. "Prophecy or Restorationism in Religious Life?" In *The
  Church and Consecrated Life: The Best of the Review,* edited by David L.
  Fleming, S.J., and Elizabeth McDonough, O.P. St. Louis, Mo.: Review
  for Religious, 1996.
Becker, Lawrence C., and Charlotte B. Becker, eds. *A History of Western
  Ethics.* 2nd ed. New York: Routledge, 2003.
Bellah, Robert N. "Habit and History." *Ethical Perspectives* 8, 3 (2001).
Bensimon, Estela M., Anna Neuman, and Robert Birnbaum. "Making Sense
  of Administrative Leadership: The 'L' Word in Higher Education." In
  ASHE-ERIC *Higher Education Report 1, 1090.* Washington, D.C.: School
  of Education and Human Development, George Washington Univer-
  sity, 1989.
Bernheim, B. Douglas. "A Theory of Conformity." *Journal of Political Econ-
  omy* 102, 5 (1994).
Blaney, Dorothy. "Who Should Pay the Bill for a Private Education?" *Chroni-
  cle of Higher Education,* April 2, 2004, B24.
Bowen, William G. *Inside the Boardroom.* New York: Wiley, 1994.
Breneman, David W. *Liberal Arts Colleges: Thriving, Surviving, or Endangered?*
  Washington, D.C.: Brookings Institution, 1994.
Bretzke, James T. *A Morally Complex World: Engaging Contemporary Moral
  Theology.* Collegeville, Minn.: Liturgical Press, 2004.
Brewer, Eileen M. *Nuns and the Education of American Catholic Women 1860–
  1920.* Chicago: Loyola University Press, 1987.
Brueggemann, Walter. *The Prophetic Imagination.* Minneapolis: Fortress
  Press, 1976.
Bryk, Anthony S., Valerie E. Lee, and Peter B. Holland. *Catholic Schools and
  the Common Good.* Cambridge, Mass.: Harvard University Press, 1993.
Buckley, Michael J. *The Catholic University as Promise and Project.* Washing-
  ton, D.C.: Georgetown University Press, 1998.

Burns, James McGregor. *Leadership*. New York: Harper and Row, 1978.

Burtchaell, James T., C.S.C. *The Dying of the Light*. Grand Rapids, Mich.: Eerdman, 1998.

Cahill, Lisa Sowle. *Sex, Gender, and Christian Ethics*. Cambridge: Cambridge University Press, 1996.

Cameron, Kim S., and Robert E. Quinn. *Diagnosing and Changing Organizational Culture: Based on the Competing Values Framework*. Reading, Mass.: Addison-Wesley, 1999.

Cantosta, David. "The Philadelphia Story: Life at Immaculata, Rosemont, and Chestnut Hill." In *Catholic Women's Colleges in America*, edited by Tracy Schier and Cynthia Russet. Baltimore: Johns Hopkins University Press, 2002.

Caspary, Anita Marie. *Witness to Integrity: The Crisis of the Immaculate Heart Community of Caifornia*. Collegeville, Minn.: Liturgical Press, 2003.

Catechism of the Catholic Church. Vatican City: Librerria Editrice Vaticana, 1997.

Cavadini, John C. "Ignorant Catholics: The Alarming Void in Religious Education." *Commonweal* 131, 7 (2004).

Chadwick, Owen. *The Secularization of the European Mind in the Nineteenth Century*. Cambridge: Cambridge University Press, 1975.

Chait, Richard P., Thomas P. Holland, and Barbara E. Taylor, *Improving the Performance of Governing Boards*. Phoenix, Ariz.: Oryx Press, 1996.

Chittister, Joan, O.S.B. *The Fire in These Ashes: A Spirituality of Contemporary Religious Life*. Kansas City: Sheed Ward, 1995.

Coburn, Carol, and Martha Smith. *Spirited Lives: How Nuns Shaped Catholic Culture and American Life, 1836–1920*. Chapel Hill: University of North Carolina Press, 1999.

Creek, Mary Immaculate, C.S.C. *A Panorama: 1844–1977, Saint Mary's College Notre Dame, Indiana*. Notre Dame, Ind.: Congregation of the Sisters of the Holy Cross, 1977.

Crowley, Joseph N. *No Equal in the World: An Interpretation of the Academic Presidency*. Reno: University of Nevada Press, 1994.

Daigler, Mary Jeremy. *Through the Windows: A History of the Work of Higher Education among the Sisters of Mercy of the Americas*. Scranton, Pa.: University of Scranton Press, 2000.

D'Antonio, William V., James D. Davidson, Dean R. Hoge, and Katherine Meyer. *American Catholics: Gender, Generation, and Commitment*. New York: Rowman and Littlefield, 2001

Deal, Terrence E., and Allan A. Kennedy. *Corporate Cultures: The Rites and Rituals of Corporate Life*. Reading, Mass.: Addison-Wesley, 1982.

DeMaria, Richard J., C.F.C. "Let's Talk Again about Poverty." *Review for Religious* 54, 4 (July–August 1995).

de Ridder-Symoens, Hilde, ed. *Universities in Early Modern Europe*. Vol. 2 of *A History of the University in Europe*. New York: Cambridge University Press, 1996.

———. *Universities in the Middle Ages*. Vol. 1 of *A History of the University in Europe*. Cambridge: Cambridge University Press, 2003.

Dinges, William, Dean R. Hoge, Mary Johnson, and Juan L. Gonzales, Jr. "A Faith Loosely Held: The Institutional Allegiance of Young Catholics." *Commonweal*, July 17, 1998.

Dreyer, Elizabeth A., "Prophetic Vision in Religious Life." *Review for Religious*, 62, 3 (2003).

Ebaugh, Helen Rose Fuchs. *Women in the Vanishing Cloister*. New Brunswick, N.J.: Rutgers University Press, 1993.

Egan, Gerard. *Working the Shadow Side: A Guide to Positive Behind-the-Scenes Management*. San Francisco: Jossey-Bass, 1994.

Ellis, John Tracy. "American Catholics and the Intellectual Life." *Thought* 30 (Autumn 1955).

Finnis, John. *Aquinas: Moral, Political, and Legal Theory*. New York: Oxford University Press, 1998.

———. *Fundamentals of Ethics*. Oxford: Clarendon, 1982.

———. *Natural Law and Natural Rights*. Oxford: Clarendon, 1980.

Fisher, James L. *Power of the Presidency*. New York: Macmillan, 1984.

Fitzgerald, Paul A. *The Governance of Jesuit Colleges in the United States, 1920–1970*. Notre Dame, Ind.: University of Notre Dame Press, 1984.

Flannery, Tony, C.S.s.R. *The Death of Religious Life?* Dublin: Columba Press, 1997.

Fogarty, Gerald P., S.J. *The Vatican and the American Hierarchy from 1870 to 1965*. Collegeville, Minn.: Liturgical Press, 1985.

Foley, Nadine, ed. *Journey in Faith and Fidelity: Women Shaping Religious Life for a Renewed Church*. New York: Continuum, 1999.

Gallin, Alice, O.S.U. *Negotiating Identity: Catholic Higher Education since 1960*. Notre Dame, Ind.: University of Notre Dame Press, 2000.

Gaiani, P. Vius, O.F.M. *For a Better Religious Life*. Staten Island, N.Y.: Alba House, 1963.

Ganns, George E., S.J. *Saint Ignatius' Idea of a Jesuit University: A Study in the History of Catholic Education*. Milwaukee: Marquette University Press, 1956.

Geertz, Clifford. *The Interpretation of Cultures*. New York: Basic Books, 1973.

Gleason, Philip. *Contending with Modernity: Catholic Higher Education in the Twentieth Century*. New York: Oxford University Press, 1995.

Gottemoeller, Doris, R.S.M. "Community Living: Beginning the Conversation." *Review for Religious* 58, 2 (March–April 1999).

———. "Has the Renewal of Religious Life Been Successful?" *Review for Religious* 55, 1 (January–February 1996).

Grisez, Germain. "A Contemporary Natural-Law Ethics." In *Moral Philosophy: Historical and Contemporary Essays*, edited by William C. Starr and Richard C. Taylor. Milwaukee: Marquette University Press, 1989.

Gutek, Gerald L. *A History of the Western Educational Experience*. 2nd. ed. Prospect Heights, Ill.: Waveland Press, 1972.

Hall, Edward. *The Silent Language*. New York: Anchor Books, 1991.

Haughey, John C., S.J. "Faculty Research and Catholic Identity." In *Theological Education in the Catholic Tradition: Contemporary Challenges*, edited by Patrick W. Carey and Earl C. Muller, S.J.. New York: Crossroad, 1997.

Hayes, Edward J., Paul J. Hayes, Dorothy Ellen Kelly, and James J. Drummey. *Catholicism and Ethics*. Norwood, Mass.: C.R., 1997.

Heaney, Stephen J. "The Catholic University Project: What Kind of Curriculum Does It Require?" In *Enhancing Religious Identity: Best Practices from Catholic Campuses*, edited by John R. Wilcox and Irene King. Washington, D.C.: Georgetown University Press, 2000.

Hegarty, Mary Loyola, C.C.V.I. *Serving with Gladness: The Origin and History of the Congregation of the Sisters of Charity of the Incarnate Word, Houston, Texas*. Houston: Bruce, 1967.

Hennessy, Paul K., C.F.C., ed. *A Concert of Charism: Ordained Ministry in Religious Life*. Mahwah, N.J.: Paulist Press, 1997.

Hesburgh, Theodore M., C.S.C., ed. *The Challenge and Promise of a Catholic University*. Notre Dame, Ind.: University of Notre Dame Press, 1994.

———. *God, Country, and Notre Dame*. New York: Fawcett Columbine, 1990.

Hittinger, Russell. *The First Grace: Rediscovering the Natural Law in a Post-Christian World*. Wilmington, Del.: ISI Books, 2003.

Hoge, Dean R. "Catholic Generational Differences: Can We Learn Anything by Identifying the Specific Issues of Generational Agreement and Disagreement?" *America* 181, 9 (1999).

Hoge, Dean R., William D. Dinges, Mary Johnson, and Juan L. Gonzales, Jr. *Young Adult Catholics: Religion in the Culture of Choice*. Notre Dame, Ind.: University of Notre Dame Press, 2001.

Hunter, James Davison. "Leading Children beyond Good and Evil." *First Things* 103 (2000).

Imbelli, Robert P. "Christ the Center." In *Examining the Catholic Intellectual Tradition*, vol. 2, edited by Anthony J. Cernera and Oliver J. Morgan. Fairfield, Conn.: Sacred Heart University Press, 2002.

Jaeger, C. Stephen. *The Envy of Angels: Cathedral Schools and Social Ideals in Medieval Europe, 950–1200*. Philadelphia: University of Pennsylvania Press, 1994.

Kant, Immanuel. *Prolegomena to Any Future Metaphysics*. Translated by Lewis W. Beck, revised by P. Carus. New York: Prentice-Hall, 1950.

Kanter, Rosabeth Moss. *Commitment and Community: Communes and Utopias in Sociological Perspective*. Cambridge: Harvard University Press, 1972.

Kennedy, Robert T. "McGrath, Maida, Michiels: Introduction to a Study of the Canonical and Civil-Law Status of Church-Related Institutions in the United States," *Jurist* 50 (1990).

———. "Note on the Canonical Status of Church-Related Institutions in the United States." In *New Commentary on the Code of Canon Law*, edited by John P. Beal, James A. Coriden, and Thomas J. Green. New York: Paulist Press, 2000.

———. "Shared Responsibility in Ecclesial Decision-Making." *Studia Canonica* (Ottawa: Saint Paul University) 14, 1 (1980).

Kennelly, Karen, C.S.J. "Women Religious, the Intellectual Life, and Anti-Intellectualism." In *Women Religious and the Intellectual Life: The North American Achievement*, edited by Bridget Puzon, O.S.U. San Francisco: International Scholars, 1996.

Kerr, Clark, and Marian Gade. *The Many Lives of Academic Presidents: Time, Place and Character*. Washington, D.C.: Association of Governing Boards of Universities and Colleges, 1989.

Kmiec, Douglas W., and Stephen B. Presser. *The History, Philosophy and Structure of the American Constitution*. Cincinnati: Anderson, 1998.

Kolakowski, Leszek. *Modernity on Endless Trial*. Chicago: University of Chicago Press, 1990.

Krier Mich, Marvin L. *Catholic Social Teaching and Movements*. Mystic, Conn.: Twenty-Third, 1998.

Kuhns, Elizabeth. *The Habit: A History of the Clothing of Catholic Nuns*. New York: Doubleday, 2003.

Landy, Thomas M. "The Colleges in Context." In *Catholic Women's Colleges in America*, edited by Tracy Schier and Cynthia Russet. Baltimore: Johns Hopkins University Press, 2002.

Langan, John P., S.J., ed. *Catholic Universities in Church and Society: A Dialogue on Ex Corde Ecclesiae*. Washington, D.C.: Georgetown University Press, 1993.

Langley, Monica. "Money Order: Nuns' Zeal for Profits Shapes Hospital Chain, Wins Fans." *Wall Street Journal*, January 7, 1998.

Lasch, Christopher. *The True and Only Heaven: Progress and Its Critics*. New York: Norton, 1991.

Lipman-Blumen, Jean. "The Age of Connective Leadership." In *On Leading Change*, edited by Frances Hesselbein and Rob Johnston. San Francisco: Jossey-Bass, 2002.

Lombo de León, Francisco, and Bart van Leeuwen. "Charles Taylor on Secularization." *Ethical Perspectives* 10 (November 2003).

MacIntyre, Alasdair. *After Virtue: A Study in Moral Theory*. 2nd ed. Notre Dame, Ind.: University of Notre Dame, 1984.

———. *Dependent Rational Animals: Why Human Beings Need the Virtues*. Chicago: Open Court, 1999.

———. *Three Rival Versions of Moral Inquiry: Encyclopaedia, Genealogy, and Tradition*. Notre Dame, Ind.: University of Notre Dame, 1990.

———. *Whose Justice? Which Rationality?* Notre Dame, Ind.: University of Notre Dame Press, 1988.

Macunovich, Diane J. *Birth Quake: The Baby Boom and Its Aftershocks*. Chicago: University of Chicago, 2002.

Madden, Mary Roger, S.P. *The Path Marked Out: History of the Sisters of Providence of Saint Mary-of-the-Woods*. Vol. 3. Saint Mary-of-the-Woods, Ind.: Office of Congregational Advancement—Sisters of Providence, 1991.

Mahoney, Kathleen A. "American Catholic Colleges for Women: Historical Origins." In *Catholic Women's Colleges in America*, edited by Tracy Schier and Cynthia Russet. Baltimore: Johns Hopkins University Press, 2002.

Markham, Donna, O.P. "Psychological Factors Influencing the Decline of and Persistence in Religious Vocations." Unpublished manuscript. Donna Markham, 1257 E. Siena Heights Drive, Adrian, Michigan, 49221.

Marshall, Catherine, and Gretchen B. Rossman. *Designing Qualitative Research*. Newbury Park, Calif.: Sage, 1989.

Marty, Martin E. *Education, Religion and the Common Good*. San Francisco: Jossey-Bass, 2000.

Mason, Patrick L., "Persistent Discrimination: Racial Disparity in the United States, 1997–1998." *American Economic Review*, 90, 2 (2002).

Massa, Mark S., S.J. *Anti-Catholicism in America: The Last Acceptable Prejudice*. New York: Crossroad, 2003.

———. *Catholics and American Culture: Fulton Sheen, Dorothy Day and the Notre Dame Football Team*. New York: Crossroad, 1999.

McBrien, Richard P., ed. *Catholicism*. San Francisco: HarperCollins, 1994.

———. *The HarperCollins Encyclopedia of Catholicism*. New York: HarperCollins, 1995.

———. "What Is A Catholic University?" In *The Challenge and Promise of a Catholic University*, edited by Theodore M. Hesburgh, C.S.C. Notre Dame, Ind.: University of Notre Dame Press, 1994.

McCormick, Richard A., S.J. "What Is a Great Catholic University?" In *Enhancing Religious Identity: Best Practices from Catholic Campuses*, edited by John R. Wilcox and Irene King. Washington, D.C.: Georgetown University Press, 2000.

McDonough, Peter. *Men Astutely Trained: A History of the Jesuits in the American Century*. New York: Free Press, 1992.

McEvoy, Thomas T. *Great Crisis in American Catholic History, 1895–1900*. Chicago: Henry Regnery, 1957.

McNamara, JoAnn K. *Sisters in Arms: Catholic Nuns through Two Millennia*. Cambridge, Mass.: Harvard University Press, 1996.

Meyers, Bertrande, D.C. *The Education of Sisters: A Plan for Integrating the Religious, Cultural, Social, and Professional Training of Sisters*. New York: Sheed and Ward, 1941.

Meyerson, Debra E. "Radical Change, The Quiet Way." In *Harvard Business Review on Culture and Change*. Cambridge, Mass.: Harvard Business School, 1999.

Mintzberg, Henry. "Managing Quietly." In *On Mission and Leadership*, edited by Frances Hesselbein and Rob Johnston. San Francisco: Jossey-Bass, 2002.

Morey, Melanie M. "Leadership and Legacy: Is There a Future for the Past?" Ed.D. diss., Harvard Graduate School of Education, 1995.

———. "The Way We Are: The Present Relationship between Religious Congregations of Women and the Colleges They Founded." In *Catholic Women's Colleges in America*, edited by Tracy Schier and Cynthia Russet. Baltimore: Johns Hopkins University Press, 2002.

Morey, Melanie M., and Dennis H. Holtschneider, C.M. "Leadership and the Age of the Laity: Emerging Patterns in Catholic Higher Education." In *Lay Leaders in Catholic Higher Education*, edited by Anthony J. Cernera. Fairfield, Conn.: Sacred Heart University Press, 2005.

———. "Relationship Revisited: Catholic Institutions and Their Founding Congregations." *Occasional paper no. 47*. Washington, D.C.: Association of Governing Boards of Universities and Colleges, September 2000.

Murphy, Terrence J. *A Catholic University: Vision and Opportunities*. Collegeville, Minn.: Liturgical Press, 2001.

Neal, Marie Augusta, S.N.D.deN. *Catholic Sisters in Transition: From the 1960's to the 1980's*. Wilmington, Del.: Michael Glazier, 1984.

Newman, John Henry Cardinal. *The Idea of a University*. New York: Image, 1959. (Originally published 1852.)

———. *The Idea of a University*. New Haven: Yale University Press, 1996. (Originally published 1852, 1889.)

Nidiffer, Jana. "New Leadership for a New Century." In *Women Administrators in Higher Education*, edited by Jana Nidiffer and Carolyn Terry Bashaw. Albany: State University of New York Press, 2001.

Oates, Mary J., C.S.J. "Sisterhoods and Catholic Higher Education." In *Catholic Women's Colleges in America*, edited by Tracy Schier and Cynthia Russet. Baltimore: Johns Hopkins University Press, 2002.

O'Brien, George Dennis. *The Idea of a Catholic University*. Chicago: University of Chicago Press, 2002.

Odozor, Paulinus Ikechukwu, C.S.Sp. *Moral Theology in an Age of Renewal: A Study of the Catholic Tradition since Vatican II*. Notre Dame, Ind.: University of Notre Dame Press, 2003.

Olsen, Glenn W. *Beginning at Jerusalem: Five Reflections on the History of the Church*. San Francisco: Ignatius, 2004.

Pedersen, Olaf. *The First Universities: Studium Generale and the Origins of University Education in Europe*. Cambridge: Cambridge University Press, 1998.

Plato. *The Republic Book 6*. Translated by H.D.P. Lee. Baltimore: Penguin Books, 1955.

Pope, Stephen J. "Natural Law and Christian Ethics." In *The Cambridge Companion to*

Christian Ethics, edited by Robin Gill. Cambridge: Cambridge University Press, 2001.

Porter, Jean. "Virtue Ethics." In *The Cambridge Companion to Christian Ethics*, edited by Robin Gill. Cambridge: Cambridge University Press, 2001.

———. *Natural and Divine Law: Reclaiming the Tradition for Christian Ethics*. Grand Rapids: Eerdmans, 1999.

———. *Nature as Reason: A Thomistic Theory of the Natural Law*. Grand Rapids: Eerdmans, 2005.

Provost, James H. "The Sides of Catholic Identity." In *Enhancing Religious Identity: Best Practices from Catholic Campuses*, edited by John R. Wilcox and Irene King. Washington, D.C.: Georgetown University Press, 2000.

Quinonez, Lora Ann, C.D.P., and Mary Daniel Turner, S.N.D.deN. *The Transformation of American Catholic Sisters*. Philadelphia: Temple University Press, 1992.

Readings, Bill. *The University in Ruins*. Cambridge, Mass.: Harvard University Press, 1996.

Reiser, William, S.J., "Reformulating the Religious Vows." *Review for Religious* 54, 4 (July–August 1995).

Reuben, Julie A. *The Making of the Modern University: Intellectual Transformation and the Marginalization of Morality*. Chicago: University of Chicago Press, 1996.

Rinere, Elissa, C.P. "Poverty: Now You See It, Now You Don't." *Review for Religious* 58, 2 (March–April 1999).

Roberts, Jon H., and James Turner. *The Sacred and the Secular University*. Princeton: Princeton University Press, 2000.

Rüegg, Walter, ed. *Universities in the Nineteenth and Early Twentieth Centuries (1800–1945)*. 4 vols. Vol. 3, *A History of the University in Europe*. New York: Cambridge University Press, 2004.

Schein, Edgar H. *The Corporate Culture Survival Guide*. San Francisco: Jossey-Bass, 1999.

———. "How Can Organizations Learn Faster? The Challenge of Entering the Green Room." *Sloan Management Review* 342 (1993).

———. *Organizational Culture and Leadership*. San Francisco: Jossey-Bass, 1992.

Schneiders, Sandra, I.H.M. *Finding the Treasure: Locating Catholic Religious Life in a New Ecclesial and Cultural Context*. New York: Paulist Press, 2000.

Schockenhoff, Eberhard. *Natural Law and Human Dignity: Universal Ethics in an Historical World*. Washington, D.C.: Catholic University of America Press, 2003.

Schuth, Katarina, O.S.F. "The Intellectual Life as a Value for Women Religious in the United States." In *Women Religious and the Intellectual Life: The North American Achievement*, edited by Bridget Puzon, O.S.U. San Francisco: International Scholars, 1996.

Scully, Timothy R., C.S.C. "What Is Catholic about a Catholic University?" In *The Challenge and Promise of a Catholic University*, edited by Theodore M. Hesburgh, C.S.C. Notre Dame, Ind.: University of Notre Dame Press, 1994.

Senge, Peter M. "Lessons for Change Leaders," In *On Leading Change*, edited by Frances Hesselbein and Rob Johnston. San Francisco: Jossey-Bass, 2002.

Stark, Rodney. "False Conflict: Christianity Is Not Only Compatible with Christianity— It Created It." *American Enterprise* 14 (October–November 2003).

Stark, Rodney, and Roger Finke. *Acts of Faith: Explaining the Human Side of Religion*. Berkeley: University of California Press, 2000.

Steinfels, Peter. *A People Adrift: The Crisis of the Roman Catholic Church in America*. New York: Simon and Schuster, 2003.

Taylor, Charles. "Justice after Virtue." In *After Macintyre: Critical Perspectives on the Work of Alasdair Macintyre*, edited by John Horton and Susan Mendus. Notre Dame, Ind.: University of Notre Dame Press, 1994.

Tripole, Martin R. "Secularism, Justice, and Jesuit Higher Education—Are They the Same?" *Review for Religious* 63, 1 (2004).

———, ed. *Jesuit Education 21: Conference Proceedings on the Future of Jesuit Higher Education*. Philadelphia: Saint Joseph's University Press, 2000.

Van Engen, John. "Historic Past or Distinctive Future?" In *The Challenge and Promise of a Catholic University*, edited by Theodore M. Hesburgh, C.S.C. Notre Dame, Ind.: University of Notre Dame Press, 1994.

Veysey, Laurence R. *The Emergence of the American University*. Chicago: University of Chicago Press, 1965.

Waters, Lindsay. "Bonfire of the Humanities." *Village Voice*, August 30, 2004.

Westley, Frances, and Henry Mintzberg. "Visionary Leadership and Strategic Management." *Strategic Management Journal* 10 (1989).

Whitehead, Alfred North. *Symbolism: Its Meaning and Effect*. New York: Macmillan, 1927.

Wilcox, John R., and Irene King, eds. *Enhancing Religious Identity: Best Practices from Catholic Campuses*. Washington, D.C.: Georgetown University Press, 2000.

Wilson, Edward O. *Consilience: The Unity of Knowledge*. New York: Knopf, 1998.

Winston, Gordon C. "Subsidies, Hierarchy and Peers: The Awkward Economics of Higher Education." *Economic Perspectives* 13, 1 (1999).

Wittberg, Patricia, S.C. *Pathways to Re-Creating Religious Communities*. New York: Paulist Press, 1996.

———. *The Rise and Fall of Catholic Religious Orders: A Social Movement Perspective*. Albany: State University of New York Press, 1994.

Wolfe, Alan. *The Transformation of American Religion: How We Actually Live Our Faith*. New York: Free Press, 2003.

Wolff, Madeleva, C.S.C. "The Education of Our Young Religious Sisters." *National Catholic Education Association Bulletin*, vol. 46 August 1949.

Wuthnow, Robert. *Meaning and Moral Order:Explorations in Cultural Analysis*. Berkeley: University of California Press, 1987.

Index

Quesadillas

Quesadillas

DONNA KELLY

Photographs by Marty Snortum

GIBBS SMITH
TO ENRICH AND INSPIRE HUMANKIND
Salt Lake City | Charleston | Santa Fe | Santa Barbara

This book is lovingly dedicated to: Kate, always an inspiration; Amy, for sweetness and love; Matt, with a big and warm heart; Jake, for all the smiles; Anne, my culinary muse; Alexys, for keen editing skills; and to Jim, truly one-of-a-kind!

First Edition
14 13 12 11 10   5 4 3

Text © 2010 Donna Kelly
Photographs © 2010 Marty Snortum

Published by
Gibbs Smith
P.O. Box 667
Layton, Utah 84041

Orders: 1.800.835.4993
www.gibbs-smith.com

Designed by Dawn DeVries Sokol
Printed and bound in China
Gibbs Smith books are printed on either recycled, 100% post-consumer waste, FSC-certified papers, or on paper produced from a 100% certified sustainable forest/controlled wood source.

Library of Congress Cataloging-in-Publication Data
Kelly, Donna.
Quesadillas / Donna Kelly ; photographs by Marty Snortum. — 1st ed.
    p. cm.
ISBN-13: 978-1-4236-0503-4
ISBN-10: 1-4236-0503-9
1. Quesadillas. I. Title.
TX836.K45 2010
641.8'15—dc22   2009026447

Contents

Introduction

Quesadilla's Roots

Simply put, the quesadilla is a delightful package of strong-flavored foods with melted cheesy goodness—all sandwiched inside crispy tortillas. It is the ultimate blend of Southwest Old World tradition and New World foods. When the conquistadores arrived in Mexico in the fifteenth century, they found the natives eating what they described as "corn cakes." These were the ancestors of what we call "tortillas" today. These natives used tortillas like the Europeans used bread—as a side dish for their meals. They also used them as utensils, as a sort of edible plate or a spoon to hold other foods while eating. The Spaniards had enjoyed pastries stuffed with fillings and eaten like a sandwich, so the transition to using tortillas instead of pastry was an easy one. The word *quesadilla* is loosely translated to English as "little cheese snack." Since the popular filling for these bundles was cheese, the term fit.

I grew up a few miles north of the Mexican border in Tucson, Arizona, where quesadillas were a staple in most households. They were a cinch for us kids to make—we just added a few handfuls of grated cheese to a tortilla, folded it over, and cooked it in a skillet until the cheese was melted and the tortilla had browned. And, with the invention of microwave ovens, quesadilla time went from mere minutes to seconds. They were the perfect after-school snack food. And the adults made fancier versions as appetizers for parties or with more fillings as a main dish.

Over the years, quesadillas have become increasingly popular in America. The foods and spices of most cultures are now often captured inside a quesadilla. The two essential ingredients are tortillas, which form the crisp outside crust, and cheese, which is necessary as the "glue" that melts and holds the quesadilla together.

Quesadillas are so simple, delicious, and easy to make that their popularity has survived centuries of time.

Cooking Techniques

There are several popular methods for making quesadillas. They can be baked, grilled, microwaved, or pan cooked, with or without oil. There are even specialty quesadilla makers available in the kitchen department of many stores. All methods use high heat to ensure the crispiness of the tortillas.

Baking

To bake quesadillas, simply put the stuffed tortillas on a wire rack that is standing on a baking sheet and place in the middle of the oven. Bake for about 20 minutes at 425 degrees. The actual baking time will vary according to how much filling is in each quesadilla. The more filling a quesadilla has, the longer it will take to bake. The goal is to have a quesadilla with the cheese fully melted, the filling heated through, and the tortilla crispy. Watch closely the last few minutes to make sure the tortillas don't become too brown. Cook until tortillas have browned and filling is cooked through. Nut- or cheese-crusted quesadillas require the baking method because the nuts and cheese loosen when turning quesadillas in a skillet.

Grilling

For grilling, place quesadillas on a hot grill with very low flames. Close cover and wait a minute or two, watching closely so tortillas don't become too brown. Turn over with a wide spatula, close cover, and grill another minute or two, or until tortillas have browned and filling is cooked through.

Microwaving

Microwaving quesadillas can be done, but you will not have a crisp, crunchy texture. If you prefer your quesadillas soft, then fill the tortillas and place in a microwave. Cook on high for about 60 seconds, then remove quesadilla, wipe plate dry, turn the quesadilla over, and cook about 60 seconds more. Actual time will vary depending on how much filling

is in the quesadilla. Cook until filling is cooked through and cheese is melted.

Toasting in a Skillet

The best method for cooking quesadillas is in a dry, covered skillet over medium heat, or in a quesadilla maker. When using a skillet, it should be dry, with no oil or butter used, in order to prevent oily or burned quesadillas. This toasting method also ensures that the filling will be cooked through, the cheese will be melted, and the tortillas will be crisp and browned. I prefer cooking quesadillas with two flat tortillas rather than one folded tortilla, because this ensures more even cooking. Choose a skillet that is just slightly wider than your tortillas. For example, use a 10-inch skillet for tortillas that are 8 to 9 inches in diameter.

Start by placing a dry tortilla in a skillet that has been heated to medium heat. Place the filling ingredients on the tortilla, making sure that there is some cheese both on the top and the bottom of the filling. This will help the quesadilla stick together. Place another tortilla on top. Cover with a tight-fitting lid. This will hold the heat in and cook the quesadilla all the way through without burning the outside of the tortillas. Let the quesadilla cook for a minute or two. Check to see if the bottom tortilla has browned. If so, turn the quesadilla over with a very wide spatula. Place lid on skillet and cook another minute or two, or until bottom tortilla has browned, filling is cooked through, and the cheese is melted.

Ingredient Tips

Since there are so few ingredients in quesadillas, be sure to buy the best quality you can find. Ingredients must generally be cooked before adding to the quesadilla, because the purpose of the final cooking of the quesadilla is not to cook ingredients but to crisp the tortillas, melt the cheeses, and heat the filling through. Slice all ingredients thinly so that the quesadilla is relatively flat and has no large lumps or bulges.

Cheeses

Cheese comes in three general categories: melting cheeses, hard cheeses, and soft cheeses. Combining types of cheeses in one quesadilla gives a greater richness than any one cheese.

In most quesadilla recipes, there is some type of cheese that melts well. This ensures that the quesadilla will be "glued" together. The most common cheeses for quesadillas are cheddar and Monterey Jack. Other types of cheeses that melt well are fontina, Havarti, Gouda, Gruyère, and mozzarella.

Hard cheeses are primarily used for strong flavor. The most common hard cheeses are Parmesan, Asiago, and Romano.

Soft cheeses are also used for flavor and can be spread or crumbled. The most common soft cheeses are goat cheese, Brie, blue cheese, Gorgonzola, ricotta, Boursin, cream cheese, and mascarpone cheese.

The salt content of cheese varies according to brand, so add salt to recipes, as desired, after tasting cheese to determine saltiness.

Tortillas

Flour tortillas are generally the best to use for making quesadillas. Corn tortillas can be used but generally do not become as crispy as flour tortillas when cooked with the usual quesadilla methods. Thinner tortillas are best, since the goal is to have a very crispy outside for the quesadillas. Try experimenting with new, flavored tortillas, such as those flavored with sun-dried tomatoes, basil, etc. You may have to adjust cooking heat or time to make sure the flavored tortillas become crispy.

If you would like to try making your own flour tortillas, try this easy and inexpensive method:

Flour Tortillas

Mix together 2 cups flour, 2 teaspoons salt, and 1 teaspoon baking powder. Cut in with a pastry blender ⅓ cup cold vegetable shortening or lard until fine crumbs. Stir in about ⅔ cup warm water until dough begins to come together. Turn out onto a floured surface and knead 3 to 5 minutes, or until smooth. Break into 8 equal pieces, and shape into balls. Cover and let rest about 2 hours at room temperature. Roll each dough ball into approximately 10-inch circles. Cook over medium-high heat on a dry skillet, about 1 minute on each side, or until lightly browned. Homemade tortillas can be stored with a sheet of wax paper between each tortilla in sealed ziplock bags for 5 to 7 days in the refrigerator or up to 3 months in the freezer.

Filling Ingredients

The wonderful thing about quesadillas is that the only essential ingredients are tortillas and cheese, and any other foods can be used as fillings. In general, all ingredients should be thinly sliced and then cooked before being used as filling.

A good general rule is that 1 to 1½ cups of filling is the perfect amount for 8- to 10-inch tortillas. If you use more, the cooking time will have to be increased to allow filling to heat through completely. Also, thicker quesadillas are trickier to eat, so you may have to eat with a fork instead of by hand.

Generally, the cheeses used in quesadillas are well salted. As a result, salt is not included as an ingredient in these recipes. Feel free to add salt and pepper to any of the savory recipes if you prefer your quesadillas on the salty side.

Another wonderful thing about quesadillas is that they are a great vehicle for using leftover meats, vegetables, and cheeses. Yesterday's pot roast or other meats, thinly sliced or shredded, make great quesadillas. They are a great way to clean out your fridge.

Since quesadillas have Southwest roots, try using spicy chiles with more mellow cheeses. Be adventurous, and you just might discover whole new food and flavor combinations that will surprise and delight you!

Sauces and Salsas

The last section of this book has recipes for delicious salsas and sauces for any quesadilla in this book, and whatever quesadillas you may come up with in the future. Any quesadilla can be topped with any number of sauces or toppings, depending on your personal preference. Use sauces that complement the quesadilla well, such as Mushroom Cream Sauce with the Mushroom Madness quesadilla, Roasted Red Pepper Sauce with the Roasted Veggie quesadilla or the Roasted Ratatouille quesadilla. The sweet or savory sauces are made to be drizzled over the top of the quesadillas just before serving or to be used as dipping sauces on the side.

Serving Quesadillas

Quesadillas should be served by cutting into wedges with a pizza cutter. They are made to be eaten with your hands. They can be served plain or with accompaniments. Popular traditional toppings include crumbled dry or grated cheese, melted cheese, sour cream, diced avocados, guacamole, diced onions, diced tomatoes or pico de gallo, and diced cilantro. Salsas and sauces can also be drizzled on top or used as a dip on the side. If you're having a quesadilla like Barbecue Chicken, try sprinkling with cilantro and serving extra barbecue sauce on the side for dipping. Or warm marinara sauce is delicious on the side of the Pizza Style quesadilla. Experiment with your own combinations—you will be surprised at how many work well together!

The Basics

The Classic

This classic quesadilla is a simple but sublime blend of cheeses and peppers.

3 large Anaheim peppers

6 ounces sharp cheddar
cheese, grated

6 ounces Monterey Jack
cheese, grated

3 ounces crumbled queso
fresco cheese

8 (9- to 10-inch) flour or
wheat tortillas

1. Blacken the skins of the peppers by grilling, broiling, or using a kitchen torch. Place in a ziplock bag and seal. Allow to stand at room temperature for about 10 minutes. Take peppers from bag and remove skins by holding under running tap water and scraping off skins with fingers. Cut peppers open and remove seeds by scraping with a spoon; dice peppers.

2. Toss cheeses together in a bowl. Lay 4 tortillas on the counter and spread about ¾ cup cheese over each. Sprinkle about ¼ cup diced peppers over top.

3. Slide one of the cheese-covered tortillas into a 10-inch skillet over medium heat. Place one of the remaining tortillas on top. Press down with a wide spatula to remove any air pockets. Cover and cook 1 to 2 minutes, checking frequently, until bottom tortilla is crisp and browned.

4. Turn over, cover, and cook 1 to 2 minutes more, or until lightly browned. Repeat this process for remaining quesadillas. Cut into wedges and serve immediately.

Makes 4 to 6 servings

Barbecue Chicken

The smoky taste of grilled chicken and smoked Gouda make this a must for your next backyard barbecue.

1 (2-pound) rotisserie chicken

1/3 cup barbecue sauce

1/2 cup minced red onion

1/4 cup minced cilantro

12 ounces smoked Gouda cheese, grated

8 (9- to 10-inch) flour or wheat tortillas

● **Suggested garnishes:**
Sour Cream Paprika Sauce (page 120) or White Cheddar Sauce (page 123)

1. Remove meat from chicken, cutting into small pieces as you go, and discarding the skin, fat, and bones. Toss chicken with barbecue sauce.

2. Toss onion, cilantro, and cheese together in a bowl. Lay 4 tortillas on the counter and spread about 1/3 cup cheese mixture over each. Spread 1 cup chicken over cheese. Sprinkle another 1/3 cup cheese mixture over top.

3. Slide one of the cheese-covered tortillas into a 10-inch skillet over medium heat. Place one of the remaining tortillas on top. Press down with a wide spatula to remove any air pockets. Cover and cook 1 to 2 minutes, checking frequently, until bottom tortilla is crisp and browned.

4. Turn over, cover, and cook 1 to 2 minutes more, or until lightly browned. Repeat this process for remaining quesadillas. Cut into wedges and serve immediately.

Makes 4 to 6 servings

BLT

What a great twist on this classic sandwich favorite!

8 slices bacon, frozen

6 ounces fontina or Monterey
   Jack cheese, grated

2 ounces sharp cheddar
   cheese, grated

8 (9- to 10-inch) flour, wheat,
   or garlic tortillas

4 ripe tomatoes, diced (seeds
   and liquid removed)

4 cups diced lettuce

¼ cup ranch or blue cheese
   dressing

1. Preheat oven to 425 degrees.

2. Let bacon thaw slightly and then dice. Spread evenly on a baking sheet and bake 10 to 12 minutes, or until bacon is browned and crisp. Remove from oven and blot dry on paper towels.

3. Toss cheeses together in a bowl. Lay 4 tortillas on the counter and spread about ⅓ cup cheese over each. Sprinkle about ¼ cup tomatoes and ¼ cup bacon over cheese. Sprinkle another ⅓ cup cheese over top.

4. Slide one of the cheese-covered tortillas into a 10-inch skillet over medium heat. Place one of the remaining tortillas on top. Press down with a wide spatula to remove any air pockets. Cover and cook 1 to 2 minutes, checking frequently, until bottom tortilla is crisp and browned.

5. Turn over, cover, and cook 1 to 2 minutes more, or until lightly browned. Repeat this process for remaining quesadillas. Toss lettuce in dressing and spread over top of quesadillas. Cut into wedges and serve immediately.

Makes 4 to 6 servings

Fajita Style

This favorite restaurant dish makes mouthwateringly delicious quesadillas.

1 pound frozen flank or top
   sirloin steak (or frozen boneless,
   skinless chicken breasts)

1 teaspoon lime zest

2 tablespoons lime juice

3 tablespoons canola oil, divided

1 tablespoon cumin

2 teaspoons chipotle chile powder

1 teaspoon salt

1 large yellow onion

2 bell peppers, any color

8 ounces Monterey Jack or
   pepper jack cheese, grated

8 (9- to 10-inch) flour or
   wheat tortillas

● **Suggested garnishes:**
Sour Cream Paprika Sauce (page 120),
Creamy Avocado Sauce (page 121), or
favorite salsa

1. Let meat stand at room temperature for 10–15 minutes. Thinly slice across the grain and then place in a ziplock bag with lime zest, juice, 1 tablespoon oil, cumin, chile powder, and salt. Marinate at room temperature for 30 minutes, turning occasionally. Sauté meat in the remaining oil in a skillet over high heat for 5 minutes, stirring constantly, until browned. Remove meat from skillet.

2. Cut onion and peppers into ¼-inch strips. Add to skillet and sauté until limp and lightly browned. Stir meat back into skillet.

3. Lay 4 tortillas on the counter and spread about ¼ cup cheese over each. Sprinkle 1 cup of the meat mixture over cheese. Sprinkle another ¼ cup cheese over top.

4. Slide one of the cheese-covered tortillas into a 10-inch skillet over medium heat. Place one of the remaining tortillas on top. Press down with a wide spatula to remove any air pockets. Cover and cook 1 to 2 minutes, checking frequently, until bottom tortilla is crisp and browned.

5. Turn over, cover, and cook 1 to 2 minutes more, or until lightly browned. Repeat this process for remaining quesadillas. Cut into wedges and serve immediately.

Makes 4 to 6 servings

Pizza Style

Everyone loves pizza—use these classic toppings, or your favorites, for rave reviews!

8 (9- to 10-inch) flour, wheat, or garlic tortillas

6 ounces mozzarella cheese, grated

1 (6-ounce) can sliced black olives, drained

½ cup diced onion

½ cup diced green bell pepper

1 (8-ounce) package pepperoni slices, whole or diced

4 ounces Parmesan cheese, grated

● **Suggested garnish:**

Warm marinara sauce

1. Preheat oven to 400 degrees.

2. Lay 4 tortillas on the counter and spread about ⅓ cup mozzarella cheese over each. Sprinkle a few black olives, 2 tablespoons onion, and 2 tablespoons bell pepper over cheese. Lay pepperoni on top, covering entire surface. Sprinkle another ⅓ cup cheese over top. Cover each with one of the remaining tortillas.

3. Brush a little water on top of each tortilla. Spread ¼ cup Parmesan cheese in an thin layer over top and press down with a wide spatula, making sure cheese is pressed into tortilla. Repeat with each quesadilla.

4. Place quesadillas, Parmesan-crusted side up, onto a wire rack standing on a baking sheet. Bake 10 to 12 minutes, checking frequently so as not to burn. Cut into wedges and serve immediately.

Makes 4 to 6 servings

Smoked Salmon

Who needs a bagel with this charming way of eating smoked salmon?!

1 (8-ounce) package cream
cheese, softened

8 (9- to 10-inch) flour or
wheat tortillas

6 ounces fontina cheese, grated

2 ounces Gruyère cheese, grated

8 ounces Nova Scotia–style
smoked salmon

½ cup diced fresh dill

2 tablespoons drained capers,
diced

1. Spread 1 tablespoon cream cheese on each tortilla.

2. Toss cheeses together in a bowl. Spread about ⅓ cup cheese over 4 tortillas. Slice salmon into strips and place on top of cheese. Sprinkle 2 tablespoons dill and ½ tablespoon capers over salmon. Sprinkle another ⅓ cup cheese over top.

3. Slide one of the cheese-covered tortillas into a 10-inch skillet over medium heat. Place one of the remaining tortillas on top, cream cheese side down. Press down with a wide spatula to remove any air pockets. Cover and cook 1 to 2 minutes, checking frequently, until bottom tortilla is crisp and browned.

4. Turn over, cover, and cook 1 to 2 minutes more, or until lightly browned. Repeat this process for remaining quesadillas. Cut into wedges and serve immediately.

Makes 4 to 6 servings

Seafood Medley

The symphony of your favorite seafood will become your own quesadilla classic!

1 pound assorted shelled raw seafood, diced (such as crab, shrimp, and scallops)

2 tablespoons butter

6 ounces fontina cheese, grated

2 ounces Gruyère cheese, grated

2 teaspoons Old Bay seasoning, or other seasoning blend

8 (9- to 10-inch) flour or wheat tortillas

1 cup diced fresh parsley

1. Sauté seafood in butter in a skillet over medium-high heat until opaque and cooked through.

2. Toss cheeses and seasoning together in a bowl. Lay 4 tortillas on the counter and spread about ⅓ cup cheese over each. Sprinkle about ½ cup seafood and a little parsley over cheese. Sprinkle another ⅓ cup cheese over top.

3. Slide one of the cheese-covered tortillas into a 10-inch skillet over medium heat. Place one of the remaining tortillas on top. Press down with a wide spatula to remove any air pockets. Cover and cook 1 to 2 minutes, checking frequently, until bottom tortilla is crisp and browned.

4. Turn over, cover, and cook 1 to 2 minutes more, or until lightly browned. Repeat this process for remaining quesadillas. Cut into wedges and serve immediately.

Makes 4 to 6 servings

Crab Cake Style

Fold the taste of New England into a quesadilla with this tasty combination of cheese, veggies, and crab.

8 ounces cooked lump crabmeat, well drained

1 tablespoon lemon juice

1/2 red bell pepper, diced

1/2 cup diced celery

1 teaspoon Worcestershire sauce

8 ounces fontina cheese, grated

8 (9- to 10-inch) flour or wheat tortillas

1. Toss crabmeat, lemon juice, bell pepper, celery, and Worcestershire sauce together in a bowl.

2. Lay 4 tortillas on the counter and spread 1/3 cup cheese over each. Spread 1 cup crab mixture over cheese. Sprinkle another 1/3 cup cheese over top.

3. Slide one of the cheese-covered tortillas into a 10-inch skillet over medium heat. Place one of the remaining tortillas on top. Press down with a wide spatula to remove any air pockets. Cover and cook 1 to 2 minutes, checking frequently, until bottom tortilla is crisp and browned.

4. Turn over, cover, and cook 1 to 2 minutes more, or until lightly browned. Repeat this process for remaining quesadillas. Cut into wedges and serve immediately.

Makes 4 to 6 servings

● **Suggested garnishes:**

Roasted Red Pepper Sauce (page 119)
or Creamy Avocado Sauce (page 121)

Carne Asada

This Southwest blend of spicy beef and cheese is great to try at any summer barbecue.

1 ½ pounds flank or top sirloin steak

1 teaspoon lime zest

¼ cup lime juice

2 tablespoons canola oil, divided

3 tablespoons Southwest Spice Rub (page 119)

8 (9- to 10-inch) flour, wheat, or chipotle tortillas

8 ounces Monterey Jack cheese, grated

2 bunches green onions, thinly sliced

1 red bell pepper, diced

1 cup diced cilantro

● **Suggested garnishes:**
Sassy Smoky Salsa (page 118),
Southwest Pesto Sauce (page 120),
or Creamy Avocado Sauce (page 121)

1. Place beef in freezer for about 20 minutes, or until mostly frozen. Remove and slice beef very thinly across the grain. Place in a ziplock bag with lime zest, juice, and 1 tablespoon oil. Let stand at room temperature for 30 minutes, turning every few minutes.

2. Drain marinade from beef. Sprinkle beef generously with spice rub and then rub into beef. Let stand for 10 minutes. Brush or spray beef with remaining oil and then grill or broil over high heat until browned.

3. Lay 4 tortillas on the counter and spread ⅓ cup cheese over each. Sprinkle green onions and bell pepper over cheese. Top with 1 cup beef and another ⅓ cup cheese.

4. Slide one of the cheese-covered tortillas into a 10-inch skillet over medium heat. Place one of the remaining tortillas on top. Press down with a wide spatula to remove any air pockets. Cover and cook 1 to 2 minutes, checking frequently, until bottom tortilla is crisp and browned.

5. Turn over, cover, and cook 1 to 2 minutes more, or until lightly browned. Repeat this process for remaining quesadillas. Cut into wedges and serve immediately.

Makes 4 to 6 servings

California Dreamin'

Avocados are a natural for quesadillas, and add a sweet, creamy goodness.

8 slices bacon, frozen

8 (9- to 10-inch) flour, wheat, or spinach tortillas

8 ounces pepper jack cheese, grated

2 large ripe avocados, peeled and sliced

1 tablespoon lemon juice

8 to 10 dried figs or apricots, diced

1 tablespoon smoked paprika

● **Suggested garnishes:**
**Roasted Red Pepper Sauce (page 119)
or Creamy Avocado Sauce (page 121)**

1. Preheat oven to 425 degrees.

2. Let bacon thaw slightly and then dice. Spread evenly on a baking sheet and bake 10 to 12 minutes, or until bacon is browned and crisp. Remove from oven and blot dry on paper towels.

3. Lay 4 tortillas on the counter and spread ⅓ cup cheese over each. Sprinkle ¼ cup bacon over cheese. Toss avocado slices in lemon juice and then spread evenly over bacon, followed by the dried fruit. Sprinkle another ⅓ cup cheese over top and a little smoked paprika.

4. Slide one of the cheese-covered tortillas into a 10-inch skillet over medium heat. Place one of the remaining tortillas on top. Press down with a wide spatula to remove any air pockets. Cover and cook 1 to 2 minutes, checking frequently, until bottom tortilla is crisp and browned.

5. Turn over, cover, and cook 1 to 2 minutes more, or until lightly browned. Repeat this process for remaining quesadillas. Cut into wedges and serve immediately.

Makes 4 to 6 servings

Shrimp on the Barbie

Grilled quesadillas on the barbecue are a favorite in the summertime—or anytime!

24 medium raw peeled shrimp

¼ cup barbecue sauce

1 cup diced zucchini

1 cup fresh or frozen corn

3 green onions, tops included, thinly sliced

1 tablespoon butter

6 ounces fontina cheese, grated

2 ounces Jarlsberg cheese, grated

8 (9- to 10-inch) flour or wheat tortillas

● **Suggested garnishes:**

Roasted Red Pepper Sauce (page 119) or Mushroom Cream Sauce (page 121)

1. Thread shrimp onto skewers and brush with a little barbecue sauce. Grill over very high heat for 1 to 2 minutes on each side, or until just opaque and lightly browned. Remove from grill. Let shrimp cool and then slice in half lengthwise, creating two thin half-moons.

2. Sauté all vegetables in a skillet in butter over medium-high heat until cooked through and moisture has evaporated, about 3 to 5 minutes.

3. Toss cheeses together in a bowl. Lay 4 tortillas on the counter and spread ⅓ cup cheese over each. Spread a layer of shrimp over cheese, covering entire surface. Sprinkle ½ cup vegetables over top, followed by another ⅓ cup cheese.

4. Place one of the remaining tortillas on top. Press down with a wide spatula to remove any air pockets. Place on a grill over low heat, close cover, and cook 1 to 2 minutes, checking frequently until bottom tortilla is crisp and browned.

5. Turn over, cover, and cook 1 to 2 minutes more, or until lightly browned. Repeat this process for remaining quesadillas. Cut into wedges and serve immediately.

Makes 4 to 6 servings

Rise 'n' Shine

Wake up your taste buds with this quick and delicious snack.

8 slices bacon

¹/₂ cup diced green bell pepper

¹/₂ cup diced yellow onion

1 large russet potato, peeled
and coarsely grated

6 large eggs, mixed with
2 tablespoons milk

4 ounces Monterey Jack
cheese, grated

2 ounces cheddar cheese, grated

8 (9- to 10-inch) flour or
wheat tortillas

● Suggested garnishes:

Roasted Red Pepper Sauce (page 119)
or White Cheddar Sauce (page 123)

1. Dice bacon and cook in a 10-inch skillet over medium-high heat. Remove bacon, blot with paper towels, and dice.

2. Sauté bell pepper and onion in bacon drippings until soft. Place grated potato in a kitchen towel and wring out. Add the potato to the pepper and onion and cook for 2 to 3 minutes, stirring only once or twice to ensure it browns. Remove vegetables from pan and then pour egg mixture into pan and scramble. Remove eggs and wipe skillet clean with a paper towel.

3. Toss cheeses together in a bowl. Lay 4 tortillas on the counter and spread ¹/₃ cup cheese over each. Divide vegetables, bacon, and eggs over cheese. Sprinkle another ¹/₃ cup cheese over top.

4. Slide one of the cheese-covered tortillas into a 10-inch skillet over medium heat. Place one of the remaining tortillas on top. Press down with a wide spatula to remove any air pockets. Cover and cook 1 to 2 minutes, checking frequently, until bottom tortilla is crisp and browned.

5. Turn over, cover, and cook 1 to 2 minutes more, or until lightly browned. Repeat this process for remaining quesadillas. Cut into wedges and serve immediately.

Makes 4 to 6 servings

New York Deli

East Coast flavors in a classic Western quesadilla!

4 tablespoons spicy brown
   mustard

1 (8-ounce) package cream
   cheese, softened

8 (9- to 10-inch) flour, wheat,
   or spinach tortillas

8 ounces Swiss cheese, grated

1 pound thinly sliced deli
   pastrami or corned beef

1 cup sauerkraut, drained

2 teaspoons crushed
   caraway seeds

● **Suggested garnishes:**
Sour Cream Paprika Sauce (page 120)
or Spicy Mustard Sauce (page 122)

1. Stir together mustard and cream cheese until smooth. Lay tortillas on the counter and spread a generous tablespoon of cream cheese mixture on each.

2. Spread ⅓ cup Swiss cheese over cream cheese mixture. Lay pastrami over cheese and then sprinkle with ¼ cup sauerkraut and some crushed caraway seeds. Sprinkle another ⅓ cup Swiss cheese over top.

3. Slide one of the cheese-covered tortillas into a 10-inch skillet over medium heat. Place one of the remaining tortillas on top. Press down with a wide spatula to remove any air pockets. Cover and cook 1 to 2 minutes, checking frequently, until bottom tortilla is crisp and browned.

4. Turn over, cover, and cook 1 to 2 minutes more, or until lightly browned. Repeat this process for remaining quesadillas. Cut into wedges and serve immediately.

Makes 4 to 6 servings

Turkey Cranberry

Savor the traditional flavors of Thanksgiving dinner in a crispy tortilla.

1 (8-ounce) package cream cheese, softened

3 tablespoons jellied cranberry sauce

8 (9- to 10-inch) flour or wheat tortillas

8 ounces smoked Gouda cheese, grated

1 cup sweetened dried cranberries, diced

½ cup diced walnuts

1 pound deli turkey, sliced into 16 slices

1. Mix together the cream cheese and cranberry sauce. Lay tortillas on the counter and spread a generous tablespoon of cream cheese mixture over each.

2. Over 4 tortillas, sprinkle ⅓ cup Gouda over cream cheese mixture followed by 2 tablespoons dried cranberries, 1 tablespoon walnuts, and another ⅓ cup Gouda. Place 2 slices turkey over cheese, covering entire surface with turkey.

3. Slide one of the turkey-covered tortillas into a 10-inch skillet over medium heat. Place one of the remaining tortillas over top, cream cheese side down. Press down with a wide spatula to remove any air pockets. Cover and cook 1 to 2 minutes, checking frequently, until bottom tortilla is crisp and browned.

4. Turn over, cover, and cook 1 to 2 minutes more, or until lightly browned. Repeat this process for remaining quesadillas. Cut into wedges and serve immediately.

Makes 4 to 6 servings

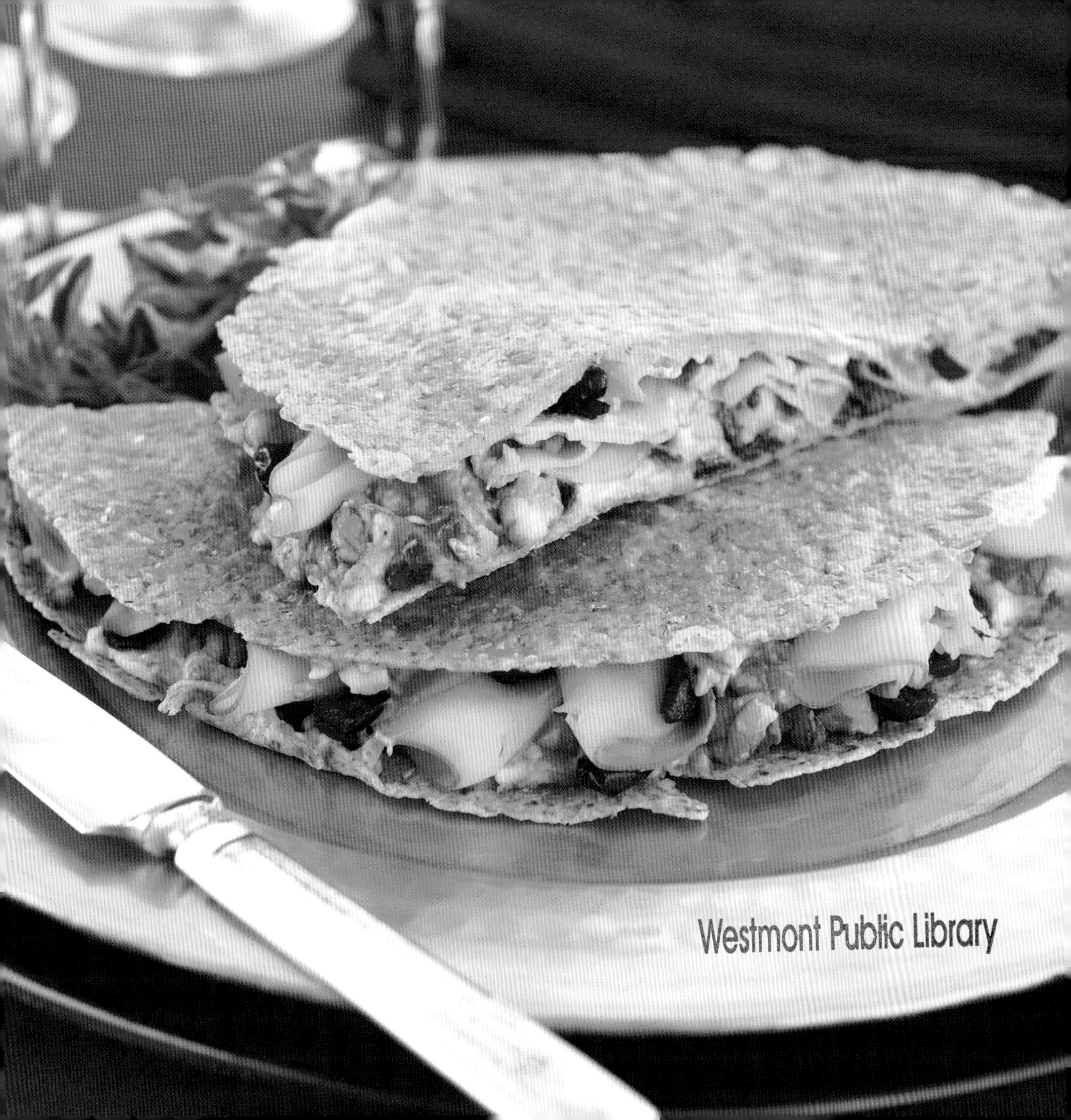

Tex-Mex

The cheesy goodness of a classic quesadilla with a Tex-Mex twist!

6 ounces sharp cheddar
   cheese, grated

6 ounces Monterey Jack
   cheese, grated

3 ounces crumbled queso
   fresco cheese

1 (4-ounce) can diced green chiles

8 (9- to 10-inch) flour, wheat,
   or jalapeño tortillas

4 cups chili

4 tablespoons sour cream

3 green onions, tops included,
   thinly sliced diagonally

1. Toss cheeses and green chiles together in a bowl. Lay 4 tortillas on the counter and spread ¾ cup cheese mixture over each.

2. Slide one of the cheese-covered tortillas into a 10-inch skillet over medium heat. Place one of the remaining tortillas over top. Press down with a wide spatula to remove any air pockets. Cover and cook 1 to 2 minutes, checking frequently, until bottom tortilla is crisp and browned.

3. Turn over, cover, and cook 1 to 2 minutes more, or until lightly browned. Repeat this process for remaining quesadillas. Cut into wedges and keep warm.

4. Heat chili and ladle 1 cup over each quesadilla. Garnish with 1 tablespoon sour cream and a few green onions. Serve immediately with a fork.

Makes 4 to 6 servings

Stacked Torte

This layered quesadilla is packed with flavors and pretty enough to serve to company.

1½ pounds ground beef
  or turkey

1 teaspoon salt

2 (10-ounce) cans red
  enchilada sauce

1 cup salsa

8 (9- to 10-inch) flour or
  wheat tortillas

2 cups fresh or frozen corn

½ cup chopped cilantro

2 (14-ounce) cans black or
  pinto beans, drained

1 cup thinly sliced green onions

4 ounces Monterey Jack
  cheese, grated

8 ounces cheddar cheese, grated

1. Preheat oven to 350 degrees.

2. Brown the ground beef or turkey in a skillet and add salt.

3. In a bowl, stir together the enchilada sauce and salsa.

4. Spray a 10-inch springform pan with nonstick cooking spray. Make six layers in pan as follows, using a little of each as you go: 1 tortilla, cooked meat, corn, cilantro, salsa mixture, beans, green onion, and cheeses. Top with the remaining tortilla.

5. Bake for 30 to 40 minutes, or until bubbly and cooked throughout. Remove from oven and let stand 5 minutes. Remove sides of springform pan and set on a round serving plate in center of table. Garnish with a little grated cheese, if desired. Cut into wedges and serve.

Makes 4 to 6 servings

Note: For a spicier version, replace some of the ground meat with chorizo.

Spicy Grilled Flank Steak

The bold flavors from the grilled steak are just right for a quesadilla.

¼ cup regular or tamari soy sauce

¼ cup ketchup

1 teaspoon red pepper flakes

3 tablespoons canola oil, divided

3 cloves garlic, pressed

1 pound frozen flank steak

1 tablespoon sesame oil

8 ounces Monterey Jack cheese, grated

½ cup thinly sliced green onions

8 (9- to 10-inch) flour, wheat, or sun-dried tomato tortillas

● **Suggested garnishes:**
Sassy Smoky Salsa (page 118), Roasted Red Pepper Sauce (page 119), and/or Southwest Pesto Sauce (page 120)

1. Place soy sauce, ketchup, red pepper flakes, 1 tablespoon canola oil, and garlic in a ziplock bag. Let steak sit at room temperature for 10–15 minutes to slightly thaw; slice thinly across the grain. Add steak slices to mixture and let marinate 8 hours or overnight. Remove steak 20 minutes before using.

2. Combine remaining oils and brush over steak. Grill over very high heat about 1 to 2 minutes on each side, or until browned.

3. Toss cheese and green onions together in a bowl. Lay 4 tortillas on the counter and spread ⅓ cup cheese mixture over each. Spread steak over cheese, followed by another ⅓ cup cheese mixture.

4. Slide one of the cheese-covered tortillas into a 10-inch skillet over medium heat. Place one of the remaining tortillas over top. Press down with a wide spatula to remove any air pockets. Cover and cook 1 to 2 minutes, checking frequently, until bottom tortilla is crisp and browned.

5. Turn over, cover, and cook 1 to 2 minutes more, or until lightly browned. Repeat this process for remaining quesadillas. Cut into wedges and serve immediately.

Makes 4 to 6 servings

Tuna Melt

This cheesy tuna classic is a combination everyone will love!

1 can (12 ounces) solid albacore
   tuna, drained

2 stalks celery, minced

$\frac{1}{4}$ cup mayonnaise

$\frac{1}{4}$ cup minced red onion

$\frac{1}{4}$ cup chopped flat-leaf parsley

2 tablespoons lemon juice

2 tablespoons diced fresh
   dill leaves

1 teaspoon Dijon mustard

8 ounces Provolone cheese,
   thinly sliced

8 (9- to 10-inch) flour or
   wheat tortillas

● **Suggested garnishes:**
Creamy Avocado Sauce (page 121)
or Spicy Mustard Sauce (page 122)

1. Mix all ingredients together except cheese and tortillas.

2. Lay 4 tortillas on the counter and spread a few slices of cheese on each, completely covering surface. Spread $\frac{1}{2}$ cup tuna mixture on top. Spread a few more slices cheese over tuna, completely covering surface.

3. Slide one of the cheese-covered tortillas into a 10-inch skillet over medium heat. Place one of the remaining tortillas over top. Press down with a wide spatula to remove any air pockets. Cover and cook 1 to 2 minutes, checking frequently, until bottom tortilla is crisp and browned.

4. Turn over, cover, and cook 1 to 2 minutes more, or until lightly browned. Repeat this process for remaining quesadillas. Cut into wedges and serve immediately.

Makes 4 to 6 servings

Chicken Caesar

Caesar salad made into a quesadilla—garlicky and fresh!

2 boneless, skinless chicken
  breasts, frozen

3 cloves garlic, pressed

2 tablespoons canola oil

4 ounces Parmesan cheese,
  divided

2 ounces Monterey Jack
  cheese, grated

2 ounces Asiago cheese, grated

1/2 cup Caesar salad dressing,
  or more to taste, divided

8 (9- to 10-inch) flour, wheat,
  or spinach tortillas

1 cup thinly sliced celery

8 cups chopped romaine lettuce

1. Thaw chicken slightly and then thinly slice across the grain. Sauté in garlic and oil in a skillet over medium-high heat until lightly browned, stirring constantly, about 5 minutes.

2. Grate half the Parmesan cheese and then toss all grated cheeses together in a bowl. Lay 4 tortillas on the counter and spread 1/4 cup cheese over each. Drizzle 1 tablespoon dressing over cheese. Spread chicken and celery over dressing. Spread another 1/4 cup cheese over top.

3. Slide one of the cheese-covered tortillas into a 10-inch skillet over medium heat. Place one of the remaining tortillas over top. Press down with a wide spatula to remove any air pockets. Cover and cook 1 to 2 minutes, checking frequently, until bottom tortilla is crisp and browned.

4. Turn over, cover, and cook 1 to 2 minutes more, or until lightly browned. Repeat this process for remaining quesadillas. Cut quesadillas into wedges.

5. Toss lettuce with dressing and spread on top of quesadillas. Shave the remaining Parmesan cheese into thin ribbons and sprinkle on top of lettuce. Serve immediately.

Makes 4 to 6 servings

Cajun Spice

Food has never been yummier down on the bayou!

8 ounces fresh or frozen and thawed okra, thinly sliced

½ large white onion, diced

1 tablespoon oil

8 ounces andouille or mild Italian sausage, cooked and diced

8 ounces raw peeled shrimp (51/60 count)

1 tablespoon Louisiana or Tabasco sauce

2 teaspoons smoked paprika

2 teaspoons Cajun spice blend

8 (9- to 10-inch) flour or wheat tortillas

8 ounces Monterey Jack cheese, grated

1. Sauté okra and onion in oil in a large skillet over medium-high heat until onion is translucent. Add sausage and shrimp, and sauté until shrimp is opaque. Add hot sauce, paprika, and spice blend.

2. Lay 4 tortillas on the counter and spread ⅓ cup cheese over each. Spread 1 cup meat and vegetable mixture over cheese. Spread another ⅓ cup cheese over top.

3. Slide one of the cheese-covered tortillas into a 10-inch skillet over medium heat. Place one of the remaining tortillas over top. Press down with a wide spatula to remove any air pockets. Cover and cook 1 to 2 minutes, checking frequently, until bottom tortilla is crisp and browned.

4. Turn over, cover, and cook 1 to 2 minutes more, or until lightly browned. Repeat this process for remaining quesadillas. Cut into wedges and serve immediately.

Makes 4 to 6 servings

Buffalo Chicken

The marriage of this "Happy Hour" classic and quesadillas is heavenly.

2 frozen boneless, skinless chicken breasts, slightly thawed

2 tablespoons butter, melted

1/4 cup Louisiana or Tabasco sauce

1 tablespoon apple cider vinegar

3 tablespoons brown sugar

1/2 teaspoon salt

8 (9- to 10-inch) flour or wheat tortillas

8 ounces sharp white cheddar cheese, grated

1 cup very thinly sliced celery

1/2 cup thinly sliced green onions

● **Suggested garnishes:**

Sour Cream Paprika Sauce (page 120)

or Creamy Avocado Sauce (page 121)

1. Thinly slice chicken across the grain. Spread in a single layer on a baking sheet sprayed with nonstick cooking spray. Whisk together butter, hot sauce, vinegar, sugar, and salt. Brush half of sauce over chicken. Broil for 5 to 8 minutes about 6 inches from heat until lightly browned, watching closely so as not to burn.

2. Turn chicken slices over with a wide spatula and then brush with remaining sauce. Broil another 3 to 5 minutes until lightly browned, watching closely so as not to burn.

3. Lay 4 tortillas on the counter and spread 1/3 cup cheese over each. Spread chicken, celery, and green onions over cheese. Spread another 1/3 cup cheese over top.

4. Slide one of the cheese-covered tortillas into a 10-inch skillet over medium heat. Place one of the remaining tortillas over top. Press down with a wide spatula to remove any air pockets. Cover and cook 1 to 2 minutes, checking frequently, until bottom tortilla is crisp and browned.

5. Turn over, cover, and cook 1 to 2 minutes more, or until lightly browned. Repeat this process for remaining quesadillas. Cut into wedges and serve immediately.

Makes 4 to 6 servings

Philly Cheesesteak

The traditional Philadelphia sandwich just went Southwest!

1 each red and green bell pepper

1 large Vidalia or white onion

1 tablespoon canola oil

1 pound frozen top sirloin or
  rib-eye steak

2 tablespoons Worcestershire
  or steak sauce

4 ounces provolone cheese,
  grated

4 ounces Monterey Jack
  cheese, grated

8 (9- to 10-inch) flour, wheat,
  or garlic tortillas

● **Suggested garnishes:**
Spicy Mustard Sauce (page 122) or
White Cheddar Sauce (page 123)

1. Slice bell peppers and onion into thin julienne strips. Sauté in oil in a large skillet over medium-high heat just until vegetables begin to soften, about 2 minutes.

2. Let steak sit at room temperature for 10–15 minutes to slightly thaw. Slice into paper thin slices across the grain. Turn skillet heat to high and add steak. Stir and cook until lightly browned. Turn off heat and stir in Worcestershire or steak sauce.

3. Toss cheeses together in a bowl. Lay 4 tortillas on the counter and spread ⅓ cup cheese over each. Spread 1 cup steak mixture over cheese and another ⅓ cup cheese over top.

4. Slide one of the cheese-covered tortillas in a 10-inch skillet over medium heat. Place one of the remaining tortillas on top. Press down with a wide spatula to remove any air pockets. Cover and cook 1 to 2 minutes, checking frequently, until bottom tortilla is crisp and browned.

5. Turn tortillas over, cover, and cook another 1 to 2 minutes, until bottom tortilla is crisp and browned. Repeat this process for remaining quesadillas. Cut into wedges and serve immediately.

Makes 4 to 6 servings

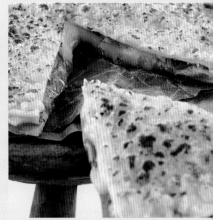

International

Old World Mexico

This old-world combo of potatoes and chorizo is scrumptious with a touch of sweet or hot peppers.

8 ounces Mexican chorizo, casings removed and crumbled

1 tablespoon butter

1 large russet potato (about $\frac{1}{2}$ pound), peeled and coarsely grated

3 cups grated cheeses, including cheddar, Monterey Jack, queso fresco, or cojita cheese

8 (9- to 10-inch) flour, wheat, or jalapeño tortillas

$\frac{1}{2}$ cup diced peppers (jalapeño or red bell pepper)

● **Suggested garnishes:**
Sassy Smoky Salsa (page 118),
Southwest Pesto Sauce (page 120),
or Creamy Avocado Sauce (page 121)

1. Sauté chorizo in a 10-inch skillet until cooked through and lightly browned. Remove chorizo and then add butter to skillet. Place grated potato in a kitchen towel and wring out to remove any excess moisture. Sauté potatoes in butter until lightly browned, stirring constantly to remove moisture; remove from heat.

2. Toss cheeses together in a bowl. Lay 4 tortillas on the counter and spread $\frac{1}{3}$ cup cheese over each. Sprinkle about $\frac{1}{3}$ cup chorizo, $\frac{1}{2}$ cup potatoes, and 2 tablespoons peppers over cheese. Sprinkle another $\frac{1}{3}$ cup cheese over top.

3. Slide one of the cheese-covered tortillas into a 10-inch skillet over medium heat. Place one of the remaining tortillas on top. Press down with a wide spatula to remove any air pockets. Cover and cook 1 to 2 minutes, checking frequently, until bottom tortilla is crisp and browned.

4. Turn over, cover, and cook 1 to 2 minutes more, or until lightly browned. Repeat this process for remaining quesadillas. Cut into wedges and serve immediately.

Makes 4 to 6 servings

Thai Peanut

Bold flavors from Thailand make this quesadilla exotic and flavorful.

1 (2-pound) rotisserie chicken

2 tablespoons grated ginger

1 teaspoon Tabasco or cayenne
   pepper sauce

$\frac{1}{2}$ cup creamy peanut butter

2 tablespoons soy sauce

2 tablespoons lime juice

8 (9- to 10-inch) flour or
   wheat tortillas

8 ounces Monterey Jack
   cheese, grated

$\frac{1}{2}$ cup thinly sliced green onions

$\frac{1}{2}$ cup diced roasted salted
   peanuts

$\frac{1}{2}$ cup chopped cilantro

1. Remove meat from chicken, cutting into small pieces as you go, discarding skin and bones. Mix together ginger, hot sauce, peanut butter, soy sauce, and lime juice. Stir into chicken.

2. Lay 4 tortillas on the counter and spread $\frac{1}{3}$ cup cheese over each. Spread 1 cup chicken over cheese. Sprinkle some onions, peanuts, and cilantro over cheese. Spread another $\frac{1}{3}$ cup cheese over top.

3. Slide one of the cheese-covered tortillas into a 10-inch skillet over medium heat. Place one of the remaining tortillas on top. Press down with a wide spatula to remove any air pockets. Cover and cook 1 to 2 minutes, checking frequently, until bottom tortilla is crisp and browned.

4. Turn over, cover, and cook 1 to 2 minutes more, or until lightly browned. Repeat this process for remaining quesadillas. Cut into wedges and serve immediately.

Makes 4 to 6 servings

Parmesan-Crusted Italian

Let your taste buds take a little trip to Tuscany with these fresh Italian country flavors.

8 (9- to 10-inch) flour, wheat, or garlic tortillas

8 ounces provolone cheese, thinly sliced

6 ounces prosciutto, thinly sliced

1 cup diced fresh basil

1 (14-ounce) can diced tomatoes with roasted garlic, drained

4 ounces Parmesan cheese, grated

● **Suggested garnish:**

Warm marinara sauce

1. Preheat oven to 400 degrees.

2. Lay 4 tortillas on the counter and place provolone cheese slices over each, completely covering surface.

3. Layer prosciutto slices in a single layer over top. Sprinkle basil and tomatoes over prosciutto. Spread another layer of Provolone cheese slices on top, completely covering surface.

4. Place one of the remaining tortillas on top. Press down with a wide spatula, making sure to remove any air pockets. Brush tortilla tops with a little water. Sprinkle ¼ cup Parmesan cheese over each, spreading evenly and thinly. Press cheese into tortillas with spatula.

5. Place quesadilla, Parmesan-crusted side up, on a wire rack standing on a baking sheet. Bake 10 to 12 minutes, checking frequently so as not to burn. Cut into wedges and serve immediately.

Makes 4 to 6 servings

Sweet and Spicy Asian

Asia meets Mexico with these delightful and playful flavors.

4 cups thinly sliced bok choy

2 cups thinly sliced red cabbage

3 green onions, cut into 2-inch
  julienne strips

2 tablespoons oil

1/4 cup hoisin sauce

2 cups shredded cooked pork

8 (9- to 10-inch) flour or
  wheat tortillas

8 ounces Monterey Jack
  cheese, grated

1 large egg, mixed with
  1 tablespoon water

1/2 cup sesame seeds

2 tablespoons olive oil or
  olive oil spray

1. Preheat oven to 400 degrees.

2. Stir-fry bok choy, cabbage, and green onions in oil in a large skillet or wok over high heat for 3 to 5 minutes, or until softened slightly and most of the liquid has evaporated.

3. In a bowl, stir hoisin sauce into pork; set aside.

4. Lay 4 tortillas on the counter and spread 1/3 cup cheese over each. Spread 3/4 cup vegetable mixture over cheese. Sprinkle on 1/2 cup pork. Spread another 1/3 cup cheese over top.

5. Place one of the remaining tortillas on top. Press down with a wide spatula to remove any air pockets. Brush tops of quesadillas with egg wash. Sprinkle on sesame seeds and brush or spray oil on top.

6. Place quesadilla, sesame-crusted side up, onto a wire rack standing on a baking sheet. Bake 10 to 12 minutes, checking frequently so as not to burn. Cut into wedges and serve immediately.

Makes 4 to 6 servings

Aloha Shrimp and Pineapple

Give your taste buds a trip to Polynesia with these fresh tropical flavors.

24 medium raw peeled and
   deveined shrimp

2 tablespoons honey

1 tablespoon butter

1 cup thinly sliced 1-inch pieces
   fresh pineapple

8 (9- to 10-inch) flour or
   wheat tortillas

8 ounces fontina cheese, grated

1 cup sweetened shredded
   coconut

● **Suggested garnishes:**
Roasted Red Pepper Sauce (page 119)
or Creamy Avocado Sauce (page 121)

1. Cut shrimp in half lengthwise making two thin half-moons and then toss in honey until evenly coated. Heat a skillet or wok to medium-high heat. Add butter to skillet and then add shrimp. Stir and cook until shrimp are opaque and then remove from pan.

2. Turn heat to high. Add pineapple to skillet, stirring constantly and scraping up bits. Cook until liquid has mostly evaporated, about 2 or 3 minutes.

3. Lay 4 tortillas on the counter. Spread the following on each: ⅓ cup cheese, ½ cup shrimp, ¼ cup coconut, ¼ cup pineapple, and another ⅓ cup cheese.

4. Slide one of the cheese-covered tortillas into a 10-inch skillet over medium heat. Place one of the remaining tortillas on top. Press down with a wide spatula to remove any air pockets. Cover and cook 1 to 2 minutes, checking frequently, until bottom tortilla is crisp and browned.

5. Turn over, cover, and cook 1 to 2 minutes more, or until lightly browned. Repeat this process for remaining quesadillas. Cut into wedges and serve immediately.

Makes 4 to 6 servings

Spicy Cuban

The taste of Cuba is a perfect fit for quesadillas! Add as little or as much spice as you like.

1 tablespoon butter

1 large plantain, sliced
$\frac{1}{8}$ inch thick

8 (9- to 10-inch) flour, wheat,
or chipotle tortillas

8 ounces Havarti cheese, grated

$\frac{1}{2}$ pound spicy ham (such as
Virginia ham), thinly sliced
and diced

1 (15-ounce) can black beans,
drained and rinsed

1 box (8 ounces) jambalaya
or Cajun style rice mix,
cooked and cooled

1 teaspoon Tabasco sauce
(or more to taste)

● **Suggested garnishes:**

Sour Cream Paprika Sauce (page 120)
or Spicy Mustard Sauce (page 122)

1. Heat skillet to medium-high heat. Add butter and sauté plantain slices in batches so they are in a single layer in the skillet. Sauté for about 1 minute on each side, or until lightly browned and softened. Remove plantains and wipe skillet clean with a paper towel.

2. Lay 4 tortillas on the counter. Spread the following over each: $\frac{1}{3}$ cup cheese, $\frac{1}{2}$ cup ham, a few plantain slices, $\frac{1}{4}$ cup black beans, $\frac{1}{3}$ cup rice, a few dashes Tabasco, and another $\frac{1}{3}$ cup cheese.

3. Slide one of the cheese-covered tortillas into a 10-inch skillet over medium heat. Place one of the remaining tortillas on top. Press down with a wide spatula to remove any air pockets. Cover and cook 1 to 2 minutes, checking frequently, until bottom tortilla is crisp and browned.

4. Turn over, cover, and cook 1 to 2 minutes more, or until lightly browned. Repeat this process for remaining quesadillas. Cut into wedges and serve immediately. Serve any remaining rice as a side dish, if desired.

Makes 4 to 6 servings

South American Chimichurri

Forget bottled steak sauce—this South American sauce pairs well with North American grilled steaks.

2 cups chopped fresh
   flat-leaf parsley

1/2 cup chopped cilantro

1/2 cup extra virgin olive oil

3 cloves garlic, chopped

2 teaspoons red pepper flakes

2 tablespoons freshly squeezed
   lime juice

2 tablespoons honey

1/2 teaspoon salt

2 (8-ounce) sirloin or tenderloin
   steaks

8 (9- to 10-inch) flour, wheat,
   or jalapeño tortillas

8 ounces Monterey Jack
   cheese, grated

1. In a food processor, blend the parsley, cilantro, oil, garlic, red pepper flakes, lime juice, honey, and salt. Place half the sauce in a large ziplock bag, add steaks, and refrigerate 2 hours or overnight.

2. Remove steaks from refrigerator and bring to room temperature, about 30 minutes. Grill over high heat until desired doneness, about 3 minutes on each side, seasoning to taste with salt and pepper. Let stand for 5 minutes and then cut into ¼-inch-thick slices across the grain.

3. Lay 4 tortillas on the counter. Spread the following over each: ⅓ cup cheese, steak slices, and another ⅓ cup cheese.

4. Slide one of the cheese-covered tortillas into a 10-inch skillet over medium heat. Place one of the remaining tortillas on top. Press down with a wide spatula to remove any air pockets. Cover and cook 1 to 2 minutes, checking frequently, until bottom tortilla is crisp and browned.

5. Turn over, cover, and cook 1 to 2 minutes more, or until lightly browned. Repeat this process for remaining quesadillas. Cut into wedges, garnish with remaining parsley mixture, and serve immediately.

Makes 4 to 6 servings

Jamaican Jerk

Fresh and spicy tastes of Jamaica shine in this flavor-packed quesadilla.

5 cloves garlic

1 Scotch bonnet or habañero chile, seeds and pulp removed

³/₄ cup ketchup

3 tablespoons soy sauce

Juice and zest of 1 lime

2 tablespoons jerk spice blend, or more to taste

10 green onions, thinly sliced, divided

6 boneless, skinless chicken thighs

1 plantain, cut into ¹/₄-inch slices

8 (9- to 10-inch) flour, wheat, or chipotle tortillas

8 ounces smoked cheddar cheese, grated

1 mango, peeled and diced

1. Place first six ingredients and half the green onions in a food processor. Process until smooth and place in a large ziplock bag. Add chicken thighs. Refrigerate at least 2 hours or overnight.

2. Bring thighs to room temperature, about 30 minutes. Grill or broil over high heat, basting with marinade until cooked through. Let stand 5 minutes and then thinly slice. Place plantain slices on skewers, brush with marinade, and grill or broil for a few minutes. Remove from heat and then dice.

3. Lay 4 tortillas on the counter. Spread the following over each: ¹/₃ cup cheese, chicken slices, 2 tablespoons green onions, 1 tablespoon mango, plantains, and another ¹/₃ cup cheese.

4. Slide one of the cheese-covered tortillas into a 10-inch skillet over medium heat. Place one of the remaining tortillas on top. Press down with a wide spatula to remove any air pockets. Cover and cook 1 to 2 minutes, checking frequently, until bottom tortilla is crisp and browned.

5. Turn over, cover, and cook 1 to 2 minutes more, or until lightly browned. Repeat this process for remaining quesadillas. Cut into wedges and serve immediately.

Makes 4 to 6 servings

Almond-Crusted Moroccan

Spiced chicken and dried apricots in a unique almond-crusted quesadilla!

1 teaspoon almond extract

8 ounces light cream cheese, softened

8 (9- to 10-inch) flour or wheat tortillas

2 ounces Gruyère cheese, grated

1 (2-pound) rotisserie chicken

2 teaspoons cumin

½ teaspoon allspice

½ teaspoon smoked paprika

1 cup diced dried apricots

1 large egg, mixed with 1 tablespoon water

1 cup minced or ground almonds

2 tablespoons olive oil

1. Preheat oven to 400 degrees.

2. Mix almond extract with cream cheese. Lay the tortillas on the counter and spread a generous tablespoon of cream cheese mixture over each. Sprinkle 2 tablespoons Gruyère cheese over 4 tortillas.

3. Remove chicken from the bones and shred with a fork. Toss with spices. Spread 1 cup chicken evenly over Gruyère cheese, covering whole surface. Sprinkle diced apricots over top.

4. Place one of the apricot-covered tortillas on a flat surface. Place one of the remaining tortillas on top, cream cheese side down. Press down with a wide spatula to remove any air pockets. Brush top of quesadilla with a little egg wash. Spread ¼ cup almonds on top and press down with spatula, making sure almonds are pressed into tortilla. Brush or spray with a little olive oil.

5. Place quesadilla, almond-crusted side up, on a wire rack standing on a baking sheet. Bake 10 to 12 minutes, checking frequently so as not to burn. Cut into wedges and serve immediately.

Makes 4 to 6 servings

Caribbean Mojo Pork

Sweet mixed with spicy is a classic Caribbean combination—all stuffed in a quesadilla.

1 pound pork loin

Mojo Marinade (page 122)

1 yellow bell pepper, cut into
 $^1/_4$-inch julienne strips

1 red onion, sliced $^1/_4$ inch thick

1 large plantain, cut into $^1/_4$-inch
 slices

2 tablespoons canola oil

8 (9- to 10-inch) flour or
 wheat tortillas

8 ounces Monterey Jack cheese,
 grated

1. Marinate pork in marinade in a large ziplock bag for 8 hours or overnight. Remove pork and grill or broil over high heat for 2 to 3 minutes per side, or until browned and crusty. Let cool to warm and then thinly slice.

2. Stir-fry the bell pepper, onion, and plantain in oil in a large skillet or wok over high heat until lightly browned and softened.

3. Lay 4 tortillas on the counter. Spread $^1/_3$ cup cheese over each. Spread 1 cup pork over cheese followed by $^1/_2$ cup sautéed vegetables. Sprinkle another $^1/_3$ cup cheese over top.

4. Slide one of the cheese-covered tortillas into a 10-inch skillet over medium heat. Place one of the remaining tortillas on top. Press down with a wide spatula to remove any air pockets. Cover and cook 1 to 2 minutes, checking frequently, until bottom tortilla is crisp and browned.

5. Turn over, cover, and cook 1 to 2 minutes more, or until lightly browned. Repeat this process for remaining quesadillas. Cut into wedges and serve immediately.

Makes 4 to 6 servings

Indian Tandoori Chicken

This Indian-inspired quesadilla takes the ho-hum out of dinner in a hurry.

½ cup plain yogurt

2 tablespoons lemon juice

2 tablespoons brown sugar

1 tablespoon paprika

1 tablespoon curry paste

1 tablespoon cumin

2 tablespoons minced fresh garlic

2 tablespoons minced ginger

1 teaspoon salt

1 teaspoon cayenne pepper

2 boneless, skinless chicken breasts

8 (9- to 10-inch) flour tortillas

8 ounces Monterey Jack cheese, grated

1 cup sliced toasted almonds

● **Suggested garnish:**
Peach Chutney (page 123)

1. Combine yogurt, lemon juice, sugar, and the spices. Place in a large ziplock bag with chicken to marinate. Refrigerate 2 hours or overnight.

2. Remove chicken and let stand 30 minutes at room temperature. Grill or broil for 8 to 10 minutes. Turn and cook 5 minutes more, or until chicken is lightly browned and cooked through. Let stand 5 minutes and then thinly slice.

3. Lay 4 tortillas on the counter. Spread the following over each: ⅓ cup cheese, ¼ cup sliced almonds, chicken slices, and another ⅓ cup cheese.

4. Slide one of the cheese-covered tortillas into a 10-inch skillet over medium heat. Place one of the remaining tortillas on top. Press down with a wide spatula to remove any air pockets. Cover and cook 1 to 2 minutes, checking frequently, until bottom tortilla is crisp and browned.

5. Turn over, cover, and cook 1 to 2 minutes more, or until lightly browned. Repeat this process for remaining quesadillas. Cut into wedges and serve immediately.

Makes 4 to 6 servings

Greek Isles

The salty goodness of classic Mediterranean ingredients is tasty in a quesadilla.

6 ounces feta cheese, crumbled

4 ounces Monterey Jack cheese, grated

8 (9- to 10-inch) flour, wheat, or sun-dried tomato tortillas

1 tablespoon butter

3 cloves garlic, pressed

1 pound frozen chopped spinach, thawed, drained, and pressed dry

½ cup pitted and minced kalamata or black olives

● **Suggested garnishes:**
Roasted Red Pepper Sauce (page 119)
or Mushroom Cream Sauce (page 121)

1. Toss cheeses together in a bowl. Lay 4 tortillas on the counter and spread about ⅓ cup cheese over each.

2. Heat a skillet to medium-high heat. Add butter and then garlic, and stir about 1 minute, or until garlic is fragrant. Add the spinach and stir constantly until most of moisture has evaporated, about 3 to 5 minutes. Spread ½ cup spinach mixture and 2 tablespoons olives on each cheese-covered tortilla. Sprinkle another ⅓ cup cheese over top.

3. Slide one of the cheese-covered tortillas into a 10-inch skillet over medium heat. Place one of the remaining tortillas on top. Press down with a wide spatula to remove any air pockets. Cover and cook 1 to 2 minutes, checking frequently, until bottom tortilla is crisp and browned.

4. Turn over, cover, and cook 1 to 2 minutes more, or until lightly browned. Repeat this process for remaining quesadillas. Cut into wedges and serve immediately.

Makes 4 to 6 servings

Vegetarian

Roasted Veggie and Goat Cheese

This combination of roasted veggies and goat cheese is simply delightful.

1 large yellow onion, peeled

2 red bell peppers, seeds and
   pulp removed

1 large bunch asparagus, bottom
   ends removed

3 small zucchini

5 cloves garlic, minced

3 tablespoons olive oil, divided

8 (9- to 10-inch) flour, wheat,
   or pesto tortillas

8 ounces goat cheese, softened

1 teaspoon salt

● **Suggested garnishes:**
Roasted Red Pepper Sauce (**page 119**)
or Mushroom Cream Sauce (**page 121**)

1. Preheat oven to 425 degrees.

2. Slice the onion, peppers, asparagus, and zucchini into 1-inch julienne strips. Place vegetables and garlic cut side down in a baking pan and brush or spray with 2 tablespoons oil. Bake for 15 minutes. Remove from oven, let cool, and then sprinkle with garlic. Return to oven for 12 to 15 minutes more, or until vegetables are softened and lightly browned.

3. Spread the tortillas evenly with the goat cheese and sprinkle salt over top.

4. Heat a skillet to medium heat. Slide one of the cheese-covered tortillas into skillet. Spread 1 cup roasted vegetables and a little garlic over top. Place one of the remaining tortillas on top, goat cheese side down. Press down with a wide spatula to remove any air pockets. Cover and cook 1 to 2 minutes, checking frequently, until bottom tortilla is crisp and browned.

5. Turn over, cover, and cook 1 to 2 minutes more, or until lightly browned. Repeat this process for remaining quesadillas. Cut into wedges and serve immediately.

Makes 4 to 6 servings

Mango Brie

The strong flavor of Brie is mellowed by the sweet mango, with a little hot pepper added for zip.

8 ounces Brie, warmed

8 (9- to 10-inch) flour or
 wheat tortillas

2 ounces Monterey Jack
 cheese, grated

3 green onions with tops,
 thinly sliced

1 small jalapeño pepper,
 seeds and pulp removed,
 minced

2 ripe mangos, peeled and
 thinly sliced

1. Spread a generous tablespoon of Brie on each tortilla. Sprinkle 2 tablespoons Monterey Jack cheese over top.

2. Sprinkle onions and a little jalapeño over 4 tortillas. Layer mango slices over top, completely covering surface.

3. Slide one of the fruit-covered tortillas into a 10-inch skillet over medium heat. Place one of the remaining tortillas on top, Brie side down. Press down with a wide spatula to remove any air pockets. Cover and cook 1 to 2 minutes, checking frequently, until bottom tortilla is crisp and browned.

4. Turn over, cover, and cook 1 to 2 minutes more, or until lightly browned. Repeat this process for remaining quesadillas. Cut into wedges and serve immediately.

Makes 4 to 6 servings

● **Suggested garnishes:**
Sour Cream Paprika Sauce (page 120)
or Spicy Mustard Sauce (page 122)

Sautéed Garlic Spinach

The garlic and spinach sautéed together with a dash of nutmeg is a delicious combination.

8 ounces cream cheese, softened

8 (9- to 10-inch) flour, wheat, garlic, or spinach tortillas

1 tablespoon butter

2 shallots, diced

3 cloves garlic, pressed

1 pound frozen chopped spinach, thawed, drained, and pressed dry

½ teaspoon nutmeg

2 ounces Gruyère cheese, grated

Salt and pepper, to taste

● **Suggested garnishes:**
Sour Cream Paprika Sauce (page 120)
or White Cheddar Sauce (page 123)

1. Spread 1 tablespoon of cream cheese on each tortilla.

2. Heat a skillet to medium-high heat. Add butter, shallots, and garlic and stir about 1 minute, or until garlic is fragrant. Add spinach and stir constantly until most of the moisture has evaporated, about 3 to 5 minutes. Remove from heat and stir in nutmeg.

3. Spread the following on 4 tortillas: 2 tablespoons Gruyère cheese, ⅔ cup spinach, and another 2 tablespoons Gruyère cheese.

4. Slide one of the cheese-covered tortillas into a 10-inch skillet over medium heat. Sprinkle with salt and pepper as desired. Place one of the remaining tortillas on top, cream cheese side down. Press down with a wide spatula to remove any air pockets. Cover and cook 1 to 2 minutes, checking frequently, until bottom tortilla is crisp and browned.

5. Turn over, cover, and cook 1 to 2 minutes more, or until lightly browned. Repeat this process for remaining quesadillas. Cut into wedges and serve immediately.

Makes 4 to 6 servings

Black and Blue

You'll love this powerful combination of strong cheese and spicy beans.

2 (15-ounce) cans black beans, drained and rinsed

1 teaspoon Tabasco sauce

2 teaspoons cumin

2 ounces Monterey Jack cheese, grated

8 ounces blue or Gorgonzola cheese, crumbled

8 (9- to 10-inch) flour or wheat tortillas

1 red bell pepper, diced

1. In a bowl, mix the beans with the Tabasco sauce and cumin.

2. Toss cheeses together in a bowl. Lay 4 tortillas on the counter. Spread ⅓ cup cheese over each. Spread ½ cup bean mixture over cheese. Sprinkle about ¼ cup bell pepper over beans. Spread another ⅓ cup cheese over top.

3. Slide one of the cheese-covered tortillas into a 10-inch skillet over medium heat. Place one of the remaining tortillas on top. Press down with a wide spatula to remove any air pockets. Cover and cook 1 to 2 minutes, checking frequently, until bottom tortilla is crisp and browned.

4. Turn over, cover, and cook 1 to 2 minutes more, or until lightly browned. Repeat this process for remaining quesadillas. Cut into wedges and serve immediately.

Makes 4 to 6 servings

Butternut Squash

The soft texture of the squash and cheese combined with the crunchiness of the pecans is delightful.

1 whole butternut squash

1 large white or yellow onion, peeled

2 tablespoons butter

1 tablespoon brown sugar

8 (9- to 10-inch) flour or wheat tortillas

8 ounces fontina cheese, grated

1 cup diced pecans

● **Suggested garnishes:**

Roasted Red Pepper Sauce (page 119) or Mushroom Cream Sauce (page 121)

1. Preheat oven to 375 degrees.

2. Cut squash in half lengthwise and remove seeds and strings. Place cut side down on an oiled baking sheet and bake 40 to 50 minutes, or until fork tender. Cool and cut into ¼-inch slices.

3. Cut onion in half and then into ¼-inch slices. Heat a skillet to medium-high heat. Add butter, sugar, and onion. Cook until caramelized, about 15 minutes, stirring occasionally; dice.

4. Lay 4 tortillas on the counter. Spread the following on each: ⅓ cup cheese, ½ cup squash, ¼ cup onion, ¼ cup pecans, and another ⅓ cup cheese.

5. Slide one of the cheese-covered tortillas into a 10-inch skillet over medium heat. Place one of the remaining tortillas on top. Press down with a wide spatula to remove any air pockets. Cover and cook 1 to 2 minutes, checking frequently, until bottom tortilla is crisp and browned.

6. Turn over, cover, and cook 1 to 2 minutes more, or until lightly browned. Repeat this process for remaining quesadillas. Cut into wedges and serve immediately.

Makes 4 to 6 servings

Roasted Garlic

If you're a garlic lover, put this on your top-ten list for favorite garlic recipes!

2 bulbs elephant garlic, or
   3 bulbs regular garlic

2 tablespoons olive oil

Salt and pepper, to taste

2 ounces Monterey Jack
   cheese, grated

6 ounces feta cheese, crumbled

8 (9- to 10-inch) flour, wheat,
   or garlic tortillas

2 green onions with tops,
   thinly sliced

1 cup toasted sliced almonds

● **Suggested garnishes:**
Roasted Red Pepper Sauce (page 119)
or Mushroom Cream Sauce (page 121)

1. Preheat oven to 350 degrees.

2. Slice garlic bulbs in half (across the diameter) and place into a square of aluminum foil, cut side up. Drizzle with olive oil. Bake 1 hour and let cool. Remove garlic cloves and mash with a fork until creamy. Add salt and pepper, to taste.

3. Toss cheeses together in a bowl. Lay all tortillas on the counter and spread garlic evenly over each. Sprinkle ⅓ cup cheese over 4 tortillas. Sprinkle some green onions and almonds over cheese. Spread another ⅓ cup cheese over top.

4. Slide one of the cheese-covered tortillas into a 10-inch skillet over medium heat. Place one of the remaining tortillas on top, garlic side down. Press down with a wide spatula to remove any air pockets. Cover and cook about 1 to 2 minutes, checking frequently until bottom tortilla is crisp and browned.

5. Turn over, cover, and cook 1 to 2 minutes more, or until lightly browned. Repeat this process for remaining quesadillas. Cut into wedges and serve immediately.

Makes 4 to 6 servings

Portobello Sun-Dried Tomato

The meaty taste of portobellos and the sweetness of sun-dried tomatoes is a perfect pair.

1 (6-ounce) jar diced sun-dried
tomatoes in oil

½ cup diced yellow onion

3 cloves garlic, minced

1 large portobello mushroom cap,
halved and thinly sliced

6 ounces Monterey Jack
cheese, grated

2 ounces Gruyère cheese, grated

8 (9- to 10-inch) flour, wheat,
or sun-dried tomato tortillas

1 cup diced flat-leaf parsley

● **Suggested garnishes:**
Roasted Red Pepper Sauce (page 119),
Mushroom Cream Sauce (page 121),
or Creamy Avocado Sauce (page 121)

1. Drain oil from jar of sun-dried tomatoes into a large skillet heated to medium-high heat. Add onion and garlic, and sauté for about 2 minutes, or until fragrant. Add mushroom slices and cook until lightly browned and liquid has evaporated.

2. Toss cheeses together in a bowl. Lay 4 tortillas on the counter. Spread ⅓ cup cheese over each. Spread ½ cup mushrooms over cheese. Sprinkle about ¼ cup parsley and ¼ cup sun-dried tomatoes over mushrooms. Spread another ⅓ cup cheese over top.

3. Slide one of the cheese-covered tortillas into a 10-inch skillet over medium heat. Place one of the remaining tortillas on top. Press down with a wide spatula to remove any air pockets. Cover and cook 1 to 2 minutes, checking frequently, until bottom tortilla is crisp and browned.

4. Turn over, cover, and cook 1 to 2 minutes more, or until lightly browned. Repeat this process for remaining quesadillas. Cut into wedges and serve immediately.

Makes 4 to 6 servings

Caprese Style

Fresh mozzarella, basil, and tomatoes is always a winning combination.

4 large ripe tomatoes, sliced into
   ¼-inch slices

1 tablespoon salt

8 (9- to 10-inch) flour, wheat,
   or sun-dried tomato tortillas

4 ounces Monterey Jack cheese,
   grated

1 large bunch basil

4 ounces fresh mozzarella,
   thinly sliced

● **Suggested garnishes:**
Roasted Red Pepper Sauce (page 119)
or Creamy Avocado Sauce (page 121)

1. Lay tomato slices in a single layer on paper towels. Sprinkle with salt. Let stand 20 minutes and then pat dry with more paper towels.

2. Lay 4 tortillas on the counter. Spread about 2 tablespoons Monterey Jack cheese over each. Spread basil leaves and tomato slices over top. Lay mozzarella slices over top, covering entire surface. Sprinkle another 2 tablespoons Monterey Jack over top.

3. Slide one of the cheese-covered tortillas into a 10-inch skillet over medium heat. Place one of the remaining tortillas on top. Press down with a wide spatula to remove any air pockets. Cover and cook 1 to 2 minutes, checking frequently, until bottom tortilla is crisp and browned.

4. Turn over, cover, and cook 1 to 2 minutes more, or until lightly browned. Repeat this process for remaining quesadillas. Cut into wedges and serve immediately.

Makes 4 to 6 servings

Three-Bean Torte

You won't miss the meat with this hearty cheese torte.

2 (14-ounce) cans black beans, drained

1 (14-ounce) can pinto beans, drained

1 (14-ounce) can white beans, drained

2 (10-ounce) cans red enchilada sauce

1 cup salsa

8 (9- to 10-inch) flour, wheat, or jalapeño tortillas

2 cups fresh or frozen corn

¹/₂ cup chopped cilantro

1 cup thinly sliced green onions

4 ounces Monterey Jack cheese, grated

8 ounces cheddar cheese, grated

1. Preheat oven to 350 degrees.

2. Stir together the beans in a bowl. Stir together the enchilada sauce and salsa in a separate bowl.

3. Spray a 10-inch springform pan with nonstick cooking spray. Make six layers in pan as follows, using a little of each as you go: 1 tortilla, corn, cilantro, sauce, beans, green onion, and cheeses. Top with the remaining tortilla.

4. Bake for 30 to 40 minutes, or until bubbly and cooked throughout. Remove from oven and let stand 5 minutes. Remove sides of springform pan and set torte on a round serving plate in center of table. Garnish with a little grated cheese, if desired. Cut into wedges and serve immediately.

Makes 4 to 6 servings

Mushroom Madness

If you love mushrooms, you have just died and gone to heaven!

12 cups thinly sliced mushrooms
(any combination of fresh
mushrooms such as portobello,
crimini, and shiitake)

3 tablespoons butter

3 cloves garlic, pressed

½ cup thinly sliced green onions,
with tops

8 (9- to 10-inch) flour, wheat,
or garlic tortillas

8 ounces regular or smoked
Gouda cheese

● **Suggested garnishes:**

Mushroom Cream Sauce (page 121)
or Spicy Mustard Sauce (page 122)

1. Sauté mushrooms in two batches, using half the butter and garlic in each batch, over medium-high heat in a 10-inch skillet until most of the moisture has evaporated and the mushrooms are lightly browned. Remove from skillet and stir in green onions. Wipe skillet dry with a paper towel.

2. Lay 4 tortillas on the counter. Spread ⅓ cup cheese over each. Spread 1 cup mushrooms over cheese. Sprinkle another ⅓ cup cheese over top.

3. Slide one of the cheese-covered tortillas into a 10-inch skillet over medium heat. Place one of the remaining tortillas on top. Press down with a wide spatula to remove any air pockets. Cover and cook 1 to 2 minutes, checking frequently, until bottom tortilla is crisp and browned.

4. Turn over, cover, and cook 1 to 2 minutes more, or until lightly browned. Repeat this process for remaining quesadillas. Cut into wedges and serve immediately.

Makes 4 to 6 servings

Caramelized Onion and Gouda

Sweet caramelized onions are the perfect flavor match for smoky Gouda.

2 medium white onions, peeled

2 tablespoons butter

1 tablespoon brown sugar

1 teaspoon white wine vinegar

1/2 teaspoon salt

8 (9- to 10-inch) flour or
   wheat tortillas

8 ounces smoked Gouda
   cheese, grated

1 cup chopped flat-leaf parsley

● **Suggested garnishes:**

Mushroom Cream Sauce (page 121)
or Creamy Avocado Sauce (page 121)

1. Slice onions into ¼-inch slices. Sauté in butter, stirring constantly, for 15 minutes over medium-high heat in a 10-inch skillet. Add sugar, vinegar, and salt, and continue to sauté until most of the moisture has evaporated and onions are browned but not mushy. Wipe skillet dry with a paper towel.

2. Lay 4 tortillas on the counter and spread ⅓ cup cheese over each. Spread ½ cup onion mixture over cheese. Sprinkle a little parsley and another ⅓ cup cheese over top.

3. Slide one of the cheese-covered tortillas into a 10-inch skillet over medium heat. Place one of the remaining tortillas on top. Press down with a wide spatula to remove any air pockets. Cover and cook 1 to 2 minutes, checking frequently, until bottom tortilla is crisp and browned.

4. Turn over, cover, and cook 1 to 2 minutes more, or until lightly browned. Repeat this process for remaining quesadillas. Cut into wedges and serve immediately.

Makes 4 to 6 servings

Spring Fling

The fresh flavors of spring vegetables are scrumptious with your favorite melted cheese.

1 bunch thin asparagus, cut into
   2-inch pieces

2 cups tiny grape tomatoes

1 bunch green onions with tops,
   thinly sliced

3 cloves garlic, minced

2 tablespoons olive oil

Salt and pepper, to taste

8 (9- to 10-inch) flour, wheat,
   or spinach tortillas

8 ounces fontina cheese or other
   mild cheese, grated

● **Suggested garnishes:**

Mushroom Cream Sauce (page 121)
or White Cheddar Sauce (page 123)

1. Spread asparagus, tomatoes, green onions, and garlic on a baking sheet sprayed with nonstick cooking spray. Brush vegetables with olive oil. Place in oven about 6 inches from heat and broil for 3 to 5 minutes, watching closely, until vegetables are cooked and lightly browned. Remove from oven and sprinkle with salt and pepper.

2. Lay 4 tortillas on the counter and then sprinkle each with ⅓ cup cheese. Spread about 1 cup vegetables over cheese. Sprinkle another ⅓ cup cheese over top.

3. Slide one of the cheese-covered tortillas into a 10-inch skillet over medium heat. Place one of the remaining tortillas on top. Press down with a wide spatula to remove any air pockets. Cover and cook 1 to 2 minutes, checking frequently, until bottom tortilla is crisp and browned.

4. Turn over, cover, and cook 1 to 2 minutes more, or until lightly browned. Repeat this process for remaining quesadillas. Cut into wedges and serve immediately.

Makes 4 to 6 servings

Three-Cheese Broccoli

The favorite combo of broccoli and cheese is extra tasty in a cheddar-crusted quesadilla.

2 tablespoons butter

4 cups diced broccoli florets

½ cup diced onion

2 ounces Gruyère cheese, grated

2 ounces Parmesan cheese, grated

6 ounces sharp cheddar cheese, grated and divided

8 (9- to 10-inch) flour or wheat tortillas

● **Suggested garnishes:**

Spicy Mustard Sauce (page 122) or White Cheddar Sauce (page 123)

1. Preheat oven to 400 degrees.

2. Heat a large skillet to medium-high heat. Add butter, broccoli, and onion. Sauté for 3 to 5 minutes, or until broccoli and onion is softened and most of liquid has evaporated.

3. Toss Gruyère, Parmesan, and all but 1 cup cheddar cheese together. Lay 4 tortillas on the counter and spread ⅓ cup cheese over each. Sprinkle broccoli mixture over cheese. Sprinkle another ⅓ cup cheese over top.

4. Place one of the remaining tortillas on top of each. Press down with a wide spatula to remove any air pockets. Brush tops of each tortilla with a little water. Spread ¼ cup of the remaining cheddar cheese on top in a thin but even layer.

5. Place quesadillas, cheddar cheese side up, onto a wire rack standing on a baking sheet. Bake 10 to 12 minutes, checking frequently so as not to burn. Cut into wedges and serve immediately.

Makes 4 to 6 servings

Roasted Corn Confetti

The browned and roasted corn adds great flavor to the other crunchy vegetables.

2 cups fresh or frozen corn

1 tablespoon butter

$\frac{1}{2}$ red bell pepper, diced

$\frac{1}{2}$ green bell pepper, diced

$\frac{1}{2}$ yellow onion, diced

8 (9- to 10-inch) flour, wheat, or chipotle tortillas

8 ounces Monterey Jack cheese, grated

● **Suggested garnishes:**

Roasted Red Pepper Sauce (page 119) or White Cheddar Sauce (page 123)

1. Heat a 10-inch skillet to medium-high heat. Add corn to dry pan and cook for 5 to 8 minutes, stirring constantly, until corn is lightly browned. Add butter, bell peppers, and onion. Cook, stirring constantly, another 3 to 5 minutes, or until onion is translucent. Wipe skillet clean with a paper towel.

2. Lay 4 tortillas on the counter and sprinkle each with $\frac{1}{3}$ cup cheese. Spread about 1 cup vegetables over cheese and sprinkle with another $\frac{1}{3}$ cup cheese.

3. Slide one of the cheese-covered tortillas into a 10-inch skillet over medium heat. Place one of the remaining tortillas on top. Press down with a wide spatula to remove any air pockets. Cover and cook 1 to 2 minutes, checking frequently, until bottom tortilla is crisp and browned.

4. Turn over, cover, and cook 1 to 2 minutes more, or until lightly browned. Repeat this process for remaining quesadillas. Cut into wedges and serve immediately.

Makes 4 to 6 servings

Roasted Ratatouille

The classic combination of roasted eggplant, squash, and onions makes delectable quesadillas.

1 large yellow onion, peeled

3 small yellow squash

3 small zucchini

1 medium eggplant

2 tablespoons olive oil

2 teaspoons garlic powder

8 (9- to 10-inch) flour, wheat,
   or garlic tortillas

8 ounces Jarlsberg or Gruyère
   cheese, grated

● **Suggested garnishes:**
Roasted Red Pepper Sauce (page 119)
or Mushroom Cream Sauce (page 121)

1. Slice onion, squash, zucchini, and eggplant lengthwise in ¼-inch planks. Cut these planks into 2-inch-long julienne strips. Place vegetables closely together, cut side down, in a baking pan and brush or spray with oil. Sprinkle with garlic powder. Broil in oven about 6 inches from heat for 3 to 5 minutes, or until lightly browned. Remove from oven and let cool.

2. Lay 4 tortillas on the counter and sprinkle with ⅓ cup cheese. Spread about 1 cup vegetables over cheese. Spread another ⅓ cup cheese over.

3. Slide one of the cheese-covered tortillas into a 10-inch skillet over medium heat. Place one of the remaining tortillas on top. Press down with a wide spatula to remove any air pockets. Cover and cook 1 to 2 minutes, checking frequently, until bottom tortilla is crisp and browned.

4. Turn over, cover, and cook 1 to 2 minutes more, or until lightly browned. Repeat this process for remaining quesadillas. Cut into wedges and serve immediately.

Makes 4 to 6 servings

Three Olive

If you love strong, exotic flavor, this is the quesadilla for you.

2 ounces Gruyère cheese, grated

6 ounces fontina cheese, grated

8 (9- to 10-inch) flour or
   wheat tortillas

4 ounces stuffed green olives,
   thinly sliced

4 ounces pitted kalamata olives,
   thinly sliced

8 ounces pitted black olives,
   thinly sliced

1/2 cup chopped flat-leaf parsley

1. Mix together the cheeses and then sprinkle 1/3 cup cheese over 4 tortillas. Toss the olives and parsley together. Spread about 1/2 cup olives over cheese and then sprinkle another 1/3 cup cheese over top.

2. Slide one of the cheese-covered tortillas into a 10-inch skillet over medium heat. Place one of the remaining tortillas on top. Press down with a wide spatula to remove any air pockets. Cover and cook 1 to 2 minutes, checking frequently, until bottom tortilla is crisp and browned.

3. Turn over, cover, and cook 1 to 2 minutes more, or until lightly browned. Repeat this process for remaining quesadillas. Cut into wedges and serve immediately.

Makes 4 to 6 servings

● **Suggested garnishes:**

Creamy Avocado Sauce (page 121)
or White Cheddar Sauce (page 123)

Desserts

Peaches and Cream

The ginger makes the peaches pop with flavor and blends well with the almond-flavored cream cheese.

2 teaspoons almond extract

12 ounces light cream
  cheese, softened

8 (9- to 10-inch) flour tortillas

4 cups (¼-inch slices) firm but
  ripe peeled peaches

2 tablespoons sugar

2 tablespoons butter

1 tablespoon fresh grated ginger

Few dashes nutmeg

Cinnamon sugar as desired

● **Suggested garnishes:**

Cinnamon Cream Syrup (page 126)
or Vanilla Cream Syrup (page 124)

1. Mix almond extract with cream cheese. Spread about 2 tablespoons of cream cheese mixture on each tortillas.

2. Toss peaches in sugar and then sauté in butter, ginger, and nutmeg over medium-high heat in a 10-inch skillet, stirring constantly to brown but not burn. Remove from skillet and wipe pan dry with a paper towel. Spread about 1 cup peach mixture over 4 tortillas.

3. Slide one of the peach-covered tortillas into a 10-inch skillet over medium heat. Place one of the remaining tortillas on top, cream cheese side down. Press down with a wide spatula to remove any air pockets. Cover and cook 1 to 2 minutes, checking frequently, until bottom tortilla is crisp and browned.

4. Turn over, cover, and cook 1 to 2 minutes more, or until lightly browned. Repeat this process for remaining quesadillas. Sprinkle with cinnamon sugar as desired. Cut into wedges and serve immediately.

Makes 4 to 6 servings

Caramel Apple

Caramel apple flavors in a crispy cinnamon-sugar tortilla crust make an easy and luscious dessert.

12 ounces light cream cheese, softened

8 (9- to 10-inch) flour tortillas

4 cups (1/8-inch slices) Granny Smith apples

3 tablespoons butter

1/4 cup brown sugar

Cinnamon sugar

Rich Caramel Sauce (page 124)

1. Spread about 2 tablespoons cream cheese over each tortilla.

2. Sauté the apples, butter, and brown sugar over medium-high heat in a large skillet for about 5 minutes, or until apple slices are soft and browned and liquid has evaporated. Spread 1 cup apple mixture over 4 tortillas.

3. Slide one of the apple-covered tortillas into a 10-inch skillet over medium heat. Place one of the remaining tortillas on top, cream cheese side down. Press down with a wide spatula to remove any air pockets. Cover and cook 1 to 2 minutes, checking frequently, until bottom tortilla is crisp and browned.

4. Turn over, cover, and cook 1 to 2 minutes more, or until lightly browned. Repeat this process for remaining quesadillas. Sprinkle with cinnamon sugar as desired. Drizzle with Rich Caramel Sauce. Cut into wedges and serve immediately.

Makes 4 to 6 servings

Mango Madness

Mango and pineapple make for a lively combination, and you'll love this unique almond crust!

1 teaspoon almond extract

1 (8-ounce) can crushed pineapple,
   drained

1 (8-ounce) package light cream
   cheese, softened

8 (9- to 10-inch) flour tortillas

1 large mango, peeled and
   thinly sliced

1 egg, mixed with
   1 tablespoon water

1 cup minced or ground almonds

2 tablespoons olive oil

● **Suggested garnishes:**
Cinnamon Cream Sauce (page 126)
or Vanilla Cream Sauce (page 124)

1. Preheat oven to 400 degrees.

2. Mix almond extract and pineapple with cream cheese. Spread about 2 tablespoons cream cheese mixture over each tortilla.

3. Spread mango slices evenly over 4 tortillas, covering the cream cheese mixture completely.

4. Place one of the remaining tortillas on top, cream cheese side down. Press down with a wide spatula to remove any air pockets. Brush top of quesadilla with a little egg wash. Spread ¼ cup almonds on top and press down with spatula, making sure almonds are pressed into tortilla. Brush or spray with a little olive oil.

5. Place quesadilla, almond-crusted side up, onto a wire rack standing on a baking sheet. Bake 10 to 12 minutes, checking frequently so as not to burn. Cut into wedges and serve immediately.

Makes 4 to 6 servings

Triple Chocolate Decadence

Chocolate, chocolate, and more chocolate—decadence stuffed in a quesadilla!

½ cup chocolate hazelnut spread

1 (8-ounce) package light cream cheese, softened

8 (9- to 10-inch) flour tortillas

8 ounces dark chocolate, broken into small pieces

12 ounces semisweet chocolate chips

Fresh raspberries, for garnish (optional)

1. Mix chocolate hazelnut spread with cream cheese. Spread a generous tablespoon of cream cheese mixture over each tortilla.

2. Sprinkle dark chocolate pieces over 4 tortillas. Slide one of the chocolate-covered tortillas in skillet over medium heat. Place one of the remaining tortillas on top, cream cheese side down. Press down with a wide spatula to remove any air pockets. Cover and cook 1 to 2 minutes, checking frequently, until bottom tortilla is crisp and browned.

3. Turn over, cover, and cook 1 to 2 minutes more, or until lightly browned. Repeat this process for remaining quesadillas. Sprinkle with chocolate chips and let sit for 1 to 2 minutes, or until melted. Spread melted chocolate chips over tortilla and garnish with raspberries if desired. Cut into wedges and serve immediately.

Makes 4 to 6 servings

● **Suggested garnish:**
Chocolate Decadence Sauce
(page 126)

Strawberry Torte

This Southwest version of strawberry shortcake is a refreshing twist on the classic American dessert.

12 ounces cream cheese, softened

2 cups sweetened whipped cream

1 teaspoon vanilla

¼ cup sugar

4 cups thinly sliced strawberries

4 (9- to 10-inch) flour tortillas

Canola oil spray

Cinnamon sugar as desired

1. Mix together the cream cheese, whipped cream, and vanilla, and chill. Mix together the sugar and strawberries, and chill for 30 minutes more.

2. Heat a large skillet to medium-high heat. Cook tortillas, one at a time in skillet for about 3 minutes total, turning over once, until lightly browned and crisp. Remove tortillas from pan and, while still hot, spray lightly with canola oil and then sprinkle both sides generously with cinnamon sugar; set aside to cool.

3. On a serving platter, make layers using the following ingredients: 1 tortilla; cream cheese mixture; strawberries. Repeat to make four total layers. Garnish with a dollop of cream cheese mixture on top. Cut into wedges and serve immediately.

Makes 4 to 6 servings

Berries and Brie

The strong flavor of Brie is mellowed by the sweet berries, making a creamy delight.

8 ounces Brie, warmed

8 (9- to 10-inch) flour tortillas

2 ounces Monterey Jack
cheese, grated

2 cups (1/8-inch slices) fresh
strawberries

1 cup fresh or frozen raspberries,
thawed

1 cup fresh or frozen blueberries,
thawed

2 tablespoons sugar

Cinnamon sugar, as desired

1. Spread 1 generous tablespoon Brie over each tortilla. Sprinkle 2 tablespoons Monterey Jack cheese over Brie.

2. Toss berries with sugar. Spread 1 cup berry mixture over 4 tortillas.

3. Place one of the berry-covered tortillas into a 10-inch skillet over medium heat. Place one of the remaining tortillas on top, Brie side down. Press down with a wide spatula to remove any air pockets. Cover and cook 1 to 2 minutes, checking frequently, until bottom tortilla is crisp and browned.

4. Turn over, cover, and cook 1 to 2 minutes more, or until lightly browned. Repeat this process for remaining quesadillas. Sprinkle with cinnamon sugar as desired. Cut into wedges and serve immediately.

Makes 4 to 6 servings

● **Suggested garnishes:**
Fresh Fruit Purée (page 125) or
Honey-Lime Fruit Salsa (page 126)

Banana Split

The '50s classic ice cream shoppe dessert is delicious folded into a quesadilla.

½ cup chocolate hazelnut spread

1 (8-ounce) package light cream
   cheese, softened

8 (9- to 10-inch) flour tortillas

4 bananas, peeled and sliced
   ¼ inch thick

½ cup diced toasted almonds

½ cup chocolate syrup

½ cup toasted almonds slivers

1 (12-ounce) jar maraschino
   cherries, drained and diced

1. Mix chocolate spread with cream cheese. Spread about 2 tablespoons chocolate mixture over each tortilla.

2. Spread banana slices over chocolate mixture on 4 tortillas, covering whole surface. Sprinkle with almonds.

3. Place one of the banana-covered tortillas in a 10-inch skillet over medium heat. Place one of the remaining tortillas on top, chocolate side down. Press down with a wide spatula to remove any air pockets. Cover and cook 1 to 2 minutes, checking frequently, until bottom tortilla is crisp and browned.

4. Turn over, cover, and cook 1 to 2 minutes more, or until lightly browned. Repeat this process for remaining quesadillas. Drizzle with chocolate syrup and sprinkle with nuts and maraschino cherries. Cut into wedges and serve immediately.

Makes 4 to 6 servings

Peanut Butter Apple

This combination makes a delicious and easy after-school snack.

²/₃ cup peanut butter

3 tablespoons honey

1 (8-ounce) package light cream
cheese, softened

2 peeled and cored large Golden
Delicious apples

8 (9- to 10-inch) flour tortillas

Cinnamon sugar, as desired

1. Mix peanut butter and honey with cream cheese. Spread about 2 tablespoons cream cheese mixture over each tortilla.

2. Grate or dice the apples and then sprinkle ½ cup over cream cheese mixture on 4 tortillas.

3. Place one of the apple-covered tortillas in 10-inch skillet over medium heat. Place one of the remaining tortillas on top, cream cheese side down. Press down with a wide spatula to remove any air pockets. Cover and cook 1 to 2 minutes, checking frequently, until bottom tortilla is crisp and browned.

4. Turn over, cover, and cook 1 to 2 minutes more, or until lightly browned. Repeat this process for remaining quesadillas. Sprinkle generously with cinnamon sugar. Cut into wedges and serve immediately.

Makes 4 to 6 servings

● **Suggested garnishes:**
Cinnamon Cream Syrup (page 126)
or Rich Caramel Sauce (page 124)

Pecan-Crusted Pear

Silky pears matched with crunchy pecans are a flavorful match.

2 tablespoons orange marmalade or other tart jam or jelly

12 ounces light cream cheese, softened

8 (9- to 10-inch) flour tortillas

4 cups (⅛-inch slices) Bartlett pears

1 large egg, mixed with 1 tablespoon water

1 cup minced or ground pecans

2 tablespoons olive oil

● **Suggested garnishes:**
Cinnamon Cream Syrup (page 126) or Vanilla Cream Syrup (page 124)

1. Preheat oven to 400 degrees.

2. Mix marmalade with cream cheese. Spread about 2 tablespoons cream cheese mixture over each tortilla.

3. Spread pear slices evenly over 4 tortillas.

4. Place one of the fruit-covered tortillas on a flat surface. Place one of the remaining tortillas on top, cream cheese side down. Press down with a wide spatula to remove any air pockets. Brush top of quesadilla with a little egg wash. Spread ¼ cup pecans on top and press down with spatula, making sure pecans are pressed into tortilla. Brush or spray with a little olive oil.

5. Place quesadilla, pecan-crusted side up, onto a wire rack placed on a baking sheet. Bake 10 to 12 minutes, checking frequently so as not to burn. Cut into wedges and serve immediately.

Makes 4 to 6 servings

Walnut-Crusted Cran-Apple

Cranberries and apples make a sweet and tart filling for this luscious dessert.

1 teaspoon cinnamon

2 (8-ounce) packages light
  cream cheese, softened

8 (9- to 10-inch) flour tortillas

2 tablespoons butter

2 tablespoons brown sugar

4 cups (⅛-inch slices) Granny
  Smith apples

1 cup dried sweetened cranberries

1 large egg, mixed with
  1 tablespoon water

1 cup minced or ground walnuts

Canola oil spray

● **Suggested garnishes:**
Cinnamon Cream Syrup (page 126)
or Rich Caramel Sauce (page 124)

1. Preheat oven to 400 degrees.

2. Mix cinnamon with cream cheese. Spread about 2 tablespoons cream cheese mixture over each tortilla.

3. Sauté apple slices in butter and brown sugar over medium-high heat in a large skillet for about 5 minutes, or until apple slices are soft and browned and liquid has evaporated. Spread 1 cup apple mixture over each of 4 tortillas. Sprinkle ¼ cup cranberries over apples.

4. Place one of the fruit-covered tortillas on a flat surface. Place one of the remaining tortillas on top, cream cheese side down. Press down with a wide spatula to remove any air pockets. Brush top of quesadilla with a little egg wash. Spread ¼ cup walnuts on top and press down with spatula, making sure walnuts are pressed into tortilla. Spray with a little canola oil.

5. Place quesadilla, almond crusted side up, onto a wire rack standing on a baking sheet. Bake 10 to 12 minutes, checking frequently so as not to burn. Repeat for each quesadilla. Cut into wedges and serve immediately.

Makes 4 to 6 servings

Cherry Crisp

With the tart cherries and the crispy coconut streusel, these are delightfully different dessert quesadillas.

2 (8-ounce) packages cream
    cheese, softened

8 (9- to 10-inch) flour tortillas

1 teaspoon almond extract

$^{1}/_{2}$ teaspoon cinnamon

2 (18-ounce) cans cherry
    pie filling

Coconut Streusel (page 125)

1. Preheat oven to 400 degrees.

2. Spread about 2 tablespoons cream cheese over each tortilla.

3. Mix together the almond extract, cinnamon, and pie filling. Spread 1 cup cherry mixture over 4 tortillas.

4. Place one of the fruit-covered tortillas on a flat surface. Place one of the remaining tortillas on top, cream cheese side down. Press down with a wide spatula to remove any air pockets. Brush tops of tortillas with a little water. Spread ½ cup Coconut Streusel on top and press down with spatula, making sure streusel is pressed into tortilla.

5. Place quesadilla, streusel side up, onto a wire rack standing on a baking sheet. Bake 10 to 12 minutes, checking frequently so as not to burn. Cut into wedges and serve immediately.

Makes 4 to 6 servings

S'mores

This gooey campfire favorite is sure to have you licking your fingers!

1 (8-ounce) package light cream cheese, softened

8 (9- to 10-inch) flour tortillas

2 cups mini marshmallows

4 (1.5-ounce) bars milk chocolate

4 tablespoons butter, melted

½ cup graham cracker crumbs

2 tablespoons sugar

Canola oil spray

1. Preheat oven to 400 degrees.

2. Spread a generous tablespoon of cream cheese over each tortilla. Sprinkle ½ cup marshmallows on top of cream cheese on 4 tortillas. Crumble chocolate bars and sprinkle evenly over marshmallows.

3. Place one of the chocolate-covered tortillas on a flat surface. Place one of the remaining tortillas on top, cream cheese side down. Press down with a wide spatula to remove any air pockets. Brush tops of quesadillas with a little butter. Mix together the graham cracker crumbs and sugar. Spread ¼ cup graham cracker mixture on top and press down with spatula, making sure mixture is pressed into tortillas. Spray with a little canola oil.

4. Place quesadilla, graham cracker–crusted side up, onto a wire rack standing on a baking sheet. Bake 10 to 12 minutes in center of the oven, checking frequently so as not to burn. Garnish with additional marshmallows, if desired. Cut into wedges and serve immediately.

Makes 4 to 6 servings

Strawberry Ricotta

An Italian cannoli dessert classic meets the quesadilla—with pleasing results.

1 teaspoon almond extract

¼ cup powdered sugar

8 ounces ricotta cheese

8 (9- to 10-inch) flour tortillas

4 cups (⅛-inch slices) fresh
   strawberry

1 cup semisweet chocolate chips

Cinnamon sugar, as desired

1. Mix almond extract and sugar with ricotta cheese. Spread 1 generous tablespoon cheese mixture over each tortilla.

2. Spread strawberries over 4 tortillas in a single layer, covering surface. Sprinkle each with ¼ cup chocolate chips.

3. Slide one of the fruit-covered tortillas into a 10-inch skillet over medium heat. Place one of the remaining tortillas on top, cheese side down. Press down with a wide spatula to remove any air pockets. Cover and cook 1 to 2 minutes, checking frequently, until bottom tortilla is crisp and browned.

4. Turn over, cover, and cook 1 to 2 minutes more, or until lightly browned. Repeat this process for remaining quesadillas. Sprinkle with cinnamon sugar as desired. Cut into wedges and serve immediately.

Makes 4 to 6 servings

● **Suggested garnish:**
Chocolate Decadence Sauce
(page 126)

Salsas and Sauces

Sassy Smoky Salsa

Juice of 1 lime (about
2 tablespoons)

2 cloves garlic

1 small bunch cilantro

2 to 3 fresh Anaheim or jalapeño
peppers, or a combination

1 bell pepper, any color

About 6 large ripe tomatoes
(to make 4 cups smashed)

2 teaspoons chipotle chile powder

1 teaspoon salt (or more to taste)

1 tablespoon olive oil

1 bunch green onions, with
tops, sliced

A little sugar, if needed

1 (6-ounce) can tomato paste,
if needed

Place lime juice, garlic, and cilantro in a food processor and blend until smooth. Remove seeds from peppers and discard; mince peppers. Cut tomatoes into quarters and squeeze out excess liquid. Mash with a potato masher, or process in a food processor until just chopped. Add chile powder, salt, and olive oil. Stir all ingredients together and let sit on counter for at least 1 hour for flavors to blend. Taste and, if necessary, add a little sugar to taste. If salsa is too runny, stir in tomato paste as needed. Cover and refrigerate for up to 10 days. Serve at room temperature.

Makes about 6 cups

Southwest Spice Rub

¹/₄ cup brown sugar

2 tablespoons onion powder

2 tablespoons garlic powder

2 tablespoons smoked paprika

3 tablespoons cumin

1 tablespoon coriander

1 tablespoon chipotle chile powder

1 teaspoon salt

Mix all ingredients in a bowl and use as directed. Store in an airtight container.

Makes 1 cup

Roasted Red Pepper Sauce

3 red bell peppers, seeds removed

Canola oil

1 (16-ounce) container sour cream

3 tablespoons tomato paste

1 tablespoon lemon juice

1 teaspoon salt

Cut bell peppers into 1-inch flattened strips and place skin side up on a baking sheet. Brush or spray with a little canola oil and broil about 6 inches from the heat for 3 to 5 minutes, or until skins are lightly browned. Place in a blender with remaining ingredients. Blend until smooth.

Makes 3 cups

Sour Cream Paprika Sauce

1 cup light sour cream

2 tablespoons lime juice

1 tablespoon honey

2 teaspoons smoked paprika

1 teaspoon cumin

Whisk together all ingredients in a bowl. Refrigerate until ready to use.

Makes about 1 cup

Southwest Pesto Sauce

2 cups chopped cilantro

$^1/_4$ cup chopped mint or basil

$^1/_2$ cup pine nuts

1 jalapeño pepper, seeds removed

1 tablespoon lime juice

1 tablespoon honey

3 cloves garlic

$^1/_2$ teaspoon salt

$^1/_2$ cup extra virgin olive oil

In a food processor, blend the first eight ingredients until smooth. Slowly pour in olive oil. Store in a covered container in the refrigerator.

Makes 1 cup

Mushroom Cream Sauce

2 cups thinly sliced crimini
mushrooms

3 tablespoons minced garlic

1 tablespoon butter

$\frac{1}{2}$ cup chicken or vegetable broth

2 tablespoons white wine vinegar

$\frac{1}{2}$ cup cream

1 teaspoon salt

Sauté mushrooms and garlic in butter for 3 to 5 minutes, or until softened. Stir in remaining ingredients and cook down until reduced by half. Blend in a blender and serve warm.

Makes 2 cups

Creamy Avocado Sauce

3 ripe avocados

3 cloves garlic

2 tablespoons lemon juice

$\frac{1}{4}$ cup mayonnaise

1 teaspoon cumin

Salt and pepper, to taste

Process all ingredients in a food processor until smooth. Refrigerate until ready to use.

Makes 2 cups

Spicy Mustard Sauce

1 cup mayonnaise

¼ cup light sour cream

¼ cup spicy brown mustard

1 tablespoon grated horseradish

Salt and pepper, to taste

Combine all ingredients together in a bowl. Refrigerate until ready to use.

Makes about 1½ cups

Mojo Marinade

1 cup pineapple juice

Juice and zest of 1 lime

Juice and zest of 1 orange

1 chipotle chile pepper in sauce, minced

½ tablespoon cumin

2 tablespoons diced fresh oregano leaves

2 teaspoons salt

Mix together all the ingredients in a bowl.

Makes 1½ cups

White Cheddar Sauce

3 tablespoons butter

2 tablespoons flour

2 cups milk

4 ounces sharp white cheddar
  cheese, grated

1 ounce Parmesan cheese, grated

Nutmeg, salt, and pepper to taste

Melt butter in a skillet over medium-high heat. Stir in flour until absorbed. Whisk in milk. Slowly add cheeses. Simmer until thickened slightly. Add a few dashes of nutmeg, salt, and pepper. Serve warm.

Makes about 3 cups

Peach Chutney

3 peaches, peeled and diced

8 ounces low-sugar peach or
  apricot preserves

2 tablespoons rice vinegar

1 tablespoon minced fresh ginger

2 green onions, thinly sliced

1 teaspoon salt

Simmer together all ingredients for 5 to 8 minutes over medium-high heat, or until thickened. Serve warm or at room temperature.

Makes about 2 cups

Vanilla Cream Syrup

1 cup cream

½ cup sugar

1 tablespoon flour

4 egg yolks

1 tablespoon vanilla

1 cup vanilla ice cream

Bring cream and sugar to a boil over medium-high heat. In a small bowl, mix together the flour, egg yolks, and vanilla. Add a few spoonfuls of the boiling cream mixture, and then add the egg yolk mixture to the cream mixture, stirring constantly for 3 minutes. Add ice cream, and continue to cook for another 3 minutes, stirring constantly until thickened. Serve warm.

Makes about 2 cups

Rich Caramel Sauce

½ cup sugar

½ cup brown sugar

½ cup cream

¼ cup butter

½ teaspoon salt

1 teaspoon vanilla

Bring to a boil the sugars, cream, butter, and salt. Boil about 1 minute to soft-ball stage, or 230 to 240 degrees. Remove from heat and add vanilla. Cool to room temperature and serve.

Makes about 2 cups

Fresh Fruit Purée

3 cups fresh fruit or berries

1 teaspoon lemon zest

1 tablespoon lemon juice

2 tablespoons pure maple syrup

2 tablespoons light corn syrup

Water

In blender, blend the fruit, lemon zest, juice, maple syrup, and corn syrup. Add water if necessary to make the right syrup consistency.

Makes about 2 cups

Coconut Streusel

$^1/_2$ cup butter

1 cup flour

1 cup light brown sugar

1 teaspoon cinnamon

1 teaspoon salt

$^1/_2$ cup rolled oats

$^1/_2$ cup sweetened coconut

$^1/_2$ cup diced walnuts

Blend together all ingredients with a pastry blender and use as directed or desired.

Makes about 3 cups

Chocolate Decadence Sauce

1 cup heavy cream

$^1/_2$ cup light corn syrup

$^1/_2$ teaspoon salt

8 ounces semisweet chocolate chips

Bring cream, corn syrup, and salt to a boil. Remove from heat and add chocolate. Let stand about 5 minutes, until chocolate is melted, and then stir. Cool to room temperature and serve.

Makes about 2 cups

Honey-Lime Fruit Salsa

4 cups diced fresh fruits, such as mango, strawberries, and kiwi

$^1/_4$ cup honey

1 teaspoon lime zest

2 tablespoons lime juice

Mix together all ingredients in a bowl. Chill and serve.

Makes 4 cups

Cinnamon Cream Syrup

1 cup sugar

$^1/_2$ cup corn syrup

$^1/_2$ teaspoon cinnamon

$^1/_2$ cup evaporated milk

In a small saucepan, combine the sugar, corn syrup, and cinnamon. Bring to a boil, stirring for 3 minutes. Remove from heat and cool 5 minutes. Stir in evaporated milk. Serve warm.

Makes about 2 cups

Index

Metric Conversion Chart

Volume Measurements		Weight Measurements		Temperature Conversion	
U.S.	Metric	U.S.	Metric	Fahrenheit	Celsius
1 teaspoon	5 ml	½ ounce	15 g	250	120
1 tablespoon	15 ml	1 ounce	30 g	300	150
¼ cup	60 ml	3 ounces	90 g	325	160
⅓ cup	75 ml	4 ounces	115 g	350	180
½ cup	125 ml	8 ounces	225 g	375	190
⅔ cup	150 ml	12 ounces	350 g	400	200
¾ cup	175 ml	1 pound	450 g	425	220
1 cup	250 ml	2¼ pounds	1 kg	450	230